GOLD COAST SCHOOLS
151 KALMUS DR., STE. E130
COSTA MESA, CA 92626

PassTrak

A Study Manual for the

Series 7

General Securities Representative Exam

ver. 911

0-884-62963-5

Longman Group USA, Inc.
© 1990. All rights reserved.

K197

Important Notice

While a great deal of care has been taken to provide accurate and current information, the ideas, suggestions, general principles and conclusions presented in this book are subject to local, state and federal laws and regulations, court cases, and any revisions of same. The reader is thus urged to consult legal counsel regarding any points of law. This publication should not be used as a substitute for competent legal advise.

ISBN: 0-884-62963-5 (PB)
       0-793-10017-8 (LL)

PPN: 3607/02

Notice Regarding NASD Qualifications Exams

The Series 7 Qualification Exam is copyrighted by the New York Stock Exchange. Each page of the examination contains the following notice:

> "The contents of this examination are confidential. Neither the whole nor any part of this examination may be reproduced in any form or quote or used in any way without the written consent of the New York Stock Exchange, Inc."

Longman Financial Services Institute, Inc. and its employees and agents honor the copyrights of the New York Stock Exchange. We specifically urge each purchaser to refrain from any attempts to remove a copy of the exam or copy or record any of the questions on the exam.

Acknowledgments

Longman Financial Services Institute, Inc. would like to acknowledge and thank the following people for their invaluable contributions to this book.

Editor:
Kimberly K. Walker-Daniels
Securities Products Manager
Longman Group USA, Inc.
Chicago, IL 60610

Technical Reviewers:
Marc Katz
LFSI, Inc.
Southfield, MI 40875

Gib Larson
LFSI, Inc.
Minneapolis, MN 55420

Neil Hitchcock
LFSI, Inc.
Minneapolis, MN 55420

Curt Dittbrenner
LFSI, Inc.
Washington, DC

Series 7 Study Manual Table of Contents

Introduction

Chapter One

Chapter Two

Debt Securities.. 2.1

Chapter Three

Corporate Debt 3.1

Chapter Four

Special Securities 4.1

Chapter Five

U.S. Government Securities... 5.1

Chapter Six

Money-Market Instruments 6.1

Chapter Seven

Issuing Securities 7.1

Chapter Eight

Trading Securities 8.1

K198

Chapter Nine

Client Accounts.. 9.1

Chapter Ten

Brokerage Office Procedures 10.1

Chapter Twelve

Economics and Analysis 12.1

Chapter Thirteen

Investment Recommendations 13.1

Chapter Fourteen

Taxation 14.1

K198

Chapter Fifteen

Government Regulations 15.1

Chapter Sixteen

Self-Regulatory Organizations 16.1

Chapter Seventeen

Municipal Securities 17.1

Chapter Eighteen

Options 18.1

Chapter Nineteen

Investment Company Products 19.1

Chapter Twenty

Retirement Planning and Annuities 20.1

Chapter Twenty One

Direct Participation Programs 21.1

PassTrak

Longman Group USA, Inc.

Introduction

to the PassTrak: Series 7

PassTrak: Series 7 Study Manual

The NASD's Series 7 Exam is a very difficult test. The concepts themselves are not that difficult, but you must show that you have a thorough understanding of and can apply those concepts. It is not possible to pass the exam merely by memorizing large volumes of facts and figures.

Test questions can be categorized by the type of reasoning and thinking required to answer them. The five categories of questions you are most likely to encounter on the Series 7 Exam are:

- **Recognition (information recall):** recognition of terms, facts, sequences, relationships, etc.
- **Comprehension:** understanding of written communications, including reports, definitions, tables, diagrams, etc.
- **Application:** application of concepts, formulas, procedures and principles to job related problems.
- **Analysis:** understanding the relationships between the various factors in a complex situation.
- **Evaluation:** evaluating data or judging the best course of action in a situation.

Although test questions may fall into more than one category, these categories can still help you decide how to approach test items and how to prepare for the exam.

Recognition. The following question is an example of a recognition or recall item: it simply requires you to recall the meaning of the term "record date."

1. AT&T has set the date that will determine which stockholders will receive an upcoming dividend. This date is called the

    ____(A) settlement date.
    ____(B) ex-dividend date.
    ____(C) ex-distribution date.
    ____(D) record date.

Comprehension. This item is an example of a comprehension item. Most questions about the Consolidated Tape will be in this category, as will questions about tables and tombstones.

2.	An order to buy Worp Corp. debentures reads: "100M 95 GTC." This order is a

____(A)	market order for 95 bonds at par.
____(B)	market order for 100 bonds at 95.
____(C)	limit order for 95 bonds at par.
____(D)	limit order for 100 bonds at 95.

Application. The next question requires the application of a specific rule in order to determine the ex-dividend date.

3.	The record date for Music Man Record Stores Inc. common stock is listed as Monday, May 10. Music Man's stock would normally go ex-dividend on

____(A)	Friday, May 14.
____(B)	Thursday, May 6.
____(C)	Tuesday, May 4.
____(D)	Monday, May 3.

Analysis. When a question must be answered by applying more than one rule or principle, it falls into the analysis category, as in the following example.

4.	A municipal bond was purchased in the secondary market on a 4.5% yield to maturity basis, and is now being sold at a price equivalent to a 5.5% yield to maturity. For tax purposes, the owner would have

____(A)	a capital loss.
____(B)	a capital gain.
____(C)	a gain that is tax-exempt.
____(D)	no gain or loss.

Evaluation. Items in the evaluation category often require a judgment as to the proper decision or course of action, as in the following case.

5.	The treasurer of a school board wishes to invest some surplus funds in a secure investment, but she will need the funds about nine months from now. Which of the following investments would be most suitable?

____(A)	call options
____(B)	municipal revenue bonds
____(C)	AAA-rated convertible debentures
____(D)	Treasury bills

The items in the last three categories require a more thorough understanding of the underlying concepts than do items in the first two categories. Once you have determined the rule, principle or concept that the question is testing, you can apply your knowledge to that particular situation. Don't try to memorize an approach to every possible situation; there will always be new situations that you have not encountered before and for which no rules exist. By understanding the underlying concepts, however, you can apply that understanding to any number of new situations.

While it will always be important to know rules and regulations (such as the maintenance requirement for short margin accounts), you need to be able to apply those rules and regulations. When reviewing questions in the Chapter Reviews and Final Exam, identify the concepts being tested and write your own rationale for the correct answer, especially for those items you might have missed.

How to Prepare for the Exam

Review the practice exams. Go over the lessons in which you missed the most questions. Research and rework the questions you missed until you understand the answers.

Complete the Final Exams. Your Final Exam gives you up-to-date material that will help you prepare for the Series 7. If you would like to do additional study, some of the best ways to use your time are:

- Review your lesson tests and exams and make sure that you now understand each question that you missed.
- If a subject still seems difficult to you, review that entire lesson. Skim the lesson first, reading the bold headings to organize your study. Reread those sections which give you the most difficulty.
- Review the glossary and review the meaning of each term.

Maintain a normal routine. In the days preceding the exam, don't change your normal work schedule. Above all, don't isolate yourself away from everyone and attempt to study for 14 hours a day. It isn't necessary, and is probably counter-productive. Instead, set up your review schedule to allow yourself adequate time for getting together with friends and getting physical exercise.

You might want to review for an hour or so the Friday night before the exam, but then relax. Get plenty of sleep. The exam is six hours long and can be very tiring.

What to Expect

The exam has 250 multiple-choice questions. You will have three hours in the morning in which to answer the first 125 questions. After lunch you will have another three hours in which to answer the final 125 questions. Most students find that they have plenty of time to finish all the questions; the Series 7 is not intended to test how fast you can answer questions.

Each month a different exam is given, but each exam is weighted in the following manner:

	Number of Questions	Percent of Questions
Advertising, Qualifying Customers, Industry Regulations	31	12%
Securities Instruments	84	33%
Handling Customer Accounts, Taxation, Margins	34	14%
Securities Markets, Order Handling, Confirmations	34	14%
Economics, Securities Analysis, Sources of Financial Information	29	12%
Portfolio Analysis, Investment Strategies, Retirement Plans	<u>38</u>	<u>15%</u>
	250	100%

Passing score. To successfully pass the Series 7 and qualify for licensure with the NASD as a General Securities Registered Representative, you must answer correctly at least 70% (175) of the 250 questions.

Chapter One

Equity Securities

Key Terms

1.3 Authorized stock

1.14 Callable

1.14 Convertible

1.15 CUSIP number

1.2 Equity

1.15 Guaranteed stock

1.4 Market value

1.4 No-par stock

1.4 Par value

1.5 Point

1.3 Preferred stock

1.10 Property dividend

1.16 Registrar

1.11 Reverse split

1.10 Stock dividend

1.11 Stock split

1.3 Treasury stock

1.7 Voting

1.10 Yield

Book value 1.4

Cash dividend 1.10

Cumulative voting 1.6

Dividend income 1.16

Fixed income security 1.12

Issued stock 1.3

Negotiability 1.15

Outstanding stock 1.3

Participating 1.13

Preemptive right 1.7

Prior preferred 1.13

Proxy 1.6

Residual rights 1.8

Senior security 1.9

Stock power 1.16

Transfer agent 1.16

Trustee 1.6

Voting Trust 1.6

K101

Equity Securities

Of all the different types of investments available to today's consumer, the one with which people are most familiar is stock and the various markets on which it is traded. The Dow Jones Industrial Average (an indicator of the general direction in which the stock market is moving) is frequently a topic of discussion on the news, in the business section of the paper, in the office and on the street.

Many people own stock in one form or another. Some received stock as a gift from a grandparent, others buy stock regularly through a payroll savings plan, some acquire stock indirectly through pension or profit-sharing programs and many purchase stock for its growth and income potential. The buying and selling of stock in its various forms constitutes a major portion of the business of many Wall Street investment firms.

Chapter One lays the groundwork for the study of stock and the stock market. In this chapter, you will be exposed to the important characteristics of common and preferred stock, the rights of stockholders, the different ways of valuing and classifying stock, the stock certificate and the transfer of stock certificates from one owner to another.

What Is Stock?

Ownership

Shares of stock represent individual pieces of ownership (or equity) in a corporation. Companies issue stock as their primary means of raising business capital and investors who buy those shares (either during the initial public stock offering or later, in the secondary market) are the owners of that company. Whatever property the business owns (that is, its assets) less the claims of its creditors (its liabilities) belongs to the owners of the business, its stockholders.

A company can also issue bonds as a means of raising capital, but the bondholders have no equity interest in the corporation; they are considered lenders, not owners.

Diversified Ownership, Centralized Management

If a company issues 100 shares of common stock, each of those shares represents a one percent ownership of that company and gives its holder one vote in its management. A person who owns ten shares of stock would own ten percent of the company (and be entitled to ten votes) and so on. In today's business world, it is not unusual to see companies that have issued ten thousand, one hundred thousand, one million or more shares of common stock. Since each of these shares carries with it the same rights and privileges of every other share, it is easy to see how conflicts could arise regarding the management of these companies by their many rightful owners, the shareholders.

For this reason, most corporations are organized in such a way that the holders of their common stock regularly vote for and elect a limited number of people to a board of directors to manage the company's business for them. By electing a board of directors, stockholders still have a say in the management of the company, but do not have to bother with the day-to-day details of its operations.

Different Types, Different Rights

In addition to its common stock, corporations will often have reasons to issue a second type of stock, called preferred stock. Although preferred shareholders also acquire equity in the corporation, they usually do not have the same voting rights as the holders of common stock. As the name "preferred" indicates, however, they do enjoy some privileges not granted common stockholders (some of the special privileges accorded the owners of preferred stock will be covered later in this chapter).

Classifying Stock by Its Holder

Authorized stock. As part of its original charter, a corporation receives authorization from the state to issue (that is, sell or distribute) a specific number of shares of stock. It must amend its charter if its board of directors ever decides that there is a need to issue more shares than are currently authorized.

Issued stock. A corporation may distribute (issue) fewer than the total number of shares authorized by the state (and many do) and reserve the excess (the unissued stock) for future needs such as:

- raising new capital for expansion;
- paying stock dividends;
- providing stock purchase plans for employees or stock options for corporate officers;
- exchanging common stock for outstanding convertible bonds or preferred stock; and
- redeeming outstanding stock purchase warrants.

Treasury stock. Treasury stock is stock a corporation has issued and subsequently repurchased from the public in the secondary market. The corporation has the privilege of holding this stock indefinitely, reissuing it or retiring it. A corporation could reissue its treasury stock to fund stock option plans or other employee bonus arrangements. Treasury stock does NOT carry the rights of other common shares, including such basic ones as voting rights and the right to receive dividends.

Outstanding stock. Outstanding stock includes any shares that have been issued by the corporation and which have not subsequently been repurchased by the company (that is, they are still in the hands of investors).

Summary. Authorized stock is the number of shares that the state has permitted the corporation to issue; issued stock is the number of shares that have actually been sold (or otherwise distributed) to shareholders. Any authorized stock that hasn't been sold or distributed is referred to as unissued stock. Stock that has been repurchased and is being held by the company is known as treasury stock. Outstanding stock represents all shares still in the possession of investors.

Putting a Value on Common Stock

As with many other retail goods, the laws of supply and demand determine a stock's price in the marketplace. A stock's market price is not the only measure of its value, however. Other measures include par value (an arbitrary value assigned to a stock by its board of directors) and book value (a figure calculated from the corporation's assets and liabilities).

Par Value

no meaning in common stock

A stock's par value is the arbitrary dollar value given to the stock by the company in its articles of incorporation. If a stock has been assigned a par value, you can usually find it printed on the face of the stock certificate. A stock's par value normally bears little or no relationship to its market price, and tends to be a small dollar amount: $1 par, $5 par, etc. The par value of a share of stock may change at some future date in the event that the company's board of directors decides to arrange a stock split.

Most states also authorize the issuance of no-par stock. Unless state statutes or the corporate charter state a minimum price for no-par stock, it can be sold for any amount. Some states require that no-par stock be given a stated value and any sale proceeds exceeding that value must be recorded as paid-in surplus. There is no discernible difference to the investor between a stock with a par value and one with a stated value.

When stock is sold, the amount of money received in excess of the par value is recorded on the corporate balance sheet as capital in excess of par (also called paid-in surplus, capital surplus or paid-in capital). In practical terms, this means that stockholders cannot be assessed at some point in the future for deficiencies in the company's operating capital.

Book Value

While par value is a stable figure, a stock's book value is not. Book value per share is a measure of how much a holder of common stock could expect to receive for each share if the corporation were to be liquidated. It is based on the difference between the value of a corporation's assets (including inventory, investments, cash on hand and facilities) and its liabilities (money owed lenders, suppliers, payroll, etc.) divided by the number of shares outstanding.

Market Value

For many people, the most familiar measure of a stock's worth is its price in the marketplace, its market value. Market value is directly influenced by supply (the number of shares available to investors) and demand (the number of shares investors would like to buy). Information about stocks and their prices (including the day's high, low and closing prices) can be found daily in many newspapers. In general, there is no direct relationship between the market value and the book value of a stock.

The market price of a stock is quoted in whole dollars plus fractions of a dollar, also known as points (1/2 point equals 1/2 of a dollar or $.50). If a stock is quoted at 25, this means that the market price for that stock is $25 per share. A stock quoted at 25 1/2 is selling for $25.50 per share.

Normally, stock prices are quoted in minimum increments of 1/8ths of a dollar (although some low-priced stocks known as "penny stocks" are quoted in fractions as small as 1/64ths).

The Rights of Corporate Ownership

Voting Rights

Holders of common stock exercise control of a corporation by electing a board of directors and by voting on corporate policy at the annual meeting. In addition to voting for members of the board of directors, shareholders are also entitled to vote on matters involving:

- issuance of senior securities;
- stock splits; and
- substantial changes in the corporation's business.

Shareholders do not have the right to vote on either the timing or the amount of cash or stock dividends. Those matters are left to the discretion of the board of directors.

Calculating the Number of Votes

A shareholder is entitled to cast one vote for each share of stock he or she owns. Depending on the bylaws of the company and on applicable state law, a stockholder may cast her votes in one of two ways. These two ways are known as statutory voting and cumulative voting.

regular voting

Statutory voting. Under the statutory voting system, a shareholder who chooses to vote in an election of members to the board of directors may cast one vote per share owned for each position.

To illustrate, if three directors are to be elected, the shareholder with 100 shares may cast from 0 to 100 votes for each of the three positions. In the event that the stockholder casts fewer than 100 votes for a candidate for one of the available seats, the remainder of those 100 votes may not be cast for another candidate for the same seat.

A candidate only needs to receive a simple majority (over 50% of the votes cast) to be elected to the board. Statutory voting tends to put majority shareholders (those who own large blocks of stock) at an advantage over investors who own smaller amounts of stock in the company.

Cumulative voting. Cumulative voting entitles the shareholder to the same total number of votes as the statutory system, but places no restriction upon allocation of those votes.

In the example above, the stockholder who owns 100 shares would have a total of 300 votes (one vote per share times the number of candidates). Under a cumulative voting system, those 300 votes could be cast in any manner the stockholder chooses. The shareholder could cast all 300 votes for a single candidate or could split them in any fashion between two or more candidates.

In companies with cumulative voting rights, minority shareholders have a better chance of electing directors, thereby gaining representation on (although not necessarily control of) the board. Election under cumulative voting requires a plurality of the votes cast (the most votes, rather than just a simple majority).

Proxies

Because stockholders of corporations sometimes find it difficult to attend annual stockholders' meetings, many vote by means of a proxy. A proxy is a legal document that can be used by a stockholder who wants to authorize another party to vote his or her shares at the meeting. Proxies must be in writing, and typically take the form of a limited power of attorney. Proxies are valid only for the specified meeting and are intended to be used to cast votes only on matters addressed at that meeting.

The voting authorization given through a proxy is revocable by the stockholder in the event he or she later chooses to attend the meeting. A proxy may also be revoked by another proxy executed at a later date by the stockholder, and all proxies become invalid at the death of the stockholder.

Parties involved in matters scheduled for discussion and vote at an annual meeting will often contact shareholders directly and solicit their proxies, in the hopes of gaining control over those votes. Shareholders have been known to receive multiple proxy solicitations if a proposal coming up for vote is at all controversial.

The Securities Exchange Act of 1934 empowered the SEC to regulate the solicitation of proxies. Corporations or individuals that solicit proxies must supply detailed and accurate information to the shareholders about the proposal(s) on which they will be asked to vote. In addition, the proxy solicitor must submit this same information to the SEC for review prior to soliciting the shareholder.

Voting Trust Certificates

In some instances (particularly in those cases where a company is having financial difficulties) management responsibilities may be temporarily transferred to an outside organization that then operates as a trustee for the company. Stockholders' voting rights may be relinquished to this board of trustees (also known as a voting trust) and the trustee (typically a commercial bank) issues voting trust certificates to shareholders in place of their stock certificates.

All of the benefits of ownership except the power to vote are retained by the stockholders. The trustee will vote those shares for as long as the voting trust is in existence. Unlike a proxy (the primary way a shareholder can transfer voting rights), the voting power transfer of a voting trust certificate is usually long-term.

Voting trust certificates trade just like stock certificates while the voting trust is in existence. At the dissolution of the voting trust, new stock certificates are exchanged for the voting trust certificates.

Nonvoting Common Stock

Under certain circumstances, companies can issue shares of nonvoting common stock. Companies that choose to issue both voting and nonvoting (or limited voting) common stock normally differentiate the issues as Class A (voting) and Class B (nonvoting) categories. Compared to issues of stock with voting rights, nonvoting stocks are usually issued in limited amounts. Issuing a separate class of nonvoting stock provides a company with a means to raise additional capital while maintaining control and continuity of management.

Preemptive Rights

First Right of Refusal

When a corporation raises capital through the sale of common stock (or securities convertible into common stock) it may be required by law or by its corporate charter to offer the securities to its common stockholders first before it offers them directly to the public. Stockholders then have what is known as a preemptive right to purchase sufficient newly issued shares to protect their proportionate ownership in the corporation. To illustrate, a person who already owns 1% of the stock of MicroScam (MCS) Corporation will have a preemptive right to purchase 1% of any new stock issue. Preemptive rights help ensure that stockholders' rights (such as voting rights) are not diluted at the issuance of new stock.

The subscription price for such an issue of additional stock (that is, the price at which existing stockholders will be able to acquire new shares) is usually lower than market value at the time the rights are offered.

Limited Liability

Stockholders cannot lose more than they have invested in the stock of a particular corporation (in other words, they cannot be forced to pay off the debts of a corporation going through bankruptcy proceedings).

Inspection of Corporate Books

Stockholders have the right to obtain lists of stockholders, receive annual reports, etc. Inspection rights do not include the right to examine the detailed books of accounts, minutes of directors' meetings or financial records.

Protection of the Corporation

Shareholders may take the company's management (including members of the board of directors) to court if they believe that it or they have committed wrongful acts that could harm the corporation.

Restraint of Illegal Acts

Shareholders may take action against the board of directors of a corporation to restrain it from acting in a manner inconsistent with the corporate charter.

Residual Claims to Assets

When a corporation ceases to exist, the stockholder, as owner, has a right to corporate assets. The right is residual in that a common stockholder may make a claim only after all debts and other security holders have been satisfied.

Risks and Rewards of Owning Common Stock

Benefits Available to Stockholders

Among the various securities issued by corporations, common stock tends to offer investors the greatest potential return. Two of the rewards people expect to receive when they invest in common stock are:

Growth. The almost unlimited potential for increase in the market price of shares owned is known as capital appreciation. Historically, ownership of common stock has provided investors with greater real returns than any other investment.

Income. Many corporations distribute a portion of their profits on a regular basis in the form of dividends. These regular distributions can be a significant source of income and are a major reason many people invest in corporate stock.

Risks of Owning Stock

Decreased or no income. Common stockholders must assume certain risks in exchange for the high profit potential of stock ownership. One of these risks is the possibility of dividend income decreasing or ceasing entirely during periods of corporate unprofitability: a corporation will usually distribute dividends to common stockholders only after satisfying the claims of other securities (such as bonds and preferred stock).

Low priority at dissolution. A second risk that holders of common stock face is that, in the event a company experiencing financial troubles goes into bankruptcy, owners of common stock have the lowest priority in claims against corporate earnings and assets. In the event of the company's dissolution, the holders of corporate bonds and preferred stock may enter claims against corporate earnings and assets before common stockholders. Because of this advantage, some refer to those investments as senior securities. Common stockholders only have what are known as residual rights to corporate assets upon dissolution.

Fall in price. A third risk of owning stock is that there always exists the possibility that other investors in the marketplace will not value the shares you hold as highly as you do. You see a reflection of this risk every day in the financial section of the newspaper as supply and demand drive the price of every stock up and down.

K101

Return on Investment

Dividends

Dividends represent the sharing of a company's profits with its owners (the stockholders). Although many investors buy stock primarily for its income (or dividend) potential, stockholders are only entitled to dividend distributions if the company board of directors votes to make such a distribution.

Cash dividends. Cash dividends are normally distributed by corporations to stockholders in the form of checks representing the stockholder's share of the company's profits (most corporations do this quarterly). Some companies take great pride in their long, uninterrupted history of regular or increasing cash dividend payments, and investors tend to view companies with consistent dividend payment histories favorably.

Stock dividends. A company may not want to pay out cash dividends from its profits, however. Often, young companies developing new products or services (or even long-established companies engaging in expansion or acquisitions) may want to use some or all of their available cash for these purposes.

To satisfy investors (and at the same time to conserve cash) a company's board of directors may declare a stock dividend instead of a cash dividend. Under these circumstances, the company issues shares of its common stock as a dividend to its current shareholders. When a stock dividend is declared, all common shareholders receive the same percentage of stock as a dividend. This way, the dividend does not increase any single investor's proportionate share of ownership in the company.

Property dividends. Sometimes, a corporation that owns securities in other companies as an investment will choose to distribute some of these securities as a property dividend. Let's take the example of a holding company that owns stock in one or more subsidiaries. The parent corporation may elect to divest itself of a subsidiary by distributing the stock it owns in the subsidiary to the shareholders as a dividend (e.g., a property dividend).

Property dividends, in some circumstances, may actually be a company product. Proctor and Gamble, as an example, could distribute shampoo as a property dividend. Property dividends are declared and identified as such and should not be confused with gifts of the sort given to stockholders who attend the annual meeting (a common practice among corporations).

Calculating Return on Investment

One way to evaluate the return on an investment in common stock is to calculate the dividend (or current) yield, the annual rate of return for an investor. If, for example,

$$\frac{\text{what you get}}{\text{what you pay}} \qquad \frac{Div's}{CMV\,1.10} \quad \%$$

the market price of a particular stock is $20 and the yearly dividend is $1.00 (a quarterly dividend of $.25), the current yield for that stock would be 5%.

Stock Splits and Reverse Splits

When a stock reaches a relatively high price (an indication of this would be a per share cost that appears to be discouraging potential investors from buying shares in the secondary market) the company's board of directors may decide to declare a stock split (which must be approved by a vote of the shareholders). This effectively reduces the price per share without placing current shareholders at a disadvantage.

main reason: increase marketability

As an example of a situation involving a stock split, let's say that stock in This Can't Be Sushi (TCBS) is selling for $100 per share, and the company declares a 2-for-1 stock split. Each existing stockholder will receive one new share of TCBS for each share held before the split. Each outstanding share has been split into two shares each valued at half as much as before. A stockholder who owns $10,000 worth of TCBS before the split (100 shares at a current market price of $100 per share) will own 200 shares worth $50 per share after the split.

To calculate the effect of a 2:1 split, you multiply the number of shares by 2/1 and multiply the price by 1/2 (notice that the value of the stockholder's position is $10,000 both before and after the split).

A reverse split has the opposite effect on the shares and the shareholders. After a reverse split, investors own fewer shares that are now worth more per share. After a 1:2 reverse split, for example, a shareholder who owned 100 shares with a market value of $5 per share now owns 50 shares worth $10 per share. Corporations sometimes do this to reduce the number of shares outstanding or to increase the earnings per share and at the same time increase the price per share.

small $5 stock companies do it.

Section Three

Characteristics of Preferred Stock

To many people, preferred stock appears to be a cross between an equity and a debt security. Although it is an equity security and represents ownership in the issuing corporation, it does not provide all of the privileges of ownership that are normally associated with common stock. Like a debt instrument, it is often (though not always) issued as a fixed income security with a stated dividend. Its price fluctuations tend to be affected more by changes in interest rates than by supply and demand. Unlike common stock, most preferred stock is issued as nonvoting stock.

Although preferred stock does not typically have the same growth potential as common stock (since its price is more likely to be affected by changes in interest rates than by changes in company profits), the owners of preferred stock generally have an advantage over common stockholders in two ways:

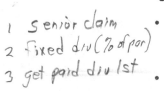

- When dividends are declared by the board of directors, owners of preferred stock receive their dividends (plus any dividends in arrears) first; and
- If a corporation goes bankrupt after paying off creditors, preferred shareholders have a prior claim on the remaining assets. Common shareholders' claims are typically the last ones paid.

Dividend Preference over Common Stock

Dividends (once they have been declared by the board of directors) must be paid to preferred stockholders before they can be paid to common shareholders. This gives holders of preferred stock a higher probability of receiving regular income than the holders of common stock.

Stated (Fixed) Rate of Return

To most owners of preferred stock, the stock's most attractive feature is its fixed dividend (although preferred stocks with variable dividends exist, they are not common). If the stock has been assigned a par value (a value normally much higher than that assigned to the corporation's common stock), it will state the annual dividend payments in terms of percentage of par value. A preferred stock with a par value of $100 that pays $6 in annual dividends would be known as a 6% preferred. No-par value preferred stock has a dividend stated in a dollar amount. A $6 no-par preferred would pay a $6 annual dividend.

Prior Claim over Assets at Dissolution

Holders of preferred stock can make a claim against the assets of the corporation (in the event of its liquidation) before common stockholders can.

Limited Ownership Privileges

Preferred stocks usually do not carry either voting rights or preemptive rights. There are exceptions, however, including those times when a company is in financial difficulty and the occasional issue of preferred stock with full or limited voting rights.

No Maturity Date or Set Maturity Value

Unlike corporate bonds (or other debt securities), preferred stock has no preset date at which it matures and/or is scheduled for redemption by the corporation.

Classes of Preferred Stock

Just as they can issue more than one class of common stock, corporations can issue more than one class of preferred. Separate classes of preferred may differ in terms of rate of dividend, profit participation privileges, or in any number of other ways. All, however, maintain a degree of preference over common stock. The classes are frequently referred to as Preferred A (prior preferred) and Preferred B (second preferred).

Prior Preferred

Prior preferred stock has a prior claim over other preferred stock in receiving dividends, as well as in the distribution of assets in the event of liquidation.

Cumulative Preferred (Deferred

One of the primary reasons investors buy preferred stock in a corporation is due to preferred stock's predictable dividend flow. Holders of preferred stock can expect payment of a predetermined amount at regular intervals. Common stockholders, on the other hand, don't have this advantage: their dividends (if they receive any at all) are paid only after all of the corporation's other debt obligations and preferred stock dividends are paid, and only when (and if) the board of directors votes to pay them.

If a corporation is experiencing financial difficulties, however, its board of directors may vote to reduce or suspend payment of dividends to both common and preferred stockholders. Common stockholders don't have any recourse if this occurs: any dividends they miss may (or may not) be made up by the corporation at a later date. An investor who has purchased cumulative preferred stock, though, has a definite advantage. Any and all dividends due will accumulate on the company's books until such time as the corporation is able to pay them. When the company is able to resume full payment of dividends, holders of cumulative preferred stock will receive the current preferred dividend plus the total accumulated dividends (dividends in arrears) before any dividends are distributed to common stockholders.

Participating Preferred

In addition to the fixed dividend characteristic of other classes of preferred stock, participating preferred stock offers its owners another benefit. These stockholders receive a share of any corporate profits that remain after all dividends due other securities are paid. The percentage to which participating preferred stock actually participates is usually printed right on the stock certificate. If a preferred stock is described as, "XYZ 6% Preferred Participating to 9%," you know that the company will pay its holders up to 3% in additional dividends in profitable years.

Owners of participating preferred stock don't participate in a corporation's profits until after payment of:

- interest to bondholders;
- dividends to other preferred stockholders;
- payment of their basic dividend rate; and,
- dividends to common stockholders.

Convertible Preferred

A preferred stock is convertible if the holder has the right to convert shares of the preferred stock into shares of common stock at some future point in time. To illustrate, a convertible preferred stock with a $100 par value might be convertible into common stock at $25 per share. For each share of $100 par value preferred an investor owns, she can exchange it for four shares of common stock. As long as the price of the common stock in this example remains below $25 per share, the preferred stockholder would have little incentive to take advantage of the conversion feature.

If the market price of this corporation's common stock were to move above $25 per share, however, the preferred shareholder could profit by converting her shares into common stock at the preset below-market conversion price. Because the value of convertible preferred is linked to the value of the common stock in this way, it tends to fluctuate more in price than do other fixed income securities.

Convertible preferred is usually issued with a lower stated dividend rate than nonconvertible preferred, due to the special advantages it offers shareholders. In addition, the conversion of preferred stock into shares of common increases the total number of common shares outstanding, thereby decreasing (or diluting) total earnings per common share.

Callable Preferred

Occasionally, a corporation may decide to issue a special class of stock known as callable (or redeemable) preferred. With this type of stock, a company retains the right to call (or buy back) the stock from investors. It does this by notifying them that it will buy the shares back from them at a specified price on a particular date. Companies often issue preferred stock with a call feature during periods of high interest rates. The right to call back the stock allows them to eliminate a relatively high fixed dividend obligation sometime in the future and sell in its stead an issue of preferred stock with a lower dividend.

Shareholders do not have to surrender their stock when it is called by the corporation, but most will since dividend payments and conversion rights generally cease on the call date. The stock will retain its par value even if it is not surrendered. In return for the call privilege, the corporation usually pays the shareholder a premium over the stock's par value at the call (such as $103 for a $100 par value stock).

Combinations ← all are possible

A corporation may decide to issue a preferred stock with more than one of the features described above. A single preferred issue can include participating, cumulative, convertible and/or callable features.

Guaranteed Stock

When payment of dividends is guaranteed by a corporation other than the issuing corporation, the stock is known as guaranteed stock. In the past, guarantees were used primarily to build large railway systems, industrial and public utility companies and allied enterprises. Since dividend payments are guaranteed by a corporation other than the issuer, guaranteed stock is considered a dual security, although it provides equity only in the issuing corporation.

Transferability of Ownership

Shares of stock are negotiable; that is, a shareholder can give away, transfer, assign or sell shares in the marketplace with very few restrictions. Because of this negotiability and the ease with which ownership of shares can be transferred, it is important to understand what a stock certificate represents, why a certificate is negotiable and how transfers of ownership take place.

The Stock Certificate

A stock certificate is physical evidence of a person's share in the ownership of a corporation and individual stock certificates may be issued for any number of shares. As an example, if an investor buys 100 shares of General Motors at one time, she will receive one certificate for 100 shares. If another investor buys 22 shares of GM, that person will receive one certificate for 22 shares.

Stock certificates contain a lot of information. Some of the information an investor can find printed on the face of a certificate includes the company's name, the names of some of its officers and directors, the name of the transfer agent, the number of shares the certificate represents, the name of the investor and more. In addition, each certificate is printed with its own, unique CUSIP (Committee on Uniform Securities Identification Procedures) number, which helps identify and track the certificate in the event that it becomes lost or stolen.

Negotiability

Negotiability (or transferability) is a key characteristic of corporate stock. It is, simply, the stockholder's right to assign, give, transfer or sell shares to another person without a third party's permission (other securities, such as limited partnership interests and certain government issues, are not as easily transferred).

K101

Anytime a stockholder wishes to transfer ownership of shares he or she owns to someone else, certain transfer procedures must be followed. To transfer ownership of any stock, the registered owner must either sign the stock certificate on the back in the place designated for the owner's signature or sign a stock power. Once the certificate or a stock power has been signed, an exchange member, authorized person of a broker-dealer or an officer of a national bank must guarantee the signature.

Transfer Procedures

Two of the parties involved in the transfer of ownership and the issuance of stock certificates are the transfer agent and the registrar. Transfer and registration are two distinct functions that, by law, cannot be performed by a single person or one department within the same institution. Issuers typically use banks and trust companies to handle these functions.

The transfer agent and the registrar are responsible for transferring and keeping records of stock ownership.

Transfer agent. The transfer of corporate stocks is supervised and certified by a transfer agent. Although most corporations employ an outside organization to act as their transfer agent, a few large corporations do their own transfer work. If a corporation does select a third party to act as its transfer agent, the agent will usually handle other duties for the corporation as well, including the distribution of information, proxies and dividends to shareholders.

The primary function of the transfer agent is to see that certificates are issued in the correct owner's name (particularly in the event of a sale of stock or after any other transfer of ownership). The transfer agent then has the certificates signed by the appropriate corporate officer(s), affixes the corporate seal, delivers them to the new owner (or transferee) and then destroys the original certificates registered in the seller's name.

For each registered shareholder, the transfer agent records the name, full address, Social Security number and the total number of shares owned.

Registrar. The maintenance of all of the various records relating to the stock certificates issued by a corporation is the responsibility of the registrar. Stock transactions requiring new certificate registration must, therefore, be routed through the registrar as well as through the transfer agent. One of the responsibilities of the registrar is to ensure that a corporation does not have more stock outstanding than can be accounted for on the company's books. Unlike the transfer agent, the registrar must be independent of the issuing corporation but, like the transfer agent, it is usually a bank or trust company.

Chapter Review

Questions

1. Which of the following represent ownership (equity) in a company?

   I. corporate bonds
   II. common stock
   III. preferred stock
   IV. mortgage bonds

   ___(A) I and IV
   ___(B) II
   _✗_(C) II and III
   ___(D) I, II, III and IV

2. Treasury stock

   I. has voting rights and is entitled to a dividend when declared.
   II. has no voting rights and no dividend entitlement.
   III. has been issued and repurchased by the company.
   IV. is authorized but unissued stock.

   ___(A) I and III
   ___(B) I and IV
   _✗_(C) II and III
   ___(D) II and IV

3. In which of the following ways may a company declare dividends?

   I. cash
   II. stock
   III. stock of another company

   ___(A) I
   ___(B) I and II
   ___(C) I and III
   _✗_(D) I, II and III

4. ABC Company currently has earnings of $4 and pays a $.50 quarterly dividend. The market price of ABC is $40. What is the current yield?

____(A)   1.25%
____(B)   5%
____(C)   10%
__X__(D) 15%

(handwritten: $\frac{Div}{price}$ .50 x 4 = $2 2/40 = 5% of 100)

5. A corporation must have stockholder approval to

__X__(A) split its stock 3 for 1.
____(B)   repurchase 100,000 shares of stock for the treasury.
____(C)   declare a 15% stock dividend.
____(D)   declare a cash dividend.

6. Limited liability regarding ownership in a large, publicly held U.S. corporation means all of the following EXCEPT *(handwritten: the one it doesn't mean)*

____(A)   investors might lose the amount of their investment.
__X__(B) investors might lose their investment plus the difference between their investment and par value.
____(C)   investors' shares are non-assessable.
____(D)   investors are not liable to the full extent of their personal property.

7. Stockholders' preemptive rights include which of the following?

____(A)   the right to serve as an officer on the board of directors
__X__(B) the right to maintain proportionate ownership interest in the corporation
____(C)   the right to purchase treasury stock
____(D)   the right to a subscription price on stock

8. Common stockholders' rights include

I.   a residual claim to assets at dissolution.
II.   a vote for the amount of stock dividend to be paid.
III. a vote in matters of recapitalization. *(handwritten: (splits etc))*
IV.   a claim against dividends that are in default.

____(A)   I
____(B)   II and III
__X__(C) I and III
____(D)   III and IV

9. When an issuing corporation provides a proxy, it is

   X (A)   providing a legal form of absentee voting, effected through a "limited power of attorney."

   (B)   providing a document authorizing a third party to buy and sell securities.

   (C)   setting company operating policy.

   (D)   offering the right to present shareholders to purchase more shares below the current market price.

10. When a corporation holds treasury stock, it has the option of

   (A)   reissuing it as debt securities.

   (B)   not disclosing it to the registrar.

   X (C)   retiring it.

   (D)   registering it under any name it chooses.

Answer Key

1. C.

2. C.

3. D.

4. B.

5. A.

6. B.

7. B.

8. C.

9. A.

10. C.

Chapter Two

Debt Securities

Key Terms

2.10 Accrued interest

2.12 Bearer

2.5 Call

2.2 Coupon

2.6 Current yield

2.5 Discount

2.11 Investment grade

2.9 Liquidity

2.5 2.2 Par

2.4 Principal

2.4 Series

2.3 Sinking fund

2.4 Trust indenture

2.6 Yield

2.8 Yield to call

Balloon 2.3

Book-entry 2.13

Call protection 2.16

Covenants 2.4

Debt service 2.4

Funded debt 2.2

Issuer 2.2

Nominal yield 2.6

Premium 2.5

Registered 2.12

Serial 2.3

Term 2.3

Volatility 2.10

Yield curve 2.9

Yield to maturity 2.6

K102

Debt Securities

Bonds of various types (including those issued by municipalities, corporations, the U.S. government and governmental agencies) are commonly referred to as debt securities; that is, they represent a loan by an investor to the issuer. In return for this loan, the issuer promises both to repay the debt at a specified date in the future and to pay the investor interest on the amount it has borrowed. Because the interest rate an investor receives is normally set by the issuer at the time the bond is issued, bonds are also referred to as **fixed income securities**.

Characteristics of Bonds

Issuers

Municipalities. Municipal securities are the debt obligations of state and local governments and their agencies. Most are issued to raise capital to finance public works and construction projects that benefit the general public (as opposed to financing the municipality's current expenses).

Corporations. Debt issued by corporations (also known as funded debt) includes both short-term debt (notes) and long-term debt (bonds). Issuing long-term debt securities is an important source of corporate capital for plant construction, equipment purchases and working capital.

U.S. government and government agencies. The federal government is not only the nation's largest borrower, it is also its most secure credit risk. The bills, notes and bonds it issues to finance operations are backed by the full faith and credit of the government and by the government's almost unlimited powers of taxation.

Purpose

Loans by investors. A bond represents an issuer's promise to repay money it has borrowed (the principal of the loan) at some point in the future. The individual bonds that make up the entire bond issue usually have a face (or par) value of $1,000.

Interest Paid by Issuer

In return for the money loaned to it by investors, the bond issuer promises to pay them interest for that loan at a fixed rate and on particular dates. Those interest payment dates are set when the bonds are issued. The interest rate (or coupon) is calculated from the par value of the bond. Interest on the outstanding loan balance of a bond accrues daily and (in most cases) is paid in semiannual installments over the life of the bond. An investor who owns a $1,000 bond that pays 7% interest will receive $70 ($1,000 x 7% = $70) in income each year in the form of two $35 semiannual installments. The final interest payment will be made on the date the bond is scheduled to mature.

Maturities

The maturity date (the date on which the loan principal is repaid to the investor) varies from bond to bond and from issuer to issuer. Investors can find bonds with a wide range of maturities in today's market. There are three basic types of bond maturity structures: term, serial and balloon.

only 2 types

Term maturity. If an issuer chooses to structure a bond issue so that the principal matures all at once, it is known as a term bond. Because all of the principal is repaid at one time, most issuers of term bonds set up a special account in which to begin accumulating the money that will be due. This special account is referred to as a sinking fund.

Serial maturity. Not all bond issuers choose to repay their bonds by making a single, lump-sum payment on the specified maturity date. Some issuers prefer to schedule repayment of the bond over a period of time and choose to structure their bond issues with serial maturities. When a bond is designed with serial maturities, portions of the bond will mature at intervals until the entire balance has been repaid. Figure 2.1 is an example of bonds issued with serial maturities.

This announcement is neither an offer to sell nor a solicitation of an offer to buy these securities. The offer is made only by the Prospectus.

New Issue / July 14th, 1994

$2,875,000
MicroScam, Inc.

8.75% Bonds
due 2004 - 2015

Amount	Due	Coupon	Yield
$350,000	2004	8.75%	8.45%
$550,000	2008	8.75%	8.50%
$650,000	2010	8.75%	8.65%
$650,000	2012	8.75%	8.75%
$675,000	2015	8.75%	9.00%

Copies of the Prospectus may be obtained in any State in which this announcement is circulated only from such of the undersigned as may legally offer these securities in such State.

Dean Emeritus, Inc.
Madre Merrill Corp.
The Kimkentu Group

AFAP Securities
Worthmore, Moola
Churn, Burn, Spurn, Inc.

Fig. 2.1 A tombstone listing serial maturities.

Balloon maturity. Occasionally, an issuer will choose to repay part of a bond's principal before the final maturity date (as with serial maturities), but pay off the major portion of it at maturity. This type of maturity schedule is called a balloon, or serial and balloon, maturity.

K102

New Issue / July 14th, 1994

$1,250,000
DataWaq, Inc.
Series Bonds

Series	Issue Date	$ Amount of Issue	Interest Rate	Maturity Date
L	Jul 1994	$400,000	7.25%	Jul 2014
M	Nov 1996	$250,000	7.35%	Dec 2016
N	Jun 1998	$400,000	7.65%	Jun 2025
O	Jul 2000	$200,000	7.50%	Jul 2030

Copies of the Prospectus may be obtained in any State in which this announcement is circulated only from such of the undersigned as may legally offer these securities in such State.

Dean Emeritus, Inc.
Madre Merrill Corp.
The Kimkentu Group

AFAP Securities
Worthmore, Moola
Churn, Burn, Spurn, Inc.

Fig. 2.2 A bond issued in series form.

Series issues. Instead of placing all of its bonds in the hands of investors at one time, any bond issuer (term, serial or balloon) may spread out its bond sales over several years — that is, issue them in separate **series**.

Trust Indenture

As established by the Trust Indenture Act of 1939, non-exempt corporate bonds must be issued under a trust indenture, a legal contract between the bond issuer and a trustee that represents the bondholders (the trust indenture is discussed more fully in Chapter Three). Although you will see a reference to the trust indenture on the face of the bond certificate, the indenture itself is a rather lengthy document that is not automatically supplied to the bondholder.

Within the trust indenture, covenants (or promises) identify the rights of the bondholders and name the entity that will act as the trustee (a bank or a trust company, usually). The trustee ensures compliance with the covenants of the indenture and acts on behalf of the bondholders in the event of a default by the issuer. The indenture also lists the qualifications and responsibilities of the trustee.

Federal and municipal governments are exempt from the provisions of the Trust Indenture Act, although municipal revenue bonds are typically issued with a trust indenture.

Debt Service

payments made each year for princ and interest

Level debt service. The two most common methods issuers use to calculate payments on a serial bond are called level and decreasing debt patterns. If the issuer chooses a level debt pattern for its repayments, each payment will be for the same dollar amount, but the portion of the payment that represents principal and the portion that represents interest will change over time. As the issuer repays the loan, the outstanding balance (the principal) will be reduced. As the principal goes down, so will the amount

Level Debt Service

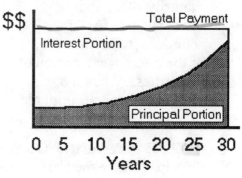

Fig. 2.3 Payments remain the same with level service.

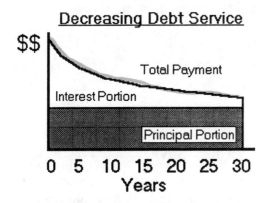

Decreasing Debt Service

Fig. 2.4 Payments decrease with decreasing service.

of interest the issuer owes. Since the issuer wants to make level payments, it will increase its repayment of principal as the interest decreases. The net result will be equal payments over the life of the bond (see Fig. 2.3).

Decreasing debt service. In the case of decreasing debt service, the issuer wants to repay the principal due to the bondholders in installments of equal size. Since these principal payments are reducing the outstanding debt, the amount of interest due is also being reduced. If the principal repayments stay level and the interest paid goes down, the total payment becomes smaller over time. The net effect is decreasing payments, illustrated by Figure 2.4.

Call Features

An issuer may reserve the right to redeem (or call) a bond issue before its final maturity date. The fact that a bond is callable will be established before it is issued (term bonds are more likely to be callable than other types of bonds). Callable bonds can often be identified by the way they are quoted. A "Jan. 1995/00" bond matures in January of the year 2000, but is callable between January 1995 and its maturity in January 2000. Interest rates on callable bonds tend to be higher than on comparable, noncallable bonds. Callable bonds can be advantageous to the issuer for the following reasons:

- If general interest rates decline, the issuer can call in bonds on which it must pay a high rate of interest and replace them with a new issue of bonds with a lower coupon.
- The issuer can call in bonds to reduce its debt when it chooses (once it has passed the initial call date).
- The issuer can replace short-term debt issues with long-term issues, and vice versa.
- The issuer can call bonds as a means of forcing the conversion of convertible corporate securities.

Pricing

Par, premium and discount. All debt securities are issued with a face (or par) value, typically $1,000. Par represents the dollar amount of the contract between the issuer and the investor and is the amount repaid to investors per bond when the bond is due. The maturity date is the point at which the issuer redeems the debt obligation at par value and interest no longer accrues.

Either before or after bonds begin to trade in the secondary market, they may sell at any price. Investors can expect to see bonds issued or trading at par, below par (that is, at a discount) or above par (at a premium). The two primary factors affecting a

K102

bond's market value are the market's perception of the investment quality of the bond and overall interest rates.

Yields

One way investors evaluate debt securities is by comparing their yields. Affecting the buyer's yield are interest rate, time to maturity, price at purchase and sale, and call features. Investors must make sure they are comparing yields calculated by the same method.

Face rate → constant

Nominal yield. A bond's nominal yield (or coupon rate) is a fixed percentage of a bond's par value (normally $1,000). It is set at issuance and printed on the face of the bond. A coupon of 6%, for instance, means the issuer will pay $60 interest every year until the bond matures.

Current yield. The interest an investor receives (the nominal yield) does not tell the whole story of potential return, however. Although the interest rate is calculated on the bond's face value of $1,000, the investor may not have paid that amount for the bond. Current yield is a measure of the return an investor receives compared to the current price of the security.

$$\frac{\text{Annual Interest}}{\text{Current Market Price}} = \text{Current Yield}$$

Fig. 2.5 Current yield formula.

Relationship of yield to price. A bond traded at par ($1,000) will have identical nominal and current yields. An investor who pays $1,000 for a 6% bond will actually receive a 6% return on investment, or $60 per year. A bond purchased at a discount will have a current yield that is higher than its nominal yield. For example, a 4 1/2% coupon bond trading at a discounted price of $750 has an annual interest payment of $45 and a current yield of 6% ($45 / $750 = 6%). Conversely, a bond purchased at a premium will have a current yield that is lower than its nominal yield. An investor who buys a 10% coupon bond trading at a premium of $1,200 receives an annual interest payment of $100 and a current yield of 8.33% ($100 / $1,200 = 8.33%).

While current yield accounts for the dollars actually invested in the bond, it does not take into account a gain or loss on the sale of the bond or whether the bond is held to maturity.

Yield to maturity. A bond's yield to maturity (or YTM) is a measure of the annual return on the investment from purchase until maturity. This measure of yield does account for the difference between the amount an investor pays for the bond and the amount the investor receives at the time the bond matures. For example, an investor who purchases a 10% coupon bond at 105 (or $1,050 per bond) can expect $100 in interest per year. If he holds that bond to maturity, he will have realized a loss of $50

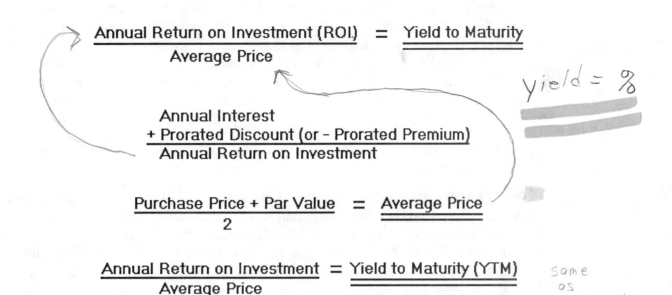

$$\frac{\text{Annual Return on Investment (ROI)}}{\text{Average Price}} = \text{Yield to Maturity}$$

Annual Interest
+ Prorated Discount (or - Prorated Premium)
Annual Return on Investment

$$\frac{\text{Purchase Price + Par Value}}{2} = \text{Average Price}$$

$$\frac{\text{Annual Return on Investment}}{\text{Average Price}} = \text{Yield to Maturity (YTM)}$$

yield = %

same as top formula

Fig. 2.6 Yield to Maturity rule of thumb.

on his investment (purchase price of $1,050 less the maturity value of $1,000). This capital loss should be taken into account when calculating the actual yearly earnings of a bond bought at a premium. Yield to maturity on a premium bond will always be lower than the nominal yield.

Two bonds with equivalent current yields may have quite different yields to maturity. Two 5% bonds purchased at 90, for example, will have different yields to maturity if they have a different number of years remaining until maturity. The reason is that the investor in the longer term bond has to wait a longer time to realize the value of the discount. Prorating the $100 discount over 10 years is the equivalent of an additional $10 per year in income. Prorating the same $100 discount over two years means an additional yield of $50 per year.

Discount Bond Yields

10-Year Bond	2-Year Bond
$50 Annual Interest + $10 Prorated Discount $60 Annual ROI	$50 Annual Interest + $50 Prorated Discount $100 Annual ROI
$\dfrac{\$900\ \text{Price} + \$1,000\ \text{Par}}{2}$ = $950 Average Price	$\dfrac{\$900\ \text{Price} + \$1,000\ \text{Par}}{2}$ = $950 Average Price
$\dfrac{\$60}{\$950}$ = .06316, or 6.3% YTM	$\dfrac{\$100}{\$950}$ = .1053, or 10.53% YTM

Fig. 2.7 The effect of time on discount bond yields.

K102

The yield to maturity of discount bonds, by contrast, is higher than the coupon rate, since the investor realizes a capital gain when the bond is redeemed at par. If an investor purchases a bond with a 10% coupon at a discounted price of 97 ($970 per $1,000 face value bond) she will receive $100 a year in interest. In addition, the investor stands to realize a gain of $30 ($1,000 value at redemption less the $970 purchase price) if the bond is held to maturity. The decrease in the bond's price helps bring its yield back into line with the yields of bonds newly issued at higher coupon rates.

Yield to maturity will differ from current yield whenever the price paid for the security differs from par value.

Yield to call. A bond may be called anytime after a call date set at the time of issuance (before that date, a bond is said to have call protection). If a bond is called early, any discount will accrue faster (resulting in a higher yield) or any premium will be lost over a shorter period (resulting in a lower yield). If the bond is callable at a premium, then the amount to be prorated is the difference between the price paid and the call price (par plus the premium).

Unless the bond issuer is paying a call premium, the yield of a bond bought at par and called away before its maturity date will remain unchanged. An investor who buys a 6% bond for $1,000 receives a 6% return on the bond for however long it is held. That fact is not changed when the issuer calls the bond and repays the $1,000 original investment.

An investor who buys a callable bond at a premium, on the other hand, stands to lose money faster if the bond is called at par before its maturity date. Since one of the reasons the bond's price is at a premium to par is because coupon rates on newly issued bonds are lower, the sooner the bonds are called away, the sooner the premium the investor paid is "lost." Less of the premium the investor paid for the bond in the secondary market will be recovered by the higher coupon rate she receives, thus the yield to call will be lower than the nominal yield, current yield or yield to maturity if the bond is called at par.

Yield to call can be calculated the same way as yield to maturity, using the rule-of-thumb method. The difference is that the discount or premium is prorated over the time remaining to the first call date (bonds may be issued with more than one call date) and the call price is used instead of the par value.

For a bond purchased at a discount, yield to call will always be greater than yield to maturity. For bonds purchased at a premium, yield to call may be greater or less than the yield to maturity depending on the relationship between the purchase price and the call price. If the purchase price of the bond is lower than the call price, then the yield to maturity will be lowest. If the purchase price is higher than the call price, the yield to call will be the lowest.

Tell Client → call bonds sold at a premium with call price less than premium.

The Relationship of Yield to Price

Bond prices and yields have an inverse relationship. As bond prices go up, yields go down (and vice versa). If a bond is trading at a discount, the current yield increases; if a bond is trading at a premium, the current yield decreases.

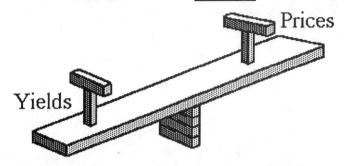

Yield and price have an inverse relationship—

as one goes up, the other goes down.

Fig. 2.8 Inverse relationship of rates and prices.

Short-Term vs. Long-Term Yields

A positive yield curve is referred to as "normal curve" due to the fact that most investors are willing to pay a higher price for the benefits of liquidity (that is, the ease with which an investment can be converted to cash without an excessive loss of principal). Short-term investments tend to be more easily bought and sold (that is, more liquid) than long-term investments of the same type and quality, so investors are generally willing to accept lower yields for shorter maturities. Conversely, investors who assume more risks by purchasing longer-term maturities (risks that include lower marketability, the effects of changing interest rates on principal, and the time-value of money) demand a higher yield in return.

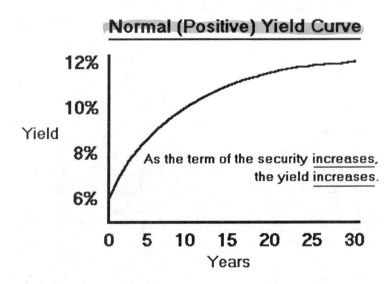

Normal (Positive) Yield Curve

As the term of the security increases, the yield increases.

Fig. 2.9 Rates rise as terms lengthen.

A yield curve is typically plotted on a graph that shows the yields of bonds of the same quality with maturities ranging from close to far away. The resulting curve allows you to analyze whether short-term interest rates are higher or lower than long-term rates in today's market.

Changing interest rates have a greater effect on bonds with long maturities than on those with short. As interest rates rise, the price of long-term bonds drops more quickly than the

K102

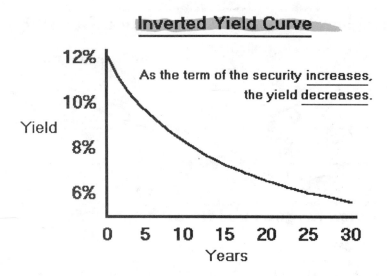

Inverted Yield Curve

As the term of the security increases, the yield decreases.

Fig. 2.10 Rates fall as terms lengthen.

price of short-term bonds. An advantage for investors willing to put money into longer-term investments is that long-term yields (and therefore prices) tend to be less volatile (changeable) than short-term yields.

At times, the yield curve is inverted and has a **negative** (or downward) slope. An inverted curve is one in which bonds with shorter maturities have higher yields than bonds of longer terms. This rather unusual situation occurs when interest rates are temporarily very high and investors expect them to decline.

Accrued Interest

Interest payments on bonds generally occur at six-month intervals. In between those dates, interest accrues without being paid. Awareness of this fact becomes important when a bond is sold and it becomes necessary to determine how much interest the seller will receive from the buyer.

Unless otherwise noted, the majority of bonds trade with accrued interest. That is, accrued interest is added to the price the buyer pays to the seller. At the next interest payment date, the buyer receives the interest due for the full six months. Accrued interest is paid from the date of the last interest payment up to, but not including, the settlement date.

Rating Bonds

Various rating services, such as Standard & Poor's, Moody's and Fitch's evaluate and publish their ratings of bond issues. (Fitch's rates corporate bonds, municipal bonds and commercial paper; White's rates municipal bonds; Standard & Poor's and Moody's rate both corporate and municipal bonds.) Moody's, Standard & Poor's and Fitch's base their bond ratings primarily on the issuer's creditworthiness; that is, the ability of the issuer to make interest and principal payments as they come due. The less likely the issuer is able to make payments as promised, the lower the rating given the bond. If the prospects are good that the issuer will be able to make the required payments and make them on time, the bond will be granted a high rating. (White's bases its ratings on a bond's marketability rather than on its creditworthiness.)

The ratings on bonds may change over time. If the issuer's ability to make interest and principal payments changes after the bond is first issued, the rating services will reevaluate the bond and make changes in their ratings as necessary.

Investment grade. The Comptroller of the Currency, the FDIC, the Federal Reserve and state banking authorities have established policies determining which securities banks can

Standard (all letters standard)
AAA

Moody (different)
Aaa

Standard & Poor's	Moody's	Interpretation
("Bank Grade" or "Investment Grade" bonds)		
AAA	Aaa	Highest rating. Capacity to repay principal and interest judged high.
AA	Aa	Very strong. Only slightly less secure than highest rating.
A	A	Judged to be slightly more susceptible to adverse economic conditions.
BBB	Baa *Triple B*	Adequate capacity to repay principal and interest. Slightly speculative.
("Speculative" or "Non-Investment Grade" bonds) JUNK		
BB	Ba	Predominantly speculative.
B	B	Issuer has missed one or more interest or principal payments.
C	Caa *Triple C*	No interest is being paid.
D *Don't Buy*	D	In default. Payment of interest and/or principal is in arrears.

Fig. 2.11 Comparing S&P's and Moody's rating systems.

purchase. A municipal bond must be considered of investment grade (that is, with a rating of "BBB/Baa" or higher) to be suitable for purchase by banks. "Investment grade" bonds are the same as "bank grade" bonds. As you can see from Figure 2.11, bonds rated BBB or Baa may involve some uncertainty, but banks may still buy them.

Finer gradations of these categories are also possible. A plus sign or minus sign in a Standard & Poor's rating would indicate that the bond falls within the top or bottom of that particular category. A1 and Baa1 are used by Moody's to indicate the highest quality bonds within those two categories. Moody's also provides ratings for short-term municipal notes, designating MIG 1 as the highest quality and MIG 4 as the lowest.

Specific criteria used to rate corporate and municipal bonds include:

- amount and composition of existing debt;
- stability of issuer's cash flows;
- ability of issuer to meet scheduled payments of interest and principal on its debt obligations;
- asset protection; and
- management ability.

Relationship of Rating to Yield

Generally, the higher the bond rating, the lower the yield. Investors are willing to accept a lower return on their investment if they expect their principal to be safe and annual interest payments more predictable.

Registration of Bonds

Coupon (Bearer) Bonds

An issuer that does not want the trouble and expense of tracking (or registering) the investors in its bonds can issue those bonds in coupon (or bearer) form. This means that no records are kept of the purchasers by the issuer, and the securities are issued without an investor's name printed anywhere on the certificate. Because coupon bonds are not registered, whoever is currently in possession of that bond is entitled to collect interest, trade the bond, or deliver it for redemption.

A bearer bond will have interest coupons attached to it: the person in possession of the bond can collect interest by simply clipping the appropriate coupon and sending (or delivering) it to the issuer's paying agent. Individual coupons represent promissory notes, payable to the bearer. When the bond matures, the bearer is entitled to submit it to the paying agent and receive the principal.

To trade bearer bonds, the buyer and seller simply exchange bonds for money: no proof of ownership is necessary. A legal change in ownership occurs when the seller delivers the certificate to the buyer. Bearer bonds are not currently being issued, though a limited number are still trading.

Registered Bonds

The most common form of bond issued today is the registered bond. When a registered bond is issued, the issuer's transfer agent keeps a record of the bondholder's name. The name of the person who purchased the bond (the owner) will appear on the face of the bond certificate.

Fully registered. When bonds are registered as to both principal and interest, the transfer agent maintains a list of bondholders and updates this roster as bond ownership changes. Interest payments are automatically sent to bondholders of record in the transfer agent's books. Before the transfer agent can transfer any type of registered bond (which it does by canceling the seller's certificates and issuing new ones in the name of the buyer), the seller must make the certificate negotiable by properly endorsing it.

Registered as to principal only. Certificates for these bonds have interest coupons attached to the bond, just like the interest coupons that come with bearer bonds. The registered bondholder clips these coupons as they come due and forwards them to the paying agent for collection. Bonds registered as to principal only have the owner's name printed on the front, although the coupons are in bearer form.

When bonds registered as to principal only are sold or otherwise transferred, they are not canceled and reissued in the name of the new owner (as are fully registered bonds). Instead, as transfers are made the names of the new owners are recorded (in order) on the bond certificate and on the registration record of the issuer. Like bearer bonds, bonds registered as to principal only are not currently being issued.

Book-Entry Bonds *no certificate ; computer entry*

An investor in a bond that has been issued in book-entry form does not receive a certificate. Instead, banks maintain computerized records of the ownership of the security.

Bond Tables

To understand bond tables, you need to know the difference between bond and basis points.

- Bond points are used to measure both bond prices and bond yields. One point is equivalent to $10, 1% of the par value of $1,000.
- Basis points are used to measure bond yields. One basis point is equal to 10 (1/100 of a percentage point or .01% of $1,000).

Bond Points vs. Basis Points

	Value	Measures
Bond Points	1%	of par ($1,000) or yield (100%)
Basis Points	.01% (.0001)	of yield

Fig. 2.12 The difference between bond and basis points.

As an example, the price of a bond that traded at 97 on Monday and 94 on Friday has decreased by three points (which translates into a dollar change of $30). The yield of another bond has increased from 4.70% to 5.10%, an increase of 40 basis points or .40% (each basis point represents 1/100 of a percentage point, so 40/100 of 1% equals .40%).

Bond yields are arranged in yield tables in The Bond Basis Book. The Basis Book contains yield to maturity tables arranged by coupon rates, time to maturity and bond prices. Generally, the coupon rates of these tables range from 0% to 12%. Each coupon table displays yields to maturity based on maturities ranging from one month to 40 years. If you know a bond's coupon rate, the length of time to maturity and its market price, you can use the tables to find the bond's yield to maturity. Conversely, if you know the coupon rate, the maturity date and the intended yield to maturity, you can determine the selling price of the bond. You can also use this table to determine the optimum selling price of a bond.

Basis means YTM

9.80 Basis

Bond Basis Book Example

Yield	14-6	15-0	15-6	16-0	16-6	17-0	17-6	18-0
			Years and months			9 1/2%		
5.00	146.02	147.09	148.14	149.16	150.16	151.13	152.08	153.00
5.20	143.41	144.41	145.38	146.32	147.24	148.14	149.02	149.87
5.40	140.86	141.78	142.68	143.56	144.41	145.24	146.04	146.83
5.60	138.38	139.23	140.06	140.86	141.65	142.41	143.15	143.87
5.80	135.95	136.73	137.50	138.24	138.96	139.66	140.34	141.00
6.00	133.58	134.30	135.00	135.68	136.34	136.98	137.60	138.21
	132.42	133.11			135	135.67		
9.40	100.78	100.80	100.81	100.82	100.83	100.84	100.85	100.86
9.50	100.00	100.00	100.00	100.00	100.00	100.00	100.00	100.00
9.60	99.23	99.21	99.20	99.19	99.18	99.17	99.16	99.15
9.70	98.46	98.44	98.41	98.39	98.37	98.35	98.33	98.31
9.80	97.70	97.67	97.63	97.60	97.57	97.54	97.51	97.49
9.90	96.95	96.91	96.86	96.82	96.78	96.74	96.70	96.67
10.00	96.21	96.16	96.10	96.05	96.00	95.95	95.91	95.86
10.20	94.76	94.68	94.61	94.53	94.47	94.40	94.34	94.28
10.40	93.34	93.24	93.14	93.06	92.97	92.89	92.81	92.74
10.60	91.94	91.83	91.72	91.61	91.51	91.42	91.33	91.24
10.80	90.58	90.45	90.32	90.20	90.09	89.98	89.87	89.78
11.00	89.25	89.10	88.96	88.82	88.69	88.57	88.46	88.35
11.20	87.95	87.78	87.62	87.48	87.34	87.20	87.08	86.96
11.40	86.67	86.49	86.32	86.16	86.01	85.86	85.73	85.60
11.60	85.43	85.23	85.05	84.88	84.71	84.56	84.41	84.27
11.80	84.21	84.00	83.81	83.62	83.45	83.28	83.13	82.98
12.00	83.01	82.79	82.59	82.39	82.21	82.04	81.88	81.72

(Handwritten annotations: "new example"; "9½ %"; "AA 9½ coupons"; "16-0 XRX"; "15-0 GE yrs"; "what are prices?"; "yield → not 7.8% on both"; "$976"; "$976.70"; "1.25/8th"; "Gov 97.16 = 16/32"; "16/32 of $10 = $5.00 + 970 $975")

Fig. 2.13 Basis books are useful in interpolation.

Interpolation

Interpolation is a method used to determine the price (or yield) of a bond from a bond table when its actual price (or yield) falls between two numbers listed. In order to calculate the yield, begin by thinking of the table as a continuous plane, with only some points on that plane visible. In between the yields and prices shown are other prices.

If you bought a 9 1/2% bond at 95 that matures in exactly 16 years and wanted to know the bond's true yield to maturity, you first scan down the column headed "16-0" (which indicates 16 years and 0 months). The true yield for the bond priced at 95 will lie between 10.00 and 10.20, the yields for the prices bracketing 95.

The yield will lie at the same relative position between 10.00 and 10.20 that 95 lies between 96.05 and 94.53. The difference between 96.05 and 94.53 in the bond table is 1.52 points, since 96.05 - 94.53 = 1.52. The 95 price is .47 points above the lower price (95 - 94.53 = .47). The bond priced at 95, therefore, represents .47 out of the total difference of 1.52 points. Since .47 / 1.52 = .309 (or 30.9%), the distance between 94.53 and 95 is 30.9% of the distance between 94.53 and 96.05.

Now you need to locate the point that lies 30.9% of the way from 10.20 to 10.00 (notice that we are using the yield numbers in the same order as we used the price numbers on the chart, working from the bottom up). That will be the yield for a bond priced at 95. Subtracting 10.00 from 10.20 gives us .20 basis points, the difference between the two yields. Now find the point lying the same proportionate distance above 10.20 that 95 lies from 94.53. To do that, multiply .20 by 30.9%, to get .06 basis points. Subtract .06 from 10.20, and you find that the yield of a bond priced at 95 is 10.14% (10.20 - .06 = 10.14).

When interpolating yields based on data found in The Bond Basis Book, remember that both the price and the yield are a proportionate distance from the top or bottom number.

Debt Retirement

ways to retire: callable → call it
maturity → it matures
convertible → convert to stock
tender offers in open market

To keep financing flexible, an issuer may reserve the right to call in its debt before the scheduled maturity date. Because the issuer's financial needs may change, an issuer may find it advantageous to retire one debt early to clear the way for new debt financing.

Calling Bonds

Call option. During periods of high interest rates, you are likely to encounter a number of bonds issued with what is known as a call feature (or call option). A call feature in a bond's trust indenture allows the issuing company to call (or buy back) the bonds from investors. The issuer does this by notifying bondholders that it is willing to buy the bonds back from them at a specified price on a particular date (frequently preset at the time the bond is issued).

Call premiums. The right to call back bonds enables issuers to eliminate a relatively high fixed interest payment and issue, in their place, bonds with a lower interest obligation. In return for the call privilege, the issuer usually pays the bondholder a premium (known as a call premium) over the bond's par value at the time of the call. A number of U.S. government bonds, municipal bonds, corporate bonds and preferred stocks are callable at some point over their terms, although some tax-exempt state and local government securities are noncallable.

Sinking fund. In order to facilitate the early retirement of bonds, many issuers establish a sinking fund. The fund is operated by the bond's trustee, which acts to protect the interests of the investors holding the bonds. A sinking fund is part of the trust indenture and may be used to call bonds, pay bonds off at maturity or buy back bonds from investors in the open market.

The issuer deposits cash (or other bonds) with the trustee. In this way, funds are always available for redeeming the bonds and the callable issue can be retired gradually. A sinking fund aids a bond's stability (even in a falling market) due to the fact that the fund itself may be an active buyer of the bonds in the secondary market.

Advantages of a call option. An issue of bonds may be redeemed in full or in part at the option of the issuer. An optional call permits the issuer maximum flexibility. Advantages of having optional call flexibility include the following:

- An issuer can replace high-interest coupon bonds with low- interest coupon bonds.
- An issuer can reduce its debt as it chooses.
- An issuer can replace short-term debt issues with long-term and vice versa.
- An issuer can eliminate bonds with unfavorable trust indenture provisions.

A mandatory call, on the other hand, may be included as part of the trust indenture and would require the issuer to call specified bonds under particular circumstances.

Call protection. Although there can be some disadvantages for investors when bonds are called, they often have some measure of protection. There is often an initial noncallable period following the issuance of the bonds (typically five or ten years). During this period, the issuer is prohibited from calling any of the bonds back from the investors. Once the call protection period has expired, the issuer may elect to call any or all of the bonds. A call protection feature in a trust indenture can be an advantage to bondholders during periods of declining interest rates.

A bond issued with a call feature presents some risks for bondholders. A callable bond paying a high rate of interest, for example, may be called when prevailing interest rates drop. If this occurs, the investor may be unable to obtain a similar yield. This disadvantage is referred to as call risk. To partially compensate investors for future interest payments they won't receive, bonds are generally called at a premium. Issuers rarely call bonds at a premium, however, if they can accomplish the same thing by purchasing them back for less money in the secondary market. U.S. government bonds are callable only at par.

Redemption of Bonds

Notice by a company that it intends to call back an issue of bonds is usually given in the newspapers and other business periodicals 30 to 90 days prior to the call. All registered bondholders are contacted directly by the issuer, but it is the investors' responsibility to be aware of these call dates. The issuer will not pay interest beyond the call date.

Refunding Bonds

Refunding an issue means retiring an outstanding issue of bonds using the money generated by the sale of a new offering. Refunding, like redemption, can be done in full or in part. Generally, an entire issue will be refunded at one time.

Refunding becomes increasingly more common as bonds approach maturity. An issuer might not have sufficient available cash to pay off the issue, or the issuer's financial plans might call for continued borrowing so that it can put its cash to other uses. When an issuer is not in a favorable financial position to refund or retire an issue, it may try to extend the maturity date. Some inducement will then have to be offered to bondholders to obtain agreement to the extension. Those bondholders who do not agree to the extension must be paid in cash.

Tender Offers

When general interest rates are down, companies may wish to redeem bonds (both callable bonds for which the call protection period hasn't expired and noncallable) and replace them with securities paying a lower rate. In a case like this, a corporate bond issuer may make a tender offer to investors for their bonds. Since the bonds are paying attractive interest rates, bondholders are not likely to tender their securities to the issuer unless the offer includes a promise to pay them a substantial cash bonus.

Chapter Review

Questions

1. A trust indenture is a contract between the

    ___(A)   issuer and investor.
    X (B)   issuer and trustee.
    ___(C)   trustee and underwriter.
    ___(D)   issuer and underwriter.

2. Bonds that mature with a smaller amount in the earlier years and a greater amount in later years are called

    ___(A)   series bonds.
    ___(B)   term bonds.
    X (C)   balloon bonds.
    ___(D)   callable bonds.

3. Which of the following are true of bonds?

    I.   Bonds represent a loan to the issuer.
    II.   Bonds give the bondholder ownership in the entity.
    III.   Bonds are issued to finance capital expenditures or to raise working capital.
    IV.   Bonds are junior securities.

    ___(A)   I, II and IV
    X (B)   I and III
    ___(C)   II and III
    ___(D)   I, II, III and IV

4. What type of bonds mature in stages over a succession of years?

    ___(A)   series
    ___(B)   callable
    ___(C)   term
    X (D)   serial

5. As the maturity date approaches, the amount of interest paid out by the issuer would be most reduced on a(n)

    ___(A)   series bond.
    ___(B)   adjustment bond.
    X (C)   serial bond.
    ___(D)   income bond.

6. A bond at par has a coupon rate

    ____(A)   less than current yield.
    ____(B)   less than yield to maturity.
    _✗_(C)   the same as current yield.
    ____(D)   higher than current yield.

7. What is the calculation for determining the current yield on a bond?

    ____(A)   Annual Interest divided by Par Value
    _✗_(B)   Annual Interest divided by Current Market Price
    ____(C)   Yield to Maturity divided by Par Value
    ____(D)   Yield to Maturity divided by Current Market Price

8. The difference between par and a lower market price on a bond is called the

    ____(A)   reallowance.
    ____(B)   spread.
    _✗_(C)   discount.
    ____(D)   premium.

9. Which of the following factors would be least important in rating a bond?

    _✗_(A)   interest rates
    ____(B)   amount and composition of existing debt
    ____(C)   stability of issuer's cash flows
    ____(D)   asset protection

10. A customer purchased a 5% U.S. government bond yielding 6%. A year before the bond matures, new U.S. government bonds are being issued at 4% and the customer sells the 5% bond. The customer

    I.   bought it at a discount.
    II.   bought it at a premium.
    III. sold it at a premium.
    IV.   sold it at a discount.

    _✗_(A)   I and III
    ____(B)   I and IV
    ____(C)   II and III
    ____(D)   II and IV

Answer Key

1. B.

2. C.

3. B.

4. D.

5. C.

6. C.

7. B.

8. C.

9. A.

10. A.

Chapter Three

Corporate Debt

Key Terms

Corporate Debt

Debt securities. Corporate bonds are debt securities. They are issued by corporations that need to raise money for working capital or for capital expenditures such as plant construction, equipment purchases, expansion, etc. and are commonly referred to as funded debt.

Unlike stockholders, corporate bondholders do not have ownership interest in the issuing corporation or a voice in management. In return for their investment, bondholders receive the corporation's promise to repay principal and pay interest on the debt. As creditors of the corporation, bondholders receive preferential treatment over common and preferred stockholders in certain instances. When a corporation files for bankruptcy, the claims of creditors (including bondholders) are settled before the claims of stockholders. For this reason, bonds are sometimes called senior securities.

Par value of a corporate bond is usually $1,000. Issues of less than $1,000 are referred to as baby bonds and are not popular with investors because they tend to be less marketable.

Maturities. Corporate bonds are normally issued with maturity dates ranging up to 40 years or more. The most common maturities are in the 20- to 30-year range. Bonds issued with maturities of less than five years are generally considered short-term (and are usually called corporate notes).

Pricing. Like most bonds, corporate bonds are bought and sold in the secondary market at par, at a premium over par or at a discount from par. Quotes on corporate bonds are stated as percentages of the principal amount of the bond. For example, a bid of 100 means 100% of par, or $1,000.

Changes in bond prices are quoted in newspapers and other business-oriented periodicals in points and a bond point is equal to $10 (1% of $1,000). A bond quote of 98 1/8 means 98 and 1/8th percent (98.125%) of $1,000. The minimum variation for corporate bond quotes is 1/8 (.125%). The price moves from 98 to 98 1/8 to 98 1/4 and so on.

Bond certificate. Each bond certificate contains the following information:

3.2

- name of issuing company;
- type of bond;
- principal amount;
- date of issue;
- maturity date;
- call feature(s);
- interest rate and payment date;
- where interest is payable; and
- reference to trust indenture.

Types of Bonds

Secured Bonds

There are two primary types of corporate bonds: secured and unsecured. The term "secured" is used when the issuer has set aside certain identifiable assets as collateral for the prompt payment of interest and the repayment of principal. In a default (that is, when the issuer has failed to meet its obligations to pay either principal or interest or both), bondholders can lay claim to the assets.

Mortgage bonds. Mortgage bonds are the most popular with investors whose primary interest is in safety of principal. Mortgage bonds are typically secured by a property pledge, lien or mortgage against the issuing corporation's real estate assets.

Collateral trust bonds. Collateral trust bonds are usually issued by corporations that own securities of other companies as investments (these other companies may be subsidiaries of the parent company issuing the collateral trust bonds or nonaffiliated independent corporations). The corporation issues bonds secured by a pledge of these investment securities as collateral. The trust indenture will usually contain a covenant requiring that the pledged securities be held by a trustee.

Collateral trust bonds may be backed by one or more of the following securities:

- stocks and bonds of partially or wholly owned subsidiaries;
- prior lien long-term bonds of the pledging company that have been held in trust to secure short-term bonds;
- another company's stocks and bonds; or
- installment payments or other obligations of the corporation's clients.

Equipment trust certificates. Railroads, airlines, trucking companies and oil companies use equipment trust certificates (or equipment notes and bonds) to finance the purchase of transportation equipment. _Rolling stock_

Title to the newly acquired equipment is held in trust (usually by a bank) until all certificates have been paid in full. Since certificates usually mature before the equipment wears out, principal is generally less than the value of the property securing the certificates.

Few other corporate securities are as strongly backed as equipment trust certificates. Though mortgage bonds are technically the safest form of corporate debt, real estate is not as easily sold as transportation equipment. Equipment trust certificates, therefore, are generally considered to offer greater safety of principal. Consequently, yields on these certificates may be quite low.

Unsecured Bonds

Debentures. Unsecured bonds have no specific collateral backing. There are two primary types of unsecured bonds: debentures and subordinated debentures. Debentures are backed by the general credit of the issuing corporation. In other words, investors simply believe that the corporation will pay its debts. The owner of a debenture is considered a general creditor of the corporation. Debentures are considered less safe than secured bonds, but safer than subordinated debentures or preferred stock. The issuing corporation promises to pay back principal and interest, just as it does with secured bonds.

underneath, below, junior

Subordinated debentures. Subordinated debentures are so called because the claims of their owners are subordinated to the claims of other general creditors, including owners of ordinary debentures. Subordinated debentures appeal to the investor because they generally offer higher income than either straight debentures or secured bonds and often have conversion features.

Guaranteed Bonds

This is like having someone cosign a loan for you

If a corporation issues guaranteed bonds, a company other than the issuer (such as a parent company to a subsidiary) has guaranteed payment of principal and interest. This effectively increases the safety of the issue.

Income Bonds

know this cold

Income bonds (also known as adjustment bonds) are sold with a promise to repay the bond principal in full at maturity. They pay interest on the bond only if the corporation's earnings are sufficient to meet the interest payment and if the payment is declared by the board of directors. Hence the name, income bonds.

chapter 11 bankruptcy, companys that come back

Income bonds are traded flat in the secondary market; that is, the bonds are bought and sold without any accrued interest paid by the buyer to the seller. Because there is no promise to repay regular fixed interest payments, income bonds usually offer higher interest rates than do other types of bonds.

hi yld

Zero Coupon Bonds

A relatively recent addition to the bond market, zero coupon bonds do not have interest coupons attached nor do the issuers make annual interest payments. Investors

20yr
$50/$1000
1000 Par at deep discount

who purchase them, therefore, do not receive interest. Instead, they purchase a bond at a price lower than the bond's $1,000 par value and can redeem it for par on the maturity date. The "interest" earned on the bond is the difference between the price paid initially and the amount received at maturity. Zero coupon bonds are issued both by corporations and by municipalities and they may be created by broker-dealers from other types of securities, including those issued by the federal government.

Even though interest is not paid until the bond matures, the investor who owns corporate or government zeroes owes income tax each year on a portion of that amount, just as though it had been received in cash. Since the annual interest is not prorated on a straight-line basis and the investor is apportioned a different amount each year, the issuer of the bond is required to send the investor an IRS Form 1099 annually showing the amount of interest subject to taxation. Final determination of the amount of taxable interest may be made by the IRS.

Long-term zero coupon bonds issued by various broker-dealers and based on securities issued by the federal government are called STRIPS (Separate Trading of Registered Interest and Principal of Securities).

accretion *difference in what you pay to what you got at maturity*

Because they do not pay interest until maturity, zero coupon bonds are more volatile in price than other fixed income securities (and don't trade with accrued interest). As noted in Chapter Two, deeply discounted long-term bonds react more sharply to interest rate fluctuations than do short-term bonds and bonds selling near par. Zero coupon bonds are the ultimate in deep-discount, long-term debt. In effect, the zero coupon bond locks in an unchanging interest rate for its entire life.

If that rate is relatively good, investors will pay dearly to receive it. If the rate is relatively low, investors will not buy the securities unless they are selling at an especially deep discount. So a decrease or increase in interest rates will cause a sharper decrease or increase in the price of a zero coupon bond than in the price of an interest-bearing bond with a similar yield.

Liquidation

Liquidation priority. The backing of a bond is of greatest concern when a corporation goes into liquidation. In such a case, strict rules are followed for paying off employees (who are paid first), creditors and shareholders of a corporation. In order of priority, liquidation occurs as follows:

- the Internal Revenue Service;
- holders of secured debt;
- holders of unsecured debt and general creditors;
- holders of subordinated debt;
- preferred shareholders; and
- common shareholders.

The Trust Indenture

The Trustee

The Trust Indenture Act of 1939 requires that a corporation appoint a trustee for its bonds, usually a commercial bank or trust company. This trustee, which represents the bondholders and is independent of the issuer, helps to prepare the issue. In the trust indenture (an agreement between the issuer and the trustee) the corporation agrees to abide by certain covenants or promises.

Certain types of securities are exempted from the provisions of the act, including securities issued by municipalities and the federal government. The act also exempts securities not issued under an indenture, as long as the total amount of securities issued by a single entity does not exceed $2,000,000 in a 12-month period (with the exception of commercial paper, which have maturities of less than 270 days).

Protective Covenants of the Indenture

The debtor corporation agrees to:

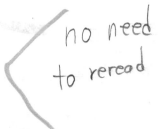

- pay the interest and principal of every bond;
- specify the places bonds or coupons can be presented for payment;
- defend the legal title to the property;
- maintain the property to ensure that business can be conducted profitably;
- do nothing that will diminish the claims of the bonds;
- insure the mortgaged property against fire and other losses;
- pay all taxes and assessments (property, income, franchises);
- maintain its corporate structure and the right to do business; and
- record the mortgage and pay any recording fees.

Agreements may also contain other promises, such as the avoidance of debt with prior lien or the prohibition of any other statutory lien with priority outstanding against the property. Covenants might also include provisions for a sinking fund, a replacement fund, maintenance of minimum working capital and requirements to be met before paying dividends on any stock.

Mortgage bonds may be issued with either open- or closed-end covenants. Bonds issued with a closed-end covenant will have senior lien (or claim) on the underlying assets, even if the corporation issues other bonds secured by the same assets. An open-end covenant permits subsequent issues to be secured by the same property and have equal liens on it.

Remedies of Bondholders

If a corporation is judged bankrupt, liquidated or fails to meet its promises in the indenture, the trustee and bondholders may take certain actions to recover losses. The agreement usually provides these remedies:

- right of entry;
- right to sell property to the highest bidder;
- right to foreclose;
- right to bring suit; and
- right to declare the principal due prior to the maturity date.

Although trustees rarely exercise these remedies, they can be forced to take action by written request from a specified proportion of the bondholders. Also included in the provisions of the indenture are:

- **Acceleration of maturity in cases of default**. If the issuer defaults, the remaining principal becomes payable immediately.
- **Release of mortgaged property**. The indenture usually allows the issuer to sell, exchange or abandon property covered in the indenture if the trustee approves and certain conditions are met.
- **Protection for bondholders in consolidations and mergers**. The successor corporation is required to assume the debt of the former corporation.

Unless the trust indenture specifies otherwise, changes in the indenture cannot be made without the unanimous consent of the bondholders.

Types of Secured Bonds

Mortgage bonds. Mortgage bonds are considered relatively safe investments. In reorganization or liquidation, mortgage bonds have "absolute priority" among claims on the assets pledged to secure them. For this reason, they are sometimes called "senior debt securities." While mortgage bonds as a whole are considered relatively safe, individual bonds will be ranked against other bonds and have high or low ratings given to them by the various bond rating organizations.

Not all mortgage bonds, however, are equal. First claim on the pledged property goes to first-mortgage bonds, second claim to second-mortgage bonds and so on.

Closed-end indentures. In a closed-end mortgage arrangement, a corporation issues the maximum number of bonds authorized in the trust indenture as first-mortgage bonds. In many cases, the company will issue all the bonds at once. Any subsequent issues will have subordinated claims on the property.

Open-end indentures. An open-ended trust indenture permits the corporation to issue more bonds of the same class later. Subsequent issues will be secured by the same collateral backing the initial issue and will have equal liens on the property.

Prior lien bonds. Companies in trouble financially sometimes attract capital by issuing mortgage bonds that take precedence over first-mortgage bonds. Before issuing prior lien bonds, a corporation must have the consent of first-mortgage bondholders.

Tracking Corporate Bonds

Bonds are listed in newspapers and other financial publications, such as *Barron's* and *The Wall Street Journal*. The following illustration is an example of a NYSE bond table as it might appear in a financial publication.

Corporate Bond Quotations
Volume $44,720,000

Bonds	Cur Yld	Vol	High	Low	Close	Net Chg.
AbbtL 7 5/8s 96	7.6	21	99 3/4	99 3/4	99 3/4	. . .
Advst 9s 08	cv	72	103 1/2	103	103	. . .
AetnLf 8 1/8s 07	8.5	15	95 3/4	95 3/4	95 3/4	-1
AirbF 7 1/2s 11	cv	32	114	112	114	+1
AlaP 9s 2000	8.9	18	100 3/4	100 5/8	100 3/4	+1/4
AlaP 8 1/2s 01	8.6	13	98 3/8	98 3/8	98 3/8	-3/8
AlaP 8 7/8s 03	9.5	65	102 7/8	102 1/2	102 1/2	-3/8

Fig. 3.1 An example of a published bond quotation.

Locate Alabama Power 9s 2000. The symbol for the bond (AlaP) and the description of the bond (9s 2000) tell us that the bond pays 9% interest and matures in the year 2000. The current yield is given as 8.9%, which indicates that the bond is selling at a premium. The "Vol" (volume) column states how many bonds traded the previous day (the day being reported). Eighteen bonds, or $18,000 par value, were traded in Alabama Power 9s of 2000.

The next three columns explain the high, low and closing price for the day. For AlaP, the high was 100 3/4, the low was 100 5/8 and the bonds closed at (last trade) 100 3/4. The net change refers to how much more or less the bond's closing price differed from the previous day's close. Alabama Power 9s of 2000 closed up 1/4 of a point, or $2.50. AlaP closed yesterday at 100 1/2 (100 3/4 - 1/4).

Chapter Review

Questions

1.   Interest payments on bonds are based upon the security's

   ____(A)   par value.
   _X_(B)   discount value.
   ____(C)   market value.
   ____(D)   book value.

2.   A 5% bond is issued at par. It is now selling at 90 and is redeemable at par. What is its owner's annual income from this investment?

   ____(A) $20
   _X_(B) $50
   ____(C) $500
   ____(D) $5,000

3.   Which of the following is commonly referred to as funded debt?

   _X_(A)   corporate bonds
   ____(B)   municipal bonds
   ____(C)   preferred stock
   ____(D)   government bonds

4.   Equipment trust certificates would most commonly be issued by

   I.   airline companies.
   II.   railroad companies.
   III. farm equipment companies.
   IV.   automobile manufacturers.

   ____(A)   II
   _X_(B)   I and II
   ____(C)   III
   ____(D)   III and IV

5.   Bonds that are secured by other securities placed with a trustee are called

   ____(A)   mortgage bonds.
   ____(B)   collateral trust bonds.
   ____(C)   debenture bonds.
   _X_(D)   guaranteed bonds.

6. In case of bankruptcy, debentures rank on a par with

  ___×___(A)   first-mortgage bonds.
  _____(B)   equipment trust certificates.
  ═ _____(C)   unsecured debts of private creditors.
  _____(D)   collateral trust bonds.

7. Bonds that are "guaranteed" are

  _____(A)   insured by AMBAC.
  _____(B)   required to maintain a self-liquidating sinking fund.
  ___×___(C)   guaranteed as to payment of principal and interest by another corporation.
  _____(D)   guaranteed as to payment of principal and interest by the U.S. government.

8. Which of the following is(are) true regarding corporate zero coupon bonds?

  I.   Interest is paid semiannually.
  ‑ II.   Interest is not paid until maturity.
  ‑ III. The discount must be prorated and is taxed annually.
  IV.   The discount must be prorated annually, with taxation deferred to maturity.

  _____(A)   I and II
  ___×___(B)   II and III
  _____(C)   I and IV
  _____(D)   II and IV

9. An indenture has a closed-end provision. This means that

  ___×___(A)   additional issues will have junior liens.
  _____(B)   the bonds must be called before maturity.
  _____(C)   a sinking fund must be established.
  _____(D)   no additional bonds may be issued.

10. Southern California Electric Company issued Mortgage Senior Lien bonds at 8 7/8, price 96.353. These bonds pay annual interest, per $1,000 bond, of

  _____(A) $96.35.
  ___×___(B) $88.75.
  _____(C) $85.51.
  _____(D) $85.00.

Answer Key

1. A.

2. B.

3. A.

4. B.

5. B.

6. C.

7. C.

8. B.

9. A.

10. B.

K103

Key Terms

Convertible Securities

Characteristics *all convertable bonds are debentures (unsecured)*

Some corporate securities may be converted by the owner into another security of the same corporation (such as stocks into bonds). These are called convertibles and are usually debentures, subordinated debentures or preferred stock.

Technically, convertible bonds are classified as debt securities. Their holders are creditors of the corporation. But debentures, in reality, are like both debt and equity securities. Though they have a fixed interest rate and a maturity date established at the time of issuance, they can also be converted into common stock of the issuing corporation.

Why Corporations Issue Convertible Securities

A corporation will add a conversion feature to its bonds and preferred stock issues to make them more marketable. During strong bull markets, when investors are interested in stocks and the market for new fixed income securities is poor, the conversion privilege makes a bond more attractive. In exchange for the investor benefits offered by a conversion feature, many corporations will pay a lower rate of interest on convertible securities.

When the bond market is strong, convertible debentures are frequently issued as a means of raising equity capital on a postponed basis. When (and if) the debentures are converted, the corporation's capitalization changes from debt to equity.

Advantages to Issuer

There are a number of reasons corporations issue convertible securities:

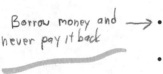
Borrow money and never pay it back →

- Convertibles can be sold with a lower coupon rate than nonconvertibles. In exchange for the conversion privilege, purchasers accept lower income.
- The company can eliminate a fixed interest charge as conversion takes place, thus reducing debt.
- A rapid increase in the number of shares in the market (such as may occur after an underwriting) could cause a drop in the price of common stock. This usually does not happen with conversions, since they take place over a longer period of time.
- By issuing convertibles rather than common stock, the corporation avoids immediate dilution of primary earnings per share.

Disadvantages to Issuer

On the other hand, issuing convertibles poses some possible disadvantages to the corporation and its shareholders:

- When bonds are converted, stockholders' equity is diluted (that is, there are more shares outstanding, so each share now represents a smaller fraction of ownership in the company).
- Since common stockholders have a voice in the management of the company, a substantial conversion could cause a shift in the control of the company.
- Reduction of corporate debt through conversion means a loss of leverage.
- The resulting decrease in (deductible) interest costs raises the corporation's taxable income; therefore, the corporation pays increased taxes as conversion takes place.

There is some uncertainty in the corporate capital structure, since there is no way of knowing when and how many of the bonds will be converted.

Advantages and Disadvantages of Convertibles for Investors

Theoretically, the convertible bondholder has the best of two markets, the investment safety of the fixed income market and the potential appreciation of the equity market. This leads to several advantages:

- As a debt security, a convertible debenture pays interest at a fixed rate and will be redeemable for its face value at maturity, provided the debenture is not converted. As a rule, interest income is usually higher and surer than dividend income on the underlying common stock. Similarly, convertible preferred stock usually pays a higher dividend than common stock does.
- If the corporation should experience financial difficulties, the convertible bondholder has priority over common stockholders in the event of a corporate liquidation.
- In theory, the market price of a convertible debenture will tend to be more stable during market declines than the price of common stock. Its value in the marketplace will be supported by current yields of other competitive debt securities.
- Since convertibles can be exchanged for common stock, their market price tends to move upward if the stock price moves up. For this reason, convertible securities are more volatile in price during times of steady interest rates than are other fixed income securities.

Critics of convertible securities contend that convertibles do not necessarily offer the best of the equity and debt markets. The critics say convertibles do not offer interest rates commensurate with lack of principal safety (nonconvertible debentures offer higher interest yields), and have a tendency to depress common stock prices because of the possible dilution effect.

Conversion Price or Ratio

Conversion price. The conversion price is the amount of par value of the convertible bond for one share of common stock. For example, Hammermill Paper has a convertible debenture with a conversion price of $40. This means each $40 worth of par value will be converted into one share of common stock. In other words, for every bond a holder converts, the bondholder would receive 25 shares of stock (a 25-to-1 conversion ratio). The conversion ratio is simply a factor of the conversion price. The conversion ratio times the conversion price will equal the bond's par value.

Conversion ratio. The conversion ratio (also called conversion rate) expresses the number of shares of common stock obtainable by converting $1,000 par value of the bonds. A debenture, for example, with a conversion price of $40 has a conversion ratio of 25 to 1 ($1,000/$40 = 25). Conversion terms are stated in the indenture agreement, either as a conversion ratio or conversion price. A preferred stock normally has a par value of $100, so a conversion price of $50 would mean a conversion ratio of 2 to 1.

Fixed or Variable

The conversion terms may or may not be constant throughout the life of the debenture. Frequently, the convertible debenture will be issued with a schedule of different conversion prices incorporated into the indenture agreement. The schedule usually calls for higher conversion prices as the debenture nears maturity because the issuer anticipates that the price of the common stock will increase in the future.

For example, a convertible debenture issued on October 1, 1970, might carry the following schedule:

Debenture Conversion Schedule

Conversion Dates	Conversion Ratio	Price
Oct.1, 1980 to Sept. 30, 1994	50 shares	$20.00
Oct. 1, 1994 to Sept. 30, 1996	49	$20.41
Oct. 1, 1996 to Sept. 30, 1998	47.5	$21.05
Oct. 1, 1998 to Sept. 30, 2000	45	$22.22

Fig. 4.1 An example of a conversion schedule.

(Note: The conversion ratio goes down as the conversion price goes up.)

When a convertible bond is originally issued, the conversion price is usually substantially higher than the current market price of the common stock. This is to discourage investors from immediately converting the bond. On the other hand, if the corporation would like to encourage conversion, the conversion price may be only slightly above the market price of the common stock when the bond is issued. Factors that affect the initial conversion rate or price are:

[handwritten margin notes:]
$1,000 par
Bond is cv in common
shares at a fixed
cv price/sh of $25
1000/25 = 40 shares

— compare —
Bond   Stock
110   : 40 sh
$1100 : $27.50 Equal
parity
if at $27.50
Stock
disparity
is
not equal

(40 to 1 Ratio)
(Sh   Bond)

- Price of the stock at the time the bonds are issued.
- Earnings prospect of the issuing company and its effect on the stock price.
- Market trend (convertibles become very popular with investors in a rising market).
- Conversion period (generally, the longer the time period, the less favorable the initial conversion rates need be).
- Amount of interest the corporation is willing to pay (a higher interest rate would encourage investors to accept a higher conversion price at issuance).

Subscription Privileges for Stockholders

Because convertibles can dilute stockholders' equity, stockholders often have a preemptive right to purchase any new security issues that are convertible to stock, usually at a subscription price below the market value of the bond. When new convertibles are issued, current stockholders will receive certificates (called rights because they represent the stockholder's preemptive right) that they can convert to bonds. These rights are themselves securities, which the holders can sell if they choose not to use them to buy the bonds.

Protective Features

Stock splits. Conversion prices may be adjusted if stock splits and stock dividends are declared on the underlying common stock during the life of the debenture.

Consider, for example, what would happen if a company declared a 2-for-1 split. First, what happens to the stock itself? If it is trading at $40 a share before the split, the market price will drop to $20 per share afterward and an investor with 100 shares of the stock will receive 200 shares of the new stock. Now, what happens to the debentures with a conversion price of $40 and a conversion ratio of 25 to 1? Much the same thing, actually. To reflect the new stock price, the conversion price drops to $20 per share. The ratio, on the other hand, doubles and becomes 50 to 1. Simply stated, after the split, it takes twice as many shares to give the bondholders an equivalent dollar value if they convert their bonds into stock. In a 3-for-1 split, the conversion price would drop to $13.33 (40 / 3) and the ratio would rise to 75 to 1. An investor converting $1,000 of bonds would need 75 shares of the $13.33 stock to equal the value of 75 shares worth $40 per share.

Changes in class of conversion securities. If common shares that are outstanding are converted into the same number of shares of another class, the conversion privilege would apply to an equal number of new shares.

Additional shares. The indenture fixes the maximum number of additional shares the corporation can issue while convertible bonds are outstanding and the minimum price at which they can be issued.

Mergers, consolidations, dissolutions, etc. If the corporation ceases to exist because of any of these situations, holders of convertible bonds lose their conversion privileges.

Calculating Conversion Parity

Investors holding convertible securities naturally are curious about which is worth more, the security they own or the security they could own by converting. Answering that question involves finding the prices that will put the two securities at parity (or equality). If the securities are not at parity, then one is worth more to the investor than the other.

Parity means that two securities (in this case, a convertible preferred stock or bond and the common stock it can be converted into) are of equal dollar value. If a corporation issues a convertible preferred stock that has a par value of $100 and is convertible at $50, then the conversion ratio is 2 to 1. The investor can receive two shares of common stock for one share of the preferred. Then the question about relative value becomes simpler: which is worth more on the market, one share of the preferred or two of the common?

Suppose, for example, that a convertible preferred is selling in the market at $104 and is convertible into two shares of common stock. The market price of the common would have to be at about $52 to have the same dollar value as (to be at parity with) the convertible preferred. Why? Because two shares of common stock at $52 per share are equivalent in value to one share of the preferred at $104 per share. If the common stock is selling below 52 (below parity) then the investor can make more by selling the preferred than by converting and selling the common. If the common is selling above 52, the investor can make more money converting to common and selling that.

You can also calculate parity the other way around, beginning with the market price of the common stock and calculating the parity price of the preferred. Knowing that the common is trading at $52 and that the convertible preferred has a conversion ratio of 2 to 1, you can multiply $52 by 2 to calculate that the preferred's parity price is $104. An investor would find a conversion profitable only if the common has a price of more than $52 (greater than one-half the preferred's price of $104).

The following formulas allow you to find the parity prices of convertible securities and their underlying common shares.

Market Price of Convertible / Conversion Ratio = Parity Price of Common

---

Market Price of Common x Conversion Ratio = Parity Price of Convertible

---

In a rising market, the market value of the convertible rises with the common stock. In a declining market, the market price of the convertible tends to level off when the yield becomes competitive with bonds that are not convertible and may not decline in price as far as the common stock.

Arbitrages Affecting the Price of Bonds

Usually, debentures will sell at a premium over their conversion parity prices. But market conditions can occur in which the conversion value of a debenture might be slightly higher than the market value of the debenture. In such instances, an immediate profit could be established by purchasing a convertible debenture and selling its common stock equivalent. This would be an arbitrage transaction. Arbitrage takes advantage of the discrepancy between the market value of the debenture and the conversion value of the debenture.

Investment Value and Conversion Value

Debt securities have investment value whether or not they are convertible. A nonconvertible debt security's investment value is based on its percentage yield as compared with yields of other investments with similar risk levels. The estimated investment value of a convertible debenture is the market price at which the security would sell if it were not convertible into common stock. When an investor buys a convertible debenture, he must always consider both the investment value of the debenture as an income security and the conversion of the debenture into equity securities. The conversion value of a debenture is the total market value of common stock into which the debenture is convertible.

Let's take the example of a convertible debenture, selling at 90, that can be converted into 20 shares of common stock. If the market value of each share is $44, the conversion value is $880 ($44 x 20). The convertible bond will usually sell at the higher of its two current values (and, in a strong market, at a premium).

Factors Influencing Conversion

Because convertible debentures often sell at a premium above parity, this premium is the major reason convertible debentures are not constantly being exchanged for common stock during a rising market. The investor interested in profit taking is better off selling his debentures rather than converting them. Another investor who is more interested in income may want to keep the convertible for its higher interest or dividend return.

Forced Conversion

Sometimes corporations create conditions that encourage the conversion of bonds. Though this is known in the industry as "forced conversion," in fact investors cannot be forced to convert securities. The issuer can, however, alter circumstances to make conversion more attractive. One way in which this can be done is by calling the bonds.

The corporation can call the bonds (assuming that they are callable as well as convertible) when market conditions are such that bondholders will find it more profitable to convert the bonds than to submit them for redemption at the call price. This will happen when the parity price is above the call price.

Say, for example, that an issue of bonds is convertible into common stock at $25 (a conversion ratio of 40 to 1) and is called at 105. The stock is currently trading at $30 per share, so by converting a bond, an investor can become the owner of 40 shares of common worth $1,200. The parity price of the bond would be 120 ($1,200 for a $1,000 par value bond). The parity price, in other words, is above the call price. The bond owner is better off to convert and sell the 40 shares of common for $1,200 than to tender the bond for redemption at $1,050.

The issuer has not, technically, forced the bondholders to convert; it has merely created conditions in which conversion is the better alternative by making an offer investors would be foolish not to accept.

Rights

A corporation, when issuing new shares of common stock, may first decide to go to existing shareholders to sell its shares before going to public investors. This may be because they believe their shareholders would be the best prospects to buy additional shares of the company or it may be because the corporation's shareholders have preemptive rights.

Preemptive rights refer to the right of an existing shareholder to purchase shares of a new issue of stock in proportion to the number of shares the investor already owns. A concern is that if new shares are issued by a corporation the present shareholders, ownership of the company will be diluted if they are not able to purchase a proportionate share of the new issue. Their voting percentage, earnings per share and net worth per share will be reduced. In addition, the additional supply of stock available to the market may cause the market price of the stock to decrease.

The rights entitle the shareholder to purchase the common stock below the current market price. This means that the rights are valued separately and trade in the secondary market during the subscription period. A stockholder who receives rights may take one of the following actions:

- Exercise the right to buy stock, thereby maintaining proportionate interest in the corporation.
- Sell the rights; since the rights certificate is a negotiable security, the investor can sell the right and profit from its market value (although by selling the right, the investor forgoes any potential profits from exercising the right and owning the stock).
- Let the rights expire, thus reducing proportionate ownership and losing the value of the rights or of the stock they could have been used to acquire.

Approval by Vote of Stockholders

Decisions to issue additional stock must first be approved by the board of directors. If the additional stock to be issued through the rights offering increases the total stock issued beyond the amount authorized in the charter, the stockholders must vote to amend the charter.

[Handwritten annotations:]

1 right/sh

(1,000,000 stock rights) → 1,000,000 sh outstanding

$$\frac{(10,000 \text{ rights})}{5,000} = 2 \text{ rts/sh}$$

10,000 sh I own
(1% owner)

500,000 new shares
× 1%
5,000 additional shares at subscription price (lower)

4.9

K104

Characteristics of Rights

Subscription Right Certificate

A rights offering is a short-term (typically 30 to 45 days) privilege and a subscription right is the actual certificate representing that privilege a stockholder receives from the corporation. One right is issued for each share of common stock the investor owns. An investor with 100 shares of common stock receives a certificate representing 100 rights.

Terms of the Offering

The terms of the offering are stipulated in the subscription rights, which are mailed to stockholders on the payable date. The rights describe the new shares to which the stockholder is entitled to subscribe, the price, the date the new stock will be issued, the rights agent that will send the subscription and the final date for exercising those rights.

Significant Trading Dates and Prices of Rights Offerings

Let's look at an example of a rights offering. On April 1, Associated Industries, Inc., which plans to raise capital by issuing stock, declares a rights offering. Holders of the common stock as of May 1st will be able to subscribe to one new share at $70 for each five shares already owned. (The stock is currently trading at $100.) The rights expire (and become worthless) on June 18.

The number of rights required to buy one new share is a factor based on the number of shares outstanding and the number of new shares offered. Assume Associated Industries, Inc. has 5,000,000 shares outstanding and it wants to issue another 1,000,000 shares. Each existing share is entitled to one right, so there will be 5,000,000 rights issued. Those rights entitle shareholders to only 1,000,000 shares, so 5,000,000 rights divided by 1,000,000 new shares means that it will require 5 rights to buy one new share. Between April 1 and June 18, the stock tables in newspapers and other publications will show two different entries for Associated Industries:

- the price of the stock itself, either with rights (cum rights) or, after the ex-date, without them (ex-rights); and
- the price of the rights, either on a when-issued basis or, after they've been issued, at the current market price (the price of the rights appears just under the stock price in the tables).

The corporation will issue rights May 8 to any stockholder of record May 1. Stock is traded cum rights up until the ex-date. An investor who purchases the stock cum rights is also entitled to receive the right.

Beginning on the fourth business day preceding the record date, common stock trades ex-rights (except in cash transactions where the buyer and seller settle on the day of the trade). This means that an investor who purchases a share of the stock does not receive a right. Rights are traded on a when-issued basis until the issuance date. Investors who do not intend to exercise their rights may sell them separately.

The Rights Agent

As you may recall from the chapters on corporate stock, corporations employ transfer agents to record the name of each shareholder as they cancel old certificates and issue new ones. The rights agent does for rights what the transfer agent does for stocks; that is, the rights agent keeps a record of who owns each right. When a right is sold, the rights agent records the name of the new owner. This function may (or may not) be performed by the same individual or trust that acts as transfer agent. You will also recall that the registrar keeps track of the number of shares of securities outstanding. This ensures that the corporation does not issue more than the authorized number of shares. The registrar does not, however, keep a list of the names of shareholders.

Standby Underwriting

In the initial offering, current stockholders may not subscribe to all the rights. The unsold rights may be offered through a broker-dealer in a standby underwriting. This will be done on a firm-commitment basis.

Value of Rights

Theoretical. From the time rights are declared until they are issued, they have only a theoretical value. This value is based on the savings investors will be able to realize by exercising the subscription rights to purchase securities below market price.

Prior to ex-date. To compute the value of a right when the stock is trading cum rights, we will use the Associated Industries example. The market price (M) of the stock cum rights is $100; the subscription price (S) is $70. The investor needs five rights and $70 to buy one new share. The five rights, therefore, earn the investor a $30 discount on a share of stock ($100 market price - $70 subscription price).

$$\frac{\text{Market Price} - \text{Subscription Price}}{\text{\# of Rights Needed to Purchase One Share} + 1} = \text{Value of One Right}$$

$$\frac{M - S}{N + 1} = \text{Value of one right when the stock is trading } \underline{\text{Cum Rights}}.$$

$$\frac{M - S}{N} = \text{Value of one right when the stock is trading } \underline{\text{Ex-Rights}}.$$

Fig. 4.2 Calculating the value of a right.

To determine the value of one right, divide the savings it represents (M - S) by the number of rights needed to purchase one share (N), plus one right (N + 1). The extra right is added to the denominator because, when the stock is trading cum rights the current market value of the stock, theoretically, includes the cost of one right.

After ex-date. On the day when the stock first trades ex-rights, the market price drops by the value of the right. The stock is now at $95. For the stock selling without rights, the divisor, in this case, is the same as the number of rights needed to purchase one share. The market price of the stock, during the time the rights are trading, will move up or down and the theoretical value will change accordingly, but on the date the stock goes ex-rights, the value can be computed as shown.

Warrants

buy 100sh TWA common until 7/1/2010 at $20/sh
com valuable if stock price above $20/sh

A warrant is a certificate giving the holder the right to purchase securities at a stipulated price from the issuer. Unlike a right, a warrant is usually a long-term instrument, affording the investor the option of buying shares at a later date at the subscription price, subject to the warrant's expiration date.

Warrants may be detachable from the underlying security or they may be nondetachable. If detachable, they trade in the market purely as speculation on the price of the underlying stock (since the warrants receive no dividends or represent any other of the rights of a corporate owner). While the exercise price is set above the market price of the stock when the warrant is first issued, the investor hopes the stock's price will increase in the market. The investor can (1) exercise the warrant and buy the stock below the price he would have to pay in the market or (2) sell the warrant in the market at a price based on the benefit the purchaser can get by exercising the warrant and buying stock below the market price.

Origination of Warrants

Warrants are usually offered to the public as a "sweetener" in connection with other securities (usually debentures) to make these securities more attractive to investors. Investors enjoy the security of owning a bond, note or preferred stock, but might also benefit from the opportunity to participate in the appreciation of the common stock. The market price of the common stock is normally lower than the exercise price stated in the warrants when they are first issued.

American Depository Receipts (ADRs)

Receipts for foreign shares

Americans buying stock of foreign corporations need not always arrange to receive the foreign certificates. Instead, the investor can, in many cases, buy American Depository Receipts (ADRs). ADRs facilitate the transfer of American investments in foreign corporations, and the ADR itself is an instrument that can, like a stock, be bought and sold in the American securities markets on an exchange or over the counter.

An ADR is a negotiable receipt for a given number of shares of stock (typically one to ten) in a non-American corporation. The foreign stock certificate that the ADR represents remains in the custody of a foreign bank and the ADRs themselves are issued by foreign branches of large commercial American banks. The stock must remain on deposit as long as the ADR is outstanding, since the ADR is the depository bank's guarantee that it holds the stock.

Registered in Name of Owner

ADRs are registered on the books of the American bank responsible for them. Dividends are sent to the registered owner. All rights normally held by common shareholders, except the preemptive right, are given to the holder of the ADR.

Subject to the Securities Exchange Act of 1934

ADRs are either sponsored or unsponsored. If the company itself creates the instrument by depositing shares with a custodian outside the United States and agrees to comply with SEC reporting requirements, the ADR is **sponsored**. Unsponsored ADRs are created when a bank buys shares and keeps them on deposit overseas with a custodian (typically a branch of the U.S. bank) and registers the ADR with the SEC.

Eurodollars and Eurodollar Bonds

Eurocurrency is a time deposit, which may be negotiable, and is denominated in a currency foreign to the local market in which the deposit is made. Thus, a deposit of U.S. dollars in a bank in London or Japan would be referred to as Eurocurrency or Eurodollars.

Eurobonds tend to be long-term debt instruments that are issued and sold outside the country of the currency in which they are denominated. Thus, a U.S. dollar denominated Eurobond is a bond sold outside the United States, but the principal and interest is stated and paid in U.S. dollars. U.S. dollar denominated Eurobonds are issued by foreign businesses, governments and U.S. corporations. Borrowers (including U.S. corporations) can reach new sources of revenue and avoid the regulatory requirements and expense of selling the bond in the domestic market. However, they generally pay a higher interest rate than they pay at home. The investor will demand a higher return since there are fewer safeguards in the unregulated Eurobond market. The unregulated, decentralized international market that deals in the various major currencies of the world, referred to as the interbank market, is a telephone/telex market conducting business around the world from individual bank trading rooms. It is from the interbank market that we get the foreign exchange rates.

[handwritten margin note: payable in dollars but not eurobonds]

Questions

1. Which of the following statements concerning convertible bonds is (are) true?

   I.   Coupon rates are usually lower than nonconvertible bonds of the same issuer.
   II. Convertible bondholders are creditors of the corporation.
   III. If the underlying common stock should decline to the point where there is no advantage to converting the bonds into common stock, the bonds will sell at a price based on their inherent value as bonds, disregarding the convertible feature.

   ____(A) I
   ____(B) III
   ____(C) I and III
   _×_(D)   I, II and III

   Use the following information to answer questions 2 and 3.

   ```
   New Issue                              July 27, 1991

              Tippecanoe Ferry Company

        12% Convertible Subordinated Debentures
                Due November 15, 1995

            Convertible into Common Stock
     at $12.50 per Share, unless previously redeemed.

                    Price 100%

         AFAP Securities, Inc.      Doowah, Inc.
        Madre Merrill, Inc.              E.S. Mutter
        Shearsome, Leavesome          Smith Baloney
        Blindem N. Robbem              Providential

      This announcement appears as a matter of record only.
   ```

2. The bonds are convertible into how many shares of common stock?

   _×_(A) 80
   ____(B) 95
   ____(C) 100
   ____(D) 105

   $$\frac{1000}{12.5} = 80 \text{ conv ratio}$$

3. On December 3, 1996, the Tippecanoe bonds were trading at 102. Therefore, the parity price of the common stock on that date was approximately

    ____(A)   12 1/4.
    ____(B)   12 1/2
    _X_(C)   12 3/4.
    ____(D)   13.

cmv / conv ratio = parity price

1020 / 80 = 12.75   OR   *If bond ↑ 2% then stock ↑ 2%*

see Q 2

4. ABC bonds are convertible at $50. If the bonds are selling in the market for 60 ($600) and the common stock is selling for $30, which two of the following statements are true?

conv ratio = 20 *(1000/50)*   *20 x $30 = $600 conv parity*

    I.   The bonds are trading below parity to the common.
    II.   The stock is selling at conversion parity.
    III. There would be a profitable arbitrage situation.
    IV. The bonds can be converted into 20 shares of common.

    ____(A)   III and IV
    ____(B)   I and II
    ____(C)   I and III
    _X_(D)   II and IV

5. ABC Corporation 6% debentures are convertible into common stock at $25 per share. The common stock is trading at 27 1/2 and the bonds are trading at 112. The corporation calls the bonds at 108 as permitted by the indenture. The bondholder should be advised to

conv ratio = 40 *(100/25)*   *40 x 27.5 = $1100 common*   *Can't sell at 112 (1120) because corp calls at 108 ($1080) bond*

    ____(A)   hold the bonds and await the call.
    _X_(B)   sell the bonds at the current market.
    ____(C)   convert the bonds into common stock.
    ____(D)   refuse to tender the bonds to the corporation.

6. A corporation issuing stock has informed its shareholders that they can buy the newly issued stock for $21.50 per share with 20 rights. The outstanding stock is currently trading at $40. To purchase a share of the stock at the subscription price takes

    ____(A) $21.50 with 21 rights.
    _X_(B) $21.50 with 20 rights.
    ____(C)   one right with $21.50.
    ____(D)   one right with $40.

7. An investor owns a stock with a CMV of $70. The company is issuing more common stock by way of a rights offering, with five rights required to buy one new share at $55 per share. The value of the rights before the security trades ex-rights is

    X (A) $2.50.
        (B) $3.00.
        (C) $5.00.
        (D) $15.00.

$$\frac{70-55}{5+1} = \$2.50 \qquad \underline{\underline{4.11}}$$

8. An investor owns a stock with a CMV of $70. The company is issuing more common stock by way of a rights offering, with five rights resquired to buy one new share at $55 per share. The stock is trading on the ex-rights date with a market value of $70. The rights now have a market value of

        (A) $2.50.
    X (B) $3.00.
        (C) $5.00.
        (D) $15.00.

$$\frac{70-55}{5} = \$3$$

9. DWAQ corporation has declared a rights offering. An investor who owns 100 shares on the record date is entitled to 100 subscription rightsto be sold on a when-issued basis. The change of ownership is recorded by the

        (A)   registrar.
    X (B)   rights agent.
        (C)   transfer agent.
        (D)   issuer.

10. Which of the following instrument do(does) not receive dividends?

    X (A)   warrants
        (B)   common stock
        (C)   preferred stock
        (D)   convertible preferred stock

K104

Answer Key

1. D.

2. A.

3. C.

4. D.

5. C.

6. B.

7. A.

8. B.

9. B.

10. A.

Chapter Five

U.S. Government Securities

Key Terms

U.S. Government Debt

The federal government not only is the nation's largest borrower but also its best credit risk. Securities issued by the U.S. government (or by governmental agencies) to finance its operations are backed by its "full faith and credit." The full faith and credit backing the U.S. government gives the securities it issues is largely based on its power to raise money through taxation.

The Public Debt Act of 1942 gave the U.S. Treasury department the authority to determine the amount and types of government securities to be sold to meet the needs of the federal budget. The Treasury, however, does not set the rate on its new issues; the marketplace does. The marketplace also dictates, to a degree, the form and features of those securities. In general, government securities are exempt from state and municipal taxation, but subject to federal taxation.

Some government securities (in particular, registered or bearer bonds) are issued in definitive form, which means that the investor receives a certificate. Others are issued in book-entry form; that is, the investor's name is stored in a computer, and the investor receives no certificate.

Marketable Government Securities

Treasury Bills

Issuance and trading. T bills are issued at a discount from par in a competitive bidding auction. They are quoted and traded in the secondary market at a discount, and are traded flat (without accrued interest). T bills do not pay interest: an investor's return on T bills is the difference between the price the investor paid and the price at which the investor sells or redeems them.

Book entry. Treasury bills are issued in book-entry form. An owner receives no certificate but a record of the purchase is kept on computer. When the T bill matures, the principal amount is sent to the owner of record. The investor, meanwhile, has the confirmation as proof of purchase.

Maturities and denominations. Treasury bills are short-term issues with maturities of one year or less. Issued in denominations of $10,000 to $1 million (in $5,000 increments), they mature in 13 weeks, 26 weeks or 52 weeks. T bills with 13 week and 26 week maturities are auctioned weekly, while those with 52-week maturities are auctioned every four weeks. At maturity, the investor can either request cash or request that the investment be rolled over into another T bill.

Pricing. Treasury bills are quoted at a discount from par. A quote of 5.50%, for example, means a T bill is selling at 5 1/2% less than its face value. For a $10,000 52-week Treasury bill, that would be a price of $9,450. A T bill quote might read as

always ↓ cheaper

follows: "Maturity April 6, bid 5.50%, asked 5.35%." The bid appears higher than the asked because the bidder wants to pay less for the bill to achieve a higher yield, and thus bids at a deeper discount from par.

Treasury Notes

Issuance and trading. T notes are interest-bearing securities that pay interest every six months. Before June 30, 1983, T notes were issued in bearer form with coupons attached. Since that time, investors have had a choice between receiving fully registered certificates, and having a record of their ownership on computer in book-entry form.

Maturities. Issued in denominations of $1,000 to $1 million, T notes are inter-mediate-term bonds maturing in one to ten years (notes typically have maturities of at least two years).

Pricing. T notes are issued, quoted and traded at a percentage of par. A quote of 98.24 on a $1,000 note means that the note is selling for 98 and 24/32% of its par value of $1,000. In this instance, .24 is not a decimal; instead, it designates 24/32 of 1%. A quote of 98.24 is equivalent to 98.75% of $1,000, or $987.50.

Redeemable at face value. At maturity, Treasury notes can be redeemed for cash at par, or they can be refunded. If a T note is refunded, the government offers the investor a new security with a new maturity date as an alternative to a cash payment for the existing securities. Bondholders may always request the principal amount in cash if they do not wish to reinvest.

Treasury Bonds

Issuance and trading. Treasury bonds constitute the smallest portion of the government's marketable debt. Interest is payable every six months. Before June 30, 1983, they were issued in bearer and registered forms. Now T bonds are sold only in registered or book-entry form.

Callable. Some Treasury bonds have optional call dates, ranging from three to five years before maturity. Before calling the bonds, however, the Treasury depart-ment must give bondholders four months notice. U.S. government securities are always called at par and never at a premium.

A bid of:	Means:	In dollars:
98.1	98 + 1/32% of $1,000	$980.3125
98.2	98 + 2/32% of $1,000	$980.6250
98.3	98 + 3/32% of $1,000	$980.9375
...	...	...
98.10	98 + 10/32% of $1,000	$983.1250
98.11	98 + 11/32% of $1,000	$983.1250
98.12	98 + 12/32% of $1,000	$983.7500

Fig. 5.1 Notes and bonds are quoted in 32nds.

Maturities. Issued in denominations of $1,000 to $1 million, Treasury bonds generally have maturities of 10 years or more. Like Treasury notes, they are issued, quoted and traded at a percentage of par value with minimum variations of 1/32 of 1%.

Flower bonds. Prior to 1971, the Treasury department issued some bonds with a special tax advantage. An investor could purchase these bonds at a discount from face value (partly due to their extremely low interest rates) and, after the investor's death, his or her heirs could redeem the bonds at face value to pay federal estate taxes. The tax advantages of these flower bonds (the name was suggestive of funeral flowers) appealed to older, wealthy investors. The last issue matures in 1998.

death anticipation bonds

must know

Cash Management Bills

Cash management bills (CMBs) are used by the Treasury to meet short-term (10 to 20 days) borrowing needs. It takes a minimum bid of $10,000,000 to purchase CMBs at auction, and CMBs are usually bought by banks and dealers and held to maturity. Before 1975, the Treasury used tax anticipation bills (TABs) to meet short-term borrowing needs; CMBs have replaced TABs.

Treasury bills	90 days to one year	$10,000 to $1,000,000	Priced on an interest rate basis	Book entry
Treasury notes	One to ten years	$1,000 to $1,000,000	Priced at a percent of par	Book entry and registered
Treasury bonds	Ten to thirty years	$1,000 to $1,000,000	Priced at a percent of par	Book entry and registered

Fig. 5.2 Marketable government securities.

Zero Coupon Securities

Brokerage firms have the permission of the Treasury department to create zero coupon bonds (Treasury receipts) from U.S. Treasury notes and bonds. Broker-dealers buy Treasury securities, then sell the principal and coupons separately to investors, pricing them at a discount from face value. You can think of a $1,000 Treasury note with a 6% coupon as a number of separate obligations; the obligation to pay $30 in six months, in a year, in a year and a half and so on to maturity; and the obligation to pay $1,000 at maturity. The broker who buys the note can resell each of those obligations separately.

The Treasury securities underlying the zero coupon bonds are held for the investor by a custodial bank. Because the underlying Treasury notes and bonds pay semiannual interest to the custodial bank, the zero coupons are issued with maturities at six-month intervals.

STRIPS. The Treasury department itself has entered the growing zero coupon bond market by issuing special bonds that an investment firm could purchase, place in escrow and then sell evidences of ownership in either the bond principal or interest to investors. These special securities became known as STRIPS, which stands for Separate Trading of Registered Interest and Principal of Securities. Treasury STRIPS are not to be confused with zero coupon bonds that broker- dealers create by "stripping" the coupons from corporate or government bonds and selling them separately. While the security underlying STRIPS is issued by the government, the actual separation and trading of its parts is performed by major banks and dealers.

Other zero coupon bonds. The original zero coupon bonds were created by brokerage firms, and tend to be identified by such memorable acronyms as TIGRs (Treasury Investment Growth Receipts), CATS (Certificates of Accrual on Treasury Securities) and LIONs (Lehman Investment Opportunity Notes) and TBRs (Treasury Bond Receipts).

low credit risk
avoid reinvestment risk

Tracking the Investment

Newspaper Listings

Daily information about U.S. government securities is available in most major newspapers. Listed in the following chart are quotes for Treasury bonds, notes and bills. Reading from left to right under "Government Bonds & Notes," or under "Treasury Bills" you can determine the coupon rate, the maturity date, the bid and asked prices, the bid change from the previous trading day, and the yield to maturity.

Government Bonds & Notes

Rate	Maturity	Bid	Asked	Bid Chg.	Yld.
8.75	Aug 94	103.30	104.10	+.16	7.70
12.62	Aug 94n	119.26	119.30	+.16	7.77
9.50	Oct 94	107.08	107.12	+.17	7.75
10.12	Nov 94	109.30	110.02	+.16	7.77
11.62	Nov 94n	116.09	116.13	+.13	7.78
8.62	Jan 95n	103.23	103.27	+.18	7.75
3.00	Feb 95	93.05	93.23	+.16	4.28
10.50	Feb 95	111.23	111.27	+.16	7.83

Decimals in bid and asked and bid changes represent 32nds. 99.04 means 99 4/32. n- Treasury note.

Treasury Bills

Maturity	Bid	Asked	Yld.
Jan 18 90	7.64	7.60	8.00
Jan 25 90	7.58	7.54	7.95
Feb 15 90	7.57	7.53	7.94
Mar 15 90	7.53	7.49	7.91
Apr 12 90	7.40	7.36	7.79
May 10 90	7.37	7.33	7.78
Jun 07 90	7.31	7.27	7.74
Jul 05 90	7.29	7.26	7.77

Treasury bill quotes are in hundredths. Price quotes are the discount from par.

Fig. 5.3 An example of bond, note and bill quotes.

Treasury Bonds and Notes

Treasury bonds and notes are quoted at a percentage of par. The first note shown in the quote above pays a rate of 12 5/8% and matures in August 1994. No letter after the year indicates the security is a bond, and an "n" indicates that it is a Treasury note. The Bid and Asked prices reflect the most recently reported over-the-counter market prices and the Bid Change indicates how much the price has changed from the last report. At the current Bid and Asked, this bond would yield 7.77%. Other government and agency issues are quoted in a similar fashion.

In the third listing under Government Bonds & Notes, the bonds have a 9 1/2% coupon rate and mature in October 1994. The bid was 107.08; the asked price was 107.12. The bonds have a yield to maturity of 7.75%.

Treasury Bills

Treasury bills are very short-term securities sold and quoted at their annualized discount rate (or yield). The maturity date is given in the first column. The second column shows the discount rate that results from the bid prices dealers will pay to buy the bills. In the third column is the ask price which, although it appears to be lower than the bid, is not. The number actually reflects the discount from par, and the discount on the asked side is smaller than that on the bid side. Under the words "Bid" and "Asked" are listed the discounts from par that investors and broker-dealers are willing to give and take for the bonds. In the preceding chart, the dollar bid on a May 10th, 1990 $1 million T bill would be $926,300 ($1,000,000 - $73,700). The dollar ask price would be $926,700 ($1,000,000 - $73,300).

The first bill in the chart matures January 18, 1990. It is being offered for sale at par less a discount computed at a rate of 7.60%, to yield 8.00%. On January 18, 1990, the bill is payable at par.

Flower Bonds

Notice that the second bond from the bottom under Government Bonds & Notes has a 3.00 interest rate, much lower than the other bonds available. It is also trading at a significant discount from par, an unusual situation for a below market-rate bond. This bond is a **flower bond**, a special type of bond issued by the U.S. government and used by investors to settle estate taxes, as discussed earlier in this chapter.

Nonmarketable Government Securities

Savings bonds differ from other government securities in that they cannot be used as collateral and are not negotiable. They are **nonmarketable securities** because they are nontransferable. They are not bought and sold on an exchange or over the counter; rather, they are purchased from the Treasury department through various issuing agents, including commercial banks and post offices. They can be redeemed only by the purchaser or by a beneficiary.

Zero coupon securities

Series EE bonds. Series EE bonds are discount bonds: bondholders earn the discount over the life of the bond and are paid the face value at maturity (although they may be redeemed before they mature). Series EE bonds are issued at 50% of their face value in denominations from $50 to $10,000 (with a minimum purchase of $25, a $50 face bond). In the early years, only small amounts of interest accrue; the bulk of the interest accrues in later years. Series EE bonds can be redeemed before maturity, but will receive a lower rate of return (giving the bondholder an incentive to hold bonds until maturity). A minimum return is guaranteed on Series EE bonds, a return tied to 85% of the average return of five-year Treasury securities. The tax on accrued interest on EE bonds can be paid annually or deferred until the bond matures. Tax can be deferred further by trading EE bonds for HH bonds.

retirement bonds

Series HH bonds. Series HH bonds differ from Series EE bonds in that they pay interest semiannually. They are designed for investors who want regular income. Series HH bonds can be purchased only by trading in Series EE bonds at maturity. Series HH bonds come in denominations of $500 to $10,000 and mature in 10 years, although the investor can redeem them at face value at any time.

Bond	Maturity	Denomination	Pricing	Form
Series EE	10 years	$50 to $10,000	Issued at a discount	Registered
Series HH	10 years	$500 to $10,000	Issued at par	Registered

Fig. 5.4 A comparison of Series EE and HH bonds.

Agency Issues

Authorization. Congress authorizes certain agencies of the federal government to issue marketable debt securities. Some of these agencies (reported daily in many newspapers) are:

- Federal Farm Credit Banks
- Federal Home Loan Mortgage Corporation (FHLMC or Freddie Mac)
- Government National Mortgage Association (GNMA or Ginnie Mae)
- Inter-American Development Bank (IADB)

Other agency-like organizations that are operated by private corporations, include:

- Federal Home Loan Banks (FHLBs)
- Federal National Mortgage Association (FNMA or Fannie Mae)

The term "agency" is sometimes used to refer to entities that are not, technically, government agencies, but do have ties to the government. The Federal Home Loan Banks, for example, are owned by the private savings and loan associations that are members of the FHLB system. Yet, the FHLB operates under federal charter and regulates its members. Whatever its technical status, therefore, it functions as a government agency. The Federal National Mortgage Association (Fannie Mae) is also privately owned but government regulated.

Yields and maturities. Agency issues sell at higher yields than do direct obligations of the federal government (partially attributable to a slightly higher level of risk), but they frequently sell at lower yields than those available on corporate debt securities. The maturities of these issues vary from very short-term to relatively long-term.

Backing. Agency issues have a very slight risk of failing to pay interest and principal because the issuing agency backs them with revenues from taxes, fees or income from lending activities. Agency issues are backed in several ways: by collateral, such as cash, U.S. Treasury securities and the debt obligations; by a U.S. Treasury guarantee; by the right of the agency to borrow from the Treasury; or, in a few cases, by the full faith and credit of the government.

Taxation. Interest on government agency issues is sometimes exempt from state and local income taxes but is always subject to federal income tax. Fannie Mae and Ginnie Mae securities, for example, are taxed at federal, state and local levels.

Federal Farm Credit Bank

The Farm Credit System is organized geographically into 12 districts and is composed of 37 banks (Federal Land Bank, FLB; Federal Intermediate Credit Bank, FICB;

and Bank for Cooperatives, COOP). The Federal Farm Credit Bank Consolidated Systemwide Securities are the joint and separate obligations of all 37 Farm Credit Banks. These institutions are all privately owned; their securities are not directly backed by the faith and credit of the U.S. government. (The Farm Credit Administration oversees the system and is an agency of the government.)

The securities, issued to fund producers of crops and livestock and provide mortgages for farm property, include discount notes (very short maturities), six- and nine-month notes, and longer term bonds. Consolidated Systemwide bonds are issued only in book-entry form.

Taxation. Farm Credit Bank issues are federally taxed, but are exempt from local and state taxes.

Federal Home Loan Bank (FHLB)

The Federal Home Loan Bank operates as a credit reserve system for the nation's savings and loan institutions, which in turn provide credit for residential mortgages. Three FHLB securities are issued, all in book-entry form and all noncallable. They are:

- short-term discount notes (with maturities of 30 to 270 days);
- interest-bearing notes (with maturities of less than one year); and
- bonds (with maturities of one to ten years).

These securities are available in denominations of $10,000, $25,000, $100,000 and $1 million. The minimum requirement for discount notes is $100,000. Interest on notes is payable at maturity; interest on bonds is payable every six months. FHLB securities are backed by mortgages, cash and other bank assets.

Taxation. Interest income from FHLB securities is federally taxable but exempt from local and state taxes.

Federal Home Loan Mortgage Corporation (FHLMC or Freddie Mac)

Directed by the Federal Home Loan Bank system, the Federal Home Loan Mortgage Corporation was created in 1970 to promote the development of a nationwide secondary market in mortgages. It does this by purchasing residential mortgages and selling its interest in them through mortgage-backed securities.

Pass-through certificates. A pass-through security is created when mortgage holders form a collection (or **pool**) of mortgages and sell certificates representing interests in the pool. The term "pass-through" refers to the mechanism of passing payments from home buyers through the mortgage holder to the investors in certificates. Both FHLMC and GNMA function in this way.

FHLMC sells two types of pass-through securities: mortgage participation certificates (PCs) and guaranteed mortgage certificates (GMCs). Investors in Freddie Mac securities receive registered certificates representing an undivided interest in the underlying pool of mortgages. The interest and principal payments from the mortgages pass through to the investors (both the principal and interest once a month with PCs and interest semiannually and principal annually with GMCs).

Taxation. All FHLMC securities are subject to full state and federal income taxation.

The Federal National Mortgage Association (FNMA or Fannie Mae) *only one*

The Federal National Mortgage Association is a publicly held corporation (not a government agency) that provides mortgage capital. FNMA purchases conventional and insured mortgages from agencies such as the Federal Housing Administration (FHA) and the Veterans Administration (VA). The securities are backed by FNMA's general credit.

Types of issues. FNMA issues debentures, short-term discount notes and mortgage backed securities (like GNMA). The notes are issued in denominations of $5,000, $25,000, $100,000, $500,000 and $1 million. Debentures (3- to 25-year maturities) have denominations from $10,000 up in increments of $5,000. Interest is paid semiannually. They are issued in book-entry form only.

Taxation. Interest from FNMA securities is taxed at the federal, state and local levels.

Government National Mortgage Association (GNMA or Ginnie Mae)

GNMA (established in 1968) is a wholly U.S. government-owned corporation that supports the Department of Housing and Urban Development. Ginnie Maes are backed by the full faith and credit of the government.

Types of issues. GNMA buys FHA and VA mortgages and auctions them to private lenders, who pool these mortgages (along with GNMA mortgages acquired from other sources) and sell pass-through certificates based on them. These certificates represent proportionate interests in the mortgages. Each month, principal and interest payments from the pool of mortgages pass through to investors (after deduction of GNMA fees). The amount of principal represented by a GNMA certificate is, therefore, constantly decreasing. In this regard, a GNMA certificate is similar to a single mortgage.

GNMA pass-throughs are popular investments, primarily because they pay a higher rate of interest than comparable Treasury securities and they are guaranteed by the federal government. GNMA also guarantees timely payment of interest and principal. Because GNMAs are backed directly by the government, risk of default is nearly zero. Yields, however, may fluctuate as prices rise and fall in relation to current interest rates. If interest rates fall, home-owners may pay off their mortgages early which affects the yield on certificates. If mortgage interest rates rise, certificates may mature more slowly.

Quoted yields for GNMAs are based on early payment, since few mortgages last for the full term. Yields are based on a 12-year prepayment assumption: that is, that the balance of the mortgage is prepaid in full after 12 years of normally scheduled payments.

Taxation. Interest earned on GNMA certificates is fully taxable at the federal, state and local levels.

Inter-American Development Bank (IADB)

The Inter-American Development Bank promotes social and economic development in member countries in Latin America by financing capital projects. The IADB may borrow from all over the world and its securities have denominations in various international currencies.

Chapter Review

Questions

1. Government bonds and notes are quoted

   ____(A) in 1/8s.
   _×_(B) as a percentage of par.
   ____(C) on a yield to maturity.
   ____(D) as a percentage of par on a discounted annualized basis.

2. The maximum maturity on a Treasury note is

   _×_(A) 10 years.
   ____(B) 5 years.
   ____(C) 3 years.
   ____(D) 1 year.

3. Which of the following are true regarding T bills?

   I.   T bills trade at a discount to par.
   II.   T bills have one year or less maturity.
   III. Most T bill issues are callable.
   IV.   T bills are a direct obligation of the U.S. government.

   ____(A) I and II
   ____(B) I, II and III
   _×_(C) I, II and IV
   ____(D) I, II, III and IV

4. Which of the following U.S. government securities states a rate of interest on its face?

   I.   Treasury bonds
   II.   Treasury notes
   III. Treasury bills

   _×_(A) I and II
   ____(B) II and III
   ____(C) I and III
   ____(D) I, II and III

5. The following is(are) true of Series EE and Series HH bonds EXCEPT *the ones that aren't:*

    I.   EE bonds do not generate interest income; HHs have a fixed coupon.
    II.   HH bonds can be borrowed against.
    III. EE bonds are registered; HH bonds are bearer bonds.
    IV. EE bonds are sold at a discount; HH bonds are sold at par.

    ____(A)   I and II
    ____(B)   I and IV
    ____(C)   II
    _X_(D)   II and III

6. Which of the following is an original issue discount obligation?

    ____(A)   GNMA certificate
    _X_(B)   T bills
    ____(C)   corporate bonds
    ____(D)   FNMA bonds

7. If you invest $10,000 in T bills over a period of years, which of the following are true?

    I.   The principal is stable.
    II.   The interest is volatile.
    III. The interest is stable.
    IV. The principal is volatile.

    _X_(A)   I and II
    ____(B)   III and IV
    ____(C)   I and III
    ____(D)   II and IV

8. 13-week and 26-week T bill auctions are held

    ____(A)   daily.
    _X_(B)   weekly.
    ____(C)   monthly.
    ____(D)   quarterly.

9. The function of the Federal National Mortgage Association is to

    _X_(A)   purchase FHA-insured, VA-guaranteed and conventional mortgages.
    ____(B)   issue conventional mortgages.
    ____(C)   provide financing for government-assisted housing.
    ____(D)   guarantee the timely payment of interest and principal on FHA and VA mortgages.

10. GNMA pass-through certificates pay interest ∧ *principle*

    X (A)   monthly.   <u>S.11</u>
    ___ (B)   quarterly.
    ___ (C)   semiannually.
    ___ (D)   annually.

K105

Chapter Review

Answer Key

1. B.

2. A.

3. C.

4. A.

5. D.

6. B.

7. A.

8. B.

9. A.

10. A.

Chapter Six

Money-Market Instruments

Key Terms

K106

Money-Market Instruments

In the financial marketplace, a distinction is made between the capital market and the money market. The capital market consists of debt and equity securities with maturities of more than one year, and provides intermediate to long-term funding for corporations, municipal and federal governments. The money market, on the other hand, consists of short-term debt issues.

Need for short-term capital. The economy cannot survive on long-term capital alone: it requires a constant flow of money, both cash and credit. Banks must be able to meet demands for currency immediately, even when that demand is unusually large. Businesses must be able to finance current operations as bills come due. Money-market instruments provide ways for businesses, financial institutions and governments to meet their short-term obligations.

Moving money. The business of the money market is to shift funds from institutions with a temporary excess of money to institutions with a temporary deficiency. Typical borrowers in the money market include the U.S. Treasury, large commercial banks, corporations, dealers in money-market instruments, and many states and municipalities. Large institutions such as banks, trust companies and insurance companies are the lenders, the buyers of money-market instruments.

Liquid and safe. Most of the debt or fixed-income securities discussed so far offer a wide range of maturities, from a few months to more than 30 years. Money-market instruments, by contrast, are fixed-income securities with short-term maturities of almost always one year or less. Because they are short-term instruments, money-market securities offer the investor a highly liquid investment that is relatively safe (most have a high credit rating).

Issuers. Money-market instruments issued by the U.S. government and its agencies include:

- Treasury bills;
- Tax Anticipation Notes (TANs);
- Federal Farm Credit Banks' short-term notes and bonds maturing in one year;
- Federal Home Loan Banks' short-term discount notes and interest-bearing notes;
- FNMA short-term discount notes; and
- Short-term discount notes issued by various smaller agencies.

Municipal money-market instruments include BANs, TANs, RANs, TRANs and PNs. Corporations and banks issue the following short-term debt instruments:

- **Repurchase agreements (repos).** Repos are very short-term sales of money-market securities by U.S. government primary dealers who repurchase the securities at a specific price and date.
- **Reverse repurchase agreements**
- **Bankers' acceptances (time drafts).** Short-term, highly liquid bills of exchange drawn on banks and used to finance exports and imports.
- **Commercial paper.** Promissory notes with maturities up to 270 days, generally issued at a discount by large, well-known businesses.
- **Prime paper.** High-quality commercial paper is sometimes called prime paper.
- **Negotiable certificates of deposit.** Certificates with fixed interest rates and minimum face values of $100,000 (although minimums of $1,000,000 and up are more common), issued and guaranteed by banks and can be traded in the secondary market.

Although they are not true money-market instruments, the following investments are usually included in discussions of them due to their short maturities:

- **Federal funds.** Very short-term (usually overnight) unsecured loans between member banks of the Federal Reserve System.
- **Brokers' and dealers' loans.** Loans by brokers and dealers to finance margin purchases, payable on demand the day after being contracted.

Types of Money-Market Instruments

Federal Funds

Banks are required to keep in reserve an amount equal to a specified percent of their depositors' money (called the reserve requirement). The term federal funds is commonly used to describe any excess money that member banks have on deposit with the Federal Reserve System. When a bank falls short of its reserve requirement, it may borrow the excess reserves of some other member bank overnight (federal funds). Interest on these overnight loans is computed at an annualized rate (360-day year) and paid daily. The rate of interest is negotiated between the banks through the federal reserve system and is called the federal funds rate.

The federal funds rate is our economy's most volatile interest rate and is an immediate indicator of short-term interest rates. The rate fluctuates from hour to hour, particularly on Wednesdays, when banks are required to have their reserve accounts up to prescribed levels. The federal funds rate is listed in the newspaper with the money rates.

Prime Rate

Prime rate refers to the interest rate that commercial banks charge their best (or prime) customers (generally, large corporations) for unsecured loans to finance inventory purchases. The rate is set by the banks themselves with larger banks generally setting the prime rate and smaller banks following suit. The prime rate has the greatest impact on our economy, since the cost of borrowing is passed on to the consumer in the price of retail goods.

Like other interest rates, the prime rate is subject to the pressures of supply and demand. When Federal Reserve Board policies are designed to make money more easily available, banks tend to drop the prime rate. When the Fed contracts the money supply, on the other hand, banks tend to raise the prime rate. In general, other interest rates are high when the prime is high and low when it is low.

Repurchase Agreements

Money-market dealers have large amounts of capital, but the security positions they take are often many times that amount. As a result, dealers must raise money to finance their transactions. One way of doing so is to sell securities temporarily, with an agreement to buy them back later. A sale of this sort is called a **repurchase agreement** (or **repo**). The agreement specifies a repurchase price and date (usually) for the repurchase. Repos typically involve government securities.

Though technically a sale of securities, a repurchase agreement is very similar to a fully collateralized loan. Instead of borrowing money and putting up securities as collateral until paying off the loan, the dealer actually sells the securities and agrees to buy them back later at a higher price. The interest on the loan is the difference between the sale price and the repurchase price. In case the dealer defaults on the agreement to buy back the securities, the "lender" (the investor making the initial purchase) holds the securities and can sell them in the open market. Repurchase agreements may be used as both money-market instruments and as instruments of Federal Reserve monetary policy. Sources of repurchase agreements include:

- U.S. government securities dealers financing their inventories;
- commercial banks raising short-term funds; and
- the Federal Reserve effecting short-term changes in member bank reserves (fine-tuning the monetary supply).

Reverse Repurchase Agreements

A reverse repurchase agreement (reverse repo) takes place when an investor sells securities to a dealer and, at the same time, agrees to buy them back at a set price and date. The difference between repurchase agreements and reverse repurchase agreements is that the dealer makes the initial sale in a repo and an investor makes the initial sale in a reverse repo.

Bankers' Acceptances

A banker's acceptance is a short-term time draft (essentially a post dated check maturing in one to 270 days) used to finance international trade. After a draft is accepted by a bank, it is sold by the bank and trades at a discount in the money market. When the acceptance matures, the current holder receives the face amount from the

1 1 yr or less (270 days) max
2 import/ex business
3 Time draft

bank. At maturity, it will be redeemed by the accepting bank at face value. These are considered to be one of the few "secured" money-market instruments, since the holder has a lien against the trade goods in the event the bank fails.

Commercial Paper

Commercial paper consists of unsecured short-term promissory notes issued in bearer form by corporations. Chief among the reasons for issuing commercial paper is to finance accounts receivable and seasonal or unusually large inventories. The primary purchasers of commercial paper are corporations, commercial banks, insurance companies and mutual funds.

Maturities of commercial paper range from a few days up to 270 days. Any security with an original maturity of less than 270 days is exempt from registration under the act of 1933 and is, therefore, less expensive to issue. Commercial paper is issued primarily by large, well-known companies with excellent credit ratings, and is therefore considered a very safe investment.

Direct paper is so called because issuers, such as General Motors Acceptance Corporation (GMAC) or Commercial Credit Corporation, sell their notes directly to the public without using the services of dealers. Direct paper is often known as finance company paper because it is most often issued by finance companies.

Dealer paper. Dealer paper is usually handled in one of three ways by the issuing corporation:

- **Outright sale**. Notes are sold directly to a dealer who sells them to individual investors.
- **Bought and sold basis**. The dealer sells the paper to an investor as agent for the issuing corporation and makes a commission on the transaction.
- **Open rate** (rarely used). A combination of the first two.

Broker Call Rate

The broker call rate is the interest rate that banks charge broker-dealers on money they borrow to lend to margin account customers. Broker call rate is sometimes used synonymously with loan rate or call money. The broker loan rate is usually a percentage point or so above other short-term rates, such as the federal funds rate and T bill rate. These loans are callable on 24-hours' notice.

Negotiable Certificates of Deposit

marketable

Certificates of deposit (CDs) are negotiable certificates that evidence a time deposit of funds with a bank at a specified rate of interest for a specified period of time. A certificate of deposit is an unsecured promissory note guaranteed by the issuing bank. Because CDs are negotiable, they can be bought and sold in secondary markets before their maturity. The minimum size of negotiable CDs included in the money market is $100,000.

A Review of Money Rates

Following is a comparison of the various money-market instruments:

- **Prime Rate.** The base rate on corporate loans at large U.S. money center commercial banks.
- **Federal Funds Rate.** Reserves traded among commercial banks for overnight use in amounts of $1,000,000 or more.
- **Discount Rate.** The charge on loans to depository institutions by the New York Federal Reserve Bank.
- **Call Money Rate.** The charge on loans to brokers on stock exchange collateral.
- **Commercial Paper.** The rate on commercial paper placed directly by General Motors Acceptance Corporation.
- **Certificates of Deposit.** Typical rates paid by major banks on new issues of negotiable CDs, usually on amounts of $1,000,000 or more. The minimum unit is $100,000.
- **Bankers' Acceptances.** Negotiable, bank-backed business credit instruments typically financing an import order.
- **Treasury Bills.** Results of auction of short-term U.S. government bills sold at a discount from face value in units of $10,000 to $1,000,000.
- **Federal Home Loan Mortgage Corporation.** Posted yields on 30-year mortgage commitments for delivery within 30 days.
- **Federal National Mortgage Association.** Posted yields on 30-year mortgage commitments for delivery within 30 days, priced at par.

Chapter Review

Questions

1. All of the following are money-market instruments EXCEPT *the one that isn't*

   ____(A) Treasury bills.
   ____(B) municipal notes.
   ____(C) commercial paper.
   __×_(D) newly issued Treasury bonds.

2. Which of the following is a money-market instrument?

   __×_(A) short-term debt
   ____(B) long-term debt
   ____(C) short-term equity
   ____(D) long-term equity

3. The maximum maturity of commercial paper is

   ____(A) 90 days.
   ____(B) 180 days.
   __×_(C) 270 days.
   ____(D) 360 days.

4. Which of the following are true of negotiable certificates of deposits?

   I.   The issuing bank guarantees the instrument.
   II.   Certificates of deposit are callable.
   III. Minimum denominations are $1,000.
   IV.   They can be traded in the secondary market.

   __×_(A) I and IV
   ____(B) II and III
   ____(C) I, II and III
   ____(D) I, II, III and IV

5. Commercial paper is

   ____(A) a secured note issued by a corporation.
   ____(B) a guaranteed note issued by a corporation.
   __×_(C) a promissory note issued by a corporation.
   __×_(D) none of the above.

6. Which of the following money-market instruments finances imports and exports?

____(A) Eurodollars
____(B) bankers' acceptances
____(C) ADRs
____(D) commercial paper

7. A banker's acceptance is a

____(A) promissory note.
____(B) capital-market instrument.
____(C) time draft.
____(D) means to facilitate the trading of foreign securities.

8. Which of the following money-market instruments is a time draft?

____(A) commercial paper
____(B) CDs
____(C) banker's acceptance
____(D) Treasury bills

9. Which of the following trade with accrued interest?

____(A) zero coupon Treasury obligations
____(B) Treasury bills
____(C) certificates of deposit
____(D) bankers' acceptances

10. A U.S. government bond dealer sells bonds to another dealer with an agreement to buy back the securities in a specified period of time. This is a(n)

____(A) repurchase agreement.
____(B) reverse repurchase agreement.
____(C) open market certificate.
____(D) open market note.

Answer Key

1. D.

2. A.

3. C.

4. A.

5. C.

6. B.

7. C.

8. C.

9. C.

10. A.

Key Terms

Issuing Securities

In general, securities come to market in one of two ways: as new issues (primary distributions) from a corporation, municipality or federal government; or in secondary trades between investors. This chapter introduces you to the market for newly issued securities, beginning with a review of the stock market crash of 1929, the calamity that precipitated the legislation now governing securities trading. As you read about those laws, you'll study the process of registering a new securities offering and the role an investment banker plays in various types of offerings. And, because offerings may be brought to market by more than one firm, you'll read about the formation and functioning of an underwriting syndicate. You will learn to distinguish between primary and secondary offerings, public offerings and private placements and competitive and negotiated bidding. Finally, you'll look at some of the differences between underwriting corporate and municipal securities.

The Regulation of New Issues

The Crash of 1929

During the early 1900s, America enjoyed a long-term bull market that promised to last forever. Attracted by the dream of easy money, Americans turned en masse to Wall Street, pouring over stock price tables and learning the language of trading operations. For the first time, the general public became a significant factor in the market; but often they purchased securities knowing little or nothing about the issuing company or its plans for spending their money.

Investors borrowed heavily (that is, they bought securities on margin). Doing so was an act of faith in the perpetual bull market and an outcome of generous credit policies that allowed investors to borrow most of the purchase price of stock. By the summer of 1929, over a million Americans held stock on margin.

The rest is familiar history. Stock prices reached new heights in early September 1929. Then things fell apart. By the third week of September tumbling prices had brought the Dow Jones averages down 19 points. A month later, averages were 50 points below the September high mark. The downward spiral of prices gained momentum, breaking through crumbling layers of anticipated buying support.

Rapidly declining prices meant investors' stocks were no longer adequate security for the loans they had taken out to buy them. Securities purchased on very low margins, therefore, were sold to raise money; and this caused even deeper drops in market prices. Dumping stock for forced sale destroyed grass-roots investors and wealthy traders alike,

7.2

including those supposedly safe investment trusts, which unloaded their holdings for whatever they could bring.

The Legislative Reaction

After the crash, the market continued to decline for several years. During that time Congress examined the causes of the debacle and passed several laws meant to prevent its recurrence. This legislation included, among others, the Securities Act of 1933, the Securities Exchange Act of 1934 and the Glass-Steagall Act of 1933.

The Securities Act of 1933. Sometimes called the Prospectus Act or the New Issues Act, the Securities Act of 1933 requires issuers of securities to provide sufficient information for investors to make fully informed buying decisions. This information must be registered with the federal government and published in a prospectus. The act outlaws fraud committed in connection with underwriting and issuing securities.

The Securities Exchange Act of 1934. The Securities Exchange Act of 1934 addresses secondary trading of securities, personnel involved in secondary trading and fraudulent trading practices. It also created the Securities and Exchange Commission (SEC, a government agency) to oversee the industry.

In 1938 the act was broadened when amended by the Maloney Act, which provides for the establishment of a self-regulatory body to help police the industry. Under the provision of the Maloney Act, the NASD regulates over-the-counter trading in much the same way the exchanges regulate their members.

The Glass-Steagall Act (Banking Act) of 1933. Securities firms were not the only financial companies to go belly-up in the early 1930s. Banks, too, went broke in vast numbers. Congress concluded that one factor in the general financial collapse was the fact that commercial bankers engaged in investment banking. In their role as commercial bankers they took deposits and financed commercial enterprises. As investment bankers they underwrote stocks, using deposits to finance their securities ventures. Losses on the investment side of the bank, therefore, affected the health of the commercial operations.

With the Glass-Steagall Act (Banking Act) of 1933, Congress attempted to erect a wall between commercial and investment banking. The act forbids commercial banks to underwrite securities (except municipal general obligation bonds) and denies investment bankers the right to open deposit accounts or make commercial loans.

The Securities Act of 1933

Registration of Securities

The 1933 act protects the investor considering purchase of new issues by:

- requiring registration of new issues that are to be distributed inter-state;
- requiring the issuer to provide full and fair disclosure about itself and the offering;
- requiring the issuer to make available all material information necessary for the investor to judge the merit of the issue;
- regulating the underwriting and distribution of primary and secondary issues; and
- providing criminal penalties for fraud in the issuance of new securities.

Registration of securities. When a corporation wants to issue its securities to the public, the SEC requires it to:

- supply detailed information about itself and its securities to the SEC; and
- supply the relevant portion of that information to the general investing public.

A registration statement disclosing material information must be filed with the SEC by the issuer. Part of the registration statement is a prospectus, which must be provided to all purchasers of the new issue. A prospectus contains much of the same information included in the registration statement but without the supporting documentation.

Municipal, government and certain other securities are exempt from the registration requirements of the Securities Act of 1933. Municipal issuers and underwriters are, however, still subject to the antifraud provisions.

Cooling-off period. If approved, the registration can become effective as soon as the 20th calendar day following the date the SEC receives it. This interim is called the cooling-off period. In practice, however, the cooling-off period is seldom 20 days; the SEC usually takes longer to clear registration statements. If it finds that the registration statement needs revision or expansion, the SEC may suspend the review and issue a deficiency letter. The 20-day cooling-off period resumes when the issuer submits a corrected registration statement.

See notebook

The Prospectus

The preliminary prospectus. During the cooling-off period, a registered representative may discuss the issue with clients and provide them with a preliminary prospectus. Also known as a red herring, the preliminary prospectus is used to **obtain indications of interest** from clients. Unlike the final prospectus, it is not an offer to sell the security, as sales may not take place until the registration becomes effective.

A red herring need not include the final price of the securities, commissions, dealer discounts or net proceeds to the company. The document is subject to amendment and must have a warning to that effect printed on its face in red ink.

The final prospectus. When the registration statement does become effective, the issuer amends the preliminary prospectus and adds information, including the final offering price and the underwriting spread. This revised report becomes the final prospectus. Registered representatives may then take orders from those customers who indicated an interest in buying during the cooling-off period.

A copy of the final prospectus must precede or accompany all sales confirmations. The prospectus should include all of the following information:

- description of the offering;
- price of the offering;
- selling discounts;
- date of the offering
- use of the proceeds;
- description of the underwriting, but not the actual contract
- statement of the possibility that the issue's price may be stabilized;
- history of the business;
- risks to the purchasers;
- description of management;
- material financial information;
- legal opinion concerning the formation of the corporation; and
- SEC disclaimer.

The SEC reviews the prospectus to ensure that it contains whatever material facts the SEC deems necessary, but it does not guarantee the accuracy of the disclosures. Further, the SEC does not approve the issue, but simply clears it for distribution. Implying that the SEC has approved the issue is a violation of federal law. Finally, the SEC does not pass judgment on the investment merit of the issue. The front of every prospectus must contain a clearly printed SEC disclaimer clause specifying the limits of the SEC's review procedures. A typical SEC disclaimer clause reads as follows:

> **These securities have not been approved or disapproved by the Securities and Exchange Commission nor has the Commission passed upon the accuracy or adequacy of this prospectus. Any representation to the contrary is a criminal offense.**

The only advertising allowed during the cooling-off period is what is commonly referred to as a tombstone, a simple statement of facts without embellishment. The tombstone (examples of which appear regularly in The Wall Street Journal) merely announces a new issue, but does not offer the securities for sale. It will usually refer to the availability of a prospectus.

The tombstone may appear before or after the effective date. Its publication may be simply a matter of record, that is, an indication that the new issue has already been sold. Issuers are not required to publish tombstones under federal law.

Due Diligence Meeting

Near the end of the cooling-off period, the underwriter holds a due diligence meeting, attended by representatives from the underwriting group, the officers and directors of the issuing corporation, their legal and accounting support staffs and the general public (if they choose to attend).

The purpose of the due diligence meeting is to make a final review of the registration statement and prospectus to ensure their complete accuracy. This involves taking into account any financial developments that occurred during the cooling-off period. In theory, the meeting provides a last chance for the underwriters to abandon the underwriting if it seems ill-advised.

The Underwriting Process

A business or branch of government that plans to issue securities usually works with an **investment banker**, a securities broker-dealer that may also specialize in underwriting new issues by helping to bring securities to market and sell them to investors.

An investment banker's functions may include:

- advising corporations on the best ways to raise long-term capital;
- raising capital for issuers by distributing new securities;
- buying securities from an issuer and reselling them to the public; and
- distributing large blocks of stock to the public and to institutions.

Competitive and Negotiated Underwritings

Competitive bids. An issuer may announce a planned offering of new securities and ask underwriters to bid on the right to distribute the new issue. The underwriter that submits the bid most beneficial to the issuer is awarded the right to underwrite the issue. This is called a competitive bid.

In a bond underwriting, the bid most beneficial to the issuer will be the lowest possible interest cost. A bond offering investors 7% interest, for example, is cheaper for the issuer to pay off than a bond offering 7 1/2%. In stock underwritings, the most attractive bid is for the highest stock price, since that raises the most money for the issuer.

Negotiated underwritings. Instead of asking for competitive bids, an issuer may choose an underwriter and negotiate the terms of the offering with that firm. The terms negotiated include the price the issuer receives for the stocks or bonds, the public offering price, and, in a bond underwriting, the coupon rate.

In both negotiated and competitive underwritings, the underwriter's profit is the difference between the price the issuer receives for the security and the public offering price. This difference is called the spread.

Underwriting agreement. After selection of an underwriter and agreement on the terms of the offering, the underwriter and the issuer sign an underwriting agreement or syndicate letter, which sets forth the terms of the offering and the obligations of the underwriter and the issuer.

Types of Underwriting Commitments

Firm commitment underwriting. A broker-dealer may make a firm commitment to purchase the securities from the issuer and then resell them to investors at the public offering price. Since the underwriter is actually purchasing the securities, it is acting as a **principal** (or dealer) in the underwriting. If the offering is not successful and some securities remain unsold, the underwriter bears the loss.

Because a firm commitment involves risks for the underwriter, the contract includes a market-out clause to relieve the underwriter of obligation if certain circumstances arise before the effective date. For example, if the government enacts a new tax law with severe effects on the issuer, the underwriter might be relieved of its responsibility to purchase the issue.

In a competitive bid, the award is always for a firm commitment underwriting. This makes the bidders especially careful not to promise interest rates so low or stock prices so high that the issue won't sell.

Best-efforts underwriting. In a best-efforts offering the underwriter acts as an agent appointed by the issuer. The underwriter commits to distributing as much of the offering as it can. If all of the securities cannot be sold, the underwriter has no financial obligation to purchase the unsold portion of the offering.

An investment banker acting as agent may also enter into an agreement with the issuer, called an **all-or-none agreement**. Under the terms of this agreement, the investment banker tries to sell the entire issue of securities for the issuer. If the entire issue cannot be sold to the public, the offering is canceled. No sale is final in an all-or-none offering until the offering is completed.

In a **mini-max agreement**, failure to sell a specified minimum amount of securities results in cancellation of the issue. After reaching the minimum, the offering continues to the sale of a specified maximum amount. Investors' funds are held in escrow until the minimum is met or the offering is terminated. No sale is final until the minimum has been reached.

Formation of the Underwriting Syndicate

Many new issues are so large that one underwriter cannot handle the entire offering amount on a firm commitment basis. One investment banker, therefore, invites others to form an underwriting syndicate to carry out the distribution jointly.

The underwriting manager. The investment banker that negotiates with the issuer is known as the underwriting manager or manager of the syndicate. The underwriting manager directs the entire underwriting process, including signing the underwriting agreement with the issuer and directing the due diligence meeting and sales process. There may be more than one manager in a syndicate (acting as co-managers).

The syndicate. The members of the underwriting syndicate make a commitment to the manager to help bring the securities to the public. In a firm commitment offering, all members of the syndicate make a commitment to distribute an agreed upon amount of the issue (their participation or bracket).

Syndicate members sign a syndicate agreement (or syndicate letter) that describes the responsibilities of the members and the manager and allocates syndicate profits. The manager drafts the agreement.

The selling group. Although the members of an underwriting syndicate agree to underwrite an entire offering, they frequently need other firms to help distribute the securities. The syndicate will then invite other broker-dealers to be members of the selling group. Selling group members act as agents with no commitment to buy securities.

Time Line for an Underwriting

Forming the syndicate. The syndicate and selling group may be assembled before or after the issue is awarded to the underwriter. In competitive bidding, the syndicate is assembled first and works together to arrive at the bid. In a negotiated underwriting, the syndicate may be formed after the issuer and the underwriting manager have negotiated the terms of the offering.

Preparing documents. The underwriter may assist the issuer in preparing the registration statement and the prospectus.

Performing due diligence. The underwriter performs due diligence by examining the accuracy of statements in the prospectus and assessing the feasibility of the project for which the funds will be used.

Selling the securities. After the final due diligence meeting and the passing of the cooling-off period, the syndicate sells the securities to the public. This process may take a few hours or several weeks.

Disbursing proceeds. When the offering has been completed, the underwriting manager allocates underwriting profits and commissions. A final accounting must be given to syndicate members for the disbursement of underwriting proceeds.

Underwriting Corporate Securities

The first successful securities underwriting in the United States is attributed to Jay Cooke. During the Civil War, he and his force of bond salesmen placed over $2 billion in U.S. government bonds with private investors throughout the North. By fostering these financial ties between government and investors, Cooke's sales force reinforced the loyalty and patriotism of many investors.

After the war ended, securities underwriting continued to be critical to the economic development of the United States. Today, publicly owned and financed corporations dominate U.S. business. Each year, the underwriting activities of investment bankers provide billions of dollars in new equity and debt financing.

Participants in a Corporate New Issue

The Securities and Exchange Commission (SEC). When a corporation issues new securities, the SEC is responsible for the following.

- reviewing the registration statement filed for the offering (accomplished during the cooling-off period between the filing date and the effective date);
- sending a deficiency letter to the issuer if the review uncovers problems, thus halting the review until deficiencies are corrected, at which point the cooling-off period continues.
- declaring the registration statement effective; that is, releasing the securities for sale.

The issuer. The issuer is the party selling the securities to raise money. The issuer:

- files the registration statement with the SEC;
- files a registration statement with the states in which it intends to sell securities (also known as "Blue-Skying" the issue); and,
- negotiates the price of the securities and the amount of the spread with the underwriter.

approves Spread

National Association of Securities Dealers. The NASD Committee on Corporate Financing reviews the underwriting "spread" to determine fairness and reasonableness of underwriting compensation.

The individual states. State security laws, also called **blue-sky laws** require state registration of new issues. Registering securities with the state is called blue-skying the issue. The issuer or investment banker may blue-sky an issue by one of the following three methods.

- **Qualification.** The issue is registered with the state independent of federal registration, meeting all state requirements.
- **Coordination.** The issuer registers simultaneously with the state and the SEC. Both registrations become effective on the same date.
- **Notification.** Certain states allow some new issues to blue-sky by having the issuers notify the state of registration with the SEC. In this case, no registration statement is required by the state, although certain other information must be filed.

The underwriter. The underwriter not only assists with registration, but also may advise the corporate issuer on the best way to raise capital. The underwriter will consider at least the following matters:

- **Whether to offer stock or bonds.** If stocks are currently selling at depressed prices, offering bonds may seem the more attractive alternative. If bonds are currently selling at high interest rates, the company may choose to issue stock.

- **Tax consequences of the offering.** The interest a corporation must pay on its bonds is tax deductible. The stock dividends it pays investors are paid out of after-tax profits.
- **Whether to go to the money market for short-term funds or the capital market for long-term funds.** If the corporation decides to go to the capital market, it will issue one of the following types of securities: secured bonds, debentures, preferred stock or common stock.

Under the provisions of the Securities Act of 1933, offering such securities normally requires registration with the SEC unless a specific exemption applies.

Types of Offerings

Initial public offering (IPO). A company's initial public offering, sometimes called "going public," is the first time that company sells stock to the public. For example, a small, privately held corporation may decide that it wants to seek a national market. To raise money for expansion without going into debt, the owners may issue stock and allow public investors to share in the ownership of their business.

(new)

Primary and secondary distributions. When a company raises capital by issuing securities, the offering is called a primary distribution, primary offering or new issue. This can be either an initial public offering or a subsequent (but still primary) distribution. In a primary distribution, proceeds of the public sale of the securities are paid directly to the corporation.

A secondary distribution involves securities owned by major stockholders (typically, founders or principal owners of a corporation). In a secondary distribution, sale proceeds go to the sellers of the stock, not to the issuer.

Combined distribution. Often, an issue is a combined distribution (sometimes called a **combined** or **split offering**). A portion of the securities are newly issued and the proceeds of the sale go to the corporation itself. The remainder of the issue is a secondary offering, proceeds of which go to the selling shareholders.

Syndicate Structure

Corporate underwriting normally takes the form of a negotiated agreement between the issuer and investment banker. This negotiated agreement is known as the syndicate letter or underwriting agreement and will be signed just prior to the effective date. An initial letter of intent is used to initiate the underwriting process between the issuer and the underwriter.

Depending upon the size of the offering, the underwriter may want to form a syndicate. The underwriting syndicate includes a syndicate manager and an association of underwriters.

The syndicate manager oversees and manages the underwriting and makes decisions according to the underwriting agreement. Responsibilities include the following:

- Executing the underwriting agreement with the issuer.
- Formulating the agreement among underwriters (also known as the syndicate letter), which establishes the underwriters' liability (Western/divided or Eastern/undivided) and compensation. This compensation, also called a spread, is the difference between the public offering price and the net proceeds to the issuer. *[handwritten: Joint & Several] [handwritten: Several liability]*
- Obtaining from each member of the syndicate a commitment to underwrite a specific amount of the issue. This amount is the individual underwriter's percentage of participation.
- Determining how many shares from its bracket each firm will sell. This portion of an underwriter's participation is called its **retention,** the shares it holds to sell to clients. The unretained portion of a firm's bracket goes into the pool of shares sold by the selling group.
- Reallocating any securities not sold by a member of the syndicate to other syndicate members with excess demand or to members of the selling group.
- Determining whether or not to establish a selling group.
- Forming the selling group to assist in the distribution of the offering. Members of the selling group sign a letter agreeing to abide by the terms of the offering, to maintain the public offering price and to maintain NASD membership. A syndicate member must have the managing underwriter's permission before selling part of the issue to a member of the selling group.

Due Diligence

Once the syndicate has been formed, the underwriting process begins. As part of the underwriting process, due diligence must be exercised by the the investment banker, which means it must:

- examine the use of the proceeds;
- perform financial analysis;
- determine the stability of the company; and
- determine whether the risk is reasonable.

Under the "Full and Fair Disclosure" requirements of the Securities Act of 1933, the underwriter is responsible for making sure the company is doing all it claims. Due diligence includes:

- a preliminary study;
- a letter of intent; and
- a general examination of other factors including industry data (major trends, major competitors, etc.), operational data (company

[handwritten in left margin: Could be tested]

history, major products, etc.), management and employee relations, financial stability and legal status of the issuer.

Cooling-Off Period

After the issuer (with the underwriter's assistance) files with the SEC for registration of the securities, a cooling-off period ensues before the registration becomes effective.

During the cooling-off period, underwriters may use the preliminary prospectus (also known as the red herring) to tell investors about the new issue that will be available after the registration's effective date. Though the underwriter can't sell the securities at this time, it can collect indications of interest (that is, indications from customers that, if and when the issue comes to market, they might be interested in acquiring shares or units) and perform final due diligence.

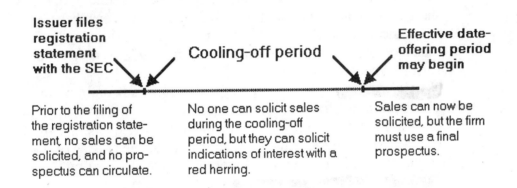

Fig. 7.1 The three phases of an underwriting.

Pricing the New Issue

The price of an issue is determined by the effective date of the registration. It is based on such factors as:

- indications of interest from the underwriter's book;
- prevailing market conditions;
- price the syndicate members will accept; and
- price/earnings ratios of similar companies.

Stabilizing the Issue

During the underwriting, the sale of large numbers of shares (especially if this causes supply to outpace demand) could drive down the market price of the securities. To stabilize the price of the security in the secondary market, the syndicate manger may buy stock through a syndicate bid, which must be placed at or below the public offering price. It would be considered manipulative to create the illusion of a hot issue by bidding the price up.

K107

Underwriting Compensation

The underwriter's compensation is the difference (or **spread**) between what the issuer receives for the security and the public offering price. Figure 7.2 illustrates what might occur if a corporation offers one million shares to the public at $10 per share with a spread on the offering of $1.00 per share.

From this $1.00, the following distributions are made:

- **Manager's fee.** This is compensation for the manager's role in the underwriting. In this example, the fee is $.10 per share or $100,000 for one million shares. The manager's fee is typically the smallest percentage of the total spread. It is not shared with other members of the syndicate. (Additional compensation may be granted to the underwriters in the form of warrants for stock, stock options or stock.) The management fee is deposited in a fund pool called the syndicate account and the managing underwriter takes its fee when the account is liquidated and the syndicate dissolved. The management fee may also be used to cover underwriting expenses, such as advertising.

- **Underwriting fee.** This percentage of the spread compensates syndicate members for the risk they assume in the underwriting. In our example, the underwriting fee might be $.15 of the $1.00 spread. The underwriting fee is allocated (at the closing of the account) to syndicate members based on their participation.

- **Selling concession or reallowance.** The remaining portion of the spread (and the largest part) is the selling concession, the amount received by whoever actually sells the shares (the manager, the syndicate member or the selling group member). In our example, the selling concession is $.75 out of the $1 per share spread.

Distributing the spread. If the managing firm sells shares directly to customers, it receives the concession ($.75), along with its underwriting fee ($.15) and management fee ($.10). A syndicate member keeps the concession ($.75) and the underwriting fee ($.15), for a net of $.90. The selling group members purchase shares from the syndicate at $9.25 and keep only the concession of $.75 per share. The breakdown of the underwriting spread is illustrated in Figure 7.2.

The amount of the spread varies with the type of issue, the strength of the market and the risk involved. It is also reviewed by the NASD's Committee on Corporate Finance for fairness and reasonableness. An underwriter's compensation will also be affected by any of the following:

- **The type of commitment.** A firm commitment earns a larger spread than a best-efforts agreement.
- **The marketability of the security.** An AAA bond will have a smaller spread than a speculative stock.
- **The issuer's business.** A stable utility stock can get by with a smaller spread than a more volatile stock.
- **The size of the offering.** In a very large offering, the underwriter can spread costs over a larger number of shares, thus the per share cost may be lower.

Who Gets What in an Underwriting

$10,000,000 in proceeds from
the sale of the issue
to the public.

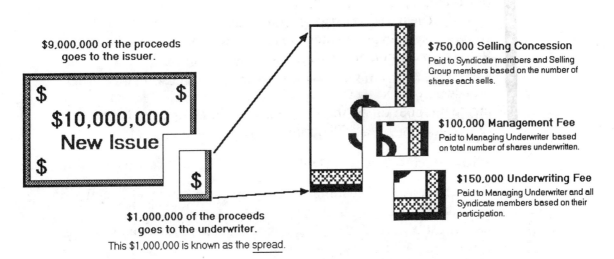

$9,000,000 of the proceeds
goes to the issuer.

$750,000 Selling Concession
Paid to Syndicate members and Selling Group members based on the number of shares each sells.

$100,000 Management Fee
Paid to Managing Underwriter based on total number of shares underwritten.

$150,000 Underwriting Fee
Paid to Managing Underwriter and all Syndicate members based on their participation.

$1,000,000 of the proceeds
goes to the underwriter.
This $1,000,000 is known as the spread.

Fig. 7.2 The spread is split among the participants.

Overallotment

The managing underwriter allocates trades according to the guidelines set forth in the syndicate letter. Occasionally, an underwriter will sell an overallotment of shares, pledging more stock than the issuing corporation has authorized for public sale.

This may sound illegal, but it isn't. Like an airline overbooking, it's an industry norm, a marketing strategy designed to distribute the most shares. An issue may be overallotted in the expectation that some trades will be canceled. The syndicate may have to buy the security in the secondary market to fill the overallotment of customer orders.

Free Riding and Withholding

With hot issues, those that rise in price quickly, an underwriter may be tempted to make a profit by withholding all or part of the issue from the public, then selling after the price has gone up. This practice, called free riding and withholding, violates the NASD Rules of Fair Practice. According to the NASD rules, if public demand exists for the issue, no securities broker-dealer may withhold securities for themselves, their families, their partners or their employees.

To determine whether or not an issue is hot, the NASD compares its price in the immediate secondary market to the public offering price. If there is enough public or institutional interest in the issue and it has the potential to trade at an immediate premium to the public offering price, it is considered a hot issue.

Hot issues may not be sold to:

- the underwriters;
- any NASD member broker-dealer;
- any person associated with any NASD member including officers, directors, registered representatives and employees;
- supported family members of a person associated with an NASD member; or
- any person financially dependent on a person associated with an NASD member.

Under certain circumstances, limited amounts of a hot issue may be sold to :

- finders, attorneys, accountants or others performing a fiduciary service for the managing underwriter;
- bank trust officers and similar senior officers of financial institutions who would be in a position to direct their firms' securities business to the broker-dealer; and
- family members of the above and nonsupported family members of any classified accounts.

The only circumstances under which hot issues may be sold to such customers are:

- the customer has a history of purchasing similar securities in the past from the broker-dealer;
- the size of the purchase is consistent with the normal investment practice of the customer;
- each such sale is of an insubstantial amount, compared to the total amount available to the customer; and
- the total of all sales of the security to all classified accounts is not disproportionate to the amount the dealer had available for sale.

The rule of thumb is that no more than 10% of the dealer's allotment of the hot issue may be sold to these accounts.

Underwriting Accounting *by under manager*

After the issue has been sold and the underwriting completed, the long process of accounting begins. This process includes:

- allocation and payment of concessions;
- determination of participation percentages of underwriting fees;
- distribution of funds in the syndicate account; and
- completion of accounting report to syndicate members.

Buying Groups

Present shareholders. Present shareholders of the issuing corporation may have a preemptive right to retain their current percentage of ownership of a new issue. Current shareholders receive certificates, called rights, which allow them to buy new stock at a subscription price that is typically below the current market price of the outstanding stock.

The general public. Securities that are not subscribed to in a rights offering by present stockholders are next offered to public investors. An investment banker will "**stand by**" to underwrite these securities. This is known as a standby underwriting or **standby offering.** It is done on a firm commitment basis: the underwriter agrees to purchase all shares not sold in a rights offering, then attempts to resell these securities to customers. The corporation may offer the new securities to the general public initially even if the preemptive right is not part of the corporate charter.

Private placements. When one or more large institutional investors express interest in a new issue, a private placement may be made instead of a public offering. Private placements occur when the institutional buyer, using an investment banker, purchases securities from the issuing corporation. Because private placements involve no sales to public investors, they are generally exempt from the registration requirements of the Securities Act of 1933.

Exemptions from the Securities Act of 1933

With certain exceptions, the Securities Act of 1933 requires the registration of new issues with the SEC. Exemptions from registration may be granted because of the nature of the issuer, the type of securities issued or the structure of the offering. The following issuers are not required to register securities offerings with the SEC:

- the U.S. government;
- state and political subdivisions (municipalities);
- nonprofit organizations; and
- banks. *domestic*

Banks are exempted from SEC registration of securities because they file information on new issues with bank regulators ,and that information is available to investors. This exemption applies only to the securities of banks, not to securities of bank holding companies. The 1933 act exempts from registration commercial paper with maturities of less than 270 days, bankers' acceptances and fixed annuity contracts. Even though neither the issuer nor the type of security is exempt, the manner of sale may qualify an offering for exemption. Exempt offerings include Regulation A offerings, intrastate offerings and private placements.

Regulation A Offerings (Reg A)

A Regulation A exemption permits issuers to raise up to $1,500,000 capital in a 12-month period without full registration. This allows a small company access to the capital market to raise a small amount of money without incurring prohibitive costs.

In a Reg A offering, instead of filing a full registration statement with the SEC in Washington, the issuer files an abbreviated notice of sale (offering circular) with the regional office of the SEC. Purchasers are provided with an offering circular rather than a full prospectus. The cooling-off period is reduced to 10 days between filing date and effective date and the issuer need not provide audited financial information. The Regulation A exemption is not available for investment companies or for oil and gas limited partnerships.

Intrastate Offerings (Rule 147)

Offerings that take place entirely in one state do not come under the SEC's jurisdiction. They are, instead, the responsibility of the state commissioner of securities.

SEC Rule 147 exempts such offerings from registration under the following conditions:

- The issuer of the securities has its principal office and receives at least 80% of its income within that state.
- At least 80% of its assets are located within that state.
- At least 80% of the proceeds of the offering are used within that state.
- The broker-dealer acting as underwriter is a resident of that state and has an office in the state.
- All of the purchasers are residents of that state (as verified by voter registration or drivers licenses).

Purchasers of an intrastate issue may not resell the stock to any resident of another state for at least nine months after the underwriting is completed.

Private Placements

Securities are not offered for sale to the general public in a private placement. Since the purpose of the 1933 Securities Act is to protect the public investor, private placements are exempt from registration and prospectus requirements. Investors in private placements are assumed to have sufficient investment knowledge and financial resources.

The SEC does not require registration of an offering privately placed with:

- officers or other "insiders" of the issuer;
- financial institutions or other similar investors who do not need SEC protection (accredited investors); and,   *rich & famous*
- a maximum of 35 individual (nonaccredited) investors.

An accredited investor is generally accepted to be one who:

- has proven a net worth of $1,000,000 or more;
- has proven an annual income of $200,000 or more; or   *(joint of 300,000 +)*
- ~~makes a purchase of $150,000 or more (as long as that purchase~~   *delete* ~~does not represent an investment of more than 20% of the investor's net worth).~~

4 page disclosure – Form D

Chapter Review

Questions

1. Which of the following are types of underwriting?

   I. firm commitment
   II. all or none
   III. standby
   IV. best efforts
   V mini-max

   ____(A) I and II
   ____(B) II and III
   ____(C) I, III and IV
   _X_(D) I, II, III and IV , V

2. In a best-efforts offering, an underwriter

   _X_(A) makes no guarantee that an offering will be sold.
   ____(B) makes a best-efforts attempt to reduce the underwriting spread.
   ____(C) guarantees a minimum price and makes a best-efforts attempt to increase that price.
   ____(D) makes a best-efforts attempt to bring the security to market within the cooling-off period.

3. A standby underwriting is used

   ____(A) for a company going public for the first time.
   ____(B) in a secondary offering.
   ____(C) in a best-efforts underwriting.
   _X_(D) in a rights offering.

4. The XYZ Company has filed an offering of 425,000 shares of common stock. One-third of the shares are being sold by existing stockholders and the balance are new shares. Which of the following are true?

   I. The XYZ Company will receive the proceeds from the entire sale.
   II. This offering is a combined distribution.
   III. The selling stockholders will receive some of the proceeds.
   IV. This offering is an exchange distribution.

   ____(A) I and II
   ____(B) I and IV
   _X_(C) II and III
   ____(D) II, III and IV

5. The principal functions of an investment banker are to

    I. distribute securities to the public.
    II. provide a secondary market.
    III. provide financing for the individual.
    IV. advise the issuer about alternatives in raising capital.

    ____(A) I and II
    ____(B) II and III
    ✗(C) I and IV
    ____(D) III and IV

6. All the following are prohibited during the cooling-off period EXCEPT *the one that isn't*

    ____(A) promising a certain amount of the issue to the customer.
    ✗(B) soliciting indications of interest.
    ____(C) taking an order.
    ____(D) accepting a check from the customer to purchase the issue.

7. The red herring typically includes all of the following EXCEPT *the one that isn't*

    ____(A) a list of officers of the company.
    ✗(B) price of the issue.
    ____(C) a list of principal underwriters.
    ____(D) number of shares.

8. The Securities Act of 1933 does all the following EXCEPT *it doesn't*

    ____(A) require SEC registration of most new issues of securities.
    ____(B) require publication of material information about the issue.
    ✗(C) provide for the establishment of self-regulatory organizations.
    ____(D) exempt certain types of securities from registration.

9. The underwriting manager is the

    ____(A) employee who supervises the underwriting activities of an investment banker.
    ____(B) broker-dealer who supervises the activity of the issuer on authority of the SEC.
    ____(C) broker-dealer that publishes the offering prospectus.
    ✗(D) broker-dealer that supervises the activity of the underwriting syndicate and selling group.

Longman Group USA, Inc.
Copyright 1989. All rights reserved.

K107

10. Which of the following are considered by an underwriter when establishing the offering price?

    I.   projected earnings for the company
    II.   likely dividends to be paid over the coming years
    III. demand for the security by the investing public
    IV. earnings multiples for other companies in the market in the same industry

    ____(A)   I and II
    ____(B)   I, II and III
    ____(C)   I, II and IV
    __X_(D)   I, II, III and IV

Answer Key

1. D.

2. A.

3. D.

4. C.

5. C.

6. B.

7. B.

8. C.

9. D.

10. D.

7.24

Chapter Eight

Trading Securities

Key Terms

Trading Securities

Wall Street is a marketplace where merchants, agents and customers of the financial industry meet to buy and sell stocks, bonds and other securities. Much buying and selling of stocks and bonds takes place on exchanges where stocks are traded in a two-way auction process. The major exchanges include:

National

- the New York Stock Exchange (NYSE);
- the American Stock Exchange (AMEX); and
- regional stock exchanges

Other trades take place in the nationwide network of broker-dealers known as the over-the-counter (OTC) market. The following material introduces you to the terminology and language of trading securities.

Role of the Broker-Dealer

Firm of NASD or/and Exchange   NOT A PERSON

Brokers. Those engaged in buying and selling securities must register as broker-dealers. Most firms act both as brokers and dealers, but not in the same transaction. Brokers are agents who arrange trades for clients and charge them a commission. The broker does not buy shares, but simply arranges a trade between a buyer and a seller.

Dealers. When firms act as dealers (or principals), they buy and sell securities for their own accounts (inventory). When selling from their inventory, dealers charge their clients a markup rather than a commission. A markup is the difference between the current interdealer offering price and the actual price charged the client. When a price to a client includes a dealer's markup, it is called the net price. The dealer doesn't just arrange a trade, but actually sells the client shares from its inventory.

See notebook

Broker	Dealer
Acts as an agent, transacting orders on behalf of the client.	Acts as a principal, dealing in securities for its own account and at its own risk.
Charges a commission.	Charges a markup or markdown.
Is not a market-maker.	Makes markets and takes positions (long or short) in securities.
Must disclose to the client its role and the amount of its commission.	Must disclose to the client its role, but not necessarily the amount or source of the markup or markdown.

Bids, Offers and Quotes

(handwritten in margin: see notebook)

A quote (or quotation) is a dealer's current bid and offer on a security. The current bid represents the highest price at which any dealer will buy, and the current offer (or asked price) represents the lowest price at which any dealer will sell. The difference between the bid and ask is known as the spread.

A typical quote might be expressed as: "Bid 63; offered 63 1/4." This means that the highest purchase price the dealer will pay is 63 and the lowest selling price the dealer will accept is 63 1/4. The spread is 1/4 point between the bid and asked. The broker could also say "63 bid; 63 1/4 ask," or, even more simply, "63 to 1/4." The following table illustrates the customer's and the broker-dealer's relationship to the quote.

	Bid	**Asked/Offer**
Quoting Dealer	Buys	Sells
Customer	Sells	Buys

Types of Markets

A market is the exchange (or system) in which trades of securities occur. There are four markets:

- The **exchange market**. The best-known exchange is the New York Stock Exchange, but there are others, including the American Stock Exchange (also in New York City) and several regional exchanges. Securities traded on an exchange have met the exchange's requirements and are said to be listed and thus eligible for margin. The exchange market is an auction market.
- The **OTC market** is a system of telephone and computer connections between broker-dealers. On the OTC market, the only stocks eligible for margin are those that have been specifically designated by the Federal Reserve Board. The OTC market is a negotiated market.
- The **third market** comprises over-the-counter trading of listed securities.
- The **fourth market**, or institutional market, is direct trading between institutional investors without the mediation of a broker-dealer. These investors are connected by a computer network called INSTINET.

(handwritten: institutional network)

(handwritten: Inventory of dealers)

The New York Stock Exchange

The following sections explain the exchange market as exemplified by the New York Stock Exchange (NYSE). Major topics include the functioning of an auction market, organization and membership of the NYSE, listing requirements, auction procedures, types of orders and the role of the specialist on the exchange.

Auction market. Exchange securities are bought and sold in an **auction market**. Although exchanges are called "stock" markets, they are also used for the trading of other securities (bonds, options, rights, etc.). Brokers representing clients or dealers buying and selling for their own accounts, bid for and offer securities on the exchange floor, an area designated for trading. Of the exchanges in the United States, by far the best known is the New York Stock Exchange.

Often called the "Big Board," the NYSE is located in New York City and it handles roughly three-fourths of all exchange transactions. The American Stock Exchange, (AMEX), which handles one-fifth of exchange transactions, is also in New York City. Stocks listed on the NYSE can also be listed on regional exchanges (such as the Midwest Exchange), but not on the American Exchange. The primary objective of the NYSE is to provide a central location for the transaction of its members' business. The exchange itself does not buy and sell stocks.

Securities traded on the NYSE must satisfy the exchange's listing requirements, and are known as **listed securities**. The exchange itself does not influence or determine prices. Its only active role is to monitor operations and to facilitate an orderly market and prevent fraudulent practices.

Both the NYSE and the AMEX begin trading at 9:30 am Eastern time each business day and close trading at 4 pm Eastern.

Organization. The New York Stock Exchange is a corporation operated by a board of directors. The board is responsible for setting policy, supervising exchange and member activities, listing securities, overseeing the transfer of members' seats on the exchange and judging whether an applicant is qualified to be a specialist.

Membership. The number of memberships, or **seats**, on the NYSE is fixed at 1,366. Since all these seats are currently owned, one must purchase a seat from a member, not from the exchange. The buying and selling of seats is done through negotiation, with approval of the entire membership. When the market is up, seats are substantially more expensive than they are in bear markets.

Technically, only individuals can own seats on the exchange. Some seats, in fact, are held in families and pass from generation to generation. Many seat ownerships,

8.4

however, are sponsored and funded by firms, which explains references to "member firms."

Only NYSE members (the individual owners of seats) can trade on the floor. These traders are of four types:

- **Commission house broker** — Also called floor brokers, commission house brokers execute orders for clients and for the firm's account.

- **Two-dollar broker** — When commission brokers are too busy to execute all of their firms' orders, they call on the services of two-dollar brokers (also known as competitive traders) to execute orders for them. The two-dollar brokers charge a commission for their services.

- **Registered trader** — Registered traders are members of the exchange who trade primarily for their own accounts. If they accept a public customer's order from a floor broker, they must give that order priority. They may not execute their own trades while holding an unfilled public order.

  spoiled rich kid

- **Specialist** — Specialists facilitate trading in specific stocks. Their chief function is to maintain a fair and orderly market in those stocks. In fulfilling this function, they act as both brokers and dealers. They act as dealers when they execute orders for their own accounts and as brokers when they execute orders left with them by other members. Specialists do not participate in every transaction in the stocks in which they specialize, but any transactions in that stock must take place in front of the specialist assigned that stock.

Allied members. Allied members are executive officers, directors or holders of more than 5% of the voting stock of a member firm. Though allied members are responsible for the supervision of their organization, they are not allowed to trade on the exchange floor.

Trading posts. On the floor of the exchange are a number of horseshoe-shaped trading posts surrounded by video display terminals. Each stock listed with the exchange is traded at a particular post. At present, the exchange has 22 posts each trading about 100 securities. At each post are the specialists, each of whom has been assigned a certain number of issues.

A commission house broker with a buy or sell order, therefore, takes the order to the post designated for that security. Around the post the broker will find a crowd, interested in the security. The "crowd" may be as small as one specialist or as large as two specialists and a group of interested brokers and dealers. The commission house broker may execute the buy or sell order in this crowd at the best available price, leave the order with the specialist to execute when the price is right or hand the order to a two-dollar broker to trade.

Exchange Listing Requirements

Listing. The initial requirements for any corporation that wants its stock listed on the NYSE are as follows.

- The market value of its publicly held shares must be at least $18 million.
- At least 1,100,000 shares must be publicly held.
- Two thousand stockholders must each hold 100 shares or more (2,000 round-lot owners).
- Corporate earnings before federal income tax must be at least $2.5 million for the latest fiscal year and at least $2 million for each of the two preceding years.

Consideration is also given to the following factors:

- whether there is national interest in the company;
- the market for its products (small. large, diversified, etc.);
- the strength and stability of the company;
- prospects for maintaining position in an expanding industry; and
- the company's prospective earnings.

Higher-than-minimum standards may apply if there is evidence of lack of public interest in the company. Such evidence might include:

- low volume on another exchange;
- lack of OTC dealer interest in the company;
- unusual geographic distribution of securities; or,
- slow growth in number of shareholders.

Delisting. The NYSE reserves the right to delist companies. For example, the exchange might stop trading the securities of a company if the number of shareholders, shares outstanding or total market value of outstanding shares fell below certain levels. The exchange may also delist companies that engage in activities adverse to investors' interests, including failure to disclose financial statements or to solicit proxies for all meetings.

Auction Procedures

To establish the best bid, a buying broker must announce a bid at least an eighth of a point higher than the current best bid. The best offer by a selling broker must be at least an eighth of a point lower than the current best offer.

There may be several bids at the same price and several offers at the same price. To provide for the orderly transaction of business on the floor, the highest bids and the lowest offers always receive first consideration.

Priority, Precedence and Parity

What happens when more than one broker enters the crowd with the same bid or offer? The specialist awards the trade in the following order:

- **Priority.** First order in.
- **Precedence.** Largest order of those submitted.
- **Parity.** Random drawing. *matched and lost or won*

Priority goes to the broker who clearly is the first to bid or offer at the best price. Only one broker can have priority. This broker must receive the first execution. The first best bid (assuming there are no subsequent bids at a higher price) always has priority. That bid maintains its priority, even if the broker who made it leaves that trading post and hands the order to another broker or to a specialist.

Precedence means that the broker who can fill the largest order gets the execution. Precedence is considered only after priority. If no bid or offer clearly is first, then the largest bid or offer takes precedence.

Parity occurs when neither priority nor precedence can be established. Parity means that everything is the same (at par). Brokers who have established the same bid or offer at the same time and can fill the same size order, must do a "match." That is, they draw straws or toss a coin. The winner receives execution.

Arbitrage

Arbitrage is a trading strategy used by specialized traders (called **arbitrageurs**) to profit from temporary price differences in between markets or securities. There are several types of transaction called arbitrage. Specialized traders who make arbitrage transactions are called arbitragers. In general, arbitragers look for ways to make a profit on temporary price disparities in the same or equivalent securities.

Market arbitrage. Sometimes a security trades in more than one market- on two exchanges, for example, opening up the possibility that the security will be selling for two different prices at the same time. When that happens, arbitragers can buy at the lower price in one market and sell at the higher price in the other.

Security arbitrage. Arbitrage trades are also possible in equivalent securities-convertible bonds and the underlying stock, for example. If conditions are right, an arbitrager may be able to convert bonds to stock and sell the stock for a profit.

Risk arbitrage. Risk arbitrage becomes possible in proposed corporate takeovers. Arbitragers buy the stock in the company being acquired and sell short the stock of the acquiring company. They do so believing that the merger will raise the stock price of the acquisition and lower the stock price of the acquirer.

Role of the Specialist on the Exchange

Qualifications. About one-quarter of the NYSE members are specialists who trade specific stocks assigned to them. Most specialists handle a number of different stocks traded at the same post. The NYSE board of directors selects specialists on the basis of their ability to keep an orderly market and on their available capital.

For efficiency, several specialists may combine their capital and form specialist units. Most of these units are partnerships or joint accounts. Therefore, when you hear the term specialist, this means a member of a specialist firm who is currently on duty.

Market maker. The specialists' primary function is to make a market or maintain a market in each assigned stock. This means that they stand ready to buy or sell a round lot of the security (as well as give a quote on that security). The specialist must have enough capital to maintain a substantial position in the security. Maintaining markets through specialists is one of the functions an exchange performs for public investors.

Agent and principal. The specialist is both agent (broker) and principal (dealer). On the floor of the exchange, specialists can act in two capacities:

- As agents (or broker's brokers), executing all orders left with them by other brokers. Specialists accept certain kinds of orders from other members (such as limit and stop orders) and execute these orders as conditions permit. For acting in this capacity, the specialist receives a commission from the other broker's firm.
- As dealers (principals), buying and selling for their own accounts. Specialists, as you saw above, buy and sell in their own accounts (as dealers) to make a market in an assigned stock. They are expected to maintain continuous, fair and orderly markets; that is, markets with reasonable price variations.

The specialist's book. A specialist's most important tool is the specialist's book, a record of limit and stop orders the specialist holds for execution. The book's contents are confidential; the entries need not be disclosed by the specialist to anyone.

Long and Short Sales

Long sale. The most common transaction is the opening or closing of a long account. The customer decides XYZ stock will appreciate in value and opens a long position by purchasing shares in the company. In this case the customer believes the stock's value will appreciate enough to allow him to sell the stock at a profit.

Short sale. Somewhat less typical is the short sale. An investor who sells short has the same profit motive as an investor who buys long, but does everything in reverse. The short-selling investor initially borrows stock from a broker-dealer, then sells the stock at the market. The investor anticipates that the price of the stock will go down enough to allow him to replace the borrowed stock at a cheaper price at a later date.

The broker-dealer, if able to find shares of that security to borrow, loans the shares to the client and lets him take his chances that the stock will indeed become cheaper in the future. The client takes a short position by selling shares of stock he does not own.

Short sales are considered risky. The seller must buy stock to repay the loan and is thus at the mercy of the market. If the stock price rises instead of falls in price, the investor may have to pay a great deal of money to buy the shares necessary to repay the loan.

	Long Position	**Short Position**
First Transaction	Buy Low	Sell High (Borrow securities and sell them.)
Second Transaction	Sell High	Buy Low (Buy back securities to replace those borrowed.)

Short Sale Rule

Orders to sell short may be executed only on a plus tick or a zero-plus tick. A plus tick is a price higher than the last different price, from 40 to 40 1/8, for example. A zero-plus tick occurs when the last trade for the security was made at the same price as the trade before, but that trade was higher than the previous trade. A trade of 40 to 40 1/8 would be a plus tick and then if the next trade was at 40 1/8, that would be considered a zero- plus tick.

Look at the sequence of prices in the illustration that follows. An order to sell short could be entered on the second, third and fourth trades.

Trade:	1	2	3	4	5	6
Price:	42	42 1/4	42 1/4	42 3/8	42 1/4	42 1/4
Tick:		+	0+	+	−	0−
Plus Tick or Zero Plus Tick	no	YES	YES	YES	no	no

Fig. 8.1 Plus ticks and zero-plus ticks.

Marking the Order Ticket

When a customer calls in an order to sell, a registered rep must inquire whether the customer is selling securities that he or she holds (a long position) or needs to borrow stock to complete delivery (a short position). The sell order ticket must be marked long, short or short-exempt (there are some exemptions from the short sale plus-tick rule): the sell short order will only be executed then at a plus tick or a zero-plus tick.

The Over-the-Counter Market

Not all trading takes place through auctions on an exchange floor. In fact, the oldest continuous securities market is the **over-the-counter market**, in which broker-dealers negotiate trades directly with one another. Although "over-the-counter" has an old-fashioned ring to it, the modern OTC market is actually a highly sophisticated telecommunications and computer network connecting broker-dealers across the country.

OTC trading is regulated by the National Association of Securities Dealers (NASD), the industry association that administers the Series 7 examination. And the computerized information system that keeps track of OTC trading is called NASDAQ, the National Association of Securities Dealers Automated Quotation service.

Securities that can be traded in the over-the-counter market include but are not limited to:

- ADRs (American Depository Receipts);
- bank stocks and insurance company stocks;
- most corporate bonds;
- municipal bonds;
- U.S. government securities;
- common and preferred stock;
- equipment trust certificates; and
- closed-end investment companies.

Mutual funds and other new issues are initially issued over-the-counter. Since open-end mutual funds are redeemed through their issuer, however, they do not continue to trade in the OTC market. To summarize:

Over-the-Counter	**New York Stock Exchange**
Securities prices are determined through negotiation.	Securities prices are determined through auction bidding.
Regulated by the National Association of Securities Dealers (NASD).	Regulated by the New York Stock Exchange (NYSE).
Broker-dealers must be registered with both the SEC and the NASD.	Broker-dealers must be registered with the SEC and be Exchange members.
Traded at many locations throughout the country.	Traded only on the floor of the NYSE.

The Role of the Broker-Dealer

Filling an order. A broker-dealer may fill a customer's order to buy securities in any of the following ways.

- The broker may act as the client's agent by finding a seller of the securities and arranging a trade.
- The dealer may buy the securities from the market maker, mark up the price and resell them to the client on a dealer basis.
- If the dealer has the securities in its own inventory, it may sell the shares to the client from that inventory.

A firm is prohibited from acting as both a broker and a dealer in the same transaction. For example, your firm cannot make a market in a stock, mark up that stock and then add an agency commission. If the firm acts as a broker, it may charge a commission. If it acts as a dealer, it may charge a markup (or markdown).

Quotations

Firm quotations. A firm quotation means that the broker-dealer is willing to buy or sell at least one trading unit (100 shares of stock or five bonds) at the quoted price. When an OTC firm makes a market in a security, the broker-dealer must be willing to buy or sell at least one trading unit of the security at its firm quote. All quotes are firm quotes unless otherwise indicated. Some typical expressions used to denote subject and firm quotes are shown on the next chart. Note that firm quotes are absolute statements, whereas subject quotes are hedged.

In a typical transaction, a trader at one broker-dealer will call a trader at another broker-dealer (a market maker) to buy XYZ. A market maker might give a another broker-dealer a quote that is firm for an hour with five-minute recall. This is a firm quote that remains good for an hour. If, within that hour, the market maker receives another order for the same security, the trader will call the broker-dealer back and give it five minutes to confirm its order or lose its right to buy that security at the price it was quoted.

The OTC market works because market makers don't back away from their firm quotes (that is, once they give a quote, they honor it). "Backing away" from a firm quotation for a round lot (100 shares) is against NASD rules

Subject quotations. Subject quotations are, as the name suggests, subject to further negotiation. The dealer or broker may or may not be willing to buy or sell the stock at exactly that price at this time. Interdealer quotations in any written form are subject quotations. A typical subject quote would be, "The stock is 32-32 1/2, subject."

Work-out quotations. A work-out quote is usually given as a range of prices within which the dealer or broker thinks it can make the trade. A broker-dealer might give a work-out quote by saying, "It looks like 30 to 33, work out."

Subject or Work-Out Market	Firm Market
It is around 40 - 41.	The market is 40 - 41.
Last I saw it was 40 - 41.	It is currently 40 - 41.
It is 40 - 41, subject.	We can trade it 40 - 41.
40 to 42 1/2, work out.	We will do it 40 - 41.

It is quoted 40 -41 (someone else)

Negotiated Trading

The OTC market is a negotiated market in which market makers may bargain during a trade. A negotiated market is competitive: your firm is competing against a number of other brokerage firms, each trading for its own inventory. Dealers communicate by phone and when a customer wants to put in an order to buy or sell securities, your firm will call one or more market makers in that security and negotiate a price.

Exchange → auction market
OTC → negotiated market

National Association of Securities Dealers Automated Quotations System (NASDAQ)

Market Makers

One of the traditional advantages of exchange trading has been ease of keeping track of information about securities. Keeping track of the price of a security traded over-the-counter by dealers across the country is a much more formidable task.

In the exchange market, you will remember, specialists act as market makers and stand ready, willing and able to trade in specified securities. In the over-the-counter market, of course, there are no exchanges and no specialists. But some OTC dealers make a market in certain securities. They keep these securities in their inventories, buying and selling them for their own profit and at their own risk. Since a broker-dealer acting as a market maker buys and sells for its own account, rather than arranging trades, it acts as a principal and not an agent. The market maker takes a position in the security by purchasing it or by selling it short (borrowing to deliver). This is called position trading. OTC securities listed with NASDAQ (about which you'll read more later) must be traded by at least two market makers.

Requirements for market-makers. In order for a firm to make a market in a particular security, it must meet certain minimum NASD standards. Among these are that the firm (or individual) must:

- be an NASD member;
- meet minimum net capital requirements;
- be able and willing to execute a trade for at least a normal trading unit at its quote;
- ensure that its quotations are reasonably related to the current market for that security;
- file daily volume reports for those securities in which it makes a market; and
- performs these functions during normal business hours.

When more than one firm makes a market in a security, the market price of that security results from competition among those firms. A registered representative who takes a client's order to buy an OTC stock turns the order over to the trader of the firm, who may contact several market makers and arrange the trade at the lowest offering price. If only one firm makes a market in a particular security, it cannot claim to be offering that security "at the market." As the only dealer in that stock, the firm (not a market of competing buyers and sellers) plays the major role in setting the price.

NASD Automated Quotations System (NASDAQ)

To bring some order into OTC trading, NASDAQ (NASD Automated Quotations System) provides a computer link between broker-dealers who trade OTC. NASDAQ lists frequently traded OTC securities in much the same way an exchange lists exchange-traded securities.

Generally, securities included in the NASDAQ system include any actively traded security registered under the Securities and Exchange Act of 1934 (including stocks, bonds, warrants, rights and convertible securities). Specifically, a NASDAQ company must have the following qualifications:

- total assets of $2 million or more;
- capital and surplus of at least $1 million;
- 100,000 or more publicly held shares;
- 300 or more shareholders;
- at least two registered and active market makers; and
- eligibility for authorization and registration under either the Securities Exchange Act of 1934 or the Investment Company Act of 1940.

In addition to these minimum requirements, the issuers of securities listed with NASDAQ must submit audited financial reports and documents and continue to meet the minimum standards required for ongoing listing.

National Market System (NMS) Stocks

Within NASDAQ, some of the larger stocks comprise the National Market System (NMS). More information is made available about NMS stocks than about other NASDAQ stocks. According to the SEC, stocks to be included in the National Market System must meet higher minimum conditions than those listed only with NASDAQ, including:

See notebook

- average trading volume (600,000 shares a month for preceding six months);
- number of publicly held shares (500,000);
- market value of their outstanding shares;
- bid on the stock of $10 or more per share;
- company net worth; and,
- total assets.

Tracking Traded Securities

Stock Tables

The securities industry divides amounts less than one dollar (referred to as a point) into eighths of a dollar, each with a value of 12 1/2 cents ($.125). Very low-priced stocks may be quoted in fractions of a dollar as small as sixteenths ($.0625 or 6 1/4 cents), thirty-seconds ($.03125 or 3 1/8 cents) and sixty-fourths ($.015625 or 1 9/16 cents).

Consolidated stock tables, which represent the most complete information, are printed in most major newspapers. Following is an example of a NYSE Composite Transactions table as it might be printed in the *The Wall Street Journal*. It reports activity for the previous day.

NEW YORK STOCK EXCHANGE COMPOSITE TRANSACTIONS
Tuesday, September 13, 1998

Quotations include trades on the Midwest, Pacific, Philadelphia, Boston and Cincinnati Stock Exchanges and reported by the National Association of Securities Dealers and INSTINET.

52 Weeks High	Low	Stock	Div	Yld %	P-E Ratio	Sales 100s	Net High	Low	Close	Net Chg.
80	40	ABCorp	.75	.1	12	3329	78	68	73	- 1 1/2
42 5/8	26 7/8	AFAP	2.40	5.6	12	x1265	42 5/8	41 1/4	42 5/8	+ 1 1/4
35	24 5/8	Anchor	1.48	4.9	36	1960	30	29 3/4	30	+ 1/4
84 1/4	40	BrlNth	2.20	3.7	13	2701	59 3/8	58 1/4	58 3/4	+ 1/2
82 1/2	39 5/8	Dsny	.32	.6	17	6211	53 3/4	52	53 1/4	+ 1 1/4
38 3/8	19 1/2	Fuqua	.24	.9	13	454	28	26 7/8	27 3/8	+ 1/4
8 3/4	3 5/8	Navistr	...	... ...	...	6484	4 1/2	4 1/8	4 1/4	...

Fig. 8.2 A typical stock quotation.

The yearly range of prices is shown in the first two columns. This range is for the previous 52 weeks plus the current week but not the latest trading day. AFAP, for example, has hit a high of 42 5/8 ($42.625) and a low of 26 7/8 ($26.875) per share. The name of the stock and the annual dividend follow the 52-week price range. The dividend is quoted as an annual dollar amount based on the most recent quarter. AFAP is paying an annual dividend of $2.40 per share. The "Yld" (or Yield) column reports the current yield of the security. For AFAP, the yield is 5.6% ($2.40 divided by 42 5/8 equals 5.6%).

The "P-E Ratio" (price/earnings ratio) is given in the column after the yield column. It is the ratio of the current price of the stock to its earnings during the past 12 months. AFAP's P-E ratio is 12.

The "Sales" column reports number of shares sold during the day. Trading is reported in round lots of 100 shares each. The entry for AFAP is 1265, which means that 126,500 shares of stock were traded the previous day. The "x" before the sales volume indicates that the stock is selling ex-dividend or ex-rights, meaning that a buyer will not receive the next dividend check.

The two columns after "Sales" list the daily range of prices, the security's high and low prices for the day. AFAP sold for a high of 42 5/8 and a low of 41 1/4. The column labeled "Close" shows the final price for the day. AFAP closed at 42 5/8, at the top of its 52-week range.

The net change in price is reported in the final column. The net change is the difference between the closing price on the trading day reported and the previous day's closing price. AFAP closed up 1 1/4 points from the previous day's (Monday's) close, which would have been 41 3/8 on that day (42 5/8 - 1 1/4 = 41 3/8).

Over-the-Counter Stock Listings

OTC stocks. Thousands of securities trade in the over-the-counter market. Most of them are traded in the region where the company does business and first went public. Daily quotations on these securities and the names of market makers who trade each of them are found in the pink sheets, which are named for the color of paper they are printed on. These are interdealer quotations and are subject to change.

OTC stocks with more widespread interest may be listed under "Additional OTC Quotes," and usually display only the bid and ask.

NASDAQ. OTC securities that have a national interest are listed on the NASDAQ system. Quotes for these securities can then be found on the quote machine, the computer that facilitates OTC trading.

Listings for more frequently traded NASDAQ securities may appear in *The Wall Street Journal*, and contain the same information supplied for listed securities.

NASDAQ (NMS). NASDAQ stocks with a very high national interest may be listed on the NASDAQ National Market System (NMS). Although these securities may be eligible for listing on an exchange, the company may choose to sell over-the-counter instead. Apple Computer is an example of a well-known company that does not list its stock on an exchange.

The Exchange Market

How the System Works

An investor in Chicago goes to a local broker, a member firm of the NYSE, and gives the registered representative a market order to buy 100 shares of XYZ Company. At about the same time, another investor in Palm Springs places a market order with a local broker, also a member firm, to sell 100 shares of XYZ stock. The orders are quickly sent to the trading departments of the respective firms and then transmitted directly to the floor of the NYSE. The firms' floor brokers, located on the trading floor, receive the orders from teletype machines serving the trading area.

Once the floor brokers receive the orders, they proceed to the trading post where XYZ is bought and sold. (Remember, each listed stock is traded at specific locations or posts and each listed stock has at least one specialist assigned to it).

At the post, brokers enter the crowd, a group of other brokers who also have orders for XYZ. "How's XYZ?" asks the broker representing the Chicago investor. "Thirty and three-eighths to three-quarters," someone (usually the specialist) responds. This is the current bid and asked quotation- the best bid is 30 3/8, the most anyone in the crowd is willing to pay; and 30 3/4 is the best offer (or the lowest price) at which anyone will sell.

The broker for the Chicago investor will try to get a better price than the offer by saying "thirty and a half for one hundred." If there is no response, the broker will raise the bid in increments of 1/8. Perhaps at 30 5/8, the Palms Springs broker yells, "Sold!" (meaning "I sold"), feeling it is the best price that can be expected at that time.

The transaction is complete; customers are notified of the execution by their registered representatives, often within minutes after the order was first sent to the floor. If there had been no offers to sell stock when the floor broker representing the Chicago investor arrived at the post, the specialist might have sold the stock from his or her own account. Similarly, if a broker brings a sell order and finds no buyers, the specialist may buy the stock for his or her own account.

Types of Orders

Clients who want to buy or sell securities can enter several different types of orders. In this section you will read about the following:

- **Market orders**: Executed immediately at the market price.
- **Limit orders**: Set a limit on the amount paid or received for the securities.
- **Stop orders**: Become market orders if the stock reaches the stop price (or the trigger price if the order is a stop-limit).
- **Stop limit orders**: Entered as stop orders and change to limit orders if the stock hits the trigger price.
- **Day orders**: Expire if not filled by the end of the day.
- **Good-till-canceled (GTC) orders**, which do not expire until filled or canceled.
- **At-the-opening** and **market-on-close orders**: Executed at the opening of trading the day after the order is placed or as close as possible to the close of trading on the day placed.
- **Not-held**: Give the broker discretion on price and time of execution.
- **Reducing orders**: Under certain conditions, automatically drop in price.
- **Fill-or-kill orders**: Must be executed immediately in full or be canceled.
- **Immediate or cancel orders**: Must be executed immediately in full or in part. Any part the order that remains unfilled will be canceled.
- **All-or-none orders**: Must be executed in full, but not immediately.
- **Contingent orders (either/or orders)**: Can't be executed until another specified order has been executed.

Market (or Unrestricted) Orders

An order that is sent immediately to the floor for execution without restrictions or limits placed on it is known as a market order. It is executed immediately at the current market price. A market order to buy is executed at the lowest offering price available; a market order to sell is executed at the highest bid price available. As long as the security is trading, a market order guarantees execution. No other type of order offers that guarantee.

Limit Orders

An order on which a client has placed a limit on the acceptable purchase or selling price is called a limit order. Limit orders are usually not executed immediately (unless the price is right). A sell order at a limit sets a minimum price at which the client is willing to sell the stock. The client will gladly accept a higher price than the limit, but not a lower one. A limit order to buy sets a maximum purchase price. The client prefers to buy at the lowest possible price, but will under no circumstances pay more than the limit price.

Executing a limit order. The commission broker takes a limit order to the floor and presents it to the trading crowd, hoping to get a price better than the limit. Even

See notebook

See notebook

though there is a specific price on the limit order, it must be executed at the most advantageous price for the client. Limit orders, therefore, can be executed only at the specified price or better.

If the order cannot be executed at the market, the commission house broker leaves the order with the specialist, who writes the trade down in the specialist's order book and watches the market for that price. Almost without exception, limit orders are left with the specialist so that they can be executed if and when price conditions meet the order limitation.

Risks and disadvantages of limit orders. Clients who enter limit orders risk missing the chance to buy or sell, especially if the market moves rapidly away from the limit. The market may never go as low as the buy limit price or as high as the sell limit price. The client accepts the risk in exchange for extra control. (This can't happen with a market order, since it is executed at the current market price.)

Sometimes limit orders are not executed even if the limit price is met. There are a couple of possible explanations for this:

- **Stock ahead.** When there are limit orders on the specialist's book for the same price, they are arranged according to when they were received. If a limit order at a specific price was not filled, chances are that another order at the same price took precedence; that is, there was "stock ahead."
- **Plus tick needed.** Limit orders to sell short may be executed only on a plus tick or a zero-plus tick. This means that even if you see a sale on the NYSE tape at your price, your limit order to sell short might not be executed because a plus tick did not occur.

Stop Orders

A stop order (also known as a stop loss order) is a trading tool designed to protect a profit or prevent further loss if the stock begins to move in the wrong direction. The stop order becomes a market order once the stock trades at or moves through a certain price, known as the stop price. Stop orders are usually left with and executed by the specialist. There is no guarantee that the executed price will be as favorable as the stop price. In this way, a stop order differs from a limit order, which does guarantee execution at the limit price or better.

In effect, a stop order is a way of saying, "Stop the market; I want to get off (or on)." The stop price triggers the order, which is then normally entered as a market order. A stop order takes two trades to execute:

- **Trigger**   The **trigger transaction** activates the trade (the trigger transaction must be at or through the stop price).

- **Execution**   The **execution transaction** completes the trade (the stop order has become a market order and is executed at the best market price).

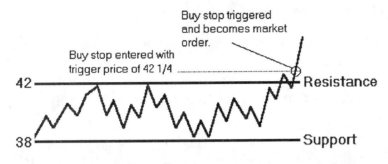

Buy stop triggered and becomes market order.

Buy stop entered with trigger price of 42 1/4 ....

42 ——————————————— Resistance

38 ——————————————— Support

Buy stop orders are entered above the market and are triggered when the market price touches or goes through the buy stop price.

Fig. 8.3 Buy stops are placed above the market.

Buy stop order. A buy stop order is always entered at a price above the current offering price. Why would an investor instruct his registered representative to place a stop order to "Buy 100 XYZ at 42 1/4 stop" when the market is at 40? An illustration is useful here: the trading of XYZ over a period of time looks like the example in Figure 8.3.

When XYZ breaks through the resistance level of 42 (a bullish event), the investor believes it will keep going up, hopes to buy at 42 1/4 and ride the stock up. Until then, the money isn't tied up.

Sell stop order. If the market is at 40 a client, who purchased the stock originally for $20 a share, might call with a stop order to sell at 37 3/4. In essence this orders says, "If the stock breaks through its support level (a bearish event), I think it will keep going down. At that point, I want out."

Buy stop orders are usually made to limit the risk of short sales. Sell stop orders are made: 1) to protect a profit (for example, a stock bought at 35 goes to 45; a sell stop order is entered at 42); and 2) to stop losses (for example, a stock bought at 45 goes to 40; a sell stop order is placed at 38). A sell stop is also called a stop loss. It makes sense, then, that a bullish buy stop order will be placed above the market and a bearish sell stop will be placed below the market.

What if the market really gets away on a stop? For example, if the market is at 40 and a buy stop is placed at 43. First, the stop is triggered. The market goes crazy and a purchase is executed at 52. Then, the market goes down and stays there for months. When a large number of stop orders on the specialist's book are triggered, a flurry of trading activity may take place as they become market orders. This activity may

Sell stop orders are entered below the market and are triggered when the market price touches or goes through the sell stop price.

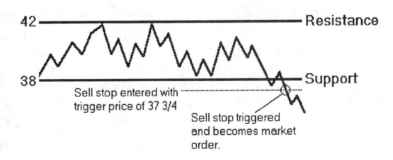

42 ——————————————— Resistance

38 ——————————————— Support

Sell stop entered with trigger price of 37 3/4

Sell stop triggered and becomes market order.

Fig. 8.4 Sell stops are placed below the market.

accelerate the advance or decline of the stock price. Consequently, the original intention of a stop order (to curtail a loss or protect a profit) is sabotaged. Such surprises may be avoided if a limit is placed on the stop order.

Stop limit order. A stop limit order is a stop order that, after being triggered, becomes a limit order rather than a market order. For example, an order that reads, "Sell 100 XYZ at 52 stop, 51 1/2 limit," means that the stop will be activated at or below 52. Ordinarily, the order then becomes a market order and shares are sold at the next available price.

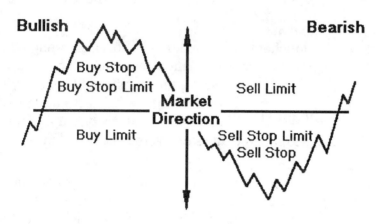

Fig. 8.5 Stop and limit orders.

However, because there is a 51 1/2 limit, the order to sell cannot be executed at less than 51 1/2. In essence, the investor is saying, "If the stock price goes down, I'd like to get out; but if it goes too far, I'd just as soon hang on until it comes around again."

Again, the execution takes the following order. First, the stop is triggered. Then, the trade is treated like any other limit order that must be executed at the limit price or better.

The buy stop, buy stop limit and sell limit orders are entered at or above the current market price. The buy limit, sell stop and sell stop limit orders are entered below the current market price.

Reducing Orders

Certain orders on the specialist's book are reduced when a stock goes ex-dividend, and these are detailed in the following paragraphs.

All orders entered below the market are reduced on the ex-date, the first date on which the new owner of stock does not qualify for the next dividend. On the ex-date, the price of the stock drops by the amount of the distribution. Orders reduced include buy limits, sell stops and sell stop limits. Without this reduction, trading at the lower price on the ex-dividend date could cause execution.

Dividend value	Reduction (equiv. fraction)	Order price less reduction	Order price after reduction
$.20	$.25 (1/4)	35 1/8 - 1/4	= 34 7/8
$.52	$.62 1/2 (5/8)	50 1/4 - 5/8	= 49 5/8
$.02	$.12 1/2 (1/8)	5 - 1/8	= 4 7/8

The **stop or limit price** is reduced by the next greatest increment of trading; that is, the amount of the dividend is rounded to the next highest 1/8.

Do not reduce, or DNR, orders may be entered by a customer. A DNR order will not be reduced by an ordinary cash dividend only. It will be reduced for other distributions, such as after a stock dividend or when a stock trades ex-rights.

The up tick for the short sale rule carries overnight. In the event of a reduction resulting from a distribution, the prior close is adjusted. For example, the stock closes on an up tick at 49 and opens ex-dividend the next day with a 1/4 point reduction (to 48 3/4). A customer could short the next morning at 48 3/4. This is a zero-plus tick. If the stock closes at a minus tick or zero-minus tick, the price the next morning must be 1/8 point higher than the reduced price of 48 3/4 for a short sale to be executed.

Reductions for stock splits (proportional reductions). To calculate the reduction in the price of an open buy order or an open stop order after a stock split, divide the market price by the fraction that represents the split. As an example, if a buy stop order has been entered for a stock at $100 and a 5-for-4 stock split has been announced, divide the $100 order price by the fraction 5/4 to find the adjusted order price of $80.

Calculating Order Adjustments for Stock Splits

Order price = $100
Stock split = 5 for 4 $100 divided by 5/4 = $80
Adjusted order price = $80   (5/4 = 1.25)

Order price = $100
Stock split = 2 for 1 $100 divided by 2/1 = $50
Adjusted order price = $50   (2/1 = 2.00)

Order price = $100
Stock split = 3 for 2 $100 divided by 3/2 = $66.67
Adjusted order price = $66.67 (3/2 = 1.50)

If a calculation results in a price that cannot be converted exactly into eighths, the order price is rounded **down** to the nearest eighth.

Other Types of Orders

Day orders. Unless marked to the contrary, an order is assumed to be a day order, valid only until the close of trading on the day it is entered by the client. If it has not been filled, it will be canceled at the close of the day's trading.

Good-till-canceled (GTC) orders. Good-till-canceled (GTC) orders or open orders, are valid until executed or canceled. However, even these orders have a specific lifetime. Regardless of the day they are entered, the specialist will cancel these orders on the last business day of April or October (that is, every six months) unless the customer renews them at that time (individual firms may clear out GTC orders as frequently as monthly). This clears the specialists' books of obsolete orders and reduces the risk of executing trades that customers have forgotten.

A GTC order that has been properly renewed or confirmed retains its original position on the specialist's book. If a GTC order is not renewed or confirmed at the appropriate time, it is canceled and must be re-entered as a new order. Investors should wait until the end of the day to change day orders to GTC orders or they will lose their place for the rest of the day.

At-the-opening and **market-on-close orders**. At-the-opening orders are executed at the opening of the market. Partial executions are allowable. They can be either market or limit orders, but must reach the post by the open of trading in that security. Market-on-close orders are executed at (or as near as possible to) the closing.

Not-held orders. A market order coded "NH" indicates that the client agrees not to hold the floor broker or the broker-dealer firm to a particular time and price of execution. This gives the floor broker discretion to choose the best time and price at which to execute the trade. Market not-held orders may not be placed with the specialist. *not held responsible, partial descretion*

Market orders must be executed immediately with the time of execution stamped on the trade ticket. The customer can expect a price close to the price just after the trade has been entered. With an NH order, the broker watches the market for a good time to execute the trade but is not held responsible for being wrong and missing a good price. Market NH orders are often large.

Fill-or-kill (FOK) orders. The commission house broker is instructed to fill the entire order immediately at the limit price or better. A broker who cannot fill the entire order immediately cancels it and notifies the originating branch office. The commission house broker will not leave the order with the specialist.

Immediate-or-cancel (IOC) orders. These limit orders are like fill-or-kill orders except that with an immediate-or-cancel order a partial execution is acceptable. The portion not executed is canceled.

All-or-none orders (AON). These orders have to be executed in their entirety or not at all. All-or-none orders can be day or GTC orders. They differ from the fill-or-kills in that they do not have to be filled immediately. On the NYSE, AON orders are prohibited for stock trades, but allowed for bonds.

Alternative (contingent) orders. An alternative (also known as an either/or, or a contingent order) is an order to do either of two alternatives for example, either sell a particular stock at a limit or sell on stop.

Order Type	Description	Exchange Orders	OTC Orders
Market	Buy or sell at the best available market price.	Most common order type on all exchanges.	Most common order type OTC.
Limit	Minimum price for sell orders, maximum for buy orders.	Handled by specialist floor broker as a day or GTC order.	Acceptable on either a day or GTC basis.
Stop	Buy orders entered above the market, sell orders entered below.	Acceptable on all major exchanges as day or GTC orders.	Not currently acceptable OTC.
Stop Limit	Stop order that becomes a limit order once the stop price has been reached or exceeded.	Acceptable on all exchanges.	Not currently acceptable OTC.

Consolidated Tape Displays

How the Tape Works

The Consolidated Tape and ticker tape symbols report trades made of NYSE- or AMEX-listed securities. The tape prints volumes and prices of securities transactions within seconds of their actual execution on the floor of the NYSE or other exchanges. The Tape displays information from two networks, the "A" and "B" networks. The "A" network includes NYSE common stocks, warrants, rights and preferred stock. These trades appear on tape without an indication of the market on which they took place; thus:

Boston	**B**	Cincinnati	**C**	INSTINET	**O**
NASD	**T**	Philadelphia	**X**	Pacific	**P**
Midwest	**M**	NYSE	**No symbol**		

The "B" network prints AMEX securities transactions that occurred on the American Stock Exchange, regional exchanges, OTC or through INSTINET. The exchange symbols do not appear on the tape, but they do appear on the Quotron terminal above the specialist's booth.

The tape reports trading conditions, operational malfunctions and special situations. When the tape is running late delete modes, such as "digits deleted," "volume deleted," and "repeat prices deleted" may be employed in periods of active trading.

K108

INSTINET. Although fourth-market (institution-to-institution) trades are not reported on the Consolidated Tape, the privately operated INSTINET system (O) trades are included, as are trades involving NASD members.

INSTINET (Institutional Networks Corporation), registered with the SEC as a stock exchange, includes among its subscribers a large number of mutual funds and other institutional investors. All INSTINET members are linked by computer terminals. Subscribers can display tentative volume, business and bid/ask quotes to others in the system.

How to Read the Tape

The ticker abbreviations (trading symbols for stocks, warrants and rights) appear at the top of the Tape. The trading symbol, the number of shares sold and the price are printed immediately below the trading symbol.

Sales of 100 shares of a given stock will be listed with the stock symbol but no quantity (T 25 1/4 for example). Sales of 200 or more shares, in which the round lot is 100 shares, will be indicated by printing the number of round lots followed by the letter "s," and then the price. Therefore, a sale of 200 shares of T would be printed T 2s25 1/4. Volume sales of 10,000 shares or more will be printed in full (10,000s, 50,000s and so on).

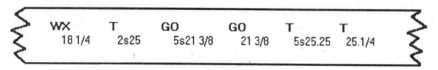

Fig. 8.6 Trades as they appear on the Tape.

The transactions listed (reading from left to right) show trades of 100 shares of WX (Westinghouse Electric) at 18 1/4, 200 shares of T (AT&T) traded at 25, followed by 500 shares of GO (Gulf Oil) at 21 3/8, followed by another 100 shares of GO at 21 3/8.

The transaction "T 5s25.25" indicates trades of 500 shares of AT&T at 25 followed by 100 shares at 25. The T 25.1/4 indicates two trades of AT&T, one at 25 and one at 25 1/4. The period could indicate that one trade has been split, meaning a sell order for 200 shares was bought by two contra-brokers.

Error reports. In the event an error was made, the Tape reports corrections. Errors can be made in pricing, volume, stock symbol, etc. For example, a pricing error report indicates that Oneida (OCQ) was incorrectly reported as being traded at 24 per share, when in fact it sold for 14 per share. Symbol errors are corrected as shown, where GT

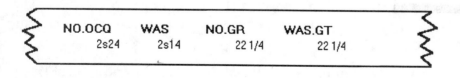

Fig. 8.7 Error messages as they appear on the Tape.

(Goodyear) was the correct symbol for the stock traded, not GR (see Fig. 8.7).

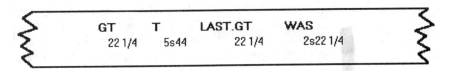

GT	T	LAST.GT	WAS
22 1/4	5s44	22 1/4	2s22 1/4

Fig. 8.8 Volume corrections also appear on the Tape.

Errors can also be made in printing volume. An incorrect report of a sale of 200 shares of Goodyear along with an example of how the correction would be printed is shown in Fig. 8.8.

Symbols used to indicate delays of any kind are as follows:

- **SLD** indicates that the exchange did not report a sale on time, so it is out of sequence on the tape. For example, a customer who sees 25 on the Tape followed by an SLD 25 1/8 might believe the price of the stock just sold is going up. In reality, however, the price may be going down: the 25 1/8 is out of sequence and should have appeared someplace before the 25.

  T 2s25 SLD (Late)

- **OPD** announces the initial transaction in a security for which the opening has been delayed.

Following are several common symbols found on the Tape:

- **SS** identifies stock trading in units of 10 shares instead of 100.
- **WI** indicates when-issued stock resulting from a stock split or stock trading when-issued.

  ABC pr 5s 115 1/4

- **RT** indicates rights.
- **WS** indicates warrants.
- **Pr** Indicates preferred stock.

Order Routing Systems

Broker-dealers use computerized order routing systems programmed to choose the destination of any order. The order may be routed to the commission house booth for handling by the exchange member that represents the broker-dealer. The exchange member (the floor broker) will present the order in the trading crowd. Notice of the execution of the order is given to the commission house booth, which, in turn, uses the communication system of the broker-dealer to notify the registered representative who notifies the customer.

At some exchanges, the order routing system may choose automatic execution for certain orders. Small market orders and small executable limit orders, for example, are sent directly to the trading post, where they are executed against orders on the specialist's book or market makers' quotes. Notice of execution is sent directly to the broker-dealer. To speed execution, the automatic execution system bypasses the commission house communication booth and the floor broker.

K108

Regardless of the name, each system has direct communication to and from the trading post. Names of the order routing and execution systems are as follows:

- **NYSE.** The NYSE uses the Designated Order Turnaround (DOT) system. "Super DOT" can process market orders for up to 2,099 shares, including odd-lot orders. An order for 2,100 + shares must be executed by the floor broker or the floor broker's delegate.
- **CBOE.** The Chicago Board Options Exchange uses the Order Routing System (ORS) to route trades to their appropriate destinations. Market orders and executable limit orders are sent to the Retail Automatic Execution System (RAES), which is a part of the ORS. Small orders are automatically executed and confirmed to the broker-dealer and market maker.
- **AMEX.** The American Stock Exchange uses Automatic Post Execution Reports (Autoper) for equity trades and the Automatic Amex-Options Switching (AutoAmos) for options transactions. The AutoAmos automatically executes trades for the four to six most active stocks of the XMI index option.
- **Other markets.** The Philadelphia Exchange uses PHLX Automated Communication and Executions System (PACE). The Pacific Exchange uses the Securities Communication Order Routing and Execution (SOREX) system.
- **Small Order Execution System (SOES).** The OTC's automated execution system (SOES) executes trades for limited amounts of NMS and NASDAQ shares. *1000 shares* All NASDAQ and NMS securities that have an active SOES market maker are eligible and the system allows participants to "lock- in" trades cleared through the system.

The Specialist

Quotations and Size

Figure 8.9 is an excerpt from a specialist's book in AFAP Enterprises, Inc. stock. The specialist enters buy orders on the left, sell orders on the right.

If you were to ask the specialist for the quote for AFAP, the reply would be, "51 1/8 to 1/2." The current quote on a stock includes the highest limit

BUY	AFP	SELL
1 MLPFS		
1 PWJC	51	
1 A.G.EDWARDS		
4 BACHE	1/8	
3 A.G.BECKER STOP	1/4	
	3/8	2 SMITH BARN STOP
		4 OPPENHEIMER
	1/2	2 TUCKER ANTHONY
		3 PIPER
	5/8	
		2 HUTTON
	3/4	
		3 DEAN WITTER
	7/8	

Page 13

Fig. 8.9 The specialist's book.

order for the bid and the lowest offer, because market orders to buy or sell can be immediately executed at those prices. Any stop orders (to buy if the bids rise to 51 1/4 and to sell if the offers fall to 51 3/8) are not included in the quote because they have not been triggered yet and therefore can't be executed.

The specialist's current quote can be translated as follows: market orders to buy stock can be immediately executed at 51 1/2; market orders to sell stock can be immediately executed at 51 1/8.

The specialist must always get the best possible price for a limit order: at the limit price or better. At times, a specialist may be prompted to give quotations that take into account other factors in addition to the orders listed in the specialist's book. Specialists often compete against other floor brokers trading in the same stock and sometimes against other specialists if a security is actively traded. Consider the following situations:

- Floor broker X enters the crowd with an offer to sell AFAP stock at 51 3/8. Although the specialist already has offers to sell at 51 1/2, the quote in AFAP will be 51 1/8 bid (represented by the specialist) and 51 3/8 offered (represented by broker X).
- If there is more than one specialist in a stock because of large volume, the specialists may compete against other specialists. The resulting quotation on a particular stock would be composed of the highest bid and the lowest offer from all the specialists' books combined.
- The specialist may offer a different quotation in an attempt to get a better price for the orders in the book.

The above situations all reflect the basic rule: the current quotation always states the best (highest) bid and the best (lowest) offer.

The specialist is allowed to reveal the number of shares available in a current quote, but is not allowed to reveal the number of shares or prices above or below the current quote. Upon request, the specialist will provide a quote and size:

- "63 1/8 to 3/8, 5-4" means 500 shares bid for at 63 1/8, 400 shares offered at 63 3/8.
- The quote and size are good only for the moment they are given. However, they provide some indication of the current price.
- This quote and size (Q&S) is from the specialist's book only and may or may not include any indications from the crowd, so the advice to a customer should include these statements: "The Q&S will change by the time an order gets to the floor," and "The size may very well be larger than indicated."

Stopping Stock

Stopping stock means a specialist guarantees that a market order will be filled at the current bid or offer. This guarantee gives the commission house broker who originated the order time to go into the crowd and try to find a better price. The commission house broker is thus assured of not missing the market while trying to find a better bid or offer for the client.

A specialist may stop stock only for the benefit of a public order. This requires no permission. In the event the price in the crowd (the members trading in that stock around the specialist's post) moves beyond the stopped price, the specialist automatically executes the order.

Specialists' Restrictions

A specialist cannot directly accept orders in stocks in which he or she specializes, from anyone except a member on the floor or a commission house broker.

Crossing Orders

A commission house broker (CHB) has just picked up two market orders for the same stock from the telephone clerk. One is an order to buy 1,000 share; the other is an order to sell 1,000 shares. The CHB wants to **cross** the two orders (use one order to fill the other).

Before crossing the orders, however, the CHB must offer the stock in the trading crowd surrounding the specialist's post at a price higher than the bid by the minimum variation (normally 1/8). So the broker goes to the post at which the stock trades and asks the specialist for a quote. Let's say, for example, the quote is 63 1/8 to 63 3/8. After deciding to cross the orders at 63 1/4, the CHB offers 1,000 shares at 63 3/8. If there are no takers, the CHB crosses the two orders at 63 1/4.

Block Trades

Member firms must forward all orders in listed securities to the NYSE floor. Those owning seats and trading on the floor claim the best market exists when all orders are channeled to one place. All trades in listed securities by member firms must take place in the auction market.

Some trades, however, are so large that the normal auction market can't absorb them in a reasonable time at a reasonable price. So the exchange specifies procedures for trades involving large blocks of listed securities.

How big is a block trade? No hard and fast definition exists, but a trade judged to be a block trade must be processed according to the following regulations:

- All block trades must be approved by the NYSE.
- The originator of a block transaction pays all costs. That is, in a distribution, the seller pays all commissions; in an acquisition, the buyer pays.
- A floor official has authority to grant permission for the specialist block.

To understand block trades, it may be beneficial to look at the size of the distribution and manner of execution. The four types of block trades, beginning with the smallest, are as follows.

Specialist block. The specialist block purchase is the smallest type of block trade and perhaps the easiest to handle. For example, if a customer wants to sell 5,000 share of T, the customer's registered representative informs a trader at the block desk of the impending transaction. The trader contacts the specialist through a floor broker. The specialist, if willing to buy the stock, makes a bid, typically a point or so below the best current bid on the auction market. The trade is done after the market and is not shown on the Tape. It is, however, reported weekly to the NYSE with the specialist's volume.

Exchange distributions or acquisitions. This block trade involves one or a few members of the NYSE. Often one firm has a large block to acquire or distribute. The firm asks one or a few other members to help find offsetting offers. After finding the offers, the members take them to the crowd and cross the orders within the current quote (after offering the securities at a price higher than the current bid).

There is no advance notice of the offer; instead, an announcement made on the Tape after the trade is completed identifies it as an acquisition or distribution (distributions are most frequent). An exchange distribution always takes place on the floor of the NYSE during market hours and involves only NYSE member firms.

Special offering or bid. Any number of NYSE firms may be involved in this type of block trade. Generally, a larger block will require a larger number of participants. An announcement is made before the transaction of a **special offer** or **bid**. An incentive is offered to the registered representative watching the tape when the price is announced. The price stipulated is net to the buyer or seller and the initiator pays transaction costs to sell (or acquire) the shares. As an incentive to complete the block trade, commissions to the selling agent are twice normal size.

This type of block trade is rarely executed because it takes a great deal of effort, especially to stabilize the price, and may take a long time. For this reason, partial completions are printed on the tape at the close of business.

Secondary distribution. Secondary distribution procedures are suitable for the largest blocks of stock, those too large for other block procedures.

Nonmember firms are invited to participate with NYSE firms in secondary distributions. An announcement is made after the market closes. The price is net to the buyer and is never higher than the closing price on the exchange. (This type of secondary distribution should not be confused with the other secondary distribution with an underwriting involving previously issued securities.)

Type of Block	Participants	Shown on Tape	When Shown	On Floor?	When Done	Price/Proceeds
Specialist block - Purchase - Sale	Only the specialist	Not shown. Reported to the exchange weekly with the volume. Shown in the specialist's position record.	Never	No	After market	Net bid usually below quote
Exchange - Distributions - Acquisitions	Only one or a few members	DIST. or ACQ. and volume	After trade only	Yes	During market	Crossed on the floor within current quote
Special - Offering - Bid	Any members	Before transaction, Spec Offer (Bid). Partial completion is printed at close.	Before and after, announced at close if not completed.	Yes	During market	Fixed net price to buyer. Syndicate formed. Price may be stabilized.
Secondary distribution	Both members and non-NYSE members	Announcement is made, volume announced, not included on tape.	After market close	No	After market	Under the current market

Fig. 8.10 A comparison of different block trades.

The Nine-Bond Rule

listed

The nine-bond rule requires that special attention be given to orders for fewer than 10 bonds. These orders must be shown on the floor of the exchange before being traded over-the-counter, where most bonds trade. The trade may be done OTC if the price is better there or if the customer requests it. Bonds that must be redeemed within 12 months, U.S. government and municipal securities are exempt from the nine-bond rule.

OTC Market Operations and Trading

In this section, you will learn more about (1) OTC market operations and trading and (2) the OTC market makers who facilitate trading activities. One difference between exchange markets and the OTC market that should be noted is that short sales are not limited by the plus-tick rule when executed OTC.

Communications

Quotation sheets. Each afternoon, OTC market makers send their interdealer quotations to the National Quotation Bureau for publication. The quotations, printed on pink paper and commonly called **the pink sheets** have six key features:

- They are devoted exclusively to OTC stocks.
- The prices are quotes, not actual transaction prices.
- The quotes are between dealers (they are interdealer: that is, not retail).
- The quotes are subject (not firm).
- For NASDAQ system stocks, the NASDAQ symbol appears right after the name of the stock.
- An "M" preceding the name of the stock means the stock is marginable.

Although pink sheet quotes are subject, a dealer who publishes a quote on a security in the pink sheets must be ready to quote a firm price for 100 shares of that security. The National Quotation Bureau also publishes corporate bond quotations call the yellow sheets.

NASDAQ System

Levels of Service

The NASDAQ system provides three levels of service. Level 1 is for registered representatives, Level 2 is for retail and institutional traders and Level 3 is for market makers. Level 3 includes all the features of Level 2, and Level 2 includes all the features of Level 1.

- **Level 1**: NASDAQ Level 1 gives only the inside quote, which is the highest bid and the lowest offer available from any of the market makers. The bid and the ask prices of the inside quote may be from different broker-dealers. The RR knows only that this

RR desktop

quotation is the best available. Because of rapid price fluctuations, the RR cannot guarantee this price to a client.

- **Level 2**: NASDAQ Level 2 provides the current quote from each market maker in the security. These quotes are firm for at least 100 shares.
- **Level 3**: NASDAQ Level 3 allows market makers to update their quotes in a security. A selling broker-dealer must update quotes within 90 seconds.

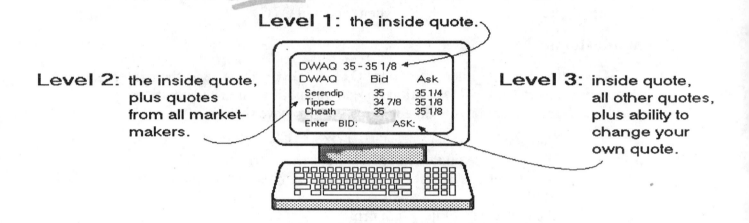

Fig. 8.11 Level 1, 2 and 3 on a quotation machine.

Generally, the NASDAQ system does not provide up-to-the-minute volume in each security, nor does it provide the price of the last sale in each security. It does, however, give the volume in each security at the end of the day.

The size of the spread between bid and ask prices changes with the amount of activity in the security and the overall risk associated with the issuer. Spreads are widest for inactive securities (and unstable issuers) and grow narrower with increased trading (and financially secure issuers).

The NASD 5% Policy

Dealers, unlike brokers, do not charge commissions, but instead sell stock at a **markup**. Because of dealer competition, there is usually a natural limit to the size of the markup that the traffic will bear. The NASD Rules of Fair Practice provide guidelines for markups, known as the 5% Markup Policy. The 5% markup policy applies to commissions as well as markups and markdowns. It does not apply to new issues or to any issue accompanied by a prospectus.

The 5% markup policy states that all commissions, markups and markdowns must be fair, reasonable and not applied discriminatorily. A broker-dealer either will charge a commission or a markup (markdown), but cannot charge both on the same trade. Because the 5% rule is a guideline only, a charge of more than 5% is not necessarily unfair, nor is a charge of less than 5% necessarily fair. Fairness of the markup depends upon the following:

- **Type of security involved**. A highly speculative stock would be expected to have a higher markup than a conservative bond because of the greater risk involved.
- **Availability of the security in the market**. Markups can be lower on active securities. In the case of an inactive security, the amount of the commissions or markup may be higher because the security is difficult to find or riskier to keep in inventory.
- **Price of the security**. The percentage of the markup generally decreases as the price of a security increases. For example, a 5% markup on a $200 stock would be $10 per share or $1,000 total. Although conforming with the 5% policy, a $1,000 markup would be considered unreasonable on this 100-share trade.
- **Amount of money involved**. A small transaction may warrant a larger markup percentage to cover handling expenses.
- **Disclosure**. If the amount of the markup is disclosed to the customer, the disclosure itself cannot be used to justify an excessive markup.
- **Pattern of markup**. Each transaction must be fair. A pattern of excessive markups will weigh against a dealer.
- **Nature of member's business**. Costs of services provided are properly considered in determining the fairness of markups (such as full-service vs. discount brokers).

Types of transactions covered. The 5% policy applies to all securities transactions in the OTC market, except exempt securities (government and municipal securities) and those made with a prospectus. The policy covers both agency and principal trades:

- **Riskless or simultaneous transaction**. A member takes no risk when buying a security to fill an order already received from a client.
- **Sale to a client from inventory**. Markup is determined by the current market (that is, the inside quote), not according to the price the dealer paid for the security.
- **Purchase of a security from a client**. Dealers mark down the price of a security purchased from a client.
- **Agency transactions**. The broker charges a commission.
- **Proceeds transactions**. When a client sells securities to a dealer and uses the proceeds to buy other securities from the same dealer, it is called a proceeds transaction. It is viewed as one transaction for markup purposes.

Basis for the markup. The markup (or markdown) is calculated from the current inside (or Level 1) price. Dealer's costs are not used to determine fairness of the markup or markdown. A dealer is required to disclose the amount of the markup to the customer for listed and NMS securities.

Confirmations

Customers must receive written confirmation of each transaction. The rules describe these confirmations in great detail. Confirmations must specify the security, trade date, settlement date, amount of accrued interest and designation of the firm as agent (broker) or principal (dealer). Confirmations for trades involving callable securities must include a statement indicating that the yield shown may be affected by the exercise of a call provision and that information concerning the call provision will be provided upon request.

Since 1983, all confirmations sent to customers must include the applicable Committee on Uniform Securities Identification Procedures (CUSIP) number, if any.

Questions

1. The New York Stock Exchange serves investors by

    ____(A)   offering securities for sale.
    ____(B)   buying securities for members.
    ____(C)   both of the above.
    _X_(D)   neither of the above.

2. Which of the following statements about the NYSE are true?

    I.   The NYSE is a corporation operated by a board of directors.
    II.   Membership on the exchange is fixed at 1,000.
    III. Allied members can trade on the floor of the exchange.
    IV.   The NYSE auction procedures are based on rules of priority, precedence and parity.

    ____(A)   I and II
    ____(B)   II and III
    _X_(C)   I and IV
    ____(D)   III and IV

3. Which of the following brokers would be allowed to trade on the NYSE?

    I.   registered representative
    II.   specialist
    III. registered trader
    IV.   commission broker

    ____(A)   I and II
    ____(B)   II and III
    ____(C)   II, III and IV
    _X_(D)   I, II, III and IV

4. All of the following are used in awarding trades on the NYSE EXCEPT

    ____(A)   priority.
    ____(B)   parity.
    _X_(C)   premium.
    ____(D)   precedence.

5. Which of the following reasons is an appropriate justification for selling a stock short?

     ____(A)   to cut losses on a long position
     ✗ (B)   to benefit from a decline in the price of the stock
     ____(C)   to benefit from a rise in the price of the stock
     ____(D)   to seek a modest potential reward with limited risk

6. The over-the-counter market is a(n)

     ✗ (A)   negotiated market
     ____(B)   auction market
     ____(C)   transfer market
     ____(D)   double-auction market

7. Which of the following are true regarding the OTC market?

    I.   It facilitates the trading of stock not listed on an exchange.
    II.   It is a connection of broker-dealers via computers and phones.
    III.   Stocks of banks and insurance companies typically trade in the over-the-counter market.

     ✗ (A)   I and II
     ____(B)   I and III
     ____(C)   II and III
     ____(D)   I, II and III

8. An over-the-counter trader attempting to buy stock is given a quote of "16-17 work out." This indicates that the quote is

     ____(A) $16 with a suggested broker-dealer markup of $1.
     ____(B)   firm.
     ____(C)   bona fide.
     ✗ (D)   approximate.

9. All of the following are usually traded over-the-counter EXCEPT

     ____(A)   mutual fund shares.
     ____(B)   foreign securities and ADRs.
     ✗ (C)   exchange-listed stocks.
     ____(D)   closed-end investment company securities.

Correction

10. Which of the following orders would not be reduced by the specialist on the ex-dividend date?

    I. buy limit orders
    II. open sell stop orders
    III. buy stop orders
    IV. sell limit orders

    _____(A)   I and II
    _____(B)   I and IV
    __✗__(C)   III and IV
    _____(D)   II, III and IV

Answer Key

1. D.

2. C.

3. C.

4. C.

5. B.

6. A.

7. D.

8. D.

9. A.

10. C.

Chapter Nine

Client Accounts

Key Terms

9.6 Beneficial owner

9.2 Custodial account

9.2 Discretionary account

9.6 Equity

9.5 Guaranteed account

9.7 JTIC

9.4 Limited trading authorization

9.3 New Accounts Form

9.4 OCC Options Disclosure Document

9.3 Street name

9.9 Uniform Gifts to Minors Act (UGMA)

Churning 9.11

Debit balance 9.6

DVP 9.3

Fiduciary 9.8

Hypothecation agreement 9.4

JTWROS 9.7

Margin account 9.6

Nominal owner 9.6

Regulation T 9.7

Trading authorization 9.2

Client Accounts

Classification of Accounts

A registered rep may handle many different types of accounts. Generally, accounts are classified by three features: ownership (and right to trade), how securities are paid for, and types of securities bought and sold in the account.

Account ownership. Procedures and relevant regulations vary according to the type of person, group or business that owns the account. The principal types of ownership are:

- individual;
- joint (for example, a husband and wife or two business associates)
- corporate; and
- partnership.

The primary types of trading authorization are:

- **Discretionary**. After receiving authority from the customer, the registered representative enters trades without having to consult the customer before each trade.
- **Fiduciary**. The individual given fiduciary responsibility enters the trades for the account.
- **Custodial**. The custodian for the beneficial owner enters all trades.

Payment method. Customers may pay for securities in one of two ways: cash only or cash plus money borrowed from the broker-dealer. In cash accounts, clients must pay the full purchase price of securities. In margin accounts, clients may borrow part of the purchase price of a security from the broker-dealer.

Securities traded. Clients must have special approval to make certain types of trades in their accounts, and additional special requirements exist for options accounts.

Opening New Accounts

Before opening any new account, the broker-dealer and registered representative must evaluate the prospective customer as to character and credit references, financial reliability and specific financial goals and objectives.

Required information. According to NYSE Rule 405 (the "Know Your Customer" rule), exchange members must exercise due diligence to learn essential facts about every customer and every account. General guidelines suggest the RR interview the client in order to obtain an inventory of the client's present securities' holdings, and discover the client's financial situation, needs and objectives.

Generally, any competent person may open an account. Anyone person declared legally incompetent may not open an account. Fiduciary or custodial accounts may be opened for minors or legally incompetent individuals.

Payment and delivery instructions. After opening an account, the client and the RR establish payment and delivery instructions. These instructions may be changed for individual transactions. For a purchase or buy order, the customer must stipulate whose name is to be on the security and who will keep the security certificate. For buy orders, customers may select any of the following payment and delivery instructions:

- **Transfer and ship**. Securities are transferred into the name of the customer and shipped to him or her.
- **Transfer and hold in safekeeping**. Securities are transferred into the customer's name but held by the broker-dealer.
- **Hold in street name**. Securities are transferred into the broker-dealer's name and held by the broker-dealer. Although the broker-dealer is the nominal owner of the securities, the customer is still the beneficial owner. "Street" here refers to Wall Street and is shorthand for the world in which the firms operate.
- **Delivery versus payment (DVP)**. Securities are delivered to a bank or depository against payment. In other words, this is a COD (cash on delivery) settlement. The broker-dealer must verify the arrangement between customer and bank or depository and the customer must notify the bank or depository of each purchase or sale.

For sell orders, the customer will give one of two instructions, hold cash at the broker-dealer or forward the cash balance on the settlement date.

Documenting New Accounts

New Accounts Form. Before opening any account the brokerage firm is required to fill out a new accounts form. The firm must record the following information:

- full name;
- address and telephone number (business and residence numbers);
- Social Security or tax identification number of client;
- occupation, employer and type of business;
- bank and brokerage references;
- how the account was acquired;
- name and occupation of person with authority to make transactions in the account;

- citizenship; and
- signatures of the representative opening the account and a principal of the firm (the client's signature is not required on a new accounts form).

The above items are required by NYSE and NASD rules. The Municipal Securities Rulemaking Board (MSRB) requires the RR to ask not only about financial objectives and background, but also to make inquiries concerning the customer's tax status.

Client information must be updated periodically as situations change. Transactions placed by the customer and judged unsuitable by the RR may still be entered by the customer. For unsuitable trades (as well as any trades requested by a customer without the rep's recommendation), the rep should note on the confirmation that the transaction was unsolicited.

Third-party accounts. Opening certain types of accounts requires additional information or documentation. If trading in the account will be done by a third party, the client must sign a trading authorization, otherwise the RR cannot open a third party account. A trading authorization gives another person power of attorney to transact business in the account. In a discretionary account, the client signs a trading authorization granting the registered rep the right to make trades that are binding on the customer. The authorization may be a limited or full trading authorization.

A limited authorization grants authority only to place buy and sell orders in the account. A full authorization grants authority to place orders and to add and withdraw assets from the account.

Margin accounts. When opening a margin account, the client signs a margin agreement disclosing the terms under which credit will be extended. The margin agreement contains a credit agreement, a hypothecation agreement and an optional loan consent.

- The **credit agreement** discloses the terms under which credit is extended.
- The **hypothecation agreement** gives the firm permission to pledge (or hypothecate) securities held on margin. The hypothecation agreement is a mandatory part of the margin agreement.
- The **loan consent agreement** gives the firm permission to lend the customer's securities.

Options accounts. When opening an options account, the customer signs a Customer Options Agreement, which explains the risks and requirements of option trading. By signing the agreement, the client ackowledges having (1) read the OCC Risk Disclosure Document, which is published by the Options Clearing Corporation and (2) understands the risks associated with trading options.

Special Situations

Numbered accounts. At a client's request, an account may be identified only by a number or symbol. These are called **numbered** (or **hidden**) accounts. In most cases, numbered accounts are used by institutions to preserve anonymity. The client must sign a form certifying that he or she owns the account(s) identified by number or symbol.

Multiple accounts. If a client wishes to open more than one individual account with a broker-dealer, the representative must obtain from the customer a statement attesting that no one else has any interest in the second and subsequent accounts and that each account unreservedly guarantees the others. (These are sometimes called guaranteed accounts.) An individual who has both a cash and a margin account, however, is considered to have only one account.

Account transfers. To transfer a client's account from one broker-dealer to another, the client signs a transfer request form. A copy of the form is sent to the original broker-dealer who will transfer the client's money and securities to the new firm.

Opening Accounts for Employees of Other Brokers

NYSE requirements. The NYSE requires prior written approval by the employer before an employee of a member firm can open a cash or margin account with another firm. If the account is approved, duplicate statements and confirmations must be sent by the transacting firm to the employer broker-dealer. Employees of the NYSE (the exchange, not member firms) also need written permission of the employer. Duplicate confirmations need not be sent to the employer.

Employees of banks, insurance companies and NASD broker-dealers need prior approval to open a margin account. (An officer of a bank or insurance company is not an employee and therefore does not require prior approval.) Duplicate confirmations do not need to be sent.

Employed By:	Margin Account	Cash Account	Duplicate Confirm
NYSE members	Prior permission	Prior permission	Yes
Exchange	Prior permission	Prior permission	No
Nonmember financial institution (nonofficer)	Prior permission	No	No
NASD	Notification (not permission)	Notification (not permission)	Upon request
MSRB	Notification (not permission)	Notification (not permission)	Upon request

NASD requirements. NASD rules do not require the employee of one NASD member firm to get the employer's permission to open an account with another NASD member. The rules do require the firm opening the account to notify the client's employer. The employee is responsible for disclosing that he or she is an NASD member when opening the account. Duplicate confirmations and statements must be sent to the employer broker-dealer only if the employer requests them.

MSRB requirements. Like the NASD, the MSRB does not require an employee of a member firm to obtain prior permission from the employer to open an account with another firm. The employer must be notified in writing that the account is being opened and must be mailed duplicate confirmations, unless requested in writing not to do so. For married persons or for joint accounts, all account opening restrictions apply if the spouse or a minor child is employed by a member firm.

Margin Accounts

With a margin account, a firm extends credit to a client for a portion of the purchase price of securities, which allows the client to **leverage** investments.

A cash account client who wants to purchase 1,000 shares of XYZ stock at $10 per share must deposit $10,000 by settlement date. In a margin account, the client must currently deposit no less than 50% of the purchase price ($5,000 initial equity, in this example) and can borrow the balance from the broker-dealer. The $10,000 purchase price of the securities the client purchased less the $5,000 debit balance (the amount borrowed from the broker-dealer) leaves the client with $5,000 in equity in the account. (The 50% initial equity requirement is subject to change.)

Relationship between client and broker. Opening a margin account changes the relationship between client and broker- dealer. The firm is the client's creditor, so all securities purchased on margin are registered in street name. The brokerage firm is called the nominal owner of the securities. The client is known as the beneficial owner.

Advantages of a margin account. The margin account offers two distinct advantages:

- The client can purchase more securities with the same amount of money or the same amount of securities with a lower initial cash outlay.
- By borrowing a portion of the purchase price, the customer can leverage an investment. (That is, the customer who buys on margin can realize the same gains as a customer who buys securities with cash, without having to put up as much money.)

For example, if the price of XYZ, purchased for $10,000, increases to $15 per share, the customer's equity in the cash account will be $15,000, representing a 50% return. In the margin account, the customer's equity will be $10,000 (the loan of $5,000 is still owed to the firm), representing a return of 100% on the initial cash outlay of $5,000. Therefore, the customer's return is magnified by leveraging the investment in a margin account (100% versus 50%).

The market could just as easily turn down, in which case the individual with a margin account would experience a magnified loss.

The Federal Reserve Board's Regulation T

Because leveraging is a two-way street, several rules apply to margin accounts. The Securities Exchange Act of 1934 grants the Federal Reserve Board (FRB) authority to regulate credit extended in the purchase of securities. The FRB established Regulation T, which sets forth the equity or margin required in a purchase of securities in a margin account. Regulation T prevents the overextension of credit in securities transactions. It also stipulates which securities may be purchased on margin.

Types of Accounts

Joint Accounts

In a joint account, two or more individuals are co-tenants or co-owners of the account. In addition to the appropriate new accounts form, a joint account agreement must be signed and the account must be designated as either Joint Tenants in Common (JTIC), or Joint Tenants with Right of Survivorship (JTWROS).

The account forms must be signed by all owners. Both types of joint account agreement provide that any or all tenants may transact business in the account. Checks must be made payable to the name(s) in which the account is registered (and must be endorsed for deposit by all tenants) although mail need only be sent to a single address. To be in good delivery form, securities sold from a joint account must be signed by all tenants.

Joint Tenants in Common. Joint Tenants in Common ownership (JTIC) provides that a deceased tenant's fractional interest in the account is retained by that tenant's estate and is not passed to the surviving tenant(s), if any. As an example, if the JTIC agreement provides for 60% ownership interest by one owner and 40% ownership interest by the other, then that is the fraction of the account that would pass into the deceased owner's estate if either owner died. The JTIC agreement may be used by more than two individuals.

Joint Tenants With Right of Survivorship. Joint Tenants with Right of Survivorship (JTWROS) ownership stipulates that a deceased tenant's interest in the account passes to the surviving tenant(s).

Partnership Accounts

A partnership is an unincorporated association of two or more individuals. The partnership, in addition to filling out the new accounts form, is required to provide a partnership agreement stating which of the partners can make transactions for the account. When a partner dies, the partnership ceases to exist. The account must be frozen and no orders accepted until proper documentation is received from the deceased's estate.

Corporate Accounts

When opening an account for a corporation, the RR must have a corporate representative complete a new accounts form. The RR must also ascertain which members of the corporation may trade in the account by having the corporation submit a Corporate Agreement for a Cash Account. The agreement, signed by the secretary of the corporation, identifies officers authorized to make transactions.

In addition to the documentation required for all margin accounts, corporate margin accounts require a certified copy of the corporate charter and bylaws authorizing a margin account.

Form	Individual		Joint		Partnership		Corporation	
	Cash	Margin	Cash	Margin	Cash	Margin	Cash	Margin
New Account Form	X	X	X	X	X	X	X	X
Margin Agreement		X		X		X		X
Joint Account Agreement			X	X				
Corporate Charter and By Laws								X
Partnership Agreement					X	X		
Corporate/Partnership Resolution					X	X	X	X
Discretionary Authorization	As needed							
Power of Attorney	As needed							
Options Agreement	As needed							

Fig. 9.1 Different accounts require different forms.

Fiduciary Accounts

When securities are placed in a fiduciary account, someone other than the owner (the person whose name is on the account) initiates trades. Perhaps the most familiar example of a fiduciary account is a trust account. Money or securities are placed in trust for one person, often a minor, but someone else must manage the account. The manager (or trustee) is a fiduciary.

A fiduciary is any person legally appointed and authorized to represent and act in another person's behalf. Fiduciaries includes:

- **Trustees** designated to administer a trust. A testamentary trustee is a trustee appointed in a decedent's will. A trustee of a living trust, also called an inter vivos trust, is appointed in a trust agreement by a living person.
- **Executors** who are designated in a decedent's will to manage the affairs of the estate.

- **Administrators** appointed by the courts to liquidate the estate of a person who died intestate (without a will).
- **Guardians** designated by the courts to handle the affairs of a minor until that minor reaches the age of majority or to handle the affairs of incompetents.
- **Custodians** of a Uniform Gift to Minors Act (UGMA) account.

Opening a fiduciary account. Opening a fiduciary account requires completion of a new accounts form for fiduciaries and acquisition of a court certificate or other acceptable document to certify the individual's appointment and authority. (With the exception of an individual acting as the custodian for a Uniform Gifts to Minors Act custodial account, no documentation of custodial rights is required here.) The registered rep for a fiduciary account must be aware of the following rules before transacting business in the account:

- Proper authorization must be given (the necessary court documents must be filed with and verified by the broker-dealer).
- Speculative transactions are generally not permitted.
- Margin accounts are permitted only if the legal documents establishing the fiduciary account authorize them.
- The prudent man rule requires fiduciaries to make prudent (wise and safe) investments.
- Many states publish a **legal list** of securities approved for fiduciary accounts.
- No authority may be delegated (a power of attorney cannot be accepted for the account).
- The fiduciary may not share in the profits of the account, but may charge a "reasonable" fee for services.

Uniform Gifts to Minors Act (UGMA). Until the Tax Reform Act of 1986 changed the favorable tax status of Uniform Gifts to Minors Act accounts (UGMAs), many people used these accounts as a means of transferring highly taxable income and capital gains to a child in a lower tax bracket through gifts of money or securities (children are normally in a low tax bracket and subject to lower taxes on most types of income). Even though the tax advantages are not as great these days, many people still use these accounts to set aside money and securities for the benefit of children.

UGMA accounts require an adult (or bank trust department) to act as a custodian for a minor (the beneficial owner). Any kind of securities may be given and there is no limitation on the dollar amount of the gift. The custodian may either be the donor or a person appointed by the donor but does not need to be a family member. A gift to a minor under the UGMA is **irrevocable**; the donor may not take back the gift, nor may the minor return the gift until he or she has reached the age of majority (which varies from state to state; check your local state laws). When the beneficiary reaches the age of majority, the securities are transferred into his or her name.

The following regulations apply to gifts of securities to minors:

- Securities delivered to a custodian or held for a custodian's account may not be listed in street name. Certificates must be registered in the custodian's name as "Custodian for (minor's name) under the (state's name) Uniform Gifts to Minors Act." The gift is considered to have been made when this registration has been completed.
- No special documentation naming the custodian is required to open a brokerage account under UGMA.
- Securities donated as a gift must be fully paid for; margin accounts are not permitted.
- Bearer securities are generally not permitted, but if they are, gifts of bearer securities must be accompanied by a Deed of Gift.
- Options may not be placed or purchased in a custodial account, because no evidence of ownership is issued to an option buyer.
- There may be only one custodian and one minor per custodial account.
- In most states, a gift under this law may not be made through a will.
- The death of the child before the age of majority terminates the custodianship. The property in the account must be delivered to the minor's estate.
- If the custodian resigns or dies, the court assigns a succeeding custodian, unless someone else has been assigned by the former custodian.
- The RR is not responsible for determining whether the appointment is valid or whether the custodian's activities are actually within his or her authority. However, the RR should determine whether securities being given are already owned by the minor.
- Cash proceeds from sales or dividends may be held in a noninterest-bearing custodial account for a reasonable period, but should not remain idle for long.
- Stock subscription rights or warrants may either be exercised or sold.

The custodian may use custodial property for the support, education and general use and benefit of the minor. The custodian is empowered to buy or sell securities in the account as long as the assets in the account remain the property of the minor.

The custodian may be compensated for reasonable services and reimbursed for necessary expenses.

Discretionary Accounts

If an account owner wants to give the registered rep authority to decide the particular security (by name and/or description), whether to buy or sell and/or the dollar amount of the security transaction, the client must first sign a trading authorization to make that account a discretionary account. Once trading authorization (sometimes known as a power of attorney) has been given, the client is legally bound to accept the registered rep's decisions. Discretionary accounts must have prior approval in writing from the broker-dealer or a registered principal representing the broker-dealer. Trades involving only time or price are not considered discretionary trades.

The NASD, MSRB, CBOE and NYSE require that discretionary accounts be reviewed frequently by an officer of the member firm. A principal of the firm must approve all trades promptly and in writing. A record must be kept of all transactions and order tickets must be marked "discretionary."

Churning. One possible abuse of discretionary authority is known as **churning**, the practice of trading excessively solely to generate commissions, rather than to make money for the customer. To prevent such abuses, the Self Regulatory Organizations (or SROs) require that discretionary accounts be reviewed frequently by an officer of the member firm.

Disclosure. The NASD and the MSRB require specific authorization by the client for the sale of a security to the account if there is a control relationship between the broker-dealer and the issuer of the security. For example, if XYZ broker is acting as an underwriter for the City of Monroe, before the broker-dealer can purchase the bond issued by Monroe for a discretionary account, XYZ must receive specific authorization from the client to do so.

Options Accounts

Initial approval for options accounts may come from the branch manager. In offices with more than three reps producing options business, the manager will be a registered options principal (ROP). If the manager is not a ROP, the manager's signature must be approved by a ROP within a reasonable time. When opening an options account, a registered rep must:

- ascertain the client's investment history and financial status;
- give or send the client the OCC Options Disclosure Document; and
- obtain the client's signature on a Customer Options Agreement, which states that the investor will abide by OCC guidelines and option exchange regulations.

The new account must be approved by a Registered Options Principal (ROP).

Accounts of Deceased Persons

In the event a client dies, any pending orders or instructions must be immediately canceled and the client's account marked with the client's name and the word "deceased." Nothing else should be done until instructions from the administrator or executor of the estate are received. Before the account is liquidated, certain documents may have to be obtained, including an affidavit of domicile (a form attesting to where a deceased person lived), a tax waiver and a death certificate.

Death of a joint tenant. Assets in the account may not be released until a death certificate and the inheritance tax waiver are presented. Transfer agents also require an Affidavit of Domicile, a form that attests to the decedent's state of residency. Additional papers may be required.

Death of a tenant in common. Assets and orders should be frozen until instructions from the survivor(s) and executor or administrator of the estate are received. Other papers in addition to the death certificate and inheritance tax waivers may be required.

Death of a partner. Since the partnership no longer exists, no further orders can be executed until the authority of the surviving partner(s) has been established.

Power of attorney. All trading authorizations cease upon the death of the client.

Account Records

The RR is responsible for maintaining books or records for each client's account as well as a record of each client's security holdings. All customer transactions are posted daily. The representative may use information from copies of the execution reports for the information necessary to keep the books current. The required information includes:

- client's name, address and phone number;
- type of account and account number;
- investment objective;
- list of all securities deposited with the firm; and
- list of all transactions.

Chapter Review

Questions

1. A brokerage firm can open an account for all of the following EXCEPT a(n)

    ____(A)   pension fund.
    ____(B)   insurance company.
    ____(C)   estate.
    _X_(D)   third party without written authorization to do so.

2. An employee of another broker-dealer would like to open an account with your firm. All of the following statements regarding the employee and the account are true EXCEPT the one that isn't

    ____(A)   the employer must receive duplicate copies of all transactions made in the account if requested.
    ____(B)   the employer must be notified of the opening of the account.
    ____(C)   the opening member must notify the employee, in writing, that the employer will be notified of the employee's intent to open the account.
    _X_(D)   the broker-dealer holding the account must approve each transaction made by the person before entry of the order.

3. A client wishes her account designated by a number, not by her name. The registered representative

    ____(A)   cannot open the account in this manner.
    _X_(B)   can open the account with a written statement of ownership from the client.
    ____(C)   can open this account with a written statement of ownership and approval from an authorized delegate of the client.
    ____(D)   can open this account without additional documentation.

4. All of the following are required on a new account form EXCEPT

    ____(A)   name.
    _X_(B)   date of birth.
    ____(C)   Social Security number.
    ____(D)   occupation.

5.   Which of the following must the registered rep attempt to obtain when opening a new account?

I.   financial status
II.   financial condition
III.   investment objective

____(A)   I and II
____(B)   I and III
____(C)   II and III
_X_(D)   I, II and III

6.   An account is owned by three partners, one of whom dies. The registered rep

____(A)   may continue to trade the account once a letter is received stating that the partner has died.
____(B)   must freeze the account's assets.
_X_(C)   must close out the account and all outstanding orders, since the death of a partner dissolves the partnership.
____(D)   may continue to trade the account only after receiving a certified copy of the partner's death certificate.

7.   Which of the following are considered fiduciaries?

I.   an executor of an estate
II.   an administrator of a trust
III.   a custodian of an UGMA account
IV.   a registered rep granted the authority to choose the security, quantity and action in a client's account

____(A)   I and II
_X_(B)   I, II and III
____(C)   II, III and IV
____(D)   I, II, III and IV

8.   A customer would like to open a custodial UGMA account for his nephew, a minor. The uncle

_X_(A)   can open the account provided the proper trust arrangements are filed first.
____(B)   can open the account and name himself custodian.
____(C)   needs a legal document evidencing the permission of the nephew's parents' approval for the account.
____(D)   can be custodian for the account only if he is also the legal guardian for the minor.

9. In a joint tenants with right of survivorship (JTWROS) account

    I. orders may be given by either party.
    II. checks must be made out in the name of the account.
    III. mail may be sent to either party.
    IV. in the event of death of one of the tenants, the surviving party assumes control of the entire account.

    ____(A) I and IV
    ____(B) II and III
    __X__(C) III and IV
    ____(D) I, II, III and IV

10. All of the following statements regarding client accounts are true EXCEPT *the one that isn't*

    ____(A) stock held in a custodial account may not be held in street name.
    ____(B) the customer who opens a numbered account must sign a statement attesting to ownership.
    ____(C) stock held under JTWROS goes to the survivor in the event of death of one of the tenants.
    __X__(D) margin trading in a fiduciary account does not require any special consideration.

Answer Key

1. D.

2. D.

3. B.

4. B.

5. D.

6. B.

7. D.

8. B.

9. D.

10. D.

Chapter Ten

Brokerage Office Procedures

Key Terms

Brokerage Office Procedures

The business of trading securities is not without its share of paperwork. As a registered representative, you are responsible for providing accurate and thorough information for processing transactions. Some of the procedures you follow are particular to your firm. Other procedures are required of all firms by securities regulations, such as the NASD's Uniform Practice Code.

Processing an Order

Several steps are involved in processing a transaction in a brokerage house. The process begins when the client places an order with the registered representative. The RR writes the order ticket and it is submitted to these departments:

- **Order department (wire room, order room).** This department transmits the order to the proper market for execution. Completed trade tickets are sent to the RR who initiated the trade and to the purchase and sales department.
- **Purchase and sales department (P&S).** This department handles all billing, typically a computerized process. It performs computations for each trade and records all transactions in a client's accounts. It mails the trade confirmation which specifies the commission and total cost.
- **Margin or credit department.** This department handles activities involving credit for cash as well as margin accounts. It computes the amount and date on which clients must deposit money.
- **Cashiering department.** This department is responsible for receiving and delivering securities and money. It issues payment only if instructed to do so by the margin department. It sends certificates to transfer agents to be transferred and registered, then forwards the certificates to clients. Most brokerage houses use a clearing corporation for such services as delivery of securities and settlement of trades.

A clearing corporation can simplify this process by providing specialized comparison clearance and settlement services. A clearing corporation, in effect, acts as a secretary-bookkeeper for a large number of broker-dealer firms. Its function is similar to the role the Federal Reserve Bank plays for its member banks. A clearing corporation totals all trades done on a daily basis for each of its participating firms. It "balances the books" of one firm against those of another.

Other departments are involved in client transactions:

- **Reorganization department**. This department handles any transactions that represent a change in the securities outstanding. This includes such actions as exchanging and/or transmitting any securities held for customers that are involved in tender offers, bond calls and redemptions of preferred stock, mergers and acquisitions.
- **Dividend department**. This department is responsible for crediting client accounts with dividends and interest payments on client securities held in the firm's name.
- **Proxy department**. This department has the responsibility for sending proxy statements to clients whose securities are held in the firm's name. It also sends out financial reports and other publications received from the issuer for its shareholders.
- **Stock record department**. This department maintains the ledger that lists the owner of the stock and the location of the certificate.
- **Controller's department**. This department is responsible for accounts payable, employee payroll and financial reports to regulatory agencies. The department also sends statements to clients.

Entering a Trade

To enter a trade for a customer, most registered reps fill out an order ticket (see Fig. 10.1) and send it to the wire (order) room. The order room is responsible for transmitting the order to the proper market for execution.

Mistakes on the part of the broker or failure to settle on the part of clients can jeopardize client relationships. According to many RRs and branch managers, the sequence of trading is most susceptible to error at two points: communication of the order between client and broker, and the transmission of the order from broker to wire operator.

Breakdowns in communication in the ordering process most often occur because of inaccurate information on the tickets. The following information is required on the order ticket:

- client identification number;
- RR identification number;
- description of the security (symbol);
- number of shares or bonds to be traded
- where the security is traded;
- action (buy, sell long, sell short);
- options (buy, write, covered, uncovered, opening, closing);
- price qualifications (at market, GTC, day order, stop order, price limit);

- type of account (cash, margin);
- settlement instruction (if not established when account was opened);
- security instructions;
- payment instructions; and
- location of certificates sold.

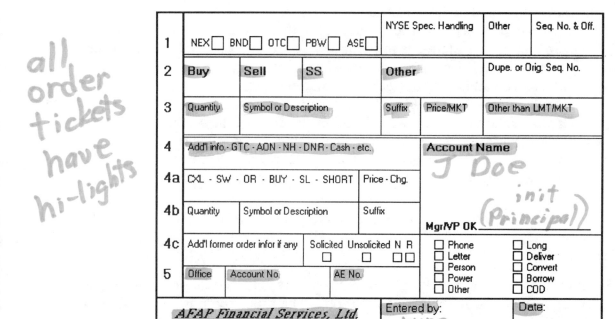

all order tickets have hi-lights

Fig. 10.1 A typical order ticket found at a brokerage.

The Report of Execution

After execution of a trade, the registered rep receives a report. The RR first checks this report of execution against the order ticket to make sure that everything was done as the client requested. If everything appears to be in order, the execution is then reported to the client. If there are any errors that appear to be due to either an incorrect ticket or a mistaken execution, they should be reported immediately to a supervisor or a manager. Never try to correct an error by making additional trades without approval from a principal of the firm.

The Route a Typical Order Takes

- Client places order with rep.
- Registered rep writes the order ticket.
- Order department receives ticket and transmits order to proper market for execution.

- Market or exchange receives order. If the order is executed, it is reported back to the firm's order department.
- Purchase and sales department computes and records all transactions, handles billing and confirmations.
- Margin department computes amount clients are required to deposit, and transmits this information to them.
- Cashiering department receives and delivers securities and money. It issues payments as instructed to by the margin department.

Checking the Confirmation

A confirmation is a printed document which confirms the trade, the settlement date and the amount of money due from or owed to the client. For each transaction, a client must be sent or given a written confirmation of the trade at or before the completion of the transaction (known as the **settlement date**). The RR receives a copy of the customer's confirmation and should check its accuracy against the order ticket.

Components of the trade confirmation include the following:

Confirmation of your order:

Order	No.	Description	Price	Amount	Inter. or tax	Reg. Fee	Commission
BOT	100	G. Heileman	28 7/8	2887.50	.00	.10	87.20

	Account No.	AE No.	AE Name	Net Amount
Trade Date 5/13/90	453-01243-1	27	Walker	2974.80
Settlement 5/20/90				

Customer Name/Address:

Ms. Jaxson Pollac
5047 W. Kenneth Ave.
Chicago   IL 60699-3287

PLEASE NOTE: On odd lot orders (orders for other than 100 share lots) on all exchanges purchases are executed at the round lot price plus a premium. Sales are executed at the round lot price less a discount.

Payment for securities bought and delivery of securities sold are due promptly and in any event on or before settlement date in order to comply with federal Regulation T and to avoid interest or premium charges.

AFAP Financial Services, Ltd. | **Please keep a copy of this confirmation for your records.**

Fig. 10.2 A typical order ticket found at a brokerage.

- **Trade date** is the day on which the transaction is made. Settlement date is usually the fifth full business day after the trade date. Industry regulations require delivery of the check (for a purchase) or security certificates (for a sale) by the settlement date. Reg T settlement (seven business days) does not appear on the confirm.

- **Account number** includes the branch office number followed by a number identifying the type of account. Types of accounts (cash, margin, short) are described briefly on the back of the confirmation.
- **AE No.** The account executive's identification number.
- **BOT** (bought) or **SLD** (sold) indicates the customer's role in the trade.
- **Quantity** shows the number of shares of stock or the par value of bonds bought or sold for the customer.
- **Description** shows the specific security bought or sold for the customer.
- **Price** is the price per share for stock or bonds before any charges or deductions.
- **Amount** is the price paid or received before commissions and other charges have been taken into consideration.
- **Commission** is added to buy transactions and subtracted from sell transactions. A commission amount usually will not appear if a markup has been charged in a principal transaction.
- **Interest or tax** shows the interest portion of a bond transaction added or the state tax subtracted on sales of stock in certain states.
- **Reg. fee** shows the Securities and Exchange Commission registration fee subtracted from the sales made on exchanges and postage.
- **Net amount** is obtained on purchases by adding expenses (commissions and postage) to the principal amount. Whether the transaction is a purchase or a sale, interest is always added whenever bonds are traded with accrued interest.

Providing Customer Account Statements

Firms are required to send each customer who has a securities position (or whose account has seen any activity) a quarterly statement showing positions and entries in that account. Most firms send a customer statement at the end of each month. Some firms mail statements monthly to clients with active accounts (accounts in which there was an entry or in which there are cash or securities), quarterly to clients with inactive accounts. The statement shows:

- all activity in the account since the previous statement;
- securities positions, long or short; and
- account balances, debit or credit.

Settlement Dates

The contract settlement date is the date on which the buyer becomes the owner (and is entitled to all dividends, voting rights, etc.) and on which the bond or stock certificates must be exchanged for money to complete a transaction. There are several different delivery contracts for corporate and government securities.

Cash trades. Cash trades are settled the same day the trade occurs (the word "cash" in "cash trade" is not to be confused with the word "cash" as used to distinguish between cash and margin accounts). Delivery is due at 2:30 pm (Eastern time) or within 30 minutes for trades completed after 2 pm.

Regular way. Most transactions settle regular way. For U.S. government securities, regular-way delivery is due the first (next) business day following the trade date. Regular-way settlement is assumed unless otherwise specified at the time the trade is done.

Regular way for corporate and municipal securities calls for settlement on the fifth business day following the trade date. To determine the fifth business day, add seven to the trade date (remember, though, that you would add extra days if a week-day holiday falls in between).

Seller's or buyer's option. Seller's option or buyer's option delivery contracts call for delivery within the number of days specified by the seller or buyer. These contracts may call for delivery no earlier than the business day following regular-way settlement, but no later than 60 calendar days after the trade date. In a seller's option, the seller will take a discount or pay a fee for delayed settlement. In a buyer's option contract, the buyer will pay a premium for setting the settlement date. A seller or buyer who wants to settle before the assigned date may do so by giving the other party one day's written notice of intention to settle early. In any event, settlement may not take place before normal regular-way settlement.

When-issued. Securities can be purchased before they have been issued or distributed, occasionally even before they are available for delivery. Such purchases are called when-issued, as-issued, when-distributed, as-distributed or if-distributed trades. In such cases, delivery is delayed until the issuing corporation has the physical certificates available for distribution. When-issued trading stops and regular-way trading begins upon issuance of the securities. All previous transactions executed on a when-issued basis are then reconfirmed for delivery. Settlement occurs five business days after the securities are available.

For transactions of when-issued securities, the confirmation will not include a total price (which depends on the amount of accrued interest) or the settlement date.

Type of Security	Delivery Contract	Time
Government bonds	Cash	Delivery by 2:30 pm on the same day as the trade
	Regular way	Delivery on the first business day following the trade date.
	Seller's/buyer's option	No sooner than the second business day after the trade date, but no later than 60 calendar days after the trade date.
	When issued	One business day after the securities are ready for delivery.
Corporate and Municipal securities	Cash	Delivery by 2:30 pm on the same day as the trade.
	Regular way	Delivery on the 5th business day after trade date.
	Seller's/Buyer's option	No sooner than the 6th business day after trade date, no later than 60 calendar days after trade date.
	When issued	Five business days after the securities are ready for delivery.

Failure To Deliver

A failure-to-deliver (or fails-to-deliver) situation occurs when the broker-dealer on the sell side of a contract has not delivered the securities to the broker-dealer on the buy side. As long as a fail-to-deliver exists, the seller will not receive payment.

Buy-In/Sell-Out Procedures

A buy-in will occur 10 business days after settlement day if the seller of a security fails to fulfill the terms of the contract to sell. When this happens, the broker-dealer "buys-in" the security to close the contract, buying the securities in the open market and then charging the seller for any loss caused by changes in the market.

When the buyer of the security fails to pay for it within the seven business days allowed by Regulation T, a sell-out will occur on the eighth day. The broker-dealer sells the security in the market and charges the client for any losses. If for good reason a buyer is unable to pay for a trade within seven business days from the trade date, the broker-dealer may request an extension from an SRO (such as the NASD).

Accrued Interest

The majority of bonds trade "and interest," which means that the buyer pays the seller the market price of the bond plus any interest accrued since the previous interest payment. Since the buyer will receive the full amount of the next interest payment (including interest that accrued while the seller still owned the bond) it is only fair that the seller be reimbursed for that portion of interest.

Most bonds pay interest every six months on either the first or the 15th of specified months. The payment dates are known as coupon dates. For example:

If the interest dates are:	The bonds are known as:
January and July 1	J & J bonds
May and November 1	M & N bonds
February 15 and August 15	F & A 15 bonds
June 15 and December 15	J & D 15 bonds

Accrued interest affects bond transactions if a bond trades between coupon dates. For example, if a J & J bond trades in March, the buyer will collect six months of interest in July from the issuer even though he or she owned the bond for only three months of that period. The buyer and seller settle this by adding the accrued interest to the cost of the buy transaction. So the buyer pays the accrued interest to the seller and then receives the full interest payment on the next coupon date. Interest begins accruing on the last interest payment date and is computed up to, but not including, the settlement date.

Corporate and Municipal Bonds

Accrued interest on corporate and municipal bonds is calculated for a 360-day year of 30-day months. For example, if an F & A corporate or municipal bond is traded regular way on Monday, March 5, the number of days of accrued interest would be:

February	30 days
March 5th trade	11 days (settles March 12)
	41 days

So interest would accrue up to but not including the settlement date of March 11 (or 5 + 6).

If an A & O corporate or municipal bond is bought or sold in a cash trade on August 16, the number of days accrued interest would be:

April	30 days
May	30 days
June	30 days
July	30 days
August	15 days (day before trade date)
	135 days

Calculating interest. Accrued interest is added to both the buyer's confirmation (the buyer owes it in addition to the purchase price) and to the seller's confirmation (the seller receives it in addition to the sale proceeds).

Accrued interest and the dated date. Calculating accrued interest is a little different for bonds bought before the first interest payment. Assume a municipal bond issue is filed and its preliminary official statement is published August 11. In that statement, the proposed bonds are described on the front page as "dated September 1." Even if the bonds are issued late in September, they begin to accrue interest on September 1. The date from which interest accrual begins is called the dated date.

Government Bonds

Calculating time. For calculating time elapsed since the most recent interest payment on a government bond, use an actual-days-elapsed method instead of the 30-day month, 360-day year method used for corporate and municipal bonds. If an F & A government bond is traded regular way on Monday, March 5, the number of days accrued interest would be:

February	28 days
March	5 days
	33 days (up to but not including the March 6th (next day) settlement date

If an A & O government bond is traded for cash on August 16, the number of days of accrued interest would be:

April	30 days
May	31 days
June	30 days
July	31 days
August	15 days
	137 days (actual days elapsed)

Calculating interest. Accrued interest is added to both the buyer's confirmation (the buyer owes it in addition to the purchase price) and to the seller's confirmation (the seller receives it in addition to the sale proceeds).

For government securities, a half-year's interest is used to calculate accrued interest. For the interest period, therefore, we calculate the proportionate amount. For government securities, accrued interest is based on a half-year period or portion of the half-year elapsed. If the time period is less than one-half year, the proportionate amount of time is figured by dividing the number of days elapsed by 184 days (the number of days in one-half year).

Ex-Dates

Previous chapters covered several different ex-dates: ex-dividend, ex-rights, ex-warrants. Since these affect the prices paid for securities, they also affect settlement procedures. To know the price to be paid in a transaction, you must know when it takes place in relation to the relevant ex-dates. The table below summarizes these dates.

Due bills. A due bill is a printed statement showing the obligation of a seller to deliver securities, rights or cash (due bill check) to the purchaser. If securities are sold shortly before the ex-date but delivered too late for the buyer's name to be put on the books by the record date, a due bill accompanies the securities. The seller owes the buyer the amount of the dividend, right or warrant received.

Transaction/Ex-Date	Definition	Duration/Expiration
Trade date	The date on which the transaction occurs.	Initiation date for all types of payment contracts. Due date for cash settlement.
Settlement date	The date on which payment must be received under NASD, NYSE or MSRB rules.	Varies according to type of delivery contract: same day for cash, five business days for regular way, 60 days for seller's or buyer's option.
Record date	The date that determines who is eligible to receive dividends or rights distributions. Fixed by the issuing corporation.	The investor must have settled the transaction to be considered the shareholder of record on the record date.
Ex-date	A date set by the Uniform Practice Committee after being informed of the distribution declaration by the issuer.	One-day period dictated by the record date for distributions. Normally four business days before the record date. Stock trades without (ex-) rights or dividends.
Ex-dividend date	The date on which stock is sold without (ex-) the right to receive the dividend.	Normally the fourth business day preceding the record date.
Ex-rights date	The date on which the seller of the underlying security is entitled to receive the stock rights.	The fourth business day preceding the record date.
Ex-warrant date	The date on which the seller of the underlying security is entitled to receive the warrants.	The fourth business day preceding the expiration of the warrant.

Rules of Good Delivery

Before a security that has been sold can be delivered to the buyer, it must be in good delivery form. It is the RR's responsibility to inquire of the seller who calls with a sell order whether the security is negotiable, in compliance with the contract of sale, can be delivered to the broker-dealer within 5 business days and is ready to be transferred from seller to purchaser.

Proper assignment. Whenever a client delivers a certificate to complete a sale, it must be endorsed exactly as the certificate is registered. Customer signatures must be guaranteed by a NYSE member firm or a bank. The only acceptable abbreviations are: Co. for "Company" or an ampersand (&) for "and." A certificate in the names of two or more persons must be endorsed for sale by every person named on the certificate.

Assignment and stock power. To comply with rules of good delivery, a registered security (like a personal check) must be assigned or endorsed. Assignment is executed on the back of the certificate or on a separate paper called a stock or bond power. One stock or bond power can be used with any number of certificates for one security (five certificates for various amounts of IBM, for example), but a separate power is required for each security: one for all the customer's IBM stock, one for all AT&T stock and so on. Stock certificates are often incorrectly endorsed, signed in the wrong place or not signed at all. Such errors delay transfer.

Risk of lost certificate. If there is a risk that the certificate may be lost, the customer should either fill in the line granting power of attorney to another party or use a stock power. A client mailing a certificate, for example, can give the broker-dealer power of attorney to transfer the title. This protects the owner if the certificates are lost or misdirected, since the securities cannot be transferred without the firm's approval.

Certificate unavailable. If the registered owner of a security does not have the certificate available for endorsement, a stock power can be used to assign the stock. The only acceptable reason for the unavailability of the stock certificate is that it is at the broker-dealer's firm (that is, the certificate is being held by the broker-dealer in the customer's name for safekeeping). No assignment is necessary if the stock is in street name.

Legal opinion. In municipal bond trading, unless the bond is traded and stamped "ex-legal" (which means without the legal opinion) the legal opinion must be printed on or attached to the bond as evidence of the validity of the bond offering. Securities traded ex-legal are in good delivery condition without the legal opinion.

Good condition of security. If a certificate is mutilated, appropriate authentication (by the transfer agent, registrar or issuer) must be obtained before the transfer agent can accept the security for replacement. If damage is so extensive that there is doubt about the authenticity of the certificate, the transfer agent will require a surety bond.

Proper denominations. Certificates must be delivered in either the unit of trading (typically 100 shares), in a multiple of the trading unit or in smaller amounts that can be combined into 100-share lots. Odd lots are separated from round-lot certificates. For example, a seller of 300 shares could deliver six 50-share certificates but not four 75-share certificates, since no combination of the 75-share certificates adds up to 100 (a round lot for most stock transactions).

This does not mean that an investor with four 75-share certificates cannot sell her securities. It does mean that her broker-dealer must send the certificates to the transfer agent to be transferred into proper denominations.

Not in the name of a deceased person. The signature of an individual becomes null and void when that person dies. The executor or administrator of the estate must endorse the certificate or furnish stock power and transfer the securities to the name of the estate before being sold.

Not a called security. Any bond or preferred stock called for redemption is not in good delivery form unless the whole issue has been called. If part of the issue is called, the securities are not in good delivery form unless identified as called at the time of the trade. Securities called after the trade date are considered in good delivery form.

Proper Assignment of Securities

Stock certificates. To be considered good delivery, securities must be properly assigned. This requires the seller to endorse the back of the certificate or a separate document called a stock or bond power.

Assignment using a stock or bond power. When a registered security is being held in the customer's name at the brokerage firm and is not available for endorsement (or when there are safety concerns) the client may sign an irrevocable stock or bond power instead of endorsing the back of the certificate.

AFAP Enterprises, Incorporated

The Company will furnish without charge to each stockholder who so requests the powers, designations, preferences and relative, participating optional or other special rights of each class of stock or series thereof of the Company, and the qualifications, limitations or restrictions of such preferences and/or rights. Such request may be made to the Office of the Secretary of the Company or to the Transfer Agent.

The following abbreviations, when used in the inscription on the face of this certificate, shall be construed as though they were written out in full according to the applicable laws or regulations:

TEN COM — as tenants in common
TEN ENT — as tenants by entireties
JT TEN — as joint tenants with right of survivorship

UNIF GIFT MIN ACT-

_____ Custodian _____
(Cust)   (Minor)
under Uniform Gift to Minors Act of
(State) _____

For value received _____ *hereby sell, assign and transfer unto*

PLEASE INSERT SOCIAL SECURITY NUMBER OR OTHER IDENTIFYING NUMBER OF ASSIGNEE

_____

_____

Please type or print name of assignee

Shares of the capital stock represented by the within Certificate and do hereby irrevocably constitute and appoint _____

_____

Attorney to transfer the said stock on the books of the within-named Company with full power of substitution in the premises.

Dated: _____ X _____
                       Sign here

                    X _____
                       If joint account, both parties must sign

Fig. 10.3 A stock power on the back of a certificate.

IRREVOCABLE STOCK OR BOND POWER

FOR VALUE RECEIVED, the undersigned do(es) hereby sell, assign
and transfer to

_____

_____

Social Security Number
or Tax Identification Number

IF STOCK, **COMPLETE** **THIS PORTION**	_____shares of the_____ stock of_____ represented by certificate(s) No.(s)_____inclusive standing in the name of the undersigned on the books of said company.
IF BONDS, **COMPLETE** **THIS PORTION**	_____bonds of_____ in the principal amount of $ _____No.(s) _____ inclusive standing in the name of the undersigned on the books of said company.

The undersigned do(es) hereby irrevocably constitute and appoint

_____

_____

**Attorney to transfer said stock or bonds as the case may be on the
books of said company, with full power of substitution in the
premises.**

Dated: _____

X _____

X _____

(Person(s) executing this Power sign(s) here)

IMPORTANT NOTICE- READ CAREFULLY

The signature(s) to this Power must correspond with the name(s) as written upon the face
of the certificate(s) or bond(s) in every particular without alteration or enlargement or any
change whatever. Signature guarantee should be made by a member or a member organization of the New York Stock Exchange, members of other Exchanges having signatures
on file with transfer agents or by a commercial bank or trust company having its principal
office or correspondent in the City of New York.

Fig. 10.4 A separate stock power.

Chapter Review

Questions

1. Which department in a brokerage firm would handle all credit transactions for a client?

    ___ ⊙ (A)   margin
    ___ (B)   cashier
    ___ (C)   purchasing and sales
    ___ (D)   reorganization

2. Once received, in what order do orders flow through a brokerage firm?

    I.   wire room
    II.   purchase and sales department
    III. margin department
    IV.   cashier

    ___ (A)   III, IV, II, I
    ___ (B)   I, IV, II, III
    ─ ___ (C)   I, II, III, IV
    ___ ⊙ (D)   II, I, IV, III

3. According to regulations, a statement for an inactive account should be sent to each client

    ___ ⊙ (A)   quarterly.
    ___ (B)   monthly.
    ___ (C)   weekly.
    ___ (D)   immediately after each trade.

4. A customer purchased a Treasury bond in a regular-way transaction on Monday, April 4. Settlement will be on   *next day*

    ___ ⊙ (A)   Monday, April 4.
    ─ ___ (B)   Tuesday, April 5
    ___ (C)   Friday, April 8.
    ___ (D)   Monday, April 11.

5. A customer purchased a Treasury bond in a regular-way transaction on Monday, April 4. The bond was a J & J bond. How many days of accrued interest will the seller receive?

    ____(A) 79
    ____(B) 80
    ____(C) 94
    ____(D) 95

6. A bond is dated June 1, 1995. The first interest payment is on January 1, 1996. How many months will the first and second interest payments cover?

    ____(A) 1 month for the first, 6 months for the second
    ____(B) 1 month for the first, 5 months for the second
    ____(C) 7 months for the first, 5 months for the second
    ____(D) 7 months for the first, 6 months for the second

7. As long as a failure-to-deliver situation exists, the seller

    ____(A) will have all accounts frozen.
    ____(B) must conduct all transactions on a cash basis.
    ____(C) will not receive payment.
    ____(D) will not receive accrued interest on bonds.

8. TRUE or FALSE. A buy-in occurs when the seller of a security fails to complete the contract according to its terms. (Circle one)

9. To be considered in good delivery form, certificates must be

    ____(A) accompanied by a preliminary prospectus.
    ____(B) called for redemption by the issuing body
    ____(C) accompanied by an assignment or stock power.
    ____(D) in the name of the deceased person, if he died after the trade date.

10. Your client has a certificate registered in his own name. To be a good delivery, the certificate must be accompanied by

    ____(A) a properly executed assignment to the brokerage firm on the reverse side of the certificate.
    ____(B) the promise that it has not been called for redemption.
    ____(C) a buyer's option.
    ____(D) the legal opinion, unless the client is selling municipal bonds.

Answer Key

1. A.

2. C.

3. A.

4. B.

5. C.

6. D.

7. C.

8. T

9. C.

10. A.

Chapter Eleven

Margin Accounts

Key Terms

11.18 Arbitrage

11.8 Credit register (CR)

11.8 Debit register (DR)

11.3 11.8 Equity

11.2 Federal Reserve Board (FRB)

11.7 Long

11.8 Maintenance margin

11.3 Margin call

11.7 Market value

11.2 Reg T call

11.6 Restricted account

11.7 Short

11.18 Short exempt

Commingle 11.7

Current market value 11.3

Debt 11.3

Excess equity 11.5

Hypothecation 11.7 11.8

Maintenance call 11.3

Margin 11.2

Mark-to-the-market 11.8

Regulation T 11.2

Rehypothecation 11.7 11.8

Retention requirement 11.10

Short-against-the-box 11.19

Special memorandum account (SMA) 11.13

K111

Margin Accounts

Economic analysts in the 1930s identified excessive and unwise borrowing to buy securities as one of the causes of the Great Depression. Buying securities with a down payment of less than the full market value is called buying on **margin**. Congress, through the Securities Exchange Act of 1934, gave the Federal Reserve Board (FRB) authority to regulate margin buying.

Under Regulation T (or **Reg T**) the FRB sets the minimum a customer must deposit (expressed as a percent of purchase price) when purchasing securities from a broker-dealer or when selling securities short. Currently, the required minimum deposit is 50%. Certain securities are exempt from the Regulation T initial margin requirement, including U.S. government securities and municipal bonds.

Marginable securities. Reg T not only limits borrowing, it also identifies which securities are eligible for purchase on margin. The brokerage firm may lend money to help a client purchase marginable securities or may accept such securities as collateral for loans for other purchases. Marginable securities include:

- stocks and bonds listed on an exchange;
- stocks listed as eligible for trading in the National Market System (NASDAQ/NMS);
- certain OTC securities designated by the FRB; and
- warrants (for listed and designated securities only).

Treasury securities are exempt from Regulation T and the initial requirements of the SROs (such as the NASD and the NYSE). Because of the relative safety of Treasury securities as investments, SROs generally require a maintenance margin of only 5% of the principal amount.

Noneligible securities. The following investment instruments (sometimes called **nonmargin securities**) can not be used as collateral for loans and must be paid for in full.

- put and call options
- common and preferred OTC stocks not designated by the FRB
- insurance contracts (not a true security)
- new issues (including mutual funds until 30 days after their initial purchase)

Initial requirements. A client buying securities in a margin account is required initially to deposit a certain percentage of the purchase cost of the security. The requirement is called the Reg T call, initial margin requirement, initial call or federal call. As previously mentioned, the current Reg T requirement is 50% of purchase price for most securities.

A broker may waive the margin call (a request for a deposit from a client to meet the Reg T requirement) if the balance due is less than $500 or the total purchase is less than $1,000.

NYSE and NASD Requirements

Initial requirement. The NYSE and the NASD also have initial margin requirements. An investor must meet the larger of either the 50% Reg T requirement or the NASD/NYSE requirement of the lesser of 100% of the cost of the securities or $2,000.

Maintenance requirement. A maintenance call (a bill for a cash deposit) is sent to a client whose account falls below the required equity level. Although the $2,000 minimum is an initial requirement, the account may also be required to maintain a minimum equity of $2,000.

If a change in market value is what caused the decline in equity below $2,000, no maintenance call will be issued. However, neither the firm nor the client may take any action which will bring the equity below $2,000 (such as borrowing money or taking a cash distribution from the account). In effect, the NYSE and NASD requirement prevents a brokerage firm from lending money to a client or permitting withdrawals of cash or securities by a client whose account equity is $2,000 or less.

For small accounts, the NASD/NYSE requirement is more stringent than Reg T. Remember that a broker can waive a Reg T call of less than $500. Because of the NASD/NYSE initial minimum requirement, this will happen only in an already established account.

When-issued securities. Purchases of when-issued securities in a margin account are subject to the same Reg T requirements as other securities purchases; if Reg T is 50%, a customer must deposit 50% when purchasing nonexempt when-issued securities on margin. When-issued exempt securities, such as municipal bonds, are not subject to these credit requirements.

Margin Accounting

A customer with a margin account is in debt to the firm; in some ways, a margin account is like a loan or a line of credit. Most homeowners have a house with a market value, debt (the amount of the mortgage left to pay off) and equity (the difference between the market value of the house and the balance of the mortgage). Similarly, a customer with a margin account has current market value (in this case, of securities), debt (the loan from the firm) and equity (the difference between market value and the loan balance).

To open a margin account, a customer must first sign the margin agreement. If the customer then makes a purchase of 1,000 shares of XYZ stock at $48 per share, there will appear a $48,000 debit in the account. The customer must deposit $24,000 in cash to meet the 50% Reg T requirement, which leaves a debit balance of $24,000, the amount the firm has loaned for the purchase.

The customer's margin account now has 1,000 shares of XYZ with a market value of $48,000, no cash, a debit balance (loan) of $24,000 and equity of $24,000 (the customer's deposit). It is very important to understand that the equity in an account does not represent a cash balance; it represents that portion of the securities fully owned by the client. The account balance would appear as follows:

Current Market Value (CMV)	$48,000
Debit (Debit Register or DR)	-24,000
Equity (EQ)	$24,000

Using Fully Paid Securities to Meet Margin Requirements

In the preceding example, a client used cash to meet margin requirements. But fully paid securities may also be used to purchase stock in a margin account.

Instead of depositing $24,000 in cash to meet the initial margin requirement, the customer could have chosen to deposit securities. When meeting margin requirements, a customer may deposit securities with a loan value equal to the debit in the account (in this case, a debit of $24,000). The loan value of a stock is the **complement** of Regulation T (if Reg T were 65%, the loan value would be 35%). The Reg T loan value of stock is currently 50% of its CMV. The customer must, therefore, deposit $48,000 worth of stock ($2 of fully-paid securities for each $1 of debt).

If the customer buys $48,000 worth of XYZ and deposits $48,000 worth of fully-paid ABC stock in the account, then 50% of the stock in the account is paid for.

CMV	$96,000
DR	-48,000
EQ	$48,000

To meet the initial equity requirement in a margin account, an equal amount of fully-paid stock must be deposited, or 50% of the CMV of the stock to be purchased must be deposited in cash. The formula for calculating the dollar amount of stock necessary to meet a Reg T call is:

$$\frac{\text{Margin call in \$}}{100\% - \text{Reg T\%}}$$

Nonrequired Cash Deposits

Any deposit of cash that is not needed to meet a margin call (such as an additional cash investment by the customer or a dividend payment by a corporation) is used to pay off part of the debit balance. Anything that reduces the debit balance increases equity. Any nonrequired cash deposit is always available for the customer to withdraw. If, for instance, a customer receives a dividend of $200, that dividend will first be applied against the outstanding debit balance. A subsequent withdrawal of the $200 will increase the debit by the same amount.

For example, if a dividend of $2 per share is paid on 1,000 shares of XYZ stock, the result is a $2,000 decrease in the debit balance and a subsequent $2,000 increase in equity.

	Before	**Dividend**	**After**
CMV	$48,000		$48,000
DR	− $24,000	$2,000	− $22,000
Equity	$24,000		$26,000
Reg T	− $24,000		− $26,000 ~~$24,000~~ (½ cmv)
Excess Equity (EE)	$0		$2,000

The increase does not represent more cash in the account (cash exists only when there is no debit balance), but becomes equity in excess of the Reg T requirement. Under Reg T, the required equity in this account is $24,000. The customer currently has equity of $26,000, with excess equity of $2,000.

The customer may withdraw this excess equity, leave it in the account to be applied against the debit balance, or use it (as extra borrowing power) to purchase additional securities. The excess equity, therefore, gives the customer buying power (or borrowing power) in the account.

The Effect of Changes in Market Value

Increase in market value. As the market value of the stock goes up, equity in the account increases; and as market value falls, equity decreases. The debit balance stays the same, until cash is either deposited to or withdrawn from the account.

If XYZ appreciates from $48 to $52 per share, the CMV of the account rises $4,000 to $52,000. The debit remains $24,000 (the customer initially borrowed $24,000 from the firm to buy the stock, and that loan doesn't change). The result is an increase in equity of $4,000 to $28,000. The increase affects the equity dollar for dollar.

was
48 K
24 K
24 K
24 K (½ cmv)
0

CMV	$52,000
DR	-24,000
Eq	$28,000
Reg T	-26,000 (½ cmv)
EE	$2,000

The Reg T requirement for this account is 50% of the CMV (which is now $52,000), or $26,000.

Using excess equity to purchase stock. The customer now has excess equity of $2,000, which can be used to purchase $4,000 of stock. (Since Reg T is 50%, $2,000 meets the initial deposit requirement for a $4,000 purchase.) To calculate how much

K111

stock a customer can purchase by using a given amount of excess equity, use the following formula:

SmART

Buying Power = Excess Equity / Reg T (50%)

If excess equity is $2,000, as in the previous example, buying power is $4,000 ($2,000 divided by .50 is $4,000). The $4,000 in new buying power represents a loan by the broker-dealer.

Withdrawing excess equity. Instead of purchasing stock with excess equity, the customer can withdraw cash equal to the excess equity. Since there is no "cash" in a margin account (short of liquidating the account), the client will increase his or her debit by borrowing the money against the increased loan value of the securities. Withdrawing the excess equity results in a fully margined account (the debit is once again 50% of the current market value).

	Before	Withdraw Cash	After
CMV	$52,000		$52,000
DR	$24,000	(+ $2,000)	$26,000
Equity	$28,000	(-$2,000)	$26,000
Reg T	$26,000 ½ cmv		$26,000 ½ cmv
EE	$2,000		$0

The difference between reinvestment or withdrawal revolves around purchasing power. Because Reg T requires only 50% equity in the account, $1 of excess equity can be used to purchase $2 of stock, but the loan value of the same $1 is only $1.

Decrease in market value. If the stock decreases in value, the equity in the account will fall dollar for dollar with the market value of the stock. The debit balance does not change: it is a record of money borrowed and cash coming into and going out of the account. The current market value (CMV) is a measure of the securities' value in the account. Equity represents the CMV minus the debit; it is the client's share of the market value.

CMV - DR = Equity

Regulation T does not require that the account be kept at a 50% margin; it requires the 50% deposit only for the initial purchase. A decrease in market value that brings equity below the Reg T requirement doesn't necessarily require an additional deposit of cash or securities. If declining market value reduces equity below 50% of CMV, the customer may not have to make a deposit. If no deposit is made, however, the account's status will change and it will become what is known as a restricted account.

Holding Customer Securities

When a customer purchases securities in a margin account using money borrowed from the broker-dealer, the securities are pledged to the broker-dealer as collateral for the loan. This process is called hypothecation of the securities. The broker-dealer, in turn, may pledge those securities to a bank as collateral for a loan for itself. This repledging is called rehypothecation of the securities.

SEC rules require a firm to take into account the client's debit balance when rehypothecating securities. The firm may pledge client securities only to a maximum of 140% of the customer's debit balance. For example, if a client has a debit balance of $10,000 in a margin account and $20,000 CMV of securities, the firm may rehypothecate up to $14,000 worth of the client's margined securities ($14,000 is 140% of $10,000).

Customers' fully-paid and excess margin securities (those securities that have not been used for hypothecation by the broker-dealer) held by a broker-dealer must be segregated from the firm's own accounts and cannot be commingled with the firm's inventory. They also may not be loaned to other customers for short sales. The broker-dealer must inform the customer that all fully-paid securities are available to the customer upon request. In the account just described, the other $6,000 worth of securities ($20,000-$14,000) are considered excess margin securities and must be segregated and not used as loan collateral.

Margin Terms

Listed below are some terms that will enable you to better understand the following discussions of margin accounts.

- **Long and short positions.** The purchase (or ownership) of stock is a long position and sale (or owing) of stock is a short position.
- **Market value.** After the trade date, securities in a margin account are valued at the current market price, referred to as the current market value

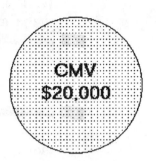

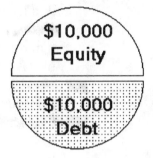

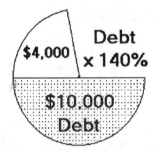

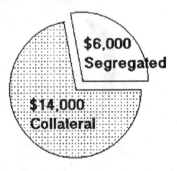

Fig. 11.1 Multiply debt by 140% for collateral value.

(CMV). The process of checking the market price and recording it in the account is referred to as "marking-to-the-market."

- **Debit balance (DR).** Debit balance (or debit register) is the amount a client owes the brokerage firm. The client pays the firm interest on any outstanding debit balance and any unpaid interest increases the investor's debit balance.
- **Credit balance (CR).** Credit balance (or credit register) is the amount of money the brokerage firm owes the client. This may be money due the client after a sale or money held in the firm's reserve account for the client. A client cannot have both a debit and a credit balance in the same account at the same time.
- **Equity.** Equity (or margin of equity) is the customer's net worth in a margin account. You can remember equity as what is owned minus what is owed.
- **Hypothecation.** Pledging securities as collateral, usually used in reference to securities purchased in a margin account.
- **Rehypothecation.** The practice used by broker-dealers of pledging a customer's margined securities to a bank as collateral for a loan to carry the customer's margin account.

Maintenance Requirements

Once the client has met the initial margin requirement, Reg T will not be a factor until the client trades or withdraws equity from the account. The client does not have to maintain equity equal to 50% of the market value of securities in the account. In most cases, a decreasing market value for the securities in the account will not obligate the client to deposit more cash (or fully owned securities) to maintain equity. But there are limits on how low equity can fall in relation to market value. These minimum maintenance requirements are set by the NASD and NYSE:

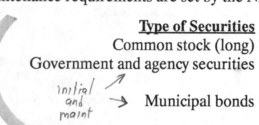

Type of Securities	Equity as a % of CMV
Common stock (long)	25%
Government and agency securities	5% ~~16%~~ of par, ~~depending on maturity~~
Municipal bonds	7% of par or 15% of CMV, whichever is greater

If a client's equity in a margin account falls below the maintenance minimum, a maintenance call will be issued to restore the equity to the proper amount. If the minimum maintenance requirement is higher than the Reg T requirement (as in the case of government and municipal securities), the minimum requirement applies initially. For both the NASD and the NYSE the initial minimum margin is $2,000 per account.

Maintenance margin and market action. If an account drops below the required minimum maintenance level, the customer will receive a maintenance call. Following is an example of the change in status of an account in which the market value of stock initially purchased at $50 falls to $30.

Stock price at $50 per share:

CMV	$5,000(100%)
DR	$2,500 (50%)
Equity	$2,500 (50%)
NYSE requirement	$1,250 (25%)

Stock price drops to $30 per share:

CMV	$3,000 (100%)
DR	$2,500 (83.3%
Equity	$500 (16.7%)
NYSE requirement	$750 (25%)

To calculate the SRO-required minimum maintenance equity, multiply the current market value by 25%. In the original transaction the client's equity is well above the 25% NYSE maintenance requirement. After the stock declines in price to $30 per share, however, the client's equity falls below the required minimum by $250 (actual current equity = $500; minimum equity = $750). The client will, therefore, receive a maintenance call for $250, which can be met by depositing cash, depositing any security acceptable to the firm, or liquidating securities in the account.

House requirements. For a number of reasons, broker-dealers often have higher minimum equity and maintenance requirements (known as **house requirements**) than do the SROs. House maintenance calls are due promptly, but most firms allow a reasonable time for payment (following the "five business days" rule of the NYSE and NASD). The following examples use the 25% NYSE and NASD requirement rather than a "house rules" figure.

Calculating Market Value at Minimum Maintenance

To calculate how low the value of securities can go in the market before a client is sent a maintenance call, use the following formula:

Learn if I have time

notebook

> Debit Balance / 75% = Market Value at Minimum Maintenance

If a customer purchases $48,000 worth of stock and deposits $24,000 to meet the 50% Regulation T requirement, the account will have the following balances:

Market value	$48,000
Debit	-$24,000
Equity	$24,000

If the market value of this stock falls to $45,000, the account balances will now look like this:

Market value	$45,000
Debit balance	-$24,000
Equity	$21,000

Using the formula, you can calculate that the market value can go as low as $32,000 before equity falls below the 25% minimum maintenance requirement:

$24,000 (DR) divided by .75 $32,000

At $32,000, the status will be:

CMV	$32,000 (100%)
DR	-24,000 (75%)
EQ	$8,000 (25%)

We know that when equity reaches the allowable minimum of 25% of CMV, the debit balance represents the remaining 75%. If the debit exceeds 75% of CMV, equity will be below maintenance and the customer will get a maintenance call.

Security	Authority	Amount
Listed stock or OTC margin stock	FRB Reg T	50%
	NYSE/NASD	25%
New issues, mutual funds, Options, nonmargin OTC stock	FRB Reg T	100%
Government and agency securities	NYSE/NASD maintenance	1-6% of par
Municipal securities	NYSE/NASD maintenance	The greater of 7% of par or 15% of CMV

Restricted Accounts

A restricted account is a margin account in which the equity is less than the Reg T initial requirement. For example, assume that Reg T is 50% and that you have a customer whose account has the following balances:

Market value	$70,000 (100%)
Debit	-$40,000 (57%)
Equity	$30,000 (43%)

When equity falls between the 50% Reg T initial margin requirement and the 25% minimum maintenance, the account becomes a restricted account. When equity falls below 50% of market value and an account becomes restricted, the Reg T retention requirement says that the client may not withdraw securities without depositing (either cash or other securities) an amount equal to 50% of whatever is withdrawn. The customer paid for half of the security purchase initially, and must now pay for the other half in order to withdraw the stock.

If an investor has a restricted margin account from which she would like to withdraw 100 shares of ATT with a $6,000 CMV, the retention requirement states that to obtain the securities, she must deposit either $3,000 in cash or securities with a loan value of $3,000. Even in a restricted margin account, Reg T permits 50% of the proceeds of any sale to be made available to the investor.

Getting into Restricted Status

There are three ways a margin account may become restricted: the market value of stock in the account could decline, the Federal Reserve Board could increase the Reg T requirement, or the brokerage firm may have waived a Reg T call for under $500.

Activity in a Restricted Account

Purchasing additional shares. If an investor wants to purchase additional shares in a restricted margin account, he must deposit either cash or securities equal to 50% of the purchase price (which is the same as saying he must meet the 50% Reg T requirement for an initial transaction). By doing so, the investor will have met his 50% Reg T requirement on the new purchase, increasing his equity in the shares owned before the purchase.

Selling shares. An investor can also sell shares held in a restricted margin account and be entitled to withdraw cash from the sale. Under the retention requirement, 50% of the proceeds of any sale must be made available to the client. However, since any sale proceeds will have been applied towards reducing the investor's debit balance, any amount subsequently withdrawn from the account will be added to his debit balance.

Sometimes the sale of securities removes an account from restricted status. If the proceeds from the sale are enough to bring the investor's debit balance down to less than 50% of the market value, then the account will no longer have a restricted status.

Cash available for withdrawal. In order to determine how much of the proceeds from a sale are available to a customer who wishes to make a cash withdrawal from a restricted account, you must make two separate calculations. For the first calculation, multiply the proceeds by 50%.

$$50\% \times \text{Proceeds of Sale} = \text{Amount Available to Client}$$

Then take into account the excess equity that might also be available for withdrawal:

$$\text{Equity} - \text{Margin Required} = \text{Excess Equity Available to Client}$$

This is an important point to remember, since you will encounter this situation in other margin problems. In effect, the amount is calculated twice: once to determine 50% of the sale proceeds that may be released to the client and a second time to determine whether excess equity is greater than the 50% figure.

Noncash withdrawals. We have already covered two examples of cash withdrawals from restricted accounts when stock is sold. Sometimes, however, customers want to make withdrawals from their accounts without selling any securities. There are two types of withdrawals that do not involve selling securities: cash withdrawals and stock withdrawals.

Cash withdrawals. A customer with a restricted margin account is entitled to withdraw cash dividends and interest. A dividend or interest payment received by the account reduces the debit. A $500 dividend, for example, reduces debit by $500 without affecting CMV. If the client withdraws that amount, the debit increases $500 and the account is back where it was before the dividend was received, as if nothing had happened.

For any other cash withdrawals, a customer with a restricted account must either deposit additional marginable securities with a loan value equal to the amount of the cash withdrawal (currently twice as much in CMV of securities must be deposited as the amount of cash withdrawn), or have SMA (which will be discussed later). The client, in effect, is borrowing against the new securities deposited.

If a customer wants to withdraw $20,000 from a restricted margin account, we already know that there is no excess equity to withdraw (having excess equity means having equity greater than 50% of the securities' CMV; being restricted means it has less than 50%). If the customer can deposit other fully paid securities in his margin account as collateral, with Reg T at 50% the maximum loan available from the broker will be 50% of the market value of the securities:

$$\boxed{\text{CMV} \times 50\% = \text{Loan Value of Securities Deposited}}$$

Stock withdrawals. If the customer wants to withdraw stock from the account and deposit money in its place, he must deposit cash equal to the retention requirement. Since the retention requirement is 50%, he will have to deposit cash equal to half the value of the securities withdrawn.

Instead of depositing cash, a customer can withdraw stock and meet the retention requirement with fully-paid stock held elsewhere. To meet the 50% retention requirement, he will have to deposit new stock with a loan value equal to 50% of the value of the stock he withdraws. In effect, with Reg T at 50%, this is a dollar-for-dollar substitution (e.g., X dollars worth of one stock for X dollars worth of another).

Same-day substitution of stock. A client with a margin account can sell one stock and buy an equivalent amount of stock without incurring a Reg T call, resulting in a **same-day substitution**. A same-day substitution works in much the same way as a stock withdrawal. Assuming that this is a restricted account or that there is no excess equity and the cost of the stock purchased exceeds the value of the stock sold, the difference between the cost of the two positions is subject to Reg T requirements. If a client sells stock for $10,000 and buys stock for $12,000, the net difference of $2,000 is subject to a call of $1,000 (50% of the excess purchase).

If the proceeds of the stock sold exceeds the cost of the stock purchased, the difference in a restricted account is still subject to the 50% retention requirement. For example, if the stock sold equaled $12,000 and the stock purchased was $10,000, the amount of cash the client could withdraw would be 50% or $1,000 (50% retention requirement times the net proceeds of $2,000).

Special Memorandum Account (SMA)

In the beginning of this chapter, you learned that clients sometimes have excess equity in their accounts, often due to increases in the market value of their stock. When excess equity does exist in a margin account, it can be credited to a separate account called a special memorandum account, or SMA. No real funds, cash or securities are actually transferred to an SMA account. It is simply a line of credit, a limit on the amount of money a customer can borrow now or in the future (similar to the credit limit placed on a credit card)

Customers of brokerage firms may withdraw funds from SMAs just as they might withdraw funds from a credit line at a bank, or take out a cash advance on a credit card. The firm doesn't charge interest on SMA (the term SMA applies to both the special account itself and to the value of the line of credit it represents), because it isn't considered money until a client uses it. When a customer withdraws or uses SMA, he or she is actually borrowing more money from the broker-dealer, thereby increasing the debit balance in his or her account. When this happens, the client will then owe interest on any amount withdrawn or borrowed.

Clients may always use the balance in their SMA unless the use (either withdrawing cash or securities, or purchasing securities) will cause the account equity to drop below the minimum maintenance (or the $2,000 minimum) requirement.

Generating SMA

An SMA balance can be generated when excess equity is credited to an SMA, or by any of the following means:

- **Nonrequired cash deposits**. If a customer's cash deposit is not required to meet a margin call, 100% of it reduces the debit and is also credited to the SMA.
- **Dividends and interest earned**. Dividends and interest received on securities in the margin account are added to the SMA. The customer can always withdraw that entire amount, even if the account is restricted.
- **Loan value**. If your client makes a nonrequired deposit of marginable stocks into an account, the loan value of that stock is credited to the SMA.

Excess equity

Suppose your client buys 200 shares of stock at $100 and deposits cash to meet the 50% Reg T requirements. Her margin account will look like this:

CMV (200x$100)	$20,000	
DR	-$10,000	
Equity	$10,000	
Reg T (50%)	$10,000	½ CMV
Excess Equity	0	
SMA	0	

If the stock increases in market value to $110 per share, this creates excess equity in her account. Excess equity can be borrowed, used to purchase additional securities, or left in the account to be credited to SMA.

CMV (200x$110)	$22,000	
DR	-$10,000	
Equity	$12,000	
Reg T	$11,000	½ CMV
EE	$1,000	
SMA	$1,000	

If the stock subsequently dropped to $95, the CMV would decline, the debit would remain unchanged, equity would decrease, excess equity would decrease, *but* SMA would remain the same. Once SMA is credited to an investor's account, only the investor's use of it can deplete it. Market or broker actions can not take away the SMA line of credit.

Stock is at $110 per share:

CMV	$22,000
DR	$10,000
Equity	$12,000
Reg T	$11,000
EE	$1,000
SMA	$1,000

Stock drops to $95 per share:

CMV	$19,000	
DR	$10,000	
Equity	$9,000	restricted
Reg T	$9,500	—50% of CMV
EE	$0	
SMA	$1,000	

Selling securities. You learned earlier that the Reg T retention requirement allows an investor to withdraw or use for additional purchases 50% of the proceeds of any sale in a margin account. If the amount is not used immediately, this amount is credited to SMA. When stock is sold in a margin account, you can calculate the new SMA balance by adding 50% of the sale proceeds to the existing amount of the SMA.

New excess equity (resulting from sale proceeds) is not added to the SMA. Excess equity and SMA are always compared and the greater of the two becomes the new SMA.

Depleting SMA

An SMA balance is depleted by all of the following:

- **Cash withdrawals** from a margin account (including the withdrawal of dividends).
- **New margin purchases**. Your customer may use the balance in an SMA to meet the Reg T requirement for purchases.
- **Withdrawing securities**. This reduces the SMA balance by 50% of the market value of the withdrawn securities. The SMA, in this case, may be used to meet a retention requirement.

In the last two cases, the SMA is used in place of a cash deposit. For a new purchase or the withdrawal of securities, the SMA is used and reduced.

Using SMA to buy stock. Previously, you saw that an investor could increase her SMA balance by selling stock from her margin account. Since SMA is a line of credit, the investor can also use it to meet the margin requirements on stock purchases. SMA gives the investor buying power. To calculate the buying power of SMA:

> SMA Balance / Reg T Requirement = Buying Power

Remember, the equation is a way of saying that for every dollar of SMA, the investor can purchase two dollars of securities when Reg T is at 50% ($1 divided by 50% = $2). If an investor uses the available SMA to buy stock, her account would change as follows:

	Before purchase:	The purchase:	After using SMA:
CMV	$10,000	$6,000	$16,000
Debit (Reg T 50%)	-$2,000	-$6,000	-$8,000
Equity	$8,000		$8,000
SMA	$3,000	$3,000	$0

The entire purchase price of the new security was borrowed from the firm, as it always is initially. The SMA is used to meet the Reg T call, but since it does not represent an actual cash deposit, it does not lower the debit when used. Since she has put no more cash in, her equity remains the same as before the purchase.

Withdrawing cash. Clients may also use SMA to withdraw (that is, borrow) money from their margin accounts. For example, if a client has a margin account with a market value of $10,000, has $2,000 in an SMA and wants to withdraw cash equal to the entire SMA balance, then the client's CMV would remain unchanged, the debit balance would increase by the amount borrowed, equity would decrease by the amount borrowed, and the SMA would be depleted.

(Reg T: 50%, NYSE: 25%, House: 30%)

	Before	After
CMV	$10,000	$10,000
DR	-$5,000	-$7,000
Equity	$5,000	$3,000
SMA	$2,000	$0

A withdrawal may not be made if it would bring the equity below $2,000 or the minimum maintenance requirement (whichever is greater). To determine how much SMA can be used without going below the 25% minimum requirement, calculate the difference between the existing and the minimum equity; that is the amount that may be withdrawn. The client cannot withdraw the full SMA balance if this action would reduce the equity in the account to an amount less than the required maintenance level. Because the SMA is not cash and using SMA for cash withdrawals increases the debit balance and reduces the equity, SMA may not be used to meet a maintenance call.

Withdrawing securities. When withdrawing securities from a restricted account, a client must meet the 50% Reg T retention requirement. This can be done with SMA, unless doing so violates maintenance requirements.

CMV	$8,000
DR	-$4,200
Eq	$3,800
SMA	$900

Notice that this account is restricted by $200. This client has $3,800 in equity instead of the $4,000 required by Reg T. When withdrawing securities, the client must either deposit 50% of the market value in cash or use SMA to meet the Reg T requirement. To calculate how much market value of securities the client can withdraw, simply divide the SMA balance ($900) by the retention requirement (50%). $900 / 50\% = \$1,800$.

$$\boxed{\text{SMA / Retention Requirement} = \text{CMV of Withdrawable Securities}}$$

The account is restricted even further, but the equity is still above the minimum requirements. After the securities are withdrawn, the account looks like this.

CMV	$6,200
DR	-$4,200
Eq	$2,000
SMA	0

Purchasing securities. Investors can use SMA to meet the Reg T requirement on new purchases. With Reg T at 50%, a customer can purchase $2 worth of securities for every $1 available in SMA. As before, SMA can only be used to purchase new securities to the extent that its use does not violate the minimum equity requirements of either the NYSE or the firm.

Activity	Effect on SMA	Remarks
Rise in market value	Increase	Only if the new excess equity is higher than the old SMA balance.
Decline in market value	No effect	After the SMA balance is established, it is not affected by a decline in market value.
Sale of securities in a margin account	Increase	The client is entitled to excess equity resulting from the sale, or 50% of the sale proceeds.
Purchase of securities in a margin account	Decrease	The margin requirement on new purchases is deducted from the SMA balance. If the SMA balance is insufficient to meet the charge, a cash deposit is required.
Deposit of cash in a margin account	Increase	The full amount of the deposit is credited to the SMA balance unless a margin call has been issued.
Withdrawal of cash from a margin account	Decrease	The full amount of the cash withdrawal is deducted from the SMA balance. Equity must remain higher than the NYSE/NASD or house equity requirement.
Deposit of marginable securities	Increase	Increased by the loan value of the security deposited as prescribed by Reg T at the time of the deposit.
Withdrawal of marginable securities	Decrease	Decreased by the retention requirement of the withdrawn stock.
Dividends or interest	Increase	100% of a cash dividend or interest (a nonrequired deposit) is credited to SMA.
Interest charges	No effect	SMA balance remains the same.
Stock dividend	Increase	SMA increases in the amount of the loan value of the securities as prescribed by current Reg T.

Purchasing Bonds in a Margin Account

Various types of bonds can be purchased in a margin account, but each has different Reg T and SRO initial margin requirements. Owners of these securities must meet SRO or house requirements for minimum equity.

Nonconvertible bonds are subject to the NYSE $2,000 initial margin requirement, although the FRB allows these securities to be treated as exempt when purchased in a margin account. Convertible corporate bonds are subject to the same Reg T requirements as marginable stocks (50%).

Type of Security	NASD, NYSE and AMEX Maintenance Requirements
Corporate bonds	Long positions: 25% of market value Short positions: 5% of principal amount or 30% of market value, whichever is greater
U.S. government debt	5% 1-6% of principal amount
Municipal debt	7% of principal amount or 15% of market value, whichever is greater

Special Arbitrage Account

This is a specialized margin account for arbitrage transactions. Three types of arbitrage situations are permitted:

- **Market arbitrage:** the simultaneous buying and selling of the same security in different markets to take advantage of a price disparity between the two markets.
- **Security arbitrage:** the simultaneous buying and selling of interchangeable or convertible securities to take advantage of a market price disparity between the two securities.
- **Risk arbitrage:** the buying and selling of securities in companies that are discussing a merger.

Margin required. Market and security arbitrage transactions never actually establish a position; buying and selling occur simultaneously. Therefore, the client is never actually long or short the security. The sale transaction is short, but it is exempt from the uptick rule and therefore called **short exempt**. In other words, the client does not have to make the sale on a plus tick or zero-plus tick, but can sell when the price is declining.

Short Sales and Margin Requirements

Regulation T initial margin requirement. A client who sells stock <u>short</u> must deposit cash in a margin account as assurance that he or she will be able to purchase the stock needed to cover the short position in the event of a price increase. The Regulation T requirement is the same for short sales as it is for long purchases. For example, if a client sells short 100 shares of stock with a market value of $48, that person would have to deposit $2,400 if Reg T were 50% (or $3,120 if Reg T were 65%). The deposit is expected promptly, but is required within seven business days.

NYSE $2,000 minimum. When opening a long margin position, a client must deposit a minimum of $2,000, but not more than 100% of the purchase price of the security. When establishing a short margin position, on the other hand, a client must always deposit a minimum of $2,000. Even if a customer sells short only $100 worth of stock, that individual must still deposit at least $2,000.

Maintenance requirement. A short sale of a low-priced stock may require a deposit greater than both the Reg T and the $2,000 minimum equity requirements. For an initial sale, the minimum requirement is effective if it is greater than the Reg T requirement.

For example, a client who sells short 1,000 shares of ABC at 2 in a new margin account must deposit $2,500 ($2.50 per share maintenance requirement). This amount is greater than the Reg T $1,000 and the $2,000 initial requirement.

Current Market Value of Stock Sold Short	Maintenance Requirement
Less than $5 per share	100% of market value or $2.50 per share, whichever is gretaer
$5 or more per share	$5 per share or 30% of market value, whichever is greater

Short Against the Box

Selling short against the box is the same as a regular short sale except that the client already owns securities identical to the securities that she borrows to sell short. A client who owns 100 shares of XYZ sells short against the box by borrowing 100 more shares of XYZ and selling them. The client still owns the first 100 shares and may or may not use them to replace the borrowed securities.

Investors borrow a stock they already own to sell short against the box primarily for tax deferral. Let's say, for example, that it's December and XYZ is trading at $50. You have a client who bought the stock in October at $40. She would like to take her profit, but doesn't want to increase her tax liability for the year. She can wait until January to sell the stock, risking a fall in price or she can borrow the stock and sell short right away. In January, she can replace the borrowed stock with the shares she has in her account. She won't be taxed on the short sale (because selling something you don't own is not a taxable event) until she replaces the borrowed stock in January.

Margin requirement. For margin purposes, the short-against-the-box position is treated as a net-zero position. That is, the investor's long position is worth exactly the same amount as the short position (same stock, same market value), so the net value of the two positions is zero. Because of this fact, there is no Reg T initial requirement when an investor establishes the short-against-the-box position. In effect, the investor deposits the certificate for the long stock instead of depositing Reg T.

Maintenance requirement. There is, however, a special maintenance requirement. The investor must deposit 5% of the market value of the long side ($250 if the market value of XYZ shares is at $50). The fact that being short against the box is treated as a net-zero position affects the long side in two more ways, (1) if the investors sells the long stock before replacing the borrowed stock, that sale is considered a short sale (the ticket is market short and the sale is not exempt from the plus-tick rule), (2) the investor may not deliver the long stock if there is a tender offer for it.

An investor can close a short-against-the-box position in either of two ways. By delivering the long position to the lender, or by buying stock to deliver to the lender.

Short Accounts

Credit balance. Clients don't borrow money for short positions. They sell securities and they make margin deposits to cover their risk, actions that put money in the account. The resulting credit balance represents actual cash (the sale proceeds plus the margin requirement), which is available when the client wants to purchase the securities to close the short position.

Equity. In a short account, equity equals the amount by which the credit balance exceeds the current market value of the securities short in the account. In a short account, the client owes the securities. Therefore, the market value is "what is owed," which is why it takes away from (subtracts from) the credit balance.

Buying power. A decline in the market value of a security below the original short-sale price may produce excess equity in a client's margin account. As with long accounts, this buying power can be preserved as SMA if not used.

Restricted accounts. Like long positions, short positions can also become restricted. In a long account, restriction can take place when the market value of a security declines below the original purchase cost. In a short account, the opposite is true: restriction can take place when a stock appreciates above the selling price.

As with a long transaction, on a short sale the brokerage firm does not have to take action unless the equity in the account is less than either the NYSE, NASD or the firm's own maintenance requirement. The account must always have equity of at least 30% of the current market value. To determine the market price at which equity equals 30% of CMV, use the following formula:

Credit Balance / 130% = Maximum Short Market Value

Effect on SMA. You will recall that in long accounts that are restricted, 50% of the proceeds of a sale can be released to SMA. This release privilege applies only to sales. When a short position is closed by purchasing securities to cover the short, however, there is no sale and no automatic 50% release. The SMA will change only if any excess equity generated by covering the short position exceeds the existing SMA balance.

Short Sale Regulations

No shorting by insiders. The Securities and Exchange Act of 1934 prohibits directors, officers and principal stockholders (insiders) from selling short or selling short against the box stock in their own companies.

Sell orders must be identified. The SEC requires that all sell orders be identified as either long or short. No sale can be marked long unless the security to be delivered is in the account of the customer or is owned by the customer and will be delivered to the broker by the settlement date. If securities owned by the client are not to be delivered to complete the sale, the client is short-against-the-box. In this case, the order must be marked short. Orders for short sales that are exempt from the plus-tick rule must be marked short exempt.

Combined Accounts

A client who has a margin account with both long and short positions in different securities is said to have a combined (or mixed) account. In combined accounts, long and short positions are netted out and viewed as a single number to determine initial margin requirements and SMA balances. You may do the calculations either by netting the accounts against each other or by calculating the long and short accounts separately and then combining the resulting figures to get the final answer.

Computing equity. Earlier in this chapter, you learned to calculate the equity for a long position by subtracting the debit balance from the market value. You have also learned to calculate the equity for a short position by subtracting the market value from the credit balance. To compute the equity in a combined account, you will use both the long and short formulas.

Reg T margin requirement. To calculate the Reg T requirement for a combined account, simply calculate the Reg T requirement for the long and short accounts separately and then combine them.

Maintenance. To calculate the SRO maintenance requirement for combined accounts, calculate the long and short positions separately, because each has a different requirement. For a long position, the NYSE requirement is 25% of the CMV. For a short position, the NYSE requirement is 30% of the CMV. (Very low-priced stock has a higher maintenance requirement.)

Buying power. The formula for calculating buying power in a combined account is the same as the formula for calculating it in a margin account CMV. When Reg T is 50%, the SMA will have a purchasing power of 2 to 1. For nonmarginable securities and options the buying power is only 1 to 1. This is just another way of saying that clients can't borrow money to buy nonmarginable securities and cannot borrow money using nonmarginable securities as collateral.

Withdrawing cash. Clients may withdraw cash from combined accounts as well as ordinary margin accounts. Remember that excess equity may be withdrawn from an account. To calculate the amount available to the client, find the excess equity in the account.

Securities	Reg T Initial Requirement	Loan Value	NYSE Maintenace Requirements
Listed equity securities, OTC margin securities, listed warrants	50% of the purchase cost or 50% of the proceeds of the short sale.	100% less the current Reg T percent (50% if Reg T is 50%, 30% if Reg T is 70%, etc.)	25% of the long market value, 30% of the short market value (for everything except low-value securities)
U.S. government obligations	Exempt: no Reg T requirement	Set by brokerage firm	5 ~~15~~% of principal amount
Municipal bonds	Exempt: no Reg T requirement	Set by brokerage firm	15% of principal amount or 7% of CMV, whichever is greater
Nonconvertible bonds	Treated as exempt from Reg T requirement	Set by brokerage firm	25% of long market value, 30% of short market value
Listed convertible bonds with and without warrants	50% of purchase cost	50%	25% of long market value, 30% of short market value

Chapter Review

Questions

1. A customer's margin account contains the following registered nonexempt securities:

   100 shares of LMN, CMV $40 per share
   100 shares of XYZ, CMV $50 per share
   100 shares of ABC, CMV $80 per share

   The account has a debit balance of $10,800 and the initial margin requirement is 50%. How much equity is in the account?

   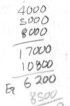

   ____(A) $4,030
   ____(B) $6,200
   ____(C) $11,050
   ____(D) $17,000

2. A customer's margin account contains the following registered nonexempt securities:

   100 shares of LMN, CMV $40 per share
   100 shares of XYZ, CMV $50 per share
   100 shares of ABC, CMV $80 per share

   The excess equity is

   ____(A) $0.
   ____(B) $2,300.
   ____(C) $6,200.
   ____(D) $8,500

3. When stock held in a margin account appreciates, which of the following increase(s)?

   I.   current market value
   II.   debit balance
   III. equity

   ____(A) I
   ____(B) II
   ____(C) I and III
   ____(D) I, II and III

4. A client chooses to leave a dividend payment in a margin account; as a result

   I. equity increases;
   II. equity decreases;
   III. debit balance increases.
   IV. debit balance decreases.

   ____(A) I and III
   ____(B) I and IV
   ____(C) II and III
   ____(D) II and IV

5. Selling a security held long in a margin account

   I. decreases the debit balance;
   II. decreases the current market value;
   III. decreases the equity;
   IV. increases the equity.

   ____(A) I and II, III
   ____(B) I and III
   ____(C) II and III
   ____(D) I, II and IV

6. A customer has opened a margin account and has signed a loan consent, hypothecation and credit agreement. Which of the following statements are true?

   I. The customer's stock will be kept in street name.
   II. A portion of the stock may be pledged for a loan.
   III. The customer will be required to pay interest on the money loaned (debit balance).

   ____(A) I and II
   ____(B) I and III
   ____(C) II and III
   ____(D) I, II and III

7. A customer purchases stock in a cash account and requests that the stock be held in "street name." The RR should inform the customer that

   ____(A) the firm can use the stock as collateral for a loan.
   ____(B) the firm may hypothecate the securities.
   ____(C) at any time, the customer can have the stock registered in his or her name.
   ____(D) the firm can loan the stock to another customer for a short sale transaction.

8. A client has a margin account with $23,000 in securities and a debit of $12,000. Which of the following are true?

    I.   The account is restricted.
    II.   The client will receive a margin call for $500.
    III. The client may withdraw securities if he deposits 50% of the securities' value.
    IV. the account has excess equity of $5,250.

    ____(A)   I and II
    ____(B)   I and III
    ____(C)   I, III and IV
    ____(D)   I, II, III and IV

Handwritten notes: CMV 23,000 / DR 12,000 / EQ 11,000 / RT 11,500 (restr) / EE 0 / maint 5750 OK

9. Your client has a margin account with market value of $3,000 and equity of $1,000. The stock drops $200 in value. The client will receive a maintenance call for

    ____(A) $0.
    ____(B) $200.
    ____(C) $750.
    ____(D) $1,000.

Handwritten notes: CMV 3000 → 2800 / DB 2000 → 2000 / E 1000 → 800 Restricted (< 2000) / RgT 1500 50% of 1400 / m call if CMV x 25% > RgT / 700 is 25% OK of 2800

10. Your client has a margin account with market value of $3,000 and equity of $1,000. The market value drops $350 in value. The client will receive a maintenance call for

    ____(A) $0.
    ____(B) $12.50.
    ____(C) $16.
    ____(D) $350.

Handwritten notes: 3000 / 2000 / 1000 / 1500 → 2650 x 25% = 662.50 / 2000 / 650 / 1325 Restricted (< 2000) / $12.50 m call

K111

Chapter Review

Answer Key

1. B.

2. A.

3. C.

4. B.

5. A.

6. D.

7. C.

8. B.

9. A.

10. B.

Chapter Twelve

Economics and Analysis

Key Terms

Economics and Analysis

Economic analysis is used to determine the overall health and vitality of our country's economy, and in particular, how the economy's ups and downs will affect investments and corporations in specific industries.

Technical analysis tends to be short-term and focuses on the technical aspects of the market, not on the fundamental soundness of particular corporations. Technicians do not select securities because of the fundamental soundness of the issuing corporation. Instead, technical analysts look at trends in the stock market, trading volumes and closing averages as if the market was independent of the larger world of the economy and the smaller world of particular corporations.

Fundamental analysis concentrates on selecting healthy companies in which to invest. To determine the economic soundness of a corporation, fundamental analysts focus on such factors as the economic and political climate, the outlook for particular industries, and the competitive position of individual companies. The fundamental analyst tends to be a long-term investor interested in appreciation potential as well as income.

Economics

Economic climate. Perhaps no single factor influences the securities market more than the economy. Business cycles, changes in the money supply, actions taken by the Federal Reserve Board to control the money supply, and a host of complex international monetary factors affect securities prices and trading.

Business cycles. Throughout our history, periods of rapid economic expansion have often followed recessions in a predictable long-term pattern called the business cycle. Long- term business cycles tend to go through four phases:

- Expansion (sometimes called recovery)
- Peak
- Contraction (also known as recession or, in the worst of times, a depression)
- Trough

It may seem like common sense to say that periods of prosperity follow hard times and hard times again yield to prosperity. But knowing when the economy is on the upward or downward slope is not always a simple matter. In the normal course of events, some industries or corporations will prosper as others fail. A long-term downward slope will be interrupted by temporary upturns that do not signal a return

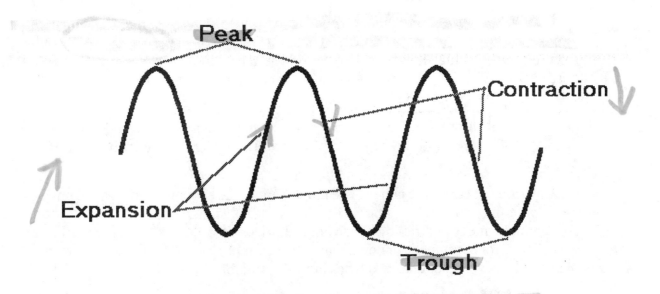

Fig. 12.1 The four stages of the business cycle.

to prosperity, and vice versa. Economists consider the following conditions when determining where we are in the business cycle. Signs of expansion include:

- increases in industrial production;
- bull stock markets;
- rising property values;
- increased consumer demand for goods and services; and
- increasing gross national product (all goods and services).

Downturns in the business cycle tend to be associated with:

- rising numbers of bankruptcies and bond defaults;
- higher consumer debt;
- bear stock markets;
- rising inventories (a sign of slackening consumer demand in hard times); and
- decreasing gross national product.

Gross National Product (GNP). The annual economic output of a nation (all goods and services) is known as its GNP (gross national product). GNP includes personal consumption, government purchases (including federal payrolls, defense spending and office supplies) and gross private investment (including new buildings, machinery and inventories). In periods of recession, the GNP declines. During expansions, GNP increases.

$$\textbf{C} \text{ (consumption)} + \textbf{G} \text{ (government spending)} + \textbf{I} \text{ (gross investment)} = \textbf{GNP}$$

When comparing the GNP of one period with the GNP of another, you must take into account price changes. Economists adjust the figures to constant dollars, rather than comparing actual dollars. Otherwise, it would be impossible to compare the GNP of recessionary periods (like the 1930s) with that of inflationary periods (like the 1970s).

According to the U.S. Commerce Department, the economy is in recession when a decline in real output of goods and services (gross national product) lasts for six months or more. A depression is a very severe downturn lasting for several years with unemployment rates greater than 15%.

Government economic policy. The movement of the economy through the business cycle sometimes creates hardships for business and consumers. Among these hardships are unemployment and rapid changes in the prices of goods and services; either up, which is bad for consumers, or down, which is bad for business. To counteract the effects of each, the government has two types of tools available:

- **Monetary policy.** The Federal Reserve Board can take action to increase or decrease the money supply.
- **Fiscal policy.** Presidential and congressional actions can affect the amount of money the government takes in and spends.

Inflation. Inflation is a persistent and measurable rise in the general level of prices. Inflation is generally associated with periods of expansion and high employment. Mild inflation is not bad. Gradually increasing prices tend to stimulate business investments and help maintain full employment and a growing GNP. But galloping inflation results in hardships for many, particularly those on fixed incomes.

Deflation. Deflation is a persistent and measurable fall in the general level of prices. During periods of deflation, production exceeds demand. Deflation usually occurs during recessions when unemployment is growing. Prices do not change at the same rate. Some rise more rapidly than others. The most prominent measure of price changes in general is the Consumer Price Index (CPI). It measures the rate of increase or decrease in consumer prices for such things as food, housing, transportation, medical care, clothing, entertainment and services. The CPI is a composite of selected consumer items in selected cities for a one-month period.

Economic Indicators

According to analysts, the economy rides a roller coaster called the **business cycle**, periods of expansion and increasing affluence alternating with hard times, during which business contracts and unemployment increase. In an attempt to improve our understanding of where we are and where we are going in the business cycle, analysts have identified certain areas of the economy called indicators. They believe that measurable movement in these indicators tends to confirm the economy's present status and predict its future direction.

Leading indicators. Leading indicators predict trends in the economy. Positive changes in these indicators (such as a bull market, expansion of the money supply, issuance of more building permits and increases in orders for durable goods or plant and equipment) indicate that the economy will improve. These are all signs that there will be more spending, production and employment in days to come. Leading indicators that economists use most often include:

- the average workweek in manufacturing;
- average weekly initial claims for state unemployment insurance compensation;
- new orders for durable goods;
- slowdowns in deliveries by vendors;
- contracts and orders for plant and equipment;
- building permits;
- changes in inventories;
- change in sensitive materials prices;
- stock prices;
- money supply (M2, which includes M1); and
- changes in business and consumer borrowing.

Coincident indicators. Coincident indicators vary directly and simultaneously with the business cycle. Leading indicators tell us where we are headed in the business cycle; coincident indicators tell us where we are. If employment, income, production and sales are down, the economy is in a slump. If they are up, the economy is, by definition, expanding. Coincident indicators include:

- nonagricultural employment;
- personal income;
- industrial production; and
- manufacturing and trade sales.

Lagging indicators. Lagging indicators, which change after the economy has altered, include:

- average duration of employment;
- ratio of deflated inventories to sales, manufacturing and trade;
- labor cost per unit of output (manufacturing);
- commercial and industrial loans outstanding; and
- ratio of consumer installment credit to personal income.

Money and Banking

A significant factor in the economy is the **money supply** (e.g., the amount of money available for consumers and business to spend). Commercial banks (as opposed to savings and loans) deal in demand deposits. A demand deposit can be either money left with the bank or borrowed from the bank. In either case the customer has the right to withdraw that sum on demand. A time deposit, by contrast, cannot be withdrawn without a delay.

By granting loans to establish demand deposits, banks create money. Assume, for example, that a commercial bank gives you a $7,000 home improvement loan. The bank

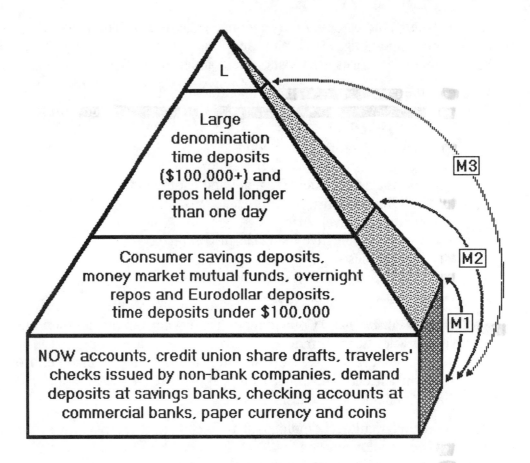

Fig. 12.2 L, M1, M2 and M3: Parts of the money supply.

will credit your checking account with $7,000, instantly creating money that you can spend.

The money you spend is deposited in other banks by the recipients. Then those banks make loans based on the deposits, which are deposited in more banks, and so on in a chain broken only when someone withdraws cash from an account. The only limit on this process is Federal Reserve Board restrictions on how much of the $7,000 (and each succeeding deposit in the cycle) the receiving bank can convert into loans.

The definition of money. "Money" means more than the cash we carry in our pockets. It also includes loans, credit and certain kinds of liquid investments. Economists divide money into four categories, depending upon the type of account in which it is kept.

- **M1.** The most readily available type of money, M1 consists of currency and demand deposits that can be converted to currency immediately. This is the money consumers use for ordinary purchases of goods and services.
- **M2.** In addition to M1, M2 includes some time deposits that are fairly easy to convert into demand deposits. These time deposits

include savings accounts, money-market funds and overnight repurchase agreements.

- **M3.** In addition to M1 and M2, M3 includes time deposits of more *Jumbo CDs* than $100,000 and repurchase agreements with terms longer than one day.
- **L.** L does not include M1, M2 or M3, but is a separate category consisting of long-term liquid assets, including T bills, savings bonds, commercial paper, bankers' acceptances and Eurodollar holdings of U.S. residents.

Most money is in demand deposits; it is checkbook money. M1, therefore, is the largest component of the money supply. M2, however, is also significant to economists and securities analysts with their eyes on credit markets.

Monetary Policies of the Federal Reserve Board

The Federal Reserve Board uses several methods of manipulating the money supply to counteract inflation and unemployment. Such actions by the Fed are based on the axioms of **monetarist theory.**

According to the monetarists, inflation can be reduced by cutting down the amount of money available for spending by businesses and consumers. The Fed has several methods of reducing the money available for banks to loan their customers at favorable rates. When individuals and businesses are unable to afford loans, they purchase fewer goods and services. And as demand for goods and services decreases, so, in theory, do the prices charged for those goods and services, thus bringing an end to inflation.

In times of unemployment brought about by a sagging economy, the Fed may expand the money supply. As businesses and consumers find more money available at reasonable loan rates, they resume borrowing and buying. In theory, this stimulates production of goods and services, resulting in the need for more laborers and thus an end to high unemployment. Unemployment is assumed to have the same cause as deflation, but may or may not be accompanied by falling prices.

The Federal Reserve System (the Fed). Monetary policy determines how the Federal Reserve Board acts to influence the money supply and, consequently, the economy. In 1913, Congress established the Federal Reserve System to regulate the U.S. banking system and the money supply. The Fed consists of 12 regional Federal Reserve Banks, with 24 branch banks and all the national and state banks that belong to the system.

The Federal Reserve Board (FRB). Under the direction of the Federal Reserve Board (which consists of seven members appointed by the president of the United States) the Fed performs the following functions:

- regulates the U.S. money supply;
- sets reserve requirements for members;
- supervises the printing of currency;
- clears fund transfers throughout the system; and
- examines members to ensure their compliance with federal regulations.

At least indirectly, the FRB determines how much money is available for business and consumers to spend and is, therefore, one of the most powerful factors in our economy. It affects the money supply by using three monetary tools:

- changes in reserve requirements;
- changes in the discount rate (on loans to member banks); and
- open-market operations (buying and selling bonds).

Reserve requirements. The Federal Reserve Bank requires that member banks have reserves equal to a certain percentage of their deposits, which can vary from 7% to 22%. As an example, if the Fed requires reserves of 14%, a commercial bank must have $14 on deposit with the Federal Reserve for every $100 in demand deposits. After depositing 14%, the bank may make the remaining 86% available for loans.

Changing reserve requirements is one way the Fed can head off inflation. To understand why, you need to look at the part reserve requirements play in the creation of money by banks.

When you spend your $7,000 loan (going back to our example), it winds up in other banks, giving them the power to create money by making further loans. If you pay $7,000 to a contractor supervising the remodeling of your house, the contractor deposits that $7,000 in his bank. The bank, which then has excess reserves, needs only part of that $7,000 to meet reserve requirements. It can loan out the rest.

If the reserve requirement is 14%, the bank must deposit about $1,000 with the Fed. It can loan out the remaining 86% (about $6,000). And that $6,000 will be deposited in another bank, creating excess reserves and the ability to loan out 86% of $6,000, and so on until that original loan of $7,000 produces almost $50,000 in bank deposits and $43,000 in credit. The amount of money available to business and consumers (the money supply) multiplies rapidly when a bank makes a loan because banks can loan more money than they take in. This is called the multiplier effect.

The multiplier effect means that loans can be extremely inflationary (e.g., too much money chasing too few goods). Conversely, too little money in circulation is deflationary and can lead to recession. Because of this, the reserve requirement gives the Fed some potential leverage over inflation and deflation. In an inflationary economy, the Fed can raise the reserve requirement, thereby reducing the multiplier effect of loans. The more money banks must keep in reserve, the less they have available to loan out. With a 20% reserve requirement, for example, that $7,000 loan would create only $35,000 in deposits and $28,000 in loans.

As profit-making enterprises, banks try to keep their reserves (which produce no income) close to the minimum. Deficiencies in reserve funds contract the money supply. The higher the reserve requirement, the faster the bank will have to remove money from circulation.

When banks borrow to meet reserve requirements, they may go directly to the Fed, which will loan them money at its discount rate. Or they can go to another member to borrow from its excess reserves. The interest rate member banks charge each other for such loans is called the federal funds rate. Since these are usually very short-term loans (overnight), the federal funds rate is quite volatile. The federal funds rate, in fact, is the most volatile interest rate indicator.

Changing reserve requirements is the Fed's least frequently used tool for combating inflation. A small change in the reserve requirement has a comparatively large influence on the money supply.

Changing the discount rate. The Fed's second most important tool for affecting the money supply is to raise or lower the **discount rate**, which is the interest rate the Fed charges its members for certain very short-term loans. If a member has a reserve deficiency, it can borrow funds from its Federal Reserve district bank. This process is sometimes called "going to the discount window."

Generally, the discount rate is close to the interest rate on U.S. Treasury bills. When the discount rate is only slightly below the T bill rate, banks that are short on reserves may borrow from the Federal Reserve instead of selling their own securities to meet reserve requirements. The effects of changes in the discount rate include the following:

- **Lowering the discount rate** tends to counteract a recessionary trend by making it easier for banks to increase their reserve funds.
- **Raising the discount rate** tends to counteract inflation by making it more difficult for member banks to increase their reserves.

Open-market operations. The Federal Reserve's most important and flexible tool is open-market operations. To conduct open-market operations, the Fed buys and sells government securities in the open market to expand and contract the money supply.

The **Federal Open-Market Committee (FOMC)** meets monthly to direct open market operations. The Fed trades only with primary dealers (about 40 of the largest banks and securities firms).

When the Fed buys securities, it **expands** the money supply; when the Fed sell securities, it **contracts** the money supply. When credit is tight and the Fed wants to expand or loosen the money supply, it buys securities such as government bonds, T bills and bankers' acceptances. The seller is usually a bank, which receives direct credit in its reserve account. If the seller is not a bank, the Fed writes a check, which eventually is deposited in a commercial bank. This process increases the reserve of the banking system, permitting more loans. Thus, by buying securities, the Fed has pumped money into the banking system, expanding the money supply.

In times of inflation, when the Fed wants to contract or tighten the money supply, it sells some of its securities. The buyer (usually a dealer bank) is charged against its reserve balance. This reduces the bank's ability to lend money, thereby tightening credit. The Fed has "pulled" money out of the system.

When the Fed buys, bank excess reserves go up; when the Fed sells, bank excess reserves go down. Since most of these transactions involve next-day payment, the effects on the money supply are immediate. And that's what makes open-market operations the Fed's most efficient tool.

Other methods. The Fed has two other methods of controlling the economy: changing margin requirements and moral suasion.

The Federal Reserve sets margin requirements, which are limitations on credit extended for the purchase of listed and certain OTC securities.

- Regulation T covers broker-dealer loans to customers.
- Regulation U covers bank loans to brokers, dealers or customers.
- Regulation G governs loans of other lenders.

By changing the margin requirements, the Fed can limit the extent to which brokers, dealers, banks and others can extend loans to purchase securities. The effect of changing margin requirements is more limited than changing reserve requirements because it affects a more limited segment of the economic community. Higher margin requirements tend to slow down the purchase of securities, thus helping put a brake on runaway inflation. Lower margin requirements make investing easier, thus helping to invigorate a flagging economy.

The board can use **moral suasion** by suggesting to member banks that its unofficial policies and banking directives be followed. It does this through warnings and speeches by board members. If moral suasion is not effective, the Fed may then have to make official policies it can enforce.

To Expand Credit During Deflationary Periods:	To Tighten Credit During Inflationary Periods:
Buy securities in the open market	Sell securities in the open market
Lower reserve requirements	Raise reserve requirements
Lower the discount rate	Raise the discount rate

Impact of Government Economic Policies

As the Fed manipulates the economy through monetary policy, the president and Congress attack economic problems through fiscal policy. The term "fiscal" refers to budgets (as in fiscal year), and fiscal policy refers to governmental budget decisions. These budget decisions can include:

- increases or decreases in federal spending;
- increases or decreases in money raised through taxation; and
- increases or decreases in federal budget deficits or surpluses.

Fiscal policy is governed by the assumptions that the government attacks inflation by policies that should reduce aggregate demand for goods and services (reducing government spending, increasing tax rates or both) and if low aggregate demand is causing unemployment, the government increases spending, reduces taxes or both.

Congress uses fiscal policies and the Fed uses monetary policy to control the severity of fluctuations in the economy. Fiscal policies are budgetary and involve changes in the amount of money the government spends, the amount of money it collects in taxes or both. The condition of the economy prompts government intervention, and government actions, in turn, help shape the economy.

The stock market. Monetary policies frequently have considerable influence on the stock market. By raising margin requirements, the Federal Reserve can restrain speculation in stocks. Even more significant, the Fed's ability to control the money supply can influence stock prices. If the Fed increases the money supply, credit is easier to obtain. And lower interest rates tend to appear bullish to the stock market.

Similarly, lowering tax rates (a fiscal measure) may stimulate spending by those individuals or businesses with more of their earnings to spend. Like easier credit, this also tends to be bullish. Raising taxes, of course, tends to have the opposite effect by reducing the amount of money available for business and consumer spending or for investment.

Interest rates. The cost of credit (interest rates) depends on supply and demand. In periods of easy money, when the credit supply exceeds demand, interest rates fall. Conversely, interest rates tend to rise when the Fed is tightening the money supply and demand exceeds supply. By influencing the money supply, the Federal Reserve also affects interest rates.

Disintermediation. Disintermediation is the flow of money from low-yielding accounts in traditional savings institutions (financial intermediaries) to higher-yielding investments in the marketplace. The process occurs when the Fed is tightening the money supply and interest rates are rising.

Business cycles. The power of the FRB to influence interest rates and expand credit has a direct impact on business. Monetary policy helps determine how much money is available for business investments. The Fed's power is considerable but not absolute. Not all commercial banks are members of the Federal Reserve System and the Fed exerts little influence over international banking. Nevertheless, financial analysts, investors and the general public watch the Fed closely, knowing its policies influence business cycles.

Government spending and taxation (fiscal policy) also influence the shape of the business cycle. Increases in government spending, as politicians are eager to tell us at election time, tends to be inflationary. Money that the government injects into the economy increases the demand for goods and services, thereby driving up their prices. Lessened government spending, naturally, has the opposite effect, tending to foster recession and unemployment.

International Monetary Factors

Balance of Payments

One important link between U.S. and international economies is the money that flows between our country and other countries. The accounting record that keeps track of all such currency exchanges is called our balance of payments.

The balance of payments may run a surplus (more money entering the country than leaving it) or a deficit (more money leaving the country than entering it). A deficit may occur when high interest rates in another country attract savings dollars of U.S. citizens or corporations. Because of this deficit, citizens of other countries accumulate more dollars than they need for their payments to us and there is an excess supply of U.S. dollars abroad.

The largest component of the balance of payments is the balance of trade, the export and import of merchandise (not services). On the U.S. credit side are sales of American products to foreign countries. On the debit side are American purchases of foreign goods that cause American dollars to flow out of the country. Until 1970, the U.S. annual trade balance was positive every year during this century: we made more money on exports than we spent on imports. Since then, we have consistently traded at a deficit. A favorable balance of trade leads to more exports than imports. An unfavorable balance of trade leads to more imports than exports.

Debit Items	Credit Items
Imports	Exports
U.S. spending abroad	Foreign spending in the U.S.
U.S. investments abroad	Foreign investments in the U.S.
U.S. bank loans abroad	
U.S. foreign aid	

International Currency Exchange Rates

When an international transaction takes place, currencies are exchanged. Foreign exchange rates are used to convert prices of goods in other currencies into dollar-denominated prices.

A currency is said to appreciate if it rises in value on the foreign exchange market (if it buys more units of foreign currencies). U.S. currency is appreciating, for example, if it buys more British pounds now than it did at some designated point in the past. If the exchange rate is 1.58 dollars to the pound, for example, U.S. tourists need $1.58 to purchase a British pound. If the exchange rate moves to 1.50 dollars to the pound, Americans will need only $1.50 to purchase a British pound.

If currency falls in value on the foreign exchange market (like the British pound in the preceding example) it is depreciating. In this case, it will buy fewer units of another country's currency. Depreciation of the U.S. dollar means that dollars are cheaper for citizens of other countries, and American goods and services would be less expensive abroad. Other countries might import more U.S. grain, tobacco, computers and other commodities, giving the United States a credit trade balance.

At the same time, goods produced by other countries become more expensive in the U.S. as that country's currency appreciates. This might discourage Americans from buying Japanese cars, Swiss watches or Brazilian coffee, reducing our debit items. So, depreciation of the dollar tends to lead to improved balance of payments.

Devaluation. Not to be confused with depreciation, devaluation occurs when a government lowers the value of a country's currency relative to gold. Depreciation is a change in the relationship between two currencies, not between a currency and gold and is determined by the marketplace, not by a government.

Eurodollars and the Interbank Market

Dollars sent abroad to pay for imports sometimes return to the United States when they are used to purchase U.S. goods, but sometimes these dollars never come home. U.S. money that migrates to Europe and has not returned becomes part of the fund of overseas U.S. currency known as Eurodollars.

Eurodollars are held mainly in European banks and in overseas branches or subsidiaries of American banks. These dollars trade in the **interbank** (or Eurodollar) market, where they are used to settle transactions payable in U.S. currency. In this market, the currency circulates free of the restrictions imposed by the U.S. in this country or by European countries on transactions in their own currencies. The interbank market is a decentralized unregulated market for international currencies, involving banks in many countries. Eurodollars in the system are loaned and spent overseas and don't come home, and it is affected by policies of U.S. and European governments.

Some securities, such as Eurodollar bonds, are denominated in Eurodollars. Other bond issues, called Eurobonds, may be paid in U.S. dollars or in the currency of the country in which they are issued. The Eurobond market is used by large multinational corporations and foreign governments.

Technical Analysis

Both types of analysis (technical and fundamental) start with the premise that price movements of the stock market can be predicted. Fundamental analysts are usually interested in the long-term behavior of investments (ranging from 6 to 18 months) in particular companies or industries. They concentrate on broad- based economic trends, current business conditions within an industry, and the quality of the stock of a particular corporation. The technical analyst, on the other hand, is more interested in forecasting short-term market trends and securities prices than in studying individual corporations. For the technical analyst, the decision to buy or sell depends almost entirely on market activity and overall market trends.

Many analysts use both fundamental and technical information in making trading decisions. Typically, they rely on fundamental analysis to determine which transactions to make and on technical analysis for timing entries and exits from the market.

Technical analysts attempt to evaluate the strengths and weaknesses of the market at a specific time. They try to predict bull markets (when investors are optimistic and prices are rising) and bear markets (when investors are pessimistic and prices are falling).

Market averages. Stock prices tend to move together. A particular stock will tend to go up in a bull market and down in a bear market. (Other factors, of course, can make a stock move against the market.) Important to technical analysts are the averages and indexes that show price changes in the securities markets. Moving averages are computed over time. One of the most frequently used averages is the 200-day moving average, which tracks the daily price of a stock for 200 days.

Trading volume. In addition to price movement, technical analysts are interested in the volume of trading. Since 1945, the annual trading volume on the NYSE has averaged between 11% and 15% of the outstanding shares of listed common stock. If volume is significantly higher or lower than average, technicians consider the market strong or weak. In general, bull markets are accompanied by a high trading volume and bear markets by low trading volume. A very low volume usually means an absence of buyers, since sellers are generally present. Therefore, volume is almost always higher when prices are going up than when prices are going down.

Advances/Declines. Analysts are also concerned with the **breadth of the market** (meaning the number of issues being traded up or down during a specific day). According to some theorists, the number of advances and declines is a significant indication of the relative strength of the market. When declines exceed advances, the market is bearish. In bull markets, advances exceed declines.

Averages and Indexes

Technical analysts use a variety of published averages and indexes to gather data on price movements and trading volumes. An average represents a price at a midpoint among a number of prices. An index compares current prices to some baseline, such as prices on a particular date.

Dow Jones averages. The most widely quoted and oldest measures of change in stock prices are the Dow Jones averages, each based on the prices of a limited number of stocks from four categories:

- industrial average (30 stocks);
- transportation average (20 stocks)
- utilities average (15 stocks); and
- composite average (the 65 stocks from the three other averages).

By far the most widely used of the various market indicators is the Dow Jones Industrial Average (DJIA). When analysts and investors speak in general about movements of the market, they are usually referring to the DJIA. The Dow Jones averages are not weighted by the relative size of an issue or corporation.

(only one)

Standard & Poor's 500. Standard & Poor's 500 stock index (S&P 500) is based on the prices of 400 industrials, 20 transportation stocks, 40 financial stocks and 40 public utility stocks. Each of these four categories is also reported separately. Standard & Poor's indexes are statistically more refined than the Dow Jones averages. The Standard and Poor's indexes offer two advantages over the Dow Jones averages: explicit weighting system and broad coverage.

Each stock is weighted according to the aggregate value of shares outstanding. The coverage is also broad: the 500 stocks represent about 75% to 80% of the aggregate value of all NYSE listed issues. The S&P 100 index is a value-weighted index of 100 blue chip stocks, such as IBM, General Motors and Xerox.

NYSE indexes. The New York Stock Exchange composite index is based on the prices of all common stocks listed on the exchange. Like the Standard & Poor's 500, it is weighted by the total value of shares outstanding for each stock. As with the Dow Jones composite and the S&P 500, industrial issues are the largest component of the NYSE Index. The index is computed and reported throughout the trading day.

NASDAQ-OTC price indexes. The NASD, through its computerized automated quotations system (NASDAQ), publishes several indexes of stocks traded over-the-counter. In addition to the NASDAQ composite index, the NASD provides group indexes for industrials, banks, insurance stock, other finance stocks, transportation issues and utilities. It is updated every five minutes.

Value Line. The Value Line composite index consists of 1,700 NYSE, AMEX and OTC stocks. In addition, Value Line offers an investment advisory service that ranks hundreds of stocks for timeliness and safety. It projects which stock will have the best or worst relative price performance over the next 12 months.

A century ago, Charles Dow and others believed that technical analysis could be applied only to the market as a whole. Analysts no longer accept this idea. Faced with the need to recommend specific issues, today's technicians attempt to analyze price movements in individual stocks.

Trendlines. While there may be daily price fluctuations, stock prices tend to move in a particular direction: upward (bull market) or downward (bear market).

Technical analysts pour over various charts and graphs, trying to find patterns that enable them to identify these primary trendlines and thus make buy or sell recommendations. They chart bull or bear trends of individual stocks by plotting the stock's trendline.

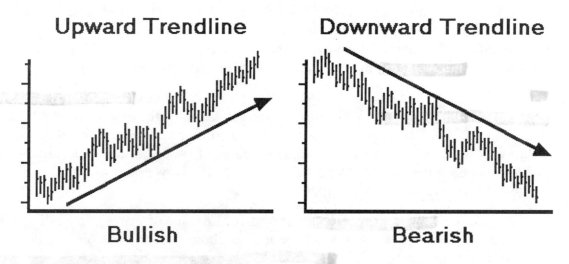

Upward Trendline   Downward Trendline
Bullish   Bearish

Fig. 12.3 Trendlines can be either bullish or bearish.

A trendline (see Fig. 12.3) connects the reaction lows in an up trend and the rally highs in a down trend. Once established, trendlines are not easily halted or reversed. Three common patterns in stock price trendlines are consolidation, reversals (head and shoulders patterns), and support and resistance levels.

If a market is staying within a narrow price range, it is said to be "consolidating." When viewed on a graph, the trendline is horizontal and is said to be moving "sideways," neither up nor down.

Reversals. A reversal indicates that an upward or downward trendline has halted and the stock's price is moving the other way. In between the two trendlines there is usually a period of consolidation, a leveling off.

One of the most difficult tasks of a technician is to recognize genuine reversal patterns. The difficulty arises because the trends, as you can see in Fig. 12.3, are actually composed of many rises and declines; further, those ups and downs may occur at

Head and Shoulders Top

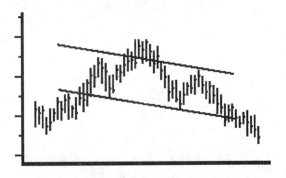

An indication of a bearish reversal of an uptrend.

Fig. 12.4 A bearish head and shoulders pattern.

different rates and for different lengths of time. Graphs of actual stock price movements, therefore, are much more complicated than the relatively straightforward charts shown here.

Because of its gently curving shape, one of the simpler reversal patterns is called a saucer (reversal of a downtrend) or an inverted saucer (reversal of an uptrend).

Another well-known, but less straightforward, reversal pattern is the head-and-shoulders pattern, named for its resemblance to the human body. Figures 12.4 and 12.5 illustrate head-and-shoulders top and head-and-shoulders bottom patterns.

Figure 12.4 is a classic head-and-shoulders top pattern, indicating a bearish trend. First, the price of the stock rises and then reaches a plateau at the neckline (left shoulder). A second advance pushes the price even higher, but then the price falls back to the neckline (head). Finally, the price of the stock rises again, but falls back to the neckline (right shoulder) and continues its down trend. This indicates that the upward trend of the stock has been reversed.

When reversed (as seen by the trendline on the right), this pattern is called a head-and-shoulders bottom and is an indication of a bullish reversal.

Support and resistance levels. Stock prices are not always in an uptrend or downtrend. Often prices hover in a narrow range for an extended period. The bottom of this trading range is known as the support level; the top of the trading range is called the resistance level.

When stocks decline to their support levels, buyers attracted by the low prices come into the market, and their buying support may tend to keep prices from declining further. When stock prices advance to resistance levels, the rise attracts sellers skeptical of continued advances. Stocks may

Head and Shoulders Bottom

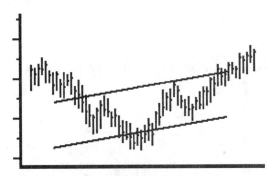

An indication of a bullish reversal of a downtrend.

Fig. 12.5 A bullish head and shoulders pattern.

K112

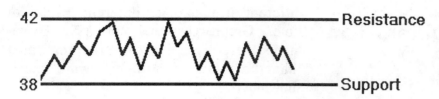

Fig. 12.6 Support and resistance levels.

continue to fluctuate for many months, testing their support and resistance levels. If the price on a particular stock penetrates either the support or resistance level, the change is considered significant.

Technically, such penetration is known as a breakout: a decline through the support level or a rise through the resistance level. Breakouts usually signal the beginning of a new upward or downward trend. Although these patterns are widely accepted, there are no hard and fast rules for chart reading. A single chart can be interpreted in different ways by different analysts.

Technical Market Theories

Technical analysts follow certain theories regarding trends in the marketplace. Two of the theories already discussed are the breadth-of-market theory (advance/decline lines) and the volume-of-trading theory. Not all technical analysts subscribe to all the theories outlined in the following discussion.

The Dow Theory. The Dow theory is used to confirm the end of a major market trend. According to the theory, there are three types of changes in stock prices: primary trends (one year or more), secondary trends (three to 12 weeks), and short-term fluctuations (hours or days).

In a bull market, the primary trend, obviously, is upward. But the stock price may still drop during the general upward trend, even for as long as twelve weeks. But the trough of that downward secondary trend should be higher than the trough of the previous downward trend. In a bear market, there may be secondary upward trends, but the highs reached during those secondary upward movements are successively lower.

According to the Dow theory, then, the primary trend in a bull

Dow Theory of Market Trends

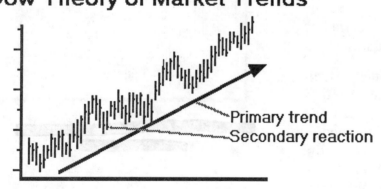

Primary trend
Secondary reaction

Fig. 12.7 Trends often go in opposite directions.

Copyright 1989. All rights reserved.

market is a series of higher highs and higher lows. In a bear market, the primary trend is a series of lower highs and lower lows. Daily fluctuations are considered irrelevant.

Figure 12.7 shows a primary upward trend interrupted by secondary downward movements. Note that the chart shows a series of successively higher highs and lows, conforming to the definition of a primary upward trend.

Any change in direction is considered deceptive unless it is mirrored by the Dow Jones industrial and transportation averages. This method lacks precision and is sometimes slow in confirming changes in market trends.

Odd-lot theory. Odd-lot trading typically is done by small investors. Followers of the odd-lot theory act on the belief that small investors invariably buy and sell at the wrong times. The prudent course of action, they believe, is opposite the trend of odd-lot trading. When odd-lot traders are buying, the odd-lot theorist is bearish. When odd-lot traders are selling, odd-lot theorists are bullish.

Short interest theory. Short interest refers to the number of shares that have been sold short and not yet repurchased. Since those short positions must be closed out with purchases, some analysts believe that short interest creates a support level for stock prices. High short interest is a bullish indicator, and low short interest is a bearish indicator. The fact that short-sale volume is usually relatively low tends to undermine the reliability of predictions based on this theory.

Confidence theory. Barron's Confidence Index is based on comparisons of yields of a group of high-grade bonds with yields of lower-ranked bonds. If the confidence index rises, investors are willing to take risks and invest in lower-rated bonds, which have higher yields. The price of lower-grade bonds increases as more investors purchase them. As a result, the yields decrease. This narrows the spread between yields on high grade and low grade bonds.

efficient market theory

Modern portfolio theory (MPT). Instead of concentrating on the evaluation of particular investments, investment managers who subscribe to MPT focus on the relationships among all the investments in a portfolio. The theory, which is supported by highly sophisticated statistical analyses, casts doubt on the ability of analysts (either fundamental or technical) to predict price movements. Adherents to MPT say that securities markets are efficient markets, meaning that securities prices react so quickly to most investment information that no analyst is likely to outsmart the market as a whole. A major emphasis of portfolio managers is selecting a mix of investments that gives the investor the highest potential return for a given amount and type of risk.

Fundamental Analysis

Industry Analysis

Once they have assessed the state of the economy, fundamental analysts look at particular industries to see which are likely to fare best as the economy proceeds along its upward or downward course. They look for industries that offer better-than-average long-term investment opportunities. Some industries are more affected by business cycles than others. Investors find it useful to distinguish between the three primary types of industries: defensive, cyclical and growth.

Defensive industries. In general, defensive industries are those least affected by business cycles. (They offer investors a defense against the inevitable downturns in the economy.) Most defensive industries involve the production of nondurable consumer goods, for example food, tobacco or utilities. Public consumption of such goods remains fairly steady, regardless of inflation or deflation. Investment in defensive industries tends to involve less risk and, consequently, less opportunity for a high return on investment.

Cyclical industries. Cyclical industries are the opposite of defensive industries: they are highly affected by business cycles and price changes. Most cyclical industries produce durable goods such as capital goods, raw materials used in manufacturing (steel, cement, aluminum) and heavy equipment. During periods of tight credit or galloping inflation, manufacturers postpone investing in new capital goods. Likewise, consumers postpone purchasing durable goods like cars. So, from an investment perspective, such industries are considered cyclical.

Growth industries. Many investors favor growth industries. These industries are growing faster than the economy as a whole because of technological changes, new products or changing consumer tastes. Computers, soft drinks and pharmaceuticals have been growth industries.

Corporate Analysis

After considering the state of the economy and the health of various industries, fundamental analysts try to select companies whose stocks offer good investment opportunities. They analyze the position of a company within its industry by looking at such matters as competitive position in the industry, prospects for growth and stability, and current financial position (as evidenced by financial statements).

To ascertain a company's ability to compete in its industry, analysts examine the company's current and probable future market share, whether it is a leader within its industry, and whether it is introducing new product lines that might increase its market share.

Fundamental analysts are concerned with the growth and stability of a company. They look at the quality of the firm's management and historical earnings trends. They plot how its projected growth compares with that of its competitors and whether its growth is stable or erratic. Analysts also examine a corporation's capitalization and use of working capital. They try to pinpoint stocks that afford maximum potential for growth, stability and profits for the investor.

Financial Statements

Fundamental analysts use the financial statements of a corporation to analyze profitability, financial strength and operating efficiency. The balance sheet can be used to analyze the solvency, liquidity and capital structure of the corporation. Analysts use the relationships between these numbers (such as the ratio of equity to total capitalization) to judge the financial health of the company.

Companies listed on the New York Stock Exchange are required to submit an annual report to each shareholder. Most listed companies also issue quarterly financial statements that include (among other financial documents) a balance sheet and an income statement. The annual report usually includes other financial reports, such as the retained earnings statement and funds statement. The balance sheet and income statement, however, are critical tools for analyzing a company's financial situation and for evaluating the viability of the company's securities investments.

Balance Sheet

The balance sheet shows what the company owns (its assets), what it owes (its liabilities), and the excess of the book value of assets over the book value of liabilities (its equity). Analogous to this is the homeowner who, in order to purchase an asset (the home), takes on a liability (mortgage). By putting down a deposit and making principal payments over time, the

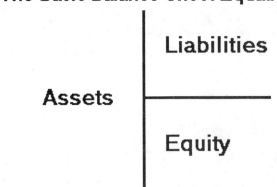

The Basic Balance Sheet Equation:

Assets | Liabilities

Equity

Assets = Liabilities + Stockholders' Equity

Fig. 12.8 The balance sheet equation.

homeowner eventually acquires equity (the difference between mortgage and market value) in the home. From the corporate perspective, the corporation buys assets with borrowed money and bonds (liabilities) plus money raised by selling stock (stockholders' equity) so the cost of assets must equal (or be in balance with) the sum of liabilities and assets.

A balance sheet reports on a company's financial position in dollars and cents. It has been compared to a snapshot of the corporation's financial condition at a given moment. It can not, therefore, tell the analyst whether the company's finances are improving or deteriorating, only how they are at any given moment in time.

Balance Sheet
MNM Corporation
as of Dec. 31, 1993

Assets

Current Assets			
	Cash and equivalents	$5,000,000	
	Accounts receivable	15,000,000	
	Inventory	19,000,000	
	Prepaid expenses	1,000,000	
	Total Current Assets		$40,000,000
Fixed Assets	Buildings, furniture & fixtures (including $10,000,000 depreciation)	$40,000,000	
	Land	15,000,000	
	Total Fixed Assets		55,000,000
Other (intangibles, goodwill)			5,000,000
TOTAL ASSETS			**$100,000,000**

Liabilities and Net Worth

Current Liabilities	_suppliers_	Accounts payable	$5,000,000	
		Accrued wages payable	4,000,000	
	Funded Debt	Current portion of long-term debt	1,000,000	
		Total Current Liabilities		$10,000,000
Long-term Liabilities		8% 20-year convertible debentures	50,000,000	
TOTAL LIABILITIES				$60,000,000
Net Worth		Preferred stock $100 par ($5 noncum conv, 200,000 shares issued)	$20,000,000	
		Common stock $1.00 par (1,000,000 shares)	1,000,000	
		Capital in excess of par	4,000,000	
		Retained earnings	**15,000,000**	
TOTAL NET WORTH				**$40,000,000**
TOTAL LIABILITIES AND NET WORTH				**$100,000,000**

Read next page

The balance sheet gets its name from the fact that its two sides must balance. This is also true for a homeowner: the value of the homeowner's asset is equal to the amount of the mortgage liability plus the equity (that is, what she owes plus what she owns). The balance sheet equation mathematically expresses the relationship between the two sides of the balance sheet mathematically.

Assets

In general, assets are listed on the balance sheet in order of liquidity. Assets most readily converted into cash are listed first, followed by less liquid assets. Balance sheets commonly include three types of assets: current assets (cash and assets easily convertible to cash), fixed assets (those not easily convertible into cash), and other assets.

Current assets. Current assets include all cash and other items expected to be converted into cash within the next accounting cycle (usually 12 months):

- **Cash and equivalents**. Cash and short-term, safe investments, such as money-market instruments, that can be sold readily.
- **Accounts receivable**. Amounts due from customers for goods delivered or services rendered that have not been paid for.
- **Inventory**. The cost of raw materials, work in process and finished goods ready for sale.
- **Prepaid expenses**. Items a company has already paid for, but has not yet benefited from, such as prepaid advertising, rents, taxes and operating supplies.

Fixed assets. Fixed assets will typically be labeled "property, plant and equipment" on the balance sheet. Unlike current assets, they cannot be easily converted into cash (that is, liquidated). Fixed assets (except for land) have limited useful lives. That is, at some point wear and tear may reduce their value to nothing. Therefore, they can be **depreciated** (their cost can be deducted from taxable income in annual installments, to compensate for loss in value). Note on the MNM balance sheet that depreciation reduces fixed assets by $10 million. That is, the assets would be valued at $50 million except for $10 million of depreciation.

Other assets. Other assets may include relatively permanent investments. MNM reported $5 million in other investments, including intangible assets. Intangible assets are nonphysical properties (including such items as formulas, contract rights and trademarks). Goodwill, also an intangible asset, is the value of a company over and above its book value. This extra sum is paid for the corporation's reputation and relationship with its clients.

Liabilities

Total liabilities on a balance sheet represent all financial claims by creditors against the assets of a corporation. Balance sheets usually include two types of liabilities: **current liabilities** (debts due within 12 months) and **long-term liabilities** (debts maturing in more than 12 months, including mortgages and long-term debt securities).

Current liabilities. Current liabilities are corporate debt obligations due for payment within the next 12 months. For MNM, these include:

- **Accounts payable**. Amounts owed to suppliers of materials and other business costs.
- **Accrued wages payable**. Unpaid wages, salaries, commissions, interest, etc.
- **Current long-term debt**. Any portion of long-term debt due within 12 months.

A balance sheet might also include as current liabilities:

- **Notes payable**. The balance due on equipment purchased on credit or cash borrowed.
- **Accrued taxes**. Unpaid federal, state and local taxes.

Long-term liabilities. Long-term debts are financial obligations that are due for payment after 12 months. Examples of long-term debts are mortgages on real property, long-term promissory notes and outstanding corporate bonds. Funded debt is any long-term debt that is payable in five years or more.

Other liabilities. A corporation may have various other obligations: deferred taxes arising from accelerated depreciation, bond premiums and other items that are not current or long-term liabilities.

Stockholders' Equity

Stockholders' equity (called net worth or owners' equity) represents the stockholders' residual claims against the assets. In accounting terms, stockholders' equity is equal to total assets less total liabilities. On a balance sheet, stockholders' equity is represented by three items: capital stock at par, capital in excess of par (additional paid-in capital) and retained earnings (earned surplus).

Capital stock at par. Capital stock includes preferred and common stock, listed at par value. Par value is the total dollar value that was assigned to stock certificates when the owners (that is, the stockholders) of a corporation first contributed capital.

Capital in excess of par. Capital in excess of par (often called **additional paid-in capital**) is the amount of money over par value that the company received for selling stock. (Par is an arbitrary value with no relationship to market price.) For example, you can see on the balance sheet that MNM issued one million shares of common stock with a par value of $1, for a total value of $1 million. It also has $4 million of capital in excess of par ($4 per share above the par value). So it actually received $5 per share for the stock.

Retained earnings. Retained earnings are profits that have not been paid out in dividends. On a balance sheet, retained earnings (also called earned surplus) represent the total of all earnings held since the corporation was formed, less dividends paid to stockholders. Operating losses in any year reduce the retained earnings from prior years.

Liquidity

Working capital is the actual amount of capital or money that a company has available to "work" with. Working capital is, therefore, a measure of a firm's liquidity (e.g., ability to transform assets into cash to meet current short-term obligations). The formula for working capital is: Working Capital = Current Assets - Current Liabilities.

Capitalization

A company's capitalization, or capital structure, refers to the sum of a company's long-term debt, stock accounts and capital in excess of par. Some authorities object that capitalization should not include long-term debt and mortgages. A company's financial structure includes additional capital, such as short-term debts and accounts payable. The income statement (or profit and loss statement) summarizes a corporation's revenues and expenses for a given fiscal period, which can be any 12-month period it designates.

Income Statements

The income statement (or profit and loss statement) summarizes a corporation's revenues and expenses for a given fiscal period. While the balance sheet presents a still picture of a corporation's financial position, the income statement is a history of the company's operations for the year, the half-year, the quarter or the month. It matches revenue against costs and expenses during the period.

**Income Statement
MNM Corporation
January 1 - December 31, 1993**

Net Sales		$60,000,000
	Cost of Goods Sold $10,000,000	
	General Operating Expenses (inc. $2,000,000 depreciation) $30,000,000	
Operating Income		$20,000,000
	Interest Expense 4,000,000	
Pre-tax Income		16,000,000
	Taxes 6,000,000	
Net Income After Taxes		10,000,000
	Preferred Dividend 1,000,000	
Earnings Available to Common		$9,000,000

The income statement is used by fundamental analysts to judge the efficiency of a company's operation. From the income statement analysts generate ratios such as operating expenses to net sales and the proportion of earnings available to common shareholders that were paid as dividends to the shareholders. The following formula illustrates typical entries on an income statement:

```
        Net sales
  -     Cost of goods sold (COGS)
  -     Operating costs (including depreciation)
        Operating profit
  +     Nonoperating income
        Total income (earnings before interest and taxes)
  -     Interest expenses
        Taxable income
  -     Taxes
        Net income after taxes
  -     Preferred dividends
        Earnings available to common
  -     Common dividends
        Retained earnings
```

Net sales. All income statements begin with net sales (sometimes called sales or revenue) for the year. Net sales are gross sales minus returns.

Costs of goods sold. Cost of goods sold (or COGS) includes outlays for raw materials, supplies, utilities and wages and labor associated with making the goods. These costs are subtracted from net sales, along with operating expenses, to calculate operating income.

Operating expenses. Operating expenses include selling and administrative expenses, research and development costs, and depreciation. These also are subtracted from net sales to arrive at operating income. MNM incurred operating expenses of $30 million, including $2 million of depreciation. Depreciation, however, is not a cash expense. It is a paper loss only, a tax deduction allowed the company to compensate for the declining value of its property and equipment as it wears out in the process of doing business. The company does not pay money for depreciation as it pays money for administrative expenses or development costs.

Operating income. Operating income (also called operating profit or operating margin) is a company's profit from the year's business operations.

```
        Net Sales
  less  Cost of Goods Sold
  less  General Operating Expenses
  less  Depreciation
        Operating Income
```

Nonoperating income. Other sources of revenue (such as interest income or dividends received) are listed separately on the income statement.

Interest expense. Interest payments on outstanding debt are not considered part of operating expenses. They are also not a part of the corporation's taxable income. To move from operating income to pretax income (the amount subject to taxes) the corporation reduces operating income by the amount of interest charges, such as interest payments to bondholders.

Net income after taxes. If dividends are paid to stockholders, they are paid out of net income. Preferred dividends are paid first and the balance is available to common shareholders.

Earnings per share. Earnings per share is calculated after payment of interest on debt securities, taxes and the payment of preferred dividends. This is the money available for payment of dividends to common shareholders. Earnings per share are computed by dividing the earnings available to common (net income after taxes less any preferred dividends) by the number of shares of common stock outstanding.

Earned surplus. Earnings not paid out in interest, dividends to preferred and common shareholders, or taxes are called earned surplus or retained earnings.

Extraordinary items. Sometimes a company will have an unusual, one-time gain or expense called an extraordinary item. MNM might, for example, sell a subsidiary or incur a large fine. Such an item would be included on the income statement below "Net Income After Taxes."

Changes That Affect Financial Statements

Balancing the balance sheet. Balance sheets must balance. This is achieved through what is known as **double-entry bookkeeping**. Every change in the financial structure of the business will require entering two changes on the balance sheet. The first change will disrupt the balance; the second change will restore the balance.

The way to keep the balance sheet in balance is to offset a positive change on one side by a positive change on the other. A company that buys an asset, for example, will raise the money for it with an increase in either liabilities or net worth; that is, by borrowing money, issuing bonds, or selling stock.

It is also possible to keep the balance by making changes on the same side of the balance sheet. A company can purchase one asset, for example, by selling another and the accountant can enter offsetting positive and negative changes on the asset side of the balance sheet. Money raised by selling stock (an addition to net worth) could be used to retire debt (a decrease in liabilities). Those two changes would keep the bottom line of the liabilities/net worth side of the balance sheet the same.

Depreciating Assets

Fixed assets, such as buildings, equipment and machinery, wear out as they are used. Because of this, they tend to decline in value (with the general exception of buildings). This decline in value is called depreciation. Depreciation is also the name of the tax deduction that compensates taxpayers for that decline in value of assets used in a business.

The depreciation deduction. Our tax laws incorporate the idea that businesses should not be taxed on expenses incurred in the operation of the business. Depreciation is an operating expense.

With some expenses (salaries for example) the business spends a certain amount of money during the year and deducts the entire amount when calculating taxable income. Depreciation is different. It isn't based on actual cash expenses paid during the year. Instead, it is a percentage of the cost of an asset. A company cannot deduct the entire cost of a building or a truck in the year of its purchase. Instead, those deductions must be spread over a number of years (the exact number depending upon the type of asset).

If a company bought machinery in 1985, for example, it might deduct a percentage of the cost of that machinery from taxes every year for the next five years. The actual amount of the deduction would be determined from tables published by the IRS. The tables would also establish that the particular asset has a life span of five years. (Whether it actually wears out in five years is beside the point. The deductions will stop then, because the entire cost of the machinery will have been recovered through the deductions.)

There are two types of depreciation: straight-line and accelerated. When depreciation is calculated by the straight-line method, the same amount is deducted each year over the useful life of the asset. Accelerated depreciation methods speed up the recovery of an asset's cost by allocating higher deductions in earlier years. As the asset's depreciable life wears on, deductions grow steadily smaller. There are several methods of accelerated depreciation, but the most common is the Accelerated Cost Recovery System (ACRS) established by the tax act of 1981 and modified in succeeding tax law changes.

Depreciation and the balance sheet. As you may have gathered from the preceding explanation, depreciation affects the balance sheet in two ways: accumulated depreciation reduces the value of fixed assets, and the depreciation deduction reduces tax liability.

The two changes balance out, so that total assets continue to equal the sum of liabilities and net worth on the balance sheet.

Valuing Inventories

Inventories include raw materials, goods in process and finished goods. Since the cost of producing goods fluctuates, the value of inventories on a balance sheet can vary, depending on the method of valuation. Accountants usually use a conservative figure, pricing inventories at either the original cost or the present market value, whichever is lower.

The two methods used to assess the value (current cost) of a company's end-of-year inventories are FIFO (first-in, first-out) and LIFO (last-in, first-out).

FIFO. FIFO, the most common valuation method, is based on the assumption that items acquired first are sold first (First In, First Out). At the end of the fiscal year, a company will have a given number of items in inventory (50,000 basketballs for example). To place a value on those basketballs requires knowing the cost of each.

During the year, however, the cost may well have changed, so that some basketballs are worth more than others. According to the FIFO method of evaluating inventory, the basketballs were sold in exactly the order received. Those remaining in inventory, therefore, were the last 50,000 to arrive at the warehouse and will be assigned the value of the most recent shipments.

During times of inflation, using the FIFO method has two consequences:

- FIFO assigns the highest possible value to inventory, since it assumes that the latest received (and most expensive) items remain unsold.
- FIFO assigns the lowest possible value for cost of goods sold, since it assumes the first (and cheapest) items are sold first.

The result of using the lowest cost-of-goods-sold amount is that a company records the highest possible profits (sales less cost of goods sold). Recording the highest possible profits, in turn, means paying the highest possible taxes.

LIFO. An alternative method, LIFO, is based on the assumption that goods acquired last are sold first (**L**ast **I**n, **F**irst **O**ut). LIFO is a more conservative approach than FIFO. In times of inflation, when prices are rising, LIFO produces a higher figure for cost of goods sold and, therefore, lowest profits for a given amount of sales. This means that using LIFO reduces the company's tax liability. When prices are falling, however, using LIFO results in higher profits and taxes than using FIFO does.

Capital Structure

A corporation builds its capital structure with four elements:

- long-term debt;
- capital stock (both common and preferred);
- capital in excess of par; and
- earned surplus (retained earnings).

The total capitalization for MNM Corporation is $90,000,000 ($50,000,000 in long-term debt, $20,000,000 in preferred stock and $20,000,000 in common shareholders' equity). Note that capital stock plus capital in excess of par plus earned surplus equals stockholders' equity (net worth).

> Total Capitalization = Long-Term Debt + Net Worth

If MNM changes its capitalization in any way (by issuing stock or bonds, for example) the effects will show up on the balance sheet. In the next sections, we'll look at how a balance sheet maintains its balance when MNM changes its capital structure in several ways.

Issuing securities. On the balance sheet displayed earlier, you could see that MNM Corporation had issued one million shares of its $1.00 par common stock. If it issues another one million shares the balance sheet will change in two ways. Net worth (stockholders' equity) will increase by the additional capital raised. And, as the stock is sold, the amount of cash assets on the opposite side of the balance sheet will also increase.

Convertible securities. When a stockholder converts one of MNM's convertible debentures into shares of common stock, the amount of liabilities decreases, while equity increases. The changes are on the same side of the balance sheet, so the bottom lines on both sides remain the same

Bond redemption. As with conversion, the redemption of bonds would reduce liabilities on the balance sheet (for MNM by $50 million). The offsetting change in this case, however, would be a decrease of $50 million in cash assets on the opposite side of the balance sheet. MNM would have $50 million less outstanding debt, but it would also have $50 million less cash to spend.

Paying dividends. The payment of dividends affects the way capitalization is reported on the balance sheet. When a cash dividend is paid, retained earnings are lowered, as is the cash balance. When a stock dividend is paid, retained earnings are lowered while the total amount of capital stock and capital in excess of par increases. Thus for a stock dividend, total capitalization does not decrease.

Most dividends are paid in cash. The declaration of a cash dividend establishes a current liability until it is paid. Once paid, it reduces current assets. In addition, a cash dividend reduces the retained earnings of the corporation at the time it is declared.

Distribution of stock dividends has no effect on corporate assets or liabilities; nor does it change the stockholders' proportionate equity in the corporation. The number of shares held by each stockholder is increased, but each share represents a smaller slice of ownership in the corporation.

In other words, there is no dilution of stockholders' equity. Dilution is a reduction in a stockholder's percent ownership in the corporation. If each stockholder receives the same percent increase in holdings, there is no change in percent ownership for anyone. From an accounting point of view, the only effect of a stock dividend is to transfer funds within the stockholders' equity accounts. The current market value of the stock dividend is deducted from retained earnings and added to capital stock accounts.

In our example, MNM Corporation issues a 10% stock dividend. This changes four entries in the net worth section of the balance sheet:

- Number of shares of common stock outstanding increases.
- Par value of outstanding common stock increases.
- Capital in excess of par increases.
- Retained earnings decrease.

Total net worth stays the same. The increases in par value and capital in excess of par are balanced by a reduction in retained earnings. Like cash dividends, stock dividends are funded from retained earnings.

Stock splits. Although corporate executives are generally delighted to see the value of the company stock go up, it is possible for a stock's price to go too high. At some point, the market value of a stock may inhibit trading. Even though a company is on sound financial footing, investors simply may not want to pay $100 a share for its stock. To reduce the price without hurting present shareholders, a company can declare a **stock split**.

In a four-for-one split, for example, the company would distribute three additional shares of new stock for each share of stock outstanding. An investor holding a round lot of 100 shares before the split would own 400 shares afterward. And, as the company splits each share into four shares, the market also cuts the per share price to one-fourth of the pre-split level. Each of the new shares, then, is worth $25 instead of $100. The shareholder's 100 shares worth $100 each become 400 shares worth $25 each. Total value doesn't change: it's $10,000 before and after the split.

Like a stock dividend, a stock split does not affect shareholder equity. On the balance sheet, only the par value and number of shares outstanding change.

Financial Leverage

Financial leverage refers to a company's ability to use long-term debt and preferred stock to increase return on common equity. A company with a high ratio of long-term debt and preferred stock to common stock is said to have high leverage.

Shareholders benefit from leverage if the return on borrowed money exceeds the debt service costs and therefore the value of common stock rises. But leverage is also risky, since increases in debt raise the possibility of default. Because leverage may increase the value of common shares, it is sometimes called trading on the equity.

As a rule of thumb, industrial companies with a debt-to-equity ratio of 30% are said to be highly leveraged. Utilities, with their relatively stable earnings and cash flow, can be more highly leveraged without subjecting shareholders to undue risk.

Financial Ratios

Financial statements alone have limited value. It would be difficult to compare the overall performances of two companies by looking only at the dollar amounts on their financial statements.

Benefits and limitations. The numbers become more meaningful when certain items from the balance sheet and income statement are combined as ratios. Financial ratios lend themselves to easy comparisons (e.g., comparisons of a company's current performance to its past performance, to its present goals, and to performances of other companies within its industry).

However, financial ratios have limitations. They are only as accurate as the numbers upon which they are based. Furthermore, standards for measuring a particular ratio are difficult to determine. Consequently, while ratios are useful, they must be viewed within the overall financial context of a given corporation.

Capitalization Ratios

Risk of bankruptcy. Analysts assess the risk that a company will go bankrupt by studying its capitalization (long-term debt plus equity) and its degree of leverage (amount of long-term debt compared to net worth).

Ratios. When assessing a company's capitalization, analysts use ratios that express the percentage of capitalization composed of long-term debt, common stock and preferred stock. Bond analysts use the following three capitalization ratios to assess the degree of safety of a corporation's bonds.

The bond ratio measures the percentage of total capitalization that is provided by long-term debt financing. It is also called the debt ratio.

The common stock ratio measures percentage of total capitalization contributed by common stockholders, including par value of stock, the amount paid for the stock in excess of par and the earnings not distributed as dividends. The preferred stock ratio measures the percentage of total capitalization that is in preferred stock.

$$\text{Bond Ratio} = \frac{\text{Long-term Debt}}{\text{Total Capitalization}} \quad (LTDebt + NWorth)$$

$$\text{Common Stock Ratio} = \frac{\text{Common Stock + Capital in Excess of Par + Retained Earnings}}{\text{Total Capitalization}}$$

$$\text{Preferred Stock Ratio} = \frac{\text{Preferred Stock}}{\text{Total Capitalization}}$$

$$\text{Debt to Equity Ratio} = \frac{\text{Total Long-term Debt}}{\text{Total Stockholders' Equity}}$$

Fig. 12.9 Several examples of capitalization ratios.

Leverage. Leverage results from the use of long-term fixed securities (such as bonds, debentures and preferred stock) to increase earnings. The debt-to-equity ratio provides a common measure of leverage.

Bond analysts often refer to the debt-to-equity ratio. A company with a disproportionate amount of debt may have difficulties meeting its interest obligations during a recession or a particularly bad year for the company. Low debt-to-equity ratios are considered more conservative than higher debt-to-equity ratios. The debt-to-equity ratio is similar to the bond ratio, which compares total long-term debt to total capitalization, rather than stockholders' equity.

Liquidity Ratios

The above ratios are primarily concerned with long-term indebtedness and the capitalization of the firm. Liquidity ratios measure the firm's ability to meet its current obligations. You've already seen one measure of liquidity, working capital. The calculation for working capital isn't truly a ratio. It is, rather, the difference between short-term assets and short-term debts. Working capital is the amount of liquid assets available to meet new short-term obligations. In addition to calculating a firm's working capital, however, analysts look at the current ratio.

Working capital is simply a dollar amount, so it can't, by itself, allow analysts to compare companies. A large company with a given dollar amount of working capital is not in the same position as a small company with the same amount. The current ratio, on the other hand, offers a basis for comparison. Companies with the same current ratio (no matter what the size of the company) have the same amount of current assets in relation to their current liabilities.

Another measure of liquidity is **quick assets**, which takes into account the size of the company's unsold inventory. While the inventory is a current asset, it isn't as liquid (as quick to convert to cash) as other current assets. Analysts use quick assets instead of current assets in the acid-test ratio.

Most accountants believe that the acid-test ratio (also called the quick ratio) is a better measure of a company's liquidity than the current ratio is. The final liquidity ratio, the cash assets ratio, measures only the cash assets (including marketable securities) in relation to current liabilities.

Efficiency Ratios

The **efficiency** of a company is a measure of how rapidly the firm is turning its inventory and accounts receivables into cash. This is

Working Capital = Current Assets − Current Liabilities

$$\text{Current Ratio} = \frac{\text{Current Assets}}{\text{Current Liabilities}}$$

Quick Assets = Current Assets − Inventory − *prepaids*

$$\text{Acid-Test Ratio} = \frac{\text{Quick Assets}}{\text{Current Liabilities}}$$

Fig. 12.10 Liquidity ratios.

measured by the inventory turnover ratio.

The inventory turnover ratio expresses the number of times a corporation's average inventory investment is turned into income dollars. Although standards vary from industry to industry, the goal is usually to increase this ratio. A low ratio indicates that the company is incurring extra expenses, such as storage costs, as well as the increased risk of having unsalable inventory on hand.

$$\text{Inventory Turnover Ratio} = \frac{\text{Net Sales}}{\text{Year-end Inventory}}$$

(handwritten "Net Sales" overwrites crossed-out "Cost of Goods Sold")

Fig. 12.11 Measuring how quickly inventory turns over.

Profitability Ratios

To measure a company's relative profitability, analysts study ratios that demonstrate how high a company's profits are in relation to its sales. These include the margin of profit ratio and the net profit ratio.

Also called the operating profit ratio, the margin of profit ratio shows the operating efficiency of a business. Why does it show operating efficiency? Because as operating costs rise, the numerator grows smaller and so does the ratio. So a low ratio indicates that costs are taking a relatively large bite out of profits.

The net profit ratio uses net income in the numerator, so it takes into account not only operating efficiency, but also the impact on a company's profits of its debt service and taxes. The greater the percentage of profits lost to taxes and interest costs, the lower the ratio. Profitability is also reflected in a firm's return on assets, which analysts measure with the following ratio.

$$\text{Margin of Profit Ratio} = \frac{\text{Operating Profit}}{\text{Net Sales}}$$

$$\text{Net Profit Ratio} = \frac{\text{Net Income}}{\text{Net Sales}}$$

$$\text{Return on Equity} = \frac{\text{Net Income (after taxes)}}{\text{Stockholders' Equity}}$$

Fig. 12.12 Measuring a company's profitability.

Asset Coverage and Safety of Income

Net asset value per bond. Analysts have devised a number of ratios to measure a firm's ability to meet its long-term debt obligations. The ratio of net asset value to number of bonds outstanding gives bondholders some information about the assets available to back up the companies' obligations to short- and long-term creditors.

Bond interest coverage. Bondholders (and other long-term creditors) need to know if the company is likely to have sufficient earnings to cover its interest payments. This can be measured by the number of times earnings before interest and taxes (EBIT) exceeds annual interest on the company's outstanding bonds.

Since the bond interest coverage ratio reveals the ability of a company to meet the interest payments on its long-term fixed obligations, it is a good measure of the solvency of a company. It is also called: interest coverage ratio, the times interest earned ratio, the fixed charge coverage ratio and the times fixed charges earned ratio.

Debt service ratio. If investors want to know the ability of an issuer to meet principal and interest payments on bonds, they can modify the bond-interest-coverage ratio by including principal payments in the denominator. This modified version of the ratio is called the debt service ratio.

Book value per share. In bankruptcy, a company sells its tangible assets and uses the proceeds to pay creditors and stockholders. Potential investors want to know how the value of tangible assets compares to the size of the company's debt and equity.

Book value of a company's assets (the amount at which they are carried on the books) is determined by deducting all liabilities and the value of any preferred stock

$$\text{Net Asset Value per Bond} = \frac{\text{Net Tangible Assets} - \text{Current Liabilities}}{\text{Number of Bonds Outstanding}}$$

$$\text{Bond Interest Coverage} = \frac{\text{EBIT} \ (Profit)}{\text{Annual Interest Payable to Bonds}}$$

$$\text{Debt Service Ratio} = \frac{\text{EBIT}}{\text{Annual Interest} + \text{Principal Payments}}$$

$$\text{Book Value per Share} = \frac{\text{Stockholders' Equity} - (\text{Par Value of Preferred Stock} + \text{Intangible Assets})}{\text{Number of Shares of Common Stock Outstanding}}$$

not likely tested

$$\text{Collection Ratio} = \frac{\text{Receivables} \times 360}{\text{Net Sales}}$$

Fig. 12.13 Coverage ratios use debt as a base.

from the company's tangible assets. Dividing this by the number of outstanding shares of common stock shows how far a company's assets might go (if they are worth their value in the books) toward reimbursing stockholders for their losses in bankruptcy.

Collection ratio. Finally, investors may also be concerned about a company's relative efficiency in collecting debts. The collection ratio roughly measures how long accounts receivable have been outstanding. As a company becomes more efficient in collecting its receivables, its collection ratio (expressed in days) decreases.

Valuation Ratios

Earnings per share. When shareholders receive the corporate annual report, they want to know whether they, as owners of the corporation, received an adequate return on their investment. Perhaps the most widely used of all accounting statistics is earnings per share, one way to compare the value of one share to the earnings per share of the company.

The concept of EPS applies only to common stock. Preferred stockholders have no claims to earnings beyond the stipulated preferred stock dividends.

Earnings per share after dilution. If a corporation has only common stock or common stock and nonconvertible bonds outstanding, the earnings per share is the only figure to be identified. If, however, a corporation has rights, stock options, warrants, convertible preferred stock or convertible bonds, the earnings per share of that corporation could be diluted through an increase in the number of shares of common outstanding. That is, the same amount of earnings available to pay common stock dividends might have to be distributed among more shares of stock. EPS is sometimes called primary earnings per share to differentiate it from earnings after dilution.

Earnings per share after dilution assumes that all convertible securities have been converted. Because of tax adjustments, the calculations for figuring earnings per share after dilution can be complicated.

Dividends per share. The dividend per share is simply the dollar amount of cash dividends paid on each common share during the year.

Price-earnings ratio. The price-earnings ratio, often abbreviated as the PE ratio, gives investors a rough idea of the relationship between the prices of different common stocks. PE is one of the most widely used ratios in the business. In a given industry, stocks with higher earnings per share generally command higher prices per share.

Growth companies usually have higher PE ratios than do cyclical companies. Investors are willing to pay more per share for stocks with promise of stable, long-term growth than for stocks that rise and fall with business cycles. Companies subject to cyclical fluctuations (like steel companies or automobile companies) generally sell at lower PE ratios. Declining industries (for example, railroads) sell at still lower ratios. Investors should beware of extremely high or extremely low PE ratios. Speculative stocks often sell at one extreme or the other.

Current yield. The current yield of a common stock, like the current yield on bonds or mutual funds, expresses the annual return on the investment as a percentage of the market value. It tells an investor only about the dividend yield, however, not the yield attributable to any long-term growth in the value of the stock.

Dividend payout ratio. The dividend payout ratio is used to measure the portion of common earnings actually paid to common shareholders as dividends.

In general, more established companies pay out the largest percentage of earnings in dividends. Utilities as a group have an especially high payout ratio. Growth companies normally have the lowest ratios, since they reinvest their earnings in the business. Companies on the way up hope to reward stockholders with gains in the value of the stock rather than with high dividend income.

(see 12.25)

$$\text{Earnings per Share (EPS)} = \frac{\text{Earnings Available to Common}}{\text{Number of Common Shares Outstanding}}$$

$$\text{Dividends per Share} = \frac{\text{Annual Dividends}}{\text{Number of Common Shares Outstanding}}$$

$$\text{Price-Earnings Ratio (PE)} = \frac{\text{Current Market Price of Common Stock}}{\text{Earnings per Share}}$$

$$\text{Current Yield} = \frac{\text{Annual Dividends per Common Share}}{\text{Market Value per Common Share}}$$

$$\text{Dividend Payout Ratio} = \frac{\text{Annual Dividends per Common Share}}{\text{Earnings per Share}}$$

Fig. 12.14 Ratios measuring return on investment.

Competitiveness (Comparative Performance)

Return on common equity. Investors are interested in how high a return on common stock investments one company offers in relation to other firms in the same industry. Rates of return 20% or higher are considered substantial. Note that the numerator of this formula is the same as that for calculating earnings per share. The denominator is the amount of equity attributable to common shareholders.

$$\text{Return on Common Equity} = \frac{\text{Earnings Available to Common}}{\text{Common Par Value + Capital in Excess of Par + Retained Earnings}}$$

Fig. 12.15 Return on equity is an industry comparison.

Analyzing Corporate Debt

Basis for Bond Ratings

Bond ratings, for the most part, are based on analytical studies of the issuing corporation's financial condition and its potential for profit. The fundamental factors studied and measured to determine a particular bond's assigned ratings are:

- **Corporate earning power.** The ability to generate profits and remain solvent.
- **Stability of income.** Corporate profitability should be predictable from year to year and not totally dependent on the economy in general.
- **Corporate asset valuation.** In the event of financial difficulties, liquidation of assets must realistically provide sufficient cash to pay debts.

The rating services apply a standard series of corporate income and balance sheet tests in making their analyses of a corporation's financial strength.

Bond-interest coverage ratio. This ratio, which you read about in the previous section of this chapter, is perhaps the most important single tool for analyzing the security of a bond. Corporations with wide margins of safety generally offer the safest bonds. A good rule of thumb is as follows: a ratio of 7 to 1 is a high degree of safety; a ratio of 2 or 3 to 1 is low.

There are, however, two caveats. First, this yardstick should be applied over a seven year period that includes both prosperous and recessionary times. In no year should the ratio fall below 5 to 1. Second, a company in a stable industry (such as a public utility) needs less stringent coverage than a company in a cyclical industry (such as steel).

$$\text{Bond-Interest Ratio} = \frac{\text{Income Before Interest and Taxes}}{\text{Annual Interest Charges}}$$

Debt

$$\text{Net Fixed Assets per Bond} = \frac{\text{Net Fixed Assets}}{\text{Number of Bonds in Funded Debt}}$$

$$\text{Bond Ratio} = \frac{\text{Value of Bonds}}{\text{Total Long-term Capitalization}}$$

Debt

Fig. 12.16 Measures of corporate debt.

Net fixed assets per bond. The amount of producing assets also indicates the soundness of a bond issue. In the previous section, we looked at net asset value per bond ratio. A more conservative measure is the ratio of net fixed assets per bond. And the most cautious method of evaluating net fixed assets is to exclude intangible assets, working capital and accumulated depreciation.

For public utility bonds, sufficient coverage usually means about 1.8 times the amount of debt in net fixed assets. If a public utility backs up each outstanding $1,000 bond with $1,800 of net fixed assets, for example, it is considered to have met this guideline.

Bond ratio. Bond ratio, the percentage of capital structure composed of bonds, is another quantitative measure used in corporate bond analysis. An acceptable model for a public utility would be:

Bonds	50%
Preferred stock	15%
Common & surplus stock	35%
Total Invested Capital	100%

In this example, the debt ratio or bond ratio is 50%. This is simply a guideline, but a utility with 60%, 15% and only 25%, respectively, would have a risky debt ratio.

Relationship to yield. Generally, the higher the bond rating, the lower the yield. Investors are willing to accept a lower return on their investment if they know that their principal is safe and interest payments are predictable. On the other hand, some bonds will sell at deep discounts, producing high yields. These bonds may have low ratings and a degree of uncertainty may surround the safety of the investment and the ability of the issuer to continue interest payments. Other bonds, however, may be selling at a deep discount because they have low coupons.

When interest rates are expected to rise, prudent investors buy very short-term instruments such as municipal notes. When interest rates are expected to decline, prudent investors buy long-term bonds. Why? First, if interest rates do decline, the bonds that will appreciate most in price are long-term bonds. Second, investors may want to "lock in" high yields for a long time because they believe they may not have another chance to receive these returns

Qualitative assessments. Analyzing bonds involves more than just numbers. Other more qualitative factors evaluated are: the stability of an industry, the strength of a company in that industry, the quality of management and the regulatory climate.

Chapter Review

Questions

1. The Gross National Product is

   _X_(A)   the sum of all goods and services produced by a nation.
   ____(B)   goods produced by a country.
   ____(C)   household goods of a country.
   ____(D)   manufactured and nonmanufactured goods.

2. A fundamental analyst would be interested in all the following EXCEPT

   ____(A)   statistics of the U.S. Department of Commerce on disposable income.
   _ₒ_(B)   daily trading volumes on the NYSE.
   ____(C)   corporate annual reports
   ____(D)   new innovations within the automotive industry

3. The balance sheet formula is

   what you own — what you owe
   is what you're worth

   ____(A)   assets = liabilities + equity.
   ____(B)   assets - equity = liabilities.
   ____(C)   assets + equity = net worth.
   _X_(D)   (assets - equity)liability = net worth.

4. Which of the following is the narrowest measure of the market?

   ____(A)   NYSE composite index
   ____(B)   Value Line index
   ____(C)   DJIA
   ____(D)   Standard & Poor's 500

5. The NYSE composite index consists of

   ____(A)   common stocks.
   ____(B)   preferred stocks.
   ____(C)   certain listed bonds.
   ____(D)   all of the above.

6. The stock index that contains securities of four hundred industrial corporations is the

____(A)   Dow Jones composite.
____(B)   NASDAQ index.
____(C)   NYSE index.
____(D)   Standard and Poor's 500.

7. What does it mean when a technical analyst says that the market is "consolidating"?

____(A)   The trendline is moving upward.
____(B)   The trendline is moving downward.
____(C)   The trendline is moving sideways.
____(D)   The trendline is moving unpredictably.

8. From a chartist's (technical analyst's) viewpoint, which of the following is true?

____(A)   Once a trendline is established, the price movement of a stock will usually follow the trendline.
____(B)   More odd-lot buying than selling is bullish.
____(C)   Heavy volume in a declining market is bullish
____(D)   Light volume in an advancing market is bullish.

9. Proponents of which technical theory assume that small investors are usually wrong?

____(A)   the breadth-of-market theory
____(B)   the short interest theory
____(C)   the volume of trading theory
____(D)   the odd-lot theory

10. Changes in which industry would be considered a "leading indicator" of economic growth?

____(A)   home appliances
____(B)   natural gas
____(C)   retailing
____(D)   new housing

Answer Key

1. A.

2. B.

3. A.

4. C.

5. A.

6. D.

7. C.

8. A.

9. D.

10. D.

Chapter Thirteen

Investment Recommendations

Key Terms

13.7 Beta coefficient

13.4 Capital risk

13.6 Constant ratio plan

13.6 Dollar cost averaging

13.8 Holding period return

13.5 Legislative risk

13.4 Market risk

13.7 Nonsystematic risk

13.5 Purchasing power risk

13.5 Suitability

Call risk 13.5

Constant dollar plan 13.6

Credit risk 13.3

Financial risk 13.3

Internal rate of return 13.8

Liquidity risk 13.5

Marketability risk 13.5

Present value 13.8

Reinvestment risk 13.5

Systematic risk 13.7

K113

Investment Recommendations

Know Your Customers

Before you can make appropriate recommendations to your customers, you must understand their financial objectives, financial status and their investment constraints. Most clients invest for one or more of five basic financial objectives.

Growth. Growth refers to an increase in the value of an investment over time. Investors seek growth in order to meet a variety of needs (retirement planning, funding a child's education, travel or a vacation home, to name a few). The most common growth-oriented investments are common stock and stock mutual funds.

Income. Many investors, particularly retirees, seek current income from interest or dividends to supplement other income. Corporate bonds, municipal bonds, government and agency securities, income-oriented mutual funds, some stocks (utilities, REITs), money-market funds, annuities and some direct participation programs (DPPs) are among the investments that can contribute additional income.

Liquidity. Some people want immediate access to their money at all times. A product is liquid if the customer can sell it quickly at face amount (or very close to it) or a fair market price without losing significant principal. Stock, for example, has varying degrees of liquidity (depending on many factors, including safety, number of shares outstanding and the market's perception of the issuer), while DPPs, annuities and bank CDs are generally considered illiquid. Real estate is the classic example of an illiquid product because of the time and money it takes to convert it into cash.

Tax relief. The Tax Reform Act of 1986 lowered the top individual income tax rate from 50% to 28% and made tax relief less important. Still, many clients seek ways to reduce their taxes. Some products, like IRAs and annuities, allow interest to accumulate tax-deferred (no taxes are paid until the investor withdraws money from the account). Other products, like many municipal bonds, offer tax-free interest income.

Safety. In general, when clients speak of "safety" they usually mean safety from credit risk or financial risk. Financial risk is the danger of losing all or part of the principal amount. As we will discuss in the next section, there are other investment risks that should be weighed as well.

Financial Status

The more you know about your clients' income, current investment portfolio, retirement plans, net worth and other aspects of their current financial situation, the better your recommendations will be. Gather information about their marital status, financial responsibilities, projected inheritances, pending job changes, and the like.

Investment Constraints

A product might be suitable for one client, but not for another, due to various investment constraints. That is why registered representatives must ask potential clients questions such as:

- What kind of risks can you afford to take?
- How liquid must this investment be?
- How important are tax considerations?
- Are you seeking long-term or short-term investments?
- What is your investment experience?
- What is your investment temperament?
- Do you get bored with stable investments?
- Can you tolerate market fluctuations?

Types of Stock

Once you know your client's financial objectives, financial status and investment constraints, you can recommend suitable investments.

Growth stocks. Stocks that have good potential for price appreciation because a company's sales and earnings are growing faster than average are known as growth stocks. Since the company retains most of its earnings for expansion, such stocks tend to pay low dividends.

Defensive stocks. Historically, defensive stocks have been unaffected by the business cycle. They are issued by industries supplying basic necessities (such as energy, food, pharmaceuticals, tobacco, etc).

Cyclical stocks. In contrast to defensive stocks, cyclical stocks rise and fall with the business cycle. Their prices tend to appreciate when the economy is strong and fall sharply as the economy turns down. Cyclical industries include automobiles, boats, appliances, housing and other durable consumer goods that people postpone buying in hard times.

Special situation stocks. Special situation stocks are stocks of a company with unusual profit potential due to nonrecurring circumstances. Examples include an expected recovery under new management, the discovery of a valuable natural resource on corporate property or the introduction of a new product.

Investment Risks

In general, the greater the risk, the greater the reward. There are several risks to consider in determining the suitability of various types of investments when building a financial portfolio.

Credit risk. Credit risk (also called financial risk or default risk) involves the danger of losing all or part of one's invested principal through failure of the issuer. Credit risk varies with the investment product. Bonds backed by the federal government or municipalities tend to be very secure and have low credit risk. Long-term bonds involve more credit risk than short-term bonds because of the increased uncertainty that results from holding bonds for many years. Preferred stocks are generally safer than common stocks. Mutual funds offer increased safety through diversification. On the other hand, penny stocks, nonbank grade bonds and some options positions can be quite risky, yet right for some customers.

Bond investors who are concerned about credit risks should pay attention to the ratings. Two of the best known rating services that analyze the financial strength of thousands of corporate and municipal issuers are Moody's Investors Services and Standard & Poor's. To a great extent, the value of a bond depends on how much credit risk investors are taking. The higher the rating, the less likely the bond is to default and, therefore, the lower the coupon rate. Clients who are seeking the highest possible yield from bonds might want to buy bonds with lower ratings. The higher yields are a reward for taking more credit risks.

Capital risk. Capital risk is the chance that investors might lose all of their money or capital under circumstances unrelated to the financial strength of the issuer. For example, when options expire out-of-the-money, buyers lose all of their capital (the cost of the premium) even though the underlying security may be very solvent.

Market risk. Both stocks and bonds involve some degree of market risk, that is, the risk that investors may lose some of their principal due to price volatility in the market. Stocks tend to be more volatile than bonds; stock prices can rise or fall dramatically due to changing investor demand.

Prices of existing bonds can fluctuate with changing interest rates. There is an inverse relationship between bond prices and bond yields. As bond yields go up, bond prices go down (and vice versa). In order to maintain a competitive yield, the market price of existing bonds drops as new bonds are issued with higher coupon rates.

All things being equal, deep discount bonds are more responsive to changes in market yields than bonds that are selling at par or at a premium. Compared to other bonds, a deep discount bond will tend to appreciate faster as interest rates fall and drop faster as interest rates rise. The most deeply discounted bonds (zero coupon bonds) are the most susceptible to market risk. Of course, clients will receive face value for their bonds at maturity. If they should sell their bonds before maturity, however, they risk losing some of their principal. This particularly affects clients who invest in bonds with long maturities. They have stable income but risk losing some principal if they sell the bonds before maturity. Further, if interest rates rise considerably after a bond is issued, the holder may be "stuck" with a low interest rate until the bond matures, which may be 20 years.

For bonds with short maturities, the opposite is true. Their price remains fairly stable since investors will not generally sell them at deep discounts or buy them at high premiums. A client's income from short maturities, however, will vary with prevailing interest rates.

Reinvestment risk. Since bond investors are typically seeking a steady flow of income, they risk not being able to reinvest their interest income or principal at the same rate. This is known as reinvestment risk and is of particular concern during periods of falling interest rates. If interest rates decline, it is extremely difficult for bond investors to maintain the same level of current income without increasing their credit risks or market risks. Zero coupon bonds are not susceptible to reinvestment risk since the bond automatically reinvests the interest at the same rate until maturity.

Call risk. Related to reinvestment risk, call risk is the risk that a bond might be called before maturity and investors will be unable to reinvest their principal at the same rate of return (or higher). When interest rates are falling, bonds with higher coupon rates are most likely to be called. Thus, investors will lose their steady stream of income. Investors concerned about call risk should look for call protection, a period of time during which a bond cannot be called. Most corporate and municipal issuers generally provide some years of call protection.

Purchasing power risk. Also known as inflationary risk, this danger is the result of rising prices. If an investment's yield is lower than the rate of inflation, the client's money will have less purchasing power as time goes on. An investor who buys a bond, preferred stock or a fixed annuity may be able to purchase far less with the invested funds when the investment matures.

Marketability risk. The marketability of the securities you recommend must be directly related to the client's liquidity needs. Government bonds, for instance, are easily marketed. On the other hand, direct participation programs are illiquid and extremely difficult to market. This is also called a liquidity risk.

Municipal securities have a regional rather than national market. Therefore, they may be less marketable than more widely held securities. White's Tax-Exempt Bond Rating Service classifies municipal securities on market factors rather than credit considerations. You might want to consult this service before recommending a municipal issue to a client who is concerned about marketability.

Legislative risk. Congress has the power to change existing laws affecting securities. For example, by changing the tax consequences of passive income from DPPs, Congress affected the viability of many deep tax shelter programs. Similarly, a client who goes short against the box to postpone capital gains might be disappointed if Congress changes the taxation of such gains. When recommending suitable investments, you should warn clients of any pending changes in the law that may affect that investment.

Suitability

Since all investments involve trade-offs, the task of the investment advisor is to select securities that will provide the right balance between investor characteristics on the one hand and investment capabilities on the other.

Selecting suitable investments to meet investor needs is both an art and a science. The process is too complex to computerize; even the most sophisticated and expensive financial plans are only partially based on a computerized model. In the final analysis, recommending investments requires the finest computer ever made: the human brain. As an investment advisor, one of your key tasks is to recommend suitable investments that best match your clients' unique characteristics.

Modern Portfolio Theory

Modern portfolio theory is a fairly sophisticated approach to investments that allows investors to quantify and control the amount of risk and return they are taking in their portfolio. It differs from traditional security analysis in that it shifts the emphasis away from analyzing the specific securities in the portfolio and, instead, relies on determining the relationship between risk and reward in the total portfolio.

Investment Strategies for Maximizing Returns

Some clients attempt to obtain maximum return on their investment portfolio and are financially and temperamentally able to withstand the risks involved with such investment strategies. Thus, they pursue what is known as aggressive policies when it comes to buying and selling securities (remember, maximizing rewards also increases the risks). Aggressive policies include:

- selecting stocks with high betas;
- buying securities on margin;
- using put and call option strategies; and
- employing arbitrage techniques.

Investment Strategies for Minimizing Risks

Other clients pursue defensive policies. They are willing to make the risk-reward trade-off and accept potentially less return in order to minimize investment risk.

Dollar cost averaging. A common defensive technique is dollar cost averaging, by which an investor makes periodic purchases of a fixed dollar amount of one or more common stocks or mutual funds. With dollar cost averaging and a fluctuating market, the average cost of the stock is always less than the average market price. The client is still not guaranteed against loss and it is fraudulent for a registered rep to imply so.

Constant ratio plan. The constant ratio plan involves keeping a portfolio balanced between equity and debt securities. The investor sets the ratio, perhaps 60% equity and 40% debt and buys and sells securities to keep the "ratio" between debt and equity securities fairly constant.

Constant dollar plan. Another defensive technique is to keep the value of a portfolio at a constant dollar amount. Assume that your client wants to keep her portfolio at a constant level of $100,000. If the value of her portfolio reaches $110,000, under the constant dollar plan the investor will liquidate $10,000 worth of securities. Conversely, if her portfolio slips to $95,000, she will buy $5,000 worth of securities. This forces the investor to sell when the market is high and buy when it is low.

By employing this technique, your client is selling as prices rise and buying as prices fall. The major problem is that, in an extended bull market, the investor keeps liquidating more and more equities to stay at the constant dollar level. Therefore she is not taking advantage of the bull stock market.

Systematic Risk and Nonsystematic Risks

When investing in securities, clients risk losing some of their principal due to fluctuations in market value. Analysts distinguish between systematic risk that is common to all stocks or bonds and nonsystematic risk that is specific to a particular stock or bond.

Systematic risk. The tendency for security prices to move together is known as systematic risk. Investors who hold securities in their portfolio cannot avoid this risk, not even through diversification. When the market is bullish, prices on individual securities tend to rise with the market. Conversely, in bear markets, the prices of individual securities tend to decline, regardless of the financial condition of the company that issued the security.

Nonsystematic risk. There is nonsystematic risk associated with the underlying investment itself. Strikes, natural disasters, operating losses and many other factors may cause the individual security's price to decline when the market as a whole is rising. On the other hand, the introduction of a new product line or an attempted takeover may cause an individual security to rise even when the market is declining. The longer and more diversified a portfolio, the less subject it is to nonsystematic risk.

Diversification. While investors can do little to avoid systematic risks or inflation, they can temper nonsystematic risks. One important investment strategy is diversification, the buying of stocks and bonds from a variety of firms in different industries. By mixing industries and the types of assets, investors are spreading their risks. A particular event (deregulation of the airlines industry, for example) will have less impact if an investor's portfolio consists of a wide assortment of securities than if the investor buys only airline stock.

Beta coefficients. Beta coefficients quantify the degree to which a stock's price changes relative to the market. Some stocks are more volatile than the market, others are less volatile. Stocks with a beta of 1 move with the market; if the Standard & Poor's index moves up 10%, the stock price will be likely to increase by approximately 10%.

If the beta coefficient is:	The stock's return will probably:
Exactly 1	Move exactly with the market
Less than 1	Move less than the market moves
Greater than 1	Move more than the market moves

In general, the greater the beta coefficient, the more risk associated with the security. High beta coefficients may indicate greater profits during rising markets, but they also mean greater potential losses during market downswings. When the market rises by 10%, a stock with a beta of 2.0 is expected to rise by 20% on the average (or fall by 20% when the market is down by 10%). Therefore, investors who are risk-averse should avoid stocks with high beta coefficients (often called "aggressive stocks"). Instead, they should consider stocks with low betas. Stocks with low betas are considered defensive and more appropriate for risk-conscious investors who understand that they are trading off some potential return for lower market risk.

Analyzing Investment Returns

Regardless of whether an investor is pursuing aggressive or defensive investment strategies, the key question is: What returns have been made on the investment in securities?

Holding period return. The easiest method (and most misleading) is to compute the holding period rate of return. This involves calculating the total return from capital gains and dividend income without taking into consideration how long the investment was held. For example, assume an investor bought 100 shares of stock at $10 per share, sold it for $15 and received $100 in dividends. This is a 60% total return ($500 capital gains plus $100 dividend income divided by $1,000 initial investment equals 60%).

A 60% return is fine if the holding period is a year or less. But if this investment were held for ten years or more, a 60% return would not be that impressive. (The investor could do better in a bank passbook savings account at 5 1/4% interest offering guaranteed safety of principal and full liquidity at any time.) Thus, the holding period return can be misleading because it fails to take into account the time value of money.

Present value. The concept of present value is based upon the "time value of money." Receiving a dollar today is preferable to receiving a dollar at some future date. Present value calculates today's value of a future payment or stream of payments, discounted at some appropriate compound interest rate. For example, assume that a customer is offered a zero coupon bond maturing in one year at $1,000. What price should the customer pay for the bond? Certainly not $1,000. Assume that the interest rate for this type of security is 5%. The price the customer would pay would be $1,000 divided by 1.05% or $952.38. This is the bond's present value.

Internal rate of return. A related concept is the internal rate of return. This theoretical investment value is most commonly used to calculate the potential return from an investment. The internal rate of return (IRR) is the discount rate at which the present value of future cash flows of an investment equal the cost of that investment. It is found by trial and error. When the present value of cash outflows (costs) equals cash inflows (returns), the investment is valued at the IRR and there will be no profits. When the IRR is greater than the investor's required rate of return, the investment is acceptable.

Chapter Review

Questions

1. Growth refers to

    ___(A)   the value of the investment increasing over time.
    ___(B)   increasing principal and accumulating interest and dividends over time.
    ___(C)   investments that appreciate tax-deferred.
    ___(D)   all of the above.

2. Credit risk involves

    ___(A)   safety of principal.
    ___(B)   fluctuations in overall interest rates.
    ___(C)   danger of not being able to sell the investment at a fair market price.
    ___(D)   inflationary risks.

3. Which of the following investments is least appropriate for a client who is primarily concerned with liquidity?

    ___(A)   preferred stock
    ___(B)   municipal bond mutual funds
    ___(C)   bank savings accounts
    ___(D)   direct participation programs

4. Bondholders risk the value of their bonds falling as interest rates rise. This is known as

    ___(A)   credit risk.
    ___(B)   reinvestment risk.
    ___(C)   marketability risk.
    ___(D)   market risk.

5. Which of the following constitutes a constant dollar plan?

    ___(A)   60% equities, 40% fixed income
    ___(B)   40% equities, 60% fixed income investments
    ___(C)   fixed amount in the portfolio regardless of market price
    ___(D)   fixed amount in fixed income investments regardless of market price

6. Which of the following securities will generate the greatest current return with moderate risk?

_____(A)   common stock of a new company
_____(B)   a security convertible into the common stock of a company
_____(C)   a fixed income security
_____(D)   an income bond

7. Municipal bonds are most suitable for

_____(A)   individual retirement accounts.
_____(B)   corporations in the maximum tax bracket.
_____(C)   pension plans.
_____(D)   individuals in the 15% tax bracket.

8. Which of the following securities carries the highest degree of purchasing power risk?

_____(A)   short-term notes
_____(B)   blue chip stock
_____(C)   long-term, high-grade bonds
_____(D)   convertible cumulative preferred stock

9. Which of the following investments would best suit a client seeking maximum liquidity and safety of principal?

_____(A)   money-market funds
_____(B)   convertible bonds
_____(C)   fixed-income mutual funds
_____(D)   oil and gas income limited partnerships

10. Which of the following considerations must you take into account when recommending suitable investments for clients?

_____(A)   client's age and marital status
_____(B)   current investment portfolio
_____(C)   investment objectives
_____(D)   all of the above

Answer Key

1. A.

2. A.

3. D.

4. D.

5. C.

6. C.

7. B.

8. C.

9. A.

10. D.

Chapter Fourteen

Taxation

Key Terms

14.6 Accrued interest

14.4 Capital gain

14.3 Constructive receipt

14.3 Earned income

14.3 Passive income

14.3 Portfolio income

14.2 Regressive tax

14.11 Tax preference item

14.7 Wash sale

Alternative Minimum Tax (AMT) 14.11

Capital loss 14.4

Cost basis 14.7

Mutual reciprocity 14.3

Pass-through 14.6

Progressive tax 14.2

Short against the box 14.8

Tax Reform Act of 1986 14.3 14.5 14.12

K114

Taxation

Taxes have been levied upon the citizens of states, countries and kingdoms since political organizations began. As these economic and political structures evolved, so have tax structures. This constant development continues today.

Congress continually alters tax laws and the Internal Revenue Service (IRS) constantly reinterprets those laws. Judicial decisions amend and sometimes reverse existing statutes. Investors tailor decisions to the current tax structures, but must remain flexible enough to change as the laws change. Taxes imposed by states and cities are less imposing than federal taxes. So investors spend more time and energy trying to understand federal taxes and to minimize their impact.

Tax Structures

Regressive vs. Progressive Taxes

Depending on how they are structured, taxes can be either regressive or progressive. Regressive taxes fall the hardest on the poorest people, progressive taxes are felt more by the rich. Sales taxes, excise taxes and gasoline taxes are regressive taxes. A flat-rate 6% sales tax, for example, is actually regressive in impact. It takes a larger fraction of the income of poor people than of the rich.

The federal government imposes two types of taxes, both of which tend to be progressive: gift/estate taxes and income taxes.

Federal gift tax. In addition to income taxes, individuals may be subject to federal gift and estate taxes. Both taxes are progressive in nature in that they rarely affect people with low incomes. A federal gift tax is imposed on gifts of cash, real property, securities and other valuables that one individual gives to another. The tax is paid by the donor. Don't confuse this gift tax with tax-deductible contributions to qualified charities. The gift tax applies only to gifts to individuals.

The Economic Recovery Tax Act of 1981 (ERTA) allowed a $10,000 federal gift tax exemption annually ($20,000 for a married couple). This means that $10,000 in cash or other assets could be given each year to each of your children or anyone else, free of any gift tax. Gifts between spouses are not subject to the federal gift tax.

Federal estate taxes. Estate taxes are imposed by a state or the federal government on assets willed to others. Under ERTA, there is no estate tax on transfers of property between spouses. There is also a $600,000 exclusion on assets left to spouses.

Grandfather dies, leaves $10,000 to me. No estate tax. Purchase dated $10/share 1000 shares use $10 Share for basis

Income Taxes

Earned income. Federal income taxes are imposed on three types of income: earned, passive and portfolio. Earned income includes salary, bonuses and income derived from active participation in a trade or business.

Passive income. Passive income and losses come from rental property, limited partnerships and enterprises (regardless of business structure) in which the individual is not actively involved in the business. For the general partner, income from a limited partnership is "earned" income; for the limited partner, such income is "passive."

The Tax Reform Act of 1986 made a significant change in the treatment of passive losses from such investments. Passive losses may be used only to offset passive income.

Portfolio income. Portfolio income includes dividends, interest and net capital gains derived from the sale of securities.

Taxation of Portfolio Income

Dividends

Cash dividends. Cash dividends paid on corporate common and preferred stock are fully taxable at the same rate as earned income by federal, state and even some local governments.

Reinvested dividends. Cash dividends are included in the investor's taxable income, even if the investor chooses to use the cash dividends to purchase additional stock. Such dividends are said to be "constructively received." Thus, even if mutual fund dividends are automatically reinvested in the fund, taxpayers still owe taxes annually on them.

Stock dividends. Corporations sometimes distribute additional shares of stock to shareholders in the form of stock dividends. Because the shareholders cannot elect to receive cash, they have no tax liability on the value of the shares when received.

Interest Income

Interest paid on debt securities is income to the bond holder. It may or may not be taxable, depending on the type of security. Based on the doctrine of mutual reciprocity, there is a reciprocal agreement between governments. The federal government does not tax state and municipal issues. In turn, state and local governments usually do not tax federal securities. Further, the debt obligations of U.S. territories and political subdivisions (Puerto Rico, Guam, the Virgin Islands) are fully exempt from all taxation.

Corporate bonds. Interest income on corporate bonds is taxable by federal, state and some local governments.

U.S. government securities. Interest income on direct federal debt is exempt from state and local taxes, but is federally taxable. Direct debt includes U.S. Treasury bills, notes and bonds. The interest on T bills is the difference between the purchase price (below par) and the sale or maturity price.

Agency obligations. The interest income on most federal agency debt, like Treasury securities, is taxable by the federal government but exempt from state and local taxes. However, some agency issues are fully taxable at all levels; these include:

- mortgage-backed securities of the Government National Mortgage Association (Ginnie Maes);
- securities issued by the Federal National Mortgage Association (Fannie Maes); and
- securities of the Inter-American Development Bank (IADB).

Municipal securities. Interest income from state and municipal debt is exempt from federal taxes. In some states, interest from municipal bonds issued within the state is exempt from state taxes. Where this exemption applies, a state resident can receive interest income that is exempt from all taxes.

Interest expenses on municipal securities. In general, interest expenses incurred to purchase securities on margin are tax deductible. An exception is interest expense incurred to buy municipal bonds. Since the income generated by the bonds is tax free, the IRS will not allow taxpayers to claim a tax deduction for interest on the investment loan.

Capital Gains (and Losses)

The sale of capital assets (securities, real estate and all tangible property) can result in a capital gain or a capital loss. A capital gain occurs when the difference between a capital asset's purchase price and its selling price is positive. If the difference is negative, it is a capital loss.

To calculate tax liability, taxpayers must first add all capital gains for the year. Then, they separately add all capital losses. Finally, they offset the totals to determine the net capital gain or loss for the year.

Net capital gains and net capital losses. If the result is a net capital gain, it is fully taxable at the same rate as earned income. Net capital losses are deductible against earned income to a maximum of $3,000 per year. Any capital losses not deducted in a taxable year may be carried forward indefinitely to lower taxable income in future years.

Individual Federal Income Taxes

The basic design of the tax return is:

	Earned income
+	Passive income (net against passive losses)
+	Interest and dividends
+/-	Net capital gains or losses
	Adjusted Gross Income (AGI)
-	Itemized deductions
-	Standard deductions
-	Personal exemptions
	Taxable income
x	Tax rate
	Tax liability

Income Tax Brackets

The Tax Reform Act of 1986 (TRA 1986) defines two tax brackets: a 15% and 28% rate. Actually, the rates are more complex than this. In the past, the U.S. income tax tables have been structured so that successively earned portions of one's income are taxed at progressively higher rates. Thus, a married couple with a combined taxable income of $35,000 would pay 15% on the first $29,750 and 28% on the remaining $5,250 in income.

However, beginning in 1988, taxpayers with taxable income over a certain level will lose the benefit of the 15% rate on lower amounts of income. For married couples filing jointly, this is accomplished by imposing an additional tax of 5% on taxable income between $71,900 and $171,090. For an unmarried taxpayer, the 5% surtax applies to incomes between $43,150 and $100,480. After those levels, a flat 28% rate applies to all taxable income.

Margin Expenses

Interest paid for securities margin loans is a tax-deductible expense. The one exception is interest expenses incurred in the purchase of municipal securities. Since the interest income is federally tax-exempt, the IRS will not allow taxpayers to claim deductions for the interest expense on municipal securities.

Investors can deduct interest expenses for other securities to the extent they do not exceed their net investment income, which includes interest income, dividends and all capital gains. The previous $10,000 limit on investment expenses is being phased out. By 1991, only net investment income will determine the amount that can be deducted annually.

Interest and Dividend Income

Dividend income from mutual funds. As discussed previously, dividend income from equity securities and interest income from taxable bonds is taxed in the year it is received. Under Subchapter M of the IRC, a mutual fund may gain exemption from taxation on income if 90% of that income is passed on to shareholders. Owners of mutual fund shares receive "dividend" checks that represent the pass-through of dividends and interest earned on the underlying portfolio. The tax consequences depend on what type of securities are in the underlying portfolio.

- Municipal bond mutual funds or unit investment trusts distribute federally tax-free dividends to shareholders.
- Dividend distributions from taxable mutual funds (for example, a corporate bond fund or a stock fund) are taxable in the year they are received by the investor. Reinvested dividends are considered "constructively received" and are also taxable in the year they are distributed.

Interest income. Interest on corporate bonds is fully taxable by federal, state and local governments. Municipal bonds generate income that is federally tax-exempt, with some exceptions. The income from U.S. government securities and most agency securities is usually exempt from state and local taxes, but not federal taxes. Exceptions to this rule are securities issued by GNMA, FNMA and IADB that are fully taxable by all levels of government.

Accrued interest. Interest income includes accrued interest received when bonds are sold between interest payment dates. The trade confirmation will disclose two amounts: the market price for the bond and the amount of accrued interest. The accrued interest is taxable income to the seller. For tax reporting, the buyer deducts the amount of accrued interest paid the seller from the total interest received. This assures that the buyer is not double taxed on that amount.

Municipal bond interest. Interest on municipal bonds issued before August 7, 1986 and on municipal bonds with a public purpose issued after that date is exempt from federal taxes. Further, interest from municipal obligations of U.S. territories (such as Puerto Rico, Guam and the Virgin Islands) is exempt from federal, state and local taxes.

Interest on a municipal bond or note may or may not be taxable for residents of the state in which the bond is issued. The tax status of municipal securities depends upon the state statutes. This consideration underscores the importance of the legal opinion. Although most municipal bonds retain their tax-exempt status, under certain circumstances, municipal securities may be taxable.

Public purpose bonds are defined by the IRC as those municipal securities issued directly by state or local governments or their agencies to meet essential government functions such as highway construction or school financing. No more than 10% of the proceeds can be used by a private entity. Such bonds are federally tax-exempt. Thus, they are more attractive to tax-conscious investors than other municipal securities that may be taxed.

Private purpose bonds may be issued by states or municipalities to meet nonessential government functions. Although still federally tax-exempt for most taxpayers, the interest on such municipal securities is a tax preference item for the Alternative Minimum Tax (discussed later). These bonds may finance:

- single-family mortgages;
- multifamily housing;
- mass transit;
- student loans;
- water, sewer and solid waste disposal facilities; and
- airports, docks and wharves.

Taxable municipal securities may be issued to finance projects that Congress did not deem essential, such as sports arenas, convention centers, trade show facilities, pollution control, parking facilities and industrial parks. Since the interest income from such bonds is fully taxable for all taxpayers, they tend to pay higher yields than other municipal securities because they have to compete with corporate bonds.

Adjusting Cost Basis

The cost basis of an investment is used to determine whether there is a taxable gain or a tax-deductible loss when the asset is sold. Because many things affect the cost basis of an asset, the IRS allows the cost basis to be adjusted for such things as stock splits or stock dividends.

Capital gains. A capital gain occurs when capital assets (securities, real estate and tangible property) are sold at a price that exceeds the adjusted cost basis. Usually, computing the capital gain or loss on an asset is a simple matter of comparing the purchase price with the selling price (less commissions).

Capital losses. Before losses can be deducted against taxable income, they must be netted against capital gains. Only $3,000 worth of losses can be deducted annually by individuals or married couples. Excess amounts may be carried forward.

Determining which shares to sell. An investor holding identical securities with different acquisition dates and different cost bases may determine which shares to sell. The IRS presumes that the first securities purchased are the first sold (first in, first out, or FIFO) unless the investor specifically instructs them otherwise.

Wash sales. Capital losses may not be used to offset gains or income if the investor sells a security at a loss and purchases the same (or substantially identical) security within 30 days before or after the trade date establishing the loss. The sale at a loss and the repurchase within a 61-day period is a "wash sale."

Substantially identical securities include stock rights, call options, the sale of short-term deep in-the-money puts, warrants and convertible securities of the same issue. The IRS compares three qualities of municipal securities in determining whether they are substantially identical: the maturity, the coupon and the issuer. The bond is

See notebook

substantially identical if all three qualities of the bond sold at a loss and the newly purchased bond are the same.

The wash sale rule only applies to realized losses. It does not apply to a realized gain. You may sell a stock to realize a gain and immediately purchase it to reestablish your position.

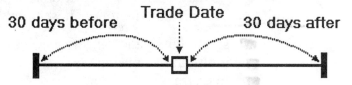

Wash Sale Rule

30 days before   Trade Date   30 days after

61 days in total including the trade date.

Fig. 14.1 The wash sale period covers 61 calendar days.

Adjusting Cost Basis on Equity Securities

Stock splits. Your client's total cost basis after a stock split remains the same. If a customer purchased 100 shares of MCS stock at $50 per share for a total cost basis of $5,000 ($50 x 100 shares), when MCS splits 2 for 1, he owns 200 shares of MCS at an adjusted cost basis of $25 per share, half of what it was originally. After the split, his total cost basis is the same as before, $5,000 ($25 x 200 shares). If he sells 100 shares in the market at $30 per share, he realizes a $5-per-share capital gain.

Stock dividends. The cost basis is not adjusted for cash dividends, but it is for stock dividends. If a customer initially bought 100 shares of TCBS for $20 per share and received a stock dividend of five shares, the new cost basis is the cost of the original shares ($2,000) divided by the new number of shares (105) or $19.05 per share. If these shares are then sold for $30 per share, she will have a capital gain of $10.95 per share.

Subscription rights. Rights involve no direct cost basis for the investor. If the rights are exercised, the cost basis for the new shares is their subscription price. However, since the rights do have value, if they are sold instead of exercised, a capital gain is incurred. The cost basis for the rights is zero.

Convertible securities. When a convertible security (either a bond or preferred stock) is converted, the original cost of the convertible security is the basis for the shares of common stock. That cost is divided by the number of shares received in conversion to obtain the cost basis per share.

Selling short against the box. The usual reason for selling short stock which the investor actually owns, called "selling short against the box," is to defer a capital gain from one year to the next. Investors do not have to report capital gains on short positions until settlement.

Mutual funds. In addition to dividend distributions (which are taxable in the year they are received), investors in mutual funds realize capital gains from two sources:

- **Distributions of capital gains passed through from the mutual fund**: taxable in the year they are distributed.
- **Gains or losses upon the sale of the shares of the mutual fund**: reported when the shares are sold. Any gain from the sale of shares is taxable in the year of the sale. Losses are deductible.

The exchange of fund shares within a family of funds is considered a sale and a purchase. Just as with shares of common stock, an investor in a mutual fund can determine which shares are sold. Unless otherwise identified, the IRS will assume that the first shares purchased are the first shares sold (FIFO accounting).

Adjusting Cost Basis of Debt Securities

Bonds may be bought at par, at a discount or at a premium. They also may be sold at par, at a discount or at a premium. Bonds will mature at par or be called at a premium. In any of these cases, capital gains or losses may be realized. An investor will not have a gain or loss on a bond if it is purchased at par and sold at par or held to maturity. Treatment of bonds bought at a premium or a discount depends upon the type of bond purchased.

Corporate bonds bought at a premium. Owners of corporate bonds bought at a premium may have two options:

- Amortize the premium annually, using a straight-line method, and deduct the amortized amount from their taxes. The cost basis of the bond is adjusted (lowered) by the amount of the premium that is amortized.
- Deduct the capital loss when the bond matures. The gain or loss upon sale of the bond is determined by the original cost basis.

Corporate bonds bought at a discount. The owner of a market discount corporate bond must accrete the discount on a straight- line basis. The basis is adjusted each year, but the income from the basis adjustment is earned at the time the bond is sold or matures.

Zero coupon bonds. Zero coupon bonds (sometimes referred to as Treasury receipts) are issued without coupons and do not pay semiannual interest. Instead, they are issued at deep discounts and the difference between the purchase price and the maturity price is considered interest income. The accrued interest is taxable each year even though it has not yet been received.

The IRS has the final determination of the acceptable amount of accrued interest to be taxed. The issuer informs the investor of that amount. The accreted interest increases the cost basis of the bond. If the bond is sold before the maturity date, the adjusted cost basis is used to determine any capital gain or loss.

Taxation of Options

Options are capital assets. Trading them involves capital gains and losses rather than ordinary income.

Option expires. An option that expires results in a capital loss for the person who paid a premium to buy it. The writer of the option, who received the premium, realizes a capital gain in that premium.

Position is closed. An option writer may decide to effect a "closing purchase," thereby ending the position of risk. An investor who originally purchased an option may wish to effect a "closing sale" and retrieve some or all of the original cost.

- A capital gain will result if the sale price of the option is greater than the purchase price. This is true even if the option was sold first and later purchased (closing purchase of a written option).
- A capital loss will result if the sale price is less than the purchase price of the option.

Option is exercised. Tax treatment of an option that is exercised is slightly more complicated than a straight capital gain or loss. When an option is exercised, one investor buys and the other sells the stock. The premium on the option affects the cost basis if the stock is being purchased or the sale proceeds if the stock is being sold.

When a call is exercised, the holder of the option buys the stock at the call's strike price. However, it also cost the investor the call premium for the right to purchase the stock at the strike price. The total cost basis on the stock, therefore, is the strike price plus the premium on the call.

A call writer has to deliver the stock at the strike price. They also received the call premium for taking the risk. The sale proceeds equals the strike price plus the call premium.

Exercising puts. When a put is exercised, the premium of the option is subtracted from the cost basis or sale proceeds of the stock.

Establishing gains or losses. When an option is exercised, you cannot automatically determine whether the investor has realized a capital gain or loss; further information is needed. If the stock is being sold through exercise, you need to know the original purchase price. If the stock is being purchased through exercise, you need to be told the price at which the investor later sells the stock.

NonEquity Option Taxation

One characteristic of nonequity options is unique. Investors holding non-equity options positions on December 31 are taxed as if the positions are closed out.

The following chart summarizes the tax consequences of options.

Investment Strategy	Option Expires	Option Exercised	Position Closed at Intrinsic Value
Buy a Call	Capital loss	Strike price + Premium = Cost basis	Capital gain or loss
Sell a Call	Capital gain	Strike price + Premium = Sale proceeds	Capital gain or loss
Buy a Put	Capital loss	Strike price - Premium = Sale proceeds	Capital gain or loss
Sell a Put	Capital gain	Strike price - premium = Cost basis	Capital gain or loss

Alternative Minimum Tax

Some taxpayers have been very successful in their use of the tax provisions to minimize taxes. For example, a person with $100,000 income from municipal bonds may incur no tax liability. To make certain that high-income taxpayers do not escape paying taxes, Congress enacted the Alternative Minimum Tax (AMT).

AMT for individuals. The AMT is a flat rate of 24%. To determine if an individual is subject to the AMT:

- add all preference items to the taxpayer's adjusted gross income;
- from this amount, subtract $40,000 (married filing jointly), $30,000 (single) or $20,000 (married filing separately);
- multiply this amount by a flat 24%. The result is the minimum tax liability. If the taxpayer's standard tax is less than this figure, the individual must pay the AMT.

Tax preference items. Certain preference items receive favorable tax treatment. These items must be added back into taxable income for the AMT, including:

- accelerated depreciation on property placed in service after 1986;
- certain costs associated with DPPs, such as research and development costs and intangible drilling costs;
- local tax and interest on investments that do not generate income;
- tax-exempt interest on private-purpose municipal bonds issued after August 7, 1986;
- untaxed appreciation on charitable contributions of appreciated property; and
- incentive stock options in excess of their fair market value.

Corporate Income Taxes

The Tax Reform Act of 1986 substantially lowered corporate tax rates to a maximum rate of 34% (from a previous maximum of 46%). At the same time, it reduced or eliminated some of the techniques that corporations have used in the past to reduce their tax burden including:

- repealing the Investment Tax Credit (ITC);
- lengthening depreciation schedules; and
- eliminating the favorable treatment of capital gains.

Provisions affecting corporate taxes. Corporations are major investors in securities. Some of the IRC provisions affecting corporations as investors include:

Dividends. Dividends paid from one corporation to another are 70% exempt from taxation. A corporation that receives dividends on stocks of other domestic corporations, therefore, pays taxes on only 30% of the dividends received. This provision encourages corporations to invest in common and preferred stock of other American corporations.

Municipal securities. As with individual taxpayers, corporations do not pay federal taxes on income received from municipal obligations. An exception is taxable municipal securities as discussed earlier.

IBM has

$1000 DIV on XRX

70% tax free

$300 taxable at 34% = $102

70% exclusion

Chapter Review

Questions

1. Which of the following bonds is totally tax-exempt?

    ____(A) Hawaii GO bonds
    ____(B) U.S. government bonds
    ____(C) Puerto Rico GO bonds
    ____(D) U.S. Steel bonds

2. Max Leveridge invests $5,000 in the following new issue:

    **OHIO
    GENERAL TELEPHONE COMPANY
    $20,000 9% debentures
    Price 97
    To yield 9.2%**

    The bonds are

    ____(A) federal and state tax-exempt.
    ____(B) state tax-exempt.
    ____(C) federal and state tax-exempt if purchased by an Ohio resident.
    ____(D) fully taxable.

3. Income from all the following securities is fully taxable at the federal, state and local levels EXCEPT

    ____(A) Ginnie Maes.
    ____(B) Treasury bonds.
    ____(C) reinvested mutual fund dividends.
    ____(D) IADB securities.

4. Losses from direct participation programs can be used to offset

    ____(A) earned income from salary or commissions.
    ____(B) portfolio income.
    ____(C) income from limited partnerships.
    ____(D) none of the above.

5. In September, an investor writes two ABC January 60 puts at 3. If the two ABC January 60 puts expire in January, what are the tax consequences for the writer?

____(A) $600 gain realized in September
____(B) $600 loss realized in September
____(C) $600 gain realized in January
____(D) $600 loss realized in January

handwritten: 2 × 300 = $600   Gain for writer
handwritten: $600   Loss for investor

6. January 1, an investor buys an XYZ Apr 50 call at 4 and an XYZ Apr 50 put at 2 1/2. Both options expire unexercised. What are the tax consequences?

____(A) $400 gain on the call, $250 gain on the put
____(B) $150 net capital gain
____(C) $150 net capital loss
____(D) $400 loss on the call, $250 loss on the put

handwritten: 400   250

7. Sally Smith buys 1 XYZ Oct 50 call at 3. She exercises the option to buy 100 shares when the market is at 60. What is the cost basis of the 100 shares?

____(A) $5,000
____(B) $5,300
____(C) $6,000
____(D) $6,300

handwritten: 5000 + 300 = $5300

8. A customer writes a July 50 put at 7. The put is exercised when the market price is 40. For tax purposes, what is the effective cost basis of the stock put to the writer?

____(A) 40
____(B) 43
____(C) 50
____(D) 57

handwritten: 50 − 7 = 43   14.10

9. Which of the following statements are true concerning the 1988 tax treatment of mutual funds?

I.   Dividend payments and capital gains distributions will not be subject to taxation as long as they are reinvested in the fund.
II. Dividend payments and capital gains are taxed at the same rate.
III. The IRS treats exchanging shares within the same family of funds as a sale and repurchase of securities.

____(A) I and II
____(B) I and III
____(C) II and III
____(D) I, II and III

10. Interest expense incurred to purchase which of the following types of securities is NOT federally tax-deductible?

____(A)   corporate bonds
____(B)   Treasury securities
____(C)   municipal bonds
____(D)   common stocks

Answer Key

1. C.

2. D.

3. B.

4. C.

5. C.

6. D.

7. B.

8. B.

9. C.

10. C.

Chapter Fifteen

Government Regulations

Key Terms

Government Regulation

The securities industry is regulated by legislation at the federal and state levels. Securities regulations are designed to protect investors by requiring proper disclosure of information and establishing procedures that safeguard against fraud and misrepresentation.

This chapter introduces the major pieces of federal legislation (the Securities Act of 1933 and the Securities Exchange Act of 1934) and later acts that expanded or amended these basic regulations.

The securities laws at the state level are known as the blue- sky laws. The Uniform Securities Act is model legislation which most states have adopted, with each state adapting the act to its specific requirements. The blue-sky laws deal with issues such as registration requirements for securities, broker-dealers and representatives.

The Securities Act of 1933

paper

The Securities Act of 1933 regulates new issues of corporate securities sold to the public. The act is also referred to as the Full Disclosure Act, the New Issues Act, the Truth in Securities Act and the Prospectus Act. It requires the registration of new issues (debt and equity) before they may be sold to the public. The main purpose of the act is to ensure that the investing public is fully informed about a security and its issuing company when it is first sold to the public. This act requires registration of new issues of nonexempt securities with the Securities Exchange Commission. It also requires that a prospectus (which contains information derived from the registration statement) be given to buyers.

When a corporation needs capital, it contacts an investment banker (underwriter) for help in raising the money. The underwriter (usually a broker-dealer firm with experience in selling new issues to the public) advises the corporation as to the type of security to issue. An agreement is signed between the issuer (the corporation) and the underwriter and the process begins.

The issuer of a security registers with the Securities and Exchange Commission (SEC) by filing a **registration statement**. This document describes the issuer's business and tells how the proceeds of the offering will be used. Technically, the issuer is the entity that files the registration statement with the SEC, but the underwriter, the expert at primary issues, generally does the actual writing of the registration statement and files the paperwork.

The filing of the registration statement starts the cooling-off period. For at least 20 days after filing, the issuer cannot sell the security to the public. During this time, the

SEC reviews the statement. If there are questions about its content, the SEC interrupts the cooling-off period by sending a deficiency letter to the underwriter. Because of delays caused by deficiency letters, the 20-day minimum cooling-off period usually lasts longer than 20 actual days.

When the SEC is satisfied with the content of the registration statement, the issue is released for sale to the public. The SEC does not approve or disapprove the securities and this fact must be displayed prominently on the prospectus.

The new issue must be registered in each state in which the underwriter wishes to sell securities. During the cooling-off period, the issue will be "blue skyed," the term applied to registration with state securities departments.

Prefiling Period

- Issuer identifies a need for capital.
- Issuer negotiates with an investment banker (underwriter) and signs an underwriting agreement.
- Underwriter, with input from issuer, prepares and files registration statement with the SEC.

Cooling-off Period

- Underwriting syndicate is formed.
- SEC reviews registration.
- SEC sends letter(s) of deficiency if warranted.
- Due diligence meetings are held.
- Red herrings are distributed.
- Indications of interest are taken.
- No actual sales may be confirmed.
- Underwriter blue-skys issue with states.
- NASD Committee on Corporate Finance reviews the planned spread.

Post-registration Period

- Brokers may confirm all indications of interest.
- Final prospectus must be sent or given to purchasers no later than when the confirmation is mailed.
- The corporation must deliver a prospectus with any sale of an exchange- or NASDAQ-listed security for 25 the first days after the effective date.

The Registration Process

Filing. The filing date (the day the issuer files the registration statement) marks the beginning of the cooling-off period, during which time the SEC reviews the statement. If the underwriter has not heard from the SEC during this period, the issue may be sold at the end of that time (although this seldom happens). The SEC will usually have questions about the content of the registration statement (or ask that corrections or clarifications be made) and will do this through a deficiency letter to the underwriter.

Because of the time it takes to make additions and corrections, the cooling-off period can in fact last several months. The SEC sometimes issues a "stop order" which demands that all underwriting activities cease. This may be done if requirements of the 1933 act have not been met or if fraud is suspected.

Cooling-off period. During a cooling-off period, the underwriter does several things. A syndicate is formed and a selling group is assembled. A preliminary prospectus (red herring) is circulated. Since the registration statement is still subject to change at this point, information contained in the red herring might also change. A notice to that effect must appear on the cover page of the preliminary prospectus. Although one of the primary purposes of the preliminary prospectus is to solicit indications of interest from investors, the preliminary prospectus will not state the price of the securities or the effective date of the offering. These two facts will not be known until immediately before the effective date.

Blue-skying the issue. In addition to being registered with the SEC, the issue must be registered with the securities commissions in each state where the underwriter wishes to sell. The state securities laws are called "blue-sky" laws. If the state securities commissions do not deny the registration, the security can be sold in each state where it was blue skyed when the SEC clears the issue. Filing a registration with various states concurrently with the SEC filing is called registration by coordination.

Due diligence meeting. Toward the end of the cooling-off period, the underwriter holds a due diligence meeting with everyone involved in the issue. Syndicate members, selling group members, all directors and partners of the issuer and any experts who contributed information to the registration statement look carefully at every aspect of the issue to be sure that everything in the registration statement is true and that important facts have not been omitted.

Effective date. The effective date of an issue is the first date on which the securities can be sold to the public. The syndicate members can then contact clients who had indicated an interest in the issue and confirm orders.

Final prospectus. The final prospectus must be delivered with each sale of a newly issued security. It must contain all the information that is found in Part I of the registration statement. Documentation of facts need not be included in the prospectus, but all information in this document must be up to date.

SEC disclaimer. One very important statement must appear on the front of every prospectus, the SEC disclaimer. The SEC disclaimer states that the SEC neither approves nor disapproves of the issue. It merely reviews the information in the registration statement and releases the issue for sale to the public.

The prospectus must be sent or given to purchasers of the issue at or before delivery of the confirmation. For new issues that are either exchange-listed or authorized for inclusion in the NASDAQ system, the prospectus must be delivered for the first 25 days after the effective date.

The Registration Statement

The registration statement must contain:

- a description of the issuer's business;
- the names and addresses of key people in the company, officers and directors, their salaries, and a five-year business history of each
- the amount of corporate securities owned by these key people and by owners of 10% or more of the company;
- the company's capitalization, including its equity and the amount of funded debt;
- a description of how the proceeds will be used; and
- whether the company is involved in any legal proceedings.

Exemptions from Registration

Exempt securities, issuers and transactions. The Securities Act of 1933 provides exemption from registration for *certain securities*. Securities of some *issuers* are exempt from registration. Some securities themselves do not need to be registered, and sometimes a nonexempt security (that is, a security which would ordinarily need to be registered when issued to the public) receives an exemption from registration because it is being sold in an exempt *transaction*.

Exempt issuers. Securities issued by *certain issuers* do not need to be registered with the SEC before they are sold to the public. Exempt issuers include:

- the federal government;
- states, counties, cities, etc. (issuers of municipal securities);
- domestic banks and trust companies;
- charitable organizations (benevolent associations);
- government agencies; and
- small business investment companies (SBICs).

Exempt securities. Certain types of *securities* that do not need to be registered include:

- commercial paper (maturing within 270 days of issuance); and
- bankers' acceptances (maturing within 270 days of issuance).

Exempt transactions. Exempt transactions include Regulation A offerings, intrastate offerings, private placements and restricted and control stock sold in compliance with SEC Rule 144.

Regulation A. A Regulation A offering allows an abbreviated type of registration for corporations raising a small amount of money. The costs of normal registration may be too high for such a small underwriting. In a Regulation A offering, no more than $1,500,000 can be raised in any 12-month period. An abbreviated registration statement is filed with the SEC, and the cooling-off period is only 10 days. An "offering circular" that is similar to, but not as detailed as a prospectus, must be distributed when Regulation A securities are sold.

Intrastate offerings (Rule 147). SEC Rule 147 stipulates that intrastate offerings are exempt under these provisions.

- The issuer must have its main office, be doing business in and have 80% of its assets in the state of issue.
- At least 80% of the proceeds of this issue must be used in the state.
- The underwriting broker-dealer must be a resident of the state.
- All of the purchasers must have their principal residence in the state. Moreover, purchasers of the issue may not sell these securities to any resident of another state for at least nine months after the close of the issue.

Regulation D (Private Placements). SEC Regulation D provides exemptions for private placements. Private placements are securities that have never been offered to the public that are placed with a small, select group of investors. They are exempt from registration and prospectus requirements of the Securities Act of 1933.

Rule 506 under Regulation D specifically provides an exemption from registration if the issue is sold to no more than 35 nonaccredited investors. An unlimited number of sales may be made to accredited investors (financial institutions or wealthy individuals, as defined by the rule). An accredited investor must have $1,000,000 in net worth or an annual income of $200,000.

The purchasers must have access to the same type of information as if the securities were being sold under prospectus in a registered offering. A private placement memorandum is supplied in place of a prospectus. The SEC must be notified of the private placement on Form D. There is no limit to the amount of capital that can be raised under Rule 506.

The purchaser in a private placement must sign a letter stating that she intends to hold the stock for investment purposes only. Private placement stock is referred to as lettered stock due to this investment letter. The certificate may bear a legend indicating that it cannot be transferred without registration or exemption (private placement stock is also referred to as legended stock).

Rule 144. Rule 144 regulates the sale of two types of securities: control securities and restricted securities. Stock which has not been registered is considered restricted stock. Rule 144 of the act stipulates the holding period, quantity limitations, manner of sale and filing procedures for restricted stock.

Control securities are owned by directors, officers or persons who own 10% or more of any type of outstanding securities of the company (or financially dependent relatives of such individuals). Restricted securities are those acquired through some means other than a registered public offering. A security purchased in a private placement is a restricted security.

notebook

Under SEC Rule 144, control securities and restricted securities can be exempted from full registration before they are sold to the public. The requirements for a sale of restricted stock under Rule 144 are:

- The securities must have been owned fully-paid for at least two years. If the securities were transferred, the new owner must own the securities for two years. In the case of a gift, the donor's holding period is added to the recipient's holding period. In case of an owner's death, the holding period is considered to be satisfied.
- Current financial information about the company must be made available to the buyer. This can be accomplished by verifying that the company is a "reporting company" which regularly files 10K and 10Q reports with the SEC.
- The person selling the securities files notice with the SEC on Form 144. The notice does not need to be filed if the sale is for less than 500 shares and less than $10,000 in value.
- The filing is effective for 90 days. If the sale has not been completed within that time (or the investor wants to sell additional shares), a new Form 144 must be filed.
- The sale of these securities cannot be advertised, no special promotion is allowed, no extra commission can be paid.
- If the securities were owned for three years or more, there is no volume limitation on the amount of restricted securities sold under Rule 144.
- If the securities were owned between two and three years, the volume of securities that can be sold is limited. The limit is the greater of 1% of all of the outstanding shares of the company or the average weekly trading volume for the preceding four weeks.

Restricted stock certificates bear a legend stating that the sale of those particular shares is restricted. When restricted stock is sold to the public in a 144 offering, that legend is removed in the transfer process.

For sale by "insiders" or sale of "control" stock, Rule 144 applies as follows:

- Corporate insiders are officers, directors or anyone who owns 10% or more of the outstanding shares of the company (or financially dependent relatives).
- If the insiders' securities are restricted (e.g., purchased in a private placement) the minimum two-year holding period applies. If the securities are not restricted, the two-year holding period does not apply. (Securities may become control securities by being purchased in the open market by a control person.)
- The volume limitation is the same as for non-insider-owned restricted stock: the greater of 1% of the outstanding shares of the company or the average weekly trading volume for the preceding four weeks.

All the other rules that apply to sales of restricted securities under Rule 144 apply to sales of securities by insiders.

Integration of offerings. The SEC may integrate (treat as one offering) any offerings by the same issuer made within a twelve-month period (beginning six months before and extending six months after the offering). An issuer who has a Regulation A offering and an intrastate offering within that time period may run the risk of the combined offerings canceling both exemptions.

Antifraud Provisions

Although a security might be exempt from the registration requirement (and regulations regarding disclosure of information), *no offering is exempt from the antifraud provisions* of the Securities Act of 1933. The antifraud or antimanipulation provisions of the act of 1933 apply to all new securities offerings, whether exempt from registration or not. Issuers must provide accurate information regarding any securities offered to the public.

The Securities Exchange Act of 1934

People

After the Securities Act of 1933 was enacted regulating primary issues of securities, attention turned to the need for regulation of secondary trading. The intent of the Securities Exchange Act of 1934 is to maintain a fair and orderly market for the investing public. It seeks to attain this goal by regulating the securities exchanges and the over-the-counter markets. Commonly called the Exchange Act, it formed the Securities and Exchange Commission (SEC) and gave the commission authority to oversee the securities markets and to register and regulate the exchanges.

According to the Securities Exchange Act of 1934, several other entities must also register with the SEC, including exchange members and broker-dealers who trade securities over-the-counter and on exchanges, and individuals who effect securities trades with the public.

The Securities Exchange Act of 1934, which has much greater breadth than the act of 1933, addressed:

- creation of the Securities and Exchange Commission;
- regulation of exchanges;
- regulation of credit by the Federal Reserve Board;
- registration of broker-dealers;
- regulation of insider transactions, short sales and proxies;
- regulation of trading activities;
- client account regulations;
- Customer Protection Rule;
- regulation of over-the-counter market; and
- Net Capital Rule.

The Securities and Exchange Commission

The SEC, created by the act of 1934, was given responsibility and authority to regulate the securities markets. The SEC is made up of five commissioners appointed by the president of the United States and approved by the Senate. One of the primary responsibilities of this group is to enforce the act of 1934.

The SEC has established rules regarding net capital requirements for broker-dealers, hypothecation of customers' securities, commingling of broker-dealer securities with those of customers, the use of manipulative and deceptive devices and broker-dealer recordkeeping. The SEC enforces the Securities Exchange Act of 1934 (and others) by providing rules and by prescribing penalties for violations.

Registration of Exchanges and Firms

Under the 1934 act, the national securities exchanges must file a registration statement. When they register, the exchanges agree to comply with and help enforce the rules of this act. Each exchange gives the SEC copies of its bylaws, constitution and articles of incorporation. Any amendments to rules must be disclosed as soon as they are adopted. The exchange must also institute and enforce disciplinary procedures for members who do not use just and equitable practices.

In addition to the registration of exchanges, the act of 1934 requires companies that list securities on those exchanges to register with the SEC. Each listed company must file quarterly and annual statements (Form 10Q and 10K, respectively) informing the SEC of its financial status (as well as other information).

Many firms with securities that are traded OTC must also register. Those with firms 500 or more shareholders and assets of $1,000,000 or more are required to do so. Exchange members who do business with the public must register as well as broker-dealers who do business over-the-counter or who use the mail (or telephone, TV, radio, etc.) to conduct their business.

The Maloney Act of 1938, an amendment to the Securities Exchange Act of 1934, permitted the establishment of a national securities association of broker-dealers transacting business in the over-the-counter market. According to the act, self-regulatory organizations such as the National Association of Securities Dealers (NASD) could be established and registered with the SEC.

There are also some exemptions from registration, including: small, local exchanges and any broker-dealers who deal only on an intrastate basis. An intrastate firm, however, cannot use the mail or other instruments of interstate commerce and still qualify for the exemption from registration.

Regulation of Credit

The act of 1934 empowered the Federal Reserve Board (FRB) to regulate margin accounts (that is, to regulate credit extended in the purchase of securities). Within FRB jurisdiction are:

- **Regulation T**: regulates the extension of credit by broker-dealers.
- **Regulation U**: deals with the extension of credit by banks.
- **Regulation G**: deals with the extension of credit by anyone else.
- **Regulation Q**: limits the rate of interest banks may pay on time deposits.

Regulation of Insider Transactions

An insider is any person who might have access to nonpublic information about a corporation. Insiders who own corporate securities must file a statement of ownership with the SEC. They may not use inside information for personal trading until that information has been made public. The SEC can levy a penalty of three times the amount of profit made (or loss avoided) if inside information is used. Short-swing profits (those occurring in six months or less) may not be retained by insiders, and can actually be reclaimed by the shareholders. Short sales or short-against-the-box positions are prohibited for insiders. Any trades of insider-owned securities are to be reported to the SEC within 10 days of the ~~trade~~ *end of the month that the trade took place.*

Regulation of Trading Activities

The activities of members of the national exchanges are regulated by the act of 1934. Members may not trade excessively for their own accounts since that would obstruct the maintenance of a fair and orderly market. Specialists on the exchanges are limited in their activities. Specialists must keep the contents of their books confidential. Only a few select officials of the exchange can see the contents, no one else.

Broker-dealers may effect a particular transaction as a broker (agent) or as a dealer (principal). They may act as either, but not both, in the same transaction. They cannot charge both a markup and a commission in the same trade. Any trading practice that manipulates the market or deceives the investing public is a violation of SEC regulations. Following are some of the act of 1934 and SEC rules concerned with manipulative practices:

- In order to prevent downward price manipulation, the SEC has ruled that short sales on exchanges can be made only on a plus tick (uptick) or zero-plus tick. Ticks refer to the prices of securities as their trades are reported on the tape. An uptick (or a plus tick) is a price that is higher than the last trade price. A zero-plus tick is the same price as the previous trade if the last change in price was an upward change.

			30 1/8	30 1/8			
30			30			30	30
	29 7/8						

Opening Sale	Down-Tick No Short Sales	Up-Tick Short Sale OK	Up-Tick Short Sale OK	Zero Plus Tick Short Sale OK	Down-Tick No Short Sales	Zero Down-Tick No Short Sales

Fig. 15.1 Short sales on up or zero-up ticks only.

- All sell orders must be designated "short" or "long." Arbitrage and odd-lot trades are exempt from the up tick rule, so tickets are marked short exempt.
- When a corporation makes a tender offer, only fully owned shares may be tendered.
- Anyone involved in a new issue of securities may not trade that company's already outstanding securities. Unsolicited orders from

customers are allowed. Stabilization of the issue during the under-writing is permitted.
- Matching, pegging and price fixing are prohibited.
- Manipulative or deceptive devices are prohibited. Such devices include enacting a series of trades in a security to make it appear as if it is actively traded, inducing the sale of a security through misleading statements, or giving out information about the actions of a person or group that might affect the price of the security.

Solicitation of Proxies

A proxy is the power of attorney given by a shareholder to another person (such as their broker-dealer or the issuing firm) which gives that person the right to vote for the shareholder. Stockholders may certainly vote their shares personally, but for those who own a fairly small number of shares, that is often impractical. The exchanges require listed companies to solicit proxies from shareholders, which ensures that all stockholders will have input into major company decisions.

Proxy solicitation is not required by the SEC, but if proxies *are* solicited, the SEC regulates the procedure. If a company solicits proxies, the SEC requires that it give information about the items that will be voted on. Before it sends out the proxies and the information, the company must allow the SEC to review the information. If, in a particular vote, control of a company is at stake (called a **proxy contest**), everyone who is a participant in the control struggle must register with the SEC. Also, anyone who is not a direct participant but who advises voters (**unsolicited advice**) must also register as a participant. All participants, actual or advisory, face criminal penalties if they fail to register.

Broker-dealers who merely answer customers' questions about a proxy contest are not considered participants.

Client Accounts

Broker-dealers may not open a margin account for customers without first disclosing to the customer the terms of the account, rate of interest, how interest is computed and conditions for charging interest. New issues (including mutual funds which, because of their continuous offering of securities, are considered new issues) may not be margined. After a customer has owned a security fully-paid for 30 days, it may be deposited in the margin account and used as collateral.

The Securities Exchange Act of 1934 also regulates the hypothecation of customers' securities. Since broker-dealers may not pledge or lend customers' securities without the customer's written consent, margin accounts must have the customer's signature. Also, the firm may not pledge more of a customer's securities than are needed to cover the loan from the bank for the margin account and may not pledge those securities for any purpose other than the client's loan.

Broker-dealers may not commingle customers' securities with those of the firm. Client securities in a margin account are held in street name, so the broker-dealer must keep meticulous records to ensure that they have accounted for all clients' margin securities.

Regulation of the Over-the-Counter Market

The Securities Exchange Act of 1934 also regulates the over-the- counter market. Broker-dealers who effect trades must register with the SEC. All registered broker-dealers have the responsibility of maintaining high standards of business conduct. They must be sure that recommendations to customers are suitable for those customers. The registered representative must inquire into the customer's financial needs, objectives, and means before recommending investments.

Every broker-dealer firm has the responsibility of supervising all associated persons. Each firm must have a written procedures manual and must designate a supervisor (principal) who is responsible for enforcing the rules in the manual.

The principal must review and approve all newly opened customer accounts and review and approve (indicating the approval by signing or initialing) every security transaction and all correspondence done by representatives. The principal must also review customer complaints.

All broker-dealers registered as over-the-counter firms must maintain customer records. Client account information includes the client's name, address, birthdate, citizenship, Social Security (or Tax I.D.) number, occupation, investment objectives and signature. The firm must keep records about all discretionary accounts, and the broker-dealer must keep on file all customer complaints and how they were handled.

The confirmation sent to customers before the completion of a trade (the settlement date) must inform the client if the firm acted as a broker or a dealer in that particular transaction. If it was an agency trade (the firm acted as a broker), the firm must reveal the amount of commission charged. When the firm acts as principal (dealer) it must disclose the amount of markup only if (1) the transaction was riskless and simultaneous, or if National Market System securities were involved or (2) exchange-listed securities were traded over-the-counter (the third market).

Excessive trading in discretionary accounts is forbidden. To monitor this, detailed reports of trades in discretionary accounts must be written after each trade and maintained in that client's records.

Net Capital Rule → *All broker/dealrs must be solvent.*

In order to ensure broker-dealer firms' solvency, the act of 1934 states that broker-dealers must maintain a certain level of net capital. A firm must not let its debts exceed 15 times its net capital. Also, customers who have cash in their accounts (a free credit balance) must be notified of this regularly (at least quarterly). That cash, as well as fully-paid securities, must be segregated and labeled as the customer's property.

Customer Protection Rule

The Customer Protection Rule (Rule 15c3-3) was written by the SEC in accordance with the Securities Exchange Act of 1934. The rule requires the following:

- A client's fully-paid securities and excess margin securities are to be segregated, actually physically set aside, and kept safely.
- Each firm must keep a reserve bank account for customers' funds.
- Securities sold by a client must be delivered within 10 business days after the settlement date. If delivery does not occur, the firm will close out that sale by "buying in" the same security to cover the undelivered certificate. In addition, in a dealer-to-dealer transaction, securities must be delivered to the contra-broker no later than 30 calendar days after settlement.

Other Federal Legislation

Regulation of the securities industry was further refined by legislation that expanded or amended the acts of 1933 and 1934. The information in this section highlights this legislation.

The Maloney Act of 1938. The Maloney Act of 1938 provided for the creation and registration with the SEC of a national securities association to regulate brokers and dealers not affiliated with an exchange. Under the provisions of this amendment, the National Association of Securities Dealers (NASD) was formed and is the only such organization currently registered with the SEC.

The Trust Indenture Act of 1939. The Trust Indenture Act of 1939 specifies that any corporate bond issue of over $2,000,000 and a maturity date more than nine months in the future must be issued with a trust indenture (a written agreement between the corporate issuer and the investors). The trust indenture contains certain covenants (or promises) that protect the bondholders. An independent trustee is appointed to ensure that the covenants are carried out; the independent trustee also participates in the drafting of the indenture. This law requires full disclosure of information in the indenture. Since this is usually a very large document, each investor does not receive a copy of the indenture, but is entitled to review a copy at the custodian bank where it is usually held.

The Investment Company Act of 1940. The purpose of the Investment Company Act of 1940 is to regulate investment companies in order to ensure that they adhere to specific rules and regulations, and to keep investors fully informed about investment company operations. The act regulates the issuance of investment company securities by setting standards for the organization and operation of investment companies, the pricing and public sale of the investments, and reporting requirements. The act is administered by the SEC. In order to comply with the act of 1940, investment companies wishing to sell their shares publicly must register with the SEC. The company must state its investment objectives in the registration statement (and in the prospectus).

An investment company, according to the act of 1940, is any company that invests and reinvests in securities. This includes an issuer that invests 40% or more of its total assets. An investment company is owned by 100 persons or more and makes a public offering of its securities. A registered investment company may not publicly offer its shares unless it has a net worth of at least $100,000.

Face-amount certificate companies. Face-amount certificates are purchased at less than face value. Upon maturity, the full face value of the certificate is paid in cash and the difference between the discount purchase amount and the maturity value is the interest earned.

Unit investment trusts. There are two types of unit investment trusts (UITs): fixed portfolio and nonfixed portfolio. A fixed UIT has a portfolio of securities that is professionally selected but not actively managed (that is, no changes are made in the fixed UIT portfolio). A typical fixed UIT will invest primarily in municipal bonds. The maturation of the last bond terminates the UIT.

A nonfixed unit investment trust is one in which the investment portfolio can be altered. The investor has certificates of ownership in the trust which, in turn, owns shares of the mutual fund (this is known as a participating trust). Participating trusts are generally referred to as plan companies.

Management companies. The third type of investment company is a **management investment company.** This type of investment company actively manages its portfolio by buying, selling and trading securities. There are two types of management companies: open-end (companies that make a continuous offering of their shares to the public) and closed-end (companies that make a single offering, and whose shares are traded on an exchange or over the counter after the offering closes). Both types can be either **diversified** or **nondiversified**.

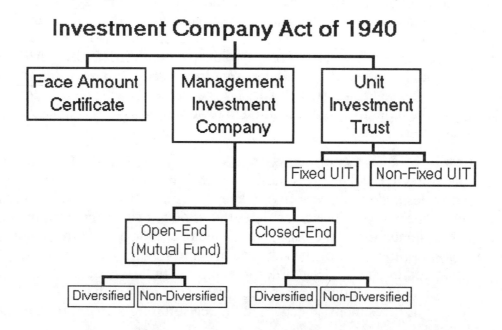

Fig. 15.2 The three types of investment companies.

Investment Advisers Act of 1940. This act requires that, if an individual is in the business of giving investment advice, actually gives such advice and charges a fee for the advice, he or she must register as an investment adviser.   *RIA licence*

Securities Investor Protection Act of 1970. The Securities Investor Protection Corporation (SIPC) was established in 1970 with the passage of the Securities Investor Protection Act. The purpose of the act is to protect the customers of securities firms that go bankrupt. SIPC is a nonprofit corporation, not a government agency, like the

Federal Deposit Insurance Corporation (FDIC) and the Federal Savings and Loan Insurance Corporation (FSLIC). Members include all broker-dealers registered under the Exchange Act of 1934, all members of national securities exchanges and most NASD members.

Each separate customer at a broker-dealer firm is covered for a maximum of $500,000 in securities and cash. Of that amount, up to $100,000 in cash is covered. Equity in margin accounts is covered up to $500,000. Commodities accounts are not covered. Customers with claims beyond $500,000 are treated as general creditors.

A person who has several accounts in her own name at one broker-dealer firm still has maximum coverage of $500,000 because the protection is $500,000 per *separate customer*, not per *account*. That customer could, however, have several accounts at one broker-dealer firm in different forms of ownership.

When a member firm is in financial trouble, SIPC requests that a federal district court appoint a trustee to supervise liquidation. The trustee's responsibilities include:

- supervising the orderly liquidation of the SIPC member;
- notifying clients of the liquidation; and
- returning clients' identifiable securities.

When notified, clients file a claim with the trustee to receive any money or securities due them.

Securities Acts Amendments of 1975. The Securities Acts Amendments of 1975 established the **Municipal Securities Rulemaking Board**. This board makes rules pertaining to the issuance and trading of municipal securities.

State Securities Regulations

In addition to federal securities regulations, each state has laws that pertain to the issuance of securities and to the trading of securities in the secondary market. State securities laws are known as blue-sky laws. The name "blue-sky" comes from a statement made by a U.S. Supreme Court justice who referred to "speculative schemes that have no more basis than so many feet of blue sky." The Uniform Securities Act serves as model legislation each state may follow or adapt to its own needs.

Most states require that broker-dealers who do business in a particular state must register with that state's securities commission. Salespeople associated with a broker-dealer must also be registered in the state (or states) where they do business.

Several states require that broker-dealers have a minimum net capital. In many states, broker-dealers must post fidelity bonds. The state securities administrators have the power to revoke the registration of a broker-dealer or the license of a registered representative if the firm or the representative has violated any of that state's securities laws.

In most states, securities must be registered before they can be sold to the public. There are three ways to register a security in a state.

- **Coordination.** This is the method used most often when securities are newly issued. At the same time the issuer files with the SEC, it files with the state. Registration in the state is automatically effective when the federal filing becomes effective.
- **Notification.** If an issuer meets certain criteria, it can notify the state that it is about to sell a security. If the state does not reply, the registration is effective on the second full business day after the filing.
- **Qualification.** If an issue cannot be registered by either coordination or notification, it might be registered by qualification. The issuer, in this case, would file with the state a registration statement that meets the state's requirements. This type of registration becomes effective when so ordered by the state securities administration.

The types of securities and transactions exempt from state securities registration requirements are similar to those exempt from SEC registration. The list includes:

- securities listed on SEC-registered stock exchanges;
- nonprofit organizations;
- insurance companies;
- banks;
- building and loan associations;
- public utilities and railroads;
- cooperative associations; and
- private placements.

Under blue-sky laws, most states require that all advertising be submitted for approval to the state securities administration.

Chapter Review

Questions

1. The Securities Act of 1933

   I. requires registration of exchanges.
   II. is called the "Truth in Securities Act."
   III. requires full and fair disclosure.
   IV. requires that debt securities be issued with a trust indenture.

   ____(A)   I and II
   ____(B)   I and III
   __·_(C)   II and III
   ____(D)   I, II and IV

2. The Securities Exchange Commission, under the Securities Act of 1933, has authority to

   I. issue stop orders.
   II. approve new issues.
   III. review prospectuses.

   ____(A)   I
   ____(B)   II
   __·_(C)   I and III
   ____(D)   I, II and III

3. In the time before a registration statement becomes effective, which of the following would be true statements?

   I. No sales may be solicited.
   II. Sales literature may not be used.
   III. Unsolicited inquiries may be answered.

   ____(A)   I and II
   ____(B)   I and III
   ____(C)   III
   __·_(D)   I, II and III

4. Which of the following are considered nonexempt offerings under the Securities Act of 1933?

  I. government securities
  II. a private placement
  III. a public offering of $2,000,000 by a brokerage firm
  IV. a sale of $5,000,000 of corporate bonds

  ____(A)   I and II
  ____(B)   I and III
  ____(C)   III and IV
  ____(D)   II, III and IV

5. Under the intrastate offering rule (Rule 147), when may a resident purchaser of the securities resell them to nonresidents?

  ____(A)   three months after the first sale made in that state
  ____(B)   six months after the last sale made in that state
  ____(C)   nine months after the first sale made in that state
  ____(D)   none of the above

6. The sale of securities in most states is regulated by

  ____(A)   interstate commerce law.
  ____(B)   intrastate commerce law
  ____(C)   blue laws.
  ____(D)   blue-sky laws.

7. Full disclosure of all material information about securities offered for the first time to the public is required by the

  ____(A)   Securities Exchange Act of 1934.
  ____(B)   Trust Indenture Act of 1939.
  ____(C)   Securities Investor Protection Act of 1970.
  ____(D)   Securities Act of 1933.

8. The provisions of the Securities Act of 1933 include

  I. regulation of offerings of new securities;
  II. prohibition of fraud in the sale of new securities;
  III. full and fair disclosure of information;
  IV. regulation of insider trading.

  ____(A)   I
  ____(B)   II and III
  ____(C)   I, II and III
  ____(D)   I, II, III and IV

9. Under the Securities Exchange Act of 1934, the SEC does which of the following?

   I.   regulates securities exchanges
   II. requires the registration of brokers and dealers
   III. prohibits inequitable and unfair trade practices
   IV. regulates over-the-counter markets

   ____(A)   I and II
   ____(B)   I and IV
   ____(C)   II, III and IV
   ____(D)   I, II, III and IV

10. The Securities Exchange Act of 1934 has some sections that deal with

   I.   regulation of investment companies.
   II. trading activities such as short sales, stabilizing and the registration of over-the-counter brokers and dealers.
   III. the form and content of the prospectus that must be given to all prospective purchasers of a security.
   IV. registration of persons engaged in the business of advising others about investment company transactions.

   ____(A)   I and II
   ____(B)   II
   ____(C)   II and IV
   ____(D)   I, II, III and IV

Chapter Review

Answer Key

1. C.

2. C.

3. D.

4. C.

5. D.

6. D.

7. D.

8. C.

9. D.

10. B.

Chapter Sixteen

Self-Regulatory Organizations

Key Terms

Self-Regulatory Organizations

National Association of Securities Dealers (NASD)

The National Association of Securities Dealers (NASD) was formed when the securities industry recognized a need for an organization that would provide standards and guidelines for the industry and would also provide self-discipline. As an amendment to the 1934 Securities Exchange Act, the Maloney Act of 1938 permitted the establishment of the NASD as a self-regulatory organization overseeing broker-dealers transacting business in the over-the-counter market.

The purposes of the NASD are to promote the securities business, standardize business practices, encourage high standards of honor and encourage self-discipline among member firms. The NASD has adopted the Rules of Fair Practice, which promote just and equitable principles of trade in order to protect investors.

To fulfill its role as a regulatory body, the NASD has outlined its policies in the *NASD Manual*. The manual describes four sets of basic rules and codes by which the OTC market is regulated.

First, the Rules of Fair Practice present guidelines on how a member firm should deal with the public. Second, the Uniform Practice Code establishes trade practices for broker-dealers as they do business with other member broker-dealer firms. Third, the Code of Procedure tells how to handle violations of NASD regulations. Fourth, the Code of Arbitration describes the method for handling disputes between member firms, registered representatives and the investing public.

National Association of Securities Dealers

Rules of Fair Practice	Code of Procedure	Uniform Practice Code	Code of Arbitration
Fair and ethical trade practices which must be followed by member firms and their representatives when dealing with the public.	How the NASD hears and handles member violations of the Rules of Fair Practice.	Established the *Uniform Trade Practices*, including settlement, good delivery, ex-dates, confirmations, DK procedures, etc.	Resolution of disagreements and claims between members, registered reps and the public. Addresses monetary claims, not violations of the Rules of Fair Practice.

[handwritten annotations: "fair to customer", "COP violators", "Same practice", "baseball players"]

Registration. The NASD by-laws define the powers of the NASD and list the registration and membership requirements for broker-dealers, principals and registered representatives. Any person who effects transactions in securities as a broker, a dealer or investment banker may register with the NASD. Qualification examinations are required for individuals who want to be principals or representatives with a member firm.

Certain circumstances can disqualify one from registration. If an individual has been suspended or expelled from another securities association or a national exchange, registration will be denied with the NASD. If the SEC has revoked or suspended a broker-dealer's license, or if a person has been convicted of a securities crime within the past ten years, the NASD will refuse registration.

NASD member firms must register each branch office when it opens and inform the NASD if a branch closes. Those individuals who act as managers, supervisors or trainers in a member firm must pass an examination and register with the NASD in their managerial (supervisory, training, officer, etc.) capacity.

People "associated with" a member firm and who trade securities for it must also register with the NASD through the employer broker-dealer firm. Registered representatives must also pass a qualifying examination before their registration is in force.

Some individuals employed with a member firm are not required to register. Persons whose function is clerical or administrative need not register. Someone employed by a broker-dealer firm trading only on a national exchange and registered with that exchange does not need to register with the NASD. Foreign employees are also exempt if they do all of their business outside the U.S with non-U.S. citizens.

A registered representative may terminate his or her registration by submitting a written resignation. The resignation is not effective for 30 days after it is submitted. If a representative wishes to work for a different broker-dealer firm, she or he must terminate registration with the old company (on a U-5 form) and apply again for registration through the new member firm (on a U-4 form for Series 7).

An individual must be registered in order to sell most nonexempt securities. Persons not registered may not receive commissions on securities sales. A registered representative who leaves a member firm (upon retirement, for example) may continue to receive commissions on business she or he had placed while employed. There must, however, be a contract to this effect before the representative leaves the firm. Heirs of a deceased representative may also receive continuing commissions on business placed by the representative if a contract exists.

Assessments. The NASD is self-supporting. It assesses member firms' registered reps and applicants to raise money to meet its expenses. The NASD's Board of Governors determines the amount of assessments, which is subject to change.

Districts. The NASD has divided the United States into 13 districts in order to facilitate operation. Each district elects a District Committee to administer the NASD codes and rules. A Committee has a maximum of 12 members who serve for three years.

Each year a District Business Conduct Committee (DBCC) is appointed by each District Committee. This group handles the trade practice complaints that may arise in each district. On the national level, the Executive Committee of the NASD, made up of members of the Board of Governors, manages the NASD affairs between meetings of the Board.

The Rules of Fair Practice

The NASD drafted the Rules of Fair Practice as a comprehensive set of guidelines and rules that require member firms (and registered representatives) to use just and equitable practices of trade. The main goals of the Rules of Fair Practice are to protect the customer by preventing fraud, market manipulation and unreasonable charges and commissions.

Advertising and sales literature. It is important to know the difference between advertising and sales literature as determined by the NASD Rules of Fair Practice. **Advertising** is any material published for or distributed through a *public medium* (such as newspapers, magazines, billboards, radio, television or telephone directories. The broker-dealer has *little or no control* over who ultimately sees a message published or broadcast in this public manner. **Sales literature** is any written communication that *does not meet the definition of advertising* (such as circulars, research reports, market letters, form letters, options worksheets, reprints of articles and seminar texts). The assumption in this case is that the broker-dealer has *some type of control* over who will ultimately see these communications.

Filing requirements. For one year after attaining NASD membership, broker-dealers are required to file advertising (but *not* sales literature) with the NASD at least 10 days *prior* to use. After this one year period, members no longer need to send their advertising to the NASD before it is issued, but must keep a file of all advertising and sales literature, indicating who prepared the material and which principal approved it. The DBCC can require a broker-dealer to continue filing advertising and/or sales literature before use even if it previously fulfilled the 12-month filing requirement.

Investment company advetising and sales literature. Advertising and sales literature for investment companies is governed by a slightly different rule. Underwriters of investment companies must file all material (not just advertising) *within* 10 days of first use. There is no 12-month rule here.

Option advertising. Advertising that pertains to options must be filed at least ten days *prior* to use unless it has been filed with another registered exchange or SRO.

Pricing OTC trades. The Rules of Fair Practice require member firms to obtain the best possible interdealer securities price for their customers (lowest buy price or highest sell price).

Receipt and delivery. When a representative takes a customer's order to purchase securities, the representative must inquire and be assured that the customer does agree to receive the securities and will pay for them at the price agreed upon. When a representative accepts a sell order from a customer, the representative must inquire and be assured that the customer has the security (in a "long" position) and can deliver it within five business days of the trade. If the security is being held in street name at another firm, the rep must verify that it is being held there before executing any sell transaction for the customer.

Forwarding information. Member firms must forward all securities-related information and proxy material received from the issuer or others to customers holding securities in street name with the member.

Free riding and withholding. When a member firm participates in a new issue distribution, the Rules of Fair Practice state that the member must make a bona fide offering at the public offering price. Failure to do so is considered **free riding and withholding**. In addition, the member may not sell part of a hot issue to any officer, partner, director or employee of the firm or to a family member of one. (Family members include spouse, parents, parents-in-law, brothers, sisters, brother- or sister-in-law, children or any relative who is economically dependent on the person associated with the member firm.)

Classified accounts. Certain other accounts holders (known as **classified accounts**) are also prohibited from purchasing a hot issue. This includes *employees* (and immediate families) of banks, insurance companies or any institution that buys and sells securities. *Directors and officers* of banks and insurance companies are not considered employees, and therefore do not fall into the category of classified accounts. Finders and those acting in a fiduciary capacity for the underwriter (attorneys and accountants) are also in the classified account group.

Exceptions. There are exceptions to the free riding and withholding rule for classified accounts. If the account (1) has a *history* of regularly buying newly-issued securities from this member firm, (2) the purchase is *comparable* in size to the normal investment practice of that account, and (3) the purchase is *insubstantial* in amount when compared to the offering as a whole, then the purchase of the hot issue would be allowed.

Recommendations to customers. The Rules of Fair Practice state that members must inquire into a customer's financial situation before making any recommendation to purchase, sell or exchange securities. The representative must determine such things as the client's other security holdings, income, expenses, financial goals and objectives. The following activities are violations of the Rules of Fair Practice:

- recommending speculative securities without finding out the customer's financial situation and being assured that the customer can bear the risk;
- excessive trading (churning) in a customer's account (whether the account is discretionary or not);
- short-term trading of mutual funds;

- setting up fictitious accounts to transact business that would otherwise be prohibited;
- making unauthorized transactions or unauthorized use of funds;
- recommending purchases that are inconsistent with the customer's ability to pay; and
- committing fraudulent acts (forgery, omission or misstatement of material facts).

NASD 5% markup policy. When the member is acting as a dealer in the over-the-counter market, the NASD has a general policy that a 5% markup (or markdown, when the customer sells securities) is acceptable. Certain factors may influence that policy:

NASD Mark-up (Mark-down) Policy

Relevant factors	Markups or mark-downs are generally higher for:	Markups or markdowns are generally lower for:
Type of security	Stocks	Bonds
Availability of security	Closely held or thinly traded securities	Actively traded or securities with a large float
Price of security	Low-priced	High-priced
Amount of money involved	Small dollar amounts	Large dollar amounts
Nature of member's business	Full service	No service

When a member acts as an agent (broker) the commission or service charge must be fair. The broker must take into account the market conditions at the time, the expense involved in making the trade (for example, difficultly in finding a buyer or seller for the other side of the trade) and the value of the member firm's service and experience.

If the amount of a markup is disclosed to the client before a transaction, the disclosure itself cannot be used to justify an excessive markup, but it will be a factor to be considered. (The NASD markup policy does not apply to prospectus offerings, that is, new issues of corporate securities and open-end investment companies.) Each transaction must be fair, but if a broker were to show a pattern of charging excessive markups, that might weigh against him.

The NASD markup policy also refers to riskless and simultaneous transactions. When a member purchases a security to fill an existing buy order from a customer, a riskless and simultaneous transaction has taken place. The member could have acted as an agent, charging a commission, but chose to act as a principal instead. In this case, the markup must be revealed to the customer.

When the member firm sells a security from its inventory, the markup must be based on the current market price, not on the price the member paid for it. In addition, when a firm buys a security from a customer, the markdown must be reasonable and based on current market price.

The member's charges for services such as safekeeping or transferring securities or collecting dividends must be reasonable and not discriminate unfairly between customers.

Reports of transactions and quotations. The Rules of Fair Practice mandate that only bona fide transactions can be reported. Any quotes given must represent a real bid or offer. No fictitious quotes are allowed. When a member or a representative makes a firm quote, that quote must be honored. A refusal to honor a firm quote is known as **backing away**, and is a prohibited practice. The member must be willing to trade at least one round lot of the security at the quoted price. All dealer quotes needn't be firm, however. Any quote can be subject to negotiation, but if it is, it must be clearly designated as "subject."

Confirmations. On confirmations sent to customers, the firm must disclose for each transaction whether it acted as a broker (agent) or a dealer (principal). A member may not act as both broker and dealer in the same transaction.

Control disclosure. If a member has a control relationship with the issuer of a security, that fact must be disclosed to customers before a transaction occurs.

Gifts and Gratuities

Shearson recommending AMEX (control)

Influencing employees of others. Members may not give business-related gifts valued in excess of **$50 per year** to employees of other member firms. This is intended to prevent a firm from using cash or gifts to unduly influence another firm's employees. Forms of entertainment that are tax deductible are allowable. Occasional meals or tickets to concerts or sports events are acceptable if the gift is business-related; season tickets are not.

NASD

Discretionary Accounts

A registered representative must have prior written authority from the customer before entering discretionary trades in that customer's account. All discretionary orders are to be promptly approved in writing by the principal and the accounts frequently reviewed by a principal of the member to prevent churning.

Customer Securities

Member firms may not lend a client's securities without written authorization and the firm may not hypothecate more of a customer's securities than is necessary to cover the customer's debt.

Members and representatives must not guarantee the customer against loss. They may not share in profits or losses of the customer's account. (In a preapproved joint account with a customer, a registered representative may share in the profits and losses in proportion to his contribution to the account.)

Member firms may deal with each other on a net basis. They may do trades with each other at less than the public offering price. At no time, however, may they deal with nonmembers (public customers or nonregistered broker-dealers) at any price less than the public offering price.

Investment Companies

The maximum sales charge for open accounts, (or single payment investment plans) is 8 1/2% of the public offering price. For an investment company underwriter to charge the maximum sales charge, the fund must offer reinvestment of dividends at net asset value (no sales charge), quantity discounts (breakpoints), and rights of accumulation.

The public offering price must be calculated as described in the prospectus. The underwriter can purchase shares of the open-end investment company only to fill customer orders, not for the underwriter's inventory.

The manager of the mutual fund must select a broker-dealer to execute portfolio transactions according to the broker-dealer's performance in that capacity. The broker-dealer's record of the mutual fund's sales should not influence the fund's manager in selecting a broker-dealer.

Supervision. Each member firm must have written procedures for supervision of associated persons. Every firm must designate a principal (a partner, officer or manager) to carry out the written procedures. The principal must review and approve all correspondence and keep a record of all securities transactions and correspondence. The member must regularly review the activities of all branch offices.

A person associated with a member must notify the employer broker-dealer in writing before participating in any private securities transactions. The registered representative must furnish the employer with duplicate offering documents. The employer broker-dealer is responsible for due diligence if consenting to private transactions of the registered representative.

If a registered rep opens an account with a broker-dealer other than his employer, the rep must (1) notify his own employer that he is opening the account and (2) tell the broker-dealer with whom the account is being opened that he is a rep with another firm. The opening broker-dealer is also responsible for informing the employing broker-dealer and must offer to send duplicate confirmations to the employer if it so requests.

Variable annuities. Sales charges for variable annuities must be reasonable. The variable annuity must sell shares on the forward pricing basis, where the price offered to the public is the price next calculated after the receipt of the order. Members may sell variable annuities only if the issuing insurance company agrees to promptly redeem the accumulation units as requested by the customer.

The Uniform Practice Code

The Uniform Practice Code standardizes trading practices among members of the NASD. All transactions done over the counter are subject to the code, unless all parties involved agree to suspend it. The Uniform Practice Code addresses itself to dealings among member firms, not dealings with the public.

Delivery of securities. For trades between broker-dealers, securities are delivered on the day of the transaction in a cash trade, on the fifth business day after the transaction for most securities and on the next business day for government securities in regular-way transactions. For seller's option trades, delivery is at expiration of a predetermined time period. The option can expire between six business days (two business days for U.S. government securities) and 60 calendar days after the trade. Buyers' option trades deliver on the day the option expires. For when-, as- and if-issued securities, delivery can take place on the day after the transaction, unless otherwise stipulated by the National Uniform Practice Committee.

Confirmations. Each broker-dealer sends to the other a confirmation (or comparison) of each trade. In a cash trade, the Uniform Comparison or Confirmation forms are exchanged on the day of the trade. In a regular-way trade they are sent no later than the business day after the transaction. In cash trades, they must be exchanged on the day of the trade. When trades between broker-dealers do not match, a "DK" ("Don't Know") form is sent. If a DK is sent, the broker-dealers involved find the error and correct it.

Good delivery. A unit of delivery for stock is 100 shares. Odd lots are considered good delivery if they total the exact number of shares sold, up to 100 shares. Securities must be in good, readable condition, and the certificates must be properly signed.

If the security is sold before an ex-date but for some reason will be delivered after the record date (for example, with seller's option), a due bill must be attached to the new certificate. A due bill is a printed statement showing the obligation of the seller to deliver securities, rights or cash to the purchaser. The seller pays transfer fees in most cases.

If the seller fails to deliver the security on time, the broker-dealer will buy the security in the open market to fulfill the seller's contract. The seller will be charged for the purchase price and all expenses related to the buy-in.

If the buyer does not pay for the securities on time or refuses to accept delivery without good cause, the broker-dealer will sell out those securities on the open market. Any losses and expenses for the sale will be charged to the buyer.

The Code of Arbitration

The Code of Arbitration provides procedures for settling disputes, claims and controversies that arise between broker-dealers, registered representatives and the public. Disputes handled through arbitration do not involve violations of regulations. If a dispute involves a public customer, the customer's written consent is necessary in order to bring the matter to arbitration. No written consent is necessary for arbitration of disagreements between people in the securities industry.

If the dispute is about an amount of $5,000 or less, it is handled by one arbitrator. Claims of $10,000 or less are heard by a panel of three arbitrators. All decisions are final; there is no appeal. Any awards made by the arbitrator must be settled within 30 days of the decision.

The Code of Procedure

Regular complaint procedure. The Code of Procedure outlines the method for handling trade practice complaints when a violation of the Rules of Fair Practice is involved. Under the Regular Complaint Procedure, the dispute is first heard by the District Business Conduct Committee (DBCC). The maximum penalty for each violation is $15,000 and a possible revocation or suspension of one's registration. Any decision of the DBCC may be appealed to the NASD Board of Governors within 15 days of the original decision. Further appeals can be taken to the SEC. Final appeal can be made to the federal courts.

Summary complaint procedure. When the Rules of Fair Practice have been broken, but no serious damage caused, this procedure must be offered by the DBCC and accepted by all parties involved. There is no hearing and no appeal. The NASD Board of Governors automatically reviews these cases. The maximum penalty is censure and/or a $2,500 fine.

Under the settlement procedure, the respondent (the party complained against) may submit a written offer of a way to settle the dispute. The offer must contain a proposed penalty that should be consistent with the violation. If the offer is accepted, it becomes effective immediately and there is no appeal.

The New York Stock Exchange (NYSE)

The New York Stock Exchange (NYSE) provides a central location at which its members can transact the business of buying and selling securities. The purpose of the NYSE is to maintain high standards of integrity among its members, who are governed by a comprehensive set of rules which promote principles of fair trade.

The New York Stock Exchange is governed by a board of directors consisting of 10 exchange members, 10 public representatives and one chairman. A member of the exchange is an individual registered with the exchange as a "member" and whose business is effecting securities trades on the floor of the exchange. Only members can effect trades on the floor of the exchange. A member firm is a company in the securities business that has at least one principal officer who is a member of the exchange. A member corporation is a member firm that is incorporated. An allied member is a person who is either a partner of a member firm or an executive officer of a member corporation or an owner of 5% or more of the stock of a member corporation. An allied member does not trade on the floor of the exchange.

There are 1,366 exchange members. Membership can be transferred from one person to another with the approval of the board of directors. There are an unlimited number of allied memberships; they are not transferable.

Registration of employees. All employees of NYSE member firms must be registered through their firm with the NYSE. The exchange can deny registration to unacceptable applicants. Registered reps who work for a member firm must exhibit high standards of business conduct and integrity, must pass an examination and must have reached the age of majority. A registered rep solicits orders from clients for the purchase and sale of securities. A registered rep cannot be employed in name only. The rep must have the intention of building a real clientele. Registered reps must, in most cases, work full-time for the firm. A part-time association might be permissible only if that arrangement would not be contrary to the public interest.

Registered reps must sign statements agreeing to abide by certain regulations. A person who wishes to become a registered representative must give the exchange a history of employment and other information. He or she must agree to read the NYSE constitution and regulations and abide by them. The prospective representative agrees to appear before committees as requested and to notify the exchange of any securities-related litigation in which he or she might become involved. The representative agrees to submit to arbitration if it should be required because of a dispute.

A prospective rep also agrees not to guarantee any customer against loss, share in a client's profits or losses, or rebate commissions. The representative can receive compensation for securities transactions only from his or her employer. Permission from the exchange is needed in order to be paid by any other firm for securities trades.

Registered representatives can be paid a salary or a commission. Bonuses are allowed with exchange approval. Department heads may share in the member firm's net profit if the exchange approves of the arrangement.

Gifts from other members to a registered rep are allowed as long as their value is $50 or less yearly. A registered rep can accept a gift from a client if it is the customary practice of that client.

A registered rep may voluntarily terminate employment by notifying the Department of Member Firms on a U-5 form and stating the reason for leaving. Transfer of registration is not permitted; a rep must resign from one employer and reapply for registration with the new firm.

Communication with the public. Any communication with the public that promotes securities trading is regulated by the exchange. Advertising, sales literature, market letters and research reports are all covered by these rules.

Communications must be truthful and in good taste. Recommendations must have a reasonable basis. If a purchase or sale of a security is recommended, the current market price must be given. If a member firm has a special interest in a security it recommends, that fact must be disclosed. For example, if the firm makes a market in a security, it has a special interest.

Past records of a security can be used to promote its sale if at least one year's history is shown and if it is stated that the past is no indication or guarantee of future performance. A testimonial is an individual's statement about his or her experience with a particular product or investment. A testimonial must be accompanied by the statement that this represents only the experience of the person making the statement and that others may not experience the same results. If the testimonial is paid for, that must be disclosed. Any projections must be labeled as estimates of future performance.

All communications with the general public must be approved by a principal of the member organization before use and kept on file with the broker-dealer for at least **three years**. Research reports must be approved by a Supervisory Analyst.

A registered representative must have prior approval from his or her employer before speaking at a seminar or lecture. The content of a speaking program must adhere to the same standards as those of a written communication. The talk should be truthful, in good taste and free of exaggerated claims.

NYSE "Know Your Customer" rule. When a registered rep (RR) opens an account for a client, the RR must learn the client's financial situation and investment objectives. The New York Stock Exchange regulates the many different types of accounts for the benefit and protection of public investors.

Accounts cannot be opened for a third party. A person can open an account for himself and give power of attorney to someone else. An adult can open an account for a minor with the minor as beneficial owner. An adult cannot open an account for another adult, nor trade for the account of another (even a spouse), without a power of attorney.

[handwritten margin notes: Seminars script on hand for 3yrs *;* Rule 405 *]*

If a customer wants to keep his securities trades confidential, he may have a "designated account" assigned a number or letter rather than a name. This is permitted if the member has on file a signed statement from the customer claiming ownership of that account.

In a "street name" account, although the customer actually owns the securities involved, the name of the broker-dealer is on the certificate. The customer is the beneficial owner of the securities and has all of the rights of ownership. The member firm must give all dividends and interest to the client and forward all proxies to the client so he can exercise his right to vote. If the client waives his right to vote (by not returning or returning a blank proxy), the member firm can then exercise that right.

Opening accounts for members. If an employee of a member firm wants to open a personal trading account with another member firm, the employee must have written permission from his or her current employer. Duplicate confirmations must be sent to the employer on request. An employee of the Exchange (not a member firm) must have the employer's written permission, but duplicate confirmations do not have to be sent. An employee of a bank or insurance company needs the employer's permission only when opening a margin account. Duplicate confirmations are not required to be mailed to the employer.

Employed by:	Permission needed to open a cash account?	Permission needed to open a margin account?	Duplicate confirms required?
Member organizations	Yes	Yes	Yes
The NYSE	Yes	Yes	No
Nonmember financial institutions (banks, insurance companies, etc.)	No	Yes	No

Exceptions to the requirement for employer's permission. An officer of a nonmember financial institution such as a bank or insurance company is not considered an employee of that firm. As an example, a bank's vice president of finance would not need the bank's permission to open an account.

Discretionary accounts. If a customer gives the registered representative written authority to choose which security to trade, to decide what action to take (buy or sell) and to decide how much to trade, the representative has discretion in the account. *Discretionary accounts are permissible.* The registered representative must receive discretionary authority from the client **before** any discretionary activity can take place. The member's principal must approve the discretionary authority before it is accepted. NYSE rules require the principal to approve all orders, but it is not necessary to do so before the order is entered. Discretionary orders must be designated as such and accounts must be reviewed frequently by the supervisory principal to prevent churning.

Reporting to Customers

Statement of account. Customers must be informed regularly about the status of their accounts. The NYSE requires that members send statements to clients at least once every quarter showing the security positions, the amount of money and any transactions that occurred in the account.

Mailing instructions. When a new accounts form is filled out, the client gives specific mailing instructions. Statements and confirms may be sent to someone other than the client (the client's agent or attorney, for example) if the client requests it in writing or if duplicate confirms are also sent to the client. A member firm may hold the customer's mail for up to two months if the customer is on vacation in the U.S., and up to three months if the client is abroad.

Incorrectly reported trades. Sometimes the details of a trade are reported to a customer incorrectly. In spite of the mistaken report, the actual trade is binding on the customer. However, if an order is executed outside the customer's limit, the trade is not binding. Member firms are required by the NYSE to undergo an annual audit by an independent accountant in order to ensure the firm's financial health.

Margin Requirements

The NYSE requires that a customer's long margin account have a minimum equity of **at least $2,000** or **100% of the purchase price**, whichever is less.

An order to sell shares must be marked either "long" or "short." If it is a long sale, the registered representative should get assurance from the owner that the securities will be delivered in a timely fashion. Short sales can be executed only on an up tick or a zero-up tick. The plus tick or minus tick carries over from the previous day's trading to the next day's opening. There is no plus tick requirement for securities sold over the counter or for U.S. governments or municipals.

Fraudulent and Manipulative Practices

The New York Stock Exchange prohibits member firms from taking part in fictitious transactions. Wash sales and matched orders are not allowed if the purpose of the transaction is to create the false impression of activity in a particular security. The NYSE also prohibits excessive trades (churning) in any account, and any manipulative operation (such as spreading rumors about a security in order to affect its price or effecting wash sales).

Other NYSE Regulations

Prepayment to the seller, that is, giving the seller the proceeds of a sale before settlement date, is usually not permitted. If there is an emergency and if the customer has not requested this in the past, it could be allowed. All prepayments are to be reported and reviewed by the main office.

Odd-lot orders are orders to trade less than a round lot of a security. A member broker-dealer can charge an extra fee for this, called an **odd-lot differential**.

The NYSE has a "nine-bond rule" which states that orders for nine bonds or less must be sent to the exchange floor to be executed unless the client requests an off-the-floor trade. The member broker-dealer cannot ask clients for off-floor (OTC), nine-bond trades. An order for 10 bonds or more may be done off the exchange floor.

A member broker-dealer cannot hypothecate (pledge) client's securities without written consent of the client. The member cannot pledge more than a reasonable value of the client's securities. The maximum amount that can be hypothecated is 140% of the customer's debit balance.

A NYSE member must forward proxies to the beneficial owners of street-name accounts. *Instructions from clients to the contrary cannot be honored.* If the client does not return the proxy within 10 business days, the member firm can vote those shares if the question is of minor importance. If the question is very important (a merger, issuance of more debt, etc.) and is a proxy contest, the member firm cannot vote the client's shares.

If the member firm offers unsolicited advice to clients in a proxy contest, then that firm must register with the SEC as a participant in the contest. If the client asks for advice, a registered representative may give an opinion without registering as a participant. If a corporation listed on the New York Stock Exchange fails to solicit proxies, it can be delisted.

Settlement dates. Securities usually settle (change ownership after a trade) in one of three ways: cash, regular way or seller's (buyer's) option. The delivery dates (settlement dates) for corporate bonds, rights, round lots of stock or odd lots of stock are as follows:

- **Cash trade**: delivery is on the trade date.
- **Regular way**: delivery is five business days after the trade date.
- **Seller's (or buyer's) option**: delivery is whenever the option says it is. It must be at least six business days but no more than 60 calendar days after the trade date.

U.S. government securities settle (deliver) as follows:

- **Cash trade**: delivery is on the trade date.
- **Regular way**: delivery is on the next business day.
- **Seller's (or buyer's) option**: delivery is whenever the option says it is. It must be at least two business days but no more than 60 calendar days after the trade date.

Ex-dates. For trades done regular way, the ex-dividend or ex-rights date is four business days before the record date. For cash transactions, the ex-date is the business day after the record date.

Bond interest. Bonds are traded "and interest," meaning that the seller of the bond receives the price for the bond and the interest due him for the portion of time he held the bond after the last interest payment. Corporate bonds and municipals calculate their interest using a 360-day year (all months have 30 days). Government securities calculate interest due using actual days elapsed. Income bonds and bonds in default trade flat; that is, no interest is due to the seller.

Due bills. If a security is traded before its ex-date and if settlement cannot occur until after the record date, then the seller will deliver the security with a due bill for the amount of the dividend (or the number of rights). Delivery of a due bill is likely to happen when a seller's option transaction is entered into near the ex-date.

Arbitration. The New York Stock Exchange Board of Arbitration hears and settles disagreements between members, allied members, member organizations and their employees. Nonmembers (customers, for example) may voluntarily submit to arbitration in a dispute with members or employees. Decisions of the arbitrators are final; there is no appeal.

Disciplinary hearing. A grievance or complaint against an employee of a member organization must be made in writing. The employee has 25 days to respond in writing. Then a hearing is held before a NYSE panel. The employee may have an attorney present. The decision of this panel can be appealed to the NYSE board of directors, but there is no appeal beyond that point. The decision of the board is final.

Listing requirements. In order for the securities of a corporation to be listed on the New York Stock Exchange, the corporation must have:

- at least 2,000 stockholders who own at least 100 shares each;
- a minimum of 1,100,000 shares which are publicly owned;
- a total market value for the publicly held shares of $18 million or more;
- pretax income for the previous year of $2,500,000 or more; and
- pretax income for the two years before of at least $2 million each year.

A corporation may ask to be delisted if 2/3 of the stockholders and the company's board of directors approve the request and fewer than 10% of the shareholders object to delisting. The exchange does not like to have companies delist voluntarily. If however, a corporation does not solicit proxies for its stockholders' meetings, the exchange itself will delist that company.

Net capital of broker-dealer firm. Under SEC Rule 15c3-1, broker-dealer firms must remain solvent; the ratio of indebtedness to net capital cannot exceed 15 to 1. If a member's net capital falls below this level, the NYSE can limit the firm's activities to protect the public.

Commissions. NYSE member firms must charge a commission for acting as a broker for trades done on the exchange, but there is no minimum rate required. The exchange prohibits member firms from fixing commission rates.

A member organization must keep its main office open for business every day that the exchange is open for business. Each office must display its certificate of membership with the NYSE. A member organization may not share its office with another broker-dealer except under special circumstances.

A member firm must obtain prior approval from the exchange in order to open a branch office. If a registered representative uses his home as an office, this is considered office of the employing firm. Every branch must be supervised by a principal who has passed the appropriate principal's examination. A very small office may be supervised by a registered representative, but that representative is still closely supervised by a principal in another office.

Although principals in branch offices are responsible for the business in their respective offices, the ultimate responsibility rests with the general partner or the directors of the member firm. The principal's supervisory duties include:

- approving new accounts;
- reviewing all correspondence, trade blotters and registered representatives' client statements;
- reviewing all transactions with clients and representatives' accounts of clients; and
- initialing all of the above items.

Other Exchanges

Other stock exchanges, such as the American, the Philadelphia and the Midwest are also self-regulatory organizations (SROs). Each exchange has developed rules and regulations to govern its members. The rules and regulations of all the self-regulatory organizations are based primarily on the statutes of the acts of 1933 and 1934.

The Federal Reserve Board

The Securities Exchange Act of 1934 gave the responsibility of regulating credit in the securities industry to the Federal Reserve Board. To fulfill this obligation, the FRB wrote Regulations T and U. Regulation T covers credit extended by broker-dealers to customers in securities transactions:

- In a cash account, the customer must fully pay for a transaction in seven business days.
- In a margin account, for an initial purchase of corporate securities, the customer must deposit or already have on deposit, 50% of the market value of the security.

Regulation U controls the credit that banks may extend to customers (mainly broker-dealers) for purchasing marginable securities.

Chapter Review

Questions

1. The NASD Uniform Practice Code was established to

   ____(A)   require that practices in the investment banking and securities industry be just, reasonable and nondiscriminatory between investors.

   ____(B)   eliminate advertising and sales literature the SEC considers to be in violation of standards.

   ____(C)   provide a procedure for handling trade complaints from investors.

   ____(D)   maintain similarity of business practices among member organizations in the securities industry.

2. Free riding and withholding refer to

   ____(A)   distributing new issues valued at amounts exceeding the cost.

   ____(B)   purchasing securities with the intent of selling them before the settlement date.

   ____(C)   a member of an underwriting or selling group failing to make a public offering of a security at the public offering price.

   ____(D)   none of the above.

3. A sell out happens when which of the following occurs?

   ____(A)   The buyer of a security fails to complete the contract according to its terms and the broker-dealer closes the contract by selling the security for the account of the buyer.

   ____(B)   The seller of a security fails to complete the contract according to its terms and the buyer closes the contract by buying the security in the best available market and charging the seller.

   ____(C)   The party who requests the transfer of securities fails to pay the transfer agent's service charges and the transfer agent sells off the securities to cover the deficit.

   ____(D)   A season ticketholder sells a single game's ticket to a scalper.

4. Disciplinary decisions of the NASD Board of Governors and appellate and review procedures are subject matters covered in the

   ____(A)   SEC bylaws.

   ____(B)   Rules of Fair Practice.

   ____(C)   Code of Procedure.

   ____(D)   Uniform Practice Code.

5. The NASD Uniform Practice Code was established to

___(A) require that practices in the investment banking and securities industry be just, reasonable and nondiscriminatory between investors.

___(B) eliminate advertising and sales literature the SEC considers to be in violation of standards.

___(C) provide a procedure for handling trade complaints from investors.

___(D) maintain similarity of business practices among member organizations in the securities industry.

6. The purpose of the Rules of Fair Practice is to

___(A) provide a means of handling trade complaints from investors.

___(B) provide a means of communication between member firms.

___(C) require that business practices be similar among all members.

___(D) promote fair and ethical trade practices for member firms to use when dealing with the public.

7. The Code of Arbitration is for

___(A) handling violations of the Rules of Fair Practice.

___(B) assuring just and equitable practices of fair trade.

___(C) establishing uniform trade practices.

___(D) handling disagreements and claims between member firms, registered reps and the public.

8. Who is permitted to transact business on the floor of the exchange?

___(A) members

___(B) allied members

___(C) floor clerks

___(D) floor officials

9. All of the following need permission to open margin accounts with a NYSE member firm EXCEPT an employee of a(n)

___(A) communications company.

___(B) bank.

___(C) broker-dealer.

___(D) insurance company.

10. Which of the following would be considered discretionary?

___(A)   an order that specifies the size of the security but leaves the choice of price and time up to the account executive

___(B)   an account where the broker has the power to decide when and what to trade without specific customer authorization for those trades

___(C)   an account where the customer has power of attorney over another individual's account

___(D)   an account where an investment adviser has power of attorney over another individual's account

Answer Key

1. D.

2. C.

3. A.

4. C.

5. D.

6. D.

7. D.

8. A.

9. A.

10. B.

VERY IMPORTANT CHAPTER

Key Terms

17.25 17.5	Ad valorem	Blue List 17.19 17.12
17.11	Bond attorney	Competitive bidding 17.9
17.4	Covenant	Daily Bond Buyer 17.12
17.23	Debt limit	Eastern account 17.13
17.6 17.25	Flow of funds	General obligation bond 17.5
17.12	Glass-Steagall Act of 1933	Gross revenue pledge 17.7
17.11 17.5	Legal opinion	Munifacts 17.12
17.9	Negotiated underwriting	Net revenue pledge 17.6
17.9	Official Notice of Sale	Official statement 17.18
17.12	Placement ratio	Price scale 17.13
17.5 17.11	Qualified opinion	Reciprocal immunity 17.2
17.3	Redemption	Refunding 17.4
17.5	Revenue bond	Sinking fund 17.3
17.17	Syndicate letter	Tombstone 17.12
17.4	Trust indenture	Unqualified opinion 17.11 17.5
17.12	Visible supply	Western account 17.13

Municipal Securities

Municipal securities represent loans to a state, a legally constituted political subdivision of a state, or a U.S. territory. They are issued, like other debt obligations, to raise capital, in this case to finance public works and construction projects (capital improvements) that benefit the general public. Some examples include construction and maintenance of streets and highways, water distribution and sewage systems, and public welfare and health services.

Safety. For safety of principal, municipal securities are considered second only to U.S. government and U.S. government agency bonds. The degree of safety, however, varies with individual issues. Municipal securities are protected, essentially, by the viability of the issuing municipality and the community in general. To bolster this relative safety, each new issue is accompanied by documentation that:

- sets forth the terms of the loan and schedule of repayment;
- attests to the issuing municipality's authority to issue the debt obligation;
- describes specific features of the issue;
- explains the intended use of the borrowed funds; and
- provides financial information about the economic health of the issuer.

Tax benefits. The interest on most municipal securities is exempt from federal income taxation. The federal government does not tax the debt obligations of municipalities; municipalities reciprocate by not taxing federal debt securities. This doctrine of reciprocal immunity was established by a Supreme Court decision. To be exempt from federal taxation, municipal securities must be issued to fund government (rather than private) activities.

In many cases, municipal bonds are also exempt from state income tax for investors who live in the state where the bond is issued or who purchase bonds issued by a territory of the United States.

The tax advantage of municipal bonds allows municipalities to offer the bonds at lower interest rates than the rates of taxable bonds. The result is that municipal securities are more attractive to investors in high tax brackets than to those in lower brackets (avoiding a 28% tax liability is more attractive than avoiding a 15% tax liability). Investors should carefully calculate the bond's overall yield, including tax savings.

Like most other bonds, municipal bonds tend to pay interest semiannually according to a schedule set at issuance.

Issuers. The three primary entities legally entitled to issue municipal debt securities are territorial possessions of the U.S. (e.g., Puerto Rico and Guam), state governments, and legally constituted taxing authorities (county and city governments and the agencies they create). Public authorities that supervise ports and mass transit systems (such as the Milwaukee Port Authority and the Ohio Turnpike Authority) also issue debt securities.

Maturity structures. The wide range of maturities available in municipal issues (from one month to 50 years or more) is another feature attractive to investors. The three types of maturity schedules common to corporate debt issues are also used by municipal issuers. These are serial, balloon and term maturity structures.

Issuers of term and serial bonds often establish a sinking fund. Into this fund is deposited money each year to provide the cash needed to pay back the bonds at maturity (or earlier) either through a bond call or through open-market purchases.

Redemption. Paying back the principal of a bond is called redemption. It may take place on or before the maturity date. If a bond is callable, the issuer can initiate early redemption. A puttable bond may be redeemed before maturity at the investor's request. It is not unusual for bonds to be issued with call provisions by the issuer. Bonds with put features are rarer.

Most large tax-exempt offerings are issued with call provisions allowing the issuer to retire the issue in whole or in part before maturity. These are referred to as in-whole or in-part calls.

Term bonds are generally called in random order. Serial bonds, on the other hand, are usually called in inverse order of their maturity, because this lowers the total interest expense. The first bonds called, in other words, will be those with the longest time to maturity, since they have the largest overall interest cost.

Calls may be mandatory (the issuer must call the bonds at a certain time) or optional. In place of a mandatory call, an issuer is often allowed to buy bonds on the open market (a procedure referred to as tendering).

An optional call provision increases the issuer's financial flexibility, allowing the municipality, for example, to retire an issue that is paying an above-market rate of interest and replace it with a low-interest issue. Callable bonds usually pay a higher rate of interest than that available on noncallable issues.

An extraordinary mandatory redemption occurs when the issuer is required to redeem all or part of an issue of bonds. This may happen, for example, when proceeds of an issue are not spent for the required purpose by a specified date or when the facility is severely damaged. The latter situation is known as a catastrophe call.

Call dates and prices are stated on the tombstone announcing the issuance of the bond and are always explained in detail in the official statement (a document fully disclosing information about the bond issue provided by the issuer). Thirty days before calling a bond, issuers generally notify investors by placing an advertisement in a financial publication. The *Daily Bond Buyer* (a trade paper published Monday through

Friday for the municipal securities industry) publishes a Called Bond List. Investors with coupon bonds must watch the financial news to find out about calls. Holders of registered bonds are notified of calls by the issuer.

Prerefunding. Refunding an issue of bonds means paying it off with the proceeds of a new issue. Sometimes bond issues are prerefunded. In a prerefunding, a second issue is sold at a lower coupon than the older bond issue prior to the first call date on the original issue. The proceeds from the second issue are placed in an escrow account and invested in U.S. government securities or held as cash, interest from which is used to pay interest on the outstanding prerefunded bonds. The original bonds will be called at the first call date and the escrowed securities will be used to redeem them.

Prerefunded (or **advance-refunded**) bonds are virtually riskless: therefore, the rating services (such as Standard & Poor's and Moody's) upgrade them to as high as a triple-A rating (the highest available). Advance refunding is a form of **defeasance** (or termination) of the issuer's obligation; prerefunded bonds are considered defeased and no longer a part of the community's debt.

Put features. A bond with a put option allows an investor the discretion to redeem a bond (put it to the issuer) at a specified price before its maturity date. There may be specified dates before and after which the investor may not exercise the put.

Trust Indenture

Although one is not required, a revenue bond's certificate usually refers to a trust indenture. The trust indenture itself is too long to be supplied to all bondholders. The covenants of the indenture are outlined in the official statement. Protective provisions include the following:

- **Rate covenant:** a promise to maintain rates sufficient to pay expenses and debt service.
- **Maintenance covenant:** a promise to maintain equipment and the facility.
- **Insurance covenant:** a promise to insure the facilities built.
- **Issuance of additional bonds:** whether the indenture is open-ended, allowing further issuance of bonds with the same status; or closed-ended, allowing no further issuance of bonds using the same collateral unless the original bondholders agree.
- **A sinking fund:** to pay off interest and principal obligations.
- **A consulting engineer.**
- **A catastrophe clause.**
- **Details of the application of the flow of funds.**
- **Outside audit of records and financial reports.**
- Any call features or requirements are also outlined in the trust indenture.

Legal Opinion

Always attached to the certificate (unless the bond is stamped ex-legal) is a legal opinion written by the bond counsel, an attorney specializing in tax-exempt bond offerings. The legal opinion states that the issue conforms with applicable laws, the state constitution and established procedures. If the bond is tax-exempt, that too will be stated in the legal opinion. The legal opinion will be issued as either a qualified opinion, that is, the bond counsel that issued it has reservations about the issue or wants it known that certain conditions exist; or as an unqualified opinion (issued by the bond counsel unconditionally).

General Obligation Bonds

There are only two major categories of municipal securities issues: general obligation bonds (GOs, bonds that are backed by the full faith, credit and taxing powers of the municipal borrower), and revenue bonds (bonds backed by revenues generated by the financed facility).

GO bondholders have a legal claim to the revenues received by a municipal government for payment of the principal and interest due them. GOs are used to raise funds for those municipal capital improvements that typically do not produce revenues (building a new city hall, for example). Their financial support is ad valorem (real estate) taxes for cities, counties and districts; sales and income taxes for states. GOs are called full faith and credit bonds.

Because general obligation bonds are backed by the taxing powers of the municipal issuer, they must be approved by taxpayers voting in a referendum; and they may be subject to certain statutory limitations.

Source of funds. General obligation bonds are backed by taxes. State-issued debt securities are backed by income taxes, license fees and sales taxes. Cities, towns and counties issue debt securities backed by property taxes, license fees, fines and all other sources of revenue to the municipality. School, road and park districts may also issue municipal bonds that are backed by property taxes.

Statutory Limitations

Legal limits on municipal debt. While GOs are backed by the taxing powers of the issuer, the amount of debt municipal governments are allowed to incur may be subject to local and state statutory debt limitations. The purpose of these limitations is to protect taxpayers from excessive tax assessments. These restrictions make the bonds safer for investors. The lower the debt limit, the less opportunity there is for excessive borrowing and default by the municipality.

Tax limits. The municipal issuer may have either limited or unlimited taxing power. Property taxes are limited by some states to a certain percentage (expressed in mills: one mill equals 1/10th of one cent) of the estimated property value or to a certain percentage increase in any single year. Bonds that are serviced by these taxes are still considered general obligation bonds, even though the taxing power is limited. These bonds are frequently called limited tax bonds.

Overlapping debt. Debt limitations of a municipality can be quite misleading if there is overlapping debt, that is, debt incurred by several taxing authorities that draw from the same taxpayers. A school district's debt, for example, is backed by taxes on the same property as debt issued by the city and the county that the district is in. The school district and the county, therefore, issue debt which overlaps the city's debt. (Debt issued by states is not included when calculating overlapping debt.)

[margin note: coterminous debt]

Revenue Bonds

Revenue bonds are payable only from the earnings of specific revenue-producing enterprises. An analysis of the quality of revenue bonds would include sources of revenue, feasibility studies, maturity structure, call provisions, application of revenues and protective covenants of the indenture. Unlike GO bonds, revenue bonds are subject to no statutory debt limits and require no voter approval.

Sources of revenue. In contrast to GOs, the interest and principal payments of revenue bonds are payable to the bondholders only from the specific earnings of revenue-producing facilities such as toll roads, bridges, college dorms and airports. They are not payable from general or real estate taxes and are not backed by the full faith and credit of the issuer. Revenue bonds are the more common type of municipal issue and can be used to finance any municipal function that generates income. The typical sources of revenue that finance the principal and interest payments to revenue bondholders include user charges for public utility facilities (such as a municipal water or sewer authority), tolls, concessions and fees from the operation of turnpikes, bridges, airports and other facilities, and rental payments under lease-rental arrangements between the issuing authority and a state or political subdivision.

Under a typical lease rental (or lease-back) bond arrangement, a municipality might create an authority or agency to build a new school building. The authority issues bonds to raise money for construction of the school, then leases the finished building to the school district. Backing for the bond is provided by the lease payments, and those payments may be made with funds raised through special taxes or appropriations, from revenues such as tuition or fees or from the municipality's general fund.

Applications of revenues. Principal and interest on revenue bonds are paid almost exclusively from money generated by the facility financed by the issue. The issuer pledges to pay the various expenses involved in a particular order, called the flow of funds.

In most cases, a net revenue pledge is used, and the first payments go for operating and maintenance expenses. The remaining funds, or net revenues, are used to pay debt service and other expenses.

Gross Revenue Pledge	Net Revenue Pledge
<u>Gross Revenue Pledge</u>	<u>Net Revenue Pledge</u>
Issuer pays debt service first (from **gross revenues**)	Issuer pays expenses first (from gross revenues)
User pays operations and maintenance (under terms of triple net lease)	Issuer pays debt service second (from **net revenues**)

If the issuer doesn't need to commit any revenues to operating and maintenance expenses first, the first disbursements go directly to debt service. When debt service is paid first, the flow of funds is called a gross revenue pledge.

The projected flow of funds is found in the feasibility statement, which presents the underwriter's assessment of the feasibility of the financial projections.

Flow of Funds in a Net Revenue Pledge

- **Gross revenues** (total receipts from operating the facility). Usually deposited in the **gross revenue fund** and then disbursed in the following order:
- **Operations and maintenance.** Used to pay current operating and maintenance expenses. Remaining funds are called **net revenues.**
- **Debt service account.** Used to pay the semiannual interest and principal maturing in the current year and serves as a sinking fund for term issues.
- **Debt service reserve fund.** Used to hold enough money to pay one year's debt service.
- **Reserve maintenance fund.** Used to supplement the general maintenance fund.
- **Renewal and replacement fund.** Used to create reserve funds for major renewal projects and equipment replacements.
- **Surplus fund.** Used for a variety of purposes, such as redeeming bonds, making tax payments, paying for improvements and betterments.

Specified revenue bonds. Special tax bonds are issued for specific projects and are payable only from the proceeds of a special tax (tobacco, alcohol or hotel room rentals). Special assessment bonds are issued to finance construction of public facilities such as streets, curbs and gutters, sidewalks and similar improvements in a specific neighborhood. The issuer assesses only the property benefiting from the improvement and services the debt with funds from the assessments.

Other Types of Revenue Bonds

Saturn example

Industrial Development Revenue bonds (IDRs or IDBs). Industrial revenue bonds and pollution control bonds are issued by a municipal authority to construct facilities or purchase equipment, which is then leased to a corporation. The authority uses money from lease payments to cover the principal and interest on the bonds.

Technically, industrial revenue bonds are issued for the benefit of a corporation. Under the Tax Reform Act of 1986, the interest on these bonds is generally taxable-since the act reserves tax exemption for public purpose, government use or municipal bonds. Some bonds remain exempt from taxation, because of the use of the proceeds or their size.

New Housing Authority bonds (NHAs). New Housing Authority bonds (NHAs), issued by local housing authorities to develop and improve low-income housing, are backed by the full faith and credit of the U.S. government. NHAs are sometimes called PHAs (Public Housing Administration bonds). Because of their federal backing, they are considered the most secure revenue bonds.

Double-barreled bonds. Double-barreled bonds are similar to both general obligation and revenue bonds. Interest and principal are paid from the earnings of the facility. The bonds are also backed by the taxing power of the state or municipality and therefore have the backing of two sources of revenue. Although they are backed by revenues from the facility, double-barreled bonds are rated and traded as GO bonds.

Moral obligation bonds. A moral obligation bond is a type of state-issued revenue bond. If revenues backing the bond are not sufficient to meet debt service requirements, the state has the authority to authorize payment on the debt through legislative appropriation. But the state's obligation is not established in law; it is a moral obligation only.

Municipal Notes

Municipal notes are short-term securities issued in anticipation of funds from another source. When received, the anticipated funds are used to pay off the notes. Interest on municipal notes is normally paid at maturity. Municipal notes fall into several categories: tax-, revenue- and bond-anticipation notes and a special class of federally backed notes called project notes.

- **Tax Anticipation Notes (TANs)** are issued by municipalities to finance current operations in anticipation of future tax receipts.
- **Revenue Anticipation Notes (RANs)** are offered periodically to finance current operations in anticipation of future revenues.
- **Tax and Revenue Anticipation Notes (TRANs)** are issued in anticipation of taxes and revenues.
- **Bond Anticipation Notes (BANs)** are sold as interim financing that will eventually be funded long-term through the sale of bonds.
- **Project Notes (PNs)** were auctioned twice monthly by the U.S. Department of Housing and Urban Development (HUD) and issued by local governing bodies. The funds provided urban renewal and low-cost housing for their communities.

Housing

Issuing Municipal Securities

No regulation (cooling off etc)

There is a uniform sequence of events leading to a new municipal issue. The issuer, upon recognition of the need for debt financing, obtains a preliminary legal opinion that will determine whether and how the bonds are to be offered. The terms of a municipal bond offering may be set by either negotiation or competitive bidding.

usually corporate

Negotiated underwriting. In negotiated underwriting, the municipality appoints an investment banker. The investment banker consults with the issuer to establish a price that is both satisfactory to the issuer and likely to ensure the underwriter a profit. Many revenue bonds are issued through a negotiated underwriting.

IDR's most common

Competitive bidding. With a few exceptions, municipal general obligation bonds must be awarded to an underwriter through competitive bidding. When a municipality publishes an invitation to bid (also known as the Official Notice of Sale), broker-dealers respond by writing to the city's attorney for information on the offering.

ADVERTISING

Using the information in the notice of sale and *The Daily Bond Buyer* about the 30-day visible supply, other municipal issues currently being offered, and the placement ratio (these terms are discussed later in this section), investment bankers form syndicates to prepare bids for the securities. Syndicates can obtain bid work sheets from The Daily Bond Buyer.

On the date indicated, the syndicate submits sealed bids outlining proposed interest rates and other conditions for conducting the underwriting. Competitive bids are usually sealed bids and are hand-delivered to the issuer by messenger. Bids delivered after the deadline are not accepted. The issuer awards the issue to the bidder offering to sell the bonds at the lowest net cost (e.g., the best combination of high bid price and low interest expense).

Official Notice of Sale. The notice of sale is usually published in *The Daily Bond Buyer* and includes the following information:

- date, time and place of sale;
- description of issues, including both total expected revenue and the uses to which the revenue will be put;
- manner in which the bid is to be made (sealed or oral bids);
- authority for the sale;
- type of bond;
- whatever good faith deposit must be enclosed with the sealed bid;
- name of the law firm (sometimes called the bond counsel) providing the legal opinion; and
- other information, including interest payment dates, denominations, registration privileges, form of bid and right of rejection.

NEW ISSUE

Ratings
Moody's: Aa
Standard & Poor's: AA

$40,000,000

Department of Water and Power of the City of Okefenokee, Rhode Island

Electric Plant Revenue Bonds, Second Issue of 1998

Amount	Due	Coupon	Yield	Amount	Due	Coupon	Yield	Amount	Due	Coupon	Yield
$350,000	2004	7%	5.00%	$850,000	2010	6.20%	5.30%	$1,200,000	2015	5.60%	100*
550,000	2005	7	5.05	900,000	2011	5.40	5.35	1,200,000	2016	5.70	100*
750,000	2006	7	5.10	1,000,000	2012	5.40	100*	1,300,000	2017	5.80	100*
750,000	2007	7	5.15	1,100,000	2013	5.40	5.45	1,300,000	2018	5.80	5.85
800,000	2008	7	5.20	1,100,000	2014	5 1/2	100*	1,300,000	2019	5.90	100*
850,000	2009	7	5.25					1,300,000	2020	5.90	5.95

* Price

$23,400,000
6.20% Term Bonds due April 1, 2038
Price 100%
(Accrued interest to be added)

The Bonds are to be offered when, as and if issued and received by the Underwriters, subject to prior sale, to withdrawal or modification of the offer without notice and to the approval of the legality by Cheathem, Billim and Runne, Bond Counsel, Chicago, Illinois. The Bonds are offered only by means of Official Statement, copies of which may be obtained from such of the undersigned as may legally offer these Bonds in this State.

Blythely, Easterner & Co.

Wedplant, King, Chef

Witti Proffe Reynolds, Inc.

Barter Masters Bobber	Madre Meryl Capital	Stern, Sterner, Sternest
Emmet, Kelly Company	Nixon, Reagan, Ford	AFAP Securities

Fig. 17.1 A typical municipal bond tombstone.

Two key pieces of information that are not included in a notice of sale are the rating of the bond and the name of the underwriter.

Conflicts of interest. Potential conflicts of interest arise if a firm acts both as underwriter and financial advisor in connection with the same issue. Consequently, the MSRB requires the following:

- A firm consulting with a municipal issuer for a fee must describe the advisory relationship in writing and disclose the amount of compensation.
- Before submitting a competitive bid, a firm acting as financial advisor to an issuer must have the issuer's consent.
- Before submitting a negotiated bid, the advisor must receive the issuer's consent and terminate the advisory relationship in writing. It must also inform the issuer of the possible conflict and disclose the source and anticipated amount of money received for participating in the issue.
- Purchasers of the securities must be informed if an advisory relationship exists or once existed.

Functions of a Municipal Bond Attorney

Law firms are employed during the underwriting process to serve as bond counsels to the issuer and to give written legal opinions as to the legality of the issues. The bond counsel (or bond attorney) is a disinterested party offering certain legal assurances to the issuer and the investor. These include assurances that the issuer is authorized to issue the bonds, that the bonds were properly announced and that the bond certificates are properly printed.

The legal opinion. One reason the issuer retains and pays for independent bond counsel is to provide an opinion on the validity of the offering. Concern over the tax status of the issue leads bond buyers to place much importance on the legal opinion. In addition to the statement about tax exemption, the legal opinion contains a description of the bonds, statements concerning the statutory basis for bond issuance, any tax limitations of the issuer and any call provisions of the issue.

The legal opinion is a bond attorney's written opinion that the issue of bonds is exempt from federal taxes, is a binding debt of the issuer and can be legally issued by the municipal authority. The legal opinion must be attached to or printed on the back of each bond certificate. A municipal bond certificate that does not have a legal opinion on it or attached to it is called ex-legal. Without the legal opinion attached, a bond certificate is not in good delivery form (unless identified as ex-legal prior to the transaction).

An **unqualified legal opinion** is the most desirable because it states that the opinion is without question or restriction, that is, without qualifications. A **qualified legal opinion** expresses reservations about the issue. A qualified opinion might state, for example, that the issuer has acquired property but may not have clear title to it.

The underwriter's counsel. The managing underwriter may choose to employ another law firm as underwriter's counsel. This firm is not responsible for the legal opinion and is employed to represent the interests of the underwriter, not those of the investors.

Sources of information on proposed issues. Information on proposed issues may be found in the following publications:

- *The Daily Bond Buyer* is an authoritative source of information on municipal bonds. Each week this newspaper publishes the **30-day visible supply** and the **placement ratio**, among other information.

- *Munifacts*, a subscription wire service, supplies prices, information about proposed new issues and general news relevant to the municipal bond market.

- *The Blue List*, a comprehensive source of information, lists current municipal bond secondary offerings of banks and brokers across the nation but does not contain information about new issues.

The tombstone. Tombstones are formal announcements of a bond offering that present basic facts about the issue. In reading a municipal bond tombstone, you should be able to identify the type of bond, the dated date (date on which bonds begin paying interest), the maturity/maturities, interest rates, minimum denominations and the syndicate manager(s).

The tombstone is not required by the SEC. It is an advertisement by the managing underwriters (usually named at the top of the list of underwriters). Other members of the underwriting group are listed below the managers, in descending order of the size of their brackets.

Glass-Steagall Act of 1933

The Glass-Steagall Act of 1933 erected a wall between commercial and investment banking, a wall that has crumbled significantly in the 1980s. Though Glass-Steagall prohibits commercial banks from underwriting most municipal revenue bonds, it allows them to underwrite GOs and new PHA bonds.

Formation of the Underwriting Syndicate

[handwritten: Same except no cooling off period]

To spread the potential risk of underwriting a large municipal securities offering, underwriters usually form a syndicate. Underwriting syndicates are typically organized as joint ventures rather than as partnerships.

Once the Notice of Sale has circulated, syndicates interested in placing a competitive bid for an issue form without involvement of the issuer. Often the same syndicate composed of the same members handles successive offerings for a particular municipality. Participants formalize their relationship by signing a syndicate letter, also called a syndicate contract or agreement among underwriters. About two weeks before the scheduled sale, the syndicate manager sends the letter to each firm for a signature of the issue. The member's signature indicates agreement with the terms of the offering. Syndicate letters include:

- level of participation of each member firm (also known as commitment);
- priority of allocation of orders;
- duration of the syndicate account;
- appointment of the manager(s) as agent for the account;
- the fee for the managing underwriter and breakdown of the spread; and
- other obligations, such as member expenses, good faith deposits, observance of offering terms and liability for unsold bonds.

A syndicates arrives at its bid through a series of meetings. Member dealers discuss the proposed price scale and the spread for the underwriters. The goal is to arrive at the best bid to the issuer (that is, the highest possible price with the lowest possible interest cost) while still enabling the syndicate to sell the bonds profitably. A final price for the bond is set at a meeting conducted just before the bid is due.

All syndicates interested in bidding on the issue send their bid forms and a good faith deposit to the issuer at the date and time outlined in the notice of sale. The issuer awards the municipal bond issue to the syndicate that offers the bonds at the lowest net interest (or true interest) cost.

Types of accounts. Syndicate liability will vary depending upon the type of account that is established. The western account is a divided account. Each underwriter is responsible for its own underwriting allocation. For example, if the underwriter is allocated 10% of the issue, its financial liability ends once it has distributed its 10% participation.

In an eastern account (or undivided account), each underwriter is responsible for a percentage of any unsold shares or bonds. An underwriter that has sold its 15%

[handwritten: Block: $100,000 worth]

allocation is still liable for 15% of any bonds or shares that remain unsold by other underwriters. If a 15% underwriter of a $10 million bond issue has sold its 15% and bonds worth $5 million remain unsold in the syndicate, the 15% underwriter is still financially responsible for 15% of the unsold bonds, in this case $750,000 of bonds. The responsibility for the unsold bonds continues until the entire issue has been sold.

Due Diligence

Municipal underwriters, like corporate underwriters, must perform an investigation of the issuer's financing proposals. With municipal revenue bonds, as with corporate securities, this due diligence investigation is taken care of with a feasibility study. The feasibility study includes information such as projected revenues and costs associated with the project and an analysis of competing facilities.

Establishing the Syndicate Bid

Know General Knowledge Only Tested

A day or two before bids must be submitted, the syndicate meets and members present their ideas about how the issue should be priced for reoffering to the public. In this preliminary meeting, the manager seeks tentative agreement from members on matters such as the price or yield of all maturities in the issue and the gross profit or underwriting spread.

The process of establishing the yield for each maturity is called "writing a scale." A scale is the list of the different maturities of the bond issue. If the coupon rate has already been determined, each maturity listed is assigned a yield. If the rate has not been set, each maturity is assigned a coupon. A normal scale has higher yields for long-term bonds. An inverted scale has higher yields for short-term bonds. The following table shows an example of a general obligation bond scale.

General Obligation Bond Scale

Amount	Matures	Coupon	Yield
$550,000	1994	7%	5.00%
$650,000	1995	7%	5.05%
$750,000	1996	7%	5.10%
$750,000	1997	7%	5.15%
$800,000	1998	7%	5.20%

The scale shows an example of a bond with a serial maturity. It has a normal curve; the bonds with later maturities have higher yields.

The underwriters also determine the premium or discount at which the bonds are to be offered. They must work the scale according to the specifications supplied by the municipality. Level debt service, for example, will require equal annual payments of principal and interest.

Competitive bids are submitted as firm commitments. Bids must, therefore, be carefully written to be competitive in the marketplace as well as with the issuer. A low bid might win but might also result in unsold bonds and a loss of capital for the underwriter.

Awarding the Issue → *Lowest net interest cost (or true)*

When bids are due, representatives of each syndicate bring the issuer sealed bids and a good faith deposit. The issuer meets in private with its attorneys and accountants to analyze each bid and to choose the one with the lowest net cost.

In split-rate bids (bids with more than one rate of interest), the interest is determined by the lowest average interest cost to the issuer. If each bid names one rate for the whole issue, the award goes to the syndicate with the lowest rate.

When the choice has been made, the winner is announced and the good faith deposits are returned to the remaining syndicates. The winning syndicate has a firm commitment to purchase the bonds from the issuer and reoffer them to the public at the agreed-upon public offering price.

Syndicate account. The syndicate account is created when the issue is awarded. The syndicate manager keeps the books and manages the account. All sale proceeds are deposited to the syndicate account and all expenses are paid out of the account. Within 60 calendar days of the completion of the underwriting, the managing underwriter must supply a detailed record of the account to all syndicate members.

Breakdown of the Spread

Management fee. The managing underwriter receives a per bond fee for its responsibility with the new issue. For example, on a $20 spread, the manager might receive $3.

Underwriting fee. Each syndicate member receives a share of the underwriting fee (or syndicate fee) according to the bracket or percentage of commitment. A typical underwriting fee might be $4 on a $20 spread. A syndicate member who committed to 10% participation would receive 10% of the total underwriting fee after expenses are paid.

Takedown. We have accounted for about a third of the spread in this underwriting. The percentage of the spread that remains after subtracting manager's and syndicate fees ($13 of the $20 in our example) is called the takedown. The takedown is the discount at which a syndicate member buys bonds from the syndicate. Members are said to buy the bonds from the syndicate "at the takedown." A member can either sell its bonds to customers at the public offering price or sell them to a dealer in the selling group at less than full price.

Concession and reallowance. A firm that is a syndicate member buys bonds from the syndicate for $987, sells them for $1,000, and earns the takedown of $13. If the firm instead sells bonds to another dealer in the selling group, it will do so at less than $1,000. The selling group dealer receives a discount called the concession from the syndicate member. Dealers are said to buy bonds from syndicate members "at the concession."

The concession can be considered a part of the takedown. When the member does not sell the bond directly, it "concedes" a portion of the takedown to the seller. The remainder is kept by the member and is called the additional takedown.

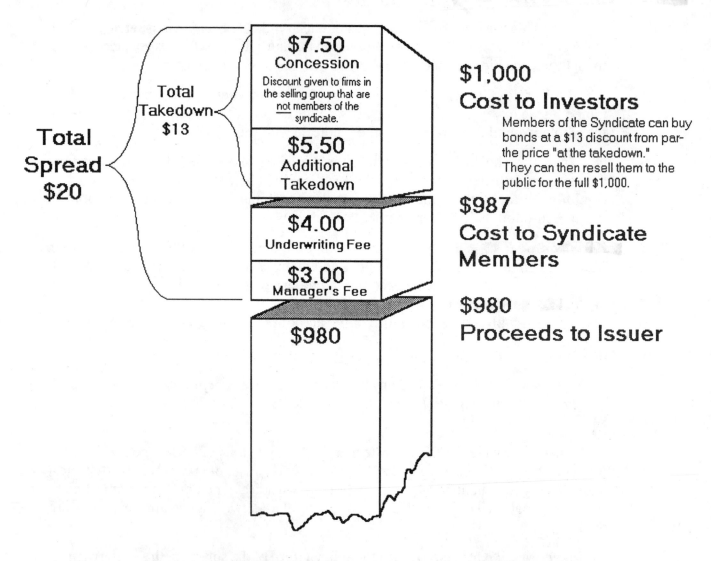

Fig. 17.2 The spread is divided among several parties.

Order Allocation

Municipal bond orders are allocated according to specific priorities. Allocation becomes especially important when a bond issue is oversubscribed. The MSRB requires that syndicates establish priority provisions for orders and that the managing underwriter submit these to all syndicate members in writing. The rule also requires managers to disclose syndicate expenses to all members and to submit, in writing, any plan for allocating securities outside of the agreed provisions. This creates an equitable situation for all syndicate members. The MSRB also establishes a time line for municipal underwritings.

K117

17.16

Longman Group USA, Inc.
Copyright 1989. All rights reserved.

The order period is a few hours or days following award of the issue, during which syndicate members submit orders to the manager. The syndicate letter must establish a priority of orders to be used for allocating the oversubscribed bonds during the order period. The normal priority is as follows:

(handwritten: Just terms)

- **Presale order**. A presale order is entered before the pricing terms of the bond have been finalized. A presale order takes priority over other types of orders. Bonds sold presale do not pay any syndicate member a takedown. The entire spread, less the manager's fee, is deposited in the syndicate account.

(handwritten: (syndicate order) big group wants to buy)

- **Group net order**. Orders designated as group net receive the next highest priority during the order period. A syndicate member who wants his customer's order to receive priority will enter the order as a group order. The member is sacrificing some commission to keep the customer happy. Profit on a group net order is also deposited in the syndicate account, which, upon completion of the underwriting, is split among members of the syndicate according to participation.

(handwritten: my clients that wont me to get all commissions.)

- **Net designated order**. The next priority is a net designated order. The customer designates how many bonds should be credited to which underwriters.

(handwritten: member (us) can buy for own inventory)

- **Member-at-the-takedown order**. The fourth priority is a member-at-the-takedown order. The firm that enters the order receives the entire takedown. The allocation procedure is usually spelled out in the letter of instructions sent to all underwriters with their written invitation to join the syndicate.

(handwritten margin box: P lease / G(s) end / (Give) / D ang / M oney)

Sale Date

After the issuer awards the offering, the managing underwriter notifies syndicate members and members of the selling group. During the order period, the syndicate manager fills orders received according to the priority established in the syndicate letter. The buyer receives confirmation of the sale either from a syndicate manager or the selling syndicate member.

The buyers of all group orders and member-related orders are disclosed to the syndicate manager when the order is submitted to the syndicate. The manager discloses these buyers to all syndicate members 10 days after the close of the order period, thereby enforcing the priority (the syndicate letter).

Payment and Delivery

Specific procedures have been established for payment and delivery of bonds. The bonds are delivered to the underwriters with a final legal opinion several weeks after the sale and the underwriters pay for the bonds on delivery. Final confirmations are mailed to clients, disclosing purchase price and settlement date. The investor pays interest accrued from the dated date to the settlement date. The underwriters then redeliver the bonds, accompanied by the legal opinion, to the investors.

After awarding an issue, the issuer customarily takes several days (sometimes as long as a month) to print the bond certificates. When the bonds are ready, the syndicate manager gives the syndicate members six business days' notice of the settlement date. On that date, the issuer expects payment and the syndicate needs its funds.

The purchase of the bonds is called a when-issued trade. After determination of the settlement date, sales between dealers or to investors are reconfirmed as regular-way trades. The syndicate gives customers (both dealers and investors) five days' notice of the settlement date. All money is supposed to change hands on the settlement date.

The settlement date should not be confused with the dated date the issuer affixes to the bond issue. The dated date, you will remember, is the point at which interest begins to accrue.

Settlement. Once the bonds have been sold, the underwriting accounts must be settled. Within 60 days after delivery of the securities, the manager must distribute profits and settle the syndicate account. The sales credit must be delivered to the members within 30 business days after the securities are delivered to the customers.

The good faith deposits of members must be returned by the manager within two business days after the settlement with the issuer or, in the case of an unsuccessful bid, within two days after the issuer returns the deposit.

Official Statement

If the final official statement is not ready when the bonds are delivered, dealers may send the preliminary official statement or may prepare and send a summary or abstract of the official statement. When the final official statement is ready, however, the dealer must send it to customers and to any industry members who request it.

Abstracts and summaries of the official statement are considered advertising. They must, therefore, be approved by a properly designated underwriting principal of the dealer before use. To ensure their availability for examination, they must be maintained in an advertising file for three years. The final and preliminary official statements (or offering circulars) are not considered advertising.

In a negotiated underwriting, the dealer is required to provide, along with the official statement, the amount of the underwriting spread, the amount of any fee the broker-dealer receives as agent for the issuer, and the initial offering price of each maturity. On or before the completion of the transaction, the broker-dealer must disclose to all customers in writing the broker-dealer's participation in the new issue, any financial advisory relationship existing between the broker-dealer and the issuer, including arrangements in which advice is given for a fee, for other compensation or for expectation of compensation, and any control relationship between the broker-dealer and the issuer (for instance, if the president of the broker-dealer is an official of the issuing authority).

Municipal Bond Transactions

Municipal bonds are bought and sold in the over-the-counter (OTC) market. Most large brokerages maintain special trading departments that deal exclusively in municipal bonds. Persons who deal in these securities are closely regulated by the MSRB. Many of the rules for trading other securities OTC are the same for municipals.

Quotations. All quotations distributed or published must be bona fide. A quote is bona fide if the dealer is prepared to trade the security at the price specified in the quote and under the conditions (if any) described in the quote. Municipal bond quotations include the following: bids or offers, requests for bids or offers, notice of bids or offers wanted. Each quote must represent the best judgment of fair market value and is subject to prior sale or change in price.

like firm

The bid price at which a dealer states its willingness to purchase securities from another dealer is called a workable indication. A dealer giving a workable indication is free to revise its bid for the securities if market conditions change. Nominal quotations are intended only as an indication of the approximate market value of a security, are provided for information purposes and are allowed if clearly labeled as such. The rules on nominal quotes apply to all municipal bond quotes distributed or published by any dealer.

Like work out

Like subject

The Blue List. The dealer's national source of information about municipal secondary offerings is a trade publication called *The Blue List*. Published daily, it lists bonds alphabetically by name and includes the number of bonds offered, the coupon rate, maturity, yield to maturity (basis price) and the name of the offering dealer. When pricing a prospective issue, dealers consult *The Blue List* for information about yields.

Broker-dealer procedures. MSRB rules govern the type of information (and promises) a broker can give to customers. For example, municipal securities brokers or dealers are required to "make reasonable and suitable recommendations to customers." This rule applies to discretionary accounts, as well as other accounts and prohibits churning (increasing commissions through excessive trading). Municipal securities brokers and dealers are prohibited from misusing municipal securities or funds held for another person, guaranteeing customers against loss, and sharing in the profits or losses of a customer's account.

Broker's broker. Some municipal brokers specialize in trading only with other municipal brokers, not with the public. They are called broker's brokers, because they generally will help a municipal broker-dealer to place an unsold portion of bonds, usually from a new issue. The broker's broker may sometimes act as a principal in order to protect the other broker's identity. The broker's broker may keep securities in an investment account but does not keep an inventory of securities to sell at a later date.

The Blue List
of Current Municipal Offerings

(A Division of Standard and Poor's Corporation)

Published every weekday except Saturdays and Holidays by
The Blue List Publishing Company, 345 Hudson Street, New York, NY 10014
Telephone 212 255-0240

The bonds set forth in this list were offered at the close of business on the day before the date of this issue by the houses mentioned subject to prior sale and change in price. Every effort is made by The Blue List Publishing Company and the houses whose offerings are shown in The Blue List to avoid mistakes and inaccuracies, but due to the fact that many offerings come in by wire and that the list is published after the offering houses have closed for the day, occasional errors are unavoidable. Neither The Blue List Publishing Company nor the offering houses take responsibility for the accuracy of the offerings listed herein.

+ Items so marked did not appear in the previous issue of the Blue List
* Prices so marked are changed from the previous issue
c Items so marked are reported to have call or option features. Consult offering house for full details.

AMT. M	SECURITY	PURPOSE	RATE	MATURITY	YIELD OR PRICE	OFFERED BY
220	ALABAMA		3.20	3/1/91	5.40	OPPENHEIMER & CO. (FT. LAU)
10	ALABAMA	HWY	3.50	1/1/94	5.90	BARR BROS & CO
30	ALABAMA	W/W	3.375	4/1/94	5.60	W. DOBBS & CO INC
25	ALABAMA	EDUC. AUTH.	6.60	3/1/01	5.40	MERRILL-WHITE
+100	ALABAMA	PUB. SCH. & COL. AU.	5.00	9/1/09	5.25	FIRST BOSTON

Fig. 17.3 A page as it might appear in The Blue List.

Confirmations. Customers must receive written confirmation of each transaction. The rules describe these confirmations in great detail. Confirmations must describe the security and list the trade date, settlement date, the amount of accrued interest and designation of the firm as agent or principal.

Amendments to MSRB Rule 15 require that a confirmation for a trade effected on the basis of dollar price must include that price and must indicate the lowest potential yield (yield to premium call, to par option or to maturity).

Confirmations for trades involving callable securities must include a statement indicating that the yield shown may be affected by the exercise of a call provision and that information concerning the call provision will be provided upon request.

This rule contains special provisions for bonds quoted or sold on a yield basis (except for dollar bonds). If sold at a premium, the broker-dealer must indicate the yield to the first call date, whichever amounts to the lower yield to the customer. In other words, the customer must be informed of the worst possible yield on a bond. The following information is also required:

- in agency transactions, the name of the party on the other side and the source and amount of any commission (the name of the other party must be disclosed on request if it isn't listed on the confirmation);

- the dated date, if it affects the interest calculation;
- the first interest payment date, if payments are not semiannual;
- whether the securities are fully registered, registered as to principal only or available in book-entry form;
- whether the securities are "called" or "prerefunded," as well as the date of maturity fixed by the call notice and the amount of the call price;
- the certificate denominations of any municipal notes and, for municipal bonds, any denominations other than standard units ($1,000 or $5,000 par value); and
- any special qualifications or factors that might affect payment of principal or interest.

Since 1983, all confirmations sent to customers must include the applicable Committee on Uniform Securities Identification Procedures (CUSIP) number, if any is assigned.

Taxation of Municipal Issues

Municipal bonds are usually priced and offered for sale at a yield to maturity (called a basis quote) rather than at a dollar price. Yield to maturity is the total return on that investment per year and takes into account both the interest paid and the premium added to (or discounted from) the par value.

Adjusting Cost Basis of Debt Securities

Bonds may be bought (and sold) at par, at a discount or at a premium. Bonds will either be called before maturity (usually at a premium) or redeemed at maturity at par. In any of these situations, capital gains or losses may be realized. An investor will not have a gain or loss on a bond if it is purchased at par and later sold at par, or held to maturity and redeemed at par. Treatment of bonds bought at a premium or a discount might differ, however, and the tax treatment will depend upon the type of bond purchased.

Municipal bonds bought at a premium. Unlike bondholders of corporate bonds bought at a premium, owners of a municipal bond bought at a premium (whether an original issue premium bond or a bond bought on the secondary market) must amortize the amount of the premium over the life of the bond. An investor buys a municipal bond at a premium because it has a higher coupon rate than more recently traded municipal bonds. Since this bond is paying tax-free income, the IRS does not allow the investor to deduct a loss on the bond if held to maturity. If sold before maturity, the cost basis must be adjusted by the amount of the amortized premium.

Original Issue Discount (OID) municipal bonds. When municipal bonds are issued at a discount, the coupon rate is not competitive with current yields on similar municipal securities. The difference between the discounted price and par, therefore, is considered additional tax-free income. If an original issue discount bond is held until maturity, the investor will have no taxable capital gain. The amount of the discount is accreted on a straight-line basis until maturity.

Municipal bonds bought at a discount (secondary market). The cost basis on a municipal bond bought at a discount in the secondary market is not adjusted. If the bond is held to maturity, the investor will realize a capital gain. If it is sold again in the secondary market, the gain or loss is determined by the difference between the bond's purchase and sale price.

Tax Benefits

The 1986 tax law changes didn't negate the most attractive feature of municipal securities (the exemption of interest from federal income tax) but did change it somewhat. Tax exemption is limited to public purpose bonds, those issued to finance projects that benefit citizens in general rather than particular private interests. Tax exemption is not granted to private-activity bonds (those which channel more than 10% of the proceeds to private parties). Further, the law now sets a cap on the amount of tax-exempt private-activity bonds each state can issue annually.

Investors considering the purchase of a tax-exempt bond should compare the yield of that security very carefully to the yields of other securities, including those that are not tax exempt. Because of the tax savings, the tax-free bond may be more attractive than a taxable bond with a higher interest rate. This will depend, in part, on the investor's tax bracket. The higher the tax bracket, the more the investor gains from the tax exemption.

In all cases, then, a tax-equivalent yield can be calculated by dividing the tax-free yield by 100% minus the investor's tax rate.

$$\text{Taxable Equivalent Yield} = \text{Tax Free Yield} / (100\% - \text{tax rate})$$

Bond Swaps

Bond swapping is a technique used by investors in municipal bonds to generate a tax loss and improve their portfolios. It involves selling bonds at a loss while simultaneously purchasing bonds similar to those sold. To avoid classification as a wash sale (and the IRS disallowing the loss for tax purposes), the new bonds purchased must differ in some respect from those sold.

Since there is a spread or difference between the bid and asked price, it is usually necessary to buy the bond with a later maturity, a lower coupon rate or a lower rating than that of the bond sold. An investor unwilling to accept some such change in his investment must be prepared to invest additional funds.

see notebook

Analysis of Municipal Bonds

An analysis of general obligation municipal bonds is conducted differently from an analysis of revenue bonds. When analyzing general obligation bonds, investors assess the municipality's ability to raise enough tax revenue to pay off its debt. With revenue bonds (as with corporate bonds), investors evaluate the likelihood that a specific facility will generate sufficient revenue to cover its operational costs and pay back the debt.

General Obligation Bonds

General wealth of the community. Since general obligation securities are backed primarily by tax revenues, they can be tested for safety by evaluating the general wealth of the community, including:

- property values;
- retail sales per capita;
- local bank deposits and bank clearings; and
- the diversity of industry in the municipality's tax base.

Holders of general obligation municipal bonds know that the issuer's taxing power will enable it to continue making principal and interest payments through all but the most severe economic circumstances.

Characteristics of the issuer. An analysis of certain factors, such as population, property values and per capita income, would constitute a quantitative analysis of the municipality. For example, a city has just announced a general obligation bond issue. According to the issue's official statement, the city is a small, incorporated city, population 50,000. Within city limits there are 10,000 homes and apartments. According to the county assessor's estimates, the market value of all nongovernmental property in the city is $1 billion. The average value of each parcel of real property is $100,000. All of this quantitative information would be taken into account in an analysis of the issuer.

An analysis of other factors, including benefits available to industries located in the area, trends toward growth or decline of population and property values and plans and projects being undertaken by the area would constitute a qualitative analysis of the municipality. A qualitative analysis of the city would examine factors such as the following: the city lies on the tollway system and has its own airport; the city has been attempting to broaden and diversify its primarily residential tax base by attracting some light industry; even though the residents have relatively high incomes and the area is growing rapidly, the community is fiscally conservative.

only GO Bonds have →

Debt limits. To protect taxpayers from excessive taxes, statutory limits may be placed on the amount of debt a municipality can assume. The state constitution and the municipality's articles of incorporation limit the amount of GO bonds that the city may issue and have outstanding. In this example, the outstanding amount of all bond issues in the city may not exceed 5% of the estimated market value of all taxable property within the city limits. This is the city's constitutional debt limit. The official statement includes information necessary to determine how close total outstanding debt, including the newly issued debt, comes to the constitutional debt limit.

The state constitution or city charter also limits the purposes for which the city may float its bond issues. The city may issue bonds to finance capital improvements as long as those bonds mature within the expected lifetime of the improvement. (The city shouldn't still owe money on a facility that has disintegrated or become obsolete.) But it may not issue securities to pay for city operations, such as snow removal.

The citizens of the city control the general obligation debt of the city. Because their taxes will service such debt, voters must approve each issue in a referendum.

Overlapping debt. Investors should take a careful look at overlapping debt incurred by issuers (such as local or statewide school districts or regional sanitation districts) that draw tax revenues from the same source. If a bond issue is to be financed from property taxes, for example, the investor needs to know how many other issuers have a claim on those revenues. The population will also be responsible for the debt they authorize the school district and the county to issue. The school district is wholly supported by the city population, because the taxing boundaries of the district are included within the city. The county debt is partially supported by city taxpayers, because the county is partially included within the city. The municipality's share of the debt issued by its political subdivisions is called overlapping debt.

The airport's terminal and other facilities are financed by city revenue bonds. Although these bonds are included in the debt statement of the city, they are self-supporting. Money to operate the airport and pay debt service on the bonds is raised by charging a fee to airport users.

Income of the municipality. From its income, the city pays interest and principal on its debt obligations. To ensure that the city has enough money to pay for the necessary police, fire and other services, principal and interest payments on its debt should not exceed 25% of annual income.

Income taxes and sales taxes are major sources of state income. Real property taxes are the principal income of the county, the school district and the city. City income includes fines, license fees, assessments, city sales taxes, hotel taxes, city income taxes, utility taxes and any city personal property taxes. But the largest source of city income is the tax on real property.

Property taxes are based on a property's assessed valuation, which is a percentage of the estimated market value. That percentage is established by each state or county and varies substantially by locale. The market value of each piece of property in the county is determined by the county assessor, who relies on recent sale prices of similar properties, income streams, replacement costs and other methods of estimating value.

Since the real property tax is based on the value of the property, it is said to be an ad valorem or per value tax. These taxes are a lien on the property, which can be seized if they aren't paid. General obligation bonds, backed by the power to tax and seize property, are considered safer than revenue bonds of the same issuer and can be issued with a lower interest rate.

Revenue Bonds

Like corporate bonds, revenue bonds are judged according to the potential for a facility to generate money to service the debt. Recently, municipalities have issued more revenue bonds and fewer general obligation bonds. Since revenue bonds are not repaid from taxes, they are not subject to statutory debt limits the way general obligation bonds are. Revenue bonds are meant to be self-supporting, but if the facility they finance does not make enough money to repay the debt, bondholders, not taxpayers, bear the risk. When assessing the quality of revenue bonds, one should consider the following factors:

- **Economic justification**. The object being built should show promise of generating revenues.
- **Competing facilities**. A facility should not be placed where better alternatives are easily available.
- **Sources of revenue**. Sources of revenue should be dependable.
- **Call provisions**. With callable bonds, the higher the call price the more attractive the bond is to the investor.
- **Flow of funds**. All funds must be sufficient to meet requirements of the project. Substantial reserve funds are a plus.

Protective covenants of the bond (trust) indenture. The face of a revenue bond certificate usually refers to a trust indenture. This is a statement of the terms of agreement between the issuing municipality and the trustee appointed to act on behalf of the bondholders.

In the trust indenture, the municipality agrees to abide by certain protective covenants (promises meant to protect bondholders). These include promises to keep orderly books, to report revenues collected, to maintain the facility and to keep rates on the facility high enough to cover all costs. The trustee appointed in the indenture supervises the issuer's compliance with the bond covenants. Municipal bonds, unlike their corporate counterparts, are not bound by the Trust Indenture Act of 1939. Most municipal securities, however, are issued with indentures.

As part of its due diligence research, the underwriter of a municipal issue will perform a feasibility study to determine such matters as whether or not the project makes economic sense and is sufficiently funded. The feasibility study appears in the official statement that describes the issue for potential investors.

Municipal Debt Ratios

The ability of a community to meet its debt obligations and retire its debt can be analyzed by applying certain ratios to the information in the debt statement and other documents. These ratios include:

- **Net debt to assessed valuation.** A ratio of 5% (that is, $5,000 of municipal debt for every $100,000 of assessed value of property) is considered reasonable.
- **Net debt to estimated valuation.** Because assessed valuation varies in different municipalities, most analysts prefer to use estimated valuation of property.
- **Debt per capita.** Larger cities can assume more debt per capita because of their diversified property base.
- **Debt service to annual revenues.** This ratio indicates whether the community is overburdened with debt service expenses (interest payments and retirement of principal). *P&I*
- **Debt trend.** This number indicates whether the ratios are rising or falling. Because bonds are long-term investment obligations, it is important to anticipate the financial position of the community in the coming years.
- **Collection ratio** (the taxes collected divided by the taxes assessed). The collection ratio is used to detect deteriorating credit conditions. *(100% best, fewest delinquencies)*
- **Coverage ratio.** Municipal bonds are evaluated on much the same basis as corporate bonds. The principal consideration is how many times annual revenues will cover debt service: the times-interest-earned or coverage ratio. With municipal revenue bonds, however, the standards are less rigorous than with corporate bonds. A coverage of 2 to 1 is considered adequate for the typical municipal revenue bond. For utility revenue bonds (sewer, water and electricity), a coverage of 1.25 times fixed charges is considered adequate. *12.35*
- **Taxes per person or per capita** (the tax income of the city divided by the city population). Taxes per capita indicates the tax burden of the population.

recognize these ratios

Interest Rate Comparisons

Municipal bond prices fluctuate more than government and corporate bond prices. Each issue, each interest rate and each maturity is a specific bond. Thousands of municipals trade, so each specific security has fewer consistent market makers. Because there are fewer market makers, the market for a specific municipal bond is thinner than the market for most corporates and governments.

Bond Ratings

Moody's, Standard and Poor's, White's (rates marketability risk) *Liquidity* and Fitch's (limited to corporate bonds) rate bonds for default risk. Moody's also rates municipal notes using a Moody's Investment Grade (MIG) rating. *1, 2, 3, 4*

The rating organizations rate only those issues that either pay to be rated or that have enough outstanding securities to generate constant investor interest. Even though a bond is not rated, it may be a safe and worthwhile addition to an investor's portfolio.

Municipal bond insurance. Issuers of municipal bonds can insure the principal and interest payments on their securities by purchasing insurance from the Municipal Bond Insurance Association (MBIA) or from the American Bond Assurance Corporation (AMBAC). Insured bonds can be issued with lower coupon rates and therefore at less cost to the issuer. Both AMBAC and MBIA bonds are rated triple-A by Standard & Poor's. Moody's does not consider insurance when rating municipal bonds.

AMBAC also sells policies to investors who want to insure the principal and interest payments from their bond portfolios. To qualify for a policy, the investor must hold "investment grade bonds" (that is, those rated at least BBB by Standard & Poor's or Baa by Moody's).

The Official Statement

To disclose to the public all pertinent information about a new issue of municipal securities, the municipality publishes the official statement. Information in the official statement includes the purpose of the issue, plan for repayment and the financial, economic and social characteristics of the issuing government. Analysts study the various documents included in the official statement to determine the financial condition of the issuer at present and in the foreseeable future.

Future financial needs. The official statement should be scrutinized for any indication of future debt requirements. The municipality would need to issue more debt if:

- its annual income is not sufficient to make the payments on its short-term (or floating) debt;
- principal repayments are scheduled too closely together;
- sinking funds for outstanding term bonds are inadequate;
- pension liabilities are unfunded; and
- it plans to make more capital improvements soon.

Issuing more debt in the near future may result in a lower bond rating, which could cause the current issue to trade at a discount.

If the financial statements and other information in the official statement are inadequate, the bonds may not be marketable or may be marketable only with higher interest rates. Inadequate financial statements should certainly raise the caution flag for investors and analysts.

The debt statement. In the official statement is a debt statement providing information useful to analysts. The first entries are estimated full valuation of taxable property, estimated assessed value of property and the assessment percentage, and the estimated population.

$$\text{Total Debt} = \text{Overlapping Debt} + \text{Net Direct Debt}$$

	Total Debt
-	Self-Supporting Debt
-	Sinking Fund Debt
	Net Direct Debt
+	Overlapping Debt
	Net Total Debt

$$\text{Net Total Debt} / \text{Population} = \text{Net Debt per Capita}$$

The next entry is the municipality's direct debt, which includes general obligation bonds, short term notes issued in anticipation of taxes or for interim financing and revenue bonds and notes.

$$\text{Net Direct Debt} = \text{Direct Debt} - \text{Self-Supporting Debt}$$

Although revenue debt is included in direct debt, it is actually self-supporting (backed by revenues from the facility it financed) and is not a burden on the municipality's taxpayers. In the debt statement, therefore, revenue debt is subtracted from direct debt to calculate net direct debt.

The overlapping debt disclosed on the debt statement is the city's proportionate share of the county debt, the school district debt, the park district and sanitary district debts. The city's total debt responsibility is the sum of the overlapping debt and the net direct debt.

See notebook

Municipal Securities Rules and Regulations

The Securities Act of 1933. The 1933 act protects the investor considering purchase of new issues by:

- requiring registration of new issues to be distributed interstate;
- requiring the issuer to provide full and fair disclosure about itself and the offering;
- requiring the issuer to make available all material information necessary for an investor to judge the merit of the issue;
- regulating the underwriting and distribution of primary and secondary issues; and
- providing criminal penalties for fraud in the issuance of new securities.

Municipal and government securities are exempt from the registration requirements of the Securities Act of 1933. Municipal issuers and underwriters are, however, still subject to the antifraud provisions.

Municipal Securities Rulemaking Board (MSRB)

Following a period of publicized investor loss due to securities fraud, the Municipal Securities Rulemaking Board (MSRB) was created in accordance with the Securities Amendment Act of 1975. Generally speaking, the act requires underwriters and dealers to protect the interests of the investor as well as their own, be ethical in offering advice and responsive to complaints and disputes.

Created after the passage of the Securities Acts Amendments of 1975, the MSRB is headed by a 15-member board. Five board members represent broker-dealer firms, five members come from banks and five are public representatives. This organization makes rules pertaining to issuing and trading municipal securities.

Like the NASD and the NYSE, the MSRB is a self-supporting, self-regulatory organization that carries out the wishes of the SEC in matters regarding municipal securities. An annual fee of $100 from each municipal securities dealer, supplemented by a fee paid for each municipal bond that is underwritten, provides the funds necessary to run this self-regulatory organization.

Unlike the NASD and the NYSE, the MSRB does not have authority to enforce the rules it makes. The rules that pertain to broker-dealers are enforced by the NASD and the SEC. The comptroller of the currency enforces MSRB rules that pertain to national banks. The Federal Reserve Board enforces MSRB rules governing any non-national banks that are members of the Federal Reserve System. The FDIC enforces these rules for non-national banks that are not members of the Federal Reserve System.

Since municipal bonds are exempt securities (they are not required to be registered with the SEC before issue), neither the MSRB nor the SEC has any authority over the issuers. The MSRB regulates the trading of municipal securities through its authority over broker-dealers and banks that underwrite and trade municipal securities.

There are three categories of MSRB rules: 1) general rules and regulations describe the policies of the MSRB; 2) administrative rules speak to the MSRB itself-how it is organized and how it functions; and 3) definitional rules give the meanings of certain terms used in the business of trading municipal securities.

General Regulations

Rule G-1. Some banks act in the capacity of municipal dealers. If a bank under-writes municipal securities, trades or sells them, it must abide by MSRB rules. Also, if a bank serves the issuer as a financial consultant, it is subject to these regulations. Providing a research or advice service for investors in municipal securities or communicating with the public in any way about investing in municipal securities would be considered activities of a municipal securities dealer.

If a bank has a "separately identifiable" department or division that does any of the above activities, it is classified as a municipal securities dealer and must comply with MSRB regulations. A "separately identifiable" division would be under the direct supervision of an officer of the bank.

Personnel Rules for Municipal Securities Firms

Rules G-2 and 3. Like other self-regulatory organizations, the MSRB has standards that must be met by people who work in the industry. No broker-dealer firm may do any municipal securities business unless that firm and all persons (the MSRB rules stipulate "natural" persons) associated with it are qualified. Those who must qualify are municipal securities principals (those who supervise or manage representatives), financial and operation principals (those who supervise the keeping of books and records) and municipal securities representatives (anyone who underwrites, trades or sells municipal securities). A municipal securities representative gives financial advice to municipal securities issuers or investment advice to investors. If you communicate with the public about municipal securities, you are acting as a representative.

To qualify as a municipal securities representative, one must pass the Municipal Securities Limited Representative Examination (Series 52) or the General Securities Registered Representative Exam (Series 7).

The MSRB has a 90-day **apprenticeship** requirement. People new to the business may not do any municipal securities business with the public during this period. They may do business with other municipal dealers if their compensation is not based on the business transacted (the apprentice could receive a salary during this time but could not receive a commission for trades made with other municipal securities dealers).

Rule G-4. The MSRB automatically disqualifies brokers or dealers if they have been expelled or suspended from any securities exchange or any other self-regulatory organization, if they have been convicted of any securities-related crime or if they have violated any part of any securities legislation.

Rule G-5. Persons in the municipal securities business must follow the MSRB rules or be subject to disciplinary action.

Rule G-7. A municipal broker-dealer firm must obtain and keep on file certain information about its associated persons. The completed U-10 Form or U-4 Form will provide all the needed information.

Rules Governing the Conduct of Municipal Securities Business

Rule G-6. Municipal brokers and dealers must have fidelity bonds on their associated persons. The required amount of the bond varies according to the size of the broker-dealer firm. Banks are not affected by this rule.

Rules G-8 and G-9. The MSRB requires firms in the municipal securities business to keep certain books and records. The firm's articles of incorporation or partnership agreements, minutes of board meetings and records of stock certificates must be kept as long as the firm exists. The firm must keep for six years:

- **blotters** (the original entries of trades and various accounts);
- records showing separate **positions** for each municipal security;
- records of all **transactions** made by the firm acting as a member of various **syndicates**;
- **customer complaints** and the firm's response; and
- detailed **account records** for each customer.

The records that must be kept for three years include:

- records of securities that have been transferred, borrowed or loaned and transactions that were not complete on settlement date;
- put options and repurchase agreements;
- transactions in which the firm acted as an agent (broker);
- transactions in which the firm acted as a dealer (principal); and
- copies of confirmations.

In addition, detailed customer account information must be kept, including:

- name and address;
- whether customer is an adult or minor;
- social security number, corporate or partnership tax ID number;
- occupation, with employer's name and address;
- signatures of the representative who introduced the account (accepted it) and of the representative's supervisory principal;
- in discretionary accounts, customer's written authorization (the principal must endorse the account and each transaction); and
- in a margin account, a signed hypothecation agreement, if applicable.

All of the above records must be kept in an **easily accessible place for at least two years**. After that, the time and effort needed to get them must be reasonable.

Rule G-16. Every municipal broker-dealer must be examined at least every 24 months to be sure that the firm is complying with MSRB regulations, SEC rules and the Securities Exchange Act of 1934. Remember, the MSRB does not enforce its own rules, so it does not examine its firms. The appropriate enforcement agency administers the examinations (i.e., NASD, FDIC, the Comptroller of the Currency, or the FRB).

Rule G-24. Municipal securities firms may not use inside information to solicit trades of municipal securities except with the consent of the issuer of the securities.

Rule G-27. Each municipal securities firm must designate a principal to supervise the firm's representatives. Each firm must have a written procedures manual. The principal of the firm must approve in writing:

- the opening of new customer accounts;
- *by end of day* every municipal securities transaction;
- actions taken on customer complaints; and
- correspondence regarding municipal securities trades.

Every firm must have a financial operations principal who maintains books and records as required by Rules G-8 and G-9.

Rule G-33. Municipal dealers must calculate accrued interest when a municipal security trades "and interest." The important thing to remember is that municipal bonds, like corporates, use a 360-day year (every month has 30 days for this calculation).

Rule G-35. The MSRB rule about arbitration is very much like the NASD and the NYSE codes of arbitration. It is for disputes between any of the participants in the municipal securities business.

Rules Governing Interactions Between Municipal Securities Broker-Dealers and Their Customers

Rule G-15. Confirmations of trades must be sent or given to customers at or before the completion of the transaction. Confirms must include:

- name, address and phone number of the broker-dealer;
- customer's name;
- detailed description of the security, including issuer, interest rate, maturity, whether it is callable, etc.;
- trade date and time of execution;
- settlement date;
- CUSIP number (if any);
- yield and dollar price;
- amount of accrued interest;
- extended principal amount (i.e., the total principal of all securities covered by the confirmation);
- total dollar amount (extended principal plus any accrued interest);

read over

- the capacity in which the firm did this trade (broker or dealer); if it is an agency transaction (broker), the name of the person on the other side of the trade must be given if requested and the amount of commission must be disclosed;
- the dated date, if it affects the interest calculation and the first interest payment date;
- the level of registration of the security (i.e., fully registered, registered as to principal only or book-entry form);
- whether the bonds are "called" or "prerefunded;" and
- any other special facts about the security traded (i.e., exlegal trade, federally taxable, odd denominations, etc.).

Rule G-17. Municipal securities broker-dealers must deal fairly with everyone in the transacting of business.

Rule G-18. Broker-dealers must try to get prices for customers that are reasonable and fair. In other words, they must try to find the lowest purchase price and the highest sale price for the customer. This rule also applies to broker's brokers, who regularly effect trades for the accounts of other municipal brokers and dealers.

Rule G-19. The municipal securities firm, through its representatives, must obtain extensive financial information about a client. From this information the representative must make recommendations that are suitable for that customer's financial situation. Even if the representative and the firm believe a certain transaction is not suitable and inform the client, the representative may do the transaction anyway if the client insists.

Discretionary accounts must be authorized in writing by the customer. The firm's principal must approve the opening of such an account. Each trade is to be reviewed and approved by the principal and the account must be checked frequently for any possible abuse of discretionary authority. Churning is prohibited.

Rule G-21. Municipal securities firms must be truthful in their advertising. They must not publish ads that are false or misleading in regard to their services, skills or products. Ads for new issues can show the original reoffering prices (even though these prices may have changed) if the date of the sale is in the ad. Each advertisement must be approved in writing prior to first use by the firm's municipal securities principal or general securities principal.

Rule G-22. Clients must be informed if a control relationship exists between the municipal firm and the issuer. A control relationship is defined as one in which the broker, dealer or municipal securities dealer controls, is controlled by, or is under common control with the issuer of the security or a person other than the issuer who is obligated, directly or indirectly, with respect to debt service on the security. For example, a mayor planning a bond issue is considered to have a control relationship if he is also a principal for a broker-dealer underwriting this issue.

The rule does not prohibit control relationships per se, but requires that broker-dealers in control situations inform their customers in writing, before settlement of the trade. If a control relationship exists, a broker-dealer cannot execute a transaction in a discretionary account without the specific authorization of the customer.

Rule G-25. Municipal securities firms may not misuse securities or money held for another person. They must not guarantee a client against loss. They may not share in the profits or losses of a customer's account (joint accounts in a private capacity are allowed).

Rule G-29. A copy of the MSRB regulations must be kept at every municipal securities broker-dealer's office. The firm must allow any customer to see the rules if the customer asks to do so.

Rule G-30. Markups or markdowns charged by municipal securities dealers must be fair and reasonable, taking into account all circumstances of the trade, such as:

- fair market value of the securities at trade time;
- total dollar amount of the transaction;
- any special difficulties in doing the trade; and,
- the fact that the dealer is entitled to a profit.

Unlike the NASD, there is no 5% guideline for markups or markdowns. Commissions charged when the firm acts as a broker must be fair and reasonable considering the circumstances relevant to the trade.

Rules Governing Municipal Securities Broker-Dealer Interactions

Rule G-12. This rule outlines the procedures for settlement of trades between municipal securities firms. Settlement dates for municipal securities are the same as for the rest of the securities industry:

- Cash trades settle on trade date.
- Trades done regular way settle on the fifth business day after the trade date.
- When-, as- and if-issued trades settle on the date on which both parties agree but not sooner than five business days after the confirmation (indicating that the settlement date is set).

Confirmations for trades between dealers are sent on the trade date or on the next business day. Confirmations between municipal broker-dealers must include essentially the same information as confirms sent to public customers (see Rule G-15). In addition, the amount of the concession, if any, must be shown. Any instructions for nonstandard delivery must be stated.

Rule G-12 also states what municipal securities firms are to do about confirmations they do not recognize. DK procedures explain how to resolve the problem.

Delivery is made in denominations of $1,000 or $5,000 for bearer bonds. Registered bonds are delivered in multiples of $1,000 par value with a maximum par value on any one certificate of $100,000. Delivery is assumed to be in bearer form unless both parties agree otherwise.

Mutilated certificates are not good delivery unless the transfer agent or some other acceptable official of the issuer will validate the security. Securities that are not in good delivery form are rejected or reclaimed (the securities are not accepted for delivery). This does not invalidate the trade. Mutilated coupons must be endorsed by the issuer or by a commercial bank. Coupon bonds must have all unpaid coupons attached in proper order.

In the case of partial call of an issue, the called securities are not good delivery unless they are identified as called when traded. Municipal securities without legal opinions attached are not good delivery unless it is specified on trade date that the transaction was ex-legal.

Rule G-12 also discusses the settlement of new issue syndicate accounts. Good faith deposits are returned by the syndicate manager to the syndicate members within two business days of settling with the issuer. Final settlement of the syndicate account must be made within 60 days after the securities are delivered by the manager to the members. Credit designated by a customer for a particular member must be delivered within 30 business days after delivery of the securities to the customer.

Rule G-13. Rule G-13 states that municipal broker-dealers can publish quotations only for bona fide bids or offers. Nominal quotes (informational only) are permissible if they are identified as such.

Rule G-14. Municipal securities broker-dealers may publicize reports of trades only if the trades actually took place. In other words, no fictitious, deceptive or manipulative reports are allowed.

Rule G-20. In order to prevent municipal securities broker-dealers from influencing employees of another firm, Rule G-20 prohibits firms from giving gifts valued at over $100 to any person in one year other than their own employees (note the difference: the NASD's yearly dollar limit is $50). Gifts of occasional meals or tickets to sporting events or concerts (not season passes) are permitted. Sponsoring of legitimate business functions is also permissible.

Rule G-28. If an employee of a municipal securities broker-dealer firm opens an account with another municipal securities firm, the MSRB regulations are similar to NASD rules. MSRB rules require the introducing broker-dealer, the firm where the employee is opening the account, to inform the employer of the new account by sending duplicate confirmations to the employer. The NASD rule states the employer must be notified only upon the employer's request.

NO BACK-SCRATCHING

Rule G-31. A municipal securities broker-dealer may not solicit business from an investment company (trading securities in the investment company's portfolio) based on the broker-dealer's record of sales of the investment company's shares.

Rule G-34. A municipal securities firm that is managing an underwriting for a new issue must, in most cases, apply for CUSIP numbers for the securities that are to be issued. An issue is eligible for CUSIP numbers if:

- the issue has a par value of $500,000 or more;
- the issue has a par value of at least $250,000 and the issuer has other outstanding debt of more than $250,000; or,
- the issuer has outstanding debt of over $500,000 and a CUSIP subscriber requests assignment of a number to an issue.

CUSIP numbers are not required for local assessment bonds or for notes that mature in one year or less.

Underwriting Rules

Rule G-11. Rule G-11 makes several statements about the sale of new-issue municipal securities during the underwriting period. Every syndicate must establish a priority for allocating orders and the conditions that might allow a change in priority. The managing underwriter sets the priority and informs the syndicate. Syndicate members must inform the manager whether an order they are submitting is for their own account, a related account, a municipal securities investment trust or its accumulation account. These types of orders would be fairly low in the order of priority.

The syndicate manager must give syndicate members a statement of expenses incurred by the syndicate in each underwriting. Another required statement shows the aggregate par value and prices of all the bonds sold from the syndicate account.

Rule G-23. The purpose of Rule G-23 is to reduce conflicts of interest in situations where the municipal securities firm acts as both a financial adviser and an underwriter for an issuer. If a firm agrees to give financial advice, or contracts for a fee to consult for an issuer about a new issue of municipal securities, that firm has a financial advisory relationship with the issuer. This advisory relationship must be described in writing. The compensation for this service must be disclosed.

If a firm acting in a financial advisory capacity wants to participate in the issue on which it has advised, it must get written consent from the issuer to submit a competitive bid. For a negotiated bid, the advisory contract must be terminated in writing and the issuer must give written consent. The former financial advisor must tell the issuer of the possible conflict of interest and must disclose to the issuer the source and anticipated amount of money received if participating in the issue. Also, if a financial advisory relationship exists or did exist between the dealer and issuer, purchasers of the securities must be informed of this fact.

Rule G-32. When a new issue of municipal securities is delivered to a customer, a copy of the official statement must accompany or precede the delivery. If it is not yet completed, a preliminary official statement is acceptable with the delivery. A summary or an abstract of the official statement is also permitted. But those two documents are considered to be advertising. They must be approved by a member of the firm before they can be distributed.

If the issue is a negotiated underwriting, the municipal firm must tell the customer the amount of the spread, the amount of any fee received if it acted as an agent in the sale and the initial offering price for each maturity in the issue.

Chapter Review

Questions

1. Municipal bonds are issued for all of the following EXCEPT

    ____(A) sewers.
    ____(B) GNMAs.
    ____(C) hospitals.
    ____(D) capital improvements.

2. In safety of principal, municipal bonds are considered second only to

    ____(A) preferred stock.
    ____(B) common stock.
    ____(C) U.S. government agency bonds.
    ____(D) FNMA securities.

3. A general obligation bond is backed by

    ____(A) tolls.
    ____(B) special taxes.
    ____(C) public housing.
    ____(D) full faith and credit of issuing municipality.

4. If interest rates rise, municipal bond prices should

    ____(A) rise.
    ____(B) decline.
    ____(C) fluctuate.
    ____(D) stay the same.

5. If a municipality appoints an underwriter to offer a new issue, the underwriting is

    ____(A) negotiated.
    ____(B) a competitive bid.
    ____(C) proportionate.
    ____(D) an eastern agreement.

6. A legal opinion on a municipal bond is prepared by

____(A)   the underwriter.
____(B)   the trustee.
____(C)   the municipality.
____(D)   an independent bond attorney.

7. All of the following are examples of short-term, tax-exempt municipal issues EXCEPT

____(A)   BANs.
____(B)   PNs.
____(C)   AONs.
____(D)   TANs.

8. Short-term municipal notes normally have all the following characteristics EXCEPT they

____(A)   mature in less than one year.
____(B)   are issued in anticipation of a bond sale.
____(C)   pay interest every six months.
____(D)   pay interest that is exempt from federal taxation.

9. The manager of a municipal syndicate is a dealer who will

____(A)   act for the underwriting group.
____(B)   take the largest position.
____(C)   act for the issuing authority.
____(D)   provide the legal opinion.

10. In a municipal securities underwriting, which of the following signs the agreement among underwriters?

____(A)   members of the syndicate
____(B)   issuer
____(C)   bond counsel
____(D)   trustee

Answer Key

1. B.

2. C.

3. D.

4. B.

5. A.

6. D.

7. C.

8. C.

9. A.

10. A.

Chapter Eighteen

Options

Key Terms

18.14 At-the-money

18.15 Bear

18.15 Call buyer

18.4 Class

18.7 Double auction market

18.3 Exercise price

18.40 Foreign currency option

18.37 Interest rate option

18.14 18.13 Intrinsic value

18.3 Non-equity option

18.8 18.4 Options Clearing Corporation (OCC)

18.7 Order Book Official (OBO)

18.5 18.2 Premium

18.18 Put buyer

18.4 Series

18.3 Strike price

18.4 Type

18.2 Write

Bull 18.15

Call 18.2

Call writer 18.17

Closing transaction 18.5

Equity option 18.3

Expiration date 18.4

Index option 18.35

In-the-money 18.13

Market maker 18.7

Opening transaction 18.5

Option contract 18.2

Out-of-the-money 18.13

Put 18.2

Put writer 18.19

Standardized option 18.6

Time value 18.14

Underlying instrument 18.2

w401

Option Contracts and the Option Markets

Calls and Puts

An option is a **contract** between two people. The purchaser (also known as the **holder, buyer** or **owner**) of the contract has paid money for the **right** to buy or the **right** to sell securities. The seller (or **writer**) of the option contract, on the other hand, has accepted money for taking on an **obligation**. The option seller **must** buy or **must** sell a particular security if asked to by the option buyer. A stock option contract (the kind we will be discussing most) represents an agreement between the two people (a buyer and a seller) to buy or sell 100 shares (a round lot) of stock.

There are two types of options: **calls** and **puts**.

- A call option is the **right** to **call** (buy) a security away from someone. You can buy that right for yourself, or you can sell that right to someone else.
- A put option is the **right** to **put** (sell) a security to someone. You can buy that right for yourself, or you can sell that right to someone else.

The buyer of an option has acquired a right.

The seller of an option has taken on an obligation.

Fig. 18.1 The difference between buying and selling.

A **call** is the right to **buy** a set amount of a specific investment instrument at a set price, for a set period of time. A **put** is the right to **sell** a set amount of a specific investment instrument at a set price, for a set period of time. The buyer of an option contract pays the seller a **premium** to take on the obligations in the contract.

Holders of option contracts (put and call buyers) have three choices. They can exercise the option (that is, use it to purchase or sell the security the contract entitles them to), let the option expire, or sell the option contract to another investor before the expiration date.

Underlying Instruments

In theory, options can be created on any item with a fluctuating market value, such as securities, houses, cars, gold coins, baseball cards or comic books. The next few sections will cover options on the following underlying instruments:

notebook

- corporate stock;
- broad and narrow-based indexes (Major Market index, Technology index, etc.);
- Treasury bonds, Treasury notes and Treasury bills; and
- major foreign currencies.

The most familiar options are those issued on common stocks, also called **equity options**. Since options are basically the same regardless of the underlying security, we'll use equity options as a general introduction. Subsequent sections of this chapter will explore the special characteristics of nonequity options (options on indexes, debt instruments and currencies).

The Option Contract

Exercise prices. An option's exercise price is the price at which the owner of the contract will be entitled to buy the underlying security, and the price at which the seller has an obligation to deliver that security. Notice that most exercise prices (also known as strike prices) in the options table following are set at intervals of $5. If the advance or decline of the price of the underlying stock warrants it, the OCC will create new options with different strike prices. For example, if a stock that is currently trading in the 70s declines significantly, the OCC might add calls and puts with exercise prices of 55 or even lower.

Options on relatively high-priced stock will have strike prices set at intervals of $10 (for example, Texas Instruments, IBM and Teledyne). Strike prices are usually multiples of $5 and $10 when issued, but may be adjusted later for stock splits and dividends

Option & NY Close	Strike Price	Calls- Last			Puts- Last		
		Jan	Feb	Mar	Jan	Feb	Mar
Adm Fam	40	1 3/8	3 5/8	r	3/16	7/8	1 1/4
41 1/8	45	1/2	1 1/2	2 1/8	3 7/8	r	1/4
41 1/8	50	r	3/8	5/8	s	s	12
AFAP Ent	30	7 7/8	9 1/8	11	r	r	1/8
37 7/8	35	3 1/8	14 1/2	6 3/4	r	1/4	1/8
37 7/8	40	3/4	1 5/8	3	3/4	7/8	r
All Swel	25	1/4	1 3/8	2	1/8	1	1 5/8
25 1/4	30	r	1/8	7/8	3 3/4	4 5/8	7
Bulln Bar	20	r	r	r	r	r	7/8
24	22 1/2	1	r	r	r	r	r
24	25	5/16	1	2 1/4	r	r	2 5/8

Chicago Board

Total call vol 1,240,086 Call open int 3,038,532
Total put vol 105,755 Put open int 941,395

Fig. 18.2 A typical stock option quotation table.

(but not for cash dividends). Sometimes, for lower-priced stocks (such as Bulln Bar in the exhibit), strike prices will be set at intervals of 2 1/2.

Expiration dates. The Options Clearing Corporation (the OCC) standardizes the expiration dates of listed options. Each class of listed options has a set of four expiration months (known as a **cycle**). An option might have expiration dates of January, April, July and October (**JAJO**); February, May, August and November (**FMAN**); or March, June, September and December (**MJSD**). Each option contract must expire on the preset option expiration day in one of those months. As one example, if the options that are currently trading are the October, January and April contracts, upon expiration of the October options, the OCC will introduce July options.

The expiration cycles were modified in late 1987 to accommodate investor preference for trading in **spot** and **nearby** expiration months. As a result, all expiration cycles feature current (spot) and next (nearby) month expirations in addition to normal quarterly expiration cycles. As an illustration of this type of trading cycle, assume that it is now January. The three option cycles would include the following:

Cycle 1:	Jan	Feb	Apr		Jul	Oct
Cycle 2:	Jan	Feb	May	Aug		Nov
Cycle 3:	Jan	Feb	Mar	Jun	Sep	Dec

Within each cycle, four expiration months are open for trading at all times: the current month, the next month, the midterm month and the distant month.

Type, Class and Series

Options are categorized by **type**, **class** and **series**.

- **Type:** There are two types of options, calls and puts.
- **Class:** All options of the same type on the same underlying security are considered as being of the same class. All AFAP calls make up one class of options, all AFAP puts make up another class of options.
- **Series:** All options of the same class with the same exercise price and the same expiration month are in the same series. All January 45 ADM puts make up one series. All January 50 ADM puts make up another series.

Long and Short Positions

The Four Basic Option Transactions

There are two types of options (calls and puts) and two types of option transactions (purchases and sales; selling is also known as writing). These can be combined in four ways by an options investor.

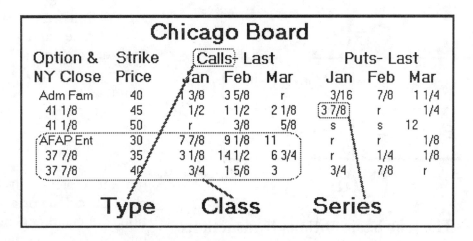

Fig. 18.3 Different option types, class and series.

Long options. The owner (buyer or holder) of an option is said to have a long position. This investor has paid money in the form of a **premium** to obtain the rights specified in the option contract.

- The investor with a **long call** has the right to **purchase** the underlying security at a specified price (strike price) at any time through the expiration date.
- The investor with a **long put** has the right to **sell** the underlying security at the specified strike price until the expiration date.

Short options. The seller (or writer) of an option is said to have a short position. This investor receives money in the form of a premium and agrees to abide by the responsibilities described in the option contract.

- The investor with a **short call** (that is, the person who sold the call) is obligated to **sell** the underlying security at the specified strike price to the holder of the long call if the option is exercised by the expiration date. For agreeing to these provisions of the contract, the writer receives the premium.
- The investor with a **short put** (that is, the person who sold the put) is obligated to **buy** the underlying security at the strike price at any time through the expiration date if the put owner exercises the option. For agreeing to the terms of the contract, the put writer receives the premium.

Every right granted to the buyer is a responsibility assumed by the writer. The writer gives up whatever the buyer gains; the writer gains whatever the buyer gives up.

Opening and Closing Transactions

When a customer enters the options market by purchasing or writing calls or puts, the order ticket is marked "opening purchase" or "opening sale." A customer who bought an option may sell that option back at any time before the option expires. That

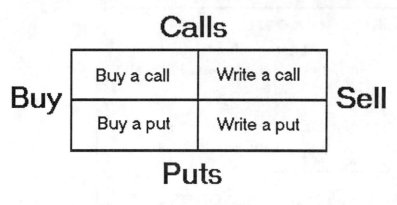

Fig. 18.4 The four basic options transactions.

second transaction is known as a closing sale, and the ticket is marked closing sale. A customer who originally sold an option may at any time before the option expires buy back the option he or she sold. That second transaction is known as a closing purchase, and the ticket is marked closing purchase. To close out a long or a short position, the customer must sell or buy back options of the same series.

Since the price of the underlying stock will change over the life of the option, an investor will probably not be able to make a closing transaction at the same price as the opening. After a closing transaction is made, the investor may find that he has made or lost money.

How the Options Market Functions

Exchange traded. Options on stock (and some other securities) trade in both exchange and over-the-counter markets. Exchange-traded options (also known as **listed** options) have standardized strike prices and expiration dates. Options are traded on the following exchanges:

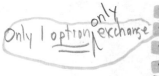
Only 1 option exchange only

- American Stock Exchange (**AMEX**)
- Chicago Board Options Exchange (**CBOE**)
- New York Stock Exchange (**NYSE**)
- Pacific Stock Exchange (**PSE**)
- Philadelphia Stock Exchange (**PHLX**)

Listing requirements. In order to qualify for listed options trading, the security underlying the option contract must meet the following requirements:

- minimum of 7,000,000 shares outstanding;
- minimum of 6,000 holders of the stock;
- volume in all markets at least 2,400,000 in the last 12 months;
- market price of at least $10 for the last three months;
- issuer in compliance with the Securities Exchange Act of 1934;
- issuer must not be in default on a dividend or interest payment; and
- issuer must have minimum net income of $1,000,000 after taxes during the last 8 months.

Delisting. If a listed option's underlying stock no longer qualifies, no new contracts can be issued. All existing contracts will trade until expiration, and can be exercised at will by the owner. Delisting will occur if:

- there are fewer than 6,300,000 shares outstanding;
- there are fewer than 5,400 holders of the stock;
- trading volume in all markets for the last 12 months falls below 1,800,000 shares;
- market price closes below $8 for last 6 months; or
- issuer does not comply with the act of 1934 or defaults on the issue.

Nonstandard options. Unlike options listed on exchanges, options traded over the counter are not standardized. Each nonstandardized option contract is created by two individuals to suit their specific needs. All of the terms are negotiated between the writer and the buyer, including the strike price, the expiration date, the premium and all other contract provisions. Because the contracts are not standard, there is little secondary market activity in OTC options.

Market maker. Options are traded by brokers who buy and sell by using hand signals and yelling out their bids or offers on the floor of an exchange in a double auction market. The exchanges employ market makers and order book officials (OBOs, sometimes known on the CBOE as board brokers) to ensure that the auction runs smoothly. The OBOs keep track of limit orders and maintain orderly markets by trading for their own accounts as market makers.

Each market maker is responsible for maintaining a fair and orderly market in the options of at least one underlying security. The market maker holds a position in the option (either long or short) and stands ready to buy or sell the option at any time. The market maker is not required, however, to support a falling market by continuously purchasing the option for his own account.

The CBOE. The CBOE uses a unique system of trading. Whereas the other exchanges employ specialists to maintain orderly markets, CBOE relies on market makers and order book officials. Each market maker is responsible for making a market in the options of at least one security. Market makers hold both long and short positions in an option and stand ready to trade at any time.

Each OBO on the CBOE maintains a record of all limit orders on a particular class of options in the order book. The OBO displays the high bids and low offers for the option and executes any open orders within the action of the trading crowd.

At the beginning of each trading day the order book official conducts an open trading rotation by asking for bids and offers on each series within a class of options. The opening rotation starts with the call series having the lowest exercise price and nearest expiration date, then moves to the call series with the same expiration date and the next highest exercise price and continues through all series of calls, and then in the same manner through all series of puts. A closing rotation is also held on the last day before the options expire (the Saturday immediately following the third Friday of the expiration month) to facilitate orderly trading prior to expiration.

Order routing systems. Broker-dealers use computerized order routing systems programmed to choose the destination of an order. The order may be routed to the commission-house booth for handling by the exchange member that represents the broker-dealer. The exchange member (the floor broker) will present the order in the trading crowd. Notice of execution of the order is given to the commission-house booth, which in turn uses the communication system of the broker-dealer to notify the registered representative and the customer.

For some orders (small market orders and small, executable limit orders) the routing system may select automatic execution. For quick action, the system bypasses the commission-house communication booth and the floor broker and sends the order directly to the trading post. Each order is executed against an order on the limit order book or a market maker's quote and the notice of execution is sent directly to the broker-dealer.

The automatic execution system of each exchange has its own criteria, special capabilities, and its own name. The CBOE has the Retail Automatic Execution System (RAES). The American Exchange (AMEX) has the Automatic Amex-Options Switching system (AutoAmos). Each has direct communication to and from the trading post.

The Options Clearing Corporation (OCC)

issuer AND, guarantor

Created by the exchanges that trade options, the Options Clearing Corporation (OCC) is the entity that standardizes option contracts, guarantees performance of the contracts, and issues options. The active secondary market in securities options is possible because of the Options Clearing Corporation. The OCC's three-part mission is to standardize options contracts, issue options to buyers and sellers, and guarantee performance of the contracts.

On exchange-traded options, the standardized strike prices and expiration months are determined by the OCC. The market itself (that is, interested buyers and sellers) determines the premiums of OCC-issued, standardized options. The services provided by the OCC make secondary trading in listed options possible. Options are issued by the OCC **without a certificate**. The investor's proof of ownership is the trade confirmation and monthly statements.

Because of the OCC, investors can easily close an open option position by selling back a long option or buying back a short one in the secondary market. The holder of a long option closes the position by making a closing sale of an identical contract. The investor who is short an option closes the position by making a closing purchase of an identical contract. In both cases, the OCC arranges the trade, so the investor doesn't have to locate a willing seller or buyer.

The Options Disclosure Document. To satisfy the prospectus requirement of the 1933 act, the OCC publishes an options disclosure document called "The Characteristics and Risks of Standardized Options." It outlines the risks and rewards associated with investing in options. An investor must receive this document from the broker-dealer prior to or at the same time they receive approval for options trading. The disclosure document must also accompany any sales literature a client receives.

Sales literature, according to the options exchanges, does not include material that is strictly educational. A disclosure document need not, for example, accompany a letter that explains covered call writing without making specific recommendations. That same educational material, however, must tell the investor where to obtain information on the risks of investing in options.

The customer must sign an options agreement within 15 days of opening an account. In this agreement, a customer states that she has read the options disclosure document and agrees to abide by the position limits and other rules of options trading. The Options Clearing Corporation also publishes a prospectus with information that is not in the options disclosure document. This prospectus must be made available to investors upon request.

OCC Rules and Regulations

Contract adjustments. The OCC does not adjust the strike price of standardized options for cash dividends. To receive a dividend, call owners must exercise their options to buy the stock before the ex-dividend date. A person who owns both stock and a put on that stock may want to exercise the put and keep the dividend paid on the stock. To do so, the investor must exercise that put on or after the ex-dividend date.

Stock splits. Options are adjusted for stock splits, stock dividends and rights offerings. When a stock splits, so does the option. If, for example, ABC stock splits two-for-one, each ABC 60 call or put becomes two ABC 30s. Each option owner therefore has twice as many contracts as before and the exercise price is one-half what it was. The aggregate (or total) exercise price remains the same.

A stock split which does not result completely in round lots is more complex. If XYZ splits three-for-two, for example, each XYZ 60 option becomes one XYZ 40 with 150 shares in the contract. Since the OCC can't, in this case, increase the number of contracts to a whole number, it adjusts the number of shares in the contract. But the effect is the same, since owning an option that gives one the right to buy or sell 150 shares is the same as owning one and one-half 100-share contracts. The exercise price becomes two-thirds what it was before.

Stock dividends. For a small stock dividend, the OCC also adjusts both the strike price and the number of shares in the contract. Adjustments to options contract prices are rounded to the nearest eighth. (In contrast, cash dividends are rounded to the next highest eighth to adjust stop and limit orders.) Neither stock splits nor stock dividends change the aggregate exercise price.

Position Limits

The OCC limits the number of options that any individual investor can hold on the same side of the market, that is, bullish or bearish positions. The options diagram is useful for recalling which positions are on the same side of the market.

Positions diagonally opposite one another across the line are on the same side of the market. In general, the OCC limits investors to the following number of equity option contracts on the same side of the market:

- 8,000 contracts: options on heavily traded stocks (at least 40,000,000 shares in the previous 6 months);
- 5,500 contracts: options on less heavily traded stocks (at least 20,000,000 shares in the previous 6 months); and
- 3,000 contracts: options on the least heavily traded stocks.

On the most heavily traded class of stock, for example, one investor could hold 8,000 long calls and 8,000 long puts or 8,000 short calls and 8,000 short puts. An investor with 4,000 long calls, however, could hold no more than 4,000 short puts, since both long calls and short puts are bullish.

Under the OCC's three-tier system of exercise limits, investors may not exercise more than the allowed number of contracts within **five consecutive business days**. The position limit on **index options** is 25,000 contracts on the same side of the market, with no more than 15,000 in the nearest term month. The exercise limit is 15,000 contracts in five days. For foreign currency options (FCOs), the position and exercise limits are the same, 50,000 contracts on the same side of the market.

Determining Position Limits

Call buyers and put writers are on one side of the market as bulls, and put buyers and call writers are on the other side of the market as bears.

Fig. 18.5 Determining market side for position limits.

Position and exercise limits apply to individuals, individuals acting in concert, and registered reps acting for discretionary accounts (among others). A group of investors cannot get around the position restrictions by intentionally splitting up a large order in order to exceed the limits set.

Important times and dates. These are the OCC's rules. Brokerage firms may establish earlier cutoff times to suit their own procedures. The key options expiration times and dates are:

10/18

- 4 pm Eastern (3 pm Central). Listed options cease trading. Trading of listed equity options ceases at 4 pm Eastern (3 pm Central) time on the business day immediately before the Saturday of expiration.

4:30 central

- 5:30 pm. Deadline for exercising listed options. After 5:30 pm Eastern time on the business day immediately before the Saturday of expiration, option holders can no longer exercise their contracts.

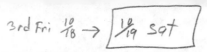
3rd Fri 10/18 → 10/19 Sat

handwritten: 10:59 central time

- 11:59 pm. Expiration of listed options. Listed equity options expire at 11:59 pm Eastern time on the Saturday following the third Friday of the expiration month. The hours between 5:30 pm the previous business day and 11:59 pm on Saturday allow firms time to clear their books by giving proper notice to the OCC.

handwritten (vertical): notebook

Assignment of exercise notice. When an option owner notifies the OCC of exercise, the OCC randomly selects a firm to which it assigns the exercise. The assignment of the exercise notice to one of its customers by the broker-dealer may be done randomly or on a first-in, first-out basis. It may not be assigned on the basis of who has the largest position or who can best afford it.

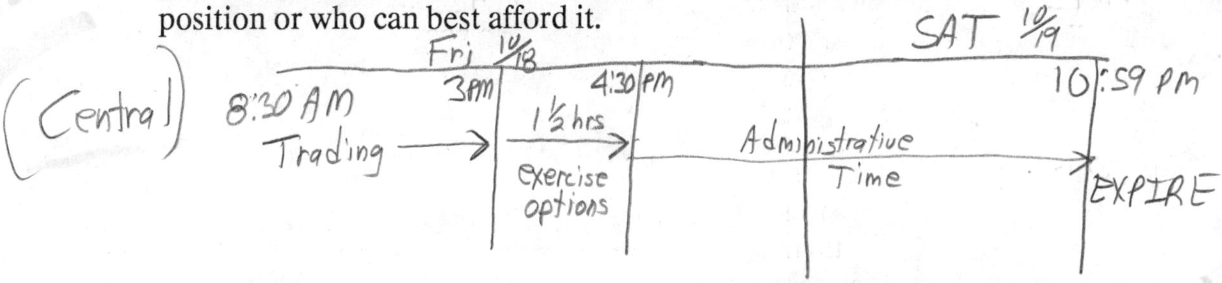

handwritten timeline:

(Central)   Fri 10/18   SAT 10/19

8:30 AM   3PM   4:30 PM   10:59 PM
Trading →   1½ hrs   Administrative Time   EXPIRE
          exercise options

18.11

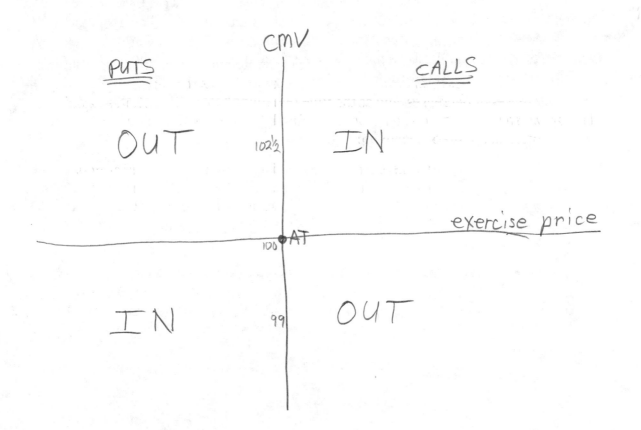

CMV

PUTS   CALLS

OUT   102½   IN

exercise price

— — — — — — — — — — 100 ●AT — — — — — — — — — — — —

IN   99   OUT

| 1 IBM Oct 100 call @ 3 |

if IBM CMV = 102½   if IBM CMV = 99

Premium   3   Prem   3
— Intrinsic   -2½   — Intri   -∅
Time   ½   Time   3
value   Value

Option Trading and Strategies: Underlying Value

The Value of an Option

How much is an option worth? The market price of an option (its premium) changes as the market price of the underlying security moves (the more volatile the underlying security, the greater the premium tends to be), as the intrinsic value of the option increases or decreases, and as the time remaining before the option's expiration date grows shorter. The option buyer, like any buyer, hopes that the premium (the option's price in the market) will increase.

When an option is worth exercising, it is called **in-the-money**. A call is in-the-money whenever the stock price exceeds the strike price. An ABC 50 call is in-the-money by seven points when the price of ABC stock is 57. A put is in-the-money whenever the stock price is less than the strike price. An ABC 50 put is in-the-money by four points when ABC stock is at 46.

An option is **out-of-the-money** when it is not worth exercising. A call is out-of-the-money if the stock price is below the exercise price. No investor will exercise an XYZ 50 call if XYZ is available at a market price of 40. A put is out-of-the-money if the stock price is above the exercise price. No investor would want to exercise an XYZ 50 put if XYZ can be sold in the market for 60.

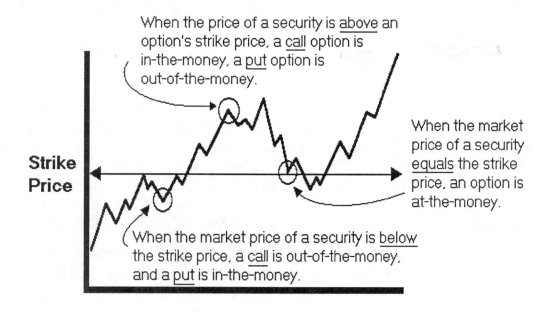

Fig. 18.6 Comparing in-, at- and out-of-the-money.

When the underlying stock is trading exactly at the exercise price of the option, the option is said to be **at-the-money.** Investors are not likely to exercise at-the-money options.

Intrinsic value. If an option is in-the-money (that is, it is worth exercising), then its premium will reflect the potential profit to be made if it is exercised. This profit potential is known as intrinsic value, and is the difference between the option strike price and the underlying stock price. The option purchaser would benefit by that amount by exercising the option.

A call option has intrinsic value when the price of the underlying stock is above the option's exercise price. A call option is worth exercising when doing so allows the option owner to buy stock below the market price. When ABC is trading at 57, a call with a strike price of 50 is in-the-money and has an intrinsic value of $7 a share. When ABC is trading at 61, an ABC call with a strike price of 50 has an intrinsic value of $11 a share. That $7 or $11 is available to the owner, who can exercise the option to buy at 50 and then sell the shares on the market at the current market price. The intrinsic value of an option (and therefore the option premium) changes as the stock price changes.

A put option has intrinsic value when the price of the underlying stock is below the option's exercise price. A put option is worth exercising when doing so allows the option owner to sell stock above the market price. An XYZ 40 put, for instance, has intrinsic value when the market price of XYZ is below 40. When XYZ is trading at 35, the owner of the 40 put can make $5 per share by purchasing XYZ stock at 35 on the market, then exercising the put to sell the stock at 40. The intrinsic value of the XYZ 40 put, therefore, is 5 when the underlying stock is at 35.

An option is out-of-the-money when it is not worth exercising, and an out-of-the-money option has no intrinsic value (although it might have some time value).

Time value. Time value is the dollars and cents an investor is willing to pay over and above an option's intrinsic value to buy and hold that option for the time remaining until the option's expiration date. An option expires on a certain date; the farther away that date is, the more time there is for a change in the price of the underlying stock. The amount of time in the contract, therefore, has value to the option buyer. A buyer, in general, is willing to pay more for a contract that has a long time to run than for a contract that is about to expire. As the option's expiration date approaches, the time value tends to diminish. On the last trading day before expiration, the time value is gone and the premium usually equals the intrinsic value. If there is no time remaining, the time value would be zero, and all remaining value would be intrinsic value.

As you can see, an option can have two kinds of value, both reflected in the premium. It can have **intrinsic value** and **time value.** In general, if you want to find the time value of an option, calculate the intrinsic value and subtract it from the time value.

premium ?

Buying and Selling Options

Though option traders sometimes pursue complex strategies, the basic reason for buying or writing options is to make money on the price movement of the underlying security (or **instrument**) during the limited life of the option contract. Those who invest in stock options are either **bullish** or **bearish** on the underlying stock. "Bullish" indicates optimism that a security or the market is going up. "Bearish" indicates pessimism; the belief that a security or the market is going down.

	Long	Short
Calls	Right to Buy Bullish	Obligation to Sell Bearish
Puts	Right to Sell Bearish	Obligation to Buy Bullish

(Buyer, Holder, Owner)　　(Seller, Writer, Grantor)

Fig. 18.7 The Bulls vs. the Bears.

Buying Calls

An equity **call option** is the right to buy 100 shares of a specific stock at a specific price for a specific period of time. If Angus buys 1 ABC November 50 call for 3, that option gives him the right to buy 100 shares of ABC at the **strike price** (or **exercise price**) of $50 per share at any time before the option expires in November. Angus paid a certain amount of money in order to acquire these rights, in this case, a premium of $300 (the "3" in the quote indicates a premium of $3 per share times the 100 shares the contract represents).

If Angus decides not to exercise his option before it **expires** (that is, if he decides not to exercise his rights to buy the underlying stock at $50 per share), he loses the entire $300 premium he paid for the option.

When Angus buys 1 ABC November 50 call at 3, he does so in anticipation that the price of the underlying stock (ABC) will go up between now and November. If he is right and ABC is trading higher than $50 (at $56, for example) near the end of October, he can still purchase 100 shares for $5,000 by exercising his call. Since the market value of those shares at 56 is $5,600, Angus has profited. The right to make that purchase cost him $300, the premium he paid for his call option. If he is wrong and the price of the stock drops below 50, he will either let the option expire (if it has become worthless) or try to sell it to someone else to recoup at least some of the premium he paid.

Options are wasting assets; the passage of time depletes their value. If an option expires unexercised, the buyer loses 100% of the premium he paid at the opening transaction.

Objectives of Call Buyers

Call buyers are generally bullish on the underlying stock. As stock prices go up, the premiums that call buyers are willing to pay also go up. Those who hold contracts with premiums that are going up may choose to exercise them or sell them on the secondary market.

Speculative profit. The most common reason for buying calls is to make a speculative profit with as little cash outlay as possible. If an investor believes that the price of ABC will rise sharply in the next several months, she compares the risks and potential rewards of buying the stock outright with simply buying a call on the stock.

If ABC is trading at $40 (for a cost of $4,000 per round lot of 100 shares), and an ABC 40 call is trading at 4 ($400 per contract), the investor could choose to buy the stock. If she buys the stock and its price goes up to $50 a share within six months, she makes a $1,000 profit, a 25% return on the original $4,000 investment. The same movement in the stock will make the ABC 40 call worth at least its intrinsic value of 10 ($1,000). If the investor had chosen instead to buy the ABC 40 call for $400, she could have realized a $600 profit ($1,000 less the $400 premium), a 150% return on her $400 investment. The option strategy provides greater leverage (a higher potential return in percent on investment).

If the stock price falls, the investor who bought stock risks the entire $4,000 purchase price (the stock could fall to $0 and become worthless). The option owner, on the other hand, could also lose her entire investment, but a $400 loss pales in comparison to a $4,000 loss.

Deferring a decision. Often investors are interested in purchasing stock in a company, but would like to put the purchase off for some period of time. By delaying the purchase, however, the investor risks having to pay much more for the stock in the event of a rise in price. To avoid the risk of paying more for a stock than the investor wants to, he could buy calls on that stock, locking in a purchase price until the option expires. This allows him to defer his decision to buy (or not to buy) the stock until near the expiration date of the option. If the market price has gone up, he can exercise his call and buy the stock below the market price. If the price has not gone up, he can let his option expire and either buy the stock more cheaply on the open market or not buy it at all.

Diversifying holdings. Investors occasionally want to profit from upward movement in the stock market without tying up a lot of cash in one or two stocks. Even with limited funds, an investor can buy calls on several stocks. Doing so allows them to profit from any rise in the option premiums (if the underlying stocks appreciate, of course). The risk in this strategy, as with all option strategies, is the loss of all or most of the premiums if the investor is wrong about stock price movements.

Writing Calls

Each option contract must have a buyer and a seller. In the previous example on buying calls, investor Angus purchased 1 ABC Nov 50 call at 3. Angus was the option buyer and paid a premium to acquire the right to **call (buy)** the stock. On the other side of the transaction was an option seller willing to take on the obligations of the contract in return for being paid the premiums. This investor **sold (wrote)** the ABC

Nov 50 call option for 3. An investor writes a call in the belief that the stock will stay the same or drop in price.

If the market price goes up, the stock could be **called away** from the call writer. That is, the call buyer might make the call writer deliver the stock at the option's strike price when the market price is considerably above that. An investor who writes 1 ABC November 50 call at 3 may be called upon to deliver 100 shares of ABC stock to the call buyer if the buyer chooses to exercise the option anytime until the expiration date of the contract. The writer will receive $5,000 if that happens (the strike price of $50 per share times 100 shares), in addition to the premiums she has already been paid.

Of course, the call writer receives a premium for writing the contract, and that reduces her net loss if she has to deliver stock. Clearly, when call writers are wrong about the price movement of the underlying stock, they may pay heavily for the error. Their potential loss, in theory at least, is unlimited, since there is no limit to how high the stock's price could rise.

Objectives of Call Writers

Call writers are generally bearish on the underlying stock. As stock prices go down, the likelihood that the call buyer will actually exercise the call against the writer decreases. If the call is still unexercised at expiration, the call writer gets to keep the premium without having to deliver the stock to the buyer.

Increased yield. Investors in many stocks use covered call writing (selling calls against stock you own) to increase the yield of their securities. By writing calls that are slightly out-of-the-money on a stock he owns, the investor stands a good chance of keeping the premiums received without having to deliver the stock. Once the expiration date of an option has passed, the investor is free to write another call against his or her stock, and receive another premium. By employing this strategy conservatively, some investors are able to increase the annual yields on their stock substantially.

Locking in a sale price. A second objective of call writers is that of locking in a sale price for a stock they hold. If an investor has already made a profit in a stock she holds, and is interested in selling if if she can get a good price for it, she could write a call at a strike price that would lock in that profit. If the price of the stock goes above the strike price of the option, the stock will be called away and the writer will receive the price she wanted for stock she was willing to sell anyway. If the stock price falls, the investor keeps the premium and the stock (lowering her cost basis in the stock in the process).

Buying Puts

An investor who buys an equity put does so in order to acquire the right to sell 100 shares of the underlying stock at the strike price anytime between the purchase and the expiration date. For this privilege, the investor pays a cash premium to the writer of the put.

Investors in puts expect that the underlying security will drop in price during the life of the option. If this bearish view is correct, the investor can then exercise the put option and sell the stock at a strike price which is higher than the market price of the stock.

The risk for put buyers is the same as the risk for call buyers. The option is a wasting asset: if it does not increase in value, it may expire worthless. The owner may lose the entire amount invested in the premium.

Objectives of Put Buyers

Put buyers are generally bearish on the underlying stock. Investors typically purchase puts because they expect the underlying security to decline in value. As stock prices go down, the premiums that bearish investors are willing to pay for put options go up.

Speculating on a decline in a stock. A put buyer may wish to profit from a decline in the price of a stock that he doesn't own. If a put holder has guessed correctly and a stock falls in price, he could go out and buy that stock cheaply on the market, exercise his put option and sell it for a higher price by putting it to the option writer. If the investor didn't want to go through the whole process of buying and selling the stock (or selling the stock short), he could just sell the put at that point and profit from the increased premium.

The potential reward increases as the stock price drops. If the stock becomes worthless, the investor will make his maximum gain, which is the exercise price less the premium paid (the investor buys the stock for $0 and sells it at the exercise price, then subtracts from his profit what it cost him to buy the option in the first place). The investor's maximum loss is the premium he paid for the option, since the investor will lose it if the stock rises and the option expires worthless.

Deferring a decision. Often investors are interested in selling the stock they own in a company, but would like to put the sale off for a period of time. By delaying the sale, the investor risks selling his stock for much less in the event of declining prices. To avoid that risk, he or she could buy puts on that stock, locking in a sale price until the expiration date of the option. This allows him to defer the decision to sell the stock until near the expiration date of the option. If the market price has gone down, he can exercise his puts and sell the stock above the market. If the price has gone up, he can still sell the stock on the open market and get a better price.

Writing Puts

Investors write puts for some of the same reasons that other investors write calls (i.e., to generate additional income). Generally, investors who write puts on stocks are bullish and think that the stock's price will stay the same or rise during the life of the option contract. In return for assuming the obligation to buy stock at the put owner's discretion, put writers receive cash premiums. The put writer is then obligated to buy stock if it is put to him at the exercise price by the put buyer.

Put writers, obviously, assume much greater risks than put buyers. Put buyers stand to lose only the premium paid if they are wrong. (It's a 100% loss of investment, but at least it's predictable.) Put writers' losses are potentially far greater than the premiums they receive (they could be forced to pay a high price for a stock that is essentially worthless). Consequently, writing options is generally appropriate only for investors who understand and can afford the risk.

Objectives of Put Writers

Put writers are generally bullish on the underlying stock. As stock prices go up, the likelihood that the put seller will exercise the put against the writer decreases. If the put is still unexercised at expiration, the put writer gets to keep the premium without having to buy the stock.

Generating a large return. The premium a put buyer is willing to pay for the option is what the put writer wants. Investors who write puts try to select securities that will rise in price, and want to take advantage of these price increases without putting up any cash (which they would have to do if they purchased the stock or calls on the stock outright). Instead, they hope the puts they sell expire unexercised so they can keep the premium. Writers benefit from the diminishing time value of the options they sell.

Buying stock below its current price. Sometimes put writers actually want the option exercised against them. They consider short puts a good way to buy stock cheap, because the premium received, in effect, reduces the cost of the stock when the stock is put to them in an exercise. If the stock is not put to them, of course, they keep the premium free and clear.

Maximum Gains, Losses and Break-Even Points

Investors who open an option position naturally want to know three things: the maximum amount he can gain, the maximum amount he can lose, and the point at which his investment will break even.

Long Calls

Maximum gain. Instead of exercising options, some investors buy options for their own investment value. As stock prices rise, the potential gain on a call option increases point for point with the value of the stock. There is no theoretical limit on the potential gains available to call owners, because there is no theoretical limit on a rise in stock price. In practice, of course, stock prices do not rise infinitely high in a finite period.

Maximum loss. On a long call, investors risk losing 100% of the premium paid. Since call buyers are bullish, you know that this will happen when the stock's market price moves below the option's exercise price and the option becomes worthless to the owner (or to anyone else).

Break-even point. A call buyer breaks even when the price of the underlying stock rises to the point where the investor could sell the option and make back the original premium he or she paid. The person who is long calls can make a profit when the current market price of her option (that is, its premium) moves above the break-even point.

Short Calls

Maximum gain. Call writers are bearish and hope the stock price will drop. If it drops below the exercise price by expiration date, the call will be worthless to the buyer and will expire unexercised. When that happens, the writer keeps the premium free and clear. No matter how low the stock price falls (even if it drops to zero) the writer's gain is limited to the amount of the premium originally received.

Maximum loss. The biggest risk an option trader can take is that a call she wrote will be exercised against her and she will have to deliver stock she doesn't own. This option position is said to be uncovered, or "naked." When a call writer has an option exercised against her, she has to deliver stock to the buyer at the exercise price. If she has to go out into the open market to purchase the stock to deliver, she may have to pay a price much higher than the exercise price of the option. As the stock price goes higher, so does the investor's potential loss. If she decides to enter a closing sale to get rid of her option, she can stop her losses from increasing. Otherwise, there is no theoretical limit on her potential loss.

Break-even point. Call writers receive the premium, so they will break even when the value of their option falls an equal amount. Since call writers are bearish, they can expect to lose money as stock prices rise. The break-even point is the same for the buyer and the writer of the same option. The person who is short the call wants the market to stay below the break-even point to make a profit.

Long Puts

Maximum gain. The buyer of a long put is bearish, and his maximum gain will occur when the price of the underlying stock reaches the lowest possible market price, which is $0. If an investor could buy the stock for $0, he could sell it at whatever strike price his put contract entitled him to by exercising the option. His maximum gain would be reduced by the premium paid in the opening transaction.

Maximum loss. A put buyer's maximum potential loss is the premium paid. On all long options, the investor pays (and risks) the premium. The worst that can happen to a put buyer is that her option will expire before it is worth exercising. This will occur at any market price above the strike price.

Break-even point. Bears buy puts. The break-even point on a put option will be reached when the market price of the stock is below the strike price by the dollar amount of the premium. At that point, the profit the put buyer could make by exercising her put (the strike price less the current market value) would equal the premium she paid.

Short Puts

Maximum gain. The writer of a put receives a premium in the opening transaction. Her greatest potential gain is that premium. When the stock price is above the exercise price, no put owner will exercise an option to sell stock, since selling on the open market offers a better return. If the stock price stays above the exercise price, the put will expire worthless and the writer will keep the premium.

Maximum loss. A put seller's maximum potential loss occurs if the stock price drops to $0. At that point, the put owner will exercise the option against the writer and make the writer buy the stock at the strike price. The put seller will have to take delivery of the stock and, since it has no market value, she is out the exercise price minus the premium received in the opening transaction.

Break-even point. Since the put seller (a bullish investor) receives the premium, she has to lose that money to break even. As a bullish investor, she will lose money with the market price below the strike price by the amount of the premium received.

Summary

The chart below provides a summary of break-even points, maximum gains and maximum losses. Rather than memorize every detail about this chart, you may find it helpful to observe the patterns that are developing. Notice that:

- The break-even point is the same for the long and short positions.
- The maximum loss when buying an option is the premium paid.
- The maximum gain when writing an option is the premium received.
- The writer's potential loss is the buyer's potential gain (and vice versa).

Position	Break-Even	Maximum Gain	Maximum Loss
Long Call	Strike price plus premium	Unlimited	Premium
Short Call	Strike price plus premium	Premium	Unlimited
Long Put	Strike price minus premium	Strike price minus premium	Premium
Short Put	Strike price minus premium	Premium	Strike price minus premium

Fig. 18.8 Each position has an opposite.

18.22

Multiple Option Strategies

Spreads, Straddles, Combinations and Hedges

Many basic option strategies are speculative, designed to capitalize on movements in the price of the underlying security. Investors also use options to enhance returns or to limit risks. This section explores investment strategies that involve **multiple option positions**. Spreads, straddles and combinations are all strategies in which an investor buys and/or sells more than one option at a time.

We will also look at strategies that **combine options with positions in the underlying security**. Investors can use various options to take advantage of a stock's price movement, regardless of the direction in which it moves. These more complex strategies are generally called **hedged positions** (simultaneous investments in options on opposite sides of the market which serve to protect one another).

Spreads

A spread is the purchase of one option and the sale of another option of the same class. Investors can establish both **call spreads** and **put spreads**. A call spread is a long call and a short call. A put spread is a long put and a short put. The two options in a spread are of the same class (both are puts or both are calls on the same underlying stock), but are of different series (they have different strike prices, expiration dates, or both).

Types of spreads. When the two options in a spread differ in strike price, the investor has established a **price spread** (or **vertical spread**). On the options table that follows you'll see that the prices are arranged vertically. When the two options differ in expiration date, the investor has established a **time** (or **calendar**) **spread**. A time spread is called a **horizontal spread** because expirations are arranged horizontally on options tables. When the options differ in both price and time, the investor has established a ~~diagonal spread~~. A line drawn between these two options would appear diagonal.

Straddles and Combinations

If an investor opens a multiple option position by purchasing a call and a put or selling a call and a put on the same underlying stock the investor has established either a **straddle** or a **combination**.

Straddles. The two options in a straddle differ only in type. The options are on the same stock, have the same strike price, and have the same expiration date. Straddles can either be long or short. A **long straddle** is the purchase of a call and a put. A **short straddle** is the sale of a call and a put. An example of a straddle would be an XYZ January 45 call and an XYZ January 45 put.

Combinations. Combinations are similar to straddles. In both, the investor is long a call and a put, or short a call and a put on the same underlying security. Unlike straddles, however, in a combination the investor purchases or sells options that differ in strike price, expiration date, or both. An example of a combination would be an XYZ January 45 call and an XYZ April 50 put.

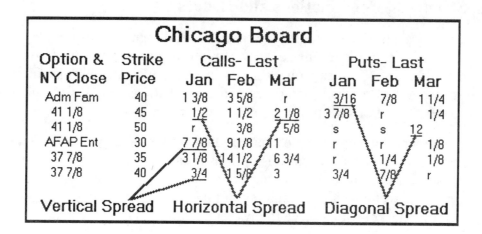

Fig. 18.9 Establishing different types of spreads.

Risks and Rewards of Multiple Option Strategies

Spreads, straddles and combinations are partially protected (or hedged) investment positions. As you saw earlier, investors who trade puts and calls take substantial risks. All option buyers risk 100% of the premium paid. Put writers may have to pay the exercise price for a worthless stock put to them by an option owner. Call writers who have not established an offsetting position take an unlimited risk.

The two options in a multiple option strategy are chosen because they are on opposite sides of the market (that is, one is considered bullish and the other bearish). Being opposites, they provide at least partial protection for each other in the event the price of the underlying stock doesn't move in the direction the investor expects. If the price of the underlying stock goes up, the bullish side of the spread, straddle or combination will increase in value and the bearish side will decrease. If the price of the underlying stock goes down, the bearish option will become more valuable and the bullish option will become less attractive to investors.

Maximum Gains, Losses and Break-Even Points

In a strategy involving a spread, the investor will see the market value (that is, the premiums) of both options increase or decrease together. If both options are calls, the premiums of both will decrease as the stock price decreases, and both premiums will increase if the stock price increases. If both options are puts, the premiums of both will decrease as the stock price increases, and both premiums will increase if the stock price decreases.

Spreads are established as either bullish or bearish. A person who anticipates a rise in the market would open a bullish spread, and an investor who believes the market will decline would open a bearish spread. Even though a spread includes options that appear to be on opposite sides of the market, if the underlying stock's price moves in the direction the investor anticipates, the overall position will be profitable.

↑ Bulls buy calls and call spreads. ↑
Bulls sell puts and put spreads. ↑

↑

Anticipated Market Direction

↓

↓ Bears buy puts and put spreads. ↓
Bears sell calls and call spreads. ↓

Fig. 18.10 When Bulls and Bears buy and

The rules for determining whether a multiple option strategy is bullish or bearish are the same as they were for single option investments. Bulls buy calls and call spreads. Bears buy puts and put spreads. Bulls sell puts and put spreads. Bears sell calls and call spreads.

An investor who establishes a spread does so for either a **net credit** or a **net debit**. An investor whose opening option transactions result in money flowing into his account begins with a net credit. An investor whose opening option transactions result in money flowing out of his account begins with a net debit. Since opening a debit spread costs the investor money initially, the investor is said to have **bought** the spread. And since opening a credit spread makes the investor money initially, the investor is said to have **sold** the spread.

Debit Call Spreads

Investor objectives. When a bullish investor establishes a debit call spread, she buys the call with the low strike price and sells the call with the high strike price. Since a call with a low strike price will be worth more in the marketplace (and will therefore have a higher premium) than a call with a high strike price, we know that more money will be flowing out of the account (for the option purchased) than will be flowing in (from the option sold). When more money flows out, you have a net debit. When you have a net debit, you bought the position.

A bullish investor buys a call or a call spread because she expects that its net market value will increase along with the underlying stock's price. If it does, she can exercise the long option of the spread (the one with the lower strike price) and buy stock below the market price, and even if the short option (the one with the higher strike price) is exercised against her, she will be able to deliver the stock she just bought and keep the difference between the strike prices. As with single option strategies, the investor can

The T Chart

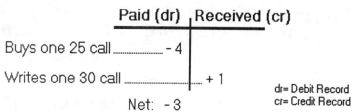

Minus (debit or dr) side of the transaction.

Plus (credit or cr) side of the transaction.

Paid (dr)	Received (cr)
Buys one 25 call .... - 4	
Writes one 30 call	+ 1
Net: - 3	

dr= Debit Record
cr= Credit Record

This is a <u>debit</u> spread. money is flowing <u>out</u> of the investor's account.

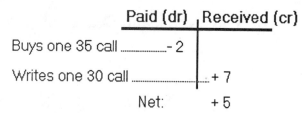

Paid (dr)	Received (cr)
Buys one 35 call .... - 2	
Writes one 30 call	+ 7
Net: + 5	

This is a <u>credit</u> spread. Money is flowing <u>into</u> the investor's account.

Fig. 18.11 Use the T chart to find debits and credits.

also choose to close out her option positions and keep the profits (or take the losses) from doing so rather than bothering to exercise the options and buy and sell the stock.

Maximum gain. The investor will realize her maximum gain anytime the stock's market price is at or above the strike price of the higher option. At that point, she will buy stock at the low strike price and be forced to sell stock at the high, and get to keep the difference between the two prices.

Maximum loss. If the stock's price falls to or below the strike price of the lower option, both calls will expire worthless. No investor will exercise a call when the stock is available in the market for less than the strike price of the option. At any price below the lower strike price, she will sustain the maximum loss because both calls will expire worthless. As a general rule, the maximum loss on any debit spread is the initial debit.

Break-even. Since an investor's maximum gain on a call spread occurs at the higher strike price (or above) and her maximum loss at the lower strike price (or below), the break-even point will obviously lie in between the strike prices. Break-even occurs when the stock's market price is above the lower strike price by the amount of the initial debit. The break-even point on a debit call spread is the lower strike price plus the initial debit.

Debit Put Spreads

Investor objectives. When a bearish investor establishes a debit put spread, he buys the put with the high strike price and sells the put with the low strike price. A put with a high strike price will be worth more to investors (and will have a higher premium) than a put with a low strike price, so more money will be flowing out of the account (for the put purchased) than will be flowing in (from the put sold).

A bearish investor buys a put or a put spread because he expects that the spread's net market value will increase as the underlying stock's price decreases. If it does, he

w403

18.26

can exercise the long put of the spread (the one with the higher strike price) and sell stock above the current market price. If the short put (the one with the lower strike price) is exercised against him, he will have to buy the stock, but by exercising the option he owns, he can then sell at the higher strike price and keep the difference. As with single option strategies, the investor can also choose to close out his option positions and keep the profits (or take the losses) rather than exercising the options.

Maximum gain. The investor will realize his maximum gain anytime the stock's market price is at or below the strike price of the lower option. At that point, he will have to buy stock at the low strike price, but can sell the stock at the high, and get to keep the difference between the two prices.

Maximum loss. If the stock's price rises to or above the strike price of the higher option, both puts will expire worthless. No investor will exercise a put when the stock can be sold in the market for more than the strike price of the option. At any price above the higher strike price, he will sustain the maximum loss because both puts will expire worthless. Again, we have the general rule: the maximum loss on any debit spread is the initial debit.

Break-even. An investor's break-even point will lie in between the strike prices. Break-even occurs when the stock's market price is below the higher strike price by the amount of the initial debit. The break-even point on a debit put spread is the higher strike price minus the initial debit.

Credit Call Spreads

Investor objectives. Bearish investors establish credit call spreads. To do so, they buy the call with the high strike price and sell the call with the low strike price. The call with a high strike price will have a lower premium than the call with a low strike price, so we know that the investor will be putting out less money for the purchase than she is taking in for the sale. When more money flows into an account than out, you have a net credit. When you have a net credit, you sold the position.

Bearish investors sell calls and call spreads because they expect the underlying stock's price to go down. If it does, both options will expire worthless, and the investor will be able to keep the net credit. If the investor is wrong and the stock goes up, the long option can be exercised to buy the stock, which will then have to be delivered against the short option. The investor will lose the difference between the two options' strike prices, but will keep the initial credit. The investor can choose to close out the positions and keep the profits (or take the losses) rather than exercising.

Maximum gain. The maximum gain on a credit call spread, as with any position established for a credit, is the initial credit. The maximum gain will occur when the stock price is at or below the **lower** strike price. Establishing a credit call spread reduces risk substantially, and is referred to as a "limited risk spread."

Maximum loss. The maximum loss on a credit call spread is the difference between strike prices less the initial credit. This occurs when the stock's price is at or above the higher strike price.

Break-even. The investor will break even when the market price of the stock is between the two strike prices. The break-even point will be the lower strike price plus the initial credit.

Credit Put Spreads

Investor objectives. Bullish investors establish credit put spreads. They buy the put with the low strike price and sell the put with the high strike price. The put with the low strike price will have a lower premium than the put with the high strike price, so the investor will be spending less money on the option with the low strike price than he is taking in on the sale of the option with the high strike price.

Bullish investors sell puts and put spreads because they expect the stock's price to go up. If it does, both options will expire worthless, and the investor will be able to keep the net credit. If the investor is wrong and the stock goes down, the investor will have to buy the stock at the high strike price, but can then exercise the other put with the lower price to sell the stock to someone else. The investor will lose the difference between the two options' strike prices, but will keep the initial credit. The investor can close out the positions and keep the profits (or take the losses) rather than exercising.

Maximum gain. The maximum gain on a credit put spread is the initial credit. This occurs when the stock price is at or above the higher strike price.

Maximum loss. The maximum loss on a credit put spread is the difference between strike prices minus the initial credit. This occurs when the stock's market price is at or below the lower strike price.

Break-even. The break-even point on a credit put spread is the higher strike price minus the net premium.

Horizontal (Time) Spreads

A horizontal spread is one established by an investor in which the option contracts have **different expiration dates**. The investor is attempting to profit from the different rates at which the time values of the premiums of the two options will erode. In most cases, the closer an option gets to expiration, the faster the time value portion of its premium will disappear.

To profit from this phenomenon, the investor would **buy** the option with the distant expiration, and **sell** the option with the near expiration. Since the premium of the contract with the near expiration will fall faster than that of the one with the more distant expiration, the spread between the premiums of the two contracts will **widen**, which will allow the investor to close out the positions at a net profit.

Spread Between Premiums

The term "spread" is sometimes used to refer to the difference between the premiums of the two options, rather than the difference between the strike prices. Strike prices don't change; premiums do. Whether investors with spreads want the premiums closer together or farther apart depends on whether the position is a credit or a debit spread.

The spread between the premiums of two options narrows if both premiums decrease, which will happen if both options become worthless (typically when one or both of the options are out-of-the-money). Investors in credit spreads keep the credit received initially if the options become worthless.

Investors with debit spreads want the spread between premiums to widen. They make their maximum gain when both options are in-the-money. They can make money by selling the long option for more than it costs them to buy back the short option. The wider the distance between the two premiums, then, the more money they can make. The widest the spread will ever be on the expiration date is the same as the difference between the two strike prices. As the market moves further in the desired direction, each option will increase equally in intrinsic value.

In a debit spread, then, the investor wants the spread (between premiums) to widen. That spread between premiums determines the amount of money the investor can make by trading or exercising the options.

Long Straddles

Objectives. Straddles are used by investors who think a stock's price is going to be volatile, but aren't sure which direction the price will take. Since both options in a straddle have the same strike price, sufficient price movement **in either direction** (that is, away from the strike price) can make a long straddle profitable for an investor.

Maximum gain. The maximum potential gain is greater for the long call than for the long put in a straddle. The call option goes up in value as the stock price rises and the stock price can rise, theoretically, without limit. The put option increases in value as the stock price drops, although the price cannot go below zero. The maximum gain for a long straddle is the maximum gain for the call.

Maximum loss. At any stock price between the strike price less the net premiums and the strike price plus the net premiums, a long straddle investor loses at least part of her money. She loses the entire premium if the options expire at-the-money, since she paid for both and neither is worth exercising or selling.

Break-even. Long straddles have two break-even points: one above the strike price, one below. A long straddle breaks even when the stock price is equal to the strike price plus or minus the debit.

Short Straddles

Objectives. An investor who writes a straddle takes the opposite view of the market from the investor who buys a straddle. The straddle writer believes the stock price will not change much and will **not** move outside the break-even points. He would like the options to remain at-the-money, where he would earn the premium he received in the opening transactions. His maximum potential loss is particularly high on the call option.

Maximum gain. The maximum potential gain for a short straddle (as with any position initially opened for a credit) is the initial premiums received.

Maximum loss. At any stock price outside of the strike price less the net premiums and the strike price plus the net premiums, a short straddle investor loses money. The maximum potential loss is greater for the short call than for the short put in a straddle. The call option price can rise without limit. The put option's risk is limited to the strike price, since the stock's price can't fall below zero. The maximum loss for a short straddle is the maximum loss for the short call.

Break-even. Short straddles have two break-even points: one above the strike price and one below. A short straddle breaks even when the stock price is equal to the strike price plus or minus the debit.

Combinations

Combinations are very similar to straddles. A **long** combination is the purchase of a call and a put on the same stock at different strike prices or expirations. A **short** combination is the sale of a call and a put at different strike prices or expirations.

Long combinations. Long combinations can be used instead of long straddles when a sharp movement in the market is expected. Long combinations are usually cheaper to establish than long straddles, since most long combinations are established when both contracts are out-of-the-money.

As an example, when ABC is at $47, an investor could purchase 1 ABC Oct 50 call at 2, and 1 ABC Oct 45 put at 2 to create a long combination. The 50 call is 3 points out-of-the-money, and the 45 put is 2 points out-of-the-money. The combined premiums of $400 reflect the time value of the two options, since neither has any intrinsic value at this point. A straddle in which one of the options was in-the-money would cost the investor more based on the higher premium attributable to the in-the-money option.

The customer will lose money if the stock price remains between 45 and 50. Both sides of the combination will expire unexercised, and the investor will be out the premiums (the maximum loss on a long combination, as with any long strategy, is the premiums paid).

The break-even points for this combination will be the strike price plus the premium for the call, and the strike price minus the premiums for the put (54 and 41 in this example).

Short combinations. Short combinations can be used instead of short straddles when no movement is expected in the market. The writer collects the premiums and keeps them if both sides expire unexercised. The break-even points for a short combination are the same as those for a long.

Strips and Straps

A **strip** is the purchase of 2 puts and 1 call on the same stock with the same terms. A **strap** is the purchase of 2 calls and 1 put on the same stock with the same terms. Strips and straps are used like long straddles in that a market movement is expected, but the direction in which it will move is uncertain. The primary difference between straddles and strips and straps is that a **strap** is marginally more bullish in strategy, and a **strip** is marginally more bearish than straddles.

Synthetic Options

Combinations of stock positions with option positions can often simulate a strategy consisting solely of an option purchase or sale. Using such a combination of stocks and options is termed a "synthetic option."

The **owner of a call** could realize unlimited gains if the stock price rises or limited losses if the stock price falls. Similar gains or losses would occur if the investor bought the stock and then purchased a put at the same strike price. The gain on the stock would remain unlimited, but the investor would be protected against loss by the put, potentially losing no more than the premiums paid for the contract.

The **writer of a call** could realize unlimited losses if the stock price rises or a limited gain if the stock price falls. The synthetic option equivalent would be the short sale of the stock and the simultaneous sale of a put on that stock (if the stock falls, the writer of the put will be exercised and will have to buy the stock, but can deliver it against the short sale).

The **owner of a put** will realize the maximum gain if the stock falls to $0, but only limited losses if the stock price rises. The same risks would apply if the investor sold the stock short and bought a call at the same price. If the price of the stock rose, the investor could exercise the call to cover the short.

The **writer of a put** has limited gain potential and realizes the maximum loss if the stock falls to $0. Similarly, if the investor bought the stock and sold a call at the same price, as the stock price rises, the call would be exercised against her, limiting her gain to the premium received. If the stock price falls, the maximum loss would still occur at a market price of $0 (partially hedged by the premium received for writing the call).

Synthetic Stock

The synthetic equivalent of being long stock is buying a call and selling a put on that stock. There is unlimited upside potential with the call, and an equivalent risk of the loss of value of the stock if it falls to $0 and the put is exercised.

The synthetic equivalent of being short stock is buying a put and selling a call. If the stock falls, there is a gain on the put (a maximum gain if the stock becomes worthless). If the stock rises, the short call would be exercised and the writer would be subject to the same unlimited losses as if he had shorted the stock.

Hedging with Options

In the preceding section on spreads and straddles, you learned about hedged strategies, those that involve positions on both sides of the market. A bullish investor may hedge his bets on the market's rise by taking a less expensive position on the bearish side of the market just in case. And a bearish investor may take a bullish position, as a kind of insurance policy.

Spreads and straddles involve only option positions, but other hedged strategies use options to reduce the risks of stock (and other security) positions.

Long Stock and Short Calls (Covered Call Writing)

Objectives of covered call writers. Although options have the reputation of being risky and speculative, covered call writing is relatively conservative. Covered call writers reduce the downside risk of long stock positions by the dollars they receive in premiums from selling the call, and the long stock position gives the call writer something to deliver if the call is exercised against him.

All conservative strategies, however, have limited profit potential. Covered call writers may have their stock called away from them at the exercise price when they could have gotten a higher price for it in the market. They trade a good rate of return and limited loss potential for a reduction in potential gain.

Rate of return. If the buyer of the call option never exercises the call against the covered call writer, the writer will never have to deliver stock at the exercise price. He will keep any premiums received, which will increase his return on his stock position.

Partial protection. An investor long a stock who is concerned about a downward move in price can reduce her break-even point on the stock position by writing a call against it. By writing calls, the premiums she receives for the options offset to some extent the downside risks of the stock. The price of her stock can fall by the same amount she received in premiums before she breaks even or begins losing money on her stock. Her risk is that the stock will take off and she will be called to deliver it at the strike price when the market price is well above that. In return for cushioning her downside loss potential, the investor loses some upside profit potential.

Long Stock and Long Puts

Hedging against price declines. If an investor owns stock, she can hedge her downside risk by purchasing puts at (or close to) the purchase price. By doing so, the investor then has the option to sell the stock she holds long by exercising the puts if the market price of the stock ever goes below the strike price. No matter how far the stock declines before the option expires, she can sell it for the exercise price of the puts. Her long stock position is hedged against a drop in price by the put options, as long as they remain in effect.

An investor could eliminate her risk altogether by purchasing puts with a strike price equaling the purchase price plus the premium she pays for them, or she could guarantee a gain by purchasing puts with an even higher strike price. The problem with that approach is that put premiums increase as their strike prices increase, and the investor limits her potential reward just as she limits her risk. Whatever profit she makes by selling the stock in a bull market will be, in effect, reduced by the amount she has spent on put premiums. To break even, the investor must be able to sell her stock for the original purchase price per share plus the premiums she paid for the puts.

If the stock increases in value, the cost of the puts reduces any profit by the premium paid for the puts. The investor breaks even if the stock trades at the purchase price of the stock plus the put premium. The long hedged position has a limited, known maximum loss and (after the cost of the insuring put is recovered) an unlimited potential gain.

Short Stock and Long Calls

Insurance to hedge a short stock position. Shorting stock means selling stock that the investor does not own, but has borrowed in order to sell and must eventually replace. The investor expects the stock's price to drop, allowing him to buy the stock at the new, lower price and use those shares to repay the loan of stock. Since there is no limit on how high the price can go, there is no limit on the short seller's loss potential.

Because of the risk, some investors hedge their short stock positions by purchasing call options. If the stock price does move against the investor by going up, he can exercise the right to buy shares of that stock at the long call's strike price, which could be anywhere from a little to a lot under the market price at that point.

Purchasing a call limits his risk to the difference between the strike price of the call (plus the premium) and the price he received for the borrowed stock. The purchase of the call reduces the overall profit potential on the short position by the amount of the premium.

Short Stock and Short Puts

A customer with a short put position may partially hedge the short position by selling short the stock at the same price.

As an example, if a customer sold short 100 ABC at 50, she could write an ABC 50 put at 3 as a partial hedge. In the event the stock declined to $0 (that is, it became worthless), the writer would be exercised on the put at a cost of $5,000. The writer could then deliver the stock received on the exercise against the short (for which she already received $5,000), thereby offsetting the loss on the put. The net effect would be that the investor would have no gain or loss on the stock, but would be able to keep the premiums received on the sale of the put.

If the stock rises in value, the investor is partially protected by the amount of money received in premiums. In this example, the stock could rise to $53 (the break-even point) before the investor would lose money.

Long Debt Securities and Long Calls

Call buying can be used in conjunction with the purchase of short-term, interest rate sensitive securities (e.g., money market instruments) as a hedge. As interest rates fall, funds tend to be shifted from money market investments to equity (stock) investments. This places downward price pressure on short-term interest rate sensitive securities and upward pressure on stock prices. Additionally, as the money market portfolio matures, the funds are reinvested automatically at lower interest rates.

Ratio Call Writing

If the owner of 100 shares of ABC writes 2 ABC July 30 calls at 3 against the stock, then the customer has established 1 covered position and 1 uncovered position. The call options were written on a **2 to 1** (2:1) **ratio** against the stock. If 3 calls were written against 100 shares, the ratio would be 3 to 1 (3:1). Ratio writing is used to increase premium income by the owner of the stock. The ratio writer is subject to the same risks and gains as a covered writer on the covered position and as a naked writer on the uncovered position(s). Ratio writing is also known as **variable hedging**.

Rolling Down a Position

A covered writer can still face a substantial loss if the price of a stock he owns declines greatly, since he is protected against a stock decline only to the extent of the premium received. As an alternative to selling the stock in the event of a decline, the investor can **roll down** the short option.

Assume the investor owns 100 shares of ABC at 40 and writes 1 ABC Jan 40 call at 5. If the market price of ABC drops to 35, then the short call is out-of-the-money, and the premium will probably have dropped to reflect this. If the premium on the option falls to $1, then the customer can buy back the option at a $4 profit per share. The customer can now sell an ABC Jan 35 call. If the price of the stock continues to fall, the investor can continue to buy and sell the calls, rolling down to a lower exercise price each time and keeping the difference in the premiums to offset the loss of the stock's value in the market.

Fully and Partially Hedged Positions

To calculate losses, gains and break-even for hedged and partially hedged positions (such as a short stock position hedged by a long call position or a short stock position partially hedged by a short put position), begin by calculating the cost of the position (paid or received). Then, to find the maximum risk and reward potentials, ask what happens when the stock price rises or drops.

Break-even points are the same whether the investor is long or short the position. The gain for the person who is long the position is the same as the loss for the person short the position and vice versa. With hedge positions, relate all strategies to stock positions first.

Nonequity Options

In theory, any item of fluctuating value can be the underlying instrument of an option. In fact, the variety of instruments underlying options has multiplied dramatically in recent years. This section will cover the characteristics of three types of nonequity options: index, interest rate and foreign currency.

Index Options

Though options on indexes are relatively new to investors, the indexes themselves are not. Indexes that measure the movements of markets or parts of markets have been around for decades. Two primary types of indexes are relevant here.

- **Broad-based indexes**. Designed to reflect the movement of the market as a whole, broad-based indexes vary substantially. Some track as few as 20 stocks; others follow the movements of more than 1,700. Options are available on the S&P 100 Index (called the OEX), the S&P 500 Index (called the SPX), the Amex Major Market Index (the XMI), and the Value Line Index, among others.
- **Narrow-based indexes**. Narrow-based indexes track the movements of market segments, such as a group of stocks in one industry, or a specific type of investment. Narrow-based indexes include the Technology Index and the Gold/Silver Index.

Options on indexes. Indexes provide information; they are not, in themselves, investments. Investors cannot buy (or sell) an actual index to profit from its changing value. Indexes do provide numerical values that are used to track other investments, however, and these values change. An investor can speculate on the direction, degree and timing of that change by purchasing or selling options on that index. Index options make it possible for investors to profit from the swings in the market or to hedge against losses that market movement can cause in individual stock positions.

Multiplier. Each index has been assigned a multiplier that is used to convert both the listed strike prices and the premiums into dollars. For the S&P 100 index (OEX), the multiplier is 100. An OEX Jan 220 call at 18 1/2 is actually worth $22,000 (220 x 100) and would cost an investor a premium of $1,850. The multiplier of 100 is easy to remember, since it is part of the name of the S&P 100 itself and because it is analogous to the 100 shares in a stock option contract.

Call options. A call on an index gives its owner the right to receive, in cash, the option's intrinsic value (the amount by which the call's strike price is below the index's "market" value) at an assigned time on the day of exercise (which is usually the open or close of trading). The S&P 500 index (SPX) uses the opening price, and the S&P 100 index (OEX) uses the closing price. In the illustration of the S&P 100 index, for example, the Jan 220 calls give call owners the right to receive the difference between 220 and 236.87, the value at the close. Because of the multiplier of 100, that amounts to $1,687.00. The writer of a call, if the option was exercised on the date listed, would owe that amount.

Put options. A put on the index gives its owner the right to "put" the index to the put writer and to receive the option's intrinsic value (the amount by which the put's strike price is above the index's

Chicago Board S&P 100 INDEX

Strike Price	Calls- Last			Puts- Last		
	Jan	Feb	Mar	Jan	Feb	Mar
200	...	38 1/2	...	1/8	2 1/8	...
205	...	...	...	1/8	2 3/4	...
210	26 3/4	...	...	1/4	3 5/8	6
215	...	...	28	3/8	4 5/8	7 3/4
220	18 1/2	22	23	5/8	5 5/8	9
225	13	16 3/4	18 1/2	1 3/16	7	11
230	8 1/2	15	20 1/4	1 15/16	8 1/2	10 1/2
235	4 5/8	12 1/4	15 3/4	3 1/4	11	13 1/2
240	2 1/4	8 3/4	12 1/2	5 5/8	13	15 5/8

Total call vol 144,244   Total call open int   395,011
Total put vol 178,177   Total put open int   319,252
The index: High 239.77; Low 231.56; Close 236.87, - 2.40

Fig. 18.12 An example of an index option table.

"market" value) at closing on the day of exercise. An OEX March 240 put, if exercised during a day when the market closed at 236.87, for example, would bring in $313 for its owner (240 - 236.87 = 3.13; 3.13 x 100 = $313). The writer of the option is obligated to pay $313. Writers lose what buyers gain (and vice versa).

Exercise settlement. Since index option writers cannot actually deliver an index to satisfy their obligations to options buyers, they deliver cash. In the preceding example, the writer of the OEX 240 put delivered $313 in cash.

Cash settlement creates a special risk, since it means that all short calls on index options are naked. A writer cannot cover a call by owning the index, as a stock option writer can cover a call by owning 100 shares of the underlying stock.

The amount that a writer must pay if exercised is based on the closing value for the S&P 100 that day, not on the value at the time of exercise. This is a risk the option holder must take. On Thursday, for example, an investor might exercise a 285 call when the index is at a high of 290.02, confident that the option is in-the-money by just over 4 points, only to watch the index fall to 282.65 at the close, leaving the option out-of-the-money by 2.35 points. During the day, a $402 gain became a $235 loss.

Dates and times. Trading of index options occurs between 10 am and 4:15 pm Eastern Standard Time. The daily exercise cut-off occurs at 4:15 pm EST. Settlement occurs one business day after exercise. In most cases, index options expire during the next three or four consecutive months. In the preceding illustration, the expiration months are January, February and March. The expiration date is the Saturday following the third Friday of the expiration month.

Index option strategies. Like stock options, index options have three major uses. An investor can profit by speculating correctly on an upturn in the market, a downturn in the market, or hedge against changes in the market.

Position and exercise limits. To prevent investors from influencing the market, the SEC establishes limits on how many index option contracts investors can establish and exercise. For index options, the position limit is 25,000 contracts on the same side of the market, and the exercise limit is 15,000 contracts in five days on the same side of the market. An investor with 10,000 long calls, for example, couldn't be short more than 15,000 puts, because long calls and short puts are on the same side of the market (both are bullish).

Interest Rate Options

Options on government debt securities are a product of the enormous growth of the federal deficit and wide variations in interest rates. Financed by Treasury bills, notes and bonds, the government's deficit creates a vast market in securities that are sensitive to changes in interest rates. Interest rate options were introduced to allow investors to profit from fluctuations in interest rates (and debt security prices) and to hedge the risks created by those fluctuations.

Investor objectives. The objectives of investors in interest rate options are similar to those of investors in stock or index options. They hope to profit from changes in the prices of debt securities (caused by fluctuations in interest rates), or to hedge existing portfolios of debt securities against price declines caused by increased interest rates. The securities underlying interest rate options have high values ($100,000 for notes and bonds and $1 million for Treasury bills), and the typical investor tends to be an institution rather than an individual.

Options on debt securities respond to changes in the price of the underlying security just as stock options do. But the

INTEREST RATE OPTIONS
FRIDAY, JANUARY 18TH, 1994

For Notes and Bonds, decimals in closing prices represent 32nds; 1.01 means 1 1/32. For Bills, decimals in closing prices represent basis points; $25 per .01 .

Chicago Board Options Exchange

U.S. TREASURY BOND- $100,000 PRINCIPAL VALUE

Underlying Issue	Strike Price	Calls- Last			Puts- Last		
		Feb	Mar	Jun	Feb	Mar	Jun
8 7/8% (ybm)	96	...	...	...	...	0.20	...
due 8 / 2017	98	...	4.19	...	...	0.28	...
	100	...	2.31	...	...	...	...
	102	...	1.30	...	...	...	...

Total call vol 221   Call open int 1,200
Total put vol 51   Put open int 1,654

5-YEAR U.S. TREASURY BOND- $100,000 PRINCIPAL VALUE

		Feb	Mar	Jun	Feb	Mar	Jun
8 1/4% (yfi)	100	...	...	...	...	0.20	...
due 8 / 2002		...	...	...	...	...	...

Total call vol 0   Call open int 206
Total put vol 30   Put open int 65

Fig. 18.13 A sample interest rate option table.

values of Treasury bills, notes and bonds move inversely to movements in interest rates. As rates go up, existing debt securities lose value. And as interest rates go down, existing debt securities gain in value. A decrease in the interest paid on newly issued bonds will cause the prices of existing bonds that pay higher interest rates to increase. Hence, interest rates have gone down and debt prices have increased.

Treasury bills. The underlying instrument for calls and puts on T bills is the most current 13-week (91-day) Treasury bill. The U.S. Treasury auctions 13-week T bills once a week. T bills are typically auctioned on Monday and issued on Thursday.

T bills are sold at a discount from par value and do not otherwise pay interest. One T bill option represents $1 million worth of some future issue of 13-week bills, rather than a specific security. This means that one cannot, technically, write a covered call on a T bill. The deliverable bills are those issued during the week of settlement, not the one current when the option is written.

An investor who writes a December 93 T bill call doesn't know the specifics of the T bill that will be current when the option expires in December. Rather, the investor expects the T bills issued closest to expiration to be trading at a price lower than 93, so that owners of December 93 calls will prefer to buy T bills at the market price rather than at the strike price of their calls. The underlying securities must be delivered on the Thursday following exercise.

To turn a T bill premium quote into a dollar figure, multiply it by $2,500. The premium is an annualized percentage of the face value, $1 million. Although one percent of $1 million is $10,000, the T bill's life span is 13 weeks, just one-fourth of a 52-week year. Annualized, therefore, each point equals $2,500 (one-fourth of $10,000). An investor interested in purchasing a T bill call quoted at a premium .5 could expect to pay $1,250.

The minimum price change in the quote for a T bill premium is one basis point, which is $25, since a basis point is .01% of face value.

Treasury notes and bonds. Treasury notes are issued for maturities of one to ten years and pay semiannual interest. Bonds, the longest term Treasury securities, are issued with maturities of ten years and up. An option on either a note or a bond represents a specific underlying security with a face value of $100,000. Upon exercise, the owner of a put or the writer of a call must deliver a note or bond from that particular issue.

Strike prices for notes and bonds are quoted at a percent of face value. One option on the 8 7/8% bond in the table, for example, has a strike price of 102. The owner of a March call on the bond can exercise the option to purchase the note for 102% of face value, which is $102,000 (plus accrued interest).

One point of premium equals 1% of the note's or bond's face value, or $1,000. In the preceding illustration, March 98 puts on the 8 7/8% notes are trading at a premium of 0.28. This does **not** mean that one call would cost a buyer $280. As you can see from the information at the top of the clipping, the premium quotes are not expressed in true decimals, but in 32nds of a point, just as Treasury notes and bonds are quoted in 32nds. A premium of 0.28, then, is equal to 28/32 of 1% of the note's face value. The premium for a March 102 call on the 8 7/8% bond is 1.30, which equals $1,000 plus 30/32 of $1,000, for a total cost to the investor of $1,937.50. The minimum change in premiums for options on notes and bonds is 1/32 of a point ($31.25).

Trading cycles. Treasury bond options trade on a March-June- September-December cycle, with three months trading at any one time. Options on Treasury notes expire in February, May, August and November. At any given time, an investor will usually be able to choose from among options expiring in three of those months.

Expiration and exercise. Expiration of interest rate options is the Saturday following the third Friday of the month. Two business days after exercise of the option, the call writer must deliver (or the put writer receive) the underlying note or bond. The investor who receives the security must pay the exercise price plus the interest that has accrued since the last payment. This time includes the date of the last payment, but does not include the date of settlement.

Accrued interest is due with the exercise price to make the transaction equitable. If the person delivering the security has actually owned it, he or she should be compensated for the interest that has accrued since the previous payment. The new owner will receive the next full interest payment as if he or she had owned the security during those months.

Hedging with long call positions. An investor who fears that long-term bond interest rates will head down and thus wants to lock in high current rates can purchase calls. If rates do decline, the price of bonds will rise. He can then exercise the call options to buy bonds below market price, or sell the calls to capture the increase in premium and use that money to buy bonds. If he is wrong and interest rates rise, he can buy his bonds at the market and let the calls expire.

Hedging with short put positions. Investors who anticipate a near-term decline in interest rates and who hold a long-term position in Treasury bonds can write puts. The investor is assuming that the puts will expire worthless when falling interest rates drive up bond prices. If she is correct, the premium received for writing the options will provide a profit without requiring the sale of the bonds themselves. If wrong, she can buy back the puts at their increased value and take a tax loss.

Hedging with long put positions. As a hedge against rising interest rates (and falling note prices), investors sometimes buy at-the-money puts on T notes. If rates do rise before the puts expire, bond prices fall and the puts increase in value. The investor can then exercise the puts to sell bonds, or he can sell the puts and take the profit on the increase in premium.

Cross hedging. Investors can use options on Treasury securities to hedge other types of debt (such as corporate or municipal debt) or even to hedge positions in interest-rate-sensitive stocks.

The hedger must use options on debt instruments with maturities that are similar to the portfolio to be hedged (short-term interest rates and long-term interest rates sometimes move in different directions). A corporate bond portfolio, for example, should be hedged with Treasury bond options. Treasury bill options should not be used because they have a short-term maturity, rather than the long-term maturity of the corporate bonds. Treasury bond options may also be used to hedge a preferred stock portfolio. Both preferred stock and T bonds are fixed-income securities and behave similarly in the market. Both decline in value as interest rates increase.

Increasing yields with call writing. To generate increased investment income on a portfolio of Treasury securities, a fund manager can write calls. If the securities remain stable in price or decrease in value, the calls (if written at- or out-of-the-money) will expire and the premium received will add to the interest income from the bonds.

U.S. Government Security Option Characteristics

<u>Underlying Security</u>	<u>Settlement Date</u>	<u>Strike Price</u>	<u>Premium</u>
$1,000,000 in current T bills	Thursday of the week after exercise	Aggregate $1,000,000 less adjusted discount	1.0 = 100 basis points = $2,500 (.01 = $25)
A specific $100,000 T note	Two business days	A percentage of face value	1.0 = 1% of face value = $1,000 (.01 = 1/32 or $31.25)
A specific $100,000 T bond	Two business days	A percentage of face value	1.0 = 1% of face value = $1,000 (.01 = 1/32 or $31.25)

Foreign Currency Options (FCOs)

Currency exchange. Any American who has traveled outside the United States has learned about currency exchange in the retail market, usually from the sometimes frustrating experience of translating the value of the U.S. dollar into the currency of another country. Currency exchange in the wholesale market of large banks, international corporations and sophisticated investors is similar in complexity and risk.

Investors trade foreign currency options for two reasons. They hope to profit from fluctuating exchange rates, and to hedge against the risks rising from fluctuating exchange rates.

Currency risk. The risk in monetary exchange arises from fluctuations in the exchange rate. On a personal scale, this is a fairly simple matter. If you go to Canada, for instance, you may be able to exchange each U.S. dollar for $1.30 Canadian. The next time you travel, your U.S. dollar might buy only $1.20 Canadian, or it might buy $1.40 Canadian.

U.S. corporations with contracts to buy or sell goods in a foreign country at a specific time have the same problem as the tourist. The dollars an American wholesaler

FOREIGN CURRENCY OPTIONS
FRIDAY, JANUARY 18TH, 1994

Philadelphia Exchange

Option & Underlying	Strike Price	Calls- Last Feb	Mar	Jun	Puts- Last Feb	Mar	Jun
50,000 Australian Dollars- cents per unit.							
ADollar	...77	r	r	r	0.35	r	r
79.56	...78	r	r	r	r	r	0.67
31,250 British Pounds- cents per unit.							
BPound	..165	r	14.10	r	r	r	r
179.44	..170	r	9.40	r	r	r	r
179.44	..175	5.10	r	r	r	1.70	3.80
179.44	177 1/2	3.15	3.90	r	r	2.40	r
6,250,000 Japanese Yen- 100ths of a cent per unit.							
JYen	..73	1.92	2.45	r	0.48	0.79	r
74.68	..74	1.40	1.95	3.0	0.75	1.15	r
74.68	..75	0.95	1.48	r	1.34	r	2.20

Total call vol 13,389   Call open int 365,373   r- not traded   s- no option offered
Total put vol 9,154   Put open int 353,817   Last is premium (purchase price)

Fig. 18.14 Option quotes on foreign currencies.

budgets to buy Swiss watches in six months may not be sufficient if the rate of exchange between U.S. dollars and Swiss francs changes in the meantime.

Characteristics of foreign currency options. The Philadelphia Exchange (PHLX) is set up to facilitate trading of options on foreign currencies. Underlying each foreign currency option is an arbitrary amount of foreign money as set by the exchange. The strike price of the option is set at a certain amount of U.S. money. Each option contract represents the right to buy or sell the foreign currency for the specified amount of U.S. money. The owner of a foreign currency option, therefore, can "lock-in" a certain exchange rate for a certain time, just as the owner of an equity option can lock in the strike price of an equity option.

If the exchange rate moves in the predicted direction, a call owner can, for the amount of U.S. money set by the strike price, purchase the amount of foreign currency determined by the contract. It's as if the traveler mentioned earlier could determine months in advance that each of his U.S. dollars would be worth $1.30 Canadian when the time came to travel.

Underlying currencies. Options are available on several foreign currencies, including British pounds, Canadian dollars, West German marks, French francs, Japanese yen and Swiss francs. As you can see from the accompanying illustration, option contract characteristics vary from currency to currency, and from exchange to exchange.

Price of the underlying currency. The left-hand column in the sample FCO table (similar to what might appear in the business section of a paper) lists current exchange rate in U.S. money per unit of the underlying currency. Exchange rates are quoted in U.S. cents per unit of the underlying currency, with two exceptions: French francs trade in tenths of a cent per franc; Japanese yen trade in hundredths of a cent per yen.

The British pound, for example, was trading at 179.44 at the end of the trading day on Friday, January 18th. A U.S. car dealer could exchange 179.44 cents ($1.79 plus 44/100ths of a cent) American for one British pound. On the same day, Japanese yen closed at 74.68- 0.7468 cents or $.007468 per yen.

w404

Contract sizes. Three quarters of a cent's worth of yen is a long way from the price of a shipment of Toyotas or VCRs. Since foreign currency options (FCOs) are designed (in large part) to meet the needs of international institutions, one option contract covers a large amount of currency. In the table, contract sizes are listed in the left-hand column, just above the exchange rate for the previous day. A call on British pounds on the PHLX represents a contract for 31,250 pounds.

For example, on Friday, January 18th, an investment officer for an American corporation purchases a PHLX March 74 call on the yen. The investor can exercise the option to purchase Japanese currency at a set price of $.0074 U.S. per yen (74/100 of a cent) at any time prior to the expiration date. Since each PHLX contract covers 6,250,000 yen, the aggregate exercise price of the option is $46,250.

If the same corporation writes a PHLX March 175 put on the British pound and is exercised, it will be required to take delivery of 31,250 British pounds at 175 U.S. cents per pound. It will pay an aggregate exercise price of $54,687.50 ($1.75 per pound x 31,250 pounds).

Premium quotes use the same units of U.S. currency employed in quoting exchange rates on the underlying instruments. To calculate both exchange rates and premium values, the value per unit is multiplied by one unit's equivalent stated in dollar terms. For example, one cent is equal to $.01. One hundredth of a cent, as for the yen contract, is stated as $0.0001.

The premium on the PHLX March 175 put on the British pound was 1.70. Since the premiums are quoted in U.S. cents, the writer will receive 1.70 cents per British pound in the contract, or $0.017 (1.70 x $0.01). Since each contract represents 31,250 pounds, a the writer will receive $531.25 ($0.017 x 31,250).

Expiration cycles. The PHLX trades foreign currency options on a three/six/nine-month schedule, and has the option of adding a 12-month contract. Several cycles may trade at one time.

Exchange Rate Quotes

West German Marks	Swiss Francs	Canadian Dollars	British Pounds	French Francs	Japanese Yen
Cents per unit of underlying currency				Tenths of cents	Hundredths of cents

Fig. 18.15 Exchange rate quotes vary among currencies.

Expiration date and last trading day. All foreign currency options expire on the Saturday preceding the third Wednesday of the month. Trading ceases at 1:30 pm EST the last business day before the expiration date (usually a Friday). The PHLX trades foreign currency options from 8:30 am until 2:30 pm EST.

Position and exercise limits. On the PHLX, position and exercise limits are 50,000 contracts on the same side of the market.

Exercise settlement. The PHLX uses the American exercise system, which allows owners to exercise their options at any time up to and including the last business day before expiration. When a foreign currency option is exercised, the owner of the put or the writer of the call must deliver the currency of the country of origin: French francs in France, Deutsche marks in Germany and so on. To make this possible, the Options Clearing Corporation (OCC) has established banking arrangements in each country.

Strategies. Investors trade foreign currency options for two reasons. They want to either profit from fluctuating exchange rates, or hedge against the risks arising from fluctuating exchange rates.

Exchange rates rise and fall because of changes in the values of both currencies involved. The changing value of the foreign currency, then, isn't the only problem for investors. The value of U.S. money may be changing as well.

The reverse also occurs. Remember that the instrument underlying the option is foreign currency. Whatever is going on with the U.S. dollar, the investor's strategy is determined by the market price of the foreign money. If the dollar is weakening, the Deutsche mark could be growing stronger. An investor would be bullish on the mark. To avoid confusion, it helps to concentrate on the underlying instrument, the foreign currency. Remember that the investor has the right to buy or sell the foreign currency, not the U.S. dollar.

When the value of the underlying instrument increases, investors use bullish strategies to profit from that increase. That means buying calls or selling puts on the currency. And when the value of the currency drops, investors sell calls or buy puts on the currency. Investors can use a variety of other strategies (including spreads) to speculate on the rise and fall of exchange rates.

Hedge strategies. The need to hedge currency exchange is a major reason for the existence of options on currencies. Companies who do business with firms overseas make commitments to spend or receive a given amount of foreign currency weeks or months in the future. Unfortunately, they cannot know precisely what the exchange value of that currency will be. So, when they purchase or sell foreign money on the spot market, they may take a beating if its value in American dollars has changed. Options on foreign currency provide a way to lessen that risk.

Margin and Tax Rules for Options

Client accounts. Options are typically bought and sold in **margin** accounts. A customer can enter into an option transaction in a **cash** account only if he or she is buying options, or is selling **fully secured and covered** calls and puts (against which sufficient stock, convertible securities, bank escrow letters, cash, certificates of deposit, or short-term government securities have been deposited). If the customer is buying an option as part of a spread, both option transactions (the long option and the short option) must be executed in the investor's margin account.

Long option positions. Although option transactions usually take place in margin accounts, options cannot be bought on margin. The option buyer must pay 100% of the purchase price of the option. Because options are **wasting assets** (in a given number of months they expire and become worthless) they would make poor collateral for margin loans. For all option purchases (whether in a cash or a margin account), the investor must pay for the purchase in full (100% of the option premium) not later than the 7th business day after the trade date.

Short option positions. **Short options positions can be covered** or **uncovered**. Margin rules take into account the fact that it's far riskier to be uncovered (naked) than it is to be covered.

Margin Requirements for Covered Options

Calls and puts may be covered in a number of different ways. Since the risk an option writer takes on can be covered (that is, the writer's obligation can be met through the purchase or sale of either the underlying security or a corresponding option), there are no margin requirements for a covered option.

A writer of an equity call option is obligated by the option contract to deliver the underlying stock when the option owner exercises the call. An investor who sells a call on a stock that he owns is described as a covered call writer. The stock covers the risk of his short option position. If the call is exercised against the writer, he can fulfill his obligation by delivering the stock he owns. Short calls may be covered in a number of ways. In a margin account, a call is covered and the writer will not be required to meet option margin requirements if he or she has deposited in the account or presents:

- the **stock** underlying the call;
- an **escrow agreement** (or **receipt**) for the underlying stock (an escrow agreement certifies that the underlying stock is held in an approved bank and will be delivered if the call option is exercised);
- a security that is **convertible** into the underlying stock;

- a **long call** on the same stock with a later expiration date, a lower exercise price, or both; or
- a **warrant** to purchase the underlying security, and the exercise price of the warrant exceeds the exercise price of the short call.

In a cash account, a call is covered and the writer will not be required to meet option margin requirements if he or she has deposited in the account or presents:

- the **stock** underlying the call option;
- an **escrow agreement** (or **receipt**) for the underlying stock; or
- a security that is **convertible** into the underlying stock.

Covered puts. Most put writers are naked. The person does not cover the risk that the stock may drop sharply in value, but simply sells a put against a deposit of cash. A put writer can cover the risk of a drop in the value of the security in several ways. In a margin account, a put is covered and the writer will not be required to meet option margin requirements if he or she has deposited into the account, presents or enters the following:

- **cash equal to the exercise price** of the put;
- a **bank guarantee letter** or **escrow agreement** in which the bank certifies it holds on deposit for the client funds equal to the exercise price of the put;
- a **short sale of the underlying stock** (and she has enough cash from the short sale to purchase the stock if the put is exercised);
- a **purchase of a put** on the same stock with a higher strike price, a later expiration date, or both.

In a cash account, a put is covered and the writer will not be required to meet option margin requirements if the writer deposits or presents:

- **cash equal to the exercise price** of the put;
- an **escrow agreement** in which a bank certifies that it holds on deposit for the client funds equal to the exercise price of the put;
- **money market securities** with a current market value equal to or greater than the exercise price of the put; or
- an **escrow agreement** for any of the above.

Margin Requirements for Uncovered Options

When an investor writes a call on a stock that he does not own, he is said to be a **naked** (or **uncovered**) writer. Naked call writing subjects an investor to greater risk than covered call writing. A naked call writer who has the call exercised against him will have to purchase securities at a current market price higher than the strike price. The put writer who has the put exercised against him will be obligated to buy securities at a strike price higher than the current market price of the stock. Because of this risk, investors must write naked (or uncovered) options in margin accounts and are required to deposit a certain percent of the dollar amount they have at risk.

As with other securities, there are both initial and minimum margin requirements for options. An investor who writes an uncovered option is required (under the **Uniform Margin Methodology**) to deposit:

- an amount equal to the current option **premium**;
- a **percentage of the market value** of the underlying security (currently **20%** of CMV for most securities, but subject to change);
- less any amount the option is **out-of-the-money**.

The writer is permitted to subtract any out-of-the-money amount since the option won't be exercised until it is in-the-money. Generally, the farther out-of-the-money the option is, the less likely it is to ever be exercised. The farther the option is in-the-money, of course, the higher the risks for the writer. It isn't necessary to alter the margin requirement to account for that risk, though, because the amount an option is in-the-money is already figured into the premium, and the premium is included in the margin requirement.

Options accounts are **marked to the market** daily. The margin requirement, in other words, is recalculated by the broker-dealer every day using the new market value of the security and the new premium on the option.

Equity options. The formula for options margin requirements is 100% of the option premium plus a percent of CMV less any amount out-of-the-money. The variable that changes (depending on the security underlying the option) is the percent of market value used. That variable changes with different types of options contracts. As discussed earlier, for equity options the margin requirement is:

Current premium PLUS 20% of the underlying security's CMV and MINUS any dollar amount that the option is out-of-the-money.

Minimum margin requirements. The minimum margin requirement becomes a concern only if the option is out-of-the-money. When dealing with an out-of-the-money option, the deposit required is the greater of the initial or minimum margin requirements. For most securities, the minimum requirement is 100% of the current premium, plus 10% of the current market value (CMV) of the underlying security (the NYSE and NASD minimum of $2,000 per account still applies). If the equity option is out-of-the-money, the minimum margin requirement is:

Current premium PLUS 10% of the security's CMV.

Required cash deposit. When an option is written, the writer receives a premium for selling the option and assuming the obligation. The dollars received in premiums for writing the option may be credited toward the required margin deposit. The cash deposit required when writing an option is therefore:

> Margin Requirement - Any Premiums Received = Required Cash Deposit.

Margin Requirements for Nonequity Options

Like margin requirements for equity options, margin requirements for nonequity options follow the **Uniform Margin Methodology**. The initial requirement is the current premium plus a percentage of the underlying market value, less any out-of-the-money amount. The minimum requirement is the current premium plus a lesser percentage of the underlying market value.

In all cases, the cash deposit required is the margin requirement minus the premium received. The accompanying table summarizes the margin requirements for uncovered options.

Options on **Treasury securities** are the single exception. For these options, the percentage of the underlying amount is a **percentage of face value**, not market value.

Option Type	Initial % of Underlying CMV	Minimum % of Underlying CMV
Equity (stock)	20% of principal	10%
Narrow-based Index	20%	10%
Broad-based Index	15%	10%
Treasury Bond	3 1/2% of principal	1/2%
Treasury Note	3% of principal	1/2%
Foreign Currency	4%	3/4%

Fig. 18.16 Margin requirements for non-equity options.

Margin on Spreads

A spread is a long position in one or more options of a given class and a short position in one or more options of a different series within the same class.

Transaction	Dr	Cr
Buy 1 AFP Sep 30 Call	-2	
Sell 1 AFP Sep 25 Call		+3
Net Credit		+1

This spread is a **credit spread** because the investor ended up with cash in hand after making both opening transactions. Credit spreads (both call or put spreads) are also known as **limited risk spreads** because the investor knows in advance his or her maximum possible loss (the difference between the strike prices is the limit of the investor's risk).

The **maintenance requirement** for a limited-risk credit spread is the dollar amount of the actual risk (e.g., the difference between the options' strike prices). The investor's **cash deposit** will be the maintenance requirement less the net premium received. For this spread, the maintenance requirement would be $500 (the maximum risk) and the cash deposit requirement would be $100 ($500-$400 net premium received).

The margin requirement for **debit spreads** is also the dollar amount of the maximum risk (for a debit spread, the maximum risk is the net debit, the amount the investor pays to open the spread). As with the purchase of any option, Reg T requires that the long option be fully paid for.

Margin Requirements for Straddles and Combinations

Purchasing a straddle means **buying** both a put and a call. **Purchasing a combination** means **buying** both a put and a call with different expiration months or strike prices. An investor who opens a long straddle or combination must deposit 100% of the combined premiums. Again, long option positions must always be paid for in full. Since the client's potential loss is limited to the combined premiums, no further margin is required even if the price of the underlying stock fluctuates.

Writing a straddle means **selling** both a put and a call. **Writing a combination** means **selling** both a put and a call with different expiration months or strike prices. The risk to a straddle or combination writer is unlimited. Unless the price of the underlying stock is exactly **at-the-money**, one of the two options will always be out-of-the-money and the other in-the-money. The margin required for short straddles and combinations is the greater of the two margin requirements for the individual options plus the current market value of the other option (that is, the other option's premium).

Margin on Option Hedges

Investors who trade options to reduce the risk on long or short stock positions also incur margin requirements. Here are four typical option hedges:

- **Long stock/short call**. The premium from the short call reduces the loss on the stock position if the stock price declines.
- **Long stock/long put**. If the stock price declines, the investor can sell the stock at the option's strike price by exercising the put.
- **Short stock/long call**. If the stock price rises, the investor can exercise the call to buy stock to replace the securities borrowed for the short sale.
- **Short stock/short put**. The premium from the short put reduces the investor's loss if the stock price rises.

Taxation of Options

Capital Gains and Losses

The sale of capital assets (securities, real estate and all tangible property) can result in a capital gain or a capital loss. A capital gain occurs when the difference between a capital asset's purchase price and its selling price is positive. If the difference is negative, it is a capital loss. To calculate tax liability, taxpayers must first add all capital gains for the year. Then, they separately add all capital losses. Finally, they offset the totals to determine the net capital gain or loss for the year.

Net capital gains and net capital losses. If the result is a net capital gain, it is fully taxable at the same rate as earned income. Net capital losses are deductible against earned income to a maximum of $3,000 per year. Any capital losses not deducted in a taxable year may be carried forward indefinitely to lower taxable income in future years.

Individual Federal Income Taxes

The basic design of the tax return is:

```
       Earned income
  +    Passive income           (netted against passive losses)
  +    Interest and dividends
  +/-  Net capital gains
       Adjusted Gross Income    (AGI)
  -    Itemized deductions
  -    Standard deductions
  -    Personal exemptions
       Taxable income
  x    Tax rate
       Tax liability
```

Income tax brackets. The Tax Reform Act of 1986 (TRA 1986) defines two tax brackets: a 15% and 28% rate. Actually, the rates are more complex than this. In the past, the U.S. income tax tables have been structured so that successively earned portions of one's income are taxed at progressively higher rates. Thus, a married couple with a combined taxable income of $35,000 would pay 15% on the first $29,750 and 28% on the remaining $5,250 in income.

However, beginning in 1988, taxpayers with taxable income over a certain level will lose the benefit of the 15% rate on lower amounts of income. For married couples filing jointly, this is accomplished by imposing an additional tax of 5% on taxable income between $71,900 and $171,090. For an unmarried taxpayer, the 5% surtax applies to incomes between $43,150 and $100,480. After those levels, a flat 28% rate applies to all taxable income.

Margin Expenses

Interest paid for securities margin loans is a tax-deductible expense. The one exception is interest expenses incurred in the purchase of municipal securities. Since the interest income is federally tax-exempt, the IRS will not allow taxpayers to claim deductions for the interest expense on municipal securities.

Investors can deduct interest expenses for other securities to the extent they do not exceed their net investment income, which includes interest income, dividends and all capital gains. The previous $10,000 limit on investment expenses is being phased out. By 1991, only net investment income will determine the amount that can be deducted annually.

Adjusting Cost Basis

The cost basis of an investment is used to determine whether there is a taxable gain or a tax-deductible loss when the asset is sold. Because many things affect the cost basis of an asset, the IRS allows the cost basis to be adjusted for such things as stock splits or stock dividends.

Capital gains. A capital gain occurs when capital assets (securities, real estate and tangible property) are sold at a price that exceeds the adjusted cost basis. Usually, computing the capital gain or loss on an asset is a simple matter of comparing the purchase price with the selling price (less commissions).

Capital losses. A capital loss occurs when capital assets are sold at a price less than that of the adjusted cost basis (less commissions). Before losses can be deducted against taxable income, they must be netted against capital gains. Only $3,000 worth of losses can be deducted annually by individuals or married couples. Excess amounts may be carried forward.

Wash Sale Rule

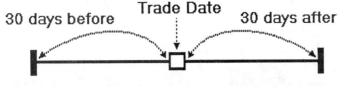

30 days before   Trade Date   30 days after

61 days in total including the trade date.

Fig. 18.17 The wash sale rule covers 61 days.

Wash sales. Capital losses may not be used to offset gains or income if the investor sells a security at a loss and purchases the same (or substantially identical) security within 30 days before or after the trade date establishing the loss. The sale at a loss and the repurchase within a 61-day period is a "wash sale."

Substantially identical securities include stock rights, call options, the sale of short-term deep in-the-money puts, warrants and convertible securities of the same issue. The wash sale rule applies only to realized losses. It does not apply to a realized gain. You may sell a stock to realize a gain and immediately purchase the security to reestablish your position.

Taxable Option Events

Options are capital assets. Trading them involves capital gains and losses rather than ordinary income. The holder (purchaser) of an option can do one of three things with that option: he can exercise the option, he can resell the option, or he can let the option expire unexercised.

Call or put option expires. An option that expires unexercised results in a capital loss for the person who paid the premium to buy it. The writer of the option received the premium and, if the option remains unexercised at expiration, realizes a capital gain from that premium.

Call or put position is closed. An investor who writes or buys an option may choose to effect a closing transaction. The tax effects of a closing purchase or sale are as follows:

- a capital gain will result if the sale price of the option is greater than the purchase price (this is true even if the option was sold first and later purchased, a closing purchase of a written option); or
- a capital loss will result if the sale price is less than the purchase price of the option.

Call option is exercised. Tax treatment of an option that is exercised is slightly more complicated than a straight capital gain or loss. When an option is exercised, one investor buys and the other sells the stock. The premium on the option affects the cost basis if the stock is being purchased or the sale proceeds if the stock is being sold.

When a call is exercised, the holder of the option buys the stock at the call's strike price. However, the investor also paid the call premium for the right to purchase the stock at the strike price. The total cost basis for the stock, therefore, is the strike price plus the premium on the call.

The call writer has to deliver stock at the strike price and received the call premium for taking the risk. The sale proceeds equals the strike price **plus** the call premium.

Put option is exercised. When a put is exercised, the premium of the option is subtracted from the cost basis (or sale proceeds) of the stock.

Establishing gains or losses. When an option is exercised, you cannot automatically determine whether the investor has realized a capital gain or loss. Further information is needed. If the stock is being sold through exercise, you need to know the original purchase price. If the stock is being purchased through exercise, you need to be told the price at which the investor later sells the stock.

Effect of Options on Stock Holding Periods

Long stock and long a put. If an individual owns stock and buys a put option on that stock, then he has effectively locked in a sale price for the life of that option. The IRS has ruled that the purchase of a put on stock held 6 months or less automatically caps that stock's holding period at 6 months. Thus, any gain on that stock will be treated as short-term.

If the stock was held over 6 months before the purchase of the put, then the holding period is unaffected. To the IRS, the fact that the holding period is already long-term is adequate proof that the investor is not attempting to turn a short-term gain into a long-term gain through purchasing a put.

If the investor has held stock for less than 6 months, buys a put and then sells that put in a closing transaction, the holding period of that stock (capped at 6 months at the purchase of the put) begins anew as of the closing date of the put sale.

Long stock and short a call. If an individual owns stock and writes an in-the-money call option on that stock, then he has virtually assured the sale of that stock by the option's expiration. The IRS has ruled that the sale of a call that is deep in-the-money (a deep in-the-money call is one that has a strike price at least 10% below the current market value of the stock) automatically caps the holding period on stock held 6 months or less at 6 months. Thus, any gain on that stock will be treated as short-term.

Writing a call that is only slightly in-the-money (a strike price less than 10% below the current market value of the stock) also caps the holding period at 6 months, but in the event a closing purchase of a call is entered, the holding period of the stock resumes.

If the stock was held more than 6 months before the sale of the call, then the holding period is unaffected. If the investor writes an out-of-the-money call, the stock's holding period is similarly unaffected.

Nonequity Options

One tax characteristic of nonequity options is unique. Investors holding nonequity option positions on December 31 are taxed as if the positions were closed out.

18.54

Chapter Review

Questions

1. As the underlying stock price increases, the premium of a call option will generally

   ____(A) increase.
   ____(B) decrease.
   ____(C) remain the same.
   ____(D) fluctuate.

   call at 50   stock ↑ 60   18.15

   *increase; because premiums
   that call buyers are willing to
   pay goes up.*

2. Which of the following investors will purchase stock if the option is exercised?

   I.   the owner of a call
   II. the owner of a put
   III. the writer of a call
   IV. the writer of a put

   ____(A) I and II
   ____(B) II and III
   ____(C) I and IV
   ____(D) III and IV

3. A call is in-the-money when the market price of the underlying stock is

   ____(A) equal to the strike price.
   ____(B) above the strike price.
   ____(C) below the strike price.
   ____(D) equal to the strike price plus or minus the premium.

4. PQR stock is trading at 25 3/4. PQR July 25 calls are trading at a premium of 2. What is the intrinsic value of these calls?

   ____(A) $0
   ____(B) $75
   ____(C) $125
   ____(D) $200

   cmv   25.75
   call   25.00
   *   .75   18.14*
   X   100 shares
   $ 75.00

K118-E

5. Which two of the following are spreads?

    I.   long 1 ABC May 40 call; short 1 ABC May 50 call
    II. long 1 ABC May 40 call; long 1 ABC May 50 call
    III. long 1 ABC August 40 call; short 1 ABC May 40 call
    IV. long 1 ABC August 40 call; short 1 ABC August 50 put

    ____(A)   I and II
    ____(B)   I and III
    ____(C)   II and III
    ____(D)   II and IV

[handwritten: Spread: same stock (class) long & short (buy & sell) either 2 calls or 2 puts; 18.23]

6. Angus Bullwether sells an XYZ March 35 call. To establish a straddle he would

    ____(A)   sell an XYZ March 35 call.
    ____(B)   buy an XYZ March 35 put.
    ____(C)   sell an XYZ March 35 put.
    ____(D)   buy an XYZ March 40 call.

[handwritten: Straddle: sell call & put or buy call & put on same security; 18.23]

7. Karen Kodiak writes an XMI 450 call at 13. The market closes that day at 462.34. Karen will break even on her short call if, on the expiration date, the index closes at which of the following prices?

    ____(A)   462.34
    ____(B)   463
    ____(C)   450
    ____(D)   437

[handwritten: 450 + 13; S&P 100 index]

8. An investor is long 10,000 OEX calls. How many OEX puts can the investor purchase?

    ____(A)   5,000
    ____(B)   15,000
    ____(C)   25,000
    ____(D)   any number

[handwritten: index: 25,000 max on either side; call buyer 10,000 / put buyer not on same side so max; 18.10]

9. In September, an investor writes two ABC January 60 puts at 3. If the two ABC January 60 puts expire in January, what are the tax consequences for the writer?

    ____(A) $600 gain realized in September
    ____(B) $600 loss realized in September
    ____(C) $600 gain realized in January
    ____(D) $600 loss realized in January

[handwritten: 2 x 300 = $600]

10. On January 1, an investor buys an XYZ April 50 call at 4 and an XYZ April 50 put at 2 1/2. Both options expire unexercised. What are the tax consequences?

    (A) $400 gain on the call, $250 gain on the put
    (B) $150 net capital gain
    (C) $150 net capital loss
    (D) $400 loss on the call, $250 loss on the put

call +400
put +250
650

Answer Key

1. A.

2. C.

3. B.

4. B.

5. B.

6. C.

7. B.

8. C.

9. C.

10. D.

Chapter Nineteen

Investment Company Products

Key Terms

19.8	Breakpoint	Closed-end company 19.3
19.10	Conduit tax treatment	Contractual plan 19.11
19.6	Custodian	Diversified management 19.4 company
19.12	Dollar cost averaging	Exchange privilege 19.9
19.2	Face-amount certificate company	Front-end load plan 19.11
19.6	Fund manager	Investment Company Act 19.2 of 1940
19.8	Letter of Intent (LOI)	Management company 19.2
19.4	Mutual fund	Net asset value (NAV) 19.7
19.3	Open-end company	Public offering price (POP) 19.8
19.13	Real Estate Investment Trust (REIT)	Right of accumulation 19.9
19.10	Selling dividends	Spread-load plan 19.11
19.6	Underwriter	Unit investment trust (UIT) 19.2
19.2	Unit of beneficial interest	Voluntary plan 19.11

Investment Companies

Investment companies are corporations or trusts that purchase securities with investors' pooled resources. The investors receive shares or units in the investment company's portfolio and the net income from the investments are distributed to individual investors proportionately. This chapter provides an overview of investment companies and then focuses on mutual funds, one form of investment company.

Classifications of Investment Companies

The Investment Company Act of 1940 was adopted by Congress as a means of regulating the formation and operation of investment companies. The act classifies investment companies into three general categories: face-amount certificate companies, unit investment trusts and management companies.

Face-amount certificate companies. Face-amount certificate companies issue a certificate that represents the issuer's obligation to pay a stated sum on a fixed, future date (such as $25,000 in 20 years from the date of issuance). The investor may purchase this face-amount certificate either by making regular payments through an installment-purchase plan or by depositing a lump sum of money. The certificate will then earn a stated interest rate over a period of time. Face-amount certificates may be backed by specific assets, such as U.S. government issues, VA and FHA mortgages, corporate debt issues or preferred stock. Usually, however, they are backed by bonds which mature when the certificates mature. In either case, principal and interest are guaranteed. When the value of the certificates is paid to the investor at maturity, the investment fund is exhausted.

Fixed portfolio

Unit investment trusts. A unit investment trust (or UIT) is an investment company organized under a trust indenture. The trust portfolio is not actively managed; that is, no decisions are made to change portfolio assets. Shares in a UIT represent interests in a portfolio of specified securities, and are commonly referred to as shares (or units) of beneficial interest. Shares are redeemed by the investor from the trustee.

A unit investment trust may be fixed or nonfixed. A typical fixed UIT may purchase a portfolio of bonds. When the bonds in the portfolio have matured, the trust is terminated. The nonfixed UIT is often used by investors interested in purchasing units on a contractual basis. The trust may purchase shares of an underlying mutual fund for the nonfixed UIT portfolio.

Management Companies

Managed investment companies actively buy, sell and trade securities which are held in their portfolios according to a specific investment objective (as stated in the company's prospectus).

Closed-end companies. A closed-end company issues a fixed number of shares in its investment portfolio. After the initial public offering, its shares are publicly traded in the secondary markets (on an exchange or over-the-counter), where supply and demand determine the price of each share in the portfolio.

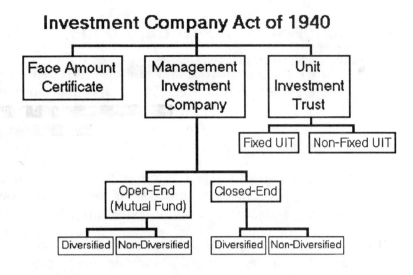

Fig. 19.1 The various types of management companies.

Closed-end management companies may issue more than one class of security (including preferred stock and bonds), but are not permitted to borrow from a bank.

Open-end companies (mutual funds). An open-end management company continuously issues new fund shares to investors who wish to buy, and redeems fund shares from investors who wish to sell. Due in part to this continuous process of issuing and redeeming shares, the capitalization of an open-end company is constantly changing. Upon request of a shareholder, open-end companies must redeem their shares at net asset value (NAV). The value of individual fund shares of the fund is determined by the fund's portfolio value (the value of its investments).

Closed vs. Open-end Management Companies

Characteristic	Open-end	Closed-end
Capitalization	Unlimited. Continuous offering of shares.	Fixed. Single offering of shares.
Issues	Common stock only, no debt securities, permitted to borrow.	May issue common, preferred and debt securities.
Shares	Full or fractional shares.	Full shares only
Offerings and Trading	Sold and redeemed only by the fund. Continuous primary offering.	Initial primary offering. Secondary trading OTC or on an exchange.
Pricing	NAV plus sales charge	CMV plus commission
Shareholder Rights	Dividends (when declared), voting	Dividends (when declared), voting, preemptive

Characteristics of Mutual Funds

Advantages to investors. Mutual funds (open-end investment companies) offer the investor several advantages. Of primary importance to fund investors is a mutual fund's guaranteed marketability. An open-end mutual fund must redeem shares presented to it by investors at the net asset value within seven days (although the company may require a written request for redemption).

A second advantage offered to investors in mutual funds is professional portfolio management. Investment decisions for the funds are made by full-time professional advisers, a luxury few investors can afford when investing independently.

Finally, mutual fund shares offer diversification. Mutual funds provide a greater degree of diversification than most private investors are able to achieve independently. Other investor advantages include the following.

- *bank*
  A mutual fund's shares are held by a custodian, which ensures safekeeping.
- The investor may purchase full or fractional shares.
- Many funds offer automatic reinvestment of capital gains distributions and dividend distributions without a sales charge.
- Most funds offer exchange privileges that permit investors to move from fund to fund within a family of funds without a sales charge. A "family" of funds is a group of funds sponsored by the same issuer, each with a different investment objective.
- Tax liabilities for the investor are greatly simplified. Each year the fund must distribute to the investor a 1099 form explaining taxability of distributions.
- The fund may offer various withdrawal plans allowing the investor choices of payment methods upon withdrawal from the fund.

Diversification. A diversified management company is defined by the Investment Company Act of 1940 as a company that has at least 75% of its assets invested in cash and/or securities, no more than 5% of its total assets invested in any one issuer, and no more than 10% of the voting securities of any one issuer. Any company that does not fit the description of a diversified company is considered nondiversified. Both open-end and closed- end companies may be classified as diversified or nondiversified.

Structure. The act of 1940 requires open-end companies to have:

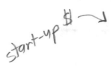

start-up $

- at least $100,000 net worth;
- at least 100 shareholders;
- clearly defined investment objective(s);
- no more than one class of security; and
- a maximum asset-to-debt ratio of 300%.

100,000,000 assets
75,000,000 diversity
5,000,000 in 1 issuer
10% voting stock max

Because open-end management companies may issue only one class of security (common stock), they are permitted to borrow from a bank. They cannot issue preferred stock or bonds, but may borrow money as long as the company's asset-to-debt ratio does not exceed 3 to 1 (that is, debt coverage by assets of at least 300%).

Rights of shareholders. Shareholders of mutual funds have several rights, which include the approval of changes in investment objectives, the approval of investment advisory agreements, voting (including proxies), and receipt of semiannual reports.

By law, an open-end investment company must redeem shares tendered to it within seven days of receipt of a written request for redemption. The price at redemption is based on the next computed NAV, which must be calculated at least once per business day. The fund may charge the investor a redemption fee, which is usually 1/2 of 1% to 2% of the NAV.

Investment objectives. Funds are available to meet the investment objective of most investors, and a mutual fund prospectus identifies the fund's objectives. The more common objectives include growth, income or a combination of growth and income.

- **Growth funds.** Growth funds invest in equity securities of companies expected to increase in value more rapidly than the overall market. Growth companies tend to retain all or most of their earnings for research and development, and reinvest profits in the company rather than pay out dividends.
- **Income funds.** Income funds seek to provide high current yield and include debt securities and equity securities of varying quality. Such funds may sacrifice safety of principal for increased potential income. The investor who selects income funds is more interested in current income than in potential growth.
- **Growth and income funds.** These funds combine growth and income objectives by diversifying their portfolios to include both equity and debt securities.
- **Balanced funds.** In a balanced fund, different types of securities are purchased according to a preset formula designed to be balanced. For example, a balanced fund's portfolio might contain 60% equity securities and 40% debt securities.
- **Bond and preferred stock funds.** The objective of bond and preferred stock funds is safety of principal and enhanced income.
- **Tax-exempt funds.** Tax-exempt funds contain instruments that produce tax-exempt income. Municipal bond funds and tax-exempt money market funds are common types of tax-exempt funds.
- **U.S. government funds.** U.S. government funds purchase securities backed by the U.S. Treasury. Investors in these funds seek current income and maximum safety.
- **Specialized funds.** These funds concentrate investments in a particular group of industries or geographic regions.
- **Dual-purpose funds.** Dual-purpose funds meet two objectives. Investors seeking income purchase income shares and receive all the interest and dividends earned by the fund's portfolio. Other investors, interested in capital gains, purchase the gains shares and

Preservation of Capital (stability)

receive all gains on portfolio holdings. The two types of shares in a dual fund are listed separately in the financial pages.

- **Special situation funds**. A special situation fund buys for its portfolio securities of companies that may benefit from a change within the company or a change in the economy. Takeover candidates and other special situations are common investments.
- **Money-market funds**. Money-market funds invest in safe, high-yield, short-term debt instruments, including Treasury bills, commercial paper, bankers' acceptances, certificates of deposit and short-term bonds. Money-market funds calculate interest daily and credit it monthly, are no-load funds, and usually offer checking privileges.

Mutual Fund Management

Similar in many ways to a corporation, a mutual fund has a board of directors, which is elected by shareholders. The board's function is to supervise the operation of the investment company. The following chart illustrates how the fund is organized.

Organization of a Mutual Fund

Manager	Custodian	Underwriter
Makes investment decisions	Holds assets	Is paid from sales charges
Paid a percent of NAV	Issues and redeems shares	Two-year initial contract
Two-year initial contract	Clerical duties	Contract renewed annually
Contract renewed annually	Is paid a fee	

Fund manager. The fund manager (usually a management company) provides investment advice and manages the portfolio. Members of the board of directors may also be members of the management team. To prevent any conflicts of interest, however, the Investment Company Act of 1940 requires that at least 40% of the board of directors have no involvement with the fund's management. The manager's fee is the largest single fund expense (an average fee is 1/2 of 1% of the fund's net asset value).

Custodian. The Investment Company Act of 1940 requires that the fund's assets be held by an independent custodian, usually a commercial bank appointed by the directors. In addition to holding fund assets, the custodian performs other clerical functions, such as receiving and disbursing money, distributing dividends, acting as registrar and receiving clients' payments. The custodian is also paid a fee, but it is less than the manager's fee.

Underwriter. The underwriter (often called the sponsor or distributor) markets fund shares, prepares sales literature and, in return, receives a percentage of the sales charge paid by the client. The underwriter's compensation is part of the sales load paid by the customer when shares are purchased. Sales fees are not part of the fund's expenses.

Determining the Value of Mutual Fund Shares

The act of 1940 requires mutual funds to calculate the value of the fund shares at least once per business day (since purchase and redemption prices are based on the net asset value of the shares). Although funds may calculate the value more often, most wait until after the close of the New York Stock Exchange. Funds must use forward pricing to determine net asset value for purchasing and redeeming shares, which means that investors who purchase or redeem shares pay or receive the price calculated next after their order is received.

Funds vary in their purchase or redemption fees. The purchase price may include an added sales charge and, on redemption, a redemption fee. If there are fees, shares are purchased at the next computed net asset value (plus sales charge) and redeemed at the next computed net asset value (less any redemption fee).

Net asset value per share. To determine the net asset value per share, the custodian bank totals the value of all assets and subtracts all liabilities, which results in the total net asset value of the fund. The *net asset value per share* is determined by dividing total net assets by the number of shares outstanding. Due to changes in the market value of the fund's portfolio, daily changes in the NAV can occur.

Marketing Methods

A fund can use any number of methods to market its shares to the public. Some marketing methods used by various firms include:

- **Fund to underwriter to dealer to investor.** The underwriter sells the shares to the dealer at net asset value plus the underwriter's concession. The dealer then sells the shares to the investor at the full public offering price.
- **Fund to underwriter to investor.** The underwriter acts as dealer and uses its own sales force to sell shares to the public.
- **Fund to investor.** These funds sell directly to the public, without the use of a sales force and without a sales charge. These funds are called no-load funds because they are sold at the net asset value. The fund pays all sales expenses.
- **Fund to underwriter to plan company to investor.** Organizations that sell contractual plans for the periodic purchase of mutual fund shares are called plan companies. Mutual fund shares are purchased by the plan company and held in trust for the purchaser under the periodic payment plan. Such plans, called contractual plans, assess a maximum of 9% in sales charges over the life of the plan.

Sales Charges

The underwriter (or sponsor) is the key salesperson for the investment company and receives a sales charge for distributing shares. Sales commissions, including any dealer concessions and sales and advertising expenses, are all part of the sales charge, which may not exceed 8 1/2% of the cost. The maximum sales load a company is permitted is reduced if the investment company does not offer automatic reinvestment of dividends and capital gains at NAV, breakpoints, or rights of accumulation.

Sales charges are added to NAV to determine the public offering price (POP) the customer pays when purchasing fund shares. Because the percentage of permitted sales charge is calculated from the POP, the formula used to arrive at the selling price is:

Know it

$$POP = NAV \times (100\% - \text{Sales Charge}\%)$$

To express the sales charge as a percentage of the public offering price, divide the sales charge (in dollars per share) by the public offering price:

$$\text{Sales Charge }\% = \text{Sales charge in dollars per share} / POP$$

Reductions in sales charges. Investors may qualify for reduced sales costs in several ways. Qualified investors may include a husband and wife in either joint or separate accounts, a parent with a minor child or a custodian for a trust account. Investment clubs or other associations formed for the purpose of investing do not qualify for the reduced charges.

Large purchases. One way a customer can qualify for a lower sales cost is through making large purchases. The prospectus contains a chart that shows reduced sales costs for larger investments referred to as a **breakpoint chart**.

Breakpoint Schedule

Purchases	Sales Cost
$1 to $9,999	8 1/2%
$10,000 to $24,999	7 1/2%
$25,000 to $49,999	7%
$50,000 +	6 1/2%

Letter of intent (LOI). Investors who do not invest a large enough amount of money at their initial purchase to qualify for a breakpoint may file a letter of intent (LOI). In the LOI they indicate their intent to invest the additional funds necessary to reach the breakpoint at sometime during the next 13 months. The LOI may be backdated by up to 90 days to include prior purchases in the total, but may not cover more than 13 months in total.

The letter of intent is a unilateral contract that is binding only on the fund. The customer must complete the investment in order to qualify for the reduced sales cost, and the fund will hold the extra shares purchased from the reduced sales load in escrow. If the client deposits the money to complete the letter of intent, he or she receives the escrowed shares.

Rights of accumulation. Another means by which qualified investors can reduce sales costs is known as rights of accumulation. Under rights of accumulation, the fund applies the investor's past purchases toward the breakpoint on the next purchase. The fund may use the greater of total purchases by the customer or the customer's account NAV in calculating the dollars to be accumulated toward the breakpoint.

Combination privilege. Funds may offer reduced sales charges to investors who invest in several members within the same family of funds by adding all of those investments together to reach a breakpoint. If available, this option will be explained in the prospectus, as will other rights offered by the fund.

Conversion or exchange privileges. Many mutual funds exist as part of a family of funds under the same management. Most funds of this type permit the investor to switch from one fund to another within the group without incurring additional sales charges. Even though there is no sales charge on the exchange, for tax purposes the IRS will consider a sale to have taken place, and the customer will have some tax liability under IRS regulations.

Distributions from Mutual Funds

Investment income. Investment income is earned from dividends paid on stocks held in the fund's portfolio, and from interest received from bonds and other debt instruments. The investment company may pay dividends to the shareholders from this investment income, but such payment must come from the net investment income. To establish the net investment income, the fund subtracts expenses from gross income.

Most mutual funds distribute dividends quarterly. These payments can be made in the form of cash or additional shares in the fund if the investor prefers to reinvest dividends. The fund must disclose to the investor the source of the dividend payment, whether from dividends or interest.

Mutual fund boards of directors set the ex-dividend date, which is usually the next business day after the record date. This is possible because the net asset value is computed daily by the fund and trades are phoned in to the distributor. An investor who orders the fund before the close of business on the record date becomes an owner of record after that day's close.

Capital gains. Capital gains are derived from selling securities held in the fund's investment portfolio. Stocks held in the fund's portfolio are expected to appreciate in value and deliver capital gains in the event the investment adviser sells them.

Capital gains distributions may not be made more often than once a year. Like investment income, they may be distributed in the form of cash or additional shares in the fund, if the investor chooses to reinvest them.

If an investor purchases fund shares just before the capital gains distribution, he or she is at a double disadvantage. Not only does the market value of the fund shares decrease by the amount of the distribution, but the investor also incurs a tax liability on the distribution. A registered representative is forbidden to encourage investors to purchase fund shares prior to a distribution because of this tax liability, and doing so is known as selling dividends.

Realized and unrealized appreciation. As with any stock purchase, an investor may profit from an investment in mutual funds when the value of the shares increases. As long as the shares are not sold, this is considered an unrealized gain. When shares are sold at a value greater than the purchase price, a gain is realized.

Tax Treatment of Investment Income

As with any other corporation, a mutual fund must pay taxes on earned net income. Because a fund's income comes from securities held in its portfolio that have already been taxed at the corporate level prior to distribution to the fund, the fund avoids additional taxes by distributing net investment income to its shareholders. In this way, triple taxation (that is, taxation of the corporation, the investment company and the mutual fund investors) is avoided.

Regulated Inv Co

Investment companies may qualify for preferential tax treatment under Subchapter M of the Internal Revenue Code if they distribute at least 90% of net investment income in the form of dividends. If the company fails to distribute at least 90% of its net investment income, it will be liable for the tax on 100% of its net. When the company distributes 90% or more of its net investment income, it is acting as a conduit, passing income through to investors (thus the term conduit or pipeline tax treatment).

Under the IRS code, the definition of net investment income is interest and dividend income minus expenses. Capital gains are not included in the calculation of net investment income.

As stated earlier, investors may take distributions in cash or in additional shares for reinvestment in the fund. In either case, the IRS requires taxes to be paid on these distributions, because the investor has constructive receipt of the distribution. The fund must disclose the source and amounts on all distributions by sending the investor a Form 1099 at the end of the year. A Form 1099, similar to a W-2, reports payments other than salary.

Shareholders are liable for taxes on capital gains distributed by the mutual fund, even when the fund retains the gains and reinvests in other securities. Usually, the company pays the tax due on the gains on behalf of the investor (similar to withholding taxes).

When investors sell their fund shares, they are liable for all taxes on the sale of shares exceeding their cost basis. Cost basis for mutual funds is the total amount invested (including any reinvested investment income) plus capital gains. This total is subtracted from the amount received from the sale to determine the taxable gain or loss at sale. Gain or loss per share may be established by the investor using one of three accounting methods:

- First-in, first-out (FIFO). The IRS assumes that FIFO is the chosen method unless the investor states otherwise.
- Last-in, first-out (LIFO).
- Share identification.

Methods of Purchasing Shares

Voluntary accumulation plans. There are two types of accumulation plans. The voluntary accumulation plan allows the customer to deposit regular periodic investments on a "voluntary" basis in preset amounts. The plan is designed to help the investor form regular investment habits while still offering some flexibility.

Contractual accumulation plans. A contractual plan differs from a voluntary plan in that the investor signs an agreement to invest an agreed-upon dollar amount over a specified period of time. Although called a contractual plan, the agreement is binding only on the company; the investor cannot be held to the contract.

Contractual plans may issue periodic plan certificates and may use either of two methods of calculating sales charges. The choice is made by the investment company and is indicated in the prospectus. The Investment Company Act of 1940 allows a maximum of 9% in sales charges by contractual plans, although for large investments, the investor may qualify for lower sales charges by meeting breakpoint minimums.

Lump-sum accounts. Lump-sum accounts are also called regular accounts. The investor buys shares in the fund by depositing the entire amount he intends to invest all at once.

Sales charges. Contractual plans may operate under one of two federal securities acts. The Investment Company Act of 1940 allows the company to charge up to 50% of the investor's deposits in the first year. These act of 1940 plans are known as front-end load plans. If a person invests $100 a month under a front-end load plan ($1,200 the first year), the company could collect $600 in sales charges the first year. The average sales charges over the life of a front-end load plan can be no more than 9%.

The Investment Company Act of 1970, which amends the 1940 act, allows the company to charge up to 20% of the investor's deposit in any one year as long as the average charges over the first four years do not exceed 16% annually. This arrangement is known as a spread-load plan. If a person invests $100 a month under a spread-load plan, and the company charged 20% of $1,200 ($240 annually) for the first three years, in the fourth year the company would be limited to $48, for an average of 16% over four years. The average sales charges over the life of a spread-load plan can be no more than 9%.

The customer has the right to early withdrawal from either plan, at no penalty, within 45 days after the custodian mails the notice of that right. The custodian must mail this notice of withdrawal rights within 60 days of the date the fund certificate is issued to the client.

Comparing Contractual Plans

Terms	1940 Act (Front-end)	1970 Act (Spread-load)
Max. sales charge (life)	9%	9%
Max. sales charge in any one year	50%	20%
Max. sales charge over four years	No limit set	16% average per year
45-day "free-look" letter	Refund of current NAV plus any sales charges	Refund of current NAV plus any sales charges
Within first 18 months	Refund of NAV plus any sales charges in excess of 15% of total payments	Refund of NAV only

If the investor terminates a spread-load plan after the 45-day right of withdrawal period, the company is allowed to keep 100% of the sales charges it has collected. The investor will receive only the net asset value of the shares in the account. The investor who terminates a front-end load plan after 45 days but before the end of the 18th month receives the net asset value of the shares in the account (the NAV) plus any sales charges deducted by the company that are in excess of 15% of the total amount the person has invested. After the 18th month, the person is entitled only to the NAV.

Plan completion insurance. Some funds offer decreasing-term group-life insurance for purchasers of contractual or voluntary plans. The custodian is named as beneficiary, and if the plan participant dies, the fund custodian receives the insurance proceeds so that purchase of fund shares contracted for can be completed and distributions made to the deceased's estate.

Dollar cost averaging. A basic advantage of contractual plans is dollar cost averaging, an investment method that requires a person to contribute money to be invested in regular amounts over a period of time. This form of investing allows the investor to purchase more shares when prices are lower and fewer shares when prices are higher. In a fluctuating market, the average cost per share over a period of time will be lower for the investor than the average price of the shares for the same period. If prices are declining, however, this will not assure the investor a profit. The example that follows illustrates how average price and average cost may vary with dollar cost averaging.

Month	Amount invested	Price per share	Number of shares
January	$600	$20	30
February	$600	$24	25
March	$600	$30	20
April	$600	$40	15
Totals	$2,400	$114	90

Average price per share equals $114 (the sum of the prices) divided by 4 (the number of purchases) for an average of $28.50 per share. The average cost per share equals $2,400 (the total investment) divided by 90 (the total number of shares purchased) for an average cost of $26.67 per share.

Real Estate Investment Trusts (REITs)

A REIT pools capital in a manner similar to an investment company. REIT portfolios, however, are comprised of professionally managed real estate holdings, typically either in direct ownership of income property or in mortgage loans. Shareholders receive dividends from investment income and/or capital gains distributions. In a REIT, income flows through to the investors but, unlike a limited partnership, losses do not.

REITs are organized as trusts or corporations where investors buy shares or certificates of beneficial interest either on stock exchanges or in the over-the-counter market. Under the guidelines of Subchapter M of the Internal Revenue Code, REITs avoid taxation by distributing at least 95% of their net investment income to investors (the requirement for investment companies is 90%).

Chapter Review

Questions

1. "Mutual fund" is a popular name for

    ____(A) all investment companies.
    ____(B) open-end investment companies.
    ____(C) closed-end investment companies.
    ____(D) any company that invests pooled funds.

2. What kind of investment company has no provision for redemption of outstanding shares?

    ____(A) open-end company
    ____(B) closed-end company
    ____(C) unit investment trust
    ____(D) mutual fund

3. The essential difference between an open-end fund and a closed-end fund is

    ____(A) the method of determining book value.
    ____(B) that closed-end funds are closed to secondary trading.
    ____(C) capitalization.
    ____(D) there is no difference.

4. An investor looking for current income would be least interested in

    ____(A) bond funds.
    ____(B) preferred stock funds.
    ____(C) common stock funds.
    ____(D) gains shares in a dual-purpose fund.

5. Money-market funds usually offer which of the following?

    I.   daily interest calculations
    I.   check writing privileges
    II.   no-load funds
    IV.   long-term growth potential

    ____(A) I and II
    ____(B) I, II and III
    ____(C) I, II and IV
    ____(D) II, III and IV

6. The custodian of the mutual fund usually does which of the following?

    ____(A)   approves changes in investment policy
    ____(B)   holds the cash and securities of the fund and performs clerical functions
    ____(C)   manages the fund
    ____(D)   does cleaning and related duties on fund's properties

7. Which mutual fund is sold at net asset value (NAV)?

    ____(A)   open-end
    ____(B)   closed-end
    ____(C)   front-end load
    ____(D)   no-load

8. In order for a company to charge the maximum sales charge of 8 1/2%, it must offer all of the following EXCEPT

    ____(A)   automatic reinvestment of dividends and capital gains at NAV.
    ____(B)   breakpoints.
    ____(C)   automatic reinvestment at POP.
    ____(D)   rights of accumulation.

9. A mutual fund is quoted at $16.56 NAV and $18.00 POP. The percentage of sales charge is

    ____(A)   7 1/2%.
    ____(B)   8%.
    ____(C)   8 1/2%.
    ____(D)   7 3/4%.

10. Redemption of a no-load fund may be made at

    ____(A)   NAV minus sales charge.
    ____(B)   POP minus sales charge.
    ____(C)   NAV plus sales charge.
    ____(D)   NAV.

Answer Key

1. B.

2. B.

3. C.

4. D.

5. B.

6. B.

7. D.

8. C.

9. B.

10. D.

Chapter Twenty

Retirement Planning and Annuities

Key Terms

Retirement Plans and Annuities

A basic goal among people who invest is to provide themselves with retirement income. Many individuals accomplish this goal through corporate retirement plans. Others set up their own plans. Still others have both individual and corporate retirement plans. Whether set up by a corporation or an individual, these plans are called qualified plans if contributions to them are tax-deductible under IRS rules; otherwise, they are nonqualified plans. Definitions of qualified and nonqualified plans are contained in the Employee Retirement Income Security Act (ERISA) of 1974.

Pension Plans

Qualified plans. According to ERISA, a contribution to a qualified plan is exempt from income tax in the year it is made. With qualified plans, the tax is deferred until the individual receives the money as income. In other words, contributions are made with before-tax dollars. Tax on that income will be due, however, when the owner of the plan receives it as income, presumably after retirement.

ERISA was passed to protect corporate and union retirement plan participants against mismanagement of retirement funds and to assure more equitable opportunity for participation. ERISA contains the following guidelines for regulation of retirement plans:

- **Participation.** If a company has a retirement plan, employees must be covered within a reasonable time, defined by ERISA as no more than three years.
- **Funding.** Funds contributed to the plan must be segregated from other corporate assets. The plan's trustees have a fiduciary responsibility to invest prudently and manage funds in a way that represents the best interests of all participants.
- **Vesting.** Employees must be entitled to their entire retirement benefit amount within a certain time period, even if they are no longer with the employer.
- **Communication.** The retirement plan must be in writing and employees must be kept informed of plan benefits, availability, account status and vesting procedure.
- **Nondiscrimination.** A uniformly applied formula determines benefits and contributions of all employees. Such a method ensures equitable and impartial treatment.

Defined benefit or defined contribution. Employer-sponsored qualified retirement plans are either defined benefit or defined contribution plans. A defined benefit plan specifies the total amount of money to be received upon retirement. A defined contribution plan specifies the amount an employer will contribute to the plan annually. With such a plan, the total amount available at retirement is unspecified because it depends on contributions and the performance of the fund's portfolio.

Nonqualified plans. Contributions to nonqualified plans, by contrast, are not exempt from current income tax. With nonqualified plans, the tax is paid in the year of the contribution. In each case, taxes on the amounts earned by the plan itself are always deferred until the owner actually receives that money as income. They are made with after-tax dollars. Because of this, money contributed to a nonqualified plan is not taxable when the owner receives it at retirement.

Individual Retirement Accounts

All employed individuals, regardless of whether they are covered by a qualified corporate retirement plan, may open and contribute to an IRA. Maximum annual contributions are subject to the following limitations:

- for an individual account, 100% of earned income or $2,000, whichever is less; and
- for a spousal account, 100% of earned income or $2,250 (divided between two accounts), whichever is less.

ERISA allows an individual who has an unemployed spouse to contribute to a separate retirement account established for the nonworking spouse (known as a spousal account).The contribution may be divided between the two accounts in any way, as long as the total contribution is not more than $2,250, and no more than $2,000 is contributed to either account.

Tax benefits of an IRA. The Economic Recovery Tax Act of 1981 allowed all IRA participants to deduct the amount contributed to their IRA from their taxable income. The Tax Reform Act of 1986 changed the deductibility for individuals who are covered by other qualified plans. If an individual is not actively participating in other qualified plans, however, the full amount of the contribution to the IRA is still deductible.

For an individual covered by another plan, the portion deductible is determined by that person's income level. For individuals whose gross income exceeds $35,000 or couples whose combined gross income exceeds $50,000, there is no allowable deduction. This is true for married couples even if only one partner is covered by a company-sponsored plan. Deductions are reduced by 10% for each $1,000 of income in the income range where there are deductible limits.

Deduction	Married: Gross Income	Single: Gross Income
Full	$0 - $40,000	$0 - $25,000
Partial (phased)	$40,000 - $50,000	$25,000 - $35,000
None	$50,000 +	$35,000 +

Payout from an IRA. IRA earnings are tax deferred until the money is received, usually at retirement. Withdrawals may not begin before age 59 1/2 and must begin by the year after the account owner reaches age 70 1/2. Withdrawals may be made in a lump sum, in varying amounts or in regular installments. Withdrawals, except contributions made with after-tax dollars (that is, nonqualified contributions), are taxable as ordinary income. Early withdrawals incur a 10% penalty, unless they occur because of the individual's death or disability. A 50% penalty is applied to accounts not meeting minimum Internal Revenue Code distribution requirements after age 70 1/2.

Excess contributions. Annual IRA contributions in excess of the maximum are subject to a 6% penalty tax if the excess is not removed by the time the taxpayer files the tax return. The penalty is applied until the excess is removed from the account.

Rollovers and transfers. Individuals may take possession of funds in a qualified plan in order to move them to another qualified plan, but may do so not more than once a year. Such a rollover into another account must be completed within 60 days of the original funds withdrawal from the qualified plan. For example, if an individual changes employers, the amount in his pension plan may be distributed to him in a lump-sum payment. He may then deposit the distribution in an IRA rollover account, where the amount deposited retains its tax-deferred status. Any portion not rolled over is subject to ordinary income tax.

Transfers of funds between qualified retirement accounts differ from rollovers in that the account owner never actually takes physical possession of the funds; the money and/or investments are sent directly from one custodian to another. There is no limit to the number of times a person can transfer investments between qualified plans.

Permissible investments. IRA investments may include stocks, bonds, unit investment trusts, mutual funds, limited partnerships, government securities, U.S. government-issued gold and silver coins, annuities and many others. Cash-value life insurance, term insurance and collectibles, however, are not permissible investments.

HR-10 Plans (Keoghs)

Contributions and eligibility. A Keogh retirement account can be opened by any self-employed individual and any full-time employees who meet minimum age and years of service requirements (age 21 and one year of service, or age 21 and three years of service if the company is vesting the employees 100% immediately upon their entry into the plan). Individuals covered by a corporate pension plan who also earn self-employment income may make contributions to a Keogh plan. For example, a stockbroker who is also self-employed teaching investment courses may deduct all Keogh contributions. IRA deductions, on the other hand, would be subject to limitations.

ERISA guidelines require employers to contribute the same percentage of income to employees' accounts as they do to their own.

The Keogh can be either a defined benefit or a defined contribution plan. For a defined contribution plan, the maximum contribution is 25% of after-contribution earnings (an effective rate of 20% of precontribution earnings) or $30,000, whichever is less. For example, on $30,000 of self-employment income, the allowable Keogh contribution would be 20% of $30,000, or $6,000. After deducting the $6,000 from $30,000, remaining taxable income is now only $24,000. The $6,000 contribution is 25% of the after-contribution income and 20% of the $30,000 precontribution earned income. Payout rules for Keoghs and IRAs are the same.

Permissible investments. Keogh investments may include stocks, bonds, unit investment trusts, mutual funds, government bonds, annuities and cash value life insurance. Term insurance and collectibles are not permissible investments.

Pension and Profit-Sharing Plans

Pension plans are corporate-sponsored employee retirement plans with virtually the same requirements that govern Keogh accounts. Pension plans are tax-exempt. Contributions to corporate pension plans are mandatory, regardless of whether the corporation has made a profit. A pension plan must be either a defined benefit or a defined contribution plan.

Qualified profit-sharing plans differ from pension plans primarily in that contributions to profit-sharing plans are not required during periods of little or no profit. The board of directors of the corporation determines whether to contribute to the profit-sharing plan, which is a defined contribution plan.

401-K Plans

A 401-K plan allows an employee to defer compensation voluntarily by placing it in a qualified retirement plan. Because of this deferral, the amount contributed is not reported as current income and, therefore, not taxed until withdrawn. Early withdrawal of funds is allowed, without penalty, for "hardship" situations (such as educational and medical expenses), and any lump-sum withdrawals qualify for ten-year income averaging. If employment changes, the 401-K participant can roll over the amount in the plan to another qualified plan.

Comparison of Qualified Retirement Plans

HR 10 (Keogh) plans and Individual Retirement Accounts (IRAs) are both tax-deferred retirement plans, designed to encourage individuals to set aside funds to provide for retirement income. Illustrations of the plans' similarities and differences follow.

Similarities

- **Tax deferral of income contributed to plans**. Taxes are deferred on the amount of contribution until the individual begins to receive distributions.
- **Tax-sheltered**. Investment income from dividends, interest and capital gains is deferred until distribution.
- **Cash-only contributions**. An investor may contribute cash, but may not contribute stocks, bonds or other securities to a plan.
- **Distributions**. Distributions may begin at age 59 1/2 and must begin by the year after the individual reaches age 70 1/2.

- **Penalties for premature withdrawal**. The individual pays income tax on the amount withdrawn during the year, plus a 10% penalty.
- **Payout**. Lump-sum distribution or regular, periodic payouts.
- **Beneficiary**. Upon the plan holder's death, payments are made to a beneficiary .

Differences

Characteristic	HR-10 Plans	IRAs
Permissible investments	Stocks, bonds, UITs, mutual funds, government securities, U.S.-minted precious-metal coins, annuities and *cash-value life insurance.*	Stocks, bonds, UITs, mutual funds, government securities, U.S.-minted precious-metal coins and annuities.
Nonpermissible investments	Term insurance and collectibles.	Term insurance, collectibles and *cash-value life insurance.*
Change of employer	Lump-sum distribution can be rolled over within 60 days into an IRA.	Does not apply.
Penalty for excess contribution	None. Excess not deductible.	6% penalty.
Taxation of distributions	Taxed as ordinary income.	Taxed as ordinary income.

Annuity Plans

An annuity is a contract between an individual and an insurance company, usually purchased for retirement income. Investors, called annuitants, contribute money to an annuity plan either in a lump sum or as periodic contractual payments. At some future time (specified in the contract), the owner of the annuity plan will begin receiving regular income distributions.

Fixed Annuities

Guaranteed return. A fixed annuity has a guaranteed rate of return. When the individual elects to begin receiving income, payout is determined by the value of the account and the annuitant's life expectancy (based on mortality tables). Payment from a fixed annuity remains constant throughout the annuitant's life. Because the minimum return in a fixed annuity is guaranteed by the insurance company, and no risk is borne by the annuitant, a fixed annuity is considered an insurance product, so in order to sell fixed annuities, a salesperson must have an insurance license.

Risks. Although principal and interest are not at risk, an investor with a fixed annuity risks loss of purchasing power because of inflation. For example, an individual who annuitized a contract in 1953 may have been guaranteed monthly payments of $375. Decades later that amount may provide insufficient income on which to live.

Variable Annuities

The investor who wants to minimize inflation risks associated with fixed annuities purchases a variable annuity contract. The money deposited in a variable annuity is invested primarily in a portfolio of equity securities (which stand a better chance of keeping pace with inflation than do investments in fixed-income securities). The annuitant, however, participates in both the greater potential gain and the greater potential risk associated with equity securities (compared to debt securities). Although the investor hopes the securities will increase in value, payouts may vary considerably as the value of the annuity units fluctuates with the value of those securities.

Separate account. Variable annuity contributions are kept in a separate account from the insurance company's investment account. Variable annuity plans do not guarantee the amount of payment because the insurance company does not guarantee the performance of the separate account. Because the risk is borne by the investor rather than the insurance company, the variable annuity must be registered under the Investment Company Act of 1940. In addition to having a valid insurance license in each state in which they do business, variable annuity salespeople must be registered with the SEC and the NASD.

Variable annuity payments. Variable annuity payments are not fixed at a certain amount, but determined by the value of the annuitant's portfolio and the mortality tables. Initial payout is used to determine the number of annuity units in the account; future payouts are determined by the fluctuating value of the annuity unit. An investor who annuitized a variable annuity in 1953 and began with monthly payments of $375 may now be receiving $1,275 per month.

Other Types of Annuity Products

Combination annuities. Some insurance companies offer a combination annuity wherein the investor contributes to both a fixed account and a variable account. The result is a guaranteed return on the fixed annuity portion and a possible higher return on the variable annuity portion.

Contractual plans. Contributions to annuities may be made in a lump sum or in installments. Installment contributions are usually made under one of two kinds of contractual plans: front-end load or spread load. Contractual plans have a maximum sales charge of 9% over the life of the plan.

403-B plans. Employees of public schools and certain nonprofit organizations may be eligible to make contributions to a tax-sheltered annuity, referred to as a 403-B plan. Contributions are made with before-tax dollars and, therefore, are taxable at the time the individual receives the income. Federal tax is deferred but FICA (Social Security) is withheld on the amount contributed to the plan. Early withdrawals from tax-sheltered annuities are subject to a 10% early withdrawal penalty.

Payout Options

Withdrawals from annuity accounts. Investors may withdraw all money from an annuity as a lump sum, but most annuitize the contract and receive a lifetime income from the insurance company. Investors may choose among several payout options:

- **Life annuity/straight life.** Clients receive monthly benefit checks over their lifetime. There are no added options or benefits, the annuitant receives the maximum payout.
- **Life annuity with period certain.** This annuity offers payment for life, with a certain period of time guaranteed. If the investor dies before the expiration of the period certain, payments go to the annuitant's named beneficiary. If the annuitant lives beyond the period certain, payments continue until the annuitant's death.
- **Joint and last survivor.** This annuity covers the lives of two people, usually a husband and wife. Payments continue as long as either annuitant lives.
- **Unit refund annuity.** This plan pays the annuitant until his or her death. If the investor dies before receiving an amount equal to the value of the account, the beneficiary receives the money remaining in the account.

Accumulation units. An accumulation unit is an accounting measure that represents the investor's share of ownership in the separate account. The value of an accumulation unit is determined in a manner identical to that used to determine the value of shares in a mutual fund. The unit value changes with the value of the securities held in the separate account and the total number of accumulation units outstanding. When payout begins, accumulation units are converted into annuity units.

Owners of accumulation units have the same voting rights afforded owners of common stock. They may elect the board of managers (who oversee the management of the portfolio) and vote on changes in investment policies.

Annuity units. An annuity unit is a measure of value used only during the payout period of an "annuitized" contract. It is an accounting measure that determines the amount of each payment to the annuitant.

The number of annuity units is calculated when the owner annuitizes the contract, that is, when payout begins. The value of the unit fluctuates with the value of the separate account portfolio. The number of units credited to the annuitant's account is based on this initial unit value and other variables, such as the payout option selected, the accumulated value of the annuitant's account, the age and sex of the individual and the assumed interest rate.

Assumed interest rate (AIR). The assumed interest rate is a basis for projecting earnings for the variable annuity. The rate provides an earnings target for the separate account and is usually conservatively estimated.

An assumed interest rate is used to project the value of an account through the annuitant's age at death as forecasted by mortality tables. Based on this value, the insurance company projects its distributions to the annuitant. It is also used when determining the number of annuity units. The higher the assumed interest rate, the higher the projected value of units and the greater the initial payment. The reverse, of course, is also true.

The AIR does not guarantee a rate of return. It is a tool for adjusting the value of an annuity unit to changes in the investment return of the portfolio of the separate account. A change in value of an annuity unit changes the amount of annuity payments. The annuitant always receives a payment equal to the value of one annuity unit times the number of units in the annuitant's account.

Fluctuating payments. After the insurance company determines the number of annuity units used in calculating the payment, the amount of each payment equals the number of units multiplied by the current value of the annuity unit. The number of annuity units used to calculate future payment remains the same. However, because the value of the units depends on the performance of the separate account, the value fluctuates and, consequently, the annuitant's payments may also fluctuate.

If an annuitant chooses an AIR that is too high, subsequent payments will continually decrease because the projections are not met by actual portfolio performance. If the AIR is too low, payments will most likely continually increase as projected returns are surpassed.

Taxation of Annuities

With the exception of 403-B plans (qualified annuities available to employees of schools and nonprofit organizations), contributions to annuities are made with after-tax dollars. Because contributions have already been taxed, the amount of the contribution is not taxable when the account is annuitized (that is, the investor is receiving retirement income). However, the earnings in the account are taxed as ordinary income at the time the investor receives the payments or lump-sum distribution.

Lump-sum withdrawals are taken out on a LIFO (last-in, first-out) basis. This means earnings are removed before the contributions. If the investor receives a lump-sum withdrawal before age 59 1/2, the portion withdrawn would be subject to a 10% penalty in addition to being taxed at the ordinary income tax rate. The penalty does not apply, however, if the amount withdrawn is due to death or disability or is part of a life-income option plan with fixed payments. After age 59 1/2, taxes are payable only on the earnings portion of the withdrawal.

Tax treatment for annuitized payments differs. The cost basis in the contract for a nonqualified plan is divided by the number of years of life expectancy (according to the mortality tables). The resultant dollar figure is considered the nontaxable amount of each year's payments. Any distribution over and above the cost basis is taxable at ordinary income rates.

Chapter Review

Questions

1. Which of the following may participate in a Keogh plan?

    I.   self-employed doctor
    II.   an analyst who makes money giving speeches on the side
    III. an individual with a full-time job who has income from free lancing
    IV.   a corporate executive who receives $5,000 in stock options from his corporation

    ____(A)   I
    ____(B)   I and II
    __°_(C)   I, II and III
    ____(D)   I, II, III and IV

2. The maximum allowable contribution to an IRA is

    ____(A) $2,250 per individual account.
    _°__(B) $2,000 per individual account.
    ____(C) $250 per individual account.
    ____(D)   none, as contributions to IRAs are no longer allowed.

3. Premature distribution from an IRA is subject to a

    ____(A)   6% penalty plus tax.
    _°__(B)   10% penalty plus tax.
    ____(C)   50% penalty plus tax.
    ____(D)   5% penalty plus tax.

4. Jay Smith earns $2,000 as a self-employed, part-time set designer. What is the maximum dollar amount of part-time earnings that he can contribute to a Keogh plan?

    ____(A) $2,000
    ____(B) $1,000
    _°__(C) $400
    ____(D) $300

5. In a variable annuity, total accumulation units are equal to

    ____(A)   one's bookkeeping value.
    _°__(B)   one's percentage of ownership of the separate account.
    ____(C)   that portion of reinvested dividends.
    ____(D)   the offering price.

6. What has the greatest effect on the value of annuity units in a variable annuity?

    ____(A)   changes in the Standard and Poor's index
    ____(B)   cost-of-living index
    ____(C)   fluctuations in the securities held in the portfolio
    ____(D)   changes in stock market prices

7. Holders of variable annuities receive the largest monthly payments under which of the following payout options?

    ____(A)   life annuity   20.8
    ____(B)   life annuity with period certain
    ____(C)   joint and last survivor annuity
    ____(D)   the same pay for all

8. Changes in payments on a variable annuity will correspond most closely to fluctuations in the

    ____(A)   cost of living.
    ____(B)   Dow Jones Industrial average.
    ____(C)   value of underlying securities held in the separate account.
    ____(D)   prime rate.

9. The owner of a non-tax-qualified variable annuity withdraws funds before the contract is annuitized. The owner would incur which of the following tax consequences?

    ____(A)   taxable income or nondeductible losses
    ____(B)   capital gains or losses   20.9
    ____(C)   tax-deferred income
    ____(D)   ordinary income in excess of basis

10. All of the following are true statements concerning the assumed interest rate (AIR) EXCEPT

    ____(A)   The AIR is used in projecting earnings for variable annuities.
    ____(B)   The higher the AIR, the lower the assumed payment.
    ____(C)   The higher the AIR, the higher the initial payment.
    ____(D)   The more conservative the AIR, the more likely the target payment will be achieved.

K120

Answer Key

1. C.

2. B.

3. B.

4. C.

5. B.

6. C.

7. A.

8. C.

9. D.

10. B.

Chapter Twenty One

Direct Participation Programs

Key Terms

21.6 Agreement of limited partnership

21.26 Basis

21.17 Cash distribution

21.20 Cost basis

21.21 21.19 Depletion

21.2 Direct Participation Program (DPP)

21.16 Equipment leasing

21.13 Intangible drilling cost (IDC)

21.8 Limited partner

21.15 Overriding royalty interest

21.28 Phantom income

21.24 21.19 Recapture

21.15 Sharing arrangement

21.17 Tax basis

Amortization 21.22

Capitalized expense 21.19

Certificate of limited partnership 21.5 21.6

Crossover point 21.28

Depreciation 21.19

Disproportionate sharing 21.15

Functional allocation 21.16

Limited liability 21.2

Oil and gas 21.13

Passive income 21.9

Real estate 21.12

Reversionary working interest 21.15

Subscription agreement 21.5 21.6

Tax credit 21.23

K121

Direct Participation Programs

Direct participation programs (DPPs), sometimes called tax shelters, are businesses organized in such a way as to enable them to pass all of their income, gains, losses and tax benefits directly to their owners. The business itself pays no tax directly, since tax liability is apportioned among the investors. Most DPPs, which are usually structured as limited partnerships (LPs), invest in real estate or oil and gas operations.

Investors in LPs typically do not receive quarterly dividends or semiannual interest payments as they would with many other types of investment securities. Instead, investors in limited partnerships may receive a tax deduction based on their share of partnership losses, and either a cash distribution or an increase in taxable income (unaccompanied by cash) based on their share of partnership income. It is this direct participation of investors in the consequences of doing business that gives direct participation programs their name.

Although DPPs are most compatible with the investment needs of wealthy, sophisticated investors, they can be an important part of many people's portfolios.

Forms of Business Organization

Individual (or sole) proprietorship. A sole proprietor (or single owner) controls a business totally, and makes all of its business decisions (hours of operation, activities, location, services offered and more). If for any reason the owner could not continue to operate the business, it probably would cease to exist. A sole proprietor is personally liable for all business debts (that is, he or she has unlimited liability), and any credit extended to the business is restricted to the sole proprietor's personal creditworthiness.

Corporation. Corporations have a continuous (and theoretically perpetual) life. Since its continued existence does not depend on one or more key individuals, a corporation won't disappear at the loss of an officer or director. To establish itself as a corporation, a business must file a certificate of incorporation with the secretary of the state in which the company's principal office is located. When accepted, this certificate becomes the corporate charter, describing the line of business the corporation will be in and giving authorization to the company to issue a certain number of shares of common stock. Corporations are able to raise large amounts of capital by selling stock to the public or by borrowing capital from investors through various debt offerings. A corporation's charter is subject to the laws of the state in which it is filed.

Corporations are the most common form of business organization, primarily because they offer their owners (the stockholders) limited liability. If a corporation goes into bankruptcy, creditors have recourse to the corporation's assets, but not to the assets of the shareholders. Stockholders are liable only to the extent of their individual

21.2

investments. In addition, corporate ownership is easily transferred because ownership of the corporation is represented by shares of stock, and transferring ownership can be accomplished by instructing a broker to buy or sell those shares.

The disadvantages to the corporate form of business are several. Formation can be complicated and costly, running from hundreds to millions of dollars. Differences in state statutes often make it difficult to transact business in states other than the state in which the company was incorporated. In addition, corporations are subject to strict government control and supervision, and are heavily taxed. Corporate earnings are subject to double taxation: a corporation first pays the corporate income tax and then investors pay taxes on dividends distributed to them by the corporation.

Subchapter S corporations. By forming a Subchapter S corporation, investors in a small business can avoid double taxation and still retain limited liability. At the end of the year, a Subchapter S corporation does not pay taxes on its profits. Instead, it computes its income or business loss and allocates each investor a proportionate (pro rata) share. Individual investors then pay taxes on the income or deduct the loss. The number of investors in a Subchapter S corporation is limited by law. A Subchapter S corporation is one type of direct participation program.

Partnerships and Limited Partnerships

Partnerships offer investors limited liability. Should the partnership default on its loans, investors could lose their entire investment (which might include a specific share of partnership debt), but they are not personally liable for other partnership debts. In this regard, partnerships resemble corporations but differ from sole proprietorships. Units of ownership in a partnership are called interests, rather than shares.

Limited partnerships (LPs) are direct participation programs that offer investors direct participation in the economic consequences of the business. Unlike corporations, LPs pay no dividends. Rather, they pass income, gains, losses, deductions and credits directly to investors. In this respect, limited partnerships resemble sole proprietorships.

Syndication and underwriting of limited partnerships. The syndicator (or syndicate manager) is the individual or firm designated to work with the general partners (GPs) of a limited partnership. The syndicator's duties include preparing the paperwork needed to register the limited partnership with the SEC; organizing and overseeing the selling syndicate (and selling group); and promoting the partnership generally. The NASD authorizes payments of up to 10% of the money raised as compensation to the syndicator for bringing the partnership to market.

Tax reporting for partnerships. Limited partnerships pass through to investors the economic benefits (growth and income) and tax consequences (deductions and write offs) of the business. If the partnership's operations result in taxable income, that amount is divided proportionally among the partners. Each investor adds that amount to his or her personal taxable income.

Maintaining partnership status. The Internal Revenue Code is the final determinant as to whether an organization qualifies for tax treatment as a corporation or as a limited partnership. Under IRS regulations, corporations may have any or all of the characteristics in the following list without affecting their tax status. Limited partnerships, however, may have no more than four of these six characteristics and still qualify for the special tax treatments afforded partnerships. The six characteristics are (in order of ease of avoidance):

Limited Part must avoid any 2 of these 4

- **Continuity of life.** This is the easiest of the corporate characteristics for an LP to avoid. The partnership agreement usually sets a date on which the partnership will be dissolved.
- **Limited liability.** Generally avoidable for an LP. GPs must make nonpartnership assets available to creditors. The liability of the LPs is limited to their investment.
- **Free transferability of interests.** Generally avoidable by most LPs. Transfer of interests to nonpartners must be approved by one or more partners (and at least one GP).
- **Centralization of management.** Hard to avoid for an LP, this can be avoided only if the general partner holds more than a 20% interest in capital or profits. Avoidance may cause conflict with state laws requiring limited partners to have no role in management.
- **Intent to do business and to divide profits** among investors. Impossible for an LP to avoid. It is one of the reasons the partnership was formed.
- **Business associates.** Impossible for an LP to avoid. A partnership must have associates because law requires at least one general and one limited partner per partnership. Without a limited partner, there is no limited partnership; without an active general partner, there is no one to run the business.

Forming a Limited Partnership

Documentation

Registration statement. To assure that a public limited partnership makes full disclosure to potential investors, federal regulations require a new partnership to file a registration statement and prospectus with the SEC in Washington, D.C. The partnership must also file with every state in which it intends to do business. A registration statement contains complete information and supporting documents that describe the partnership. The SEC reviews the filing for thoroughness, misstatements and misrepresentations of material fact. The SEC does not pass judgment on the soundness of the offering as an investment.

Prospectus. The prospectus (which is drawn from the registration statement) provides material information about the partnership and the general partner. It must include information about each property, the management, the GP's history with similar projects, potential conflicts of interest, risks and any pertinent financial data.

The prospectus must disclose the proposed use of any offering proceeds, including offering, syndication, organization and acquisition costs. Under NASD regulation and state law, these front-end fees are limited to 10%.

Subscription agreement. An investor interested in purchasing a limited partnership unit signs a subscription agreement, which includes a statement of the investor's net worth and annual income, and a power of attorney appointing the GP as the agent of the partnership. The subscription agreement, with the subscriber's money, is merely an offer to buy and becomes effective only when signed by the GP. The GP may decline the subscriber's offer if the offering has sold out or if the subscriber's net worth or income are insufficient.

Certificate of limited partnership. To be legally recognized as an LP, a business organization must file a certificate of limited partnership in its home state, usually with the office of the secretary of state. The primary purpose of the certificate is to let creditors know which partners are liable for the partnership's debts (the GPs) and which partners have limited liability (the LPs). Unless a certificate is filed, all partners may be treated as general partners; that is, investors may be denied limited liability. The certificate of limited partnership includes the following information:

- the partnership's name;
- the partnership's business; for example, to drill for oil or to construct office buildings;
- the principal place of business, often the GP's address;
- the amount of time the partnership expects to be in business;
- the size of each limited partner's investment and any additional investment expected;
- when each investor's contribution will be returned (if a time has been set);
- each LP's share of the profits or other compensation;
- whether and under what conditions an LP can assign (sell or donate) an interest;
- whether LPs may admit additional LPs;
- whether some LPs will have priority over others in contributions or compensation;
- whether upon the death or incapacity of another GP, remaining GPs may continue the business; and
- if granted, the right of an LP to request compensation in property instead of cash.

Amendment of the certificate. The certificate of limited partnership must be amended within 30 days after discovery of an error or after any changes that would make information in the certificate incorrect. Such changes would include:

- changes in membership (such as loss of a member);
- alteration of the sharing arrangement (division of benefits between GPs and LPs);
- increase or decrease in a partner's contribution; or
- change in the nature or direction of the partnership's business.

Agreement of Limited Partnership. The partnership agreement is a contract that provides guidelines for operation and describes rights and responsibilities of the general and limited partners. A general listing of the rights and obligations covered in a partnership agreement is included in the following section.

business plan

Documenting a Limited Partnership

- **Certificate of Limited Partnership.** The certificate serves to inform creditors and provides a means of complying with state statutes. Identifies the partnership, contributions of members, the sharing arrangements, the partnership's term, and provisions for changes in membership.
- **Agreement of Limited Partnership.** The contract that establishes guidelines for the operation of the partnership. Defines the roles of the general and limited partners.
- **Registration statement.** Notifies the SEC of the creation of a new public limited partnership. Contains a complete description of the partnership's business intentions.
- **Prospectus.** Part of the registration statement and the only valid offer to sell a limited partnership. Contains all of the information necessary for an investor to make an informed investment decision about the partnership.
- **Subscription agreement.** Finalizes the sale of a partnership interest when signed by the general partner. Grants power of attorney to the general partners.

Investors in a Limited Partnership

A limited partnership must have at least one general partner (GP) and one limited partner (LP). The general partner runs the business. Limited partners are passive investors with no management responsibilities and with limited liability. A certificate of limited partnership filed with the secretary of state lists the status of each investor as a limited or general partner.

Depending on the type of partnership, there can be anywhere from a handful to thousands of limited partners. In some partnerships, the general partner is not an individual or group of individuals, but a corporation. Some corporations act as general partners for several partnerships.

In a private placement limited partnership, a small number of limited partners contribute large amounts of money. As the name implies, private placements are not advertised to the general public. Limited partners tend to be wealthy investors with substantial investment experience.

In a public offering limited partnership, there are a larger number of investors, each of whom makes a relatively small contribution of capital to the business ($2,000-$5,000 is a standard minimum contribution). Because these partnerships can be publicly advertised, are relatively large, may attract investors with smaller budgets and less investment sophistication, they are more tightly regulated and are subject to more stringent federal registration and prospectus requirements.

General Partner

The general partners (which can be one or more individuals, another partnership or a corporation) are the active investors in a limited partnership, and assume responsibility for all aspects of the partnership's operations. GPs assemble the investors' capital, select assets for investment and actively manage the business of the partnership after assets have been acquired. Like sole proprietors, general partners are involved in all of the partnership's decision making. The general partner will:

- make decisions that bind the partnership;
- buy and sell property for the partnership;
- manage the partnership property and money;
- supervise all aspects of the partnership's business; and
- maintain a 1% financial interest in the partnership.

In the event that a general partner becomes incapacitated, the business may or may not be able to continue. On the other hand, a general partnership enjoys one major advantage over a sole proprietorship: the partners can combine resources and liabilities to obtain credit.

During the operating phase of a limited partnership, the GP earns money by charging a management fee, by acting as partnership or property manager for a fee, or by earning commissions on the purchase or sale of partnership property. There is a potential conflict of interest when the GP performs management functions and is responsible for establishing the compensation for doing so.

Unlike limited partners who have limited liability, the general partners have unlimited liability and are therefore personally liable for all partnership business losses and debts. The partnership's creditors may seek repayment from the GP and may go after the GP's personal assets.

The general partner has a fiduciary relationship to the limited partners. That is, the GP has been entrusted with the LPs' capital and is morally and legally bound to use that capital in the investors' best interests. The GP must manage the business in the partnership's best interest, to avoid the appearance of improper use of assets and to avoid conflicts of interest.

Limitations on the general partner. According to standard language in partnership agreements, the general partner may not prevent the ordinary flow of partnership business, assign or possess (sell or buy) a partnership property for purposes other than those in the best interest of the partnership, or compete with the partnership for personal gain.

In addition, there are other activities the GP may not undertake unless specifically authorized to do so by the partnership agreement. He or she may not admit a new general or limited partner to the partnership (the limited partners must unanimously agree to the admission, unless the agreement gives the GP authority to admit new members) or continue the business of the partnership if a general partner dies, retires or becomes otherwise incapacitated.

The general partner is also forbidden to confess a judgment against the partnership without the written authorization of the limited partners. This means that the general partner may not agree to the terms of a legal judgment against the partnership unless the limited partners authorize such agreement. The GP is compensated under specific terms of the partnership agreement and is forbidden compensation beyond the limits of that agreement.

Limited Partner

Along with one or more general partners, a partnership often includes one or more limited partners (LPs). Limited partners are passive investors who assume no part of the management responsibilities or decision making, and are therefore usually not held personally and individually liable for the general indebtedness of the partnership.

Not long ago, DPPs were thought of as tax shelters because of the tax advantages they offered the limited partners. LPs passed certain allowable deductions directly through to the investors. Partnership losses were often apportioned among investors, enabling them to claim those losses as deductions on their personal tax forms.

Under current tax law, limited partners are classified as passive investors: any income they receive from a partnership is passive income, and any losses passed through to them are passive losses. An investor may use a tax loss from a partnership only to offset income from another passive investment. Investors with no passive income in the year they receive passive losses cannot deduct the losses (neither stock dividends nor wages are classified as passive income).

Limited partners may receive cash distributions and capital gains from partnerships. The total yield of a partnership investment takes into account all potential rewards: tax deductions, cash distributions and capital gains. Investors must consider all potential rewards (not just tax write-offs) when looking to invest in a limited partnership. Investors should choose limited partnerships because they appear to be sound business ventures (that is, they are economically viable) and not because they promise to generate tax losses.

Like corporate stockholders, limited partners have limited liability. That is, if the business goes bankrupt, investors may lose only their investment, including any money borrowed on behalf of the partnership for which they are personally liable. A limited partner who exceeds legal boundaries by actively participating in business management may lose limited liability. The limited partner may, however, assist the partnership in areas such as construction or maintenance services because these are not considered management actions and do not threaten limited liability.

Rights and responsibilities. The basic obligation of the limited partner is to provide capital. The limited partner has the right to:

- vote on the admission of a new general partner;
- sue the general partner;
- vote on the sale or refinancing of partnership property; and
- inspect partnership books and records.

In special circumstances the limited partners may be required to vote, an act called exercising the partnership democracy. A vote may be taken to permit the GP to act contrary to the agreement of limited partnership or confess a judgment against the partnership. The chart following summarizes the roles and responsibilities of the general and limited partners.

Characteristics	General Partner	Limited Partner
Responsibilities	Organizes and manages the partnership business. Acts on behalf of the limited partners.	Provides capital for partnership's business.
Rights	Can legally bind the partnership.	Can receive justified returns. Monitor the partnership. Can sue or remove GP. Can petition a court to dissolve partnership.

K121

Limitations

Cannot prevent the ordinary flow of partnership business.	Cannot participate in the management of partnership business.
Cannot assign or possess partnership property for purposes other than those of the LP.	Cannot act on behalf of the partnership.
Cannot compete against the LP for personal gain.	Cannot knowingly sign a certificate containing false information.
Can receive only the compensation specified in the agreement.	Generally cannot make loans to the LP.
Cannot admit new GPs or LPs or continue the LP after the loss of a GP unless specified in the LP agreement.	Cannot have his or her name appear as part of the LP's name.

Dissolving a Limited Partnership

In most cases, limited partnerships "close up shop" on the date specified in the partnership agreement. Specifying a termination date helps avoid the corporate characteristic of "continuity of life." Sometimes partnerships close down before the specified date. In addition to avoiding continuity of life overtones, early shutdown may occur if a general partner dies, retires or becomes mentally incompetent (unless the partnership agreement specifies that the partnership will continue despite these circumstances); if the limited partners holding a majority interest endorse a decision to dissolve the partnership; or if the partnership sells, or otherwise disposes of, all assets.

Dissolution of a partnership and settlement of accounts. When the partnership dissolves, the general partner must cancel the certificate of limited partnership and settle accounts in this order:

- secured lenders;
- other creditors
- limited partners, first for their claim to a share of profits, and second for their claims to a return of contributed capital;
- general partners, first for fees and other claims not involving profits or capital, second for a share of profits, and third for capital return.

Advantages and Disadvantages of the LP

The DPP investor enjoys several advantages: 1) an investment that is managed by others, 2) a flow-through of income and expenses, and 3) limited liability. The greatest disadvantage is lack of liquidity. Because the secondary market for DPPs is limited, investors who want to liquidate frequently cannot locate a buyer for their interests. When Congress changes tax laws, new rules can cause substantial damage to limited partners, who may be locked into illiquid investments that lose their tax advantages.

The participant will also find it difficult, although not impossible, to change general partners. The GP is not subject to annual election. Nor will investors find it easy to fire the GP, even if the partnership business is operating at a loss. Although most investors do not want day-to-day management responsibilities, they want to be able to voice their opinions effectively if profits and sales are poor. Corporate investors make their opinions felt by voting at annual meetings; the LP doesn't have that right.

Conflicts of interest for the general partner(s). Because the GP is involved with daily operations, he or she must use utmost good faith in managing the business in the partnership's best interest. The GP must always be alert to potential conflicts of interest (and other hazards). For example, a GP with an inventory of drilling prospects might be tempted to keep the best and sell the others to the partnership. Similarly, the GP must resist the temptation to compete improperly with the partnership, for instance by building apartments next door to the partnership's property and renting his own units first.

Improper use of partnership assets is another pitfall GPs must avoid. The GP may not commingle the funds of various partnerships, for example, and may not commingle partnership funds with his or her personal funds. The GP may lend money or property to the partnership but may not borrow from the partnership. Such conflicts of interest add risk to the partnership venture and must be disclosed in the offering documents.

ADV

DPP's Don't pay TAX

Limited Liability for clients

DISADV

Lack of Liquidity

Possible bad GP

If GP dies, DDP is dissolved (If only 1 GP)

Types of Limited Partnership Programs

Though limited partnerships might be formed to run any type of business, generally they invest in only a few areas such as those in which the tax incentives and economic benefits are greatest. In this section, we will look at the features, advantages and disadvantages of the real estate, oil and gas, and equipment leasing programs that in recent years have made up the vast majority of limited partnerships. Limited partnerships have also invested in coal mining, agriculture, timber, breeding and livestock (primarily cattle and race horses), art objects and cable TV, but such programs have always constituted a small percentage of existing DPPs.

Real Estate LPs

Real estate limited partnerships meet a number of different investment objectives. The primary benefit is strong growth potential through appreciation of properties. Some partnerships distribute income too, and in many (but not all) real estate programs, the cash distributions are sheltered from taxes by deductions for mortgage interest and depreciation. There are three types of real estate programs: new construction, existing properties and raw land.

New construction. A new construction program builds new property. The principal advantage of such programs is the potential for appreciation. Successful construction and development of a property can increase its value many times over. The reward potential of new construction, however, is offset by certain disadvantages. Some disadvantages to new construction are possible cost or time overruns, no established track record for new property (history of success in renting, for example), the difficulty of finding permanent financing, and an inability to deduct current expenses during construction period.

Investments in new construction are more speculative than investments in existing property. For example, the investor who takes over a successful rental property or office building runs much less risk than the partnership that sets out to build. New construction may be hampered by several factors: bad weather; strikes; uncertain occupancy levels; unexpected costs; and, not least, uncertainties as to whether a new building will attract occupants.

Existing properties. Programs based on existing properties with a track record are generally safer and more conservative than new construction programs. Income and expenses are easier to estimate, and cash flow can begin immediately. Potential disadvantages include greater maintenance or repair expenses than for new construction, expiring leases that may not be renewed, and existing low-rent arrangements that may bring less revenue than desired. (The existence of low-rent leases should be disclosed and reflected in the purchase price.)

Raw land. Raw land has little to offer beyond appreciation potential- although that can be substantial. Because undeveloped land offers neither income nor depreciation deductions, it is not a tax shelter. If the purchase is leveraged, the partnership will actually lose money to debt service and to taxes. All of the benefits of owning raw land are delayed until the sale of the property.

REITs

A Real Estate Investment Trust (REIT) is a company that manages a portfolio of real estate investments in order to earn profits for shareholders. REITs are often traded publicly. DPPs and REITs are similar in that both allow gains and profits to pass through to investors. The REIT investor, however, cannot deduct operating or capital losses.

To avoid being taxed as a corporation, the REIT must receive 75% or more of its income from real estate and must distribute 95% or more of its taxable income to shareholders. Unlike DPPs, REITs became more, rather than less, attractive to investors as a result of the 1986 tax law changes.

Oil and Gas LPs

Investors select the type of oil and gas program that provides the benefits they desire at the level of risk they can tolerate. All oil and gas drilling programs are speculative, with exploratory drilling posing the greatest risks. Income programs, which invest in producing wells, are the least risky oil and gas investments.

Exploratory drilling. Exploratory drilling programs (often called wildcatting) have a single objective, to locate undiscovered reserves of oil and gas. To do this, mineral rights are acquired (usually by the GP) for the limited partnership. The cost of mineral rights relates to the proximity of producing wells (the nearer a producing well the more expensive the rights). Exploratory wells are drilled entirely on speculation that oil is present. Exploratory drilling programs offer high risk and high reward. Very few wells drilled actually produce, but if one does it can be very profitable.

The principal tax advantage of exploratory drilling programs is the write-off of intangible drilling costs (IDCs). 100% of these write-offs are generally taken the first year of operation. IDCs include labor, drilling rig rental and fuel.

Developmental drilling. Developmental drilling programs target areas of proven reserves and plan new well drilling near existing fields. Mineral rights cost more than in exploratory drilling programs, but IDCs are somewhat lower. Because of the proximity of pipelines or storage tanks, other tangible costs are lower, too. In general, there is less risk and less reward potential in developmental than with exploratory programs. Both share the same potential tax advantages, although cash distributions are unlikely during the early stages of a developmental program.

Income programs. This type of oil and gas program would be appropriate for the investor whose goal is income. If oil and gas prices are increasing, an income program can provide immediate, reliable cash flow. The partnership buys the value of the oil in the ground, with the expectation that it can sell it and receive income that is sheltered by depletion allowances (depletion allowances enable investors to recover costs of mineral rights). Income programs buy and market proven reserves of oil and gas. They do not explore or develop and do not pass on write-offs from IDCs.

Comparison of the Different Types of Oil and Gas Programs

Characteristic	Exploratory	Developmental	Income
Cost of mineral rights	Low	Medium	High
IDCs	High	Medium	None
Tangible costs	High	Medium	None
Risk/Reward	High	Medium	Low
Immediate tax write-offs	High	High	Low

The search for oil. The search for oil can be viewed as a three-stage process. The initial step is for someone, usually the general partner, to acquire mineral rights to a property that geologists believe may contain oil (the mineral rights are separate from the right to occupy the surface of the property). The owner of the land typically retains a royalty interest in any minerals extracted from it and sold by the partnership.

The amount spent to acquire mineral rights is not immediately deductible as a business expense. Instead, it becomes part of the partnership's capital expenditures to be recovered by the depletion allowance if drilling produces a successful well.

Drilling can be categorized in one of two ways: exploratory or developmental. Exploratory drilling occurs on land that has never produced oil. Developmental drilling programs sink wells into proven reserves to a depth that has produced a previous strike. Exploratory drilling offers very high risks and very high reward potential. Developmental drilling is less risky than exploratory, but the profit potential is lower as well.

The second stage in the search for oil is the actual drilling. After selecting property and acquiring mineral rights, the partnership invests its capital in drilling for oil. Drilling generates two types of expenses: tangible and intangible. Both give rise to deductions, but the partnership recovers the costs in different ways. Tangible costs (those incurred through purchasing equipment) are recovered with depreciation deductions spread over a period set by the tax code. Intangible costs (expenditures on labor and other services) are usually deducted in the year incurred, although the partnership can elect to deduct them over the life of the well (which the IRC defines as 10 years).

Stage three of the oil search involves extracting the oil from the ground. If drilling is successful (or if the partnership buys a producing well), the drillers reinforce the walls of the well with casing and pump oil into storage tanks or into a pipeline. Again, this involves tangible costs (the cost of the casing) that can be recovered through depreciation.

As the partnership sells the oil pumped out of the ground, it can claim depletion deductions to recover the costs of acquiring mineral rights. Each limited partner calculates his or her own share of these depletion deductions as well as the method by which the deductions are calculated (the investor can select the higher of cost depletion or percentage depletion).

Cost depletion is based on the amount of reserves sold and is limited to the original cost of the reserves. Percent depletion, on the other hand, is a fixed percent (currently 15%) of income from the well and is not limited by the investor's basis in the property. A limited partner may well claim percentage depletion deductions in excess of the cost of the reserves.

Sharing arrangements. There are different methods of sharing costs and revenues associated with oil and gas programs. The limited partner's intent is to bear as little cost and get as many benefits as possible, consistent with providing the general partner an incentive for improving the partnership's profitability. This is accomplished through various sharing arrangements.

Overriding royalty interest. A person with a royalty interest takes no risks but gets a share of the revenues. The landowner who sells mineral rights to a partnership, for example, commonly retains a royalty interest. The landowner with a royalty interest does not participate in the business or share risks, but does receive a portion of the income from a successful well. The general partner who holds an overriding royalty interest incurs no costs, but receives a specified percentage of oil revenue. Unlike the landowner with a royalty interest, the GP with an overriding royalty interest is involved in the business and stands to lose money if the venture fails.

Reversionary working interest. The general partner bears none of the program's costs, but does not receive its share of revenues until the limited partners have recovered their capital.

Only used in private programs

Net operating profits interest. The general partner bears none of the program's costs, but is entitled to a percentage of net profits (net profits are revenues less expenses). The net-profits-interest is figured prior to deducting the depletion allowance.

Disproportionate sharing. With this type of arrangement, the general partner bears a relatively small percentage of expenses and is entitled to a relatively large percentage of revenues.

Carried interest. The general partner shares tangible drilling costs with the limited partners but pays no part of the intangible drilling costs (IDCs). The limited partners, therefore, are carrying the general partner who shares in revenues from the beginning. In a sense, it is advantageous to bear intangible, rather than tangible, costs. IDCs generate current deductions, whereas tangible costs must be depreciated over the property's life.

Tangible / untangible [handwritten]

Functional allocation. This is the most common sharing arrangement. The general partner bears tangible costs, and the limited partners bear IDCs. Revenues are shared.

Oil and Gas Sharing Arrangements

Know the five by name and least most common [handwritten margin note]

Form	Cost paid by GP	Revenues received by GP
Overriding Royalty Interest	None	1/16 to 1/8 of gross revenues when production begins
Reversionary Working Interest	None	1/16 to 1/8 of gross revenues after limited partners have recovered their investment
Net Operating Profits Interest	None	1/16 to 1/8 of net revenues when production begins
Disproportionate Sharing	Usually 25% of deductible and nondeductible costs	Usually 50% of revenues
Functional Allocation	All nondeductible costs	Usually 40 to 50% of revenues

Combination Oil & Gas Programs [handwritten]

Equipment Leasing LPs

Some DPPs purchase equipment that they then lease to other businesses on a long-term basis. Each investor receives a share of the income from the lease payments and a proportional share of operating expenses, interest expense and depreciation. Because equipment (unlike real estate or undeveloped mineral reserves) rarely appreciates, tax-sheltered income is the primary objective of these programs. Since the 1986 tax changes, however, equipment leasing no longer guarantees the investment tax credit (ITC) once allowed to purchasers of machinery and equipment. Once a very attractive feature of these programs, the ITC has not been allowed since January 1987.

Limited Partnership Tax Accounting

Partnerships, as you learned earlier, are not subject to a tax on their income. In this respect, they are unlike corporations, which must pay a corporate income tax. The partnership's tax liabilities pass through to the investors. This does not mean, however, that partnerships are exempt from reporting requirements. Like other businesses, they must account to the IRS for their receipts, profits and taxable income, including the deductions to which they are entitled.

Taxable income is not to be confused with cash distributions. It is simply a dollar figure recorded on accounting ledgers and tax forms. A pro rata share of taxable income, then, is not a benefit to the limited partner. On the contrary, an investor in the 28% bracket who is assigned a $1,000 share of partnership income will owe the federal government an additional $280 for the year whether or not she received any cash from the partnership.

Passive gains and losses. If the partnership shows a loss, a share of that amount will be passed along to each investor. This loss may benefit the investor if it qualifies as a tax deduction. Remember that for tax purposes, losses passed along to limited partners are called passive losses because limited partners are passive investors who do not take an active role in the business.

Under the tax code, passive losses may be deducted only from passive income. Investors receive passive income from investments they do not manage, including limited partnership interests. An investor who receives a loss from one LP could, for example, deduct it from income received from another LP. That investor could not, however, deduct the loss directly from other types of income which are not classed as passive (such as wages, salary or corporate dividends).

Partnerships may also pass along cash distributions based on the partnership's profits. A partner may, in fact, receive a cash distribution (or return of capital), even when the partnership shows a tax loss (and assigns a share of it to each partner). Therefore, a cash distribution, unlike a pro rata share of income, is a benefit flowing from the partnership to the partner.

Tax basis. Each item passed through by the partnership affects the investor's tax basis in the investment. Tax basis, which begins as the cash paid for a partnership interest, is a record of the amount a partner has invested in the partnership. After the initial payment, any economic benefits passed through to the investor decrease that original basis, just as if the partnership had returned some of the investor's capital contribution. Any economic disadvantages, such as a share of taxable income, increase basis as if the partner had put more money into the business.

Basis is a very important part of DPP investing. An investor's tax basis determines how much loss the investor can write off in a year and how much taxable gain will be assigned the investor when the partnership sells its assets.

Each year, the IRS must receive a Form 1065 from the partnership, specifying the partnership's annual income, gains, losses, deductions and credits. Because the partnership itself is not a taxpayer, Form 1065 is for informational purposes only. Included in this form are a number of schedules, among them Schedule K-1. Each limited partner's share of income and loss is itemized on Schedule K-1, a copy of which is sent to the partner.

Partnership tax reporting. Every year, the partnership's accountant must fill out two tax forms: Form 1065, "U.S. Partnership Return of Income," and Schedule K-1, "Partner's Share of Income, Credits, Deductions, etc." Form 1065 provides the IRS with a thorough record of the financial consequences of the partnership's business for the year. It includes gross receipts, cost of goods sold, gross profit, ordinary income or loss and so on. Form 1065 is for information purposes only. It is simply a record of financial transactions during the year and it implies no tax liability for the business.

Schedule K-1 is a component of Form 1065. The partnership accountant must fill out a Schedule K-1 for each partner. Included on the schedule are all relevant items, especially the limited partner's share of the partnership's ordinary income or loss.

If there is income from the partnership, the investor adds it to other passive income received that year. If there is a loss, the partner subtracts it from passive income. The investor then includes total passive income with other taxable income on Form 1040. Partnership losses, therefore, reduce taxable income only to the extent that they reduce passive income.

Expenses. When calculating their taxable income, businesses are generally entitled to deduct the ordinary and necessary expenses incurred in making a profit. Rules governing the amount and timing of such deductions vary. The two broadest categories of business expenses are current expenses (or simply expenses) and capital expenses.

The cost of an item with a useful life of one year or less is a current expense. In general, partnerships (like corporations or individual proprietors) deduct these expenses from profits when computing taxable income for the year. In the language of the tax code, costs deducted in the year incurred are expensed. For accounting purposes, the following items are expensed:

- operating expenses;
- annual interest expenses;
- management fees;
- state, local and payroll taxes; and
- intangible drilling costs (IDCs).

The cost of any of these items is used in full as a deduction when calculating taxable income. In a real estate limited partnership, for example, all expenses incurred in operating furnaces, interest on mortgage debt, fees paid to building managers and taxes would be deducted from rents or leases when calculating taxable income.

Intangible drilling costs (IDCs). IDCs include items such as labor used in drilling a well. Because labor is not a tangible asset, it doesn't depreciate. Therefore, it is not added to capital costs and depreciated over a number of years. If the project produces nothing, the partnership loses every cent invested in this particular IDC because intangible items have no salvage value.

Partnerships generally expense IDCs in the first year or two of operation, but they may choose, instead, to amortize the deductions over the life of the well. When oil and gas partnerships terminate, investors may have to pay back a portion of the deductions allowed for IDCs. (Paying back a deduction is called recapture, which will be discussed later.)

Capitalized Expenses

In addition to funds spent on the current expenses of running the business, a partnership also has capital expenses for items that will benefit the business for the long term. Capitalized expenses include major assets (assets with a life of more than one year), such as buildings, land, machinery, certain fees and (for oil and gas or mining operations) minerals. Unlike current expenses, capital costs can't be deducted fully in the year they are incurred. Instead, such costs can usually be deducted, a fraction at a time, over a period of years.

For real and personal property, deductions are based on the principle that the asset depreciates in value each year. Deductions for the cost of minerals (such as oil and gas) are based on the fact that the business depletes the supply of its asset over time. In theory, then, businesses are allowed to deduct from their income an amount that represents the depreciation in value of tangible assets or the depletion of a mineral resource. In fact, depreciation and depletion deductions are usually based on a formula, not on the specific amount by which an item's value has decreased during the year.

Some capital costs are not recovered through depreciation or depletion, but are deductible under a specific amortization schedule. Other capital costs are not deductible at all. Methods for recovering the cost of capitalized expenses include depreciation, depletion, amortization and expenses capitalized but not recovered.

Depreciation. Businesses can deduct the entire cost of most tangible items, including real estate, machinery and equipment, race horses, ball players and other items not ordinarily considered business equipment. But they can't deduct 100% of these costs in the year the item is purchased. Instead, they deduct a portion of the cost each year over the item's useful (or depreciable) life.

In general, depreciation deductions are spread over an item's useful life in one of two ways, either straight line (the same amount is deducted each year), or accelerated (in which deductions start high and decline over the item's life).

In theory, tangible assets lose a portion of their value during each year of use, resulting in depreciation (a familiar example is the declining value of a car). For accounting purposes, depreciation is an annual expense. By the end of an item's useful life, it will either be worthless or have some relatively small salvage value. The tax code supports the assumption that businesses should not have to pay tax on money lost each year due to depreciation of their assets.

In fact, depreciation deductions are usually not tied to a calculated loss in value. A limited partnership that owns an airplane, for example, doesn't have to check the market value of the plane each year at tax time to compare depreciation with the previous year. The IRS publishes tables that list the depreciable life of assets (five years in the case of an airplane) and the percentage of their value that can be deducted each year. A partnership's accountant simply checks the tables and deducts the appropriate percentage when calculating the partnership's taxable income.

Accelerated depreciation offers an advantage over straight-line depreciation by allowing a partnership to deduct the maximum amount as quickly as possible, thus accelerating deductions. Accountants use several formulas in calculating accelerated deductions, but the most common method is the Accelerated Cost Recovery System (ACRS). Under ACRS, the IRS provides tables that specify the allowable deduction for each year of an asset's life. The IRS also defines the life span of different categories of tangible assets as follows:

- Real property: capitalized and depreciated over 27 1/2 years. Depreciation of real property includes buildings but not land, because land doesn't wear out.
- Personal property (machines and equipment): capitalized and recovered through depreciation over a time period determined by the IRS. Different categories of equipment have different depreciable lives.

Each depreciable asset has a cost basis, which is its value for purposes of depreciation. When the partnership's accountant calculates the year's depreciation on a building, for example, she multiplies the allowable percentage times the building's cost basis. In simplistic terms, cost basis is merely the purchase price of the building, but in tax accounting, it becomes more complex. Cost basis includes the purchase price, any real estate commissions, title search fees, attorney's fees and certain other costs. Therefore, these elements make up the cost basis for calculating depreciation deductions.

Some assets are not included in cost basis. That is, they are part of the partnership's capital expenditures, but do not qualify for depreciation deductions. Cost basis does not include the value of the land or any buildings bought only to be demolished, expense deductions that reduce depreciation or the amortized costs of rehabilitated low-income housing.

Land doesn't wear out and lose value; therefore, it is not depreciable. Buildings purchased by the partnership for demolition also are nondepreciable. After they've been demolished, they will no longer be part of the partnership's assets. In some cases, part of an asset's cost will be deducted as an expense or amortized (cost of low-income housing rehabilitation, for example). Such costs are excluded from basis so that they are not deducted twice.

Adjusted basis. Cost basis begins as cost (e.g., all long-term expenditures related to buying, building or developing property). As time passes, however, the original basis may be adjusted for certain capital expenditures related to the asset. Improvements that make a partnership's assets more valuable are included in cost basis. But routine maintenance expenses (considered current expenses) are not. The partnership doesn't capitalize and depreciate them but deducts them all in the year they are paid. For instance, adding a room on one's house increases cost basis because doing so makes it a different and more valuable asset. Mowing the lawn, however, does not because mowing is maintenance, a routine expense of owning that particular type of asset.

So cost basis begins as cost, but is adjusted for certain expenditures that make it a more valuable asset. When a partnership sells an asset, the capital gain or loss on the sale is the difference between the adjusted basis and the sale price.

Depletion. Mineral resources, such as oil and gas, are a special kind of capital asset. They don't just wear out and lose value, they actually disappear (they are depleted) as the partnership extracts and sells them. The tax code allows a special kind of deduction, called depletion, to compensate the partnership (or any qualifying owner) for the disappearance of the source of its profits.

Frequently the depletion deduction is viewed as a tax benefit available only to the oil industry, but that's not the case. The deduction is a mineral depletion allowance and is available to any industry that extracts and sells mineral resources (including oil, gas, coal, gold, uranium, oyster shells and timber).

In contrast to depreciation deductions, which are used by the partnership to reduce taxable income distributed to partners, depletion deductions are passed directly to the partners. Each limited partner receives a depletion deduction reflecting his or her share in the well or mine. Depletion deductions can be calculated two ways, through cost depletion and through percentage depletion.

Cost depletion compensates the investor for the original purchase price of the amount of oil sold during the year. Percentage depletion is percentage of income from the well. The two amounts can vary significantly. Large producers must use cost depletion. Percentage depletion may be used only by small producers (fewer than 1,000 barrels of oil per day).

Cost depletion. The cost depletion allowance is tied to the partnership's initial cost for the oil that is sold during the tax year. If a limited partnership buys oil reserves estimated at 200,000 barrels, for $1 million ($5 per barrel), a partner with a 1% share of the partnership owns 1% of $1 million worth of oil, or $10,000 worth.

If during the first year the partnership recovers and sells 20,000 barrels of its oil, the LP's 1% share of this oil would be 200 barrels. The oil cost $5 per barrel initially, so that 200 ~~gallons~~ barrels represents an investment of $1,000, and the LP's cost depletion

[handwritten margin note: Know there are 2 way]

[handwritten note below text: barrels]

deduction is $1,000. If the partnership eventually sells all the oil, the LP's accumulated deductions will add up to $10,000, the entire initial cost of the LP's oil.

Cost depletion is very much like depreciation or any other expense. The deduction is a straightforward reimbursement for money spent on the purchase of the asset. The limited partner spends $10,000 purchasing oil reserves and, if the partnership sells the entire supply of oil, receives $10,000 in cost depletion deductions.

If the estimate of oil reserves was inaccurate and the partnership sells more than 200,000 barrels, the allowable depletion deduction is still limited to the investor's original cost.

Percentage depletion. The percentage depletion allowance is not related to the cost of the partnership's reserves. Instead, it is a percentage of annual income from the well. If an investor's partnership sells 10,000 barrels and receives $20 per barrel, which is an income of $200,000, her 1% share of that annual income is $2,000. Her percentage depletion deduction will be 15% (currently the legally prescribed percentage). Her allowable deduction, therefore, is $300 (15% of $2,000).

In our example, the investor's cost depletion allowance of $500 substantially exceeds her percentage depletion allowance of $300. Percentage depletion is not limited by the investor's basis in the oil reserves, however. In reality, percentage deductions usually exceed cost deductions because of adjustments to the basis used to calculate cost depletion and, in some cases, percentage depletion deductions taken over the life of a partnership may actually exceed the amount of money the investor paid for a share of the reserves.

The investor usually finds percentage depletion more favorable because percentage depletion deductions over the life of the investment may exceed invested capital. Cost depletion deductions, by contrast, are limited to the total cost of the reserves.

Limits on percentage depletion. Though percentage depletion deductions may be more advantageous, the tax code limits their applicability in four ways:

- only new drilling qualifies for percentage depletion;
- only small, independent producers (1,000 barrels of oil or 6 million cubic feet of gas per day) can use percentage depletion (most LPs qualify as small producers);
- organizations substantially involved in refining or marketing petroleum, as well as in drilling, cannot use percentage depletion; and,
- percentage depletion deductions cannot exceed 50% of income from the well or 65% of income from all sources.

Amortization

Amortization means writing off an expense over a number of years, for example, repaying a mortgage. Certain expenses incurred during the early life of a partnership are amortized over a period of time rather than expensed in the first year. This is advantageous because in later years, income is offset by these amortization expenses.

Partnerships are always looking for ways to move write-offs up to the earlier phases of investment. Prepaying interest, however, no longer accomplishes that goal. Prepaid interest must be amortized over the life of the loan, not deducted in the year paid. In addition to prepaid interest, the IRS now normally requires prepaid fees to be amortized over the life of the service purchased, not deducted in the year of payment.

Brokerage fees and commissions paid when acquiring a mortgage aren't considered a form of currently deductible expense. Instead, they're treated as capital costs to be amortized during the life of the loan. Sometimes a partnership hires an agent to locate renters for a new building. Fees paid to the agent are called rent-up fees. They are amortized and deducted over the rent-up period, the time it takes to find renters for the units in the building.

Expenses incurred in organizing a partnership are considered to have a long-term value, so they are not currently deductible. Therefore, legal, accounting and filing fees paid while organizing a partnership must be amortized over at least 60 months (five years).

Expenses Not Recovered

Some LP expenses are not recoverable through deductions or amortization. Syndication costs are those incurred while promoting and selling the partnership and are distinct from organizational expenses. Syndication expenses are not deductible. Distributions of profits to the general partner are not an expense to be deducted from income for tax purposes and are, therefore, not deductible by limited partners. The builder's profits are not deductible because they are considered to be a share of partnership profits, in essence a distribution to a partner.

Tax Credits

Tax advantages discussed so far (expense write-offs, depreciation and depletion) are all tax deductions, used to reduce the amount of income subject to tax. A tax credit, by contrast, is an amount of money subtracted from tax liability rather than income. Tax credits are available on certain types of real estate, including low-income housing and certified historical structures. They are also available on some types of energy conservation equipment and on the costs of research and development.

rewards direct reductions in taxes

Deferral and Recapture

Deferral. Tax deductions are not necessarily permanent. When the partnership sells its property (or the limited partner sells an interest), deductions taken previously sometimes result in a higher tax payment. Specifically, they resurface as increased taxable liability on sale proceeds. Because a limited partner may eventually have to pay taxes on an amount equal to the sum of the deductions, we say that depreciation provides tax deferral. Depreciation puts off a tax liability to a later date; it doesn't necessarily eliminate the liability altogether.

Deferral was illustrated earlier in connection with depreciation deductions on equipment. You saw that depreciation deductions reduce the adjusted basis, thus increasing gain on sale (gain on sale is the difference between adjusted basis and sale proceeds).

As adjusted basis goes down by the amount of depreciation deductions, gain on sale goes up by the same amount. If the partnership takes $1,000 in depreciation deductions, adjusted cost basis goes down $1,000 and, therefore, gain on sale goes up $1,000. So the investors escape taxes on $1,000 of income during the partnership's life, but are taxed on an extra $1,000 gain when the partnership sells the depreciated property.

If the gain on the sale is less than the difference between the adjusted basis and the sale proceeds, the partnership is liable only for the difference between the adjusted basis and the sale price. As an example, if a partnership pays $1,000 for equipment, takes $500 in depreciation deductions, has no other adjustments to basis, and sells the equipment for $750, the partnership reports a taxable gain on only the $250 difference between the $500 adjusted cost basis ($1,000-$500 in deductions) and the $750 sale proceeds. This is the extent of its tax liability.

Recapture. Under some circumstances, a portion of any gain on sale is taxable as ordinary income instead of as a capital gain. This is called recapture. It is the government's way of taking back special tax advantages, either deductions or credits. When this meant the loss of the capital gains tax break (that is, before the 1986 tax law changes), recapture was a significant disadvantage. Now the difference between recapture and deferral is mainly a technical matter. We need to look at recapture of accelerated deductions on real estate, IDCs and tax credits.

Recapture of accelerated depreciation. Recapture applies to excess depreciation, which is accelerated depreciation that is greater than straight-line depreciation. Excess depreciation (and, therefore, recapture) occurs only if the property is disposed of prematurely.

If a partnership that has owned a building for six years has taken accelerated depreciation deductions totaling $20,000, and if their deductions would have been only $12,000 had used straight-line depreciation, they would have excess depreciation of $8,000 ($20,000-$12,000). If the building is sold for a gain of $40,000 over the adjusted cost basis, the excess depreciation of $8,000 is subject to recapture at sale and taxed as ordinary income. The remaining $32,000, is taxed as a capital gain.

Recapture of IDCs. If a partnership sells an oil well before the normal amortization period (five years) ends, the IRS will recapture any previously expensed IDCs. That is, any gain on sale will be treated as ordinary income, not capital gain, up to the amount of previous IDC deductions. If the partnership's gain is less than its IDC deductions, the IRS will be unable to recapture the entire amount. If the gain exceeds IDC deductions (and there are no other recapturable items) an amount equal to the deductions will be treated as ordinary income; the rest will be capital gain.

Recapture of tax credits. A tax credit, as you read earlier, is an amount subtracted from tax liability rather than from taxable income. Therefore, when a credit is recaptured, it is added to the tax owed, not to the taxable income.

Tax Reporting for Limited Partners

Distributive Shares of Revenues and Expenses

Partnerships allocate to each investor a percentage (distributive share) of their revenues for the year. This is not a cash distribution, simply an accounting procedure. If each investor has a 2% interest in the partnership, and the partnership's revenues are $5 million, they will be assigned a $100,000 share of that revenue. Before they receive any of that amount, the partnership will use it to meet expenses.

Similarly, they are apportioned a certain amount of the partnership's expenses. Again, this doesn't mean investors are out-of-pocket those expenses; it is a paper transaction. Actual payments to meet those expenses will be made from revenues or invested capital.

Expenses are broken down into operating, interest and depreciation expenses. These are all deductions allowed by the Internal Revenue Code. Operating and interest expenses are cash obligations that the partnership will meet with its revenues (if they are sufficient).

Depreciation, on the other hand, is not a cash obligation. It is a deduction based on the loss in value of partnership property. The partnership doesn't actually owe money for that depreciation, so the amount of revenue available for reinvestment of cash distributions is not actually reduced by that amount. Depreciation is a paper loss, not an actual expense.

Passive income and loss. If the total expenses listed on an investor's K-1 (including depreciation) exceed their share of revenues, for tax purposes that is the amount of their loss. According to the tax rules established in 1986 this is a passive loss and can be used as a deduction from passive income.

Cash flow. We noted earlier that the tax accounting procedures recorded on Schedule K-1 do not describe actual payments from the partnership to your clients or from them to the partnership. Money may wind up in their pockets, even if their distributive shares of the partnership's revenues and expenses are a net loss. Depreciation can turn a paper loss into positive cash flow.

The depreciation allowed by the Internal Revenue Code, unlike operating and interest expenses, is not tied to an actual cash outlay by the partnership. It is a "loss" only on paper. So the investor's share of revenue is reduced only by the operating and interest expenses. This can result in a positive cash flow ($100,000 revenues less $60,000 in cash expenses, for example). The partnership may distribute part or all of this cash flow to the limited partners as a return of capital.

Tax Basis

You've seen the term basis used in connection with depreciation. It has a similar use in relation to the individual investor, though here it is often called tax basis.

Wherever it appears, basis is an accounting term for the cost of an item. Basis can fluctuate according to the economic consequences of ownership.

The limited partner's tax basis represents the investor's interest in the partnership. It is the amount the partner has at risk. Although a limited partner does have limited liability, it is possible to lose the amount contributed to the partnership, plus any liability assumed on partnership debt.

Any cash contributed to a partnership is included in the limited partner's tax basis. If a limited partner signs a promissory note committing to additional contributions in the future, that also becomes part of the tax basis. During the life of the investment, basis will go up if the partner contributes further to the partnership. It will go down if the partnership returns capital to the partner or provides other economic benefits, such as tax deductions.

The tax basis is used to determine maximum allowable tax deductions. A partner can deduct losses up to, but not exceeding, the tax basis (although a partner may deduct passive losses only against passive income).

Establishing the basis. The investor's initial basis includes cash contributions, recourse debt (including promissory notes signed by the LP) and nonrecourse debt (only in real estate).

Recourse debt is debt for which the LP is liable in the event that the partnership defaults. The lender has recourse to the LP's cash and other assets. Recourse debt is always included in basis because the LP is always at risk for the entire amount. If the business goes bad, the LP may have to come up with money to repay the lender in the form of another cash contribution to the partnership.

Nonrecourse debt is secured only by the investors' assets in the partnership. In bankruptcy, therefore, the lender has no recourse to the LP's personal, nonpartnership assets. Only the GP may be assessed for repayment of the loan. In other words, the LP is not at risk for nonrecourse debt.

In all limited partnerships except real estate ventures, nonrecourse debt is not a part of the investor's tax basis. This is a substantial advantage for real estate investors, because the increased basis means a higher limit on deductions. The investor may, for example, have a basis consisting of a relatively small cash contribution and a relatively large share of nonrecourse mortgage debt. That allows the investor to write off (against passive income) a tax loss equal to cash contributions plus the share of nonrecourse debt. Yet the investor never risks having to contribute more capital to cover that debt if partnership revenues are insufficient to do so.

The LP's tax basis is not a constant number. It may change yearly according to the performance of the partnership. Anything the LP contributes increases basis (just as putting money into a bank account increases the value of the account). Anything returned from the partnership to the LP decreases basis (just as withdrawing from a bank account decreases the value of the account).

Increasing the basis. New contributions of cash or property, assumed recourse debt (plus nonrecourse debt for real estate partnerships) and undistributed shares in partnership income increase risk of loss and therefore increase tax basis. The first two items are obvious. Contributing more cash or assuming a greater share of the partnership's debt increases basis, just as the original contributions established basis.

The third item, however, may cause some confusion. Doesn't income flow from the partnership to the partner and, therefore, decrease basis? No. Remember that undistributed income is a paper gain only. The partnership keeps that income to pay its expenses; the partner may never see it. Therefore, it is not in any sense, a return of capital that the partner originally contributed to the business. Instead, it is a further contribution to the partnership, rather like a reinvested dividend. Furthermore, undistributed partnership income poses an increased risk to the limited partners, because the partnership puts the money back into the business and risks losing it. Undistributed income, therefore, increases basis.

Decreasing the basis. Basis is decreased by any distributions of cash or property, release of debt and distributions of partnership loss. Distributions of cash or property from the partnership are considered a return of the capital initially contributed. The more capital returned to the partner, the less money the investor has at risk. If the basis has decreased to zero because of earlier adjustments, any further distributions are considered taxable income.

Similarly, any release or repayment of debt also lowers the partner's risk and, therefore, tax basis. The less debt the investor is responsible for, the less money the investor can lose if that debt must be repaid.

Receiving shares of partnership losses results in tax deductions for limited partners, if they have passive income from other sources. Because basis is, among other things, the limit on an investor's tax deductions, it stands to reason that each deduction lowers the basis.

If the investor takes deductions equal to the original tax basis (with no other adjustments), the basis decreases to zero. The investor can then take no deductions until some other adjustment raises the basis above zero. It is impossible to have a negative basis. Losses beyond the basis for a given year are carried forward to be used when basis increases.

Phantom Income and the Crossover Point

The early years of a limited partnership may often show a tax loss with a positive cash flow. This happens because of noncash expenses, such as depreciation and depletion, and because of large deductions for the high interest payments typically charged in the early years of a mortgage repayment schedule.

After the partnership has been operating a number of years, these favorable conditions may be reversed. Partners may see no cash distributions, but have taxable income. The loan payments may be mostly principal, which is not deductible as an expense. The bulk of depreciation allowable may have been taken through accelerated deductions, or the depletion allowance may be minimal. The partnership may then have little or no cash flow, but may be declaring taxable income. Such taxable income not backed by a positive cash flow is referred to as phantom income. The point at which the partnership begins to show a negative cash flow with a taxable income, rather than positive cash and tax deductions, is called the crossover point.

Most partnerships are designed with a limited life span. They often plan to sell the partnership assets before reaching the crossover point.

Analysis and Evaluation of LPs

Investors considering a DPP should look at the offering documents to assess the economic soundness of the program. Cash flow is most important, because if the program cannot generate sufficient cash flow to support operations, the program will fail and the tax benefits will be recaptured. Recapture as a result of program failure and foreclosure by the lender is the worst of both worlds, because the investor loses both the original investment and the tax benefits. To gauge the possible success of this program, one should pay particularly close attention to the sponsor's track record and experience, as disclosed in the prospectus.

Promoters structure DPPs to meet various objectives. When the tax stance of the promoters is too aggressive or without economic purpose in the view of the final judge (the Internal Revenue Service), the program will be considered an abusive tax shelter. If the IRS judges the program to be abusive, it disallows deductions; assesses back taxes, interest and penalties; and, in some cases, charges the promoter with criminal intent to defraud.

Investors should try to match their current and future objectives with the stated objectives of the program. A person seeking taxable passive income should not be investing in an oil or gas exploratory drilling program.

Because DPPs are illiquid, investors must be willing and able to commit money for a long time. Investors also need substantial net worth and income to meet suitability requirements specified by general partners (the signed subscription agreement submitted to the GP includes information about the investor's net worth or net income).

"Basis" (how much at risk)

UP
1. Contribution (cash, check, etc)
2. share of recourse debt
   a) In real estate, share of non-recourse debt. (mort)
3. income retained in the partnership

DOWN
1. distribution (from DPP)
2. paying off loans
3. losses (passive of course)

Chapter Review

Questions

1. "DPP" stands for which of the following?

    ____(A) Direct Placement Program
    _o_(C) Direct Participation Program
    ____(B) Directed Profits Program
    ____(C) Direct Participation Program
    ____(D) Directors' and Principals' Program

2. Which of the following forms of business involves the greatest risk to the owner?

    _o_(A) sole proprietorship
    ____(B) general partnership
    ____(C) corporation
    ____(D) limited partnership

3. Which of the following has the greatest liability?

    _o_(A) general partner
    ____(B) limited partner
    ____(C) corporate shareholder
    ____(D) trustee

4. The person who organizes and registers a partnership is known as a(n)

    _o_(A) syndicator.
    ____(B) property manager.
    ____(C) program manager.
    ____(D) underwriter.

5. Raw land is a(n)

    ____(A) speculative investment.
    _o_(B) conservative investment.   21.13
    ____(C) balanced investment.
    ____(D) income-producing investment.

6. All of the following could be benefits of a long-term equipment-leasing direct participation program EXCEPT

    ____(A)   steady income from rental payments.
    ____(B)   operating expenses to offset revenues.
    ____(C)   cost recovery deductions.
    ____(D)   capital appreciation.

7. Which of the following would not generate IDCs in an oil drilling program?

    ____(A)   labor costs
    ____(B)   the cost of casing the well
    ____(C)   fuel costs
    ____(D)   geologist's fees

21.13

8. Which of the following generates deductions for oil and gas programs but not for real estate programs?

    ____(A)   depreciation
    ____(B)   depletion
    ____(C)   interest expense deductions
    ____(D)   operating expenses

9. In which of the following sharing arrangements will limited partners bear all of the deductible and nondeductible costs?

    I.   overriding royalty interest
    II.   disproportionate sharing arrangement
    III.   reversionary working interest
    IV.   carried interest

    ____(A)   II and IV
    ____(B)   I and III
    ____(C)   I, III and IV
    ____(D)   I, II, III and IV

10. An investor should consider which of the following to be potential sources of conflict of interest for the sponsor of an oil and gas program?

    I.   underdeveloped adjacent sponsor leases
    II.   loans by the program to the sponsor
    III. sponsor's compensation rates
    IV. commingling of program funds

    ___(A)   I
    ___(B)   III
    ___(C)   I, II and IV
    ___(D)   I, II, III and IV

Chapter Review

Answer Key

1. C.

2. A.

3. A.

4. A.

5. A.

6. D.

7. B.

8. B.

9. B.

10. D.

A

Abandon: The act of not exercising or selling an option before its expiration.

Accelerated Cost Recovery System (ACRS): An accounting method used to recover the cost of qualifying depreciable property placed in service after 1981. The ACRS system replaced the old "CLADR" system of depreciation. The ACRS system allows recovery of the entire cost of the property without adjustment for salvage value. Deductions are based on percentages prescribed in the Internal Revenue Code.

Accredited Investor: As defined in Rule 502 of Regulation D, an accredited investor is any institution or individual meeting certain minimum net worth requirements as an investor for the purchase of securities qualifying under the Regulation D registration exemption.

Accretion of Bond Discount: An accounting process whereby the initial cost of a bond purchased at a discount is increased to reflect its basis as the bond's maturity date approaches.

Accrual (Accounting): A method of reporting income when earned and expenses when incurred, as opposed to reporting income when received and expenses when paid. (See: Cash Basis Accounting)

Accrued Interest: Interest that is added to the contract price of a bond transaction. This interest has accrued since the last interest payment up to but not including the settlement date. Exceptions are income bonds, bonds in default and zero coupon bonds.

Accumulation Unit: An accounting measure (net asset value) that represents a contract owner's proportionate unit of interest in a separate account (the portfolio) during the accumulations (deposit) period. (See: Separate Account)

Acid Test Ratio: A more stringent test of liquidity than current ratio. It is calculated by adding the sum of cash, cash equivalents and ac- counts, and notes receivable and dividing that sum by the total current liabilities. (See: Current Ratio)

Acquisition Fee: The total of all fees and commis- sions paid by any party in connection with the selection or purchase of property by a program. The cost is added to the basis in the asset for the purpose of depreciation and calculating gain/loss on sale.

Active Crowd: That section of the New York Stock Exchange that trades the actively traded bonds. Syn: Free Crowd.

Actuals: The physical commodity being traded as opposed to the futures contracts on that commodity.

Adjusted Basis: Basis adjusted by additions and subtractions to reflect deductions taken with respect to the property and capital improve- ments to the property. Adjusted basis is used to compute gain or loss on the sale or other disposition of property.

Adjustment Bond: (See: Income Bond)

Administrator: Someone authorized to liquidate the estate of an intestate decedent. An Ad- ministrator is appointed by the court.

ADR: (See: American Depository Receipt)

Ad Valorem Tax: A tax based on the value of proper- ty (real property and/or personal property). Property taxes are the major source of revenues for local governing units. (See: As- sessed Value; Mill Rate)

Advance/Decline Line: A technical analysis tool rep- resenting the cumulative total of differences between advances and declines of security prices. The advance/decline line is con- sidered the best indicator of market move- ment as a whole.

Advance Refunding: A new municipal bond is is- sued, the proceeds of which will be used to refinance an existing issue prior to the exist- ing issues' maturity or call date. The proceeds of the new issue will be invested and the principal and interest earned used to pay the principal and interest of the securities being refunded. (See: Defeasance; Pre-refunding)

Agency Basis: Securities sold through normal broker transactions, executed through a national dealer market. The broker is acting for the account of others.

Agency Transaction: The broker-dealer is acting for the accounts of others by buying or selling securities on behalf of customers. Securities sold through normal broker transactions, executed through a national dealer market.

Agency Issues: Debt securities issued by authorized agencies of the federal government. These issues are backed by the issuing agency itself, not the full faith and credit of the U.S. Government (except GNMA and Federal Import Export Bank).

Agent: An individual acting for the account of others. Syn: Broker.

Allied Member: A general partner of an NYSE member firm who is not an NYSE member, an owner of 5% or more of the outstanding voting stock of an NYSE member corporation or a principal executive director or officer of a member corporation. Allied members don't own seats on the New York Stock Exchange.

All-or-None Offering: A brokerage firm agrees to devote its best efforts to sell an offering, but if a portion of the issue cannot be sold, then the entire offering is canceled.

All-or-None Order (AON): An order in which the floor broker is instructed to execute an entire order in one transaction (no partial executions).

Allowances: (See: Quality Allowances)

Alternative Minimum Tax (AMT): An alternate tax computation which includes certain "tax preference" items that are added back into adjusted gross income for determining the AMT. The alternative minimum tax is paid if it is higher than the regular tax liability for the year. The tax is a flat 20%. The regular tax and the amount by which the AMT exceeds the regular tax is paid.

AMBAC: The AMBAC Indemnity Corporation, which offers insurance on the timely payment of interest and principal obligations of municipal securities. Bonds insured by AMBAC usually receive a AAA rating from the rating services.

American Depository Receipt (ADR): A negotiable receipt for a given number of shares of stock in a foreign corporation. An ADR is bought and sold in the American securities markets just as stock is traded.

Amortization: Paying off the debt (principal) over a period of time in periodic installments. Amortization is also defined as the ratable deduction of certain capitalized expenditures over a specified period of time.

Amortization of Bond Premium: An accounting process whereby the initial price of a bond purchased at a premium is decreased to reflect the basis of the bond as it approaches maturity.

Annuity: A contract between an insurance company and an individual. It generally guarantees lifetime income to the person on whose life the contract is based in return for either a lump sum or a periodic payment to the insurance company. (See: Immediate Annuity; Deferred Annuity; Fixed Annuity; Variable Annuity)

Annuity Unit: The accounting measure used to determine the amount of each payment to an annuitant during payout of the annuity.

AON: (See: All-or-None Order)

Appraisal: A written opinion of the value of property prepared by a qualified independent appraiser of the types of property which are the subject of the appraisal.

Appreciation: The increase in value of an asset.

Arbitrage: Effecting sales and purchases simultaneously in the same or related securities to take advantage of a market inefficiency; two assets improperly priced relative to one another. (See: Market Arbitrage; Security Arbitrage)

Arbitrager: One who engages in arbitrage.

Assessed Value: The value of property as appraised by a taxing authority for the purpose of levying taxes. Assessed value may equal market value or a stipulated percentage thereof.

Assessments: Additional amounts of capital which a participant may be called upon to furnish beyond the subscription amount. Assessments may be mandatory or optional. Assessments are limited to the original subscription amount and must be called within 12 months.

Asset: Anything that an individual or a corporation owns.

Assignment: 1) A document accompanying or part of a stock certificate signed by the person named on the certificate for the purpose of transferring the certificate title to another person's name. 2) The act of identifying and notifying an account holder that an option held short in that account has been exercised by the option owner. (See: Stock Power)

Assignee: A person who has acquired a beneficial interest in one or more units from a third party but who is neither a substituted limited partner nor an assignee of record.

Associated Person (AP): A person associated with a broker/dealer in the capacity of sales person, manager, director, officer, partner, etc. An individual who performs strictly clerical or administrative functions is not considered an associated person. Syn: Broker; Registered Representative.

Assumed Interest Rate (AIR): A base for projecting payments from a variable annuity, the AIR is not a guarantee. Assumed interest rates offered by companies vary. Naturally, the higher the assumption, the higher the initial benefit and vice versa. The importance of the assumed interest rate as a base for projection rests with the fact that, once selected, the account must earn that rate to maintain the initial benefit level.

At-the-Close: A customer's order that specifies it is to be executed at the close of the market or of trading in that security. If the order is not executed at the close, it is canceled. The order does not have to be executed at the closing price. (See: At-the-Open)

At-the-Money: An option in which the underlying stock is trading precisely at the exercise price of that option. (See: In-the-Money)

At-the-Open: A customer's order that specifies it is to be executed at the opening of the market or of trading in that security. If the order is not executed at the opening, it is canceled. The order does not have to be executed at the opening price. (See: At-the-Close)

Auction Market: A market in which buyers enter competitive bids and sellers enter competitive offers simultaneously. The New York Stock Exchange is an auction market. Syn: Double Auction Market.

Audited Financial Statements: Financial statements of a program, corporation or issuer including the profit and loss statement, cash flow and source and application of revenues statement and balance sheet which have been audited by an independent certified public accountant.

Authorizing Resolution: The document enabling a municipality or state government to issue municipal securities. The resolution provides for establishment of a revenue fund in which receipts or income is deposited.

Authorized Stock: The number of shares of stock that a corporation is permitted to issue. This number is stipulated in the corporation's state-approved charter and may be changed by a vote of the corporation's shareholders.

B

Backing Away: The failure of an OTC market maker to honor a firm bid and asked price.

Backwardation: (See: Inverted Market)

Balance Sheet: A report of a company's financial condition at a specific time.

Balanced Fund: A type of mutual fund whose stated investment policy is to have at all times some portion of its investment assets in bonds and preferred stocks as well as common stock. Therefore, there is a balance between the two classes, equity and debt. (See: Mutual Funds)

Balloon Maturity: A maturity schedule for an issue of bonds wherein a large number of the bonds come due at a prescribed time (normally at the final maturity date). This kind of maturity schedule is a type of serial maturity. (See: Maturity Date)

BAN: Bond Anticipation Notes, short-term debt instruments issued by a municipality to be paid from proceeds of long-term debt issued.

Bank Guarantee Letter: The document supplied by an approved bank in which the bank certifies that a put writer has sufficient funds on deposit at the bank to equal the aggregate exercise price of the put.

Banker's Acceptance: A money-market instrument used to finance international and domestic trade. A banker's acceptance is a check drawn on a bank by an importer or exporter of goods and represents the bank's conditional promise to pay the face amount of the note at maturity (normally less than three months).

Base Grade: The standard grade of a commodity on which a futures contract is based.

Basis: 1) The cost of property. 2) The difference between the spot or cash price of a commodity and a futures contract price of the same commodity. Basis is usually computed between the spot and the nearby futures contract.

Basis Point: 1/100 of 1% of yield (e.g., 1/2% = 50 basis points).

Basis Quote: The price of a security quoted in terms of the yield the purchaser can expect to receive.

Bearer Bond: (See: Coupon Bond)

Bear Market: A market in which prices of securities are falling or are expected to fall.

Best-Efforts Offering: An offering in which an investment banker agrees to distribute as much of the offering as possible and any unsold securities are retained by the issuer.

Beta Coefficient: A means of measuring the volatility of a security or portfolio of securities in comparison with the market as a whole. A beta of 1 indicates that the security's price will move with the market. A beta higher than one indicates that the security's price will be more volatile than the market; a beta of less than one that it will be less volatile than the market as a whole.

Bid: An indication by an investor, trader or dealer of a willingness to buy a security or a commodity. Syn: Quote; Quotation. (See: Offer)

Bid Form: The form submitted by underwriters in a competitive bid on a new issue of municipal securities. The underwriter states the interest rate, price bid and the net interest cost to the issuer.

Block Trade: A trade of 10,000 or more shares.

Blue Chip Stock: The issues of normally strong, well-established companies that have demonstrated their ability to pay dividends in good times and bad times.

The Blue List: A daily trade publication for the secondary market that lists the current municipal bond offerings of banks and brokers nationwide.

Blue Sky: To qualify a securities offering in a particular state.

Blue Sky Laws: The nickname for state regulations governing the securities industry.

Board of Directors: A unit that governs the NYSE, composed of 20 members who are elected for a term of two years by the general membership of the NYSE. Also, individuals elected by shareholders to establish corporate management policies. A board of directors decides, among other items, if and when dividends will be paid to stockholders.

Board of Governors (NASD): The body that governs the NASD, composed of 27 members elected by both the general membership and board itself.

Board Order: A customer's order that becomes a market order as soon as the market touches or breaks through the order price. Board orders to buy are placed below the current market. Board orders to sell are placed above the current market. Syn: Market-If-Touched Order (MIT).

Bona Fide Quote: A quote from a dealer in municipal securities who is willing to execute a trade under the terms and conditions stated at the time of the quote. (See: Firm Quote)

Bond: An evidence of debt issued by corporations, municipalities and the Federal government.

Bond Anticipation Note: (See: BAN)

Bond Attorney: The attorney(s) retained by an municipal issuer to give opinion concerning the legality of a municipal issue. Syn: Bond Counsel. (See: Legal Opinion of Counsel)

Bond Buyer Index: Indexes published by The Bond Buyer of yield levels of municipal bonds. The indexes are indicators of yields which would be offered on AA and A General Obligation (GO) bonds with 20-year maturities and Revenue bonds with 30-year maturities.

Bond Fund: A type of mutual fund whose investment policy is to provide stable income with a minimum of capital risks. It invests in both bonds and preferred stock. (See: Mutual Fund)

Bond Quotes: Corporate bonds are quoted on a percentage of par with increments of 1/8, where a quote of 99 1/8 represents 99.125 percent of par ($1,000), or $991.25. Bonds may also be quoted on a yield to maturity basis.

Bond Ratio: The percentage of a company's invested capital that is provided by long-term debt financing. It is found by dividing the face value of the outstanding bonds by the invested capital. Syn: Debt Ratio.

Bond Swap: A technique used by investors in municipal bonds that involves the sale of a bond or bonds at a loss and the simultaneous purchase of entirely different bonds in a like amount, with comparable coupons or maturities.

Book-Entry: Securities sold without delivery of a certificate. Evidence of ownership is maintained on records kept by a central agency, such as the Treasury on the sale of Treasury bills. Transfer of ownership is recorded by entering the change on the books.

Book Value per Share: A measure of the net worth of each share of common stock. It is calculated by subtracting the intangible assets and preferred stock from total net worth and then dividing by the number of shares of common outstanding. Syn: Net Tangible Assets per Common Share.

Break-Even Point: The market price the stock must reach for the option buyer to avoid a loss if he or she exercises. For a call, it is the strike price plus the premium paid. For a put, it is the strike price minus the premium paid.

Break-Even Point- Straddles: There are two break-even points on straddles that are calculated by adding and subtracting the total premium from the exercise price on the straddle.

Break-Even Long Hedges: Break even occurs when the market price of the stock equals the purchase price of the stock plus the premium paid for the put.

Break-Even Short Hedges: Break even is the short sales price minus the premium paid to buy the call.

Break-Even Call Spreads: Break even can be calculated by adding the net premium to the lower strike price.

Break-Even Put Spreads: Break even can be calculated by subtracting the net premium from the higher strike price.

Breakout: The movement of a security's price through an established support or resistance level.

Breakpoints: The schedule of discounts offered by a mutual fund for lump sum or cumulative investments.

Breakpoint Sale: The sale of mutual fund shares in quantities just below the level at which the purchaser would qualify for reduced sales charges. Breakpoint sales are a violation of the NASD Rules of Fair Practice.

Broad Tape: The news wires from which price and background information on securities and commodities markets can be gathered.

Broker: 1) An individual or firm that charges a fee or commission for executing buy and sell orders submitted by another individual or firm. 2) The role of a broker firm when it acts as an agent for a customer and charges the customer a commission for its services. Syn: Agent.

Broker's Broker: A specialist handling orders for a commission house broker. A floor broker on an exchange or a broker-dealer in the OTC market acting on behalf of (as an agent for) another broker in executing a trade. (See: Correspondent Broker)

Broker's Fidelity Bond: Bonds required by NYSE Rule 319 for all employees, officers and partners of member firms to protect clients against acts of misplacement, fraudulent trading and check forgery.

Broker's Loans: Money loans made to brokerage firms by commercial banks and other lending institutions for financing margin account debit balances.

Bucketing: Accepting customers' orders and using firm or other customers' positions or orders to offset them without executing them immediately through an exchange.

Bullion: Ingots or bars of gold assayed at .995 fine or higher.

Bull Market: A market in which prices of securities are moving or are expected to move higher.

Buyer's Option: A settlement contract that calls for delivery and payment according to the number of days specified by the buyer. (See: Seller's Option)

Buy-In: The procedure that occurs when the seller of a security fails to complete a contract to sell according to its terms. The buyer can close the contract by buying the securities in the open market and charging them to the account of the seller who failed to complete the contract.

Buying a Hedge: The purchase of futures options as a means of protecting against an increase in commodities prices in the future. (See: Hedge- Long)

Buying Power: The dollar amount of securities a client can purchase using only the SMA balance in an account and without depositing additional equity.

C

Calendar Spread: Spreads between options with the same exercise price but different expiration dates. Syn: Horizontal Spread.

Call: An option contract giving the owner the right to buy stock at a stated price within a specified period of time.

Callable Bond: A type of bond issued with a provision allowing the issuer to redeem the bond prior to maturity at a predetermined price. (See: Call Price)

Callable Preferred Stock: A type of preferred stock that carries the provision that the corporation retains the right to call in the stock at a certain price and retire it. (See: Preferred Stock; Call Price)

Call Buyer: Investor who pays a premium for an option contract and receives the right to buy, during a specified time, the underlying security at the specified price.

Call Date: The date after which the issuer of a bond has the option to redeem the issue at par or at par plus a premium.

Call Loan: A collateralized loan of a brokerage firm having no maturity date which may be called (terminated) at any time and has a fluctuating interest rate recomputed daily. Generally, the loan is payable on demand the day after the loan has been contracted. If not called, the loan is automatically renewed for another day. (See: Broker's Loans; Loans for Set Amounts)

Call Loan Rate: The rate of interest a brokerage firm charges its margin account clients on their debit balances.

Call Price: The price paid (usually a premium over the par value of the issue) for preferred stock or bonds redeemed prior to maturity of the issue.

Call Protection: A provision limiting the right to call an issue. Normally stated in terms of time (five years, ten years and so on) from original issue before the issuer may exercise the call provision. (See: Call Provision)

Call Provision: The written agreement between an issuing corporation and its bondholders or preferred stockholders, giving the corporation the option to redeem its senior securities at a specified price before maturity and under specified conditions.

Call Spread: When an investor buys a call on a particular security and writes a call with a different expiration date, different exercise price or both, on the same security.

Call Writer: Investor who receives a premium and takes on, for a specified time, the obligation to sell the underlying security at the specified price, at the call buyer's discretion.

Cancel Former Order: An instruction by a customer to cancel a previously entered order (CFO).

Capital: Accumulated money or goods used to produce income.

Capital Appreciation: A rise in the market prices of assets owned.

Capital Contribution: The gross amount of investment in a program by a participant, or all participants, not including any units purchased by the sponsors.

Capital Gain: The gain (selling price minus cost basis) on an asset.

Capitalize: An accounting procedure whereby the taxpayer records an expenditure as a capital asset on its books instead of charging it to expenses for the year.

Capital Market: That segment of the securities market that deals in instruments with more than one year to maturity, that is, long-term debt and equity securities.

Capital Stock: The total stated value or par value of all outstanding preferred stock and common stock of a corporation.

Capital Structure: The composition of long-term funds (equity and debt) a company has as a source for financing. (See: Invested Capital)

Capital Surplus: Money a corporation receives in excess of the stated value of the stock at the time of sale. Syn: Paid-In Surplus. (See: Par Value)

Capitalization: The sum of a company's long-term debt, capital stock and all surpluses. Syn: Invested Capital. (See: Capital Structure)

Capitalization Ratios: Ratios revealing the percentage of bonds, preferred stock or common stock to total capitalization.

Carrying Broker: (See: Clearing Broker)

Carrying Charge: All costs associated with holding or storing a commodity, including interest, insurance, rents, etc.

Carrying Charge Market: The situation that exists when the difference in price between delivery months of a commodity in the futures markets covers all interest, insurance and storage costs.

Carryover: Any part of the supply of a commodity (particularly crop production) carried over from one year to the next.

Cash Account: An account in which a client pays in full for securities purchased.

Cash Assets Ratio: The most stringent test of liquidity. It is calculated by adding the sum of cash and cash equivalents and dividing that sum by the total current liabilities.

Cash Basis Accounting: An accounting method whereby revenues and expenses are accounted for when received or paid, rather than earned or incurred. (See: Accrual Accounting)

Cash Commodity: The actual, physical good being traded rather than a futures contract on that good.

Cash Flow: Money received by a business minus money paid out. Cash flow is also equal to net income plus depreciation/depletion.

Cash Market: Transactions between buyers and sellers of commodities that entail immediate delivery of and payment for a physical com-

modity. Syn: Cash and Carry Market. (See: Futures Market)

Cash Price: The market price for goods to be delivered and paid for immediately.

Cash Securities Equivalents: Treasury bills, certificates of deposit, money-market funds (and so on) which are extremely liquid and readily converted into cash.

Cash Transaction: A securities settlement contract that calls for delivery and payment on the date of the trade, due by 2:30 pm EST (or within 30 minutes of the trade if made after 2 pm) in New York.

Cashiering Department: The department within a brokerage firm that receives and delivers securities and money to and from other firms and clients of the firm. Syn: Security Cage.

Casing: Heavy steel pipe cemented to the wall of the hole drilled to reinforce the well when it reaches a certain depth.

Catastrophe Call: Redemption of a bond due to disaster, e.g, a power plant built with proceeds from an issue burns to the ground.

CBOE: (See: Chicago Board Options Exchange)

CCC: (See: Commodity Credit Corporation)

CD: (See: Negotiable Certificate of Deposit)

CEA: (See: Commodity Exchange Authority)

Certificate of Deposit: (See: Negotiable Certificate of Deposit)

CFTC: (See: Commodity Futures Trading Commission)

CFO: (See: Cancel Former Order)

Change: The change from the previous day's settlement price.

Chartist: A securities analyst who uses charts and graphs of the past price movements of a security to predict its future movements. (See: Technical Analyst)

Chicago Board Options Exchange (CBOE): The first national securities exchange for the trading of listed options.

Christmas Tree: The assembly of valves, gauges and pipes at the well head of an oil or gas well.

Churning: Excessive trading in a customer's account. The term suggests that the registered representative ignores the objectives and interests of clients and seeks only to increase commissions. Syn: Over-Trading.

Class: All options of the same type (e.g., all calls or all puts) on the same underlying security.

Clearing Broker: A broker-dealer that clears its own trades, as well as trades of Introducing brokers. A clearing broker-dealer can hold customers' securities and cash.

Clearing Corporation: The Clearing Corporation of the Chicago Board of Trade, through which transactions in futures and option contracts are settled, guaranteed, offset and filled. The Clearing Corporation positions itself between the buyer and the seller in a contract, becoming the buyer for all sellers and the seller for all buyers. It settles all transactions at the end of each business day and is the guarantor of all contracts.

Clearinghouse: 1) An agency of a futures exchange, through which transactions in futures and option contracts are settled, guaranteed, offset and filled. The clearinghouse may be an independent corporation or exchange-owned. 2) A member firm of the Clearing Corporation. (See: Clearing Corporation)

Close: The price of the last transaction for a particular security on a particular day. The midprice of a closing trading range.

Closed-End Lien: A provision of a bond issue preventing the issuer from issuing additional bonds having an equal claim to the same collateral or revenues.

Closed-End Management Company: A management company that sells a fixed number of shares in the company. The market price of the shares is determined by supply and demand and not by their net asset value. The shares may be traded on an exchange or OTC market.

Closing Purchase Transaction: Closing out an opening sale by buying options of the same series.

Closing Range: The relatively narrow range of prices at which transactions took place in the closing minutes of the trading day.

Closing Sale Transaction: The transaction that takes place when an investor who owns an option closes out the position in that option by selling it.

Code of Arbitration: The Code of Arbitration exists to provide a method of handling securities-related disputes or clearing controversies between members, public customers, clearing corporations or clearing banks. Any claim, dispute or controversy subject to arbitration is required to be submitted to arbitration.

Code of Procedure: The Code of Procedure is the NASD's procedure for handling trade practice complaints. The NASD District Business Conduct Committee (DBCC) is the first body to hear and judge complaints. Appeals and review of DBCC decisions are handled by the NASD Board of Governors.

Collateral Trust Bond: This form of debt is backed by stocks and/or bonds of another issuer. The collateral is held by a trustee for safekeeping. Syn: Collateral Trust Certificate.

Collection Ratio: A rough measure of the length of time accounts receivable have been outstanding. It is calculated by multiplying the receivables times 360 and dividing that amount by the net sales. For municipal bonds, the collection ratio is calculated by dividing taxes collected by taxes assessed.

Combination: An option position that represents a put and a call on the same stock in which the investor has neither purchased a straddle nor sold a straddle.

Combined Account: A customer account who has cash, long and short margin positions in different securities.

Combined Distribution: An offering in which a portion of the securities are newly issued securities and a portion are previously issued securities. It is a combination of a primary distribution and a secondary distribution. Also used to describe the simultaneous offering of different classes of securities (e.g., common stocks, bonds). Syn: Split Offering.

Commercial Bank: An institution that accepts deposits and makes business loans.

Commercial Paper: An unsecured short-term promissory note issued by well-known businesses chiefly for financing accounts receivable. It is usually issued at a discount reflecting prevailing market interest rates. Maturities range up to 270 days.

Commingling: Failure to clearly identify and segregate securities carried for the account of any customer which have been fully paid or which are excess margin securities.

Commission Broker: A member eligible to execute orders for customers of his member firm on the floor of the exchange. Syn: Floor Broker.

Commission House: A registered member firm of a given commodity exchange that handles customer accounts and transactions on that exchange. Syn: Wire House; Brokerage House; Futures Commission Merchant.

Commodity: Any bulk good traded on an exchange or in the cash (spot) market such as metals, grains, meats, etc.

Commodity Credit Corporation: A government-owned and sponsored corporation whose purpose is to aid American agriculture through price support programs, controlling supplies and controlling foreign sales.

Commodity Exchange Authority (CEA): The predecessor of the Commodities Futures Trading Commission established by the U.S. Department of Agriculture to administer the Commodities Exchange Act of 1936.

Commodity Futures Trading Commission (CFTC): The federal regulatory agency established by the Commodity Futures Trading Commission Act of 1974 to administer the Commodity Exchange Act. The five CFTC Commissioners are appointed by the President (subject to Senate approval).

Commodity Pool Operator (CPO): An individual or organization involved in the solicitation of funds for the purpose of pooling them to invest in commodities futures contracts.

Commodity Trading Advisor (CTA): An individual or organization that makes recommendations and issues reports on commodities futures or options trading for a fee.

Common Stock: An equity security that represents ownership in a corporation. This is the first security a corporation issues to raise capital. (See: Equity)

Competitive Bidding: The submission of sealed bids by rival underwriting syndicates that want to be awarded the privilege of underwriting the issue of securities. Competitive bidding normally is used to determine the underwriters for issues of general obligation municipal bonds. Required by law in most states for general obligation bonds over $100,000.

Concession: The allowance (profit) that an underwriter allows a broker-dealer who is not a syndicate member. The broker-dealer will purchase the security at public price minus the concession. Syn: Reallowance.

Confidence Theory: A technical theory that analyzes the confidence of investors by comparing the yields on high-grade bonds to the yields on lower-rated bonds.

Confirmation: A bill or comparison of trade that is sent or given to a customer on or before the settlement date.

Congestion: A narrow price range within which a commodity's price trades for an extended period of time.

Consolidation: The narrowing of the trading range for a commodity or a security. Technical analysts consider consolidation an indication that a strong price move is imminent.

Constant Dollar Plan: An investment technique where a constant sum of money is invested regardless of the price fluctuation in a security. The objective is to average out the prices of securities purchased.

Constant Ratio Plan: A method of investment in which an investor tries to maintain a predetermined ratio of debt to equity and makes purchases and sales to maintain the desired ratio.

Contango: (See: Normal Market)

Contra Broker: The broker on the other side of a transaction.

Contract: One unit of trading in futures.

Contract Grade: The exchange-authorized grade of a commodity that can be delivered against a contract.

Contractionary Policy: A fiscal policy that has as its end the decrease (contraction) of the money supply.

Contract Market: A Commodity Futures Trading Commission-designated exchange on which a specified commodity can be traded.

Contract Month: The designated month in which a particular futures contract may be satisfied by making delivery (the contract seller) or taking delivery (the contract buyer).

Contractual Plan: For mutual funds, a type of accumulation plan in which the investor makes a firm commitment to invest a specific amount of money in the fund during a specific time. Syn: Penalty Plan; Prepaid Charge Plan. (See: Mutual Fund; Front-end Load; Spread-Load Option)

Contract Unit: The unit of delivery specified in a futures contract.

Control Persons: A director, officer or other affiliate of an issuer, or a stockholder who owns at least 10% of any class of a company's outstanding securities.

Control Securities: Securities owned by a director, officer or other affiliate of the issuer, or by a stockholder who owns at least 10% of any class of a company's outstanding securities. Who owns the securities is the factor that determines that specific securities are control securities, not the securities themselves. Public offerings of control securities must comply with SEC Rule 144.

Conversion: The conversion of income taxable at ordinary income rates into gain taxable at long term gains rates.

Conversion Parity: The state of having two securities (one of which can be converted into the other) of equal dollar value.

Conversion Price: The amount of par value exchangeable for one share of common stock. This term really refers to the stock price and means the dollar amount of the bond's (or preferred stock's) par value that is exchangeable for one share of common stock.

Conversion Ratio: The number of shares per $1,000 debenture (or preferred stock) that the holder would receive if the debenture were converted into shares of common stock. Syn: Conversion Rate. (See: Debentures)

Conversion Value: The total market value of common stock into which a debenture (or preferred stock) is convertible. (See: Convertible Bond; Debenture)

Convertible Bond: A type of debt security (usually in the form of a debenture) that can be converted (exchanged) into equity securities of the issuing corporation, that is, common and preferred stock. (See: Debenture)

Convertible Preferred Stock: A type of preferred stock that offers the holder the privilege of exchanging (converting) the preferred stock into common stock at specified prices or rates. Dividends may be cumulative or noncumulative. (See: Preferred Stock; Cumulative Preferred Stock; Noncumulative Preferred Stock)

Cooling-Off Period: The period (minimum 20 days) between the filing date of a registration statement and the effective date of the registration. In practice, this period varies in length.

Co-partnership Account: An account in which the individual members of the partnership are empowered to act on behalf of the partnership as a whole.

Corporation: A form of business organization in which the total worth of the organization is divided into shares of stock, each share representing a unit of ownership. By law, it has certain rights and responsibilities. It is characterized by a continuous life span and the limited liability of the owners.

Correspondent Broker-Dealer: A broker-dealer who performs services (transactions) for another broker-dealer in a market or locale in which the first broker-dealer has no office.

Cost Basis: Money on which taxes have been paid. A return of cost basis is a return of capital and not subject to tax.

Cost of Carry: All out of pocket costs incurred by an investor while holding an open position in a security, including margin costs, interest costs, opportunity costs, etc.

Cost-Push: A type of inflation caused by higher production costs (e.g., wages).

Coterminous: Municipal entities that share the same boundaries (e.g., school district and fire district) which can issue debt separately. (See: Overlapping Debt)

Country Basis: The local cash (or spot) market price in comparison to the nearby futures price at the Chicago Board of Trade.

Coupon Bond: A bond without the name of the owner printed on its face and with coupons representing semiannual interest payments attached. Coupons are submitted to the trustee by the holder to receive the interest payments. Syn: Bearer Bond.

Coupon Yield Rate: The interest rate stated on the face of a bond representing the amount of interest paid by the issuer on the principal of the issue. Syn: Nominal Yield; Stated Yield.

Cover: Futures purchased to offset a short position, or being long actuals when shorting futures.

Coverage: For revenue bonds, a measure of safety for payment of principal and interest. Coverage is the multiple of earnings which exceed debt service plus operating and maintenance expenses payable for a time period.

Covenants: Promises or restrictions of an issuer made part of a trust indenture (bond contract). Examples include: rate covenants which establish a minimum revenue coverage for a bond; insurance covenants which require insurance on a project; maintenance covenants requiring maintenance on a facility constructed by the proceeds of a bond issue.

Covered Call Writer: An investor who writes a call and owns some other asset that guarantees ability to perform if the call is exercised.

Covered Put Writer: An investor who writes a put and owns some other asset that guarantees the ability to perform if the put is exercised.

CPI: (See: Consumer Price Index)

CPO: (See: Commodity Pool Operator)

Cracking Spread: A spread established with long crude oil futures and short heating oil or gasoline futures (cracking is the term used to describe the process by which crude oil is turned into distillates).

Credit Agreement: An agreement signed in conjunction with a margin agreement, outlining the conditions of the credit arrangement between broker and client.

Credit Balance (CR): The amount of money remaining in a client's account after all commitments have been paid in full.

Credit Risk: This risk, like financial risk, involves the safety of one's principal. The term is generally associated with bonds, and the risk is that the issuer will default in the payment of either principal or interest. Syn: Default Risk.

Cross Hedge: Hedging a futures contract risk with a different but related commodity.

Cross Trade: A manipulative practice where customers' buy and sell orders are offset against each other off the floor of the exchange and the resultant transaction is not recorded with the exchange.

Crush Spread: A spread established with long soybean futures and short soybean oil and meal futures (crushing is the term used to describe the process by which soybeans are turned into oil and meal).

CTA: (See: Commodity Trading Advisor)

Cum Rights: Stock trading with rights. (See: Ex-Rights)

Cumulative Preferred Stock: A type of preferred stock that offers the holder any unpaid dividends in arrears. These dividends accumulate and must be paid to the holder of cumulative preferred stock before any dividends can be paid to the common stockholders. (See: Preferred Stock)

Cumulative Voting Rights: A voting procedure that permits shareholders to cast all of their votes for any one director, or to cast their total number of votes in any proportion they choose.

Current Assets: Assets that are in the form of cash or are expected to be converted into cash within the next 12 months in the normal course of business.

Current Liabilities: A corporation's debt obligations due for payment within the next 12 months.

Current Market Value: The current market price of the securities in an account, based on the closing prices on the previous business day.

Current Ratio: A measure of liquidity that is calculated by dividing the total current assets by the total current liabilities. Syn: Working Capital Ratio.

Current Yield: The annual dollar return on a security (interest or dividends) divided by the current market price of the security (bonds or stock).

Custodian: The institution or person responsible for protecting the property of another. Mutual funds have custodians responsible for safeguarding certificates and performing clerical duties. (See: Mutual Fund)

Custodian of a Minor: One who manages a gift of securities to a minor under the Uniform Gifts to Minors Act. Also, someone who takes charge of an incompetent's affairs.

Customer Statement: A statement of a customer's account showing positions and entries. The SEC requires that a customer statement be sent quarterly, but customers generally receive them monthly.

Cycle: A particular set of months of maturities for listed options. For instance, January, April, July and October make up a cycle.

D

Dated Date: The date on which interest on a bond issue begins to accrue.

Day Order: An order that is canceled if it is not executed on the day it is entered.

Day Trader: A trader in securities or commodities who opens all positions after the opening of the market and offsets or closes out all positions before the close of the market the same day.

Dealer: The role of a brokerage firm when it acts as a principal in a particular trade. A firm is acting as a dealer when it buys or sells a security for its own account and at its own risk and then charges the customer a markup or markdown. Syn: Principal.

Debenture: A debt obligation backed by the general credit of the issuing corporation. (See: Convertible Bond)

Debit Balance (DR): The amount of money a client owes a brokerage firm.

Debt to Equity Ratio: The ratio of total debt to total stockholder's equity.

Debt Ratio: The percent debt in relation to total capitalization of a corporation. Syn: Bond Ratio. (See: Capitalization Ratio)

Debt Security: An evidence of debt issued by corporations, municipalities and the Federal government.

Debt Service: Annual amount needed to pay interest and principal (or the scheduled sinking fund contribution) on an outstanding debt.

Declaration Date: This is the date on which the company declares an upcoming dividend.

Deduction: Items or expenditures subtracted from gross income and adjusted gross income to arrive at taxable income, thus reducing the amount of income which is subject to tax.

Deed of Trust: (See: Trust Indenture)

Default: 1) Failure to pay interest and/or principal promptly when due. 2) Failure to perform on a futures contract as required by an exchange.

Default Risk: (See: Credit Risk)

Defeasance: A corporation or municipality removes debt from its balance sheet by issuing a new debt issue or creating a trust to be funded by assets, typically U.S. Government securities that will generate enough cash flow to provide for payment of interest and principal on the debt issue removed from the balance sheet (refunded). (See: Advance Refunding; Prerefunding)

Defensive Industry: An industry that is relatively unaffected by business cycles, such as the food industry or the utility industry.

Defensive Issue: Issues of established companies in industries relatively unaffected by business cycles. Syn: Defensive Stock.

Deferred Annuity: An annuity contract that guarantees payment of income, installment payments or a lump-sum payment to be made at an agreed upon future time. (See: Annuity)

Deficiency Letter: A list of additions or corrections that must be made to a registration statement before the SEC will release an offering to the public. The SEC sends a deficiency letter to the issuing corporation. Syn: Bed-Bug Letter.

Deflation: A persistent fall in the general level of prices.

Delivery: The change in ownership or control of the actual commodity in exchange for cash in settlement of a futures contract.

Delivery Point: The location or facility (storage, shipping, etc.) to which a commodity must be delivered in order to fulfill a commodities contract.

Delivery Month: The month specified for delivery in a futures contract.

Delivery vs. Payment (DVP): A type of payment for securities: a customer delivers the certificates to a bank designated by the customer, and the bank makes the payment on delivery of the certificates. Institutional customers most frequently use this method of payment.

Delta: Delta is a term used to describe the responsiveness of option premiums to a change in the price of the underlying asset. Deep in-the-money options have a delta near one; these show the biggest response to futures price changes. Deep out-of-the-money options have very low deltas.

Demand: The consumers' desire and willingness to pay for a good or service.

Demand-Pull: A type of inflation resulting from excessive money supply increasing the demand for goods (i.e., too much money, too few goods).

Depletion: An allowance deducted as an expense to enable the recovery of the cost of a natural resource (coal, oil, gas, quarries, etc.). Two methods of depletion are allowed: cost depletion and percentage depletion.

Depreciation: An expense allowed for the recovery of the cost of qualifying property. With currency exchange rates, a decrease in the value of a particular currency relative to other currencies. (See: ACRS)

Depreciation Expense: A noncash expense charged against earnings to recover the cost of an asset over its useful life. Depreciation (recovery) is a bookkeeping entry which does not require the outlay of cash.

Designated Order: Orders of a specified minimum size to be executed (and commissions paid to) by a dealer designated by a client. (Generally in reference to municipal bond transactions). The size of the order establishes its priority for subscription to an issue.

Development Well: A well drilled within an area of proven oil and/or gas reserves.

Diagonal Spread: The simultaneous purchase and sale of options of the same class but with different exercise prices and different expiration dates.

Dilution: A reduction in earnings per share of common stock. Dilution occurs through the issuance of additional shares of common stock and conversion of convertible securities.

Direct Debt: The percentage of an issuer's debt evidenced by outstanding bonds and notes.

Direct Participation Program (DPP): A program which provides for flow-through tax consequences regardless of the structure of the legal entity or vehicle for distribution including, but not limited to, oil and gas programs, real estate programs, agricultural programs, cattle programs, condominium securities, Subchapter S corporate offerings and all other programs of a similar nature, regardless of the industry represented by the program or any combination thereof.

Discount Bond: A bond selling below par. (See: Premium).

Discount Rate: The interest rate charged to member banks that borrow from the nine Federal Reserve Banks.

Discretionary Account: An account in which the principal (beneficial owner) has given a registered rep authority to make transactions in the account at the registered rep's discretion. The registered rep may use discretion about price (buy or sell), time, and choice of securities (bought or sold). Orders must be marked DE (discretion exercised) or DNE (discretion not exercised).

Disposable Income (DI): The sum that people divide between spending and personal saving.

Disproportionate Sharing Arrangement: In a disproportionate sharing arrangement, the sponsor will share costs of the program, but will receive a disproportionately higher percentage of revenues. An arrangement would have the sponsor paying 10% of program costs and receiving 25% of revenues. The sponsor shares in dry hole costs and investors share in both deductible and non-deductible costs.

Distant Contract: Of two or more futures contracts, the contract with the longest time remaining to expiration.

Diversified Management Company: A management company that has at least 75% of its total assets in cash, receivables or securities invested, no more than 5% of the total assets are invested in the voting securities of any company, and no single investment represents ownership of more than 10% of the outstanding voting securities of any one company.

Dividend: A distribution of the earnings of a corporation. Dividends may be in the form of cash, stock or property (securities owned by a corporation). The board of directors must declare a dividend.

Divided Account: (See: Western Account)

Dividend Payout Ratio: A ratio used to analyze a company's policy of paying cash dividends, calculated by dividing the dividends paid on common stock by the net income available for common stockholders.

Dividend Yield: The annual percentage of return that an investor receives on either common or preferred stock. The yield is based on the amount of the annual dividend divided by the market price (at the time of purchase) of the stock. (See: Dividend; Current Yield)

DJIA: (See: Dow Jones Industrial Average)

DK: An acronym for "don't know," indicating a lack of information about a transaction or a record of transaction between broker-dealers.

DNR: (See: Do Not Reduce)

Dollar Bonds: A term used to describe municipal bonds that are quoted and traded on a basis of dollars rather than yield to maturity. Term bonds, tax-exempt notes and Public Housing Authority bonds are dollar bonds. Municipal serial bonds are quoted on a YTM basis.

Dollar Cost Averaging: A system of buying fixed dollar amounts of securities at regular fixed intervals, regardless of the price of shares. This method may result in an average cost that is generally lower than the average price of all prices at which the securities were purchased.

Do Not Reduce (DNR):   An order that stipulates that the price of limit or stop orders should not be reduced as a result of cash dividends.

Double Barreled Bond: A municipal revenue bond backed by the full faith and credit of the issuing municipality as well as by pledged revenues. (See: General Obligation Bond; Revenue Bond)

Dow Jones Industrial Average: The most widely used market indicator, composed of 30 large, actively traded issues.

Dow Theory: A technical market theory with which some people try to interpret long-term trends in the stock market by analyzing the movements of the Dow Jones industrial averages.

DPP: (See: Direct Participation Program)

Dry Hole: Any well which is plugged and abandoned without being completed or which is abandoned for any reason without having produced commercially for 60 days.

Due Bill: A printed statement showing the transfer of a security's title or rights, or showing the obligation of a seller to deliver the securities or rights to the purchaser. Used as a demand for dividends due a buyer when the transaction occurs before the ex-dividend date.

Due Diligence: The careful investigation by the underwriters necessary to ensure all material information pertinent to an issue has been disclosed to the public.

Due Diligence Meeting: A meeting between an issuing corporation's officials and representatives of the underwriting group held for discussing details of the pending issue of securities. These details include the registra-tion statement and the preparation of prospectuses.

Duplicate Confirmation: A copy of a client's confirmation that a brokerage firm sends to an agent or an attorney if a client requests it in writing. Clients must receive copies unless they specify in writing that they do not wish to receive them. (See: Confirmation)

E

Earned Income: Income that is derived from personal services, such as wages, salary, tips, commissions and bonuses. (See: Unearned Income)

Earned Surplus: (See: Retained Earnings)

Earnings-Per-Share (EPS):   The net income available for common stock divided by the number of shares of common stock outstanding.

Earnings-Per-Share Fully Diluted: The earnings per share calculated assuming convertible securities (convertible preferred stock, convertible bonds) have been converted.

Eastern Account: Liability for the distribution of an issue of securities is undivided, each member of the underwriting syndicate is responsible for a proportionate share of securities remaining unsold. (See: Western Account)

Economic Risk: The risk related to international developments and domestic events.

EE Savings Bonds: Non-negotiable government debt issued at a discount from face value. The difference between purchase price and the value of the bond upon redemption determines the interest rate. Currently, EE bonds pay a variable rate of interest linked to 85% of the rate paid on five-year treasury securities.

Effective Date: The date the registration of an issue of securities becomes effective. The underwriter confirms sales of the newly issued securities after this date.

Efficient Market Theory: A theory based on the assumption that the stock market efficiently processes information. This theory postulates that new information, as it becomes known, is reflected immediately in the price of the stock and, therefore, stock prices represent "fair" prices.

Elasticity: The responsiveness of consumers and producers to a change in prices. A large change in demand or production resulting from a small change in price for a good would be considered an indication of elasticity. Small or no change in production or demand following a change in prices would be considered an indication of inelasticity.

Endorsement: The signature on the back of a certificate by the person named on the certificate as the owner. Owners must endorse certificates when transferring them to another person's name.

EPS: (See: Earnings-Per-Share)

Equipment Trust Certificate: A debt obligation backed by equipment. The title to the equipment is held by an independent trustee (usually a bank), not the company. Equipment trust certificates are generally issued by transportation companies, such as railroads. Syn: Equipment Trust; Equipment Note or Bond. (See: New York Plan)

Equity: Ownership interest of common and preferred stockholders in a corporation. Also, the client's net worth in a margin account. Also, what is owned less what is owed. (See: Common Stock; Preferred Stock; Margin Account)

Equity Interest: When used with respect to a corporation, equity interest means common stock and any security convertible into, exchangeable or exercisable for common stock. When used with respect to a partnership, equity interest means an interest in the capital or profits or losses of the partnership.

Escrow Receipt: The certificate provided by an approved bank, which guarantees that the indicated securities are on deposit at that bank and will be delivered if the option is exercised.

Excess Equity: The amount of money in a margin account that is in excess of the federal requirement. Syn: Excess; Regulation T Excess.

Exchange: Organized exchanges where commodities, futures and securities transactions occur.

Exchange Distribution: A block trading procedure in which a block of stock is crossed on the floor of the exchange with no prior announcement on the broad tape.

Exchange Offer: An offer to exchange one type of security for another.

Exchange Privilege: An investor who has invested in one fund may transfer to another fund under the same sponsor without incurring an additional sales charge. Syn: Conversion Privilege.

Exchange Rate: The price at which one country's currency can be converted into that of another's.

Ex-Date: The first day buyers are not entitled to receive distributions previously declared. The ex-date is usually four business days before the record date.

Executor: Someone authorized to manage a brokerage account for an estate. An executor's authority is established by the last will of the decedent.

Exempt Security: A security exempt from the registration requirements (although not the anti-fraud requirements) of the Securities Act of 1933. Examples include U.S. Government and Municipal Securities. Syn: Exempted Security.

Exercise: To implement the rights of an option or warrant. For example, a call holder exercises a call by implementing the right to buy 100 shares of the underlying stock at the agreed-upon price.

Exercise Price: The price per share at which the holder of a call, option or warrant may buy (or the holder of a put may sell) the underlying security. Syn: Strike Price; Striking Price.

Ex-Legal Trade: A municipal issue trading without a legal opinion of counsel accompanying the bond. An ex-legal trade must be designated as such at the time of the trade.

Expansionary Policy: A fiscal policy that has as its end the increase (expansion) of the money supply.

Expense Ratio: A ratio used to compare the efficiency of a mutual fund. The ratio is calculated by dividing expenses of operation by the fund's net assets.

Expiration date: The specified date on which the option becomes worthless and the buyer no longer has the rights specified in the contract.

Ex-Pit Transaction: Trades executed outside of the normal exchange trading ring or pit.

Exploratory Well: A well drilled either (a) in search of a new and as yet undiscovered pool of oil or gas, or (b) with the hope of substantially extending the limits of a pool already developed.

Ex-Rights: Stock purchased without rights.

Ex-rights Date: The date on or after which stocks will be traded without subscription rights.

Ex-Warrants: The date on or after which the buyer of a security is no longer entitled to warrants that will be distributed to the security's owners.

F

Face Amount Certificate Company: The certificates issued by an investment company (debt instruments) that obligate it to pay an investor a stated amount of money (the face amount) at a specific time. The investor pays into the certificate in periodic payments or in a lump sum.

Face Value: (See: Par Value; Principal)

Farm Out: An agreement whereby the owner of a leasehold or working interest agrees to assign his interest in certain specific acreage to the assignees, retaining some interest such as an overriding royalty, offset acreage or other types of interest, subject to the drilling of one or more specific wells or other performance as a condition of the assignment.

FCM: (See: Futures Commission Merchant)

Feasibility Study: A study to determine if a proposed municipal project will generate sufficient funds to cover operation of the project and debt service. Generally required before the issuance of a municipal revenue bond.

Fed: (See: Federal Reserve System)

Federal Funds: Reserves of banks and certain other institutions greater than the reserve requirements or excess reserves. These funds are available immediately.

Federal Funds Rate: The interest rate charged by one institution lending federal funds to another.

Federal National Mortgage Association (FNMA): A publicly held corporation whose common stock is traded on the NYSE. FNMA purchases conventional mortgages and mortgages guaranteed by the Federal Housing, Veterans Administration and Farmers Association Home Administration. Syn: Fannie Mae; FNMA.

Federal Reserve Board: A seven-member group appointed by the President (subject to approval by Congress) to oversee operations of the Federal Reserve System.

Federal Reserve System: The central bank system of the United States. Its chief responsibility is to regulate the flow of money and credit. Syn: The Fed.

FGIC: The Financial Guaranty Insurance Corporation, an insurance company offering insurance on the timely payment of interest and principal on municipal securities and municipal unit trusts.

Fiduciary: A person legally appointed and authorized to represent and act on another's behalf.

FIFO: (See: First-In, First-Out)

Fill-or-Kill Order (FOK): An order that instructs the floor broker to fill the entire order immediately or "kill" (cancel) the entire order. A partial fill is not acceptable.

Filing Date: The day on which a registration statement is filled with the SEC.

Final Prospectus: The prospectus delivered by an issuing corporation that includes the price of the securities, the delivery date, underwriting spread and other material information.

Financial Risk: The risk associated with the safety of one's principal related to the ability of an issuer of a security to meet either principal, interest or dividend payments.

Firm Underwriting Commitment: An underwriting in which the underwriters commit to buy the entire issue and assume all financial responsibility for any unsold shares.

Firm Quote: The actual price at which a trading unit (such as 100 shares of stock or five bonds) of the security may be bought or sold.

First-In, First-Out: A method of assessing a company's inventory in which it is assumed that the first goods acquired are the first to be sold. (See: Last-In, First-Out)

Fiscal Policy: Federal tax and spending policies set by Congress and/or the White House.

Five Percent Markup Policy: The NASD's general guideline for the percentage markup, markdown and commissions on securities transactions.

Fixed Annuity (Annuity Guaranteed): An annuity contract in which the insurance company makes fixed dollar payments to the annuitant for the term of the contract (usually until he or she dies). Syn: Guaranteed Dollar Annuity; Fixed Dollar Annuity. (See: Annuity)

Fixed Assets: Tangible physical properties owned by a corporation that are used in the production of the corporation's income.

Flat: A term used to describe bonds traded without accrued interest. The bonds are traded at the agreed-upon market price only.

Floating Debt: Obligations payable on demand or having very short maturities.

Floor Broker: (See: Commission Broker)

Floor Trader: An exchange member who enters transactions only for his or her own account from the floor of the exchange. Syn: Local.

Flow of Funds: The priority for payment of revenues collected.

Flow-Through: A term used to describe the way income, deductions and credits resulting of income from the activities of a business are applied to individual tax and expenses returns as though each incurred the income and deductions (expenses) directly. (See: Limited Partnership)

Flower Bond: A type of Treasury bond that can be used to settle estate taxes. Flower bonds tend to trade at discounts due to their low coupon rates.

FNMA: (See: Federal National Mortgage Association)

FOK: (See: Fill-Or-Kill Order)

FOMC: The Federal Open Market Committee. The committee makes decisions concerning the Fed's open market operations. (See: Open Market Operations)

Forced Conversion: A process used by a corporation that strongly encourages a convertible bondholder to exercise the conversion option. Often conversion is forced by calling the bonds when the market value of the stock is higher than the redemption price offered by the corporation. (See: Redemption)

Foreign Fund: (See: Specialized Fund)

Foreign Currency: The currency of another country than the one in which the investor resides. Options and futures contracts trade on numerous foreign currencies.

Forward Contract: A cash market transaction in which a future delivery date is specified. Forward contracts differ from futures contracts in that the terms of forward contracts are not standardized and are not traded in contract markets.

Forward Market: Non-exchange trading of commodities specifying delivery at some future date.

Forward Pricing: When pricing mutual fund shares, the valuation of the portfolio occurs at least once per day and orders to purchase or redeem shares are completed at the valuation following the order placement.

Fourth Market: The trading of securities directly from one institutional investor to another without the services of a brokerage firm. Syn: Instinet.

Fractional Share: A portion of a whole share of stock. Fractional shares used to be generated when corporations declared stock dividends, merged or voted to split stock. These days it is more common for corporations to issue the cash equivalent of fractional shares to investors. Mutual fund shares are frequently issued in fractional amounts.

Free Riding: The illegal extension of credit for the purpose of trading securities.

Free Riding & Withholding: A violation of the NASD Rules of Fair Practice, it is the failure of a member participating in the distribution of a new issue to make a bona fide public offering at the public offering price for an issue that is "hot." A hot issue is one which opens in the secondary market at a premium to the public offering price.

Front-End Load: 1) Fees and expenses paid by any party for any services rendered during the program's organizational or acquisition phase including front-end organization and offering expenses, acquisition fees and expenses and any other similar fees designated by the sponsor. 2) A system of sales charge for contractual plans that permits up to 50% of the first year's payments to be deducted as sales charge. Investors have a right to withdraw from the plan but there are some restrictions if this occurs. (See: Contractual Plan; Sales Charge)

Frozen Account: An account requiring cash in advance to buy and securities in hand to sell.

Full Disclosure Act: Another name for the Securities Act of 1933.

Full Trading Authorization: Authorization for someone other than the customer to have full trading privileges in the account, which includes making purchases, sales and withdrawals.

Fully Registered: A bond registered as to both principal and interest.

Functional Allocation: This sharing arrangement is formulated around the types of costs which exist in an oil & gas program. Investors are responsible for intangible costs and the sponsor is responsible for tangible (capitalized) costs. The revenue sharing arrangement reflects the percentage of the costs in the program.

Fundamental Analysis: A method of securities analysis that tries to evaluate the intrinsic value of a particular stock. It is a study of the overall economy, industry conditions and the financial condition and management of a particular company.

Fund: With mutual funds, the entity responsible for general administration and supervision of the investment portfolio.

Funding: The conversion of floating debt into bonded debt. (See: Floating Debt, Funded Debt)

Funded Debt: All long-term financing of a corporation or a municipality, that is, all outstanding bonds maturing in five years or longer. Syn: Bonded debt.

Funds Statement: A financial statement that analyzes why a company's working capital increases or decreases.

Fungibility: Having the same value, quality. A security which is freely transferable with another security and can be used in place of the security traded is considered a fungible security.

Futures: Exchange-standardized contracts for the purchase or sale of a commodity at a future date.

Futures Commission Merchant (FCM): An individual or organization engaged in the solicitation or acceptance of orders and the extension of credit for the purchase or sale of commodities futures.

Futures Contract: A standardized, exchange-traded contract to make or take delivery of a particular type and grade of commodity at an agreed upon place and point in the future. Futures contracts are transferrable between parties.

Futures Exchange: A centralized facility for the trading of futures contracts.

Futures Market: A continuous auction market in which participants buy and sell commodities contracts for delivery at a specified point in the future. Trading is carried on through open outcry and hand signals in a trading pit or ring. (See: Cash Market)

G

General Obligation Bond: A type of municipal bond backed by the full faith, credit and taxing power of the issuer for payment of interest and principal.

General Partner: A partner in a partnership who is personally liable for all debts of the partnership and who partakes in the management and control of the partnership.

General Partners (GPs): An association of two or more entities forming to conduct a trade or Partnership business. The partnership does not require documents for formation and the General Partners are joint and severally liable for the partnership's liabilities.

GNMA: (See: Government National Mortgage Association)

GNP: (See: Gross National Product)

Good Delivery: A security that is negotiable in compliance with the contract of the sale and ready to be transferred from seller to purchaser.

Good Faith Deposit: A deposit by underwriters bidding for a municipal issue required to ensure performance by the low bidder. The requirements are stipulated in the Official Notice of Sale sent to prospective underwriters, the amount required is usually 2% to 5% of the bid.

Good-Till-Canceled Order (GTC): An order that is left in force until it is executed or canceled. Syn: Open Order.

Government Bond: An obligation of the U.S. government, backed by the full faith and credit of the government, and regarded as the highest grade or safest issue (i.e., default risk free).

Government National Mortgage Association: A wholly owned government corporation that issues several types of securities backed by the full faith and credit of the U.S. Government. Syn: Ginnie Mae; GNMA.

Grade: The specified quality of a commodity.

Grantor: The writer or seller of an option or contract.

Gross Processing Margin (GPM): The difference between the cost of soybeans and the revenue from the resultant meal and oil after processing.

Gross National Product: The total value of goods and services produced in a society in one year which includes consumption, government purchases, investment and exports minus imports.

Gross Revenue Pledge: Debt service is the first payment to be made from revenues received from a municipal project. (See: Net Revenue Pledge)

Growth Fund: A type of diversified common stock fund that has capital appreciation as its primary goal. It invests in companies that reinvest most of their earnings for expansion, research or development. The term also refers to growth income funds that invest in common stocks for both current income and long-term growth of both capital and income. (See: Diversified Common Stock Fund; Mutual Fund)

Growth Stock: A relatively speculative issue, often paying low dividends and selling at high price to earnings ratios.

Group Net Order: Orders received by an underwriting syndicate for the benefit of the syndicate. Commissions (takedown) are paid to members according to their participation in the syndicate.

GTC: (See: Good-Till-Canceled Order)

Guaranteed Bond: A debt obligation in which a company other than the issuing corporation guarantees payment of interest and principal on the bond.

Guaranteed Dollar Annuity: (See: Fixed Annuity)

Guaranteed Stock: Generally, a preferred stock that has divided payments guaranteed by a corporation other than the issuing corporation but remains the stock of the issuing corporation. Guaranteed stock is considered a dual security.

H

Haircut: The formula used to calculate the discounted value of securities in a broker-dealer's possession in the computation of net capital.

Head and Shoulders: A technical trading pattern that has three peaks resembling a head and two shoulders. The stock moves up to its first peak (the left shoulder), drops back, then moves to a higher peak (the top of the head), drops again but recovers to another, lower peak (the right shoulder). A head and shoulder formation after a substantial rise would indicate a market reversal. An inverted head and shoulders would indicate an advance.

Heating Oil: #2 Fuel oil.

Hedge: 1) Investing to reduce the risk of a position in a security (typically the risk of adverse price movements), normally by taking a protecting position in a related security. 2) The protective position taken.

Hedge-Long: Long securities or actuals positions protected by long put positions.

Hedge-Short: Short securities or actuals positions protected by long call positions.

High: The highest price a security or commodity reaches during a specified period of time.

Holding Company: A company organized to invest in and manage other corporations.

Holding Period: Starts the day after a purchase and ends on the day of the sale.

Horizontal Spread: (See: Calendar Spread)

Hot Issue: An issue that sells at a premium over the public offering price. (See: Free Riding & Withholding)

Housing Authority Bond: A type of municipal bond issued by local public housing authorities to redevelop and improve certain areas. Syn: Public Housing Authority Bond (PHA).

House Maintenance Call: A brokerage firm's demand that a client deposit money or securities when the client's equity falls below the brokerage firm's minimum maintenance requirement which is higher than that set by the NYSE.

Hypothecation: The pledging of client's securities as collateral for loans. Brokerage firms hypothecate client's securities to finance their margin loans to customers.

I

Identified Shares: The particular shares from a multiple position of the same security that a client identifies as being the share that he or she wants delivered for sale.

Immediate Annuity: An annuity contract purchased for a lump sum (single premium) that starts to pay immediately following its purchase. (See: Annuity)

Immediate-or-Cancel Order (IOC): An order instructing the floor broker to execute immediately. Any portion of the order that remains unexecuted is canceled.

Inactive Crowd: That section of the New York Stock Exchange that trades the inactive bonds. Syn: Cabinet Crowd; Can Crowd.

Income Bond: A debt obligation that promises to repay bond principal in full at maturity. Interest on these bonds is paid only if the corporation's earnings are sufficient to meet the interest payment and if the payment is declared by the board of directors. These bonds are usually traded flat. Syn: Adjustment Bond. (See: Flat)

Income Fund: A type of mutual fund that seeks to provide a stable current income from investments by investing in securities that pay interest. (See: Mutual Fund)

Income Statement: A financial statement that summarizes a corporation's revenues and expenses for a specific fiscal period.

Indication of Interest: An investor's expression of conditional interest in buying an upcoming securities issue after the investor has reviewed a preliminary prospectus. An indication of interest is not a commitment to buy.

Individual Retirement Account (IRA): A qualified tax-deferred retirement plan for employed individuals. Allows a contribution of 100% of earned income up to a maximum of $2,000 per year. Some or all of the contribution may be tax deductible, depending on the individual's compensation level and coverage by other qualified retirement plans. (See: Qualified Retirement Plan)

Industrial Development Bond (IDB): Municipal security issues, the proceeds from which a state or municipal authority uses to finance construction or the purchase of facilities to be leased or purchased by a private company. The bonds are backed by the credit of the private company and often are not considered an obligation of the issuing municipality.

Industry Fund: (See: Specialized Fund)

Inflation: An increase in the general level of prices.

Initial Margin Requirement: The amount of equity a customer must deposit when making a new purchase in a margin account. The Regulation T requirement is currently 50% for equity securities. The NYSE and NASD initial requirement is an equity of $2,000 but not more than 100% of the purchase cost. (See: Margin)

Initial Public Offering (IPO): The original sale of a company's securities to the public.

Insider: Anyone who has nonpublic knowledge (material information) about a corporation. Insiders include directors, officers and stockholders who own more than 10% of any class of equity security of a corporation.

Instinet: (See: Fourth Market)

In-Street-Name Account: An account in which the customer's securities are held in the name of the brokerage firm.

Intangible Asset: An asset that is not physical, such as a copyright or good will.

Intangible Drilling Development Expense: An expense in the drilling operations for oil and gas, such as labor, fuel or other non-tangible costs. These costs may be expensed in the year incurred or capitalized and depleted at a later date.

Interest Coverage Ratio: A ratio describing the safety of a corporate bond. The ratio is calculated by dividing operating income by interest expense. The ratio reveals the multiple of income to interest expense. The higher the multiple the less risk there is of default on interest payment.

Interest Rate Risk: Risk associated with investments relating to sensitivity of price or value to fluctuation in current level of interest rates.

Interlocking Directorate: Two (or more) corporate boards of directors that have individual directors who serve simultaneously on both.

Internal Rate of Return (IRR): That rate of discount at which the present value of future cash flows is exactly equal to the initial capital investment.

International Arbitrage: A purchase and/or sale of a security on a securities exchange effected for the purpose of profiting from the difference between the price of the security on that exchange and the price of that security on a securities market not within or subject to the jurisdiction of the U.S. government

In-the-Money: An option that has intrinsic value: for example, a call option in which the stock is selling above the exercise price or a put option in which the stock is selling below the exercise price. (See: Intrinsic Value)

Intrastate Offering: A conditional offering of unregistered securities limited to companies that do business in one state and sell their securities only to residents of that same state (SEC Rule 147).

Intrinsic Value: The mathematical value of an option. For example, a call option is said to have intrinsic value when the stock is trading above the exercise price.

Introducing Broker: A broker-dealer that does not hold investor's money or securities. Instead, it "introduces" those accounts to a clearing broker-dealer which then handles all cash and securities for those accounts.

Inventory Turnover Ratio: A ratio that measures the efficiency with which a company can sell and replace its inventory, calculated by dividing the net sales by the inventory.

Inverted Yield Curve: A chart that shows long-term debt instruments having lower yields than short-term debt instruments. (See: Normal Yield Curve)

Investment Advisor: Anyone who, for compensation (a flat fee or percent of assets managed), offers investment advice. For Investment Companies, the advisor has the day-to-day responsibility of investing the cash and securities held in a mutual fund's portfolio. The advisor must adhere to the objective as stated in the fund's prospectus.

Invested Capital: The sum of a company's long-term debt, capital stock and all surplus. Syn: Capitalization; Capital Structure.

Investment Banker: A financial middleman who raises capital for corporations and municipalities.

Investment Banking: The business of underwriting issues of securities, of buying or selling securities as a dealer or of buying and selling securities on the order and for the benefit of others as a broker.

Investment Company: A company engaged primarily in the business of investing and trading in securities, including face-amount certificate companies, unit investment trusts and management companies.

Investment Company Act of 1940: Congressional legislation enacted to regulate investment companies. It requires any investment company in interstate commerce to register with the SEC.

Investment Company Act Amendments of 1970: An amendment to the Investment Company Act of 1940. It requires a registered investment company issuing periodic payment plan certificates (contractual plans) to offer all purchasers withdrawal rights and purchases of front-end load plans surrender rights.

Investment Company Act Amendments of 1975: Amendments to the Investment Company Act of 1940. In particular, that sales charges must relate to the services the fund provides shareholders.

Investment Grade Security: A security with a rating (S&P, Moody's, etc.) of BBB/Baa or above.

Investment Objectives: The goals a client hopes to achieve through investing.

Investment Tax Credit: A credit against tax calculated as a percentage of cost for investment in depreciable, tangible personal property which has a minimum useful life of three years. The basic amount deductible is ten percent of the qualified investment.

Investment Value: The market price at which a convertible security (usually a debenture) would sell if it were not converted into common stock. (See: Convertible Bond; Debenture)

Invitation for Bids: The "advertising" for bids to be submitted for the underwriting of a bond issue. Invitations are published in The Daily Bond Buyer, newspapers, journals and Munifacts.

In-Whole-Call: The call of a bond issue in its entirety by the issuer as opposed to the redemption of issues based on a lottery held by an independent trustee.

IRA: (See: Individual Retirement Account)

IRA Rollover: The reinvestment of assets an individual receives as a lump-sum distribution from a qualified tax-deferred retirement plan. The individual may reinvest either the entire lump sum or a portion of that sum. (See: Individual Retirement Account)

Issued Stock: Stock that has been sold to the public.

Issuer: The corporation or municipality that offers its securities for sale. Also, the creator of an option (the issuer of an OTC option is the option writer, the issuer of a listed option is the OCC).

J

Joint Account: An account in which two or more individuals act as co-tenants or co-owners of the account. The account may be joint tenants in common or joint tenants with rights of survivorship. (See: Tenants in Common; Joint Tenants With Rights of Survivorship)

Joint Tenants with Rights of Survivorship: Also known as JTWROS, a form of ownership that requires that a deceased tenant's fractional interest in an account be retained by the surviving tenant(s). It is used almost exclusively by husbands and wives.

Joint Venture: The joining of two or more persons in a specific business enterprise rather than in a continuing relationship, as in a partnership.

JTIC: Joint Tenants In Common. (See: Tenants in Common)

Junior Lien Debt: A bond backed by the same collateral backing a previous issue, having a junior claim to the collateral in the event of default. (See: Closed-End Pledge; Open-End Pledge)

K

Keogh Plan: A qualified tax-deferred retirement plan for persons who are self-employed and unincorporated or who earn extra income through personal services aside from their regular employment. Syn: H.R. 10 Plan. (See: Qualified Retirement Plan)

L

Last-In, First-Out (LIFO): A method of assessing a company's inventory in which it is assumed that the goods acquired last are the first to be sold. (See: First-In, First-Out)

Legal Investments (Legal List): The list of securities prescribed by statute for use in fiduciary accounts.

Legal Opinion of Counsel: Regardless of the type of municipal bond issued, the bond must be accompanied by a Legal Opinion of Counsel. The opinion of counsel affirms the issue is a municipal issue and interest is exempt from federal taxation, among other items.

Legislative Risk: Risk associated with the impact of changes in law on investment.

Lending at a Premium: Charging the borrower of securities (short seller) for the loan of the securities. The charge is stated in terms of dollars per 100 shares per business day.

Lending at a Rate: Paying interest on the money received in connection with securities loaned to short sellers.

Letter of Intent (LOI): A signed purchase agreement under which a fund can sell shares to an investor at a lower overall sales charge, based on the total dollar amount of the intended investment. A letter of intent is valid only if the investor completes the terms of the purchase agreement within 13 months from the time this agreement is signed. An LOI may be backdated 90 days. Syn: Statement of Intention.

Level Debt Service: Principal and interest payments remain essentially constant from year to year over the life of the issue.

Level One: The basic level of NASDAQ service. It provides registered representatives with the up-to-the-minute inside bid and asked quotations on hundreds of over-the-counter stocks through a desk-top quotation machine. (See: NASDAQ)

Level Three: The highest level of NASDAQ service. It provides up-to-the-minute inside bid and asked quotations, the bids and askeds of each market-maker for a security, and allows each market maker to enter changes in those quotes through a desk-top quotation machine. (See: NASDAQ)

Level Two: The second level of NASDAQ service. It provides up-to-the-minute inside bid and asked quotations, and the bids and askeds of each marker-maker for a security through a desk-top quotation machine. (See: NASDAQ)

Leverage: The use of borrowed capital to increase earnings. Syn: Trading on the Equity.

Leverage Transaction Merchant (LTM): An individual or organization registered with the CFTC and permitted to engage in off-exchange trading of selected futures instruments.

Liabilities: Debts owed by an entity, a legal obligation to pay. Current liabilities are debts payable within 12 months, long-term liabilities are debts payable over a period of more than 12 months.

LIFO: (See: Last-In, First-Out)

Limit Order: An order that is to be executed only at a specific price or better. Syn: Limit or Better.

Limited Partnership: A form of business organization in which one or more of the partners is liable only to the extent of the amount of dollars each has invested. Limited partners are not involved in management decisions, but enjoy direct flow-through of income and expenses. (See: Flow-Through)

Limited Partner: A partner who does not participate in the management or control of a partnership and whose liability is limited for partnership debts to the amount invested in the partnership. Syn: Passive Investor; Participant.

Limited Partnership Agreement: The Articles of Limited Partnership of each limited partnership. The agreement forms the contract between the limited and general partners stating the rights and responsibilities of each.

Limited Tax Bond: A general obligation bond where the security of the bond provided by the issuer's taxing power is limited to a specified maximum rate.

Limited Trading Authorization: Authorization for someone other than the customer to have trading privileges in the account. It is limited to purchases and sales. Withdrawal of assets is not allowed.

Limit Order: A customer's order with instructions to buy a specified security below a certain price or sell a specified security above a certain price.

Liquidity: The ease of which something can be bought or sold (converted to cash) in the market place. A large number of buyers and sellers and a high volume of trading activity are important components of liquidity.

Liquidity Ratios: With a corporation, a measure of the company's ability to meet its current obligations. For investments, the ability to convert the asset into cash without an appreciable loss on the investment. The ratio compares current assets to current liabilities. (See: Current Ratio)

Listed Option: An option that can be bought and sold on a national securities exchange in a continuous secondary market. Syn: Standardized Option. (See: OTC Option)

Listed Securities: Securities that are traded on a national securities exchange such as the New York Stock Exchange.

Loan Agreement: A lending agreement between a brokerage firm and a client that permits the brokerage firm to lend a client's securities. This is a part of the margin agreement. Syn: Consent to Lend Agreement.

Loaned Flat: Securities loaned to short sellers without an interest charge.

Loans for set amounts: A type of broker's collateral loan that requires a brokerage firm to deposit new collateral before it can obtain a new loan when additional funds are needed. (See: Broker's Loans; Call Loans)

Local Basis: (See: Country Basis)

Long: The state of owning a security, a contract or a commodity. A purchase of a 5 May Wheat contracts would be referred to as **going long** May Wheat. The speculator would have a **long** position.

Long Market Value (LMV): The current market value of securities a customer owns.

Long Term Gains (Loss): The taxable gain (or loss) on a capital asset that an investor has owned for more than six months.

Loss Carryover: The capital loss that is carried over to later years for use as a capital loss deduction.

Low: The lowest price a security or commodity reaches during a given period of time.

M

M1: A narrow definition of money supply that includes all coins, currency, demand deposits (checking accounts) and NOW accounts.

M2: A broader definition of money supply that includes all coins, currency and checking deposits; time deposits; savings deposits and non-institutional money-market funds.

M3: M2 plus large time deposits, institutional money-market funds, short-term repurchase agreements and certain other large liquid assets.

Maintenance Call: (See: House Maintenance Call; NYSE Maintenance Call)

Maintenance Excess: The difference between the equity in an account and the NYSE minimum margin (25% long and 30% short). (See: Equity; NYSE Maintenance Requirement)

Maintenance Requirement: (See: NYSE Maintenance Requirement)

Major Market Index (MMI): A 20 stock index designed to track the Dow Jones 30 industrials. The MMI is comprised of fifteen of the Dow Jones 30 and five other large NYSE listed stocks.

Make a Market: The action of a broker-dealer firm when, on a regular basis, it holds itself out to other firms as ready to buy or sell a particular over-the-counter stock for its own account. Accepts the risk of holding the position in the security.

Management Company: An investment company that manages a portfolio of various types of securities. (See: Diversified Management Company; Nondiversified Management Company; Closed-End Management Company; Open-End Management Company)

Managed Offering: The offering for a sale of securities in which the sponsor utilizes a dealer manager to hire soliciting dealers.

Management Fee: A fee paid to a sponsor of a program for management and administration of the program.

Managing Partner: The sponsor when acting in its capacity as managing partner under the articles of partnership establishing the partnership.

Manager, Fund: With mutual funds, the entity responsible for investment advisory services. (See: Mutual Fund)

Mandatory Call: Redemption of bonds by an issuer based on a predetermined schedule or happening of an event. (See: Catastrophe Call)

Margin: The amount of equity as a percent of current market value in a margin account. (See: Regulation T; Margin Call; Equity)

Margin Account: An account in which a brokerage firm lends a client part of the purchase price of the securities. (See: Regulation T; Special Arbitrage Account)

Margin Call: A demand for a client to deposit money or securities when a purchase is made in a margin account. Syn: Federal Margin; Federal Call; Call; Reg T Call; T Call; or Fed Call. (See: Margin; Initial Margin Requirement)

Margin Department: The department within a brokerage firm that computes the amount of money a client must deposit in both margin and cash accounts.

Margin of Profit: A ratio used to determine the operating efficiency of a business, calculated by dividing the operating profit by the net sales. Syn: Profit Margin.

Margin Risk: The risk that an investor will be required to deposit additional cash if security positions the individual has are subject to adverse price movements.

Mark to the Market: Adjusting the value of an account to the current market value of the security positions in the account. Current valuation of market value and equity.

Markdown: The difference between the best (highest) current bid price among dealers and the actual price that a dealer pays to a customer.

Market Arbitrage: The simultaneous purchase and sale of the same security in different markets to take advantage of a price disparity between the two markets.

Market-If-Touched Order (MIT): An order that only becomes a market order if the market touches (or hits) the specified price. A buy MIT order is placed below the current market, and a sell MIT is placed above the current market.

Market Maker (Principal): A dealer willing to accept the risk of holding securities to facilitate trading in a particular security or securities. (See: Make a Market)

Market-Not-Held Order: A market order for a sizable amount of stock that gives the floor broker discretion about the price or timing of the execution of the order. Syn: Market NH.

Market Order: An order that is to be executed at the best available price.

Market Out Clause: The standard clause in a firm commitment underwriting agreement that relieves the underwriter of its obligation to underwrite the issue under certain unusual circumstances, such as unexpected bad news just before or after the offering date.

Market Risk: Risk due to day-to-day fluctuations in prices at which a security can be bought or sold. Syn: Systematic Risk.

Market Value: The price an investor will buy or sell each share of common stock or each bond at a given time. Market value is determined by the interaction between buyers and sellers in the market.

Market Value on the Trade Date: The gross amount of a long purchase (including commissions) or the net proceeds of a short sale.

Market Value per Share: The current price at which a stock is trading in the open market.

Marketability: The ease with which a security can be bought or sold. Having a readily available market for trading.

Markup: The difference between the best or lowest current offering price among dealers and the actual price that a dealer charges its customer.

Married Put: An investor buys a stock and the same day buys a put on that stock and specifically identifies that position as a hedge. The holding period starts on the day of the purchase and does not end until the stock is sold, through the exercise of the put or otherwise.

Matching Orders: Simultaneously entering identical (or nearly identical) orders for the purchase or sale of a security to create the appearance of active trading in the securities.

Maturity Date: The date on which the principal is repaid to the investor. (See: Principal; Par Value)

Maximum Loan Value: The maximum amount a broker dealer can loan a customer for the purchase of securities. For example, if Reg T were 65%, the maximum loan would be 35%. Syn: Loan Value.

MBIA: Municipal Bond Insurance Association, an association of insurance companies offering insurance as to timely payment of principal and interest when due on qualified municipal issues. Issues with MBIA insurance are rated AAA.

Member: One of the 1,366 individuals owning a seat on the New York Stock Exchange. Also, any broker or dealer admitted to membership in the NASD. (See: Member Firm; Allied Member)

Member Firm: A firm in which at least one of the principal officers is a member of the New York Stock Exchange, another organized exchange or a clearing corporation.

Member Order: Orders by syndicate members for their retail and institutional clients. Each syndicate member receives the commission on orders filled by the syndicate manager. Member orders generally have the lowest priority during the order period. (See: Designated Order; Presale Order)

Membership: The members of the New York Stock Exchange, another exchange or a clearing corporation.

Mill Rate: The tax per dollar of assessed value of property ($.001).

Minimum Subscription Amount: The minimum amount to which a person must initially subscribe in a new offering of a DPP program.

Minus Tick: An execution price below the previous sale. A short sale may not be executed on a minus tick. Syn: Down tick.

Mixed Accounts: A margin account having both long and short positions in different securities. (See: Margin Account)

Monetary Policy: The policies and actions of the Federal Reserve Board that determine the rate of growth and size of the money supply, which in turn effects interest rates.

Money Market: The securities market that deals in short-term (less than one year) debt.

Money-Market Fund: An open-end investment company investing in money-market instruments. Generally sold with no load, the fund offers draft writing privileges and low opening investments.

Moral Obligation Bond: A revenue bond issued with nonbinding legislative authority to apportion monies for shortfalls in revenues backing the bond.

Mortgage Bond: A debt obligation secured by a property pledge. These are liens or mortgages against the issuing corporation's properties and real estate assets.

Municipal Bond: A debt security issued by a state, municipality or other subdivision (such as a school, park, sanitary or other local taxing district) to raise money to finance its capital expenditures. These might include construction of highways, public works or school buildings.

Municipal Bond Fund: A type of mutual fund that invests in municipal bonds either operating as a unit investment trust (units of interest in an existing portfolio of tax-exempt bonds) or as an open-end fund. (See: Unit Investment Trust; Open-End Management Company; Mutual Fund)

Municipal Broker's Broker: A broker acting for other brokers in the municipal market. The broker's broker does not take positions in the issue nor does the broker transact orders for the public. (See: Broker's Broker)

Munifacts: A news wire service for the municipal bond industry, a product of The Bond Buyer.

Mutual Exclusion Doctrine: The doctrine that established the federal tax exemption status of municipal bond interest. This doctrine says that states and municipalities must not tax government-owned properties. The federal government reciprocates by excluding local government properties from federal taxation. Syn: Reciprocal Immunity; Mutual Reciprocity.

Mutual Fund: A type of investment company that offers for sale or has outstanding securities that it has issued which are redeemable on demand by the fund at current net asset value. All owners in the fund share in the gains or losses of the fund. Syn: Open-End Management Company.

Mutual Fund Custodian: Usually a national bank, trust company or other qualified institution that physically safeguards securities. It does not manage investments; its function is solely clerical.

N

Naked Call Writer: Any investor who writes a call without owning the underlying stock or other related assets that would enable the writer to deliver the stock should the option be exercised. Syn: Uncovered Call Writer.

NASD: (See: National Association of Securities Dealers)

NASD By-Laws: The body of laws that describes how the NASD functions, defines its powers and determines the qualifications and registration requirements for brokers.

NASD District Business Conduct Committee: A committee composed of up to 12 NASD members from within a district who serve as administrators for the district. The NASD is divided into 13 local districts to maximize the degree of local administration. The

DBCC has original jurisdiction for hearings and judging complaints.

NASD 5% Markup Policy: A guideline about reasonable markups, markdowns and commissions for secondary over-the-counter transactions. Syn: Markup Policy.

NASDAQ: (See: National Association of Security Dealers Automated Quotation System)

National Association of Securities Dealers Inc.: The self-regulatory organization (SRO) for the over-the-counter market. The NASD was recognized as the SRO for the OTC market by the Maloney Act of 1938.

NASD Automated Quotation System: The nationwide electronic quotation system for up-to-the-minute bid and asked quotations on approximately 4,000 OTC stocks.

NASDAQ 100: A 100 stock index of the largest 100 non-financial stocks on NASDAQ weighted by capitalization.

NASDAQ National Market System (NMS): These are 200 of the most actively traded OTC stocks within the 4,000 stocks quoted on NASDAQ. Trades are reported as they occur.

National Futures Association (NFA) The self-regulatory organization (SRO) of the commodities futures industry to which all futures exchange members, commodity trading advisers (CTAs) and commodity pool operators (CPOs) must belong. The NFA is responsible to the CFTC.

NAV: (See: Net Asset Value)

Nearby Contract: Of two or more futures contracts, the contract with the shortest time remaining to expiration. Syn: Nearby Delivery (Month)

Negotiable Certificate of Deposit: A negotiable certificate that evidences a time deposit of funds with a bank. It is an unsecured promissory note normally issued in $100,000 denominations.

Negotiated Underwriting: Underwriting in which a brokerage firm consults with the issuer and arrives at a consensus about the most suitable price and timing of a forthcoming securities offering. (See: Competitive Bidding)

Net Asset Value (NAV): The value of a mutual fund share determined by deducting the fund's liabilities from the total assets of the portfolio and dividing this amount by the number of shares outstanding. This is calculated once a day, based on the closing market price for each security in the fund's portfolio. Syn: Bid Price. (See: Mutual Fund)

Net Change: The difference between the closing price on the trading day reported and the previous day's closing price. In OTC transactions, it refers to the difference between the closing bids.

Net Current Asset Value per Share: The calculation of book value per share that excludes all fixed assets. (See: Book Value per Common Share)

Net Income to Net Sales: A ratio that measures the after-tax profitability of a company. It is calculated by dividing the net income by the net sales. Syn: Net Profit Margin; Profit After Taxes; Net Profit to Sales; Return on Sales; Profit Ratio.

Net Investment Income: The sum of dividends, interest, rents, royalties and short-term gains minus investment expenses. For mutual funds, net investment income represents the source for dividend payments.

Net Revenue Pledge: A revenue pledge is contained in the trust indenture. A net revenue pledge is a pledge of revenues funding a bond after payment of operating and maintenance expenses. (See: Revenue Pledge)

Non-Accredited Investor: An investor not meeting the net worth requirements of Regulation D. Non-accredited investors are counted for purposes of the 35 investor limitation under Rules 505 & 506 of Regulation D.

Net Profits Interest: In a net profits interest arrangement, the sponsor shares in revenues after payments for royalties and operating expenses have been made. This payment is made to the sponsor receiving no other interest in the program (such as an overriding royalty) for packaging the deal. Net profits interests are limited to private placements.

Net Tangible Assets per Bond: This measures the amount of producing assets behind each corporate bond. It is calculated by dividing the net tangible assets by the funded debt. Syn: Book Value per Bond.

Net Worth: (See: Stockholders' Equity)

New York Plan: A financing method for the purchase of equipment similar to a conditional sale, a company purchases equipment by issuing bonds, as the bonds are paid off, the company acquires full title to the equipment. (See: Equipment Trust Certificate)

New Issues Act: Another name for the Securities Act of 1933.

Nine Bond Rule: The NYSE rule that requires orders for listed bonds in quantities of nine bonds or less to be sent to the floor of the NYSE before being traded in the OTC market.

No-Load Fund: A mutual fund whose shares are sold without a sales charge added to the net asset value. (See: Net Asset Value; Sales Charge; Mutual Fund)

Nominal Quote: A quotation given for informational purposes only.

Nominal Yield: The interest rate that is stated on the face of a bond. Syn: Coupon Rate. (See: Coupon Yield; Stated Yield)

Nominee: The person in whose name securities are registered if that person is other than the beneficial owner. This is the role of the brokerage firm when customer securities purchased on margin are registered in street name.

Noncumulative Preferred Stock: A type of preferred stock that does not have to pay any dividends in arrears to the holders. (See: Preferred Stock)

Nondiversified Management Company: A management company that is not restricted in its choice of securities or by the concentration of interest it has in those securities. (See: Diversified Management Company)

Non-Managed Offering: A method of distributing direct participation program interests. Rather than organizing a syndicate to distribute the interest, the program sponsor will contract with individual broker-dealers to offer the interests to the public. A wholesaler (broker-dealer) is often hired by the sponsor to arrange selling agreements with each firm.

Non-Recourse Financing: Financing in which the property is made security for the debt, but there is no personal liability on the part of the borrower.

Non-Specified Property Program: A program where, at the time a securities registration is ordered effective, less than 75% of the net proceeds from the sale of program interests are allocated to the purchase, construction or improvement of identified properties, or to a program in which the proceeds from any sale or refinancing of properties may be reinvested. Reserves shall be included in the non-specified 25%.

No-Par value: Stock issued without a stated value. (See: Par Value)

Normal Yield Curve: A chart that shows long-term debt instruments having higher yields than short-term debt instruments. (See: Inverted Yield Curve)

Numbered Account: An account titled with something other than a client's name, such as a number, symbol or special title. The client must sign a form designating ownership of the account.

NYSE Maintenance Call: A demand for a client to deposit money or securities if the client's equity falls below the NYSE minimum maintenance level. (See: Equity)

NYSE Maintenance Requirement: The minimum amount of equity that must be maintained in a margin account at all times according to NYSE rules. The minimum maintenance for corporate securities is 25% of the current market value for a long position.

O

OB: (See: Limit Order)

OCC: (See: Options Clearing Corporation)

OCC Disclosure Document: The disclosure document published by the Options Clearing Corporation that must be provided to every investor at the time the investor is approved for standardized options trading.

OCO: (See: One Cancels Other)

Odd Lot: An order for less than the normal unit of trading (normally 100 shares for stock).

Odd Lot Differential: The price differential that is often charged when an odd-lot order is executed on an exchange (usually the charge is 12.5 cents [1/8 of a point] per share).

Odd-lot Theory: A technical theory based on the assumption that "the public is always wrong." According to the theory, if odd-lot sales are up, it is probably a good time to buy.

Offer: An indication by an investor, trader or dealer of a willingness to sell a security or a commodity. Syn: Ask; Quote; Quotation. (See: Bid)

Offering Circular: A document that contains information about a corporation's issue of securities. The information included is similar to that made available in the prospectus, but abbreviated. Its use is restricted to Regulation A offerings. (See: Regulation A Offering)

Offering Price: With mutual funds, the price an investor will pay per share. The offering price is the NAV plus a sales charge (for funds that have a sales charge). Syn: Current Price. (See: Net Asset Value; Mutual Fund)

Official Notice of Sale: Notification of bidding sent to prospective underwriters specifying bid procedures including date, time and place of sale, description of the issue, maturities, call provisions and the amount of good faith deposit required.

Official Statement: A statement concerning the municipal issue offered (disclosing the underwriting spread, fees received by brokers for acting as agents of the issuer and initial offering price of each maturity) prepared by the underwriter from information provided by the issuer.

Offset: To enter an equivalent but opposite closing transaction. To offset an initial purchase, a sale would be made. To offset an initial sale, a purchase would be made.

Oil Depletion Allowance: A percentage of revenue from oil production allowed as a deduction from gross revenues generated from the sale of oil and gas. The percentage allowable is 15% (subject to certain limits).

Oil & Gas Program: A direct participation program which has its primary purpose oil and gas exploration, development or purchase of production.

One-Cancels-Other (OCO): A dual order submitted with two sets of instructions. At the moment either order is executed, the other order is canceled.

Open-End Management Company: A management company that continually issues new shares. Its shares are redeemable on any business day at the net asset value. Open-end management companies may sell only common stock. Syn: Open-End Investment Company; Mutual Fund.

Open-End Pledge: A provision in the trust indenture allowing the issuer to use collateral backing a bond for future borrowing. New creditors have the same claim on the collateral as existing creditors.

Open Market Operations: The buying and selling securities (primarily government or agency debt) by the Federal Open Market Committee (FOMC) for increasing or decreasing the level of bank reserves to effect control of the money supply.

Open Order: (See: Good-Till-Canceled Order)

Opening Purchase Transaction: Entering the options market by buying calls or puts.

Opening Range: (See: Range)

Opening Sale Transaction: Entering the options market by selling calls or puts.

Operating Ratio: The ratio of operating expenses to net sales, the complement to the profit margin.

Option: The right to buy (or to sell) a specified amount of a security (stock, bonds, futures contracts, etc.) at a specified price within a specified time. An option represents a right acquired by the purchaser, but is only an obligation on the part of the option seller.

Option Agreement: The agreement a customer must sign within 15 days of being approved for options trading. In it the client agrees to abide by the rules of the listed options exchanges and not to exceed the exchanges' position or exercise limits.

Option Term Adjustments: The automatic adjustments that are made to the terms of an option on the ex-dividend date when a stock pays a cash dividend (if OTC) or a stock dividend or if there is a stock split.

Options Clearing Corporation (OCC): The OCC is the organization through which the various options exchanges clear their trades. It supervises the listing of new options. The OCC is considered the issuer of standardized options.

Order Department: The department within a brokerage firm responsible for transmitting an order to the proper market for execution. Syn: Wire Room; Order Room.

Original Issue Discount (OID): A bond issued at a discount from face value at maturity. The bond pays no interest but the discount is taxed as if received annually as ordinary income. (Syn: Stripped Bonds)

OTC Option: A put or call option that is not listed on an options exchange. All terms of the contract are negotiated between buyer and seller.

Out-of-the-Money: Refers to an option that has no intrinsic value. For example, a put option in which the stock is selling above the exercise price or a call option in which the stock is selling below the exercise price.

Outstanding Stock: Issued stock minus treasury stock (stock reacquired by the issuing corporation). Stock which is in the hands of the public.

Overbought: A technical analyst's opinion that more and stronger buying has occurred in a market than the market fundamentals would justify.

Overlapping Debt: Results when property in a municipality is subject to multiple taxing authorities or tax districts each having tax collection powers and recourse to the residents of that municipality.

Overriding Royalty Interest: An interest in the production of an oil and gas well carved out of the working interest without liability for any costs of extraction. A form of sharing arrangement in an oil and gas direct participation program paid to someone other than the mineral rights owner. Generally paid to the sponsor.

Oversold: A technical analyst's opinion that more and stronger selling has occurred in a market than the market fundamentals would justify.

Owners Equity: (See: Stockholders Equity)

P

Paid-in Capital: That portion of stockholders' equity that has been generated through issuing stock above its stated value or through assets that have been received as gifts. Syn: Paid-in Surplus.

Parallel Shift: A movement in a yield curve up or down approximately the same percentage for all maturities.

Parity: In an auction, parity refers to all brokers who have an equal standing in terms of the bidding procedure. The intrinsic value of a convertible security in terms of the common stock into which it can be converted.

Partial Call: The call by an issuer of a portion of a bond issue outstanding prior to the maturity date.

Participant: Anyone who represents stockholders for or against management in a proxy contest. The purchaser or holder of an interest in a direct participation program. (See: Limited Partner)

Participating Preferred Stock: A type of preferred stock that offers the holder a share of the earnings remaining after all senior securities have been paid. This payment is made in addition to the fixed dividend received. Dividends may be cumulative or noncumulative. (See: Preferred Stock; Cumulative Preferred Stock; Noncumulative Preferred Stock; Convertible Preferred Stock)

Par Value: An arbitrary dollar value assigned to each share of stock at the time of issuance. The principal amount (face value) of a bond

on which interest is calculated. Syn: Stated Value.

Pass-Through Certificate: A security backed by a pool of conventional (or VA & FHA) mortgages, the principal and interest payment received by the pool are passed through to the certificate holder. Payments may or may not be guaranteed. (See: Government National Mortgage Association; Federal National Mortgage Association)

Pattern: A repetitive series of price movements on a chart use by a technical analyst to predict future movements of the market.

P/E: (See: Price/Earnings Ratio)

Pegging: Effecting transactions in a security for fixing or stabilizing the price of the security above the established offering price.

Percentage Depletion: A method of depletion whereby a percentage of gross income from the property is deductible.

Philadelphia Plan: A type of financing for equipment trust obligations that involves a vendor delivering equipment to a trustee. The vendor receives equipment trust certificates that are sold to investors. The railroad leases the equipment and pays a periodic rental fee, which covers interest installments and principal when due. When all rental payments are made, the title is transferred to the railroad.

Pink Sheets: The daily quotation sheets that publish the interdealer, wholesale quotes for over-the-counter stocks.

Placement Ratio: A ratio compiled by The Daily Bond Buyer indicating the number of new municipal issues that have sold within the last week.

Plus Tick Rule: The SEC regulation governing the market price at which a short sale may be made. No short sale may be executed at a price below the price of the last sale. Syn: Up tick Rule. (See: Zero Plus Tick)

Points: (See: Quotes- Bond & Stock; Basis Point)

POP: Public Offering Price (See: Offering Price)

Position: A position is described as either the amount of a security (shares, contracts, bonds, etc.) owned (a long position) or owed (a short position) by an individual. A dealer will also take positions in specific securities to maintain an inventory to facilitate trading.

Position Limit: The limitation established by the listed options exchanges that prohibits an investor from having a position of more than a specific number of contracts on the same side of the market.

Position Trading: 1) A dealer acquiring or selling an inventory in a security. 2) A commodities speculator who buys or sells positions in the futures markets as a means of speculating on long-term price movements. (See: 1) Dealer; Principal; Make a Market; 2) Spreader; Scalper)

Precedence: In an auction, the ranking of bids and offers according to size (the number of shares in a bid or offer).

Preemptive Right: The legal right of stockholders to purchase new stock in proportion to their holdings before the new stock is offered to the public.

Preferred Dividend Coverage: A financial ratio used to determine the margin of safety with which the fixed dividend requirements are covered for a preferred stockholder. Computed by dividing preferred dividends by net income.

Preferred Stock: An equity security that represents ownership in a corporation. It has a fixed dividend, with dividend and asset preference over common stock. Generally carries no voting rights.

Preliminary Prospectus: Any prospectus that is distributed during the cooling-off period that includes the essential facts about the forthcoming offering except for the underwriting spread, the final public offering price and date the shares will be delivered. Syn: Red Herring.

Premium: Market price of an option. The cash price that the option buyer pays to the option writer.

Premium Bond: A bond that sells above par (above 100% of $1,000). That is, the purchase price of the bond is greater than the par value (principal amount). Also, the selling price of an option. (See: Par Value; Principal)

Pre-Sale Order: An order communicated to the syndicate manager prior to formulation of the bid. If the syndicate wins the bid, the order is already considered sold. A pre-sale order normally has the highest priority in a municipal underwriting.

Price/Earnings Ratio: The ratio of the current market value of the stock divided by the annual earnings per share. Syn: P/E Ratio.

Price Spread: A spread involving the purchase and sale of two options on the same stock with the same expiration date but with different exercise prices. Syn: Money Spread; Vertical Spread.

Primary Earnings-per-Share: The earnings per share if all rights, stock options and warrants have been converted (if their total conversion will cause at least a 3% increase in the number of shares outstanding). Syn: EPS Fully Diluted.

Primary Offering: A corporation's offering of stock, or a municipality's offering of bonds to the public. Proceeds of the offering go directly to the corporation or municipality. Syn: Primary Distribution.

Prime Rate: The interest rate that commercial banks charge their prime or most credit worthy customers. Those are generally large corporations.

Principal: One who position trades in the secondary market or in the primary market; this designation includes sole proprietors, officers, directors or partners of a company or managers of offices of supervision. Also, an investment banker who assumes risk by actually buying securities from the issuer and reselling them. (See: Dealer)

Principal Transaction: The broker-dealer or bank dealer buys stocks or bonds from customers and takes them into its own inventory. It then sells stocks or bonds to customers from its inventory.

Prior Preferred Stock: A class of preferred stock that has prior claim over other preferred stock in receipt of dividends as well as in distribution of assets in the event of liquidation. (See: Preferred Stock)

Priority: In an auction, the first person to bid or offer at a given price establishes priority. Only one person can have priority.

Private Placement: An offering complying under Regulation D (Rule 505 and Rule 506). Generally speaking, the offer of an unregistered security to no more than 35 nonaccredited investors and/or an unlimited number of accredited investors.

Profitability: The ability of a company to generate a level of income and gains in excess of expenses.

Profitability Ratio: Ratios describing profit or income as a percent or multiple of sales.

Program Interest: The limited partnership unit or other indication of ownership in a direct participation program.

Program Management Fee: A fee paid to the sponsor or the persons for management and administration of the program.

Progressive Tax: A tax that takes a larger fraction of the income of high-income people. The best example is the graduated income tax.

Project Notes: Short-term debt instrument issued in anticipation of a later issuance of public housing authority bonds.

Property Management Fee: The fee paid to a sponsor or other person for day-to-day property management services in connection with a real estate program's real property project.

Prospect: An area in which a partnership intends to acquire an oil or gas interest or property.

Prospectus: The legal document that must be given to every investor who purchases registered securities in an offering. It describes the details of the company and the particular offering. Syn: Final Prospectus.

Prospectus Act: Another name for the Securities Act of 1933.

Proxy: In order to vote on corporate matters, a shareholder must be in attendance at the annual meeting. If the shareholder is unable to attend, the shareholder may still vote by proxy. A proxy is given in writing, authorizing another to vote for the shareholder according to the shareholder's instructions.

PHA: Public Housing Authority Bond (See: Housing Authority Bond)

Public Offering Price (POP): The price of new shares established in the issuing corporation's prospectus. Also, the price to investors for mutual fund shares.

Purchase and Sales Department: The department within a brokerage firm that computes commissions and taxes, and sends confirmations to client. (See: Trade Confirmation)

Purchasing Power Risk: The risk that a certain amount of money will not purchase as much in the future as it does today due to inflation. Syn: Inflation Risk.

Put: An option contract that gives the owner the right to sell a specific number of shares of stock at a specified price within a specified time.

Put Bond: A bond requiring the issuer to purchase the bond at the bondholder's discretion, normally at prescribed times. Syn: Tender Bond.

Put Buyer: Investor who pays a premium for an option contract and has, for a specified time, the right to sell the underlying security at the specified price.

Put Spread: An investment in which an investor purchases one put on a particular stock and sells another put on the same stock, but with a different expiration date, different exercise price or both.

Put Writer: Investor who receives a premium and takes on, for a specified time, the obligation to buy the underlying security at the specified price, at the put buyer's discretion.

Q

Qualified Legal Opinion: A conditional opinion of the legality or tax exempt status of a municipal bond. (See: Legal Opinion of Counsel)

Qualified Retirement Plan: Retirement plans that qualify under Sections 401 and 501 of the Internal Revenue Code. Syn: Approved Plan. (See: Individual retirement Account; Keogh Plan)

Quality Adjustment: The amount a settlement price is adjusted on a futures transaction when the delivered commodity differs from that specified in the original contract.

Quick Ratio: A test of a company's liquidity computed by dividing current assets (cash, cash equivalents and receivables) by current liabilities.

Quotation: The bid and offer of a particular security.

Quotes (Bond): Like stock, bond prices are also quoted in the financial press and most daily newspapers. Corporate bonds are quoted in eighths. Government bonds are quoted in 32nds. The quotes for corporate and government bonds are a percentage of the bond's face value ($1,000). Municipal bonds may be quoted on a dollar basis or on yield to maturity.

Quotes (Stock): Most stocks traded are quoted in the financial press or most daily newspapers. A stock is quoted in points, with each point equal to $1. The price of the stock is further broken down into eighths of a point where 1/8 = 12.5 cents.

R

RAN: Revenue Anticipation Notes, municipal notes issued in anticipation of revenues to be received.

Range: The security's low price and high price for a particular trading period (e.g., close of the day's trading, opening of the day's trading, day, month, year).

Rate Covenant: Revenue coverage minimums set in the trust indenture for payment of maintenance, debt service and reserve requirements to establish safety margins on the issue.

Ratings: Bonds are rated for safety by various organizations such as Standard & Poor's and Moody's. These firms rate the companies issuing bonds as to their ability to repay and make interest payments. Ratings range from AAA or Aaa (the highest) to C (representing a company in default).

Rating Services: Companies such as Moody's or Standard & Poor's which rate various debt and preferred stock issues for safety of payment of principal, interest or dividends. The issuing company or municipality pays a fee for the rating. (See: Ratings)

Ratio Writing: An option position in which the investor writes more than one call option for every 100 shares of the underlying stock (or for every call option) that he or she owns.

R Coefficient: A statistical measure of how closely the movements of a security's price tracks with the movements of the market.

Real Estate Investment Trust (REIT): An investment trust that operates through the pooled capital of many investors who buy its shares. Investments are either in direct ownership of income property or mortgage loans.

Real Estate Program: A direct participation program which has for its purpose the expenditure of a determinable sum of money for the investment in and/or the operation of real property for a gain.

Recapitalization: Converting a short-term liability into a long term liability.

Recapture: The treatment as ordinary income of gain which should otherwise be capital gain on the sale or other disposition of a capital asset, because of previous deductions from ordinary income which are now treated as being excessive or otherwise not allowed.

Reciprocal Immunity: (See: Mutual Exclusion Doctrine)

Record Date: The date established by the issuing corporation that determines which stockholders are entitled to receive dividends or rights distributions.

Recourse Financing: Financing in which the taxpayer is personally liable for the debt.

Red Herring: (See: Preliminary Prospectus)

Redemption: The return of a client's interest (net asset value) in a mutual fund. By law, redemption must occur within seven days.

Registered as to Principal Only: A bond on which the name of the owner is printed, but which has unregistered coupons payable to the bearer.

Representative: A person who is registered with the appropriate exchanges and/or self-regulatory organizations to transact business with public customers for his or her firm.

Retiring Bonds: Calling in the bonds by a notice in the newspaper, by purchasing bonds in the open market or by repaying bondholders the principal amount at maturity.

Redemption Notice: A notice that a company or municipality is redeeming (or calling) a certain issue of bonds.

Refinancing: Issuing equity, the proceeds of which are used to retire debt.

Refunding: A method of retiring an outstanding bond issue using the money from the sale of a new offering. This may occur before maturity (advance refunding) or at maturity (refunding).

Regional Fund: (See: Specialized Fund)

Registered Bond: A bond on which the name of the owner appears on the certificate.

Registered Options Principal (ROP): The officer or partner of a brokerage firm who approves in writing certain accounts for certain types of options transactions.

Registered Representative: Someone who has passed the General Securities Examination, is an employee of a firm licensed as a broker-dealer and solicits orders for the purchase or sale of securities for the employer's clients, including subscriptions for investment management services furnished by the employer. Syn: RR; Account Executive; Stockbroker.

Registered Secondary Distribution: An offering of pre-owned securities issued with a prospectus. Proceeds of the offering go to someone other than the issuer. Syn: Secondary Distribution.

Registered Trader: A member of an exchange who primarily trades for a personal account and at personal risk.

Registrar: An independent organization or part of the corporation charged with the responsibility of seeing that the corporation does not have more stock outstanding than is accounted for on the corporation's books.

Registration Statement: Before non-exempt securities can be offered to the public, they require registration under the Securities Act of 1933. The registration statement must disclose all pertinent information concerning the issuer and the offering. This statement is submitted to the SEC in accordance with the requirements of the Securities Act of 1933.

Regular Way: A settlement contract that calls for delivery and payment on the fifth business day following the date of trade. This is the usual type of settlement. For government securities, regular way is the next business day.

Regulated Investment Company: An investment company granted special status by Subchapter M of the Internal Revenue Code allowing the flow through of tax consequences on a distribution to shareholders.

Regulation A: The securities regulation that exempts small public offerings from registration (those valued at no more than $1.5 million worth of securities offered during a 12-month period).

Regulation D: Securities regulation that exempts from registration certain small offerings and sales to specified individuals during a 12-month period. (See: Private Placement)

Regulation G: The Federal Reserve Board regulation governing the extension of credit by persons other than banks, brokers or dealers. (See: Regulation T; Regulation U)

Regulation Q: The Federal Reserve Board regulation that establishes how much interest banks may pay on savings accounts.

Regulation T: The Federal Reserve Board regulation governing the credit brokerage firms and dealers may extend to clients for the purchase of securities. Regulation T also governs cash accounts.

Regulation U: The Federal Reserve Board regulation governing loans by banks for the purchase of securities. Call loans are exempt from Reg U. (See: Brokers Loans; Time Loans; Call Loans)

REIT: (See: Real Estate Investment Trust)

Reinvestment: For mutual funds, distributions (dividends and gains) are reinvested in the fund to purchase additional shares instead of receiving distributions in cash.

Reoffering Scale: The prices or yields at which municipal securities are sold to the public by underwriters of a municipal offering.

Repurchase Agreement: A sale and attendant agreement to repurchase the securities sold at a higher price on an agreed-upon future date. The difference between sale price and repurchase represents the interest earnings. Syn: Repo.

Reserves: The money that a bank has in its vault or on deposit with the Federal Reserve Bank. A bank is required to maintain a certain percentage of reserves as set by the Fed.

Resistance: Used in technical analysis to describe the top of a stock's trading range.

Restricted Account: A margin account in which the equity is less than the Regulation T initial requirement. (See: Margin Account; Equity; Initial Margin Requirements in Regulation T)

Restricted Securities: Unregistered non-exempt securities acquired either directly or indirectly from the issuer or an affiliate of the issuer in a transaction that does not involve a public offering. (See: Holding Period)

Retail Transaction: A trade in which a client buys an over-the-counter stock from a broker-dealer or sells one to a broker-dealer. (See: Wholesale Transaction)

Retained Earnings: The amount of net income that remains after all dividends have been paid to preferred and common stockholders. Syn: Reinvested Earnings; Earned Surplus.

Retained Earnings Ratio: The ratio of retained earnings to the net income available for common. It is the complement of the dividend payout ratio. (See: Dividend Payout Ratio)

Retention: The securities that an underwriter sells directly to its own clients. The securities that it underwrites but does not retain are turned back to the manager to be sold by another firm.

Retention Requirement: The proportion of sale proceeds that must be retained to reduce the debit balance if securities are sold from a restricted margin account. The retention requirement is 50%. (See: Restricted Account)

Revenue Bond: A bond whose interest and principal are payable only from specific earnings of an income-producing (revenue-producing) enterprise. (See: Municipal Bond)

Reversionary Interest: An interest in a program the benefits of which accrue in the future upon the occurrence of some event.

Right: A security representing a stockholder's right to purchase new securities in proportion to the number of shares already owned.

Syn: Subscription Right Certificate. (See: Preemptive Right)

Rights of Accumulation: The right to apply reduced sales loads (breakpoints) based on the dollar position held by the investor in a mutual fund.

Rights Offering: An offering that gives each shareholder an opportunity to maintain a proportionate ownership in the company before the shares are offered to the public.

Riskless Transaction: An over-the-counter transaction in which a brokerage firm buys or sells a security to fill an order previously received from a client for the same security. Although the firm is technically acting as a principal in this trade, it is relatively "riskless" because the purchase and the sale are consummated almost simultaneously. Syn: Simultaneous Riskless Transaction.

Rolling Forward: (See: Switching)

ROP: (See: Registered Options Principal)

Royalty Interest: The royalty interest is the right of the mineral rights owner to receive a share in the production of the resource, if and when production begins. The royalty interest retained is free from costs of production.

Rule 144: Covers the offering of two kinds of securities: control securities and restricted securities. (See: Control Securities; Restricted Securities)

Rules of Fair Practice: NASD rules that detail how member firms deal with the public.

S

Sales Charge: With mutual funds, the amount added to the net asset value of mutual fund shares. The investor will pay the NAV and the sales charge, which equals the offering price. Syn: Sales Load. (See: Net Asset Value; Offering Price; Mutual Fund)

Sale Leaseback: A method of raising cash, whereby the seller sells property to the buyer and leases it back from him.

Scalper: A commodities trader who buys and sells many commodities contracts during a single day in the anticipation of profiting from small price fluctuations. Scalpers rarely carry positions from one day to the next, and their buying and selling activity contributes greatly to the liquidity of the commodities markets. (See: Spreader; Position Trading)

Secondary Distribution: An offering of previously issued securities usually owned by a major stockholder such as a company founder. This offering does not increase the number of shares of stock outstanding. Also, a block trading procedure for very large blocks. It is executed off the floor of an exchange after the market closes. Syn: Secondary Offering.

Securities Act of 1933: Federal Legislation requiring the full and fair disclosure of all material information about the issuance of new securities.

Securities Exchange Act of 1934: Federal legislation that established the Securities and Exchange Commission. Its purpose is to provide regulation of securities exchanges and the over-the-counter markets, and to protect investors from unfair and inequitable practices.

Securities and Exchange Commission (SEC): The commission created by Congress to protect investors. This commission enforces the Securities Act of 1933, the Securities Exchange Act of 1934, the Trust Indenture Act of 1939, the Investment Company Act of 1940, the Investment Advisers Act of 1940 and others.

Securities Investor Protection Corporation (SIPC): A nonprofit membership corporation created by an act of Congress to protect clients of brokerage firms that are forced into bankruptcy. Membership is composed of all brokers and dealers registered under the Securities Exchange Act of 1934, all members of national securities exchanges and most NASD members. SIPC provides customers of these firms up to $500,000 coverage for their cash and securities held by the firm (although coverage of cash is limited to $100,000).

Security Arbitrage: The simultaneous purchase and sale of related or convertible securities to take advantage of a price disparity between the two securities.

Segregation: The separation of client-owned securities and those securities owned by the brokerage firm. (See: Commingling)

Seller's Option: A settlement contract that calls for delivery and payment according to the number of days specified by the seller. Settlement occurs from six business days to the expiration of the option.

Selling a Hedge: The sale of futures options as a means of protecting against a decrease in commodities prices in the future. (See: Hedge- Short)

Selling Concession: The portion of the underwriting spread that is paid to a selling group member on the securities it sells to the public during an offering.

Selling Dividends: The illegal practice of inducing clients to buy mutual fund shares by implying that a pending distribution will benefit them. Also, combining dividend and gains distributions in the calculation of current yield.

Selling Group: Brokerage firms that sell securities in an offering but that are not members of the underwriting syndicate.

Sell Out: A procedure that occurs when a buyer fails to accept delivery of securities as stipulated in a contract. The seller can close the contract by selling the securities at the best available price and holding the buyer liable for the price of the securities and the resulting transaction costs.

Senior Lien Debt: A bond issue sharing the same collateral backing as other issues but having a prior claim to the collateral in the event of default.

Separate Account: With a variable annuity contract, the account in which the insurance company invests funds paid by contract holders. The funds are kept separate from the company's general investment account. (See: Annuity; Accumulation Unit)

Serial Maturity: A type of maturity schedule in which parts of an outstanding issue of bonds mature at intervals until the issue's final maturity date. Most municipal bonds are serial bonds. Syn: Serial Bonds.

Series: Options of the same class that have the same exercise price and the same expiration date.

Series Bonds: Bonds issued in a scheduled series of public offerings. They have the same priority claim against corporate assets.

Series EE Bonds: A nonmarketable U.S. government savings bond issued at a discount from par.

Series HH Bonds: A nonmarketable interest-bearing U.S. government savings bond that is issued at par.

Settlement: The completion of a securities trade through the delivery of the security (or commodity) for cash or other consideration.

Settlement Date: The date on which a transaction must be settled (exchange of cash for securities).

Sharing Arrangement: Method of determining responsibility for expenses and right to share in revenues between the sponsor and limited partners.

Short: The state of having sold a security, a contract or a commodity. A sale of a 10 September silver contracts would be referred to as **going short** September silver. The speculator would have a **short** position.

Short Against the Box: The sale of security that the seller owns but prefers not to deliver. Done in an arbitrage account.

Short Exempt Transaction: Short sale in an arbitrage transaction that is exempt from the SEC plus tick rule.

Short Interest Theory: A technical theory that measures the ratio of short sales to the volume in a stock. A high ratio of short interest is considered bullish.

Short Sale: The sale of a security that the seller does not own or any sale consummated by the delivery of a security borrowed by or for the account of the seller.

Short-Term Capital Gain (Loss): The taxable gain (or loss) on a capital asset that is owned for six months or less.

Sinking Fund: A fund established by a corporation or a municipality into which money is regularly deposited so that the corporation or municipality has the funds to redeem its bonds, debentures or preferred stock.

Sinking Fund Call: The early redemption of bonds from the proceeds of the sinking fund set up for this purpose.

Sole Proprietorship: A form of business organization in which a single owner has total control over his or her own business and makes all the managerial decisions.

Special Assessment Bond: Revenue bonds payable only from assessments on property owners benefiting from the service or improvements provided by the proceeds from the bond issue.

Special Arbitrage Account: A type of margin account for arbitrage transactions. (See: Market Arbitrage; Security Arbitrage)

Special Bid: (See: Special Offering)

Specialist Block Purchase (Sale): A block trading procedure for smaller blocks in which the specialist purchases (or sells) the block in a private transaction.

Specialized Fund: A type of mutual fund that tries to achieve its investment objectives by concentrating its investments within a single industry or group of related industries.

Special Memorandum Account: A notation on a customers general or margin account. Funds are credited to the SMA on a memo basis and the SMA is used much like a line of credit with a bank. The SMA preserves the customer's right to use excess equity.

Special Offering: A block trading procedure in which a block of stock is offered for sale after a prior announcement on the broad tape.

Special Situation Fund: A type of mutual fund that invests in companies in special situations, such as firms undergoing reorganization or firms considered to be "takeover" candidates.

Special Tax Bonds: A type of municipal bond that is payable only from the proceeds of a special tax, other than ad valorem taxes. (See: Municipal Bond)

Speculation: The buying and selling of goods or securities solely for the purpose of profiting from those trades and not as a means of hedging or protecting other positions.

Sponsor: Any person directly or indirectly instrumental in organizing, wholly or in part, the partnership or who will manage or participate in the management of the partnership.

Spot Commodity: The actual good as it is being traded as opposed to futures or options on that good.

Spot Market: A market in which goods are traded for immediate delivery and immediate payment.

Spot Price: The actual price a particular good can be bought or sold for at a specified time and place.

Spread: With a quotation, the spread is the difference between the bid and offer. With options, simultaneously having a long and a short option position within the same class, but not the same series.

Spreader: A commodities trader who attempts to profit from the price differences between commodities, markets or delivery months. A commodities arbitrageur. (See: Scalper; Position Trading)

Spread-Load Option: With mutual funds, a system of sales charges for contractual plans. It permits a decreasing scale of sales charges with no more than 20% of the cost deducted in any one year and no more than an average of 16% of the cost deducted in a consecutive 48 month period. The maximum which may be deducted over the life of the plan is still 9%. Rights of withdrawal exist for 45 days, during which time, the client may receive a return of all sales charges deducted plus the current value of the account. After 45 days the client is entitled to the current NAV only.

Stabilizing: Occurs when a dealer appointed by the managing underwriter buys a security at or below the public offering price to prevent the price from dropping sharply.

Standard & Poor's 500: A market indicator composed of 400 industrial stocks, 20 transportation stocks, 40 financial stocks and 40 public utility stocks.

Standby Underwriter: A brokerage firm which agrees to purchase any part of an issue that has not been subscribed to through a rights offering.

Statement of Intention: (See: Letter of Intent)

Statutory Voting Rights: A voting procedure that permits a shareholder to cast one vote per share owned for each director.

Step Out Well: A well or prospect adjacent to a field of proven reserves.

Stock Ahead: A limit order at a specific price that is not filled because other orders at that same price were entered before that order.

Stock Certificate: Written evidence of ownership in a corporation.

Stock Dividend: (See: Dividend)

Stock Power: A standard form that duplicates the back of a stock certificate. It is used if the registered owner of a security does not have the certificate available for signature endorsement. (See: Assignment)

Stock Split: A reduction in the par value of stock by issuing additional stock. A reverse split increases the stocks par value by reducing the number of shares outstanding.

Stockholder's Equity: It is calculated by subtracting total liabilities from total assets. Syn: Net Worth; Owners' Equity.

Stop Limit Order: A stop order that becomes a limit order once the market price reaches or passes the specific price stated in the stop order. (See: Stop Order)

Stop Order: 1) An order by the SEC that suspends the sale of securities to the public. 2) An order that becomes a market order when the market price of the security reaches or exceeds the specific price stated in the stop order.

Stopping Stock: A specialist has guaranteed execution at a specific price for a public order submitted by a floor broker.

Straddle: Either a long or short position in a call and a put on the same security with the same expiration date and the same exercise price.

Straddle-Long: Buying a call and a put on the same stock with the same strike price and expiration.

Straddle-Short: Writing a call and a put on a stock with the same strike price and expiration.

Straight-line Depreciation: A method of depreciation by which a corporation writes off the cost of an asset in equal amounts each year over the asset's useful life.

Strangle: A strangle is a combination of a put and a call where both options are out-of-the-money. A strangle can only be profitable if the market is highly volatile and makes a major move in either direction.

Strap: A strap is the purchase of 2 calls and 1 put on the same security with the same terms.

Street Name: Securities held by the brokerage firm in its own name but owned by a client are referred to as being held in "street name." Syn: In-Street-Name.

Strengthening Basis: A narrowing of the spread between the cash (spot) price and the futures price of a commodity.

Strike Price: The price at which the underlying security will be sold if the option buyer exercises his or her rights in the contract. Syn: Exercise Price.

Strip: A strip is the purchase of 2 puts and 1 call on the same security with the same terms.

Strip Bond: A bond stripped of its coupons and repackaged and sold at a deep discount which will mature at full face value.

Stripper Well: A well producing fewer than 10 barrels of oil per day. Stripping a field is pumping occasionally and letting the field rest in between the pumping periods.

Subject Quote: A quote that does not represent actual offers to buy or sell when prices are quoted. It represents an indication of how the market stands. Syn: Nominal Quote.

Subordinated Debenture: A debt obligation that has unsecured junior claims to interest and principal subordinated to ordinary debentures and all other liabilities of the issuing corporation. (See: Debenture)

Subordinated Interest: One which is junior to the rights of participants until such time as they have received cumulative distributed cash or net revenues in an amount at least equal to their capital contribution.

Subordinated Reversionary Working Interest: In this type of sharing arrangement, the sponsor bears no drilling cost and does not share in revenues until investors achieve payout. Payout is when the investor receives all monies invested plus a predetermined rate of return (normally 6% compounded annually). At payout, the program sponsor will then receive a percentage of the revenues generated and share in additional expenses.

Subscription Agreement: An agreement whereby an investor agrees to purchase securities and in addition agrees to become a limited partner and abide by the limited partnership agreement.

Subscription Amount: The total dollar amount for which a participant in a direct participation program has subscribed for his participation in the program.

Subscription Right: A stockholder's privilege of having the first opportunity to purchase new stock issued by the corporation so that the stockholder may retain his or her proportionate ownership in the corporation. Generally, the price for subscription stock is lower than the current market value. (See: Preemptive Right; Right)

Support: A phrase used in technical analysis to describe the bottom of a stock's trading range.

Switching: Closing or offsetting a position specifying one delivery (futures) or expiration (options) month and opening a position for the same commodity or security in another, more distant month. Syn: Rolling Forward.

Syndicate: A group of broker dealers formed to handle the distribution and sale of an issuer's security. The typical syndicate formed has several firms managing the underwriting effort. Each member of the syndicate is then assigned the responsibility for the sale and distribution of a portion of the issue. (See: Eastern & Western Accounts)

Systematic Risk: The risk inherent to all securities of the same type (commodities, stocks, bonds, etc.) that cannot be eliminated through diversification or similar strategies. Syn: Market Risk.

T

Takedown: The discount at which a syndicate member buys securities from the syndicate. (See: Concession)

Taxability: The risk of the erosion of investment income through taxation.

Tax Swap: (See: Bond Swap)

TAN: Tax Anticipation Notes, short-term municipal debt securities to be paid off from tax revenues.

Technical Analysis: A method of securities analysis that analyzes statistics generated by market activity, such as past prices and volume. Technical analysis does not attempt to measure a security's intrinsic value.

Tenants in Common (JTIC): A form of ownership directing that, upon the death of one tenant, the decedent's fractional interest in the joint account be retained by the estate. This form of ownership may be used by any two or more individuals. Syn: Joint Tenants in Common.

Tender Offer: An offer to buy securities for cash or cash and securities.

Term Maturity: A type of maturity in which the entire bond issue matures on a single date. Syn: Term Bonds. (See: Maturity Date)

Testamentary Trustee: Someone authorized to administer a trust, including brokerage accounts, created by a decedent. The authority of the testamentary trustee is created by the last will of the decedent who created the trust.

Third Market: The trading of listed securities in the over-the-counter market.

Time Loan: A collateral loan of a brokerage firm that matures on a date agreed upon by lender and the borrower and has a constant interest rate for the duration of the contract. (See: Brokers' Loans)

Time Spread: A spread that involves different expiration dates but the same exercise price. Syn: Calendar Spread; Horizontal Spread.

Time Value: Refers to any current market value of an option above and beyond its intrinsic value. (See: Intrinsic Value)

Tombstone: An advertisement that announces a securities offering. It identifies the name of the issuer, the type of security, the underwriters and where additional information is available.

Trade Date: The date on which a transaction occurred.

Trading Authorization: (See: Full Trading Authorization; Limited Trading Authorization)

TRAN: Tax and Revenue Anticipation Note, a short-term municipal debt security.

Transfer Agent: A person or organization responsible for recording names of registered shareholders and the number of shares owned, seeing that the certificates are signed by the appropriate corporate officers, affixing the corporate seal and delivering securities to the transferee.

Treasury Bill: A marketable, short-term (90 days to one year) U.S. government debt security issued through a competitive bidding process at a discount from par value. There is no fixed interest rate.

Treasury Bond: A marketable, long-term (10 to 30 years), fixed-interest U.S. government debt security.

Treasury Note: A marketable, medium-term (one to 10 years), fixed-interest U.S. government debt security.

Treasury Stock: Common stock that has been issued and reacquired (purchased) by the corporation from the public at the current market price.

Trendline: The line that traces a stock's movement by connecting the reaction lows in an upward trend or the rally highs in a downward trend.

Triangle: A pattern on a chart that shows a narrowing of the price range in which a security is trading. The left side of the triangle typically shows the widest range and the right side narrows to a point.

Trust Indenture: The written agreement between a corporation and its creditors that details the terms of the debt issue. These terms include such things as the rate of interest, the maturity date, the means of payment and the collateral. Syn: Deed of Trust; Trust Agreement.

Trust Indenture Act of 1939: The legislation requiring all publicly offered non-exempt debt securities be registered under the Securities Act of 1933 and issued under a trust indenture.

Trust in Securities Act: Another name for the Securities Act of 1933.

Trustee of a Living Trust: Someone who administers a trust, including brokerage accounts, created by a living person. The authority is created by a trust agreement, not a will.

Two Dollar Broker: A member of an exchange who freelances by executing the orders for various member firms when their own floor brokers are especially busy. The broker charges a commission for services. The amount of the commission is negotiated.

Type: Refers to whether an option is a put or a call option.

U

Uncovered Call (Put) Writer: An investor who writes a call (or put) without owning the underlying security or some equivalent security. Syn: Naked Writer.

Underlying Security: The futures or securities that are bought or sold when an option is exercised, or on which an option is based.

Underwriter: The entity responsible for marketing stocks, bonds, mutual fund shares and so on.

Underwriting: The procedure by which investment bankers channel investment capital from investors to corporations and municipalities.

Underwriting Manager: The brokerage firm responsible for organizing a syndicate, preparing the issue, negotiating with the issuer and the underwriters and allocating stock to the selling group. Syn: Manager of the Syndicate; Managing Underwriter; Manager.

Underwriting Spread: The difference between the public offering price and the price the underwriter pays to the issuing corporation. Syn: Underwriting Discount.

Underwriting Syndicate: A group of brokerage firms that agrees in writing to cooperate in a joint venture to distribute a particular offering of securities. Syn: Syndicate.

Undivided Account: (See: Eastern Account)

Unearned Income: Income that is derived from investments and other sources not related to personal services. Examples of unearned income include interest from a savings account, bond interest and dividends from stock. Syn: Passive Income. (See: Earned Income)

Uniform Gifts to Minors Act (UGMA): The act that permits gifts of money and securities to be given to minors and allows adults to act as custodians for minors.

Uniform Practice Code: The NASD code that governs a firm's dealing with other brokerage firms. It serves to make these dealings uniform.

Unit Investment Trust: An investment company that has its own portfolio of securities in which it invests. It sells interest in this portfolio in redeemable securities. They include two types: fixed (no portfolio changes are made); and non-fixed (portfolio changes are permissible). Unit investment trusts are organized under a trust indenture, not a corporate charter.

Unqualified Legal Opinion: A legal opinion of a security given without condition.

Unsecured Bond: (See: Debenture)

Unspecified Property Program: (See: Blind Pool)

V

Variable Annuity: A type of annuity contract in which the insurance company makes variable dollar payments for the term of the contract. (See: Annuity)

Variable Ratio Plan: A defensive policy plan in which the investor makes purchases and sales on the theory that the higher the stock prices are, the riskier they are, whereas bond prices tend to be more stable. Therefore, the ratio of stocks to bonds is decreased as the market rises and increased as the market falls.

Vertical Spread: (See: Price Spread)

Visible Supply: 1) The disclosure of all municipal securities known to be coming to market within the next 30 days that is published in The Daily Bond Buyer. 2) All supplies of a commodity in licensed warehouses.

Volatility: The speed and extent to which the price of a security or commodity rises and falls within a given period of time.

Volume of Trading Theory: A technical theory that tries to confirm a strong or weak market by measuring the volume of trading.

Voting Trust: The transfer of common stock voting power to a trustee.

Voting Trust Certificate: A certificate evidencing transfer of shares into a voting trust. The certificate does not carry the right to vote the shares.

W

Warrant: A security giving the holder the right to purchase securities at a stipulated price. This is usually a long-term instrument, affording the investor the option of buying shares at a later date at the subscription price, subject to the warrant's exercise.

Wash Sale: The purchase of the same (or substantially identical) security within 30 days before or after the sale establishing the loss. The claimed loss will be disallowed.

Weakening Basis: A widening of the spread between the cash (spot) price and the futures price of a commodity.

Western Account: Syndicate members and dealers are liable for the sale of the securities allocated to them only. Syn: Divided Account. (See: Eastern Account)

When-Issued Contract: A settlement contract that calls for delivery on a day set by the NYSE (for securities listed on the NYSE) based on when the issuing corporation will have the physical certificates available for distribution. For unlisted securities, the NASD sets the delivery date.

When-Issued Security: A security offered for sale in advance of the issuance of the security by the issuer.

Wholesale Transaction: A trade in which a broker-dealer buys an over-the-counter stock from another broker-dealer. (See: Retail Transaction)

Withdrawal Plan: A client may request the systematic withdrawal of his/her account periodically. Withdrawals may be based on a fixed dollar amount, fixed number of shares, fixed percentage or a fixed period of time. The plan is normally a free service offered by a mutual fund.

Working Capital: A measure of liquidity calculated by subtracting current liabilities from current assets.

Working Interest: An operating interest entitling the holder to a share of production under an oil and gas lease which carries with it the obligation to bear corresponding share of all costs associated with the production of income.

Workout Quote: A type of subject quotation in which a brokerage firm estimates the price that it thinks it can get if given reasonable time to enter the market and to find the stock to buy or sell.

Writer: The seller of an option. Syn: Holder; Seller; Guarantor.

X Y Z

Yellow Sheets: Pages that the National Quotation Bureau publishes daily and that contain wholesale quotations of dealers for corporate bonds.

Yield: The rate of return on an investment, generally expressed as a percentage of the current price. Syn: Current Yield; Dividend Yield. (See: Coupon Yield; Current Yield; Yield to Maturity)

Yield Curve: Graphic representation of actual or projected yields of fixed income securities.

Yield to Call: The rate of return on an investment that accounts for the cash difference between a bond's acquisition cost and its proceeds in addition to interest income calculated to the earliest date that the bonds may be called in by the issuing corporation.

Yield to Maturity: The rate of return on an investment that accounts for the cash difference between a bond's acquisition cost and its maturity proceeds as well as interest received from owning the bond.

Zero Coupon Bond: (See: OID; Strip Bond)

Zero Plus Tick: A sale made at a price equal to the price of the last sale but higher than the last different price.

Zero Minus Tick: A sale made at a price equal to the price of the last sale but lower than the last different price.

Gloss.40